101 SOCIAL WORK CLINICAL TECHNIQUES

101 SOCIAL WORK CLINICAL TECHNIQUES

Dr. Francis J. Turner

Dr. William Rowe

With contributions from

Dr. Nancy Riedel Bowers, Dr. Alex Polgar,
Dr. Mark Ragg

OXFORD
UNIVERSITY PRESS

OXFORD

UNIVERSITY PRESS

Oxford University Press is a department of the University of Oxford.
It furthers the University's objective of excellence in research, scholarship,
and education by publishing worldwide.

Oxford   New York
Auckland   Cape Town   Dar es Salaam   Hong Kong   Karachi
Kuala Lumpur   Madrid   Melbourne   Mexico City   Nairobi
New Delhi   Shanghai   Taipei   Toronto

With offices in
Argentina   Austria   Brazil   Chile   Czech Republic   France   Greece
Guatemala   Hungary   Italy   Japan   Poland   Portugal   Singapore
South Korea   Switzerland   Thailand   Turkey   Ukraine   Vietnam

Oxford is a registered trademark of Oxford University Press in the UK and certain other
countries.

Published in the United States of America by
Oxford University Press
198 Madison Avenue, New York, NY 10016

Library of Congress Cataloging-in-Publication Data
Turner, Francis J. (Francis Joseph)
101 social work clinical techniques / Dr. Francis J. Turner and Dr. William Rowe.
pages cm
Includes bibliographical references and index.
ISBN 978-0-19-530054-3 (pbk. : alk. paper)
1. Social case work.   2. Social service—Practice.   I. Rowe, William (William S.)   II. Title.
HV43.T797 2013
361.3—dc23
2012043263

1 3 5 7 9 8 6 4 2
Printed in the United States of America
on acid-free paper

To all our clients, from whom we have learned much and hopefully we have given at least a little!

Contents

PART THREE • THE WAY AHEAD

Foreword

SOCIAL WORK GRADUATE STUDENTS, CLINICAL SOCIAL WORKERS IN practice, and social work educators often express their desire for a book that will quickly help them to identify social work techniques for use with clients expressing a range of common psychosocial problems that bring them into our agencies and practices. Over the years, we have refrained from bringing them this resource, relying instead on helping them use the *Diagnostic and Statistical Manual of Mental Disorders,* showing them the relationship between theory and practice, and most recently relying upon evidence-based practice. Each of these practices is valid and useful for educating students and ourselves about the best ways to intervene with and on behalf of their clients.

In this book, *101 Social Work Clinical Techniques*, Francis Turner and William Rowe, nationally known experts in clinical social work practice and research, have finally brought to us a volume of readily available social work techniques that have been shown to be useful in clinical social work practice. This book focuses on specific and generic clinical work techniques that may be understood conceptually and used appropriately in practice, independent of the specific theoretical orientation one may use in practice.

The authors distinguish between technique and related concepts, such as methods, process, and skills, and show how these techniques were developed and used through the history of social work practice. The title refers to 101 techniques, but the authors readily acknowledge that the number of techniques available for clinical social workers is not finite. The techniques presented in this volume are ones that have been debated, written about, and generally have become part of our practice wisdom. This does not in any way diminish the fact that many of these techniques have also been studied empirically and found to be effective for clients experiencing clinical symptoms such as depression or anxiety.

The book is composed of brief chapters for each of the techniques. It is not designed to provide an exhaustive listing of all techniques. They are presented as specific techniques belonging to one of ten categories. In addition, the authors identify more generic techniques separately to include behavioral techniques, music-based interventions, play therapy, and standardized instruments, with their own examples. Last, the authors assess a "risk factor" from minimal to high that assesses the potential risk of using these techniques with clients. This is a critical prerequisite using many of the techniques, given that some of them require additional training and specialization to be used appropriately with clients.

The format for each of the chapters is as follows. First the technique is described and defined, followed by a brief summary of its origins. The type of technique it is and the technique itself are then discussed in relation to its usefulness in social work practice. Risk factors are then presented and described, as are the required skills and knowledge necessary to use the technique. Last, two case summaries in which the technique has been applied are presented to demonstrate appropriate uses of the technique by the clinician. Each chapter concludes with a robust reference list and additional sources that the reader may consult for more information about the technique.

Drs. Turner and Rowe's wish for this book is that it stimulates interest in the use of these techniques and also provides opportunities for clinicians to independently examine and learn more about the literature underlying their use. They also hope that the volume as a whole will enhance our discussion of these techniques in clinical practice, thereby enriching our knowledge as a social work community. Last, they hope that it raises our awareness about the risks and possible misuses of some techniques, which should help us identify where our own gaps in knowledge and practice might be. This helps to ensure we do not engage in practice techniques that we are ill prepared to implement.

I found *101 Social Work Clinical Techniques* to be an insightful and delightful read. I learned about the origins of many techniques that I have used in practice and taught in courses. The book also encouraged me to think more critically about the usefulness of our rich practice history and tradition.

In this book, Turner and Rowe have given us a wonderful contribution to the development of our practice skills, and have also given the field something that it has requested over the years. I encourage you to dig into this book and enjoy it as much as I did.

Bonnie L. Yegidis, PhD

Introduction

THE PRINCIPAL GOAL OF THIS VOLUME IS TO PRESENT TO STUDENTS AND beginning practitioners a spectrum of techniques that have been found to be useful by various colleagues in practice situations and that have been discussed in our practice literature. Over our years of teaching clinically oriented students, we have commonly heard pervasive queries such as, "But what do I do when I am with a client?" "I have been well taught in one or more several theories, but I don't know yet how to apply them except in a very diffuse manner." To date the field of social work does not seem to have given technique a high priority.

We have written this book in the hopes that, as we continue to develop, we will give more attention in our practice to the concept that technique is of key importance.

In general terms, *technique* refers to that spectrum of actions we consciously do for, with, and to clients in the process of a professional intervention. That is, the term describes those actions that we consciously take as a part of our professional contact with clients.

It presumes that almost everything we do in working with a client in a psychosocial intervention is a technique, although it is not always recognized as such. If this is so, then it is important that we give much greater attention to the concept and reality of technique than is currently reflected in our literature.

At first we thought it would be adequate to develop and publish a list of the activities mentioned in our literature that we use in practice and that have been identified as techniques. This did not prove difficult. In a very short time we developed a listing of over a hundred specific activities differentially used by social workers and discussed in the literature. This process led us to an awareness that there were many more than a hundred. To show our understanding of this, we decided to use the number 101 to reflect our understanding that this was only an incomplete beginning.

As we became more immersed in this process, it became apparent that one of the problems in identifying our techniques came from our inconsistent use of the term. At times we appear to co-identify the term with such concepts as method, process, skills, objectives, activities procedure, interventions, and actions. Hence it was clear that in discussing the term and its place in practice and the literature, we needed to address this inconsistency. We needed a working definition of technique; we undertake this task in the first chapter.

As we began to look at the range of techniques, we also came to realize that, although we tend to think most techniques emerge from particular theories, in fact they emerge from a variety of sources.

Over the years considerable emphasis has been placed in our writings, teaching and supervision on the critical importance of the helping relationship and the powerful role it plays in our interaction with clients. Where we haven't given sufficient attention is in helping our colleagues and future colleagues understand that the process of developing therapeutic relationships requires us to use specific techniques. This we do in an idiosyncratic manner.

Hence it is timely that a volume on technique has been prepared. The generally accepted view of our practice welcomes the idea of a multimethod and multitheory approach as the desired profile of a social worker's knowledge and skill. The enrichment that comes from our growing interest in diversity of all types has enhanced our understanding of the human condition in its rich variety of forms, and has provided an appreciation of the multiple ways that humans can be influenced. We continue to expand our knowledge of the complex interactions of persons and social systems and the potential that emerges from this diversity.

As we seek to integrate our knowledge of diversity with our own development, one of the important sources of potential of this book will be to further operationalize and legitimize the term *practice wisdom*. We know that practitioners work from a self-perceived theoretical base. However, along with theory each of us develops highly honed skills to enhance our ability to interact effectively with clients. To expand these abilities we need to learn to identify and describe precisely as clinicians what is done with whom in what situation, and thus learn to identify the differential impact of our various actions—that is, our techniques. To enhance more precisely what we do, we need to work toward a common vocabulary and understanding of what impact our various techniques have on what kind of person and situation.

We can see several uses to which this book can be put.

1. We hope it gives some colleagues interest in trying some of the described techniques that they have not used before.
2. We hope the risk rating for each technique will alert us to use only those various techniques that are within our known level of competence.
3. We also hope the various readings will lead some colleagues to pursue the identified literature and, in some instances, to read further and expand the scope of their practice when appropriate.
4. We hope that we all share with our profession the experience we have had with given techniques, whether listed or not.
5. It is our hope that the book will lead to an overall interest in the concept and reality of the place of technique in our practice.
6. Most important, we hope to emphasize that there are risks involved in the misuse of certain techniques unless one is properly trained and, when necessary, supervised.

In summary, what this book is not!

1. It is not a final listing of social work techniques, but a sampling of some that are found in the literature.
2. It does not purport to present a final definition of technique, but one that builds on a standard definition from a social work perspective. Instead, it is seen as a step to precision.

3. It is not a collection of all the techniques that have emerged from the tenets of clinical theories.
4. It is not a listing of the techniques that are necessarily the best or most effective.
5. It is not a listing of only those techniques that have a sound research base.

WHAT THIS BOOK IS

It is a collection of professional activities that in our view merit the title of *technique*.

The book is presented as a resource to clinical social work students and colleagues to give them a clearer understanding of the nature, definition, range, and richness of our technique repertoire.

ACKNOWLEDGMENTS

AS WE COME TO THE END OF THIS PROJECT, WE ARE AWARE OF AND grateful to the many people who helped us move this project throughout its various phases. It is difficult to attempt to list them all, lest we overlook some. If so, we apologize.

Of course we are grateful to the various people at Oxford University Press who worked directly with us, such as Maura Roessner, Nicholas Liu, and Dana Bliss. In so doing we are aware that there were many behind the scenes with whom we did not have direct contact but who helped. As well, we are grateful to our four colleagues, Dr. Alex Polgar, Dr. Nancy Riedel Bowers, Anna Lee Bowers, and Dr. Mark Ragg. Their contributions were critical. We greatly appreciate the work of Carlos Pereira, who aided in the struggle over various editions and the vagaries of computers and emails.

Another critical group was those senior colleagues and master's and doctoral students who assisted in the preparation of case samples that were added to each technique in the various drafts. A special thanks goes out to graduate assistants Cassandra Gonzalez and Ahed Mando, both of whom worked on the project well past graduation. To all others as well we are collegially appreciative and grateful.

Specific and Generic Techniques
Types and Risks

101 SOCIAL WORK CLINICAL TECHNIQUES

PART ONE

TECHNIQUES IN SOCIAL WORK PRACTICE: AN OVERVIEW

Social work clinical practice consists of a series of activities; a series of things we do with, to, and for our clients. It is our knowledge and skill in making skillful use of the range of activities and resources available to us that makes our practice more or less effective. The specific activities of which our practice consists is what we call our *techniques*.

The goal of this book is to assist social work students and practitioners in enhancing the richness and effectiveness of their practice by focusing on the concept of technique. This will be helpful for two reasons. First, it will provide some balance to the evidence-based protocols that many agencies now require by adding practice wisdom and experience to formal intervention programs; that is, it will focus on what we do. Second, it will help expand our understanding and use of the range of activities upon which we can draw in seeking the goals we set with and for our clients.

Although techniques are important in the practice of any profession, surprisingly this term has not been a notable one in the lexicon or literature of our profession. For example, it is not viewed as important in the indexes of most of our major texts. It is often not listed in indexes at all, and when it is, there are often only one or two uses of the term noted.

This is strange, because all social work clinical practice, as in all human service professions, consists of a series of planned activities by the social worker; in other words, a series of techniques, whether recognized or not. To practice responsibly and effectively, one should be aware of the techniques being used and have a knowledge-based rationale for their use. We think that part of the reason we have avoided the word is because it appeared to make our practice too mechanical rather than building on our values and theories.

Technique is a valid word. It is a powerful word. It is a word that needs to have a precise meaning in our practice. It is a word that helps us operationalize select components of our theories. Hence it is an essential word for us as we move ahead to better understand and evaluate our practice. As our practice becomes more complex and diverse it is important that we also move to an increased precision in our professional vocabulary.

Certainly over the decades we have strived to identify and evaluate the things we do in practice, and to ensure that what we did in treatment was built on our respective knowledge bases. But for the most part we did not refer to these activities as techniques and hence did not make the process a precise one. Rather, as mentioned, we have tended to use the term *technique* coterminously with such concepts as *method, procedure, activity,* and *intervention,* thus diminishing its precision. We talk about the need for precision in our practice, but often use imprecise terminology to describe its components.

Our practice continues to be enriched by the impact of new theories, more sophisticated research, the advances coming from our commitment to diversity, and a greatly expanded openness to inter- and intraprofessional influences. As our practice becomes more complex and diverse, it is important that we also move to an increased precision in our professional glossary.

In examining the use of the term *technique* over the decades, it is apparent that, unlike other terms in our repertoire, this one was never out of favor. Most of our principal authors use it in discussing various aspects of treatment, but do so in a manner that implies it is not viewed as an important term. Rather, it seems to be viewed as one that all professionals understand when talking about various components of treatment, and hence one that need not be defined in any precise way.

A good example of this can be found in a book edited by Cora Kasius titled *Principles and Techniques in Social Casework* (Kasius, 1950). Although the book purports to address the topic of techniques, apart from two exceptions its chapters have little to do with technique. What Dr. Kasius meant by *technique* is not addressed. Instead, the tenor of the articles presumes that the term is an important one with a common understanding that needs no further elaboration. Later, in 1957 Perlman gave us a definition of technique that stresses the idea that a technique is the individualistic way in which each of us translates the principles of methods into practice (p. 158).

Overall the usage of the term is sparse, with an occasional, veiled admonition that we must not become overly technique oriented and that technique always needs be tied to a theoretical base.

Howard Goldstein (1973, p. 19), in his seminal work *Social Work Practice: A Unitary Approach,* gave us a definition of technique and examples of what he meant by it. The important facet of this work is that he sees *technique* as a term used to identify the very objective things we do in our practice, including such things as "conducting meetings, collecting data and record-ing." It thus comes closer than previous writings do to a more precise meaning of the term.

This theme picks up on an earlier one by Mary Richmond, when she spoke of the "warp and woof" component of our practice. By this she underscored that much of what we do with clients involves very day-to-day actions. These are critical to helping people, but do not have the glamour of the many identified techniques used in other professions, which we think partially explains why we have tended to avoid the term.

One or two of the various discussions of technique in the social work literature express a subtle concern that too much emphasis on technique might make us overly "technical" in our practice, by implying that this would lead us to view the goal of treatment as finding a specific cluster of techniques listed in a directory each time a particular situation is encountered. In other words, there would be a recipe for all occasions. Conversely, it is our view that techniques are to be viewed as tools, each of which is to be viewed as being usable in a variety of ways, appropriate to various situations or problems.

In recent years a shift can be seen toward a more frequent use of the term *technique* in social work literature, both books and articles. This seems to be at least partially related to social work's increasing comfort with interprofessional mutual influences. In so doing we find in the litera-ture of allied professions a considerable emphasis on utilizing the term *technique* and frequently giving various lists of techniques. Nevertheless, a tendency to avoid use of the term continues with a preference for the term *intervention,* which does come close to the meaning of technique but not exactly.

As our understanding of the wide range of things we do with, to, and for clients expands, so too does our realization that their importance rests in their effectiveness, not in the degree of sophistication, source, complexity, or technological attributes they are viewed as possessing. Thus we are becoming more aware that some of our most mundane activities may be, in partic-ular situations, our most powerful.

For example a slice of pizza shared with a client can be just as effective therapeutically as the most sophisticated of techniques. The test for us is to know the power of food as a technique for the right person at the right time, in the right place, and under the right circumstances. Our challenge is thus to clarify our understanding of what is meant by technique and to begin the process of cataloguing these actions.

TOWARD A DEFINITION

Although as yet there does not appear to be full consensus in our literature on what is meant by technique, there is now a sufficient number of usages that reflect formal definitions, as found in dictionaries, to conclude that we are moving toward a more precise definition. Based on a review of these trends, we have formulated a definition that will serve us for the remainder of the book.

First, technique clearly refers to those things we do directly for, with, and to clients as ways of achieving some aspect of mutually identified goals for them. It is an action that is observable; that is, I need to be able to note when you are making use of a particular technique just as you need to be able to observe when I am doing so.

A technique should also be understandable from some body or bodies of theory that are a part of our profession's knowledge base. This does not mean that each of us will utilize a particular technique from the same theory base. For example, I might make use of a particular technique from a cognitive perspective, and my colleague might use one from an existential base. The important factor is that in using the technique, each of us has a theoretical base to explain our use of it, even though we both are doing the same thing.

A technique also requires the quality of replicability. That is, it is something that can be learned and taught to others. In this way it can become a part of the armamentarium of the profession.

It goes without saying that a technique must be ethical. Included in this is some degree of professional legitimization. As yet we do not have such a formalized procedure for techniques. However, within the sociology of the profession there is a range of ways in which something becomes a recognized part of the profession's body of tools.

Building on these characteristics, we define a technique in social work as "**the artistic use of some practical object or activity by a social worker as a component of treatment aimed at achieving an identified outcome. Such action or object is replicable by others, is ethical, has a level of professional approbation, and is understandable from a relevant theoretical perspective.**"

ORIGINS OF TECHNIQUES

As we view techniques as the tools or instruments of our practice, we would assume that many, (if not most) techniques emerge from theories, which of course they do. However, this is not to imply that various theories own various techniques, even if they have originated from that particular theory.

Just as we have become comfortable with the concept of permeable boundaries between theories, so too are we coming to understand the same permeability of techniques. In this way, adherents to different theories will find different uses for the same technique.

Techniques also originate in the practice of various methods, and, as with theories, many of them then become a part of all social work methods. In the same way, many techniques that originate in other professions can be understood and utilized by social work practitioners, as with many behavioral techniques.

Techniques emerge from research, both in the formal sense of testing out new ideas in a measurable manner, but also in an informal practitioner manner, such as when someone says to herself/himself, "I wonder if...." Thus our own idiosyncratic selves can be a source of new techniques, bearing in mind always the responsibility to ensure something is ethical and that one can claim it has some degree of professional legitimacy. (Some of this legitimacy often comes from the approbation of the profession's gurus.)

Techniques also emerge from cultural and ethnic diversity. In recent years we have learned much from clients and colleagues with different diversity profiles about ways in which social work is practiced in other cultures, and how they can be applicable to our own practice.

In summary, although techniques originate from a diversity of social systems, they are an entity of their own. Our professional challenge is to learn to use each responsibly in various ways to accomplish a diversity of specific therapeutic goals.

We stress this point to avoid the position that there is a specific use for each technique, and that if I want to achieve a particular goal I will only use this technique. Obviously certain techniques will have more specificity of use than others, but as we continue to view them as tools that enrich our ability to apply theories, we will undoubtedly find many uses for each.

Before we turn to a discussion of our "101 techniques," two comments are necessary. First there is no magic in the figure 101. We used this title to avoid giving the idea that this is a closed list. As we searched the literature for techniques to add to our list, we concluded that, rather than just 101 techniques, there may in fact be many hundreds of them extant in our profession not yet identified, let alone catalogued. Thus we see this work only as a beginning step toward a more complete listing of social work techniques—a listing that will never end as our theories and practice continue to develop.

Similarly, we need to speak to the question of how to classify techniques, a challenge that emerged as we collected our material for this book. It was clear from the beginning that there are different kinds of techniques in our current body of practice. It is also our view that at this time we are probably not ready to move to a definitive formal classification schema. Early in our deliberations we attempted to formulate just such a schema, and in an early draft of the book we presented the 101 techniques according to the type of technique into which we adjudged them to fall. Eventually we decided that this would not be useful for this project. Rather, what we have done is to assign a number to each technique that corresponds to the following list of techniques. This is not a closed listing. As we address more attention to this, we will undoubtedly find other and more precise categories of techniques. This first step, however, will assist us in linking theories to techniques and in giving direction to how we select techniques for specific treatment goals.

From our observations to date we concluded that techniques fall into 10 categories. They are:

1. General techniques related to the use of self in interviewing.
2. Techniques where the social worker does something specific with the client in an interview.
3. Techniques where the client is asked to do something specific in the interview.
4. Techniques using tangible objects directly with the client.
5. Techniques making use of particular persons directly with the client.
6. Techniques making use of technology.
7. Techniques where the social worker makes specific use of the setting for a therapeutic goal.

8. Techniques where the client is encouraged to do something specific outside of the interview.
9. Techniques where the social worker acts on behalf of the client outside of an interview.
10. Techniques that originate from Native American, Alaska Native, and First Nations peoples and the traditions and practices of other cultural groups.

There is one further question of classification that has proven to be particularly challenging for this project: how to address the question of specific and generic techniques. It was clear in our review of techniques that, apart from any other approaches to classification we might take, one approach had to be considered. It relates to how we should classify such things as behavioral techniques, of which there are probably some 200 or more distinct methods, along with many standardized instruments. Any listing of social work techniques, no matter how preliminary, must include some reference to these. At this time, we are not able to list them all in a project such as this. Our decision on how to best deal with this challenge was to include brief discussions of four so-called generic topics under a separate section of our technique listing—Music, Play, Projective Instruments, and Behavioral Techniques—and to include three specific techniques from each.

Last, one theme emerged as we examined the range of techniques, which we refer to as the *risk factor*. It became obvious to us that the use of some techniques versus others varied widely in their potential risk to clients. Some techniques only require an attentive, concerned, beginner-level professional to be used safely, whereas other techniques require skilled, knowledgeable, supervised practitioners. We currently do not have a precise measure for each technique. What we did do was to make a judgment for each of the listed techniques on a 4-point scale ranging from low risk (A) to high risk (D). We saw this as a first step in assessing risk and hope that as we give this concept more attention, we can get more precise.

Clearly the risk associated with each technique will differ from client to client. Attempting to assign a "risk score" to them in any highly generalized way thus creates an aura of objectivity that could be misleading. Just as clearly, however, some of the techniques we have addressed require more knowledge, skill, and sensitivity to use responsibly than others.

For example, one of the techniques used by some social workers that we have included is hypnosis, a technique that clearly requires more knowledge training and consultation than "learning to listen" to a client in an attentive, helping way, another one of our 101 cluster. By applying a 4-point score to our 101 techniques, we want to alert colleagues to the fact that they must be constantly conscious of the fact that our interventions with clients are going to have different impacts, and that we must be alert to this fact. Our assigned score only indicates our perceived sense of potential risk inherent in each technique from a generic perspective. But our practice also requires a separate assessment of whether this judgment applies or does not apply in a particular case. It is our expectation that as we give this concept of risk more attention, patterns will emerge that will help us to make this a more precise factor.

SOME COLLEGIAL CLOSING COMMENTS

We would hope that as we become more conscious of how the ways we help clients—as well as the ways in which we intervene with them—can cause pain and harm, we will be able to develop more accurate and precise risk scales.

As researchers, we certainly embarked on this project out of a perception that, as a doing profession built on a very rich body of theory, social work had done little to identify how our theoretical base can best be put into practice. This we do by being sensitive to what we do when we are with clients, and how these actions are or are not related to what we know.

We hope that this book will be used by practitioners seeking to enhance their practice skills by enriching their interventions with an expanded repertoire of techniques that we have come to use differentially. We also hope it will be of particular use to students and beginning colleagues.

We see the book being used in several other ways. If we have viewed practice correctly, it is a work that should help us perceive practice world in a broader, more operational way. Not only should these data help us think more precisely of what specific things we do in particular cases, but our spectrum of techniques also should help us better understand the range of things that are not part of our practice repertoires. That is, we hope our 101 techniques will present a range of other things that we might do that will fit specific clients in much richer way than what we are doing now.

The 101 techniques also help us in a more generic way to expand our interventional profile, and to break out of fixed patterns of responding to clients, thus making us more effective and differentially responsive to them.

We are well aware that there are many more techniques than the 101 we have identified. As we get more "technique sensitive," it is our hope that this list will expand and that we will begin to find a richer understanding of patterns of clustering, which will show when various techniques are more helpful and—most important—when they are not and with whom.

The book has been arranged to be as useful as possible to our colleagues. The list of techniques in the previous section is presented alphabetically, to reflect our position that we view all to be of equal importance; it is how we use and understand them that makes them differentially useful. Each technique has been assigned a number of from 1 to 10 to help users understand where the technique fits into our matrix of technique types. Each is also assigned a letter ranging from A to D to aid the user in understanding our judgment of the possible harm that can be done by misusing the technique.

With the discussion of each technique we have included a brief list of references to demonstrate that the technique has professional legitimacy and deserves to be included. And last, each technique includes one or two examples of its direct use. The material for the examples has been provided by experienced practitioners, and of course has been considerably disguised and altered to prevent any possibility of identification.

Overall, our goal is to enrich our practice by beginning to build a wider and broader bridge between the use of theory to a more deliberate use of techniques.

Types of Techniques

1. General techniques related to the use of self in the interview.

2. Techniques where the social worker does something specific with the client in the interview.

3. Techniques where the client is asked to do something specific in the interview.

4. Techniques using tangible objects directly with the client.

5. Techniques making use of particular persons directly with the client.

6. Techniques making use of technology.

7. Techniques where the social worker makes specific use of the setting for a therapeutic goal.

8. Techniques where the client is encouraged to do something specific outside of the interview.

9. Techniques where the social worker acts on behalf of the client outside of the interview.

10. Techniques that originate from Native American, Alaska Native, and First Nations peoples and the traditions and practices of other cultural groups.

RISK CATEGORIES

A—Minimal Risk
B—Slight Risk
C—Moderate
D—High Risk

REFERENCES AND ADDITIONAL SOURCES

Goldstein, H. (1973). *Social work practice: A unitary approach.* Columbia, SC: University of South Carolina Press.

Kasius, C. (Ed.). (1950). *Principles and techniques in social casework.* New York: Family Association of America.

Perlman, H. H. (1957). *Social casework a problem solving process.* Chicago and London: University of Chicago Press.

PART TWO

101 SOCIAL WORK TECHNIQUES

SPECIFIC TECHNIQUES

Advice

DESCRIPTION

Advice as a technique refers to deliberate actions on the part of the social worker to convey to the client verbally and overtly a wish that he or she do or not do something in relation to some aspect of the client's situation.

ORIGINS

It is a technique that has not had a high status in our discussions of treatment. In our professional tradition, the popular position has been that we ought not to give advice to clients. Such actions on our part are viewed as diminishing client autonomy and self-determination. Advice is viewed as an imposition of the social worker's values on the client.

Its origins as an acceptable technique are unclear in that it has long been considered (and still is, by some) not to be good practice. However, experienced clinicians know that, in spite of this tradition, there are times when our professional opinion about some aspect of our clients' lives requires that we convey to them our view as to what they should or should not do.

WHY THIS IS USEFUL TO SOCIAL WORK

Despite our discomfort with the practice over the years, it has become evident that, at times, we do draw on our knowledge, expertise, experience, and understanding of the client and their situation to attempt to influence their actions through giving advice. We do this to help them avoid pursuing or continuing a particular act or pattern of action that, in our estimation, would produce or continue a problem or be dangerous to themselves or others.

HOW THIS IS USEFUL TO SOCIAL WORK

Advice is a technique in our repertoire that draws on the power and influence of the worker on the client to have them proceed in a particular manner when it is likely that they are not going to take the needed action on their own. This is done to avoid situations or actions that could be detrimental to the client or significant others in their lives. Indeed, at times matters of life or death could be at stake.

RISK FACTORS

In using this technique, it is essential that we understand both our own need or wish to give advice and our own reluctance to do so. This ensures that our use or nonuse of advice giving does not become a way of meeting our own needs rather than clients'.

Another practice challenge for the social worker in regards to this technique occurs in situations where we are dealing with a client who perceives the therapeutic process as one in which she or he will be given advice on how to manage their lives. This is a common perception of therapy for many beginning clients. In such situations, we are seen as the experts in a particular field, and the client looks to us for this expertise in the form of advice giving. We can then easily be drawn into ineffectual or inappropriate uses of the technique.

At times, failing to make use our of advice can have detrimental effects for a client and his or her significant others. This can happen when the client is engaged in or planning to engage in behavior that is illegal or dangerous to the client or someone in his or her life.

Advice giving is a powerful technique when skillfully and appropriately used, but it is fraught with uncertainty. We therefore view it as having a high risk factor.

REQUIRED SKILLS AND KNOWLEDGE

Effective use of this technique requires considerable skill and understanding of the client and their situation. The way we will give advice will range from such comments as, "I wonder what would happen if you did so and so?" to a firm "Mr. Jones, it is imperative that you do such-and-such and do so immediately." Clearly, in giving advice we will need to select the appropriate level for the situation, preferring to use a more gentle form of advice giving than something more direct and laden with authority.

Because of our longstanding tradition of not giving advice, social workers sometimes pretend to themselves that we are not advising, when in fact we are and the client is recognizing our intervention as advice. Thus the use of, "I wonder what would happen …" will be seen by many clients as our giving advice when we did not intend to do so. The important thing here is that we are clear in our own minds when we are giving advice and when we are not.

Beginning workers often misuse this technique in their strong wish to help clients move to a more healthy level of functioning or to attain identified treatment goals more quickly. This is especially risky when one is working from a problem-solving perspective. The solution to the client's problem may be quite obvious, but the client may not be ready or able to take the necessary steps. In our wish to have the client move ahead, we can be easily tempted to advise them about what they need to do.

Because of the continuing perception that we do not and ought not to give advice, there has been little research on the use of advice as a technique. Advice giving needs to be studied in detail because of its potentially powerful effect in both a positive and negative direction. Because it is so powerful, we ought not to avoid using it, lest by failing to develop our advice-giving skills, we also fail our clients when they most need them.

Case Summary One

Erica is currently attending therapy sessions to try and cope with the negative effects of a recent breakup.

SOCIAL WORKER: What would you like to discuss during session today?

ERICA: I am still writing e-mails to my ex-boyfriend. I can't seem to stop. I just keep thinking that he'll write me back eventually.

SOCIAL WORKER: If you're trying to get over this relationship, it is probably not a good idea to continue contacting him. You've stated in the past that when you write to your ex-boyfriend and you don't receive a response back, you become depressed and start to regress in the progress that you've made. I wonder what would happen if you stopped writing to him.

ERICA: I have no idea what would happen. I feel this compulsion to write to him every few days. It feels like if I don't write to him I am going to explode or something.

SOCIAL WORKER: I wonder what would happen if, when you felt that way, instead of writing to him you did something else. Maybe instead of writing to your ex-boyfriend, which produces negative feelings, you could write about your feelings in a journal or call a trusted friend to talk about how you're feeling. These are more positive ways of coping with the compulsive, exploding feeling you said you are having.

ERICA: If you think it will help, I am willing to try it.

Erica's social worker did not think that she would stop writing to her ex-boyfriend on her own, but knew it was not healthy for her and was causing her unnecessary problems. Her social worker's understanding of her situation and the way she functions allowed her social worker to present Erica with advice in a way that the social worker knew she would best receive it. Erica views her social worker as a professional with expertise and she gladly took the advice given to her.

Case Summary Two

Dave is attending therapy sessions to treat what he describes as intense feelings of worry and sadness. Through the course of treatment, Dave told his social worker about some physical symptoms he has been experiencing. Dave reports that he attributes these symptoms solely to anxiety.

SOCIAL WORKER: During your last session we discussed the fact that you were experiencing headaches quite frequently and having a hard time falling asleep at night. We also talked about the impact these symptoms were having on your life. Before you left that day, we discussed you getting checked out by your doctor. Were you able to do that?

DAVE: No, I haven't been to the doctor yet. I just haven't had the time. I'll get to one eventually. I'm sure I'm only experiencing those symptoms because I'm an anxious person. I worry and get nervous and I react physically. That's all there is to it and that's why I'm here: to fix that.

SOCIAL WORKER: While this could be true, it is still imperative that you see your primary care physician as soon as possible to rule out a medical reason for your symptoms. If you continue experiencing these symptoms and you don't find out what is causing them, it could be very dangerous for you. If the symptoms come from a medical issue, but you don't get it treated because you think they only come from an emotional problem, it could really be harmful to you.

DAVE: I think you're right. You do make some good points. I promise I will call my doctor when I get home to make an appointment. I'll make sure that I get checked out before our next session.

SOCIAL WORKER: I'm glad to hear you say that. It is important to make sure you are healthy physically, mentally, and emotionally.

There are times in the therapeutic relationship when it is appropriate or even necessary for a social worker to offer his or her professional advice or opinion about what should or should not be done in a client's life. Although Dave seemed convinced that his symptoms were merely reactions to his feelings, his social worker was not so sure. According to the social worker, it is not clear whether the physical symptoms Dave is experiencing are due to his feelings of anxiety or because of some medical reason that could be dangerous to him. The social worker's professional position and perceived expertise in the therapeutic relationship allowed him to offer advice that was well received by his client.

REFERENCES AND ADDITIONAL SOURCES

Anderson, H. (2001). Postmodern collaborative and person-centred therapies: What would Carl Rogers say? *Journal of Family Therapy, 23,* 339.

Beck, A. T. (1995). *Cognitive therapy: Basics and beyond.* New York: Guilford Press.

Galvin, K., Sharples, A., & Jackson, D. (2000) Citizens Advice Bureaux in general practice: An illuminative evaluation. *Health and Social Care in the Community, 8*(4), 277–282.

Corey, G., Corey, M., & Callahan, P. (1998). *Issues and ethics in the helping professions*. Pacific Grove, CA: Brooks/Cole.

Couture, S. J., & Sutherland, O. (2006). Giving advice on advice-giving: A conversation analysis of Karl Tomm's practice. *Journal of Marital and Family Therapy, 32*(3), 329–344.

Ellis, A. (2001). *Overcoming destructive beliefs, feelings, and behaviors*. Amherst, NY: Prometheus Books.

Ingram, R. E., & Scott, W. D. (1990). Cognitive behavior therapy. In A. S. Bellack, M. Hersen, & A. E. Karzin (Eds.), *International handbook of behavior modification and therapy* (2nd ed., pp. 53–65). New York, NY: Plenum.

Haley, J. (1987). *Problem-solving therapy* (2nd ed.). San Francisco, CA: Jossey-Bass.

Hepworth, D. H., Rooney, R. H., & Larsen, J. (1997). *Direct social work practice* (5th ed.). New York: Brooks/Cole.

Heritage, J., & Sefi, S. (1992). Dilemmas of advice: Aspects of delivery and reception of advice in interactions between health visitors and first time mothers. In P. Drew & J. Heritage (Eds.), *Talk at work: Interactions in institutional settings* (pp. 359–417). Cambridge, England: Cambridge University Press.

Kirschenbaum, H., & Henderson, V. L. (1989). *Carl Rogers reader*. Boston, MA: Houghton Mifflin.

Mosak, H., & Maniacci, M. P. (1998). *Tactics in counseling and psychotherapy*. Itasca, IL: Peacock.

Northen, H. (1995). *Clinical social work knowledge and skills* (2nd ed.). New York, NY: Columbia University Press.

Prochaska, J. O., & Norcross, J. C. (2003). *Systems of psychotherapy: A transtheoretical analysis* (5th ed.). Pacific Grove, CA: Brooks/Cole.

Shebib, B. (2000). *Choices: Practical interviewing and counseling skills*. Needham Heights, MA: Allyn & Bacon.

Turner, F. J. (1996). *Social work treatment: interlocking theoretical approaches*. New York, NY: Free Press.

Vehviläinen, S. (2001). Evaluative advice in educational counseling: The use of disagreement in the "stepwise entry" to advice. *Research on Language and Social Interaction, 34*, 371–398.

Advocacy

DESCRIPTION

This technique addresses those skills we utilize to involve ourselves in some aspect of the client's external reality in cases where some form of systemic change that will benefit the client, or that he or she needs, is being sought.

ORIGINS

Advocacy is of course a major method of social work practice and needs to be considered as such in discussions of practice. This twofold thrust of our profession, one to alter societal factors and the other to change individuals, has always been one of its strengths, even though at times the duality creates misunderstanding of the profession both within and without. In addition to understanding the complexities of a client's social system so we can seek macro changes, it is also sometimes useful for us to employ the technique of advocacy to intervene in some specific way in that social system.

WHY THIS IS USEFUL TO SOCIAL WORK

This technique is especially important for social work clinical practice because of our understanding that clients' problems often arise from stresses or difficulties in their external life, and they lack either the ability to bring about change by skillful manipulation of one or another systemic component, or the understanding of how to do so. It is one of the few professions in which equal focus is given to bringing about change in a client's reality as well as change in the client.

HOW THIS IS USEFUL TO SOCIAL WORK

This technique is useful in situations where, with the client's permission, we take action in some particular system or specific life situation. This might be a situation where we intervene with a school, a city official, or a landlord, or in any number of systemic problems of day-to-day life in which a person or family can become involved where a social worker's intervention can be useful and influential. In each situation, the required intervention or action is something that, in our judgment, the client is not able to undertake himself or herself. This judgment is based on our conviction that we can put forward the client's position more clearly, objectively, persuasively, and effectively than the client could on his or her own.

The power of this technique that assists us in seeking a favorable change for the client comes from the power inherent in the social work role; the setting we represent; our skills in writing, speaking, or negotiating; or even just being a part of the human service system. We need to remember that we bring to situations our knowledge of how bureaucratic systems function and the occasional advantage of dealing directly with a significant other in the client's life.

Although we speak of the technique of advocacy as something we do ourselves, in some situations it may be more effective to involve someone else who can speak on the client's behalf. This decision will be based on our skill in assessing the situation, in deciding with the client if using someone else might enhance the possibility of a more favorable outcome or change in a situation, and, if so, in deciding on the skills and resources needed to bring about the desired outcome.

At times, even though we or some chosen colleague has been designated to speak for the client in a specific situation, it may happen that the client will be present with us. For example, this might occur when a client is being heard by some type of review panel or committee that has discretion over the requested outcome.

Although advocacy is a technique in its own right, the format in which we utilize it can vary greatly. Our strategy may cover a spectrum ranging from an informal discussion of the matter over lunch with a colleague, to a formal, written brief or presentation to a legislative body with the power to make a decision regarding the client.

RISK FACTORS

This specific use of advocacy as a clinical technique has a moderate to high degree of risk that we need to keep before us. One risk is that our actions could bring attention to the client that might have a secondary negative impact, either immediately or in later contact with the component of the client's social system in which we have become involved on his or her behalf.

There is also the risk that the advocacy actions in which we engage might result in harm to the client's right to confidentiality. This may be highly stressful for the client, even though we might feel good about changing the system.

We need also be sure that we have the necessary knowledge and skills to act on the client's behalf, in particular through systems such as courts or government bodies, so that we do not cause further difficulties for the client.

REQUIRED SKILLS AND KNOWLEDGE

It is our knowledge of systems, and our skill at seeking alternatives and assessing situations from a systems perspective, that prepare us to make this technique powerful and effective.

In actually employing this technique, it is essential that we know that the client wishes us to act for them, and that the goal is more likely to be achieved if someone else acts for the client.

In viewing advocacy as a clinical technique, we need to be assured that it is the client who is seeking a particular goal and not us. There is always the risk that we might use advocacy because of our own wish to change some situation, rather than the client's. The two are not mutually exclusive, of course, but it is essential that it is the client's wishes that are taken into account.

Case Summary One

Pete is a child doing poorly in school. Pete's mother constantly has been receiving phone calls from the school requesting that she pick him up because of his misbehavior. Pete has been suspended several times, and both the school and Pete's mom have become fed up with the situation. Pete was recently tested for and given a diagnosis of ADHD. He is currently taking prescribed medications, but the school is unaware of this. The school has scheduled a meeting and Pete's mother is worried that they will try to throw him out of school. She has invited his social worker to the meeting to act as an advocate for Pete.

Pete, his mother, his social worker, his teacher, and his guidance counselor all met for a team meeting.

GUIDANCE COUNSELOR: We are here to discuss Pete's disruptive behavior in the classroom and his educational future.

MOM: I would like Pete to remain in this school, and I would also like to end his frequent suspensions.

SOCIAL WORKER: I have had several sessions with Pete and his mother. Originally, the school believed that Pete was just acting out, but testing has confirmed a diagnosis of ADHD.

TEACHER: His behavior in the classroom is unacceptable. It does not allow him or any of the other students to listen and learn effectively.

SOCIAL WORKER: Now that Pete has been assigned a diagnosis of ADHD, he takes prescribed medication and receives therapy to alleviate his symptoms.

MOM: Yes, I give him one pill in the morning and it should last throughout his school day. He should be able to concentrate more now.

SOCIAL WORKER: Also, we would like to see Pete placed in a smaller classroom where he has fewer distractions and is able to receive a little more one-on-one attention.

GUIDANCE COUNSELOR: Now that we have received this information, we can start the paperwork to accommodate Pete's needs.

Having Pete's social worker attend the meeting and advocate for his education provided necessary support for his mother, and helped to reinforce her needs in a professional way. In this meeting, Pete's mom wasn't seen as just another parent frustrated with the school and wanting it to stop bugging her at work. The social worker's comments and professional opinions were taken seriously because they came from an objective third party.

Case Summary Two

Kate has been attending therapy sessions for about three months. Recently she experienced a setback in her treatment caused by a traumatic event that occurred in her family. At this point in her treatment, Kate has asked to be seen weekly, and her social worker agrees that weekly sessions would be beneficial, at least for a few months. However, Kate's insurance will only authorize her to be seen by her social worker twice per month. It is the agency's general policy to see clients only as often as their insurance will authorize. If a client wants to see a social worker more often, it is their responsibility to pay full price for sessions. The agency's sliding fee scale is usually supposed to be offered only to clients who have no insurance coverage at all. Kate is a single mother who works hard to provide for her family, and she cannot afford to pay full price for therapy sessions.

SOCIAL WORKER: We both agree that at this point in time it is in your best interest to attend therapy sessions weekly. However, you have mentioned that you are unable to pay for services that aren't covered by your insurance.

KATE: Yes, that's correct. I work so hard to provide for my family on my own and unfortunately I just can't afford the price of the extra sessions.

SOCIAL WORKER: Well, I am happy to tell you that I was able to advocate on your behalf and get my supervisor to agree to allow you to pay for your extra sessions according to the agency's sliding fee scale and what you can afford to pay.

KATE: I can't believe it. That is amazing. I don't have a lot of money, but I really need these extra sessions. Thank you so much.

In this case, Kate's social worker was able to advocate on her behalf to obtain an authorization that will help to provide the services necessary for Kate's well-being. The advocacy of Kate's social worker demonstrated that her social worker's supports her and is in agreement with Kate's treatment desires.

REFERENCES AND ADDITIONAL SOURCES

Bowes, A., & Sim, D. (2006). Advocacy for black and minority ethnic communities: Understandings and expectations. *British Journal of Social Work, 36*, 1209–1225.

Brydon, K. (2010). Social work advocacy in Singapore: some reflections on the constraints and opportunities. *Asian Social Work and Policy Review, 4*(3), 119–133.

Clark, E. J. (2007). Advocacy: Profession's cornerstone. *NASW News, 52*(7), 3.

Compton, B., Galoway, B., & Cournoyer, B. (2005). *Social work processes* (7th ed.). Pacific Grove, CA: Brooks/Cole.

Davis, C., Baldry, E., Milosevic, B., & Walsh, A. (2004). Defining the role of the hospital social worker in Australia. *International Social Work, 47*(3), 346–358.

Davis, C., Milosevic, B., Baldry, E., & Walsh, A. (2005). Defining the role of the hospital social worker in Australia: Part 2. A qualitative approach. *International Social Work, 48*(3), 289–299.

Dorfman, R. A. (1996). *Clinical social work: Definition, practice, and vision.* New York: Brunner/Mazel.

Egan, G. (2007). *The skilled helper* (8th ed.). Belmont, CA: Thomson Brooks/Cole.

Faust, J. R. (2008). Clinical social worker as patient advocate in a community mental health center. *Clinical Social Work Journal, 36*(3), 293–300.

Forster, R. (1998). Patient advocacy in psychiatry: The Austrian and Dutch model. *International Social Work, 41*(2), 155–167.

Gehart, D., & Lucas, B. (2007). Client advocacy in marriage and family therapy: A qualitative case study. *Journal of Family Psychotherapy, 18*(1), 39–56.

Goldstein, E. G. (2007). Social work education and clinical learning: Yesterday, today, tomorrow. *Clinical Social Work Journal, 35*, 15–23.

Haynes, K., & Mickelson, J. (2000). *Affecting change: Social work in the political arena* (4th ed.). New York: Songman.

Heinonen, T., & Spearman, L. (2006). *Social work practice: Problem solving and beyond* (2nd ed.). Toronto, Ontario: Tompson/Nelson.

Hepworth, D. H., Rooney, R. H., & Larsen, J. A. (2002). *Direct social work practice: Theory and skills* (6th ed.). Pacific Grove, CA: Brooks/Cole.

Herbert, M., & Levin, R. (1996). The advocacy role in hospital social work. *Social Work in Health Care, 22*(3), 71–83.

Herbert, M., & Mould, J. (1992). The advocacy role in public child welfare. *Child Welfare, 71*(2), 114–130.

Hoefer, R. (2006). *Advocacy practice for social justice.* Chicago, IL: Lyceum Books.

Kirst-Ashman, K., & Hull, G. (2006). *Understanding generalist practice* (4th ed.). Belmont, CA: Thomson Brooks/Cole.

Kiselica, M. S., & Robinson, M. (2001). Bringing advocacy counseling to life: The history, issues, and human dramas of social justice work in counseling. *Journal of Counseling & Development, 79*(4), 387–397.

Lens, V., & Gibelman, M. (2000). Advocacy, be not forsaken: Retrospective lessons from welfare reform. *Families in Society, 18*(6), 611–620.

Mitchell, J., & Lynch, R. S. (2003). Beyond the rhetoric of social and economic justice: Redeeming the social work advocacy role. *Race, Gender & Class, 10*(2), 8–26.

McLaughlin, A. M. (2009). Clinical social workers: Advocates for social justice. *Advances in Social Work, 10*(1), 51–68.

Miley, K. K., O'Melia, M., & DuBois, B. (2007). *Generalist social work practice: An empowerment approach* (5th ed.). Boston, MA: Allyn & Bacon.

Pearlmutter, S. (2002). Archiving political practice: Interpreting individual need and social action. *Journal of Progressive Human Services, 13*(1), 31–51.

Poulin, J. (2005). *Strength-based generalist practice: A collaborative approach*. Belmont, CA: Brooks/Cole-Thomson Learning.

Schneider, R. L., & Lester, L. (2000). *Social work advocacy: A new framework for action*. Belmont, CA: Brooks/Cole.

Segal, E., Gerdes, K., & Steiner, S. (2007). *An introduction to the profession of social work: Becoming a change agent*. Belmont, CA: Brooks/Cole.

Sheafor, B. W., & Horejsi, C. R. (2008). *Techniques and guidelines for social work practice* (8th ed.). Boston: Allyn & Bacon.

Simpson, G. A., Williams, J. C., & Segall, A. B. (2007). Social work education and clinical learning. *Clinical Social Work Journal, 35*, 3–14.

Tahan, H. A. (2005). Essentials of advocacy in case management. *Lippincott's Case Management, 10*(3), 136–145.

Van Voorhis, R., & Hostetter, C. (2006). The impact of MSW education on social worker empowerment and commitment to client empowerment through social justice advocacy. *Journal of Social Work Education, 42*(1), 105–121.

Walker, S. (2004). Community work and psychosocial practice: Chalk and cheese or birds of a feather? *Journal of Social Work Practice, 18*(2), 161–175.

Willard, C. (1996). The nurse's role as patient advocate: Obligation or imposition? *Journal of Advanced Nursing, 24*, 60–66.

Woods, M. E., & Hollis, F. (1990). *Casework: A psychosocial therapy* (3rd ed.). New York: McGraw-Hill.

Agency Structure

DESCRIPTION

Although ordinarily we do not think of the variables of our agency or practice setting—with all its history, traditions, structures, resources, reputation, policies, and sponsorship—to be treatment resources, there are occasional opportunities to draw on these variables as techniques in our practice.

ORIGINS

Probably the first discussions in the literature of the influence of agency structure on the treatment process are to be found in the functionalist literature of the 1940s. In this era, the challenges of working in the authoritative milieu of child protection were examined, and methods for how one could practice "casework" in a positive and effective way by making the structure itself a positive treatment technique were found.

The concept of building upon the administrative structure of an agency as an enabling resource is once again receiving consideration. For example, the current climate of third-party restrictions on the amount, frequency, and types of service available to clients in particular situations often require us and the client to work in a climate with a range of inherent restrictions.

The same kinds of challenge emerge in settings where a part of the social worker's responsibility is the issuance of financial or "in kind" resources, for which the regulations are often very strict. In these instances, from the beginning the setting partly shapes the climate in which the helping process takes place. The setting has a similar effect in settings such as the military, where the strong influence of tradition, authority, rank, and protocol is a reality.

Although the common perception among practitioners has been that these type of socio-administrative realities are limiting variables, in fact they can be turned into helpful realities when viewed as techniques.

WHY THIS IS USEFUL TO SOCIAL WORK

Few if any life situations do not impose some limitations on all of us. Thus, learning to live within societally imposed limitations is a part of reality that we all have to come to terms with in our maturational journey. Helping clients to do so can be very enabling for them. In this way, our practice settings can be seen as miniature life realities, and when the opportunity presents itself in treatment, a client can be helped to see how their reaction to the limits of an agency may well reflect the way they react to their day-to-day, multiphase limitations. Learning to cope with agency limitations with our help, as well as learning how to tap the potential of the agency's mores, can be a useful way for clients to learn to deal with other life situations.

HOW THIS IS USEFUL TO SOCIAL WORK

In considering how agency structure can be a limiting factor in treatment from a negative perspective, it is important also to remember that there may be many positives in the agency that can be converted into helping techniques. For example, the overall climate of an agency may be very oriented toward outreach and support, an experience to which the client may not be accustomed. If the social worker and client examine this attitude and learning experience together, it may well improve in a supportive, nourishing way the client's perception of other systems that might be available. The same would apply to the reputation of the setting, a positive aspect that may well make a client feel more secure.

There are many aspects of our settings that can serve to make people feel wanted, respected, understood, challenged, and empowered simply through the overall impact of the physical setting that understands the importance of the small, positively sensitive attributes of the setting and its policies and procedures.

We have all experienced situations where some clients will blame us and insist that we or others change the agency's regulations or limiting policies. Others will see such factors in a pessimistic or fatalistic way and assume that nothing can be done. Still others will see these qualities as further proof that the system is against them. Helping a client focus on these reactions can, in some instances, be the essence of our impact on a client. We can help then see that this understanding can be carried over into their daily life, in the form of a more positive and less problematic manner of dealing with systemic limitations.

RISK FACTORS

This technique has a low risk factor; however, mistakes can be made. From our perspective the risk of building inherent time limitations into our practice profile is that clients, aware that there is only a certain amount of time available, may push themselves too hard, when what they need is the opportunity to process their way through very complex material. Alternatively, we may push too hard in our wish to be as helpful as possible in the time available. Although setting limitations may be helpful overall, any of them can become very unhelpful and do real harm to a client.

There are further serious and inherent risks in working within the reality of agency restrictions related to various components of treatment. For example, we might disagree with various limitations that our agencies impose on us, and we might convey these attitudes directly, overtly, or subtly to the client. When this happens, the treatment process can begin to take on a mutual anti-setting quality that may seriously interfere with what the client needs and wants and can use from the setting. That is, our own negative feelings about the aspects of the agency could begin to impact the relationship.

REQUIRED SKILLS AND KNOWLEDGE

In summary, we need to learn to assess, as did the functionalists of yore, to what extent the parameters of policy and practice in our work settings are a reality both for us and for particular clients' needs and goals. We must do this with a focus on the strengths and limitations of the setting from the perspective of each client, and with an aim to ascertain how we might deliberately build on these realities to enhance our ability to help.

One of the positive results of very stringent restrictions (e.g., on the number of contacts permitted for particular situations) is that we have learned that, in some instances, we and the client can accomplish much more in brief contacts than was once thought. One secondary payoff of such a reality is that it provides an opportunity for a client to enhance their general skill at using time in other life situations. Thus it is important in our assessment of a client that we consider the possibility that the agency structure might be an influencing variable and build on it, whether it be positive or negative.

Case Summary One

Chris has been seeing his current social worker for about a month and a half. He has had other social workers in the past, but stopped attending sessions shortly after starting.

SOCIAL WORKER: So, Chris, how are you doing today?

CHRIS: I'm great. I love coming to your office. It's so bright and cheerful.

SOCIAL WORKER: Well, I'm glad it is a pleasant experience for you.

CHRIS: Yes, me too. I'm not used to such a positive atmosphere. As soon as I walk in I'm greeted by the receptionist, who always has a smile on her face. Coming to this agency makes me feel welcomed and supported. It brightens my entire day.

SOCIAL WORKER: You said that you're not used to seeing such a positive atmosphere. What are you used to?

CHRIS: I'm used to seeing negativity everywhere I go. I've been to similar agencies and it just seemed like the employees didn't really want to be there. Plus the atmosphere was kind of bleak and dull, no artwork on the walls or anything. I couldn't keep going back to those places for too long. The way this agency is structured and clients are taken care of is just wonderful. As a client I can really tell that the staff members and agency as a whole care about me. It is part of what keeps me coming back for services.

SOCIAL WORKER: I'm happy to hear that you feel comfortable coming to our agency and you feel supported by the staff. Perhaps we can look at this as a learning experience. Although you have felt some agencies were unsupportive and had a negative atmosphere, hopefully you realize that other agencies can have the same positive and supportive atmosphere that you feel our agency does.

CHRIS: Definitely. Coming here has kind of given me a renewed faith in the system and how it operates.

In the past Chris was unable to continue attending therapy sessions more than a few weeks due to what he felt was a negative atmosphere and unpleasant experience. He reports that he is able to progress in treatment at his current agency due to their positive structure. According to Chris, the agency's environment, staff, policies, and procedures all work together to make him feel wanted, respected, understood, supported, and empowered.

Case Summary Two

Ben is a middle-aged man who has never received therapy before. He recently started attending therapy sessions to work on managing his anger and decreasing his impulsive behavior.

BEN: I have to admit, I was really nervous about coming to see a social worker.

SOCIAL WORKER: That seems to be a common statement from clients. How do you feel now that you've been attending therapy sessions for a few weeks?

BEN: I feel good about attending therapy. I don't think I needed to be nervous.

SOCIAL WORKER: What helped to ease your nervous feelings?

BEN: What really helped me was your agency's reputation in the community. It was comforting to hear friends and family members tell me that if I was going to attend therapy sessions, then this is the place to come.

SOCIAL WORKER: That's great. What was it about our reputation that made you feel more comfortable?

BEN: Mainly, that your social workers are very experienced and are dedicated to helping their clients. Also, the fact that your agency provides office hours made to accommodate their clients' needs and lifestyle. To me, that shows your agency's commitment to their clients and desire for clients to be successful.

SOCIAL WORKER: I'm glad that our agency structure helped you to feel better about seeking treatment. It is very important that you feel supported in your journey towards reaching your treatment goals and I'm glad that our agency was able to provide that for you.

CLIENT: Me too. Honestly, if I hadn't heard such wonderful things about your agency I probably would've been too fearful or skeptical to seek treatment. Now I know that with the structure of your agency, treatment will be beneficial to my life.

The structure of the agency where Ben decided to attend therapy sessions provided him with a sense that the agency cared for and supported their clients. This understanding helped Ben feel comfortable enough to seek the treatment that he wanted, and gave him the confidence to know that he could successfully reach his treatment goals. This experience also helped Ben realize how important reputations can be. Ben is used to being known as an impulsive man with a bad temper. However, he has transferred his knowledge of the agency's reputation to his own life, and currently he is working on stopping and thinking about what he says and does more often.

REFERENCES AND ADDITIONAL SOURCES

Cigno, K., & Gore, J. (1999) A seamless service: Meeting the needs of children with disabilities through a multi-agency approach. *Child and Family Social Work, 4,* 325–335.

Friedländer, W. A. (1976). *Concepts and methods of social work.* (2nd ed.). Englewood Cliffs, NJ: Prentice-Hall.

Perlman, H. H. (1957). *Concepts and methods of social work.* Chicago, IL: University of Chicago Press.

Robbins, S. P. (1983). *Organization theory: The structure and design of organizations.* Englewood Cliffs, NJ: Prentice-Hall.

Turner, F. J. (1996). *Social work treatment: Interlocking theoretical approaches.* New York: NY: Free Press.

Analysis of Obstacles

DESCRIPTION

Analysis of obstacles refers to those precise activities of the social worker where we help the client focus on identifying things, situations, or people that may impede their ability to carry out particular activities identified in the therapeutic process, and then strategize ways with the client to avoid or minimize such obstacles.

ORIGINS

Social workers have always helped clients consider issues or factors that would impede their movement in a particular direction. However, it was with the advent of problem-solving theory, then task-oriented therapy, and still later solution-based therapy, that this activity took on a more formal role in treatment as a distinct technique.

WHY THIS IS USEFUL TO SOCIAL WORK

This technique is a most useful one to our practice in several ways. First, many clients we meet in contemporary practice have not learned how to anticipate difficulties in their lives that could have been avoided if they had foreseen them. When such difficulties do arise in their day-to-day living, serious disruptions in their equilibrium, far beyond the inherent intensity of the upsetting factor, can occur. One of the life skills that seems to be absent in their lives is learning to plan ahead. This process includes learning to identify or review potential obstacles that might interfere with carrying out a planned task.

HOW THIS IS USEFUL TO SOCIAL WORK

We know from our practice that it is often not enough just to work out with a client what they are going to do about a particular situation, but also to help them think about things that might occur that would impede the decided-upon task. Not only does this process help with regard to a particular planned course of action in treatment, but, once the skill is learned, it can have a secondary payoff for the client in daily life.

One of the possible outcomes of working with the client to identify obstacles is that, in the process of analyzing obstacles related to a particular decision or course of action, the mutual deliberation may lead to a decision not to move ahead with the course of action under consideration. This can, of course, be of considerable assistance to the client, as it may well deter them from a situation that, if followed, could have had serious consequences for the client or significant others in their lives.

RISK FACTORS

This technique has a moderate degree of risk. It implies a level of social worker knowledge that may be over-exaggerated both by the worker and the client. That is, in examining the pros and cons of a particular situation with the client, both parties might misread the situation and come up with an incorrect conclusion about some aspect of the situation.

This is, of course, a risk in all therapy. It is a reality that helps us remind ourselves that, in actively participating in this type of process with the client, mistakes will be made. This can make us overcautious about using this technique. Such caution may lead us to avoid helping the client in an analytic process at a time when it is greatly needed and sought. It is one of the many realities of our practice that keeps us humble and careful.

REQUIRED SKILLS AND KNOWLEDGE

The process of obstacle analysis is, for the most part, a cognitive exercise in which clients and worker participate together. The worker's input is often in the form of questions such as, "What are you going to do if… ?"

Obviously all possible situations that may stop a client from moving in a specific duration cannot and need not be examined. The worker's input is important here, as we are able to make use of our knowledge of similar situations to suggest important things the client has not thought about or is unaware.

Overly emphasizing a "What if?" style of examination could in itself be immobilizing. We are most helpful when we focus on the ordinary kinds of obstacles that a person might meet in particular situations. In addition to analyzing obstacles, social workers' suggestions, support, and encouragement are also needed.

Case Summary One

David has been in therapy for several months now and has recently started to work toward his goal of obtaining employment. David has been out of work for the past several months after being fired from his last job. David felt very low after losing his job and lacks self-worth. He has now reached the point where he can no longer survive economically without employment.

> SOCIAL WORKER: David, you've decided to start working toward your goal of obtaining employment. Let's try to think about some obstacles that might hinder you from achieving your goal so that you can work through them.
>
> DAVID: Okay.
>
> SOCIAL WORKER: What things do you think would impede your progress toward gaining employment?
>
> DAVID: Well, I'm probably not going to be the best candidate for any job that I apply for. Plus, I get very nervous around people in positions of power because I feel they are so much better than I am. What if the hiring manager laughs in my face and tells me to leave his office? I don't think I could handle that.
>
> SOCIAL WORKER: All right, I think you've identified a big obstacle, your negative self-talk. If you don't value yourself it's hard for anyone else to. What if you looked at yourself differently? You have a lot of things going for you. I understand your fear of rejection, but let's look at each job interview as a learning experience and as practice to have an even better job interview the next time.

By analyzing the obstacles that could impede David's progress toward his goal, the social worker was able to reframe and relabel the obstacles to make them into an opportunity for David rather than a problem. Together they were also able to confront and work on improving David's feelings of worthlessness and his fear of rejection before they hindered his chances of achieving his goal of gaining employment.

Case Summary Two

Tracy recently started attending therapy sessions with her 5-year-old son, Trevor. Tracy and her son meet with their social worker both individually and as a family. Trevor has repeatedly been characterized as a "problem child" and was kicked out of several preschools he attended. Tracy's long-term goal is for Trevor to be able to control his behavior and emotions enough to appropriately express himself in school and at home.

> TRACY: This has got to stop. His temper tantrums are getting worse and worse. Plus his demands are getting greater.
>
> SOCIAL WORKER: The first goal you decided on, to help reach your long-term goal, was to stop giving in to Trevor's temper tantrums. Throughout our last few individual sessions we

have reviewed many strategies for disciplining, setting limits, and avoiding power struggles. It sounds like you are ready to put these strategies into action. Is that correct?

TRACY: Yes, definitely. I used to think that things might get better or that he would just grow out of these tantrums, but it's not happening. I am very ready to start working towards my first goal.

SOCIAL WORKER: Great, I know you can do this. We'll work together one step at a time until we reach your long-term treatment goal. For now, let's discuss some obstacles you might encounter while trying to reach your first goal.

TRACY: Well, some nights I have to work late. Then, when I get home Trevor becomes very upset and starts throwing a temper tantrum if I don't immediately give him his every desire. I'm so tired after I come home from work that most of the time it's just easier to give Trevor what he's asking for, which I've learned only reinforces his tantrums.

SOCIAL WORKER: Okay, so your goal is to stop giving in to Trevor's temper tantrums as a way to extinguish this behavior, and also so that he will understand that tantrums will not get him what he wants. What if you start implementing the strategies we've discussed and his tantrums get worse? Or what if you are really tired while he is having a tantrum and just don't feel like following through with the discipline strategy?

TRACY: I know it's not going to be easy, but like you said earlier I can do this. Also, I understand that the change is not going to occur overnight, I have to stay consistent with Trevor. I don't care how tired I am after work; I just have to keep reminding myself that it will be worth it in the end.

Through analyzing the obstacles that Tracy might encounter while trying to achieve her goal, she is able to anticipate difficulties and try her best to avoid them or at least manage them better. The social worker's support and encouragement while discussing potential obstacles empowers Tracy to feel confident enough to overcome the obstacles she might face while achieving her goal. Analyzing obstacles in this situation will also help Tracy learn to plan ahead and to improve her problem-solving skills in other aspects of her daily life.

REFERENCES AND ADDITIONAL SOURCES

Beyer, M. (1986). Overcoming emotional obstacles to independence. *Children Today, 15*(5), 8–12.

Ellis, A., & Dryden, W. (1997). *The practice of rational emotive behavior therapy* (2nd ed.). New York, NY: Springer.

Lash, S. J., & Blosser, S. L. (1999). Increasing adherence to substance abuse aftercare group therapy. *Journal of Substance Abuse Treatment, 16*(1), 55–60.

McLean, L. S. (2002). Overcoming obstacles: Therapeutic success despite external barriers. *Primary Care Companion Journal of Clinical Psychiatry, 4*(1), 27–29.

Nezu, A. M., Nezu, C. M., & Lombardo, E. (2003). Problem-solving therapy. In W. T. O'Donohue, J. E. Fisher, & S. C. Hayes (Eds.), *Cognitive behavior therapy: Applying empirically supported techniques in your practice* (pp. 301–307). Hoboken, NJ: Wiley.

Peterson, M. L. (2002) Treatment planning with individuals. In A. R. Roberts & G. J. Greene (Eds.), *Social workers' desk reference* (pp. 320–323). New York, NY: Oxford University Press.

Reid, W. J. (1996) *Task-centered social work*. In F. J. Turner (Ed.), *Social work treatment: Interlocking theoretical approaches* (4th ed., pp. 69–93). New York, NY: Free Press.

Thorne, F. C. (2006). Directive psychotherapy: XVI, situational analysis. *Journal of Clinical Psychology, 4*(3), 290–298.

Art

DESCRIPTION

Although one can understand art as a generic methodology of practice that can be viewed as a unique approach to therapy under the title of art therapy, it can also be treated as a specific technique comprising a part of our overall cadre of treatment techniques. In this regard, the power of art to touch all of us in a cognitive, emotive, and revelatory way is being drawn upon.

ORIGINS

The use of art as a technique emerges from the experience of using drama as a therapeutic medium and the understanding that, like drama, art can touch us in a variety of ways that can assist the therapeutic process.

WHY THIS IS USEFUL TO SOCIAL WORK

Art is a useful technique because of its ability to convey or elicit strong feelings, responses, and memories of both a positive or negative nature in the viewer. It is also a resource that is readily available in printed or electronic formats.

HOW THIS IS USEFUL TO SOCIAL WORK

Just as existing art can influence a viewer, creating art can help clients express themselves. In this way, having clients make their own sketches or drawings can be a form of expression on the part of its creator. This activity often can help clients express significant material that is related to problem areas in their lives, past or present.

More precisely, a knowledgeable social worker can make use of specific pictures by having clients tell stories about them, give their own interpretation of them in a personal way, or talking about the impact of selected pictures on them. This can help elicit difficult content from the client, which can be cathartic for the client and useful diagnostically. Such material can help clients to understand themselves and their histories in a growth-enhancing way. Having a client draw pictures outside of the therapeutic setting and then discuss them in therapy can also be productive and helpful diagnostically.

Art can be used as an occasional technique in several other ways. One that is not often viewed as a component of practice but that can be useful is to help a client or client group expand their horizons by learning and experiencing the pleasures of viewing art. This can be done separately from a direct therapeutic goal, but rather as a pleasurable, satisfying, and growth-enhancing process.

At another level, we can use art as a form of what we might call therapeutic distraction. There are persons we meet socially who can best talk about sensitive areas when they are engaged in some physical activity such as drawing—or, perhaps from the an artist's perspective, doodling.

We can use this rather common habit in our therapy by providing clients with the resources to do so in our interviewing setting, as simple as they need to be. Some clients may be more comfortable and less restricted in an interview situation when they are able to use this form of tactile diversion or screen in a security- or comfort-producing manner. In such situations, we probably ought not to attempt to view this type of artistic expression in a diagnostic or interpretive way, but rather to see the technique as a way of reducing stress and facilitating the helping relationship.

RISK FACTORS

Using art is a technique with a low risk factor.

REQUIRED SKILLS AND KNOWLEDGE

To make effective use of art as a therapeutic technique requires a level of understanding or knowledge by the social worker about art and its variations and general impact on the viewer.

Case Summary One

Hope is a 12-year-old female attending therapy sessions following her parents' divorce. Her mother felt that she was having a hard time handling the transition from living in a two-parent household to now living primarily with her mother. Due to the divorce, Hope has infrequent contact with her father and other relatives on his side of the family. Her mother has informed Hope's social worker that she has become more worrisome at home, her school performance has declined, and she is acting out more at home and school.

SOCIAL WORKER: Hope, you told me you enjoy drawing. I would like you to draw a picture representing your life before the divorce and another one representing life after your parent's divorce.

HOPE: Okay.

SOCIAL WORKER: Now, tell me about what you drew.

HOPE: Well, for the picture before the divorce I drew my mom, dad, and me standing outside our home with the sun shining brightly in the sky. The picture after the divorce is my mom and me sitting in my house alone and it's storming outside.

SOCIAL WORKER: Explain to me why it is sunny in one picture and storming in the other.

HOPE: Before my parents got divorced and my dad moved out it was always so happy and bright. I got to see my dad every day and we always had family around. Now it's so gloomy. I barely ever see my dad, and his family, forget about it.

Using art as a technique, the social worker was able to elicit feelings from Hope that she might not have been able to express otherwise. Hope has been attending therapy sessions for several months now and is learning how to appropriately express her emotions related to the divorce in many different settings in her life. Hope has also been using art outside of her therapy sessions as a way to cope with some of the intense emotions she feels surrounding the divorce.

Case Summary Two

Christian is 24-year-old male about to attend his third therapy session. Christian recently went through a breakup with his long-term girlfriend. His mother recommended therapy after seeing how sad her son had become and his loss of interest in activities that used to bring him joy. In previous sessions, Christian has been very guarded and mentioned that he feels uncomfortable sharing too much personal information with other people. However, during the initial intake interview Christian did mention that he enjoys painting. He stated that he has always loved to paint, but hasn't felt like painting recently. For the current session, Christian's social worker has decided to ask him to paint during the session for assessment purposes.

SOCIAL WORKER: In a previous session you mentioned that you love to paint. I'm wondering if you might be willing to paint something during our session today.

CHRISTIAN: Yeah, I guess so. I wouldn't expect to paint during a therapy session, but it could be fun.

SOCIAL WORKER: I would like you to paint a picture of your support system. Identify the people who help you with your problems and worries, the people you trust, and the people you can go to when you need help. You don't have to paint actual people if you don't want to; you can use your own creativity. You can paint the way they make you feel by using certain colors to represent certain people in your life. There is no right or wrong way to complete this painting activity.

CHRISTIAN: I can do that. (He begins to paint.)

SOCIAL WORKER: How do you feel while you are painting?

CHRISTIAN: I actually feel good. It was easy to decide which person I would paint first. What I'm painting right now represents my mom. She is one person I can always count on and I know I can go to for anything. She is a wonderful lady. Also, I forgot how much of a stress reliever painting can be for me. I am definitely going to have to paint more often.

In this case Christian's social worker decided to use art as an assessment tool and a way to identify Christian's support system. The social worker knew that Christian enjoys painting so he is able to use it as a less confrontational or intimidating way of getting him to talk about his family and other sources of support. Painting during the session helped Christian feel more comfortable and at ease in his surroundings, so he was able to let his guard down and share more personal information with his social worker.

REFERENCES AND ADDITIONAL SOURCES

Aiken, L. R. (1996). *Rating scales and checklists: Evaluating behavior, personality, and attitude.* New York, NY: Wiley.

Andsell, G., & Pavlicevic, M. (2001). *Beginning research in the arts therapies.* London, England: Jessica Kingsley.

Aldridge, D. (1994). Single-case research designs for the creative art social worker. *The Arts in Psychotherapy, 21*(5), 333–342.

Anderson, F. (2001). Benefits of conducting research. *Art Therapy: Journal of the American Art Therapy Association, 18*(3), 134–141.

Betts, D. J. (2003). *Creative arts therapies approaches in adoption and foster care.* Springfield, IL: Charles C. Thomas.Betts, D. J., & Laloge, L. (2000). Art social workers and research: A survey conducted by the Potomac Art Therapy Association. *Art Therapy: Journal of the American Art Therapy Association, 17*(4), 291–295.

Bloomgarden, J., & Netzer, D. (1998). Validating art social workers' tacit knowing: The heuristic experience. *Art Therapy: Journal of the American Art Therapy Association, 15*(1), 51–54.

Carolan, R. (2001). Models and paradigms of art therapy research. *Art Therapy: Journal of the American Art Therapy Association, 18*(4), 190–206.

Deaver, S. P. (2002). What constitutes art therapy research? *Art Therapy: Journal of the American Art Therapy Association, 19*(1), 23–27.

Edwards, D. (1993). Why don't arts social workers do research? In H. Payne (Ed.), *Handbook of inquiry in the arts therapies: One river, many currents.* (pp. 7–15). London, England: Jessica Kingsley.

Farris-Dufrene, P. (1989). *Art therapy guidelines and practices.* Mundelein, IL: American Art Therapy Association.

Feder, B., & Feder, E. (1998). *The art and science of evaluation in the arts therapies.* Springfield, IL: Charles C. Thomas.

Franklin, M., & Politsky, R. (1992). The problem of interpretation: Implications and strategies for the field of art therapy. *Arts in Psychotherapy, 19*, 163–175.

Gantt, L. M. (1998). A discussion of art therapy as a science. *Art Therapy: Journal of the American Art Therapy Association, 15*(1), 3–12.

Gilroy, A., & Lee, C. (1995). *Art and music: Therapy and research.* London, England: Routledge.

Hagood, M. M. (1990, Spring). Art therapy research in England: Impressions of an American art social worker. *Arts in Psychotherapy, 17*(1), 75–79.

Henzell, J. (1995). Research and the particular: Epistemology in art and psychotherapy. In A. Gilroy & C. Lee (Eds.), *Art and music: Therapy and* research (pp. 185–205). London, England: Routledge.

Julliard, K. (1998). Outcomes research in health care: Implications for art therapy. *Art Therapy: Journal of the American Art Therapy Association, 15*(1), 13–21.

Julliard, K., Gujral, J., Hamil, S., Oswald, E., Smyk, A., & Testa, N. (2000). Art-based evaluation in research education. *Art Therapy: Journal of the American Art Therapy Association, 17*(2), 118–124.

Junge, M. (1989). The heart of the matter. *Arts in Psychotherapy, 16,* 77–78.

Junge, M. B., & Linesch, D. (1993). Our own voices: New paradigms for art therapy research. *Arts in Psychotherapy, 20*(1), 61–67.

Kapitan, L. (1998). In pursuit of the irresistible: Art therapy research in the hunting tradition. *Art Therapy: Journal of the American Art Therapy Association, 15*(1), 22–28.

Kaplan, F. (1998). Scientific art therapy: An integrative and research-based approach. *Art Therapy: Journal of the American Art Therapy Association, 15*(2), 93–98.

Kaplan, F. (2000). *Art, science, and art therapy: Repainting the picture.* London, England: Jessica Kingsley.

Kaplan, F. (2001). Areas of inquiry for art therapy research. *Art Therapy: Journal of the American Art Therapy Association, 18*(3), 142–147.

Lantz, J., & Gyamarah, J. (2002). Using art in short term existential psychotherapy. *Journal of Brief Therapy, 1*(2), 155–162.

Linesch, D. (1992). Research approaches within master's level art therapy training programs. *Art Therapy: Journal of the American Art Therapy Association, 9*(3), 129–134.

Linesch, D. (1995). Art therapy research: Learning from experience. *Art Therapy: Journal of the American Art Therapy Association, 12*(4), 261–265.

Lusebrink, V. B., Rosal, M. L., & Campanelli, M. (1993). Survey of doctoral work by art social workers. *Art Therapy: Journal of the American Art Therapy Association, 10*(4), 226–234.

Matlo, H. C. (2002). Integrating art therapy methodology in brief inpatient substance abuse treatment for adults. *Journal of Social Work Practice in the Addictions, 2*(2), 69–83.

Malchiodi, C. A. (1995). Does a lack of art therapy research hold us back? *Art Therapy: Journal of the American Art Therapy Association, 12*(4), 218–219.

Malchiodi, C. A. (Ed.). (1998). Art therapy and research [Special issue]. *Art Therapy: Journal of the American Art Therapy Association, 15*(1 & 2).

McCaffrey, R. (2007). The effect of healing gardens and art therapy on older adults with mild to moderate depression. *Holistic Nursing Practice, 21*(2), 79–84.

McNiff, S. (1986). Freedom of research and artistic inquiry. *The Arts in Psychotherapy, 13*(4), 279–284.

McNiff, S. (1987). Research and scholarship in the creative arts therapies. *The Arts in Psychotherapy, 14*(4), 285–292.

McNiff, S. (1993). The authority of experience. *The Arts in Psychotherapy, 20*(1), 3–9.

McNiff, S. (1998). *Art-based research.* London, England: Jessica Kingsley.

McNiff, S. (1998). Enlarging the vision of art therapy research. *Art Therapy: Journal of the American Art Therapy Association, 15*(2), 86–92.

Oppawsky, J. (2000). Utilizing drawings when working with adults in therapy. *Journal of Psychotherapy in Independent Practice, 2*(1), 49–61,

Payne, H. (1993). *Handbook of inquiry in the arts therapies: One river, many currents.* London, England: Jessica Kingsley.

Rosal, M. L. (1989). Co-perspective: Master's papers in art therapy: Narrative or research case studies? *The Arts in Psychotherapy, 16*(1), 71–75.

Rosal, M. L. (1998). Research thoughts: Learning from the literature and from experience. *Art Therapy: Journal of the American Art Therapy Association, 15*(1), 47–50.

Schaverien, J. (1995). Researching the esoteric: Art therapy research. In A. Gilroy & C. Lee (Eds.), *Art and music: Therapy and research* (pp. 21–34). London, England: Routledge.

Tibbetts, T. J. (1995). Art therapy at the crossroads: Art and science. *Art Therapy: Journal of the American Art Therapy Association, 12*(4), 257–260.

Wadeson, H. (1980). Art therapy research. *Art Education, 33*(4), 31–35.

Wadeson, H. (Ed.). (1992). *A guide to conducting art therapy research.* Mundelein, IL: The American Art Therapy Association.

Wadeson, H. (2010). *Art psychotherapy* (2nd ed.). Hoboken, NJ: Wiley.

Wadeson, H. (2010). *Art therapy practice: innovative approaches with diverse populations.* New York, NY: Wiley.

Audio Recordings

DESCRIPTION

Audio recording resources are a common facet of contemporary technology with several interesting and useful possibilities for therapy. They are an omnipresent societal resource that permits us to record voices and sound in an inexpensive highly portable and easily manipulated manner.

ORIGINS

It is difficult to identify the theoretical or sociological origin of using audio recordings in our practice. Perhaps when we realized that this technology was useful as an instrument of personal communication, and that much of our intervention takes place verbally, we began to experiment with them as treatment tools that could enhance our interactions with clients in different ways.

WHY THIS IS USEFUL TO SOCIAL WORK

Because from a psychosocial basis the nature of our treatment mostly involves verbal communications, either with clients or others in their lives, any resource that will enhance our ability to do so is an important resource for us. Three distinct advantages of audio recording that make it a particularly useful therapy technique are its prevalence in society, its facility of use, and its low cost, which makes it accessible to a large component of society.

HOW THIS IS USEFUL TO SOCIAL WORK

There are several ways in which audio recordings can be considered a treatment technique. The first is where we draw on the helping, pedagogical, and therapeutic potential of the hundreds of commercial self-help or teaching audio resources. We can use these to assist clients in achieving some specific therapeutic goal, such as helping them learn to relax, meditate, or listen to an interview.

We can also make use of the many commercial audio recordings that address various personality or behavioral issues or some particular problem. Many of these recordings are formatted in a popular teaching manner. In a related way, exposing the client to the wealth of audio material can open up an area of learning or entertainment of which they were not aware, which can generally bring new levels of personal satisfaction to their lives.

Audio recordings can also be used in a more direct therapeutic way. By recording some or all of our client interviews and making the audio available to them, it gives clients an opportunity to reflect in private on various aspects of the interview that may have been particularly significant to them.

For some clients it is very important to review an interview and its contents in a way that allows them to raise particular points in subsequent sessions. As with video, audio can also be reviewed with the client to identify and reinforce gains in treatment.

Although video brings the visual factor into the equation, some clients would find this a distraction and are better able to respond to a solely auditory stimulus. This is similar to the way we close our eyes to screen out the visual and concentrate on the auditory component of communication, either to understand something better or just to listen to our favorite music. Likewise, some clients will find hearing some aspect of a process rather than seeing it more helpful.

A further use of audio recording is to serve as a reinforcement after termination. For example, there may be a particular interaction that was significant for a client. A recording of this interaction can remind the client of this important experience in their lives and help them maintain their progress in some important life area.

Social workers can use audio recordings in a similar way, when we want to review them to better understand what the client was telling us or to sort out some particular complex component of the process. They can also be used to send a verbal message to a significant person in a client's life for whom a written message may not be feasible.

RISK FACTORS

This technique has a low risk factor. It is understood, however, that not all clients would be interested in our using this resource and would be very uncomfortable if we used it. Clearly the client must have a choice, and they can choose not to have interviews recorded. There is also the question of confidentiality of material, and the responsibility to have a clear understanding as to how recordings will be maintained once they have been created. One interesting indirect fact of audio recording is that, in some parts of the world, the necessary equipment for playing it back might be expensive or not readily available to a client.

REQUIRED SKILLS AND KNOWLEDGE

When using audio recordings as a component of treatment, it is important that we address such features as ease of use so that the equipment is not intrusive and does not require our attention. The client should know where the equipment is in our interviewing locale so that there is no aspect of surprise or a suspicion that something is being done that the client is unaware of. At all times the client needs to be able to have the recording stopped or to have some or all of a recording erased if, for example it contains material that they want nobody ever to hear. The client also needs to know what happens to audio recordings once they have been created.

Case Summary One

Amber is a high school student who has been meeting with a social worker for a few weeks. Amber presented with symptoms of anxiety. She describes herself as extremely overwhelmed, nervous about the future, and feeling stressed out all the time. Part of Amber's treatment goals were to learn to relax.

> SOCIAL WORKER: Amber, do you have access to a cassette player?
> AMBER: Yes, I have one in my car as well as in my house.
> SOCIAL WORKER: We have been talking a lot about relaxation techniques and meditation during the past few sessions. I have an audio tape that I would like you to take home and listen to when you get a chance. This tape is designed to bring the listener to a state of relaxation and to teach meditation skills.
> AMBER: That sounds great. I look forward to listening to it.
> SOCIAL WORKER: Also, in the future you can check out other useful audio tapes at your local library.
> AMBER: Oh yes, that is true. How wonderful.

Listening to these audio tapes opened Amber up to an area of learning about relaxation of which she had not been previously aware. The availability of the audio tapes allowed Amber to use this new knowledge when it was convenient for her. They also provided Amber with the opportunity to listen to the information repeatedly as a way to reinforce the skills.

Case Summary Two

Jay is a senior in college. He has been attending therapy sessions for a few months due to issues with low self-esteem. After graduating in the next several weeks, he wants to pursue a career in business. Jay is nervous about the process of interviewing and obtaining employment. One of his treatment goals is to increase his self-esteem and to portray confidence while interviewing for jobs. As a way to help achieve this goal, the social worker has decided to ask Jay how he feels about recording the therapy sessions, during which they will practice interviewing skills.

> SOCIAL WORKER: During the next few sessions, we are going to work towards your goal of becoming more confident during job interviews by practicing interviews during our sessions.

JAY: Okay. I am nervous, but excited to practice. I'm looking forward to starting my career after graduation. I'm just very nervous about the whole process of getting a job.

SOCIAL WORKER: What I would like to do, if it is okay with you, is to audiotape our practice interviews during our next few sessions. We can listen to the audiotapes of your practice job interviews during the following session and discuss the progress you've made and any changes you would like to make in your interview approach. Then, you will be able to bring the tapes home with you to review as you determine necessary.

JAY: Yes, I'm fine with that. It sounds like a great idea. I think it will be very helpful for me to practice interviewing and be able to review the interviews any time I want to.

Audiotapes are a good technique for helping Jay achieve his treatment goal because they are easy to use and provide the ability to listen to the recorded material as many times as necessary. Replaying the tapes during future sessions will let Jay and his social worker hear how confident Jay sounds during each practice interview, as well as the overall progress that he has made. It will also allow them to consider any changes that might need to be made to his interviewing style. Additionally, they will allow Jay to listen to his practice interviews outside of his therapy sessions multiple times and reflect privately on his performance.

REFERENCES AND ADDITIONAL SOURCES

Bogolub, E. B. (1986). Tape recorders in clinical sessions: Deliberate and fortuitous effects. *Clinical Social Work Journal, 14*(4), 349–360.

Fox, R. (1982). The personal log: Enriching clinical practice. *Clinical Social Work Journal, 10*, 94–102.

Hill, F. E., & Harmon, M. (1976). The use of telephone tapes in a telephone counseling program. *Crisis Intervention, 7*, 88–96.

Know, R., Butow, P. N., Devine, R., & Tattersall, M. H. N. (2002). Audiotapes of oncology consultations: Only for the first consultation? *Annals of Oncology, 13*, 622–627.

Makaskill, N. D. (1996). Improving clinical outcomes in REBT/CBT: The therapeutic uses of tape-recording. *Journal of Rational-Emotive and Cognitive Behavior,14*(3), 199–207

Moore, T. E. (1995). Subliminal self-help auditory tapes: An empirical test of perceptual consequences. *Canadian Journal of Behavioural Science, 27*(1), 9–20.

Neumann, J. K. (1981). Self-help depression treatment: An evaluation of an audio cassette program with hospitalized residents. *Behavior Social Worker, 4*, 15–16.

Perr, H. M. (1985). The use of audiotapes in psychotherapy. *Journal of the American Academy of Psychoanalysis, 13*, 391–398.

Reed, A. (1969). Using a tape recorder in counseling alcoholics. *Pastoral Psychology, 20*, 45–49.

Authority

DESCRIPTION

In viewing authority as a clinical technique, we are drawing upon the authority inherent in the professional role and how to tap its potential as a positive therapeutic resource.

ORIGINS

Although not picked up in the general practice literature, the functional school understood and promulgated an understanding of the role of authority in practice, especially how the authority inherent in the structure of the agency and its societal mandate affected the nature of the helping process. Over the decades, however, the concept of authority as a positive technique has generally been eschewed, and this societal reality has been viewed only in negative terms.

This has come about for a variety of reasons. All of us have seen or know about the terrible abuse of authority in many bureaucratic systems, abuses that have caused considerable suffering to many. Because of these abuses, the idea of using authority in a positive manner generally has been avoided or overlooked.

Rather, we have attempted to foster a value that denies the existence of authority in our relationships with our clients. We presume that our goal in treatment was to develop relationships that are based on equality. Indeed, the idea of a power-neutral therapeutic relationship is probably an impossibility.

However, as the social sciences have studied the concept of authority from a more neutral perspective, we have begun to understand that there are many forms of authority. All of these can be used in both positive and negative ways. Our task in therapy is to understand the various components of authority that may be inherent in our client relationships and to learn how to build on these in a positive way.

WHY THIS IS USEFUL TO SOCIAL WORK

Authority is a tremendous utility to our practice because of its omnipresence. As we have learned to understand this we realize that the very fact of being a professional in a societally recognized setting, and of having the title of social worker, bring understanding, respect, and acceptance from society. This societal recognition includes the awareness, acceptance, and comfort that, as professionals in the human services, we are authorities in a particular component of human knowledge and the techniques involved in the helping process. Along with this comes the authority to use such techniques. Society does not accord this authority in an unchallenged way, however; it acknowledges it only reluctantly, and often challenges it rightly.

HOW THIS IS USEFUL TO SOCIAL WORK

The professional authority that is inherent in the client–social worker relationship can bring tremendous security to some people when, for instance, some aspect of their reality is understood and supported in a positive way. Because of this, there are many ways in which an awareness of our authority and the client's perception and acceptance of it can be of great benefit.

We use our authority to convey to the client our conviction that they have the ability to take some particular action. We use it to give the client assurance and support. We often use it to refer clients to other resources, and we also use it when we are seeking to empower our clients.

Although we may not always appear to be functioning in an authoritative manner, virtually everything we do with, for, and to our clients is done under the umbrella of the professional's authority. Our skill is in knowing and understanding this component of the relationship and ensuring that it functions in a positive way.

RISK FACTORS

The use of authority in practice needs to be considered a high-risk technique because of its potential for misuse and, indeed, abuse. Such errors usually arise out of a perceived wish to help clients move in a particular direction that we believe will help them, even though they may not be ready to do so.

REQUIRED SKILLS AND KNOWLEDGE

Awareness of and sensitivity to the myriad ways in which authority can be used in practice protects us against its overuse or misuse. It also requires that we understand the client's perception of authority from their own history. This is important because every time we give a client information, express an opinion, answer a question, or venture an interpretation or explanation, such actions are cloaked in authority even though we might think they are not. What we view as a casual comment can be viewed by the client as a certainty, underscored by professional authority.

Because we are aware of the inherent risks in using authority, overall we try to use it in a positive and constructive way. Indeed it may be that we err on the side of underuse. In this way, we sometimes fail our clients and attempt to function as if we were powerless out of a fear of misusing authority. In so doing we can send confusing messages. Thus it is important that we see authority as a technique, not as a weapon.

The critical factor in using this technique is to recognize its various forms, assess its role in our own lives and in a given therapeutic relationship, and be aware when we are drawing on it as an overt component of treatment. We should stay humble and be on guard when using our authority, but when skillfully used it can have a great impact on our work with clients.

Case Summary One

Molly is a single mother of an adolescent girl, Melony. Both have been seeing a social worker following Melony's sexual assault 6 months earlier. Melony's father lives out of state, and up to this point in treatment he did not know Melony had been assaulted.

MOLLY: Oh, my husband called me yesterday and I decided to tell him about what happened to Melony.

SOCIAL WORKER: How did that go?

MOLLY: I was hoping he would be supportive, but he just blamed me for what happened. He said it was my fault that she was assaulted.

SOCIAL WORKER: Do you agree with what he said? Do you think it was your fault that Melony was assaulted?

MOLLY: Well, sometimes I wonder. At times I think it is my fault and other times I don't blame myself. However, I always tell Melony that it is not her fault. I know it was not Melony's fault. Just because she skipped school doesn't mean that this should have happened to her.

SOCIAL WORKER: Well I'm glad to hear you say that you know Melony is not to blame for what happened. You are exactly right and it is so wonderful for you to tell her that. In addition to that, I want you to know that you are not to blame either. It is in no way your fault that this happened to her.

MOLLY: Yes, I know you are right. I guess I just have to remember that.

Molly was hoping to receive some much-needed support from her ex-husband after feeling so isolated for months. She was crushed when all she received from him was unnecessary blame. Fortunately, through the authority of her social worker she was reminded that her daughter's assault was in no way her fault. The confidence and authority of her social worker's words allowed her to feel understood and supported. It also served as a way to empower her and reinforce her ability to support her daughter through this trauma.

Case Summary Two

Pam is a young adult attending therapy sessions due to family conflict issues. She is still living at home with her parents while she completes her college education. Pam reports that she is finding it more and more difficult to concentrate on her studies because of the constant disputes occurring at home. Pam and her parents are attending therapy sessions with the hope that they can learn conflict resolution and anger management skills to decrease the frequency and intensity of arguments and to increase positive interactions among family members.

SOCIAL WORKER: Hi Pam. How have you been since our last session?

PAM: I've been okay. My mom and I got in another fight last week. She came in my room without knocking again and I just blew up at her. I felt bad about it later, but at the time I just couldn't help but to yell at her. I was so mad.

SOCIAL WORKER: Tell me more about how you've been feeling.

PAM: Honestly, lately I've doubted my ability to control my anger. I don't know if I can achieve this goal. I've been this way for so long, I can't expect to be different now. It's all so overwhelming. Between school demands and my home life I feel so frazzled sometimes.

SOCIAL WORKER: Pam, I understand your frustration and that you are feeling overwhelmed, but I know you can do this. You will be able to achieve your goal if you continue to work hard and take it one step at a time. We can take it as slow as you need to and the small changes you make in your life will suddenly amount to achieving your goal.

PAM: You sound so sure that I can do it.

SOCIAL WORKER: I am very sure that you can do it.

PAM: You make it sound so attainable too. I guess I know that I can achieve my goal. I just need to be reminded sometimes.

In this case the social worker was aware of and understood his professional authority in the social worker–client relationship, and he was able to use that authority as a technique to empower Pam to achieve her treatment goals. Pam has an inherent respect and acceptance of her social worker's authority. She sees him as possessing a special knowledge because of his professional position. This respect and acceptance of his authority brings Pam a sense of comfort and empowerment when her social worker encourages her and informs her that she can achieve her goals.

REFERENCES AND ADDITIONAL SOURCES

Bransford, C. L. (2005). Conceptions of authority within contemporary social work practice in managed mental health care organizations. *American Journal of Orthopsychiatry, 75*(3), 409–420.

Coady, N., & Lehman, P. (2007). *Theoretical perspectives for direct social work practice: A generalist-eclectic approach.* New York, NY: Springer.

Fusco, L. J. (2002). The techniques of intervention. In F. Turner (Ed.), *Social work practice: A Canadian perspective* (pp. 234–236). Toronto, Ontario: Pearson.

Gambrill, E. (2001). Social work: An authority-based profession. *Research on Social Work Practice, 11*(2), 166–175. doi:10.1177/104973150101100203

Hayes, F. D. (1969). The use of authority. *Australian Social Work, 22*(2), 13–18.

Hepworth, D. H., Rooney, R. J., & Larsen, J. A. (2009). *Direct social work practice: Theory and skills* (8th ed.). Pacific Grove, CA: Brooks/Cole.

Hutchison, E. D. (1987). Use of authority in direct social work practice with mandated clients. *The Social Service Review, 61*(4), 581–598.

Kadushin, A., & Harkness, D. (2002). *Supervision in social work.* New York, NY and Chichester, England: Columbia University Press.

Staples, L. (1984). *Roots to power: A manual for grassroots organizing.* New York: Praeger.

Shulman, L. (2008). *The skills of helping individuals, families, groups, and communities* (6th ed.). Pacific Grove, CA: Brooks/Cole.

Turner, F. J. (1996). *Social work treatment: Interlocking theoretical approaches* (4th ed.) New York, NY: Free Press.

Yelaja, S. A. (1971). *Authority and social work: Concept and use.* Toronto, Ontario: University of Toronto Press.

Brainstorming

DESCRIPTION

Brainstorming is a useful technique for finding solutions to questions, issues, or problems for which the client does not currently have a clear direction to follow. It is a component of and is closely related to the problem-solving process, and involves the client in both an emotive and cognitive creative manner.

ORIGINS

Brainstorming emerged from several theories, including existential, problem solving, Gestalt, task-centered, and client-centered theory. Each of these has helped us view the therapeutic process as a creative process that draws upon the range of ways in which humans seek creative solutions to life's challenges.

WHY THIS IS USEFUL TO SOCIAL WORK

Brainstorming is an important technique for social workers because it not only helps clients find useful and acceptable solutions to life situations, but it also equips them with a new tool for day-to-day living. It is also useful because it involves the client very actively in the therapeutic process and presents the social worker and therapy in a quasicollegial manner,.

HOW THIS IS USEFUL TO SOCIAL WORK

During brainstorming, the client—whether singular or part of some dyad, family, or group—is led to interact with the social worker in a search for possible solutions to the posited challenge in as free and open a way as possible. That is, when considering alternatives clients are asked to work from as broad a base as they can, regardless of practicality, appropriateness, feasibility, or logic, to identify the widest spectrum of solutions they can envision. To impose a structure upon this formal use of brainstorming, each idea that emerges in the process is noted in some format visible to all (e.g., a blackboard, flip chart, or screen), even if only a single client is involved.

No idea is to be discounted because of its apparent foolishness or impracticality. The goal is to tap the creative function of the persons involved and to lead them beyond their accustomed constraints of thinking about solutions, so they can attempt to find alternatives they may not have considered. Thus the process serves to create previously unseen solutions from the ideas that emerge. Its strength lies in its freedom from the usual societal, logical, or value-based restraints and its ability to open people up and free them from the accustomed frameworks, patterns, and restrictions in which much thought takes place.

Once a period of brainstorming has concluded, the person or people involved then turn to the process of bringing some order to the possible identified solutions. Sometimes this can be done in a fairly unstructured way; at other times the ideas are classified along various norms, such as practicality, safety, legality, unreality, cost, and the like. From this process it is hoped that a possible solution will emerge. In situations when there is more than one client, a further plan may be needed for all parties to come to a consensus or rank how appropriate or practical the chosen solutions are.

Of course, this process does not always lead to an acceptable solution to the problem under consideration. However, it does frequently open up alternatives that have not been considered or lead to a review of earlier solutions that have been rejected.

Some people find it difficult to brainstorm, especially if they have rather stringent cognitive structures and are not accustomed to stepping outside of them. They may therefore find the process not to be useful.

Once some clients become comfortable brainstorming, it may serve them well in other life situations by expanding their ability to consider a broad range of alternatives when solving problems. One of its challenges is that the brainstorming process can take on a game-like structure or aura, rather than being experienced as a serious effort at seeking workable and acceptable solutions to life's challenges.

RISK FACTORS

Although this technique does not have a high risk factor, we need to be sure that the person is capable of this type of multiphasic process. We also need to be sure that it does not impinge on their values. Furthermore, we must be careful not to shape the process to meet our own needs, wishes, and goals for the client. There is also a risk that clients might offer a solution they hadn't previously considered that is illegal, unethical, or dangerous and pursue it with negative consequences.

REQUIRED SKILLS

When using this technique, we need to be careful that we do not take over the process, out of a wish to get it started in a productive way. It is also important not to allow the process to continue too long, lest it become a way for the client to avoid moving to some plan of action. In a multiple-client situation, we also need to ensure that the process not take on a game-like atmosphere by conveying that this is a very serious activity and an important part of a therapeutic process.

Case Summary One

Sandra is a busy professional woman who recently started having difficulty sleeping. This is very troubling for her, and she does not know what to do to alleviate the problem.

SOCIAL WORKER: So, what brings you here today?

SANDRA: I can't sleep at night and it's starting to affect my daily functioning. I try and try to fall asleep, but I end up just lying in bed for hours, restless and aggravated. I want to fall asleep and stay asleep all night and wake up feeling rested.

SOCIAL WORKER: It sounds like this is very frustrating for you, and I can certainly understand your need to resolve this problem. Let's try brainstorming to find solutions for your problem. I want you to say any and every solution that comes to your mind without analyzing or evaluating it—we'll do that later.

SANDRA: Well, I've thought about taking sleeping pills, but I'm not sure about that. I guess I could try to decrease the amount of caffeinated drinks I consume close to bedtime. I could also engage in a few relaxation techniques before lying down and trying to sleep.

SOCIAL WORKER: Those are all very good ideas. I would suggest seeing your primary care physician to rule out any medical reasons for your sleep disturbance, too. Also, maybe you could write down your sleeping habits in a journal and we could evaluate them for certain patterns that are hindering your sleep. We could also discuss the possibility of feelings of anxiety or depression at bedtime that may lead to sleep problems.

SANDRA: Oh, and maybe if I don't watch television in my room, that will help, because I tend to get sucked into the program and stay up later than I wanted to. I could try to go to bed a little earlier, too. Keeping a bedtime routine could help me, instead of the chaos I'm used to living with.

SOCIAL WORKER: Now that we have brainstormed and thought of so many possibilities, let's evaluate them and determine the best solutions for your situation.

Brainstorming with the social worker gave Sandra the opportunity to think of ideas that she might not have thought of on her own, and also provided her with more possible solutions. Sandra was so frustrated by her problem that she might not have been able to think of as many possible solutions without being prompted by the social worker. The brainstorming session will ultimately lead Sandra to a plan that she can follow to solve her problem.

Case Summary Two

In the past month, David has moved into a new home and accepted a promotion at his job. Although he is happy with these situations, he reports feeling extremely stressed lately. David states that he doesn't know what to do and feels like he has no clear direction to follow to ease his tension. He is attending therapy sessions to learn coping skills for the stress he feels.

Social worker: How have you been feeling this week, David?

David: I am still very stressed out and I've been feeling more pressure lately. The house still isn't unpacked and my promotion came with so many new responsibilities. I'm at the end of my rope. I need help. I just don't know what to do.

Social worker: You have a lot going on in your life right now, and changes or transitions, even positive ones, can certainly cause some anxiety. I understand why you would feel stressed. Let's work together to search for possible solutions.

David: Okay, that sounds great. How do we do that?

Social worker: Brainstorming can be a freeing and open way to come up with ideas to cope with stress. To start, just throw out any ideas that pop into your head. Don't sit and overly think about or analyze what you could do and why it would or wouldn't work. We will write down every idea presented and then review them and refine all of the possible identified solutions. The point is to be creative, think outside the box, and consider options that maybe we normally wouldn't.

David: Here goes nothing. Umm, I could go out with my friends when they go to the park. We could play a game of football or throw a Frisbee around. That would probably take my mind off of everything for a while. I like to sing. I could take my wife to the movies. I could watch a show I like on television. I enjoy kayaking. I could just sit, clear my mind, and relax for a few minutes each day.

Social worker: Yes, those are all great. I've also heard of people writing in a journal, reading, going for a walk, or playing with a pet.

David: Yeah, playing with my dog usually does calm me down. I've thought about painting or drawing, too—those could be stress relievers. Laughing is always good, too.

Social worker: Just look at how many possible solutions we were able to brainstorm. Next, let's review our list and come up with an action plan.

Using brainstorming as a technique allowed David to find useful and acceptable solutions to coping with the tension he's been experiencing. It also equipped him with a new tool to use in his everyday life for other situations that he encounters. Furthermore, brainstorming allowed David to participate actively in the therapeutic process. It freed him from his usual pattern of thinking, and expanded the number and types of solutions he came up with. It opened up alternatives that he might not have thought of otherwise.

REFERENCES AND ADDITIONAL SOURCES

Baruah, J., & Paulus, P. B. (2011). Category assignment and relatedness in the group ideation process. *Journal of Experimental Social Psychology, 47*(6), 1070–1077.

Blot, K. J., Zarate, M. A., & Paulus, P. B. (2003). Code-switching across brainstorming sessions: Implications for the revised hierarchical model of bilingual language processing. *Experimental Psychology, 50*(3), 171–183.

Brandell, J. R. (2010). *Theory & practice in clinical social work* (2nd ed.). Thousand Oaks, CA: Sage.

Brown, V. R. & Paulus, P. B. (2002). Making group brainstorming more effective: Recommendations from an associative memory perspective. *Current Directions in Psychological Science, 11*(6), 208–212.

Coady, N., & Lehman, P. (2008). *Theoretical perspectives for direct social work practice: a generalist-eclectic approach* (2nd ed.). New York, NY: Springer.

D'Zurilla, T. J., & Nezu, A. M. (1999). *Problem-solving therapy: A social competence approach to clinical intervention* (2nd ed.). New York, NY: Springer.

Kirst-Ashman, K. K., & Hull, G. H. (2009). *Understanding generalist practice.* (5th ed.) Belmont, CA: Brooks/Cole.

Kottler, J. (1994). *Advanced group leadership.* Pacific Grove, CA: Brooks/Cole.

Osborn, A. F. (1963). *Applied imagination: Principles and procedures of creative problem solving*(3rd ed.). New York, NY: Scribner's.

Ronen, T., & Freeman, A. (2007). *Cognitive behavior therapy in clinical social work practice.* New York, NY: Springer.

Zastrow, C. (1993). *Social work with groups* (3rd ed.). Chicago, IL: Nelson-Hall.

Zastrow, C. (2009). *Social work with groups: A comprehensive workbook* (7th ed.). Belmont, CA: Brooks/Cole.

Brokering

DESCRIPTION

Brokering is the actions of a social worker that aim to assist particular clients in locating and making use of available resources deemed to be of aid or utility to them. It is akin to the techniques of advocacy and resource location, but is sufficiently distinct to be viewed separately.

ORIGINS

Seeking resources for clients and helping them use them effectively has been a part of social work from its earliest days. From the beginning, the profession was aware that no individual social worker, setting, or agency could provide the total range of psychosocial services many of our clients need. Indeed, they often require the services of several help settings, at times simultaneously.

A broad range of various kinds of social services has developed over the years in our society, creating a rich network of helping resources but also creating a complex, uncoordinated, and frequently labyrinthine structure. Even today, much time and effort is expended in the process of minimizing unnecessary duplication of services, shuttling of clients from service to service, and the repetition of processes such as providing a history or establishing eligibility.

Because a wide spectrum of resources that provide help exists in many communities—sometimes numbering in the hundreds and, in larger communities, the thousands—practitioners quickly become aware that the very existence of such a broad diversity of resources can itself be stress producing and widely confusing to clients. It has also become obvious that a necessary technique for any practitioner in a metropolitan area was to understand this diversity and to develop the skills to structure the optimum profile of helping resources for a client with a minimum of additional stress.

WHY THIS IS USEFUL TO SOCIAL WORK

Brokering is a particularly useful technique for us because the helping systems in our society have become highly complex and extensive. To find one's way through this morass of resources requires highly developed skills. However, when skillfully navigated, the range of helping resources can be rich and powerfully effective. In fact, one of the most important forms of assistance we frequently provide to clients is the very act of helping them find their way through the system in a positive manner.

HOW THIS IS USEFUL TO SOCIAL WORK

The strength of brokering lies in our ability to understand just how difficult it can be for some of our clients to involve themselves in a new situation, especially one that appears complex and daunting. Even though they may recognize cognitively the possible advantages of being involved in a new service, emotionally this may be a troubling and frightening experience for them.

One of the advantages of the helping resources that exist in our society is the broad sweep of assistance that is available. However, one of the challenges of this network is that knowing about these resources and accessing them can be a very stressful experience, requiring a high level of skill on the social worker's part.

RISK FACTORS

Brokering does not carry a high degree of risk, except what may arise from our failure to accurately assess clients' needs, perceptions, and feelings about the resources being sought, and the actual service that the resource being brokered provides.

REQUIRED SKILLS AND KNOWLEDGE

There are two components to this technique. The first focuses on the work involved in preparing and assisting clients in their use of an available resource or group of resources, and the second addresses our activities in preparing, involving, and assisting the resource so it provides the sought-after service.

Both facets of this technique require similar (although not identical) knowledge and skills. The knowledge required of the client rests primarily upon our diagnostic process, which helps us to understand who clients are, what they need and want, their potential to make use of a resource, who can best provide what they need and want, and the best way to help clients connect to it.

From the perspective of the person, setting, or resources whose services we are trying to obtain for the client, we need to be very clear about their policies, procedures, and eligibility requirements and that our client will fit them. This is often where we move from a brokering to an advocacy role. We also need to ensure that the targeted referral or resource has sufficient information about the client to proceed with the request. This requires us to provide, within the dictates of confidentiality, whatever information is needed for them to make a positive decision to move ahead.

In formulating this series of evaluations, we also need to assess what possible barriers there might be from the client's perspective. This can include their own understanding of the resource in question, their perceived reputation of the service, what their significant others might think that could support or hinder their decision, their perception of its possible value to them, what information the new resource will have, and what information we will need to provide. We need to be aware of their feelings about its appropriateness for them, and of reality factors such as location, distance, accessibility, values, availability, and possible costs.

We also have to be thoroughly cognizant of what information the client will need to provide, what documents they might require, and what procedures they might expect. We need to ensure the client understands these as far as they are able. This process of preparing the client and addressing possible areas of concern may be very complex and require considerable time and effort on our part.

A further facet of the broker role entails our remaining available during the process to be ready to deal with any difficulties that may arise on the part of the resource, the client, or both in the process of cementing the referral.

Overall brokering entails an anticipatory, watchdog function. The social worker must be prepared to take action if necessary to help the new process get started in as positive and facilitating a way as possible. It calls for alertness on the part of the social worker and an ability to move quickly when the situation demands.

Case Summary One

Sophia is diagnosed with bipolar disorder and takes medication to control her symptoms while regularly attending therapy sessions. Sophia recently lost her job and, along with that, her health insurance. Her prescription medication is about to run out, and she is concerned about what will happen if she cannot take her medication. The social worker is concerned about the success of her treatment coming undone if she cannot afford to refill her prescription.

SOCIAL WORKER: It is very important that you continue to take the medication prescribed for your bipolar symptoms.

SOPHIA: Yes, I know and I agree. However, I lost my health insurance and I cannot afford the prescription.

SOCIAL WORKER: Have you looked into alternative health care plans now that you're unemployed?

SOPHIA: Yes, but they are all too expensive.

SOCIAL WORKER: Sophia, did you know that you are eligible for free health care through the Medicaid program? How do you feel about applying for that to cover the cost of your prescriptions?

Sophia: I didn't know that. It would be great to have free health care until I find another job, but I'm nervous about the process of applying. I don't know what to do or where to go.

Social worker: While you're in my office let's get on the computer and complete the online application for Medicaid. After they receive your application, they will contact you to schedule an interview. We can also print a list of all of the required documents you'll need for your Medicaid interview.

Sophia was feeling so overwhelmed from losing her job and needing to find a way to purchase her prescriptions that she was having a hard time finding health care that would help her situation. The social worker was able to help her by using her knowledge of community resources and sharing them with Sophia. She was also feeling so helpless in her situation that she thought she was incapable of making it through the process alone. The social worker really helped her feel secure and hopeful that she could obtain the medication that she needed.

Case Summary Two

Rosemary is a 55-year-old grandmother with temporary custody of her two grandchildren. The children's father (Rosemary's son) is currently incarcerated. Rosemary has characterized the mother as unstable. She states that the mother left the children with her one afternoon and never came back. She has been unable to reach their mother and has no idea where she could be. As a result of their new living situation, Rosemary decided that it would be a good idea for the three of them to meet with a social worker. Rosemary is unsure how long the children will be living with her.

Social worker: During our last session you mentioned needing more support and resources to help with raising your grandchildren.

Rosemary: Yes, that's absolutely correct. I've raised my children and they have been out of the house for many, many years now. I should be visiting and having fun with my grandchildren, not raising them. Trying to access services can be so confusing and overwhelming. I need help, not more aggravation.

Social worker: I recognize everything you've done to make this transition as smooth as possible for your grandchildren. You're right, trying to get help can make you feel confused and overwhelmed, which is why I would like to help you navigate the system.

Rosemary: That would be absolutely wonderful. I would be so appreciative.

Social worker: Over the past week I have been in contact with the supervisor at a kinship center in town. The center works to assist relative caregivers with a wide range of needs. I already made sure that you are eligible for the program and the supervisor said that you may contact her directly to be enrolled in the program. If you'd like, we can review the center's website together right now and go over any questions or concerns that you have.

Rosemary: Sounds good to me.

SOCIAL WORKER: Also, I will be available throughout the process of you accessing this resource. Remember, I am just a phone call away. If you have any questions or concerns feel free to call me.

ROSEMARY: Thank you so much.

Not all of the services that Rosemary desires can be provided in the same setting. However, navigating the aid system seemed so overwhelming and daunting to Rosemary that it was difficult for her even to begin to involve herself in accessing resources. Therefore, brokering was an essential and useful technique to ensure that all necessary services would be provided. Through brokering, Rosemary's social worker was able to help her find her way through the system of resources in a helpful manner and link her with a resource appropriate to her situation.

REFERENCES AND ADDITIONAL SOURCES

Berkman, B., & D'Ambruoso, S. (2006). *Handbook of social work in health and aging.* New York, NY: Oxford University Press.

Budgen, D., Turner, M., Kotsiopoulos, I., Zhu, F., Russell, M., Rigby, M., … Layzell, P. (2003). Managing health care information: The role of the broker. In *From grid to health grid: Proceedings of health GRID* (pp. 3–16). Oxford, England: IOS Press.

Dorfman, R. A. (1996). *Clinical social work: Definition, practice, and vision.* New York, NY: Brunner/Mazel.

Dowson, S., & Greig, R. (2009). The emergence of the independent support broker role. *Journal of Integrated Care, 17*(4), 22–30.

Gambrill, E. (2001). Social work: An authority-based profession. *Research on Social Work Practice, 11*(2), 166–175. doi:10.1177/104973150101100203

Kirst-Ashman, K. K., & Hull, G. H. (1993). *Understanding generalist practice* (pp. 493–520). Chicago, IL: Nelson-Hall.

Leece, J., & Leece, D. (2010). Personalisation: Perceptions of the role of social work in a world of brokers and budgets. *The British Journal of Social Work, 40*(7), 1–20. doi:10.1093/bjsw/bcq087

Scourfield, P. (2010). Going for brokerage: A task of "independent support" or social work? *The British Journal of Social Work, 40*(3), 858–877. doi:10.1093/bjsw/bcn141

Singh, N. N., McKay, J. D., & Singh, A. N. (1999). The need for cultural brokers in mental health services. *Journal of Child and Family Studies, 8*(1), 1–10. doi:10.1023/A:1022949225965

Williams, C., Soydan, H., Johnson, M. (1998). *Social work and minorities: European perspectives.* New York, NY: Routledge.

Zastrow, C. (2009). *Social work with groups: A comprehensive workbook* (7th ed.). Belmont, CA: Brooks/Cole.

Zastrow, C. (2010). *Introduction to social work and social welfare: Empowering people* (10th ed.). Belmont, CA: Brooks/Cole.

Zastrow, C., & Kirst-Ashman, K. K. (2009). *Understanding human behavior and the social environment.* Belmont, CA: Brooks/Cole.

Case Management

DESCRIPTION

The goal of case management is to coordinate a cluster of services for people with multiple needs in a way that maximizes the impact of the various services and minimizes the complexities for the client by having a single person manage them.

In case management, an individual client's needs are assessed and profiled by a single managing agency or social worker. Then, through a process of negotiation, brokering, lobbying, networking, and coordination by the case manager, a package of services that are deemed the best fit for the client's identified needs is organized and implemented.

ORIGINS

Social workers have long been aware of the complexity of services with which many of our clients become involved—often in a way that becomes overwhelming—and they have made efforts to minimize their problems.

One such effort is case management, a model of service delivery that originated in the early 1980s whose structure and conceptual base can be used when serving as a technique for individual situations. As a service model, case management emerged principally out of the deinstitutionalization movement as a way of responding to large numbers of people with multiple service needs attempting to function in situations where services were highly isolated, uncoordinated, and scattered.

WHY THIS IS USEFUL TO SOCIAL WORK

There is perhaps a quality of naiveté in suggesting that this type of strategy could be implemented without a formal case management structure in place. However, it can be useful as a technique for a single case. Case management can not only result in the client being better served, but also use all parties' time, services, and resources much more economically. From an individual case perspective, this technique functions best on a short-term basis. Case management fits the reality of how social services are actually structured, which, even in smaller communities, has historically been complex and uncoordinated.

HOW THIS IS USEFUL TO SOCIAL WORK

As an individual technique, it should be used in situations where there are no case management services available, but where our client has multiple needs only available through a network of resources.

RISK FACTORS

Case management has a moderate risk factor from the client's viewpoint. Although it can be of tremendous assistance and effectiveness, it can also create stress and strain for the client. These problems emerge from an uncoordinated helping system that supposedly exists to remove road-blocks, fulfill needs, and solve problems.

There is also the possibility that we may view the process of maneuvering through the complexities of person, policies, and procedures so daunting that we decide not to proceed. A further risk in using case management arises from the possibility that, in building the necessary network of services, our own role becomes minimized, a fact that we may not comfortably accept, to the extent that we decide to remain as the principal social worker to the detriment of the client.

REQUIRED SKILLS AND KNOWLEDGE

In deciding to implement this form of coordinated approach to serve a particular client, it is not necessary that we be the designated case manager. For any number of reasons it might be much more effective to have some other person or representative of another service function in this role.

Our task is to facilitate a process that ensures a coordinated effort is made to assist the client with multiple needs. We do this by providing the optimal profile of services in a manner that reduces the difficulties of multiple relationships and duplication of efforts with a degree of coordination. We seek a plan that minimizes the extent to which the client needs to find their own way through a jungle of bureaucratic and often contradictory services in which clients often becomes underserved.

When using this technique in a once-only situation, our principal task is to seek consensus for why a case management process is needed. This would include identifying a person within the network to function as the case manager and take on the responsibility of working toward an assessment of need and the required coordination of services. The skills required to put this type of an independent structure in place are those involved in the techniques of collaboration, brokering, and advocacy.

What makes this technique a separate and distinct technique from collaboration and brokering is the goal of developing a formal structure, albeit temporary with an agreed-upon designated ad hoc case manager to whom is delegated responsibility and the ability to coordinate the needs, efforts, and resources for a single case.

Case Summary One

Terry is a single mom working hard to support her young son. She has a good support system in her family, but most of them live a few hours away. Terry does not currently own a car and relies on her sister, who lives close by, to take her where she needs to go.

SOCIAL WORKER: It's been a while since I've seen you. How has everything been the past few weeks?

TERRY: It's been okay, but I have been dealing with a few stressors lately.

SOCIAL WORKER: What's been going on?

TERRY: Right now my sister is really busy at work and isn't able to drive me to my therapy appointments. It's been hard to find a way to get here, which is why I've had to cancel my appointment the past few weeks. I've also had to miss a few days of work for the same reason. My job has been really understanding so far, but I don't know how long that will last. Plus, I am starting to have child care issues. My babysitter is moving to another state. I don't know what I am going to do with my son when she moves. I can't go to work or come to therapy if I don't have child care for my son.

SOCIAL WORKER: From what you're saying, I'm hearing that you currently need resources for transportation and child care. Is that correct?

TERRY: That is correct. I can't always rely on my sister for rides and I don't always have the money to take a cab or buy a bus ticket. The money I do have is usually already spent on bills or food.

SOCIAL WORKER: I have some information about resource options that might be helpful to meet your needs. Would you like to look at the information together now?

TERRY: Yes, that would be great. Any help is much appreciated.

During this session Terry's social worker is able to listen to Terry and be aware of her multiple needs. Her social worker works to perform the function of a case manager as a way to ensure that all of her service needs are being met. Having one person manage all of her needs helps to simplify the process of navigating resources and referrals. Also, by acting as her case manager, her social worker will help her attend therapy sessions more consistently.

Case Summary Two

Greg is attending therapy sessions for grief counseling following the unexpected death of his best friend. After his friend's death, Greg found it hard to get up and go to work daily, so he quit his job. He also states that it has been hard for him interact with others lately, so he has been isolating himself in his apartment. During therapy sessions Greg and his social worker have discussed Greg's need for employment, financial assistance until he obtains employment again, a grief support group, and social relationships. With everything that Greg is going through, his social worker believes that it will be in his best interest to use case management as a technique to help him access services, instead of trying to have him navigate the system of services by himself.

SOCIAL WORKER: During our previous sessions, we have discussed your need for multiple services located outside of this agency. I know that you are dealing with a lot in your life right now and it is hard for you to even think about trying to find and access resources which will be helpful to you. For these reasons, I think it would be an advantage to you if we used case management as a way to link you with those services. Do you feel comfortable with that idea?

GREG: I think that would be fine. Can you explain to me how it would work?

SOCIAL WORKER: We would take time during a therapy session to assess your service needs, and then I would take on the responsibility of coordinating services to meet your needs. Throughout the process we would make sure that we are always in agreement about your needs and working together for your benefit. If you agree, we can start during today's session.

GREG: That sounds good to me. I definitely have multiple needs right now and I require all the help and support I can get.

SOCIAL WORKER: Great. For the next few weeks we will designate a portion of our therapy sessions to your case management needs.

In this example, Greg's social worker will also be working as his case manager for a short period of time because there are no other case management services available to meet Greg's needs. Using case management as a technique in this situation will result in a better served client, and also a better use of time, services, and resources for all parties involved. It will also ensure that Greg does not experience additional stress, strain, or confusion while accessing services designed to meet his needs.

REFERENCES AND ADDITIONAL SOURCES

Burns, T., Fioritti, A., Holloway F., Malm, U., & Rossler, W. (2001). Case management and assertive community treatment in Europe. *Psychiatric Services, 52*, 631–636.

Cohen, E. L., & Cesta, T. G. (2005). *Nursing case management: From essentials to advanced practice applications* (4th ed.). St. Louis, MO: Elsevier Mosby.

Erdmann, Y., & Wilson, R. (2001). Managed care: A view from Europe. *Annual Review of Public Health, 22*, 273–291.

Gursansky, D., Harvey, J., & Kennedy, R. (2003). *Case management: Policy, practice and professional business*. New York, NY: Columbia University Press.

Hardcastle, D. A., Powers, P. R., & Wenocur, S. (2004). *Community practice: Theories and skills for social workers* (2nd ed.). New York, NY: Oxford University Press.

Holloway, F., & Carson, J. (2001). Case management: An update. *International Journal of Social Psychiatry, 47*(3), 21–31.

Liu, C., Leung, C. A., Li, S., Chi, I., & Chow, W. N. (2004). An experience of social work case management for frail elders in Hong Kong. *Geriatrics & Gerontology International, 4*(Suppl. 1), S173–S177.

Massie, D. K. (2004). Psychosocial issues for the elderly with cancer: The role of social work. *Topics in Geriatric Rehabilitation Cancer Issues Related to the Older Person, 20*(2), 114–119.

Moxley, D. (1989). *The practice of case management*. Newbury Park, CA: Sage.

Roberts, A. R., & Watkins, J. M. (2009). *Social workers' desk reference* (2nd ed.) New York, NY: Oxford University Press.

Rose, S. M. (1992). *Case management and social work practice*. New York: Longman.

Rosen, A., & Teesson, M. (2001). Does case management work? The evidence and the abuse of evidence-based medicine. *Australian and New Zealand Journal of Psychiatry 35*, 731–746.

Rothman, J. (1991). Guidelines for case management: Toward empirically based practice. *Social Work, 35*, 520–528.

Rothman, J. (1992). *Guidelines for case management: Putting research to professional use*. Itasca, IL: F. E. Peacock.

Vanderplasschen, W., Rapp, R. C., Wolf, J. R., & Broekaert, E. (2004). The development and implementation of case management for substance use disorders in North America and Europe. *Psychiatric Services, 55*(8), 913–922.

Vourlekis, B. S., & Robert R. G. (1992). *Social work case management*. New York, NY: Aldine.

Young, S. (2009). Professional relationships and power dynamics between urban community-based nurses and social work case managers. *Professional Case Management, 14*(6), 312–320.

Zastrow, C. (2009). *The practice of social work: A comprehensive worktext* (9th ed.). Belmont, CA: Brooks/Cole.

Ziguras, S. J., & Stuart, G. W. (2000). A meta-analysis of the effectiveness of mental health case management over 20 years. *Psychiatric Services, 51*, 1410–1421.

Challenge

DESCRIPTION

The challenge technique describes those targeted therapeutic efforts intended to inspire clients to consider or reconsider some component of their life, either to change something in their beliefs or perception, or to take or not take actions that help or hinder them and their life situation.

ORIGINS

This is one of several techniques—with which social work is becoming increasingly comfortable—that derives legitimacy and effectiveness from the support, authority, sensitivity, and power of the therapeutic relationship. Over the years, social workers have been quite uncomfortable with the concept of power and its translation into techniques such as giving advice or challenging. This discomfort emerges from a perception that power is negative in and of itself. In recent years, our understanding of power in the helping relationship has become more sophisticated, and with it an understanding that it is the misuse of power that we need to avoid, not power itself.

WHY THIS IS USEFUL TO SOCIAL WORK

Challenge is an important technique because it meets the needs of many clients who have the ability to move ahead in their lives but have no one to give them the supportive "push" they need.

We know from our own lives that there are times when a person we respect or a close friend challenges us with regard to some aspect of our lives, and does so in a manner that maintains the strength of the relationship—indeed, it can even strengthen it. We can probably remember occasions when, even though we initially may have been less than pleased at the challenge, we later came to appreciate how useful and important it was.

A friend is often able to get us to take a more healthy or objective look at some part of our reality by means of a well-phrased and well-presented challenge. Indeed, as we look at such an event in our personal lives, we realize that it was the friend who did not challenge us when we needed it who let us down. In addition to our friends, we also know how important it has been in our lives for understanding teachers, other professionals, or significant others to put challenges to us. This same dynamic and opportunity is frequently available to us in our relationships with clients.

HOW THIS IS USEFUL TO SOCIAL WORK

We make use of this technique for several reasons. We use it either to help a client expand or modify their view of some facet of their lives, or to learn to understand the views or actions of others. This potentially can help them avoid risk of harm to themselves or others. We also use it to help a client consider the implications of some proposed change in their life or to find the courage to take some significant action. This technique can be used in diverse ways, ranging from a very gentle verbal nudging about some aspect of the client's psychosocial situation, to a more assertive intervention on the social worker's part. One reality for many of our clients is that they have not been challenged along their life's odyssey. Neither have they been challenged about perceptions or behaviors that produce problems, or to take developmental steps that will contribute to more mature functioning.

RISK FACTORS

Challenge should be viewed as having a moderate to high degree of risk. In using this technique, we need to be as certain as possible that we do not fall into the all-too-present trap of inflicting our ideas of what we view as best for a client upon him or her in the form of a challenge. It is especially risky for the relationship when a confrontation is viewed from the client's perspective as a fear that "my worker won't like me if I do not go along with this challenge he has given me."

There are several other possible situations where this technique could produce a problem. These include when the client is not interested in the proposed change, is not ready to change, or is unable to change in the area under consideration.

REQUIRED SKILLS AND KNOWLEDGE

It is a technique that is used in a diverse manner ranging from a gentle verbal nudging of the client in regard to some aspect of their psychosocial entities to a more assertive level of intervention by the worker.

The decision to challenge a client is based on a diagnostic judgment of the importance and timing of the desired change in the client's perceptions or actions. This includes a careful assessment of the degree of discomfort such a challenge may create for the client, as well as their ability to cope with such discomfort.

This technique requires a considerable level of self-awareness on the social worker's part to be certain that the area of challenge will help the client rather than be irritating, frustrating, or a strain on the relationship. There is also the possibility that the challenge may represent an inappropriate projection of the social worker's wishes and values.

Power has had an important place in our maturational histories from our earliest days, sometimes positively and sometimes negatively. Thus, in considering the use of challenge in our client work, it is essential that we consider possible transference factors that may be present in any challenge we deliver.

Case Summary One

Jack is a high school student. His mother reports that she believes he is lazy and has no direction in his life. Due to his mother's concerns, Jack started meeting with a social worker after school.

> **Social worker:** Jack, what do you think about the concerns your mother has for you?
> **Jack:** She's wrong. It's not that I'm lazy. I just know that I will never amount to anything, so why bother trying?
> **Social worker:** You believe that you will never amount to anything. Are you sure about that? Can you definitively say that you will never amount to anything? Isn't there a possibility that you could be successful, even if it is at a little something?
> [After several moments of silence and some serious thinking by Jack:]
> **Jack:** Well, I guess it's not fair to say that I will never amount to anything. It just doesn't seem very likely sometimes. I guess there could be a chance that I could be a little successful at something, one day.
> **Social worker:** I'm glad to hear you say that.

During this session, the social worker was able to challenge Jack's unhelpful and unproductive beliefs about his future and get him to consider alternatives. Changing this belief was a first step toward changing the rest of his life. Being challenged in this therapeutic setting was helpful to Jack and his life situation.

Case Summary Two

Christina is a young adult who reports living a sheltered life. She states that as a child she felt isolated from her peers because her mother worried too much and often didn't let her go out with her friends. After Christina moved out of her mother's home, she started going out a lot and meeting new people. She says that her mother continues to nag her with her worries even though she isn't living with her anymore. Christina reports that she goes out every weekend and has recently started going out at least two or three nights a week. The mornings after she goes out, it is hard for her to wake up and she ends up being late to work. Her performance at work is also beginning to decline because she is so tired from being out all night.

SOCIAL WORKER: How has everything been going lately?

CHRISTINA: Pretty much everything has been going fine, except that my mother is still bothering me. She's worried that I'm throwing my life away or something. I keep telling her that everyone my age goes out to clubs. That's what I'm supposed to do. It's no big deal.

SOCIAL WORKER: You mentioned last week that you've received a warning at work due to your persistent lateness and declining job performance, and that if this behavior continues you will be fired. I'm curious, are your friends also in jeopardy of losing their jobs?

CHRISTINA: Well, no.

SOCIAL WORKER: Hmm. Are they going out every weekend and several nights during the week like you are?

CHRISTINA: No. During the week I usually end up going out alone. I still have a good time though. It's hard to find a friend that I can go out with every weekend, too.

SOCIAL WORKER: So maybe this isn't what you're supposed to do—it seems like more of a choice. It appears as though your statement at the beginning of the session isn't entirely accurate and that everyone your age isn't going out to clubs. Also, it does seem like a big deal if it's interfering with your work. What would you do if you got fired? How would you survive?

CHRISTINA: Wow, I never thought of that. I guess I never actually thought that they would really fire me. I'd probably lose my apartment and have to move back in with my mom.

SOCIAL WORKER: I wonder if you might reconsider your previous statement and think about decreasing the number of nights per week that you go out.

CHRISTINA: I think I might have to. You made some good points that I've never considered before.

Challenging Christina's belief about her partying behavior allowed her to consider the consequences of her partying habits and rethink her current behavior. Challenging is an effective technique in this case because of the support, authority, sensitivity, and power in the therapeutic relationship. By using challenging as a therapeutic technique, Christina's social worker was able to give her a supportive push in the right direction to empower her to improve her current situation.

REFERENCES AND ADDITIONAL SOURCES

Kimball, R. O. (1990). Empowerment: How and why they work: Special report: Challenging teens in treatment. *Adolescent Counselor, 4*(2), 18–22.

Pfirman, E. S. M. (1988). The effects of a wilderness challenge course on victims of rape in locus-of-control, self-concept, and fear. *Dissertation Abstracts International, 49*/07-B, 2870. (University Microfilms No. AAD88–18574)

Sheafor, B. W., Horejsi, J. C. R., & Gloria, A. H. (Eds.). (1997). *Techniques and guidelines for social work practice* (4th ed., p. 480). Toronto, Ontario: Allyn & Bacon.

Clarification

DESCRIPTION

This technique encompasses those efforts on the part of the social worker to bring clients to a broader understanding of particular significant aspects of their lives. Clarification helps clients better understand the interconnectedness of various components of their reality, rather than mistakenly assigning single causes or reasons to some aspect of their lives, or to wrongly estimate the importance of any significant component of their reality such as a boss or a misunderstanding wife. This technique has a strong cognitive element, but it is often useful at a point where a client has been venting about some life situation and now appears ready to view the issue in a less emotionally charged manner.

ORIGINS

Through the years of clinical social work practice, clarification has become almost second nature to us, to the point that at times we scarcely recognize it as a distinct technique. Nevertheless, practitioners have come to recognize that, as important as it has always been for clients to achieve insight in a psychodynamic sense, many of the problems they met in their everyday lives stem from an overly narrow or constricted view of various aspects of their reality. In her analysis of interview content, Hollis clearly recognized that this treatment component was very different from insight in the classical sense and realized how important this type of enhanced understanding for the client.

WHY THIS IS USEFUL TO SOCIAL WORK

This is a very useful technique for our practice because many of the difficulties our clients bring to sessions stem from uncertainty, misunderstanding, and confusion about various significant aspects of their lives. Helping a client deal with these realities, the "warp and woof" components of daily living that Mary Richmond described, can be just as liberating for the client as the psychic advantages of dealing with unconscious material.

Often, a client can only deal with their more deep-seated emotional material after they have been able to put their lives in order in a way that flows from understanding the nature and source of their issues. In many instances, however, this is not necessary, because it is frequently the less dramatic aspects of daily life that are their sources of trauma, anxiety, and loss of control.

HOW THIS IS USEFUL TO SOCIAL WORK

We meet many situations in practice where a considerable part of a client's difficulties stem from a lack of understanding of some facet of their lives. For example, a wife may be convinced that her husband no longer loves her, when in fact his emotional responses come from the imminent possibility that he might lose his job. A woman may think her job stress comes from unreasonable demands her boss places on her, when it actually derives from her concern over a health issue. Likewise, an adolescent may believe her teacher is pushing her too hard, not realizing she is actually trying to help the student.

There is clearly an educational component to this technique. Its effectiveness stems both from the client's wish to be helped and from the level of wisdom, power, and expertise they ascribe to the worker.

In deciding to use clarification in some particular situation, it is necessary to ensure that the issue being clarified is something the client is able to use in a helpful fashion. Certainly the richness of our experience, and the knowledge of how systems influence one another in many of our clients' lives, provide us with a broad perspective that can be of great assistance to clients who are ready for this technique.

RISK FACTORS

Clarification has a moderate level of risk; hence, we must be careful not to overuse it, because it can easily play into our own needs. It is precisely our ability to influence clients through the power of the relationship that creates this risk. We can easily fall into the trap of being the expert and enjoy the power and wisdom that some clients attribute to us, to the point where we use clarification too often.

We also need to be very sure of ourselves and how we perceive the interconnected life aspects we are seeking to clarify for the client. This caution is necessary to avoid inappropriately leading the client to behavior or conclusions that are either incorrect or may produce further problems.

Often we are not certain where the client specifically needs further clarification, and our process must begin with mutual exploration. However, what we often think of as exploration might be viewed by the client as an opinion or giving advice. Comments such as, "I wonder, Mrs. M., if such-and-such is important here?" can be easily seen as an opinion, which the client may views in a much more directive fashion than we intend.

REQUIRED SKILLS AND KNOWLEDGE

In deciding to use clarification for some particular situation, it is necessary to ensure that the area of clarification is something that the client is able to use in a helpful fashion.

Certainly the richness of our experience and the knowledge of systemic inter-influences in the lives of many of our clients provides us with a richness of purview that can be of great assistance to many if and when the client is ready for such clarifications.

As mentioned earlier effective use of clarification requires a deep understanding of the client and the spectrum of significant systems and roles in his or her reality. We also need to understand how such systems relate to and influence one another. It is our skill in biopsychosocial assessment that leads us to a diagnosis of the significant profile of the client's reality that can make clarification useful. The skills in assessment involve careful use of questions, suggestions, and direct sharing of opinions.

When skillfully employed, clarification can have a dramatic impact on our clients' lives by helping them form a clearer picture and understanding of various aspects of their reality. This often leads to a much more objective and productive use of their energy and interest in continuing with treatment to achieve goals mutually agreed upon between the therapist and client.

Case Summary One

Monica is a young adult who left home to attend a university in another state. She recently began feeling "not quite right," so she decided to seek the help of a professional.

SOCIAL WORKER: How has everything been over the past week?

MONICA: It's the same as usual. I get so bored in the evenings after classes. There's never anything to do. It makes me feel so blah.

SOCIAL WORKER: How do you usually spend your time?

MONICA: I try to fill my time by watching television and reading any magazines I might have around. I don't do anything exciting.

SOCIAL WORKER: Remind me, how long ago did you start school?

MONICA: Umm, about two months ago.

SOCIAL WORKER: So this is a fairly new and unfamiliar situation for you?

MONICA: Yes, I'd say so.

SOCIAL WORKER: It seems as though you are uncomfortable with your new situation. I wonder if you are feeling lonely and wishing you had someone to spend time with you and fill that feeling of emptiness. Does that sound right?

MONICA: Wow, that is exactly it. I never realized it before. It makes sense, though. I've never been away from my home or my family for more than a week. Now I'm living in a new city, starting college courses for the first time, and all without my family by my side.

The clarification that Monica's social worker provided her with gave her a sense of freedom. This allowed her to begin understanding where her unsettled feelings stem from. Once she knew this, she could then start working toward changing those negative feelings.

Case Summary Two

Anthony is a 12-year-old boy. His mom has brought him to therapy sessions because she believes he has anger management problems. Anthony states that he is angry because he thinks his mom is trying to ruin his life and always keeps him from having fun.

SOCIAL WORKER: Anthony, how do you feel about coming to see me for therapy sessions?

ANTHONY: I don't mind coming and talking to you. You're nice, smart, and you know what you're talking about.

SOCIAL WORKER: Your mom tells me she is concerned about how you are expressing your anger at home. What do you think about that?

ANTHONY: It's all her fault. She doesn't let me do anything. She's ruining my life and it makes me feel so angry when she doesn't let me do what I want.

SOCIAL WORKER: I remember last session you told me that you went to your friend's birthday party that weekend and had a lot of fun. Also, before that you mentioned how much fun you had at the mall with your cousins. What kinds of activities are you referring to that your mother doesn't let you do?

ANTHONY: There was this go-kart race that I wanted to go to with some friends from school, but my mom wouldn't let me go.

SOCIAL WORKER: Did she just say that you couldn't go or did she give you a reason why she didn't want you to go?

ANTHONY: I know she said something about people getting hurt, but I wasn't really listening because I was so upset that I couldn't go. Plus, there was that time I couldn't go with my older brother to a rock concert because my mom said it wasn't safe for me to go. She's so unreasonable sometimes.

SOCIAL WORKER: From what you've told me it seems as though your mom does let you have fun with your friends sometimes. However, it sounds like when there is a concern for your safety she doesn't feel comfortable letting you go out. I wonder if she's really not trying to ruin your life. I wonder if she's just trying to take care of you and ensure that you remain safe and healthy.

ANTHONY: What you're saying does make sense. Maybe I have been a little hard on my mom. She's only trying to look out for me.

Anthony was having a difficult time dealing with the fact that he isn't allowed to do everything that he wants to. He was misunderstanding his mom's reasoning for not allowing him to attend certain events. By using clarification as a technique, the social worker was able to assist Anthony in understanding alternative possibilities instead of assigning a single cause to his mom's actions. The social worker was able to use this technique effectively because she had a full understanding of Anthony's situation, and because Anthony assigns a significant level of wisdom, power, and expertise to his social worker. Clarification helped Anthony get a better picture and understanding of his reality.

REFERENCES AND ADDITIONAL SOURCES

Hepworth, D. H., Rooney, R. H., & Larsen, J. (1997). *Direct social work practice* (5th ed., pp. 155–156). New York, NY: Brooks/Cole.

Hollis, F., & Woods, M. E. (1981). *Casework: A psychosocial therapy* (3rd ed.). New York, NY: Random House.

Northen, H. (1995). *Clinical social work knowledge and skills* (2nd ed., p. 153). New York, NY: Columbia University Press.

Woods, M. E., & Florence, H. (2000). *Casework: A psychosocial therapy* (5th ed., p. 119). New York: McGraw-Hill.

Collaboration

DESCRIPTION

We are often most helpful to a client by planning and building with them a network of resources that meets the complexities of their present situation beyond what we ourselves are able to provide directly. This is achieved by our use of collaborative techniques.

ORIGINS

Collaboration has no clearly identifiable conceptual route or origin, apart from a general awareness from the profession's earliest days that much of our work in treatment is based on our psychosocial orientation when we are involved in such activities. Social workers also realized early on that the development and implementation of required helping networks required specialized skills.

Different theoretical orientations have variously stressed the importance and relevance of these activities. However, virtually all descriptions of practice credit the benefits of working collaboratively with other people and things (e.g., specialized knowledge, tangible resources, expertise, access to programs) outside the classical therapeutic relationship.

WHY THIS IS USEFUL TO SOCIAL WORK

Apart from the primary help that collaborative activities can provide, they can also bring the client a greatly expanded network of caregivers. This can have both a developmental and ego-enhancement side effect, as the client comes to realize that there are people, resources, and services that are interested in them and can care for them. The very experience of having a cluster of helpful people assists many clients in understanding and using skills to function in complex communities and their lives outside treatment.

HOW THIS IS USEFUL TO SOCIAL WORK

There are several ways in which we collaborate for the client. For example, we may involve a significant person in the client's life, another professional, a colleague in our own setting, or a group of other community resources available to us or to the client. One of the strengths of a collaborative strategy is that each person or system involved brings something not available in the primary client relationship.

In some situations, a second social worker can be brought in for a limited time. In this way, we may involve a colleague who has specific information about a resource or whose experience with a particular technique can be of particular use to our client. Before doing so, it is important to make clear who is the primary social worker, and who is the adjunct for that particular role or function.

Collaboration can be a short- or long-term process, depending on how extensively the primary social worker needs to to draw upon the helping potential of other services, resources, or skills. They may be ended once they have contributed sufficiently to the situation. Collaborative resources may also be used for a much longer, ongoing basis. In these situations, the worker must clarify and optimize the primary therapeutic process for the client.

There is much about collaboration as a technique that is similar to case management (see p. 65). However, there are differences that make them separate techniques. Case management clearly requires extensive collaboration, but collaboration does not always include case management. The factor that distinguishes the two is the question of administrative leadership. From the standpoint of responsibility, each component of the collaborative structure functions in an autonomous way, whereas in case management there is a clearly identified leadership structure.

RISK FACTORS

In working in a collaborative arrangement with other colleagues, the risk of relationship problems is high. In situations where two or more professionals are involved there can be rivalries (although subtle and unrecognized) for the client's attention. If the client is being seen separately by several people, there is the possibility that the client may relate differently to each one in a manner that creates problems for both the professionals and the client.

A further area of potential risk comes from the possibility that, although our intentions in developing a plurality of helping resources may be good, the very diversity of services in a client's life may confuse and stress the client. Overall, however, this is not a high-risk technique.

REQUIRED SKILLS AND KNOWLEDGE

The challenge in using this technique is that it is very easy for the client to get lost amid the differential expectations of multiple interacting systems, which can be quite intricate and demanding in various ways. We also need to be careful that our clients do not enter or get put into situations where there are contradictory expectations and goals for them to meet. The primary social worker and others involved therefore will require strong collaborative skills.

Case Summary One

Jenny presented with frequent panic attacks. She went to the social worker's office because she thought they were due to an anxiety disorder.

SOCIAL WORKER: Jenny, why don't you tell me what brings you to my office?

JENNY: I've been having panic attacks lately.

SOCIAL WORKER: How do you characterize your panic attacks?

JENNY: It's like a strong fear that comes on suddenly for no reason, I start sweating and shaking, it becomes hard for me to breathe, and I feel sick to my stomach.

SOCIAL WORKER: I'd like you to see your primary care physician for a physical exam and to rule out any medical reasons for your panic attacks. Can you provide the name and phone number of your doctor?

JENNY: Yes, I have his business card in my wallet.

SOCIAL WORKER: If you sign this release form, I will be able to exchange information with your doctor regarding your panic attack symptoms and the results of your physical exam.

JENNY: Okay, I'll sign the release form and make an appointment with my physician tomorrow.

SOCIAL WORKER: Let's make a follow-up appointment for two weeks from now to allow enough time to receive the information from your doctor.

The social worker instructed Jenny to see her physician because panic attacks can occur as a result of some general medical conditions. It is important for the social worker to collaborate with Jenny's doctor to find out the results of her examination and discuss anything medical that might be causing her panic attacks before looking at the possibility of some type of anxiety disorder. The social worker must collaborate directly with the physician to avoid passing information through the client, which can be partial and therefore intentionally or unintentionally misleading.

Case Summary Two

Ron is an older adult attending therapy sessions to deal with transition and grief issues. This past year, Ron's wife died of cancer. Following her death, Ron's adult son, Mike, suggested that Ron move in with him so he would be close in case of an emergency. Ron and Mike don't have any other family living in the area, and Mike has a very demanding job. During previous sessions Ron has described feeling lonely and sad about the loss of his wife, home, and everyday routine. Following Ron's disclosures over the past few weeks, his social worker decided that it would be beneficial to Ron's treatment to collaborate with his son, Mike.

SOCIAL WORKER: Mike, thank you for joining our session today. We're happy to have you here.

RON: I really appreciate you being here.

MIKE: It's no problem. I want to do everything I can to help out my dad. That's one of the reasons I suggested that he come live with me.

SOCIAL WORKER: How have things been since your dad moved in?

MIKE: Overall I think they've been great. I really enjoy having him with me. Right now I'm just feeling a little overwhelmed and stressed out. I'm pretty much the only close family that my dad has left. I want to be there for my dad, but work is demanding a lot from me right now.

SOCIAL WORKER: Ron, would you like to tell Mike what you've been telling me about how you've been feeling lately?

RON: Yes. Mike, I'm happy to be close to you and to not be living alone. However, sometimes I still feel lonely and I get sad when I think about losing your mom, my home, and my everyday routine all so quickly.

MIKE: I had no idea you felt like that, Dad.

RON: Well, I don't want to burden you. It's not your fault or your problem. I know you're busy with work.

SOCIAL WORKER: Mike, your dad and I have discussed the idea of linking him with a service which will provide companionship for your dad and maybe ease some of your stress during those times when you are swamped with work. What do you think about that?

MIKE: I think that sounds great. If that's what my dad wants I completely support it. I didn't even know services like that existed.

RON: I think it would be nice to have someone to talk to and play cards with. Maybe go up to the store with every once in a while.

The collaboration between the social worker, Ron, and Mike reminded Ron how much his son cares about him and the support he has from him. It provided an opportunity for Ron and Mike to discuss and try to understand each other's feelings. Also, through this collaboration, the social worker, Mike, and Ron were able to determine that the best solution for Mike and Ron's situation was to collaborate with a respite worker who will act as a companion to Ron and alleviate some of the pressure Mike feels. The collaboration with the respite worker will provide Ron with an expanded network of supportive and caring persons in his life and aid in the therapeutic process.

REFERENCES AND ADDITIONAL SOURCES

Altshuler, S. J. (2003). From barriers to successful collaboration: Public schools and child welfare working together. *Social Work, 8*(1), 52–63.

Chuang, E., & Lucio, R. (2011). Interagency collaboration between child welfare agencies, schools, and mental health providers and children's mental health service receipt. *Advances in School Mental Health Promotion, 4*(2), 4–15.

Fortner, J., & Walsh, S. R. (2002). Coming full circle: Family therapy and psychiatry reunite in a training program. *Families, Systems, & Health 20*(1), 105–111.

Graham, J. R., & Barter, K. (1999). Collaboration a social work practice method. *Families in Society, 80*(1), 6–13.

Hackstaff, G. L., & House, S. T. (1990). Development of a collaborative geriatric program between the legal system and a social work-directed program of a community hospital. *Social Work in Health Care, 14*(3), 1–16.

Hanna, K., & Rodger, S. (2002). Towards family-centred practice in paediatric occupational therapy: A review of the literature on parent-social worker collaboration. *Australian Occupational Therapy Journal, 49*(1), 14–24.

Leathard, A. (2003). *Interprofessional collaboration: From policy to practice in health and social care.* New York, NY: Brunner-Routledge.

Mulroy, E. A., & Shay, S. (1997). Nonprofit organizations and innovation: A model of neighborhood-based collaboration to prevent child maltreatment. *Social Work, 42*(5), 515–524.

Netting. F. E., & Williams, F. G. (1996). Case manager-physician collaboration: Implications for professional identity, roles, and relationships. *Health and Social Work, 21*(3), 216–224.

O'Neal, G. S. (1993). Preventing conflict: Encouraging collaboration among students, faculty, and family. *Social Work in Education, 15*(2) 83–89.

Parton, N., & O'Byrne, P. (2000). *Constructive social work: Towards a new practice.* New York, NY: St. Martin's Press.

Poulan, J. (2002). *Collaborative social work: Strengths based generalist practice.* Itasca, IL: Peacock.

Raeymaeckers, P., & Dierckx, D. (2012). How can we study the integration of networks among human service organizations? Some lessons from organization sociology. *European Journal of Social Work, 4*, 484–502.

Roberts, V. (1994). Conflict and collaboration, managing intergroup relations. In A. Obholzer & V. Roberts (Eds.), *The unconscious at work: Individual and organizational stress in the human services/ by members of the Tavistock Clinic "Consulting to Institutions" workshop* (pp. 187–196). London, England: Routledge.

Scott, D. (2005). Inter-organisational collaboration in family-centred practice: A framework for analysis and action. *Australian Social Work, 58*(2), 132–141.

Singh, A. M. (1999). Shamans, healing and mental health. *Journal of Child and Family Studies, 8*(2), 131–134.

Tapper. D., Kleinman, P., & Nakashian, M. (1997). An interagency collaboration strategy for linking schools with social and criminal justice services. *Social Work in Education, 19*, 176–188.

Weinstein, J., Whittington, C., & Leiba, T. (2003). *Collaboration in social work practice.* New York, NY: Jessica Kinglsey.

Wells, R., Chuang, E., Haynes, L. E., Lee, I., & Bai, Y. (2011). Child welfare agency ties to providers and schools and substance abuse treatment use by adolescents. *Journal of Substance Abuse Treatment, 40*(1), 26–34.

Compliment

DESCRIPTION

This technique encompasses the use of compliments in the therapeutic process as a way of helping clients enhance their self image.

ORIGINS

Social workers have long known and understood that an important requirement for the development of a healthy ego structure is the receipt of positive acknowledgement of successes and achievements from significant people in one's life. This has always been an important component of any of the various theories that have influenced our practice development, although it is probably most closely identified as a specific technique in Gestalt and client-centered therapy. Transactional analysis also develops this concept in the terminology of positive and negative strokes.

WHY THIS IS USEFUL TO SOCIAL WORK

Most of us who have matured in a reasonably healthy way are accustomed to giving and receiving compliments as a part of our normal interaction with significant others in our lives. However, we quickly learn in our practice experience that there are many people in society who have rarely, if ever, been complimented on achievements of any type, and that this gap in their histories has seriously affected their development and functioning.

Nevertheless, one of the things that we frequently seem to forget to do in our practice is to compliment our clients on various aspects of their lives. We know, for example, that support is a technique we frequently use, and that complimenting a client is a form of support, but it is sufficiently different from general support for it to be considered on its own merits.

HOW THIS IS USEFUL TO SOCIAL WORK

The receiving of compliments or "positive strokes" can be a very powerful agent in helping people achieve and enhance a positive image of themselves and the ability to make use of their talents and abilities. Compliments can also lead people to do things in a manner that brings them further support, encouragement, and reward from those they view as being significant in their lives. In this way, such compliments can help some clients invest more intensely in a therapeutic process.

On occasions when we have complimented a client on some psychosocial gain they have made, we can then move beyond giving compliments to leading the client to reflect with us on the role or lack of role that compliments play in their lives. This in turn can help them understand how this piece of personal history can greatly affect the way they see themselves and others in their lives, and how they interact with people.

A secondary gain of communicating this type of positive reward is that some clients will learn to incorporate such rewarding actions into their relationships with other people, which in turn can result in further appreciation from them. This can boost the clients' ego and alter their behavior.

In addition to using compliments as a reward within the treatment process itself, complimenting aspects of clients' lives outside of treatment can also have a positive effect. For many of our clients who are just surviving on a day-to-day basis, recognizing this situation can be a major personal victory. These clients often are not themselves aware of the magnitude of their achievement of simply living from one week or month to the next. Frequently such persons received little or no appreciation from people in their lives with whom they interact—if indeed there are any. Receiving such compliments or strokes can be a powerful agent in helping them to achieve and enhance a positive self-image.

RISK FACTORS

In general, this technique is low risk. For some highly damaged persons, it could well be that an overuse of compliments by us could provoke anxiety, eliciting feelings of doubt and suspicion. Such situations can weaken the therapeutic relationship rather than strengthening it.

REQUIRED SKILLS AND KNOWLEDGE

The process of giving compliments in therapy can be as simple as a positive nod or saying, "Well done" at an appropriate place in an interview, to formally recognizing a client's success via some ceremonial action. We often forget that the very process of coming to and remaining in therapy can be very difficult for some. Being aware of this and acknowledging it to the client through positive encouragement can have a powerful positive significance for them.

Case Summary One

Howard is a young man attending therapy sessions because he was physically and emotionally abused by his father. He recently moved out of his parents' house and wants to heal from his traumatic childhood. He currently reports feeling discouraged, and he is unable to identify many of his personal strengths and resources.

SOCIAL WORKER: Hello, Howard. What brings you here today?

HOWARD: I don't know how I am going to get over what has happened in my life.

SOCIAL WORKER: Tell me about your life.

HOWARD: My father started beating me around the age of ten. This abuse continued throughout the years until I moved out of the house a few months ago.

SOCIAL WORKER: Did anyone else know about this abuse?

HOWARD: No, he was very good about hiding it. He was able to hurt me without leaving big marks and he never did anything bad when my mom was around. I never told my mom about it because I was afraid she wouldn't believe me and then the beatings would get worse.

[Howard continues telling his social worker the story of his childhood and other relevant background information. The social worker then ends this session by complimenting Howard.]

SOCIAL WORKER: It was very brave of you to open up to me today. I want to thank you for your courage and motivation to come to session and share your story with me.

This complimentary expression by the social worker had a powerful positive significance for Howard. It helped him feel appreciated for his efforts and made him invest more in the therapeutic process. The compliment also acted as a form of support for Howard from his social worker, which made Howard feel more at ease and less anxious about attending sessions.

Case Summary Two

Shirley is an adolescent girl attending therapy sessions because her parents are going through a divorce. After her parents' announced that they were divorcing, Shirley started experiencing intense emotional reactions and feelings of sadness and low self-worth at home and school. Additionally, her mother reports that Shirley is losing interest in school activities and frequently forgets to complete her homework.

SOCIAL WORKER: Hi, Shirley, I'm so glad to see you here today. Were you able to chart your feelings over the past week like we discussed last session?

SHIRLEY: Yes, I have it right here. I wrote down the date and time and then I wrote how I was feeling and what happened to provoke those feelings.

[Shirley and her social worker review the assignment together.]

SOCIAL WORKER: This is great work, Shirley, very impressive.

SHIRLEY: I just did what you told me to. It's no big deal.

SOCIAL WORKER: No, Shirley, you made a choice to do something which will be beneficial to your treatment. You made the effort to complete the activity and you did a wonderful job. I'm proud of the progress you've made.

As a result of her parents going through a divorce, Shirley has felt angry and sad, in addition to feeling low self-worth and a lack of confidence. She has also mentioned that she feels ignored by both of her parents because they are more concerned with themselves and getting a divorce than with anything going on in her life. Hearing a compliment from her social worker provided Shirley with an enhanced positive image of herself. It also helped her to feel more capable about completing other tasks in her life. Shirley enjoyed receiving a compliment from her social worker, and it enabled her to become more invested in the therapeutic process and to continue to make decisions that will lead to the achievement of her treatment goals.

REFERENCES AND ADDITIONAL SOURCES

Corcoran, J. (2002). Developmental adaptations of solution-focused family therapy. *Brief Treatment & Crisis Intervention, 2*(4), 301–313.

Foxx, R. M., McMorrow, M. J., & Bittle, R. G. (1985). Teaching social skills to psychiatric inpatients. *Behaviour Research and Therapy, 23*(5), 531–537.

Petr, C. G. (2004). *Social work with children and their families: Pragmatic foundations* (2nd ed.). New York, NY: Oxford University Press.

Roes, N. A. (2002). *Therapeutic techniques for engaging challenging clients.* New York, NY: Haworth Press.

Taylor, E. R. (2009). Sandtray and solution-focused therapy. *International Journal of Play Therapy, 18*(1), 56–68.

Trepper, T. S. (1993). *101 interventions in family therapy.* New York, NY: Haworth Press.

Wall, M. D., Kleckner, T., Amendt, J. H., & Bryant, R. D. (1989). Therapeutic compliments: Setting the stage for successful therapy. *Journal of Marital and Family Therapy, 15*(2), 159–167.

Wardhaugh, R. (2009). *An introduction to sociolinguistics* (6th ed.). Malden, MA: Blackwell.

Zastrow, C. (2009). *The practice of social work: A comprehensive worktext* (9th ed.). Belmont, CA: Brooks/ Cole.

Computer

DESCRIPTION

This technique focuses on ways in which computers can be used as therapeutic resources in direct practice.

ORIGINS

In a very few years, computers have assumed an important role in social work practice that verges on the essential. Initially, the use of technology of any kind was not seen as being of particular use in social work practice, the emphasis being on the power of the in vivo therapeutic relationship. However, our theoretical base has expanded and helped us to understand that if something was ethical, useful, and within our competence, it should be a part of practice. As a result, comfort with examining and using various technical resources in direct practice soon grew.

In many ways, the acceptance of the telephone in practice assisted in this. For a long time, practitioners only saw the phone as an administrative resource. We soon discovered that much therapeutic work in fact could be and was being done over the phone. As the prevalence and influence of computers rose in our society, social workers have gained a greater appreciation for their treatment potential.

WHY THIS IS USEFUL TO SOCIAL WORK

The ability of computers to communicate with virtually anyone anywhere, their ubiquity, and their capacity to instantly store and retrieve masses of relevant information make them a powerful therapeutic resource. The things a computer can do very strongly enable much of what we aspire to do for our client.

HOW THIS IS USEFUL TO SOCIAL WORK

The number of clients across the world that we meet in practice who are computer literate has grown very quickly. This will only accelerate in the years ahead.

Computers have been put to various uses in social work practice: aiding assessment and diagnosis, record keeping, and enhancing human contact. A particularly important contemporary use of computers in direct practice relates to their power to retrieve information and knowledge. Using Internet search engines, social workers and clients can can seek out information on their own or together about some aspect of the client's situation or problem, or, in a parallel way, about resources that can assist in specific categories of need, or to complete client tasks.

Computers can also be used in self-assessment, when we have the client complete various scales, questionnaires, or standardized instruments to expand their self-awareness in some area of their life. Some data have indicated that many persons will be more open and honest when completing a computer-administered instrument than when it is administered by a social worker. In this way, a computer can provide positive reinforcement when the client is modifying some behavior or learning a new skill.

A further therapeutic potential of the computer lies in helping people contact others virtually instantaneously all over the world. This often can be done in an anonymous fashion in such things as chat rooms, group discussions, or one-on-one communications. This can help individuals expand their circle of human contacts.

As with the telephone, the computer, through the potential of e-mail, is a most convenient way of conveying information and support to clients while facilitating clients' ability to keep in touch with us. We know from experience that some people are ready to discuss very complex and intimate matters through the medium of e-mail, which can at times be made into a productive technique.

RISK FACTORS

As powerful and helpful as the self-help potential of the computer may be, we know it is a resource with a very high risk factor, one that can have serious negative outcomes in such areas as providing incorrect information or developing and fostering problematic or even dangerous relationships. For many of our clients the world of computers is an important part of their lives, whereas others fear and avoid them.

REQUIRED SKILLS AND KNOWLEDGE

If computers are to be a part of a particular plan of intervention, it is essential that we have a thorough understanding of the safety issues involved in the resources being considered. We also need to know the role that computers may or may not already be playing in a client's life. We also need to know whether a client views computers as potential resources in a helping process, and to ensure that our own interest and enthusiasm about the potential of this technique does not exceed the client's in this regard.

Computers are a powerful and virtually worldwide reality in our practice lives, one with a very high potential in the therapeutic process whose full dimensions have yet to be assessed. It is important that we continue to explore its potential as a therapeutic technique, while remaining conscious of our responsibility not to let our enthusiasm overshadow our awareness of their inherent limitations and risks.

Case Summary One

Nadine is a young woman who just moved to a new state to attend the local university. She has never been away from her family for this long before and is having a hard time adjusting to her new life circumstances. Nadine reports feeling isolated and unsupported in her new surroundings.

NADINE: The longest I've been away from my sister and parents was a few nights for sleepovers and stuff. I didn't realize how hard this would be. I was expecting college to be fun and exciting. Instead I feel upset and down all of the time.

SOCIAL WORKER: You have gone through a major change in your life. It is normal to have these feelings when you are adjusting to such a difference. It sounds as though your feelings about the situation have come as a pretty big shock to you.

NADINE: Yes, definitely. I barely get to talk to my family anymore. I thought I wouldn't miss them because I would be busy with classes and stuff all the time, but I miss them like crazy. I especially miss the bond that my sister and I shared.

SOCIAL WORKER: When is the last time you spoke to your sister?

NADINE: It's been over a month and when we do speak it's very brief and superficial conversation. I'm used to seeing her every day and talking to her several times throughout the day.

SOCIAL WORKER: What do you think is the reason behind the two of you not communicating?

NADINE: It's hard to sit down and find a good, solid amount of time to speak to her. I keep thinking about how I need to call her and then I never find a good time to do it.

SOCIAL WORKER: You mentioned in a previous session that you are very good with computers and enjoy using the Internet. I wonder if you and your sister might have better luck communicating through the computer, using e-mail or a social networking site. Is your sister good with computers too?

NADINE: I never even thought of that before. She is great with computers. I do have a school e-mail account and I could ask my parents if it would be okay for her to create a free e-mail account. Plus it would be easier to write to her any time of the day or night based on my school schedule than to have to call at a decent hour. I think this could work, and now I will be able to keep up with what is going on in her life and we can stay closely connected.

Because the social worker knew that Nadine was proficient in using computers and enjoyed using the Internet, he was able to suggest its use as an alternative to keeping in phone contact with her sister. This will allow Nadine to continue the close bond she has with her sister and improve her daily outlook. By using the computer, Nadine and her sister can exchange pictures, updates, and words of encouragement.

Case Summary Two

Jeff has recently started attending therapy sessions. He is a young adult whose brother committed suicide a few months ago. He reports having trouble sleeping and concentrating, and he feels lonely and sad most of the time.

JEFF: Most people have no idea what I'm going through, and I feel like I can't talk to the ones who do. I don't want to tell my family about how I'm feeling, because I might make them feel worse than they already do. What if they are having an okay day and I call them to talk about my brother and bring them down? I would feel so guilty.

SOCIAL WORKER: I understand what you're saying. However, it is important that you have an outlet for your feelings outside of our therapy sessions. How are you with computers?

JEFF: I'm good with computers. I use a computer at work and I have one at home. I enjoy going on the Internet. I also use my computer often to write e-mails and prepare documents for work.

SOCIAL WORKER: There is a website I would like to share with you. I think it will be very helpful to you. It has a wealth of resources, information, and support for survivors coping with the loss of a loved one who committed suicide.

JEFF: That sounds like something that would be useful to me.

SOCIAL WORKER: I believe it will be. You have the freedom to retrieve the information any time, day or night and you can choose to access the information alone or with others. While you're here we can look at the website together so that you become familiar with it.

Computers are a relevant and powerful therapeutic technique because they hold the ability to retrieve an abundance of information and knowledge on various topics. Including the computer in Jeff's treatment provided him with support, an outlet for his feelings, and an information source to help in his grieving process. It also has the added benefit of allowing Jeff to access a resource designed to meet his specific need any time he desires.

REFERENCES AND ADDITIONAL SOURCES

Abell, M. L., & Galinsky, M. J. (2002). Introducing students to computer-based group work. *Journal of Social Work Education, 38*(1), 39–54.

Brennan, P. F., Moore, S. M., & Smyth, K. A. (1992). Alzheimer's disease caregivers' uses of a computer network. *Western Journal of Nursing Research, 14*, 662–673.

de Graaf, H. (1993). Computer use in social work: Pioneers and innovators. *International Journal of Sociology and Social Policy, 10*(4/5/6), pp. 241–250.

Finn, J. (1995). Use of electronic mail to promote computer literacy in social work undergraduates. *Journal of Teaching in Social Work, 12*(1/2), 73–83.

Finn, J., & Lavitt, M. (1994). Computer-based self-help for survivors of sexual abuse. *Social Work With Groups, 17*(1), 21–46.

Freddolino, P. P. (1998). Building on experience: Lessons from a distance education MSW program. *Computers in Human Services, 15*(2/3), 39–50.

Galinsky, M. J., Schopler, J. H., & Abell, M. D. (1997). Connecting group members through telephone and computer groups. *Health and Social Work, 22*(3), 181–188.

Gustafson, D. H., Hawkins, R., Boberg, E., Pingree, S., Serlin, R. E., Graziano, F., & Chan, C. L. (1999). Impact of a patient-centered, computer-based health information/support system. *American Journal of Preventive Medicine, 16*(1), 1–9.

Grinnell, R. M., & Unrau, Y. A. (2007). *Social work research and evaluation: Foundations of evidence-based practice* (8th ed.). New York, NY: Oxford University Press.

Monnickendam, M., & Markus, E. J. (1997). Effects of a practice-centered, cognitive-oriented computer course on computer attitudes: Implications for course content. *Social Work & Social Sciences Review, 6*(3), 175–185.

Kilgussk, A. F. (1977). Therapeutic use of a soap opera discussion group with psychiatric in-patients. *Clinical Social Work Journal, 5*, 58–65.

Ko, J. W. (2011). *Alzheimer's disease and related disorders caregiver's acceptance of a web-based structured written emotional expression intervention* (Doctoral dissertation, University of Iowa). Retrieved from http://ir.uiowa.edu/etd/2729

Mitchell, J., Howell, C., Turnbull, D., & Murphy, M. (2005). Computer-assisted group therapy for the treatment of depression and anxiety in general practice. *Primary Care Mental Health, 3*, 27–39.

Recupero, P., & Rainey, S. E. (2005). Forensic aspects of e-therapy. *Journal of Psychiatric Practice, 11*(6), 405–410.

Rubin, L., & Livesay, H. (2006). Look, up in the sky!! Using superheroes in play therapy. *International Journal of Play Therapy, 15*(1), 117–133.

Tower, K. D. (2000). Fashionably late? Social work and television. *Journal of Technology in Human Services, 16*, 63–79.

Weinert, C. (2012). Social support in cyberspace for women with chronic illness. *Rehabilitation Nursing, 24*(4), 129–135.

Consciousness Raising

DESCRIPTION

Consciousness raising describes those activities of the social worker that help clients achieve a much broader understanding of themselves, their situation, and their relationship to the larger social system, as well as their ability to influence these systems.

ORIGINS

Over the decades, much of social work practice has involved helping clients better understand themselves and their situations in a manner that leads to change and more improved functioning in their own lives and those of significant others. Recently, as the profession has become more sensitive to the concepts of power and empowerment, and the related concepts of disempowerment and oppression, the dimensions of this strategy in clinical work have expanded.

Much of the concept behind this technique emerged from feminist thinking and Paulo Freire's theory of liberation theology. Under these influences, along with those of systems theory and role theory, our awareness of how systems and subsystems interact has taught us that we cannot divide practice along a micro-macro matrix except on a convenient but imprecise conceptual basis. This perception has made us realize that, just as clients are greatly influenced by a spectrum of various systems, they can also change such systems, and that we can help them to do so as a part of our clinical work with them.

WHY THIS IS USEFUL TO SOCIAL WORK

Consciousness raising is useful to us because it brings a greatly expanded understanding of and sensitivity to the social realities of our clients, rather than focusing only on them. The technique clearly reflects our psychosocial base. Thus, in addition to helping clients as individuals, when appropriate we can also expand their understanding of various aspects of society (e.g., abuse, oppression, or poverty), and explain their sources and societal or personal influences.

In practice, this technique involves the use of such activities as reading, speakers, film discussion groups, and other didactic strategies. Any medium can be used that facilitates teaching and finding ways to help clients first understand, and then become more involved in, societal change.

Although frequently thought of only as a group technique, there are important roles for this technique in work with individuals and families. The goal is always to help people learn to understand the systems in which they live, and how they are influenced by them and can participate in changing them.

In addition to helping people to learn more about their significant social systems and their various effects on them, this type of understanding can be a form of self-liberation and empowerment. This occurs as people learn that there are things they can do about their social reality, rather than just reacting to it or learning to live with it. This enhanced perception on the client's part can help him or her develop a better self-image and enhanced sensed of power.

One of the desired effects of conscious raising is to help individuals and small groups get outside of themselves and to look outward, leading to a commitment to find ways of engaging in social action activities at both a micro or macro level. Part of this education is to begin to understand how various social conditions such as poverty, disempowerment, and cultural and social factors have influenced them and their efforts to adjust to these conditions.

RISK FACTORS

Consciousness raising carries a moderate level of risk. Part of this risk emanates from the possibility that the worker or practice setting might be committed to a particular topic or project and assume the client has the same degree of investment, concern, enthusiasm, and passion about it. In so doing, the client's individual needs may be subordinated to the larger issue. This misuse of the technique is magnified when the issue targeted for change takes on the characteristics of an ideology for the social worker or agency involved, leading them to forget or subsume the client's needs, goals, and commitment.

REQUIRED SKILLS AND KNOWLEDGE

This technique requires a high degree of worker involvement and activity. It also requires a high level of self-awareness, to ensure that our commitment to social action, stemming from our own value considerations, does not take precedence, rather than focusing only on where the client is or is ready to go.

Case Summary One

Isabella is a high school student approaching her graduation. She has spent most of her life hearing messages that are harmful to her self-esteem. Isabella feels powerless, as if she were not able to make decisions for herself. She wants to do great things with her life, but feels like she can't.

SOCIAL WORKER: What would you like to talk about today?

ISABELLA: Well, I am about to graduate from high school and I am very discouraged about my future after graduation.

SOCIAL WORKER: Tell me about your discouragement. What makes you feel that way?

ISABELLA: After I graduate, all I will get to do is clean houses all day. I don't want to do that. Why do men get all the good jobs?

SOCIAL WORKER: What leads you to believe that men get all the good jobs?

ISABELLA: Well, in my school the males are always given the best opportunities. My mom is a housekeeper and her mom was a housekeeper. My friends tell me that females always make less money than males anyway. Everything on television shows successful men making all the money. I'm just supposed to be pretty and make my man happy.

SOCIAL WORKER: Isabella, you do not have to accept that as your life. Those are statements used by society that influence young females like you. You can choose to work toward overcoming these societal messages and changing the way society views women.

ISABELLA: How would I work on doing that?

SOCIAL WORKER: The fact that you're a female does not mean you have to be a housekeeper. You can work toward being whatever you want to be. Don't let society's messages hold you back from trying to achieve your dreams.

Talking to the social worker provided Isabella with some much-needed encouragement and awareness. Isabella was influenced by so many different sources telling her "the way it is" that she just accepted it as her unhappy existence. Following her session with the social worker, Isabella has a newfound sense of empowerment and is starting to believe that she has more options for the rest of her life.

Case Summary Two

Charles has lived with the oppression of poverty his entire life. He began seeing a social worker because he is convinced there is something wrong with him that needs fixing. Charles states that he wants a better job and a better life for his family, but he has no idea where to start or what he can do. His social worker has decided to use consciousness raising as a technique to help him understand the larger system in which he lives, rather than solely focusing on himself.

SOCIAL WORKER: So, Charles, tell me more about what you believe is hindering you from obtaining the employment you desire.

CHARLES: I can't do anything. I'm not qualified for the jobs I want. I've never had and will never have the opportunity to go to college. I must be stupid. There's something wrong with me.

SOCIAL WORKER: Instead of looking at something being wrong inside of you, let's look at your life situation. You grew up in an impoverished neighborhood with limited opportunities for recreation or academic growth beyond what you received during the school day. A person can only work with what they have.

CHARLES: We barely had money to pay the rent and keep food on the table. There was no way my parents could afford to register me or my siblings for sports or any kind of after school program. So what you're saying then is that there's not necessarily some problem with me, but a problem with my circumstances?

SOCIAL WORKER: Yes, but fortunately you are able to change your circumstances. There are resources out there to help you rise above the limitations that you were raised with. I have a book chapter here that I would like you to read. It's about a young man who grew up with similar circumstances as you and became a very successful businessman. I believe it will help you get started in your journey.

CHARLES: Wow, that sounds great. I'm excited to read it. I don't want my children to have to go through what I have. I need to change things now.

Using consciousness raising as a technique helped Charles to stop focusing on what he saw as self-imposed inadequacies. Instead of beating up on himself he was able to better understand himself, his situation, and the larger systems of which he is part. This understanding will lead Charles toward making changes in his social reality rather than just accepting what he thought was his fate. Following this therapy session, Charles started feeling more liberated and empowered because he realized that he can actually participate in changing the way he lives.

REFERENCES AND ADDITIONAL SOURCES

Adolph, M. (1983). The all-women's consciousness raising group as a component of treatment for mental illness. *Social Work With Groups, 6*, 117–132.

Brandell, J. R. (2010). *Theory & practice in clinical social work* (2nd ed.). Thousand Oaks, CA: Sage.

Bricker-Jenkins, M. (2002). Feminist issues and practices in social work. In A. R. Roberts & G. J. Greene (Eds.), *Social workers' desk reference* (pp. 131–136). Oxford, England: Oxford University Press.

Donaldson, L. P. (2004). Toward validating the therapeutic benefits of empowerment-oriented social action groups. *Social Work With Groups, 27*(2/3), 159–175.

Greene, R., & Greene, R. R. (2008). *Human behavior theory & social work practice* (3rd ed.). New Brunswick, NJ: Transaction.

Leonard, P. J. (1996). Consciousness-raising groups as a multicultural awareness approach: An experience with counselor trainees. *Cultural Diversity & Mental Health, 2*(2), 89–98.

Montenegro, M. (2002). Ideology and community social psychology: Theoretical considerations and practical implications. *American Journal of Community Psychology, 30*(4), 511–527.

Parker, W. M. (1998). *Consciousness raising: A primer for multicultural counseling* (2nd ed.). Springfield, IL: Charles C. Thomas.

Reger, J. (2004). Organizational "emotion work" through consciousness-raising: An analysis of a feminist organization. *Qualitative Sociology, 27*(2), 205–222.

Shorr, S. I., & Jason, L. A. (1982). A comparison of men's and women's consciousness raising groups. *Groups, 6*(4), 51–55.

Sowards, S. K., & Renegar, V. R. (2004). The rhetorical functions of consciousness-raising in third wave feminism. *Communication Studies, 55*(4), 535–552.

Weitz, R. (1982). Feminist consciousness raising, self-concept, and depression, *Sex Roles, 8*(3), 231–241.

Consultation

DESCRIPTION

Consultation refers to when a social worker calls upon the knowledge and expertise of others—be they in our own profession, an allied one, or outside both categories—who might be of assistance to us or the client about some aspect of a case.

ORIGINS

Consultation has long been a part of social work practice. It emerged as a therapeutic technique from our experience that our clients' problem areas may stem from a lack of knowledge or understanding of available resources and the ways they might be helpful. Our understanding of systems and how they interface with one another, our sensitivity to the concept of permeable or semipermeable boundaries between systems, and our knowledge of the impact they can have on clients' lives are what lead us to seek helpful resources that may be of great assistance to them.

WHY THIS IS USEFUL TO SOCIAL WORK

This technique is of critical importance in our practice as we learn just how complex the lives of many of our clients are and how complex the helping network can be. This complexity is often the source of clients' problem behavior. As our appreciation for the influences that various systems and subsystems in a client's life expands, and as we constantly strive to be aware of aid resources in our own network, we learn how consultation can help us better assist the client.

HOW THIS IS USEFUL TO SOCIAL WORK

We often consult with others to learn what resources they can provide that we cannot. Similarly, we may consult them to provide sought-after professional expertise that is outside our scope of practice. The form that such consultations take can be quite diverse. It could be a brief conversation about some aspect of a case to learn information that neither the client nor we have available. This can often be done with the client present. At other times, consultation can be a very formal action on our part, where appointments are needed, documents prepared, information shared, and specific questions formulated in the areas where we are seeking assistance.

One direct form of consultation that can be of particular assistance is when the person who we wish to consult is presented to the client as not only having some special knowledge but as being more senior in the system. Telling a client that you would like to consult with your supervisor, or with someone else in the system with more specialized knowledge, can often give the consultation further credibility. On occasion it may impress the client that their social worker's supervisor has been involved in their case.

RISK FACTORS

Consultation has a low risk factor. However, one area in which social workers should watch for difficulties is when there aspects of the client's relationship with the consultant conflict with their relationship with their primary social worker, which can put strain on the ongoing process. Also, this is a technique in which our own professional self-image can intervene, in that we might be reluctant to consult out of a fear that it will be seen as weakness on our part.

REQUIRED SKILLS AND KNOWLEDGE

Obviously, a constant challenge in our practice is to continually educate ourselves about the ever-changing network of helping resources and how available they are to our clients. More specifically, we need to strive to understand our clients formal and informal systems and networks, and where and how they may intersect in a way that is helpful to the client.

One of the judgment calls we need to make in drawing on the strength of this technique is its potential impact on clients and the therapeutic relationship. For some clients, suggesting a consultation may be viewed as a sign of ineptitude on our part, indicating that we are not sufficiently competent to deal with their case. More often, though, when we clearly present our rationale for consultation to clients, they see it as a strength, just as when our physician tells us that he or she wants a further opinion about our condition, we view it positively. Indeed, it is something in which we often take pride. Our social work consultation can be presented in the same way.

In some instances, the person with whom we are consulting may wish to meet with the client, to formulate their separate opinion about the area where we are seeking assistance. In such situations we need to ensure that the client is fully prepared for the referral process and is informed about why the consultation is being sought, and to tell him or her something about the person with whom the client will be meeting.

Case Summary One

Tiffany originally began seeing a social worker because she is changing careers, which forced her to move to another state and away from her family and friends. Tiffany told the social worker that she is feeling a lot of stress due to this transition. She is also nervous about starting a new career that she is not familiar with and being so far away from her family. During one of their sessions, Tiffany revealed that she used to be addicted to pain pills, but has not had access to them since she moved and is starting to go through withdrawal.

TIFFANY: I don't want to be a slave to pills anymore. I had a close friend who hooked me up with them, but now that I've moved away I can't get them as easily. Now is the time to quit. I need your help. Can you tell me where to go or what to do?

SOCIAL WORKER: I will help you, but I am not an expert in this area so I am going to consult with my supervisor to make sure that I provide you with the most accurate information. I will call my supervisor into the session right now if that is all right with you.

TIFFANY: That's fine with me.

SOCIAL WORKER: [to supervisor] Thank you for coming in to meet with us. Tiffany is currently going through withdrawal from pain pills and would like help in overcoming her addiction. I told her that I was not very familiar with this area, and that we could consult with you. Do you have any information or resources that you can provide Tiffany with?

SUPERVISOR: Yes I do. I will go back to my office and find some information that will be helpful to you. Also, when I bring the information we can talk more about your symptoms and how you are feeling.

TIFFANY: [to both social worker and supervisor] Thank you so much.

Consulting with the supervisor allowed the social worker to provide relevant information to Tiffany in an area where the social worker was not very familiar, instead of just telling Tiffany that he could not help her or trying to help without the requisite knowledge and skills. By taking the time to seek a consultation, the social worker showed Tiffany that she was committed to working with her and he truly cared about her recovery.

Case Summary Two

Diane is attending therapy sessions to deal with anxiety issues. During one of her therapy sessions, Diane shared that she recently and unexpectedly became the guardian for her nephew, who has been diagnosed with Asperger's syndrome. She states that a major source of anxiety and stress for her is not knowing what services are available for her nephew or how best to care for him.

DIANE: I love having my nephew with me and I want to be his guardian, but I just feel like I don't know what to do for him. He is diagnosed with Asperger's disorder and I know that he has special needs, I just don't know how to find out what they are or how to access services for him.

SOCIAL WORKER: In this instance, I think it would be most beneficial to you if I consulted with my colleague about this matter. I know a social worker at another agency who specializes in providing treatment to children on the autism spectrum. She will be able to provide you with the most accurate information about Asperger's disorder and give you the best options for seeking services for your nephew.

DIANE: That would be fantastic. Having an expert tell me where to go and what to do would alleviate so much stress and help me feel better about caring for my nephew.

SOCIAL WORKER: With your permission, I can call my colleague right now to get information and resources for you and your nephew.

DIANE: Great. Let's do it.

Diane was in need of specific information that her social worker could not provide to her. By using the consultation technique in this case, he or she provided Diane with the knowledge and expertise that she needed. It showed Diane that her social worker understood her needs and was dedicated to helping her meet them. It also made Diane feel important and more invested in her treatment.

REFERENCES AND ADDITIONAL SOURCES

Beaulieu, E. M. (2002). *A guide for nursing home social workers.* New York, NY: Springer.

Bentley, K. J., & Walsh, J. (2001). *The social worker and psychotropic medication: Toward effective collaboration with mental health clients families and providers* (2nd ed.). Belmont, CA: Wadsworth.

Caplan, G. (1970). *The theory and practice of mental health consultation.* New York, NY: Basic Books.

Clare, M. (1991). Supervision and consultation in social work: A manageable responsibility? *Australian Social Work, 44*(1), 3–10.

Coche, J. (1989). Consultation in group therapy with children and adolescents. *Journal of Independent Social Work, 3*(4), 99–109.

Drisko, J. W. (1993). Special education teacher consultation: A student-focused, skill-defining approach. *Social Work in Education, 15*(1), 19–28.

Kadushin, A. (1977). *Social work consultation.* New York, NY: Columbia University Press.

Kadushin, A., & Buckman, M. (1978). Practice of social work consultation: A survey. *Social Work, 23*(3), 372–379.

Lounsbury, J. W., & Hall, D. Q. (1976). Supervision and consultation conflicts in the day-care licensing role. *The Social Service Review, 50*(3), 515–523.

Mannino, F., MacLennan, B., & Shore, M. (1975). *The practice of mental health consultation.* Adelphi, MD: National Institute of Mental Health.

Mercer, S. O., & Garner, J. D. (1981). Social work consultation in long-term care facilities. *Health & Social Work, 6*(2) 5–13.

Meyers, J., Parsons, R., & Martin, R. (1979). *Mental health consultation in the schools.* San Francisco, CA: Jossey-Bass.

Munson. C. E. (2002). *Handbook of clinical social work supervision.* (3rd ed.). Binghamton, NY: Haworth Press.

Peterson, C. L. (1977). Consultation with community care facilities. *Social Work in Health Care, 2*(2), 181–191.

Rapoport, L. (1995). Consultation in social work. In R. Edwards (Ed.), *Encyclopedia of social work* (17th ed., Vol. 1, pp. 193–196). Washington, DC: National Association of Social Workers.

Reamer, F. G. (2006). *Social work values and ethics.* (3rd ed.). Chichester, England: Columbia University Press.

Rosenberg, E. B., & Nitzberg, H. (1980). The clinical social worker becomes a consultant. *Social Work in Health Care, 5*(3), 305–312.

Sowers, K. M., White, B. W., & Dulmus, C. N. *Comprehensive handbook of social work and social welfare: The profession of social work.* Hoboken, NJ: Wiley.

Strand, V. C., & Badger, L. (2007). A clinical consultation model for child welfare supervisors. *Child Welfare, 86*(1), 79–96.

Walsh, J. A. (1990). Using external consultants in social service agencies. *The Journal of Contemporary Social Services, 71*(5), 291–295.

Waltman, G. H. (1989). Social work consultation services in rural areas. *Human Services in the Rural Environment, 12*(3), 17–21.

Williams, M. (1971). The problem profile technique in consultation. *Social Work, 16*(3), 52–59.

Zastrow, C. H. (2008). *Social work with groups: A comprehensive workbook* (7th ed.). Belmont, CA: Brooks/Cole.

Zischka, P., & Fox, R. (1985). Consultation as a function of school social work. *Social Work in Education, 7*(2), 69–79.

18

Contract

DESCRIPTION

The use of a formal contract between a client and social worker concerning some aspect of the therapeutic process has been found to be highly useful in contemporary practice. Although the idea of a contract has had a rather long history in clinical practice, it is only in recent years that it has been highlighted as an important clinical technique. As with other types of contract, it describes a process that leads to a formal commitment between worker and client to carry out specific components of a therapeutic process to achieve specific goals.

ORIGINS

Although over the decades there has been some use of contracts in practice it was learning theory that provided its most solid theoretical base. Two other theoretical sources that further reinforced the effectiveness of specific commitments between client and social worker are task-centered therapy and planned brief treatment. What these theories added to our understanding of the power of this technique is to make it a mutual and precise process. Not only do we include in the contract what the client is going to do, but also what specific things the social worker will do to facilitate the agreed-upon goals of the intervention.

WHY THIS IS USEFUL TO SOCIAL WORK

Because much of the material dealt with in practice involves helping clients address problems in their lives, the use of a contract helps the client clearly identify and specify these problems as quickly as possible and rank them in order of precedence. In addition, by focusing on what both parties can and cannot do, the contract provides a structure for this process.

One of the important outcomes of this search for specificity is to help the client translate generic objectives, such as "I want to be more mature," into specific ones. These in turn may require that we identify those objectives that contain subordinate activities. In other words, we need to identify the actions and behaviors that will be most useful to the client.

One of the biggest advantages of using a contract is that the process can lead the client and worker to use their time more economically. However, if the question of economizing time is overly stressed, the technique can detract from a more successful outcome.

From its overall impact on the profession, use of the contract technique has been very helpful as a means of bringing greater discipline and structure to much of our practice. It also helps us establish much more specific objectives with many clients.

HOW THIS IS USEFUL TO SOCIAL WORK

One frequent use of a contract is to have it focus on the treatment process in general. It can list such things as the planned number of interviews, their time and place, general purpose and goals of therapy, fees, and client expectations, as well as the practitioner's professional responsibilities. In some instances an agency will use a generic contract covering these topics with all clients. More commonly, it is the practitioner's choice as to whether a contract is judged to be potentially useful. It is the latter case that is our interest here.

Another use of a contract that sometimes emerges during the treatment process is when the client agrees to do certain things outside of the interview. The function of such a contract is to make the components of the intervention as tangible as possible and to ensure that the expected actions are within the potential of the client and his or her resources. To be effective, such contractual matters need to be as specific as possible and in a format that can be evaluated.

Thus, statements such as, "I agree to try harder" ordinarily are not useful commitments. Rather, we look for more specific commitments, such as, "I agree to praise Johnny whenever he does his homework." In such instances, reviewing the contracted issues with the worker is essential. Often the very task of working toward specificity can have beneficial outcomes for the client.

Sometimes clients and social workers make contract-like commitments worker verbally. These can be helpful, but a written contract is a much more powerful format because it gives a greater sense of concreteness and objectivity to the process.

A contract clearly can and must be renegotiated as the client's life or situation changes, as new treatment objectives emerge, or when an extension or shortening of the established therapy period becomes necessary. However, this should not be done unilaterally.

RISK FACTORS

One risk in using this technique is moving too quickly with a client by letting our own enthusiasm or perception of where the client ought to be going lead us ahead of him or her. This is especially possible when practicing under the constraints of short-term or brief therapy. If this happens, we may have to relaunch the therapeutic process.

REQUIRED SKILLS AND KNOWLEDGE

The use of a contract presumes, of course, that the client is capable of thinking, planning, and implementing a set of clear objectives. It also presumes that all intervention will be of a problem-solving nature. We need to remember that there are clients who are not yet ready to solve problems, but instead want the opportunity to discuss, think about, and clarify various existential matters. In such instances, proposing a contract that includes very specific goals may be counterproductive.

Case Summary One

Simon is seeking treatment due to some concerns with his anger management. Simon has always been characterized as verbally and physically aggressive, and recently lost his job for yelling and swearing at his boss. His social worker has agreed to treatment on the condition that they set up a formal contract between the two of them. Simon has agreed to develop such a contract.

Therapeutic Contract With Simon Smith
Date: September 22, 2008

Long-term goal:
I will express anger through appropriate verbalizations on a consistent basis.
Short-term objectives:
I will attend therapy sessions as scheduled, weekly for six months.
Social worker will teach ways to effectively handle a disagreement.
Social worker will teach "stop and think" techniques.
Social worker will teach effective communication strategies.
I will discuss my feelings with others instead of becoming physically destructive.
I will increase my participation in positive peer-group activities.
Client Signature:_____
Social Worker Signature:_____

Using a contract allowed Simon and his social worker to agree on treatment goals and objectives and work together toward completing them. It provided a clear goal and specific objectives to achieve, and stated who was responsible for each activity.

Case Summary Two

Lucy is starting therapy with a new social worker. According to her records, Lucy has a history of being terminated from treatment for not showing up for her appointments consistently. In the beginning phase of treatment, Lucy and her new social worker cooperate to develop a contract that focuses on aspects of the treatment process. The purpose of this contract is to keep Lucy more invested in treatment and prevent her case from being closed before goal completion.

Therapeutic Contract With Lucy Jones
Date: November 26, 2010

As the client I agree to:

Attend therapy sessions every Wednesday promptly at 6:00 p.m. for at least six months.

Call in advance to reschedule a therapy appointment if I am not able to attend a session.

Complete assigned therapeutic exercises and homework.

Be open and honest with my social worker.

As the social worker I agree to:

Be available for therapy sessions every Wednesday promptly at 6:00 p.m. for at least six months.

Provide an environment for conducting therapy sessions where the client can feel safe to be open and honest.

Keep all information discussed during therapy sessions confidential unless I am required by law to disclose certain information.

Work together with the client to develop and achieve treatment goals.

*If the terms of this contract are not upheld, both parties understand that treatment may be terminated for lack of compliance.

Client Signature:_____

Social Worker Signature:_____

The use of a contract as a formal commitment between Lucy and her social worker helped Lucy become more invested and engaged in the therapeutic process. The written contract also provided a greater sense of solidity to each party's responsibilities.

REFERENCES AND ADDITIONAL SOURCES

Clark, J. J., Godlaski, T., & Leukefeld, C. (1999). Case management and behavioral contracting: Components of rural substance abuse treatment. *Journal of Substance Abuse Treatment, 17*(4), 293–304.

Collins, J. (1977). The contractual approach to social work intervention. *Social Work Today, 8*, 13–15.

Estes, R. J., & Henry, S. (1976). The therapeutic contract in work with groups: A formal analysis. *Social Service Review, 50*(4), 611–622.

Fox, R. (1983). Contracting in supervision: A goal oriented process. *The Clinical Supervisor, 1*(1), 37–49.

Greene, G. J. (1989). Using the written contract for evaluating and enhancing practice effectiveness. *Journal of Independent Social Work, 4*(2), 135–155.

Haber, D. (1993). Health contracts with older adults. *Clinical Gerontologist, 14*(2), 44–49.

Haber, D. (2001). Promoting readiness to change behavior through health assessments. *Clinical Gerontologist, 23*(1–2), 152–158.

Haber, D. (2003). *Health promotion and aging: Practical applications for health professionals* (3rd ed.). New York, NY: Springer.

Haber, D., & Looney, C. (2000). Health contract calendars: A tool for health professionals with older adults. *The Gerontologist, 40*(2), 235–239.

Haber, D., & Rhodes, D. (2004). Health contract with sedentary older adults. *The Gerontologist, 44*(6), 827–835.

Hepworth, D. H., Rooney, R. J., & Larsen, J. A. (2010). *Direct social work practice: Theory and skills* (8th ed.). Pacific Grove, CA: Brooks/Cole.

Johnson, C., Nicklas, T., Arbeit, M., Webber, L., & Berenson, G. (1992). Behavioral counseling and contracting as methods for promoting cardiovascular health in families. *Journal of the American Dietetic Association, 92*(4), 479–481.

Leslie, M., & Schuster, P. (1991). The effect of contingency contracting on adherence and knowledge of exercise regimen. *Patient Education and Counseling, 18*(3), 231–241.

Loomis, M. (1982). Contracting for change. *Transactional Analysis Journal, 12*(1), 51–55.

Maluccio, A., & Marlow, W. (1974). The case for contract. *Social Work, 19*(1), 28–35.

McCoyd, J. L. M. (2010). The implicit contract: Implications for health social work. *Health & Social Work, 35*(2), 99–106.

Neale, A. (1991). Behavioral contracting as a tool to help patients achieve better health. *Family Practice, 8*(4), 336–343.

Rothery, M. A. (1980). Contracts and contracting. *Clinical Social Work Journal, 8*(3), 179–187.

Rothman, J. (1998). *Contracting in clinical social work.* Chicago, IL: Nelson Hall

Seabury, B. A. (1974) The contract: Uses and abuses, and limitations. *Social Work, 21*(1), 16–21.

Torrance, J. (2003). Autism, aggression, and developing a therapeutic contract. *American Journal of Dance Therapy, 25*(2), 97–109.

Zayas, L. H., & Katch, M. (1989). Contracting with adolescents: An ego psychological approach. *Social Casework, 70*(1), 3–9.

19

Cue Cards

DESCRIPTION

Cue cards, sometimes called *crisis cards,* are a technique in which the client and social worker together identify a series of steps or actions that can be taken to deal with some problematic aspect of life outside of the interview situation. These identified steps are then transferred to some type of easily carried and accessible medium, such as index cards or an iPod, that is kept at hand and can be consulted when a particular situation arises.

ORIGINS

Although this technique did not emerge from any one specific theory base, there is a strong learning theory and behavior modification aspect to it. Some of the thinking that spawned it comes from the idea of task implementation in task-centered treatment.

The technique also has similarities to the practices of 12-step programs that help addicted people live on a day-to-day basis by regularly doing certain things. This includes a commitment to a set of structured actions to be taken to avoid the identified problematic behavior.

WHY THIS IS USEFUL TO SOCIAL WORK

The underlying concept or thrust of this technique is to equip a client with a set of helpful behaviors outside of the interview situation. These are to be called upon in specific areas of life that cause problems. The cards provide a concrete tool that aids in developing the habit of taking effective and immediate positive action when confronted with a challenging situation that, in the past, has been a source of difficulty. It is a process of continuing the commitment to improve made during sessions outside the interview room.

HOW THIS IS USEFUL TO SOCIAL WORK

The strength of the cue card technique is the understanding that, in helping the client develop a written list of steps to be taken, the actions he or she has developed in the process of ongoing therapy are made more concrete. For example, we may be working with a husband on a problem he is having with his wife that requires a different set of habitual responses. We would work out with this client a series of steps that he can take when the situation under consideration arises, with the understanding that in such situations he will follow this plan.

This technique is not restricted to working with individuals; it also can be used with families or couples. In such instances, decisions are negotiated in the interview over how a particular problem or situation can be dealt with differently, and steps can be identified and agreed upon for each individual to carry out when the situation arises.

This type of highly structured activity is something quite novel to some people. If adopted by a client in a positive way, the "cards" can lead them to develop positive habits not only in reference to the problem under consideration, but also in other life situations.

In using this technique, the worker must provide strong support and encouragement. This is especially so when the client has failed to put earlier plans into action when asked, with negative results. This can lead to a sense of failure and result in the client not wishing to try again.

Although for some clients it is sufficient to write out the steps in an informal way, for others having them typed up in a formal manner by the agency can lend an air of importance to the process that can be enabling for the client, not unlike the importance that we give to a prescription that our physician writes.

RISK FACTORS

The cue card technique may appear quite simple and unsophisticated, especially for social workers who, in their own lives, are accustomed to making lists of things to do and how to do them. However, for many clients this type of built-in structure does not exist in their lives, and using it will require a long process of trial and error in a supportive, encouraging milieu.

This technique has low risk unless a worker inappropriately introduces it to a client who is not able to function in this manner. It may also be that the behavior being addressed is not amenable to this type of programmed activity, which can result in a feeling of failure.

REQUIRED SKILLS AND KNOWLEDGE

An important component of using this technique effectively is working with the client to identify actions that are known to be helpful in dealing with the situation under consideration. The social worker contributes to the process by developing the list of stimuli with the client in a manner that fits the client's strengths, interests, abilities, behavior patterns, and available resources.

The development of the cue card list is not something that can be done quickly. The process requires intensive work in getting to know the client and systems, resources, and abilities that are available. The process of developing the action list itself can be highly enlightening for the client as they come to terms with possible positive steps and learn what will and won't be effective.

The list that emerges needs to be highly personalized. What might be an effective escape or substitute action for one client may be unsuitable for another. Because of this, the worker cannot rely on cue sets developed with other clients; knowing what has worked in other situations can be drawn upon, but not in a recipe-like manner.

The steps are usually arranged in some form of hierarchical order that moves from simpler actions or thoughts to more complex ones. They can also be a list of alternatives depending on the triggering situation and the resources available in the client's life—that is, if the client cannot do Step 1, he or she will move immediately to Step 2.

Case Summary One

Johnny started seeing a social worker recently when his mother brought him in following his suspension from school. Johnny was known as the class clown and was constantly getting in trouble for displaying disruptive, attention-seeking behaviors. At school Johnny would interrupt the teacher continuously by making funny noises and yelling inappropriately.

SOCIAL WORKER: Johnny, I'd like you to complete an activity with me. Okay?

JOHNNY: Yeah, sure.

SOCIAL WORKER: I have these index cards and I want to write a few sentences and perhaps draw a few pictures on them for you.

JOHNNY: What are they for?

SOCIAL WORKER: The next time you are in class and you feel the urge to yell or act in a way that is going to get you in trouble, I want you to look at these cards so you can remember what to do.

JOHNNY: So I get to keep them?

SOCIAL WORKER: Yes, but only if you are responsible with them. On this card, let's draw a stop sign, a hand, and let's write "stop and raise my hand." When you feel like yelling out to the teacher, look at your card and then stop and raise your hand until the teacher calls on you.

JOHNNY: I think I can do that.

Using the cards to involve Johnny in the process of recognizing appropriate behavior will increase the likelihood of him exhibiting the appropriate behavior. Also, it will help to Johnny to have the cards with him in school to serve as a reminder when he feels his disruptive and impulsive behaviors starting. In this instance, a discussion with the teacher and the parents is necessary in order to ensure that they support Johnny's use of the cue cards and can positively reinforce him when he uses them appropriately.

Case Summary Two

James is attending therapy sessions at the suggestion of his work supervisor. Recently, James has had confrontations with several coworkers. Following arguments with them, James usually throws objects off of his desk.

James's physical aggression has escalated over the past few weeks due to these encounters. He has already received a verbal warning from his supervisor, and if his behavior remains the same he will be fired. James's social worker will use cue cards as a technique to provide James with alternative ways to de-escalate after disagreeing with a coworker.

SOCIAL WORKER: James, tell me more about what happens after you experience a confrontation with a coworker.

JAMES: I don't even know how to describe it. I just feel so angry. My body starts to feel warm and I tense up. I hate the way it makes me feel.

SOCIAL WORKER: How do you usually react once you start feeling that way?

JAMES: That's when I start throwing things off my desk as a way to release the tension. I just throw stuff at the wall or on the floor, which I think is better than hitting a coworker.

SOCIAL WORKER: While I agree that it's a good idea not to hit your coworkers, I also know that if you continue throwing things off your desk you are going to lose your job. Is that something that you are okay with?

JAMES: No, I can't lose my job. That's why I agreed to come to therapy. I need help. I don't know what else I can do.

SOCIAL WORKER: I know you can do this. Let's work together to come up with alternative strategies for de-escalating after an argument with a coworker. After we identify the steps or actions you can take in that situation, then we can write them down on index cards so that you can keep them with you to reference in challenging situations. What do you think about that?

JAMES: I think that sounds like a good idea. It's helpful to come up with ideas together. Plus, having those ideas written down in a way that I can carry them around with me is great.

Using cue cards as a technique provides James with a concrete tool to take positive actions during challenging situations and to avoid his usual problematic behaviors. The process of making the cards was enlightening for James, and having the cue cards to refer back to will help him remember the effective, positive actions to take during future problem-producing situations. Using the cue cards and implementing the strategies written on them can lead James toward developing positive habits in other life situations as well.

REFERENCES AND ADDITIONAL SOURCES

Berkman, B., & D'Ambruoso, S. (2006). *Handbook of social work in health and aging.* New York, NY: Oxford University Press.

Bowen, C. J., & Howie, P. M. (2002). Context and cue cards in young children's testimony: A comparison of brief narrative elaboration and context reinstatement. *Journal of Applied Psychology, 87*(6), 1077–1085.

Brennan, L., Giovannetti, T., Libon, D. J., Bettcher, B. M., & Duey, K. (2009). The impact of goal cues on everyday action performance in dementia. *Neuropsychological Rehabilitation, 19*(4), 562–582.

Charlop-Christy, M. H., & Kelso, S. E. (2003). Teaching children with autism conversational speech using a cue card/written script program. *Education and Treatment of Children, 26*(2), 108–127.

Friedberg, D., McClure, J. M., & Hillwig, G. (2009). *Cognitive therapy techniques for children and adolescents: Tools for enhancing practice.* New York, NY: Guilford Press.

Goldman, R. S., Axelrod, B. N., & Tompkins, L. M. (1992). Effect of instructional cues on schizophrenic patients' performance on the Wisconsin Card Sorting Test. *The American Journal of Psychiatry, 149*(12), 1718–1722.

Johnson, S. L. (2009). *Social worker's guide to posttraumatic stress disorder intervention.* Burlington, MA: Elsevier.

Joseph, L. M., & Hunter, A. D. (2001). Differential application of a cue card strategy for solving fraction problems: Exploring instructional utility of the Cognitive Assessment System. *Child Study Journal, 31*(2), 123–136.

Kazantzis, N., Deane, F. P., Ronan, K. R., & L'Abate, L. (2005). *Using homework assignments in cognitive behavior therapy.* New York, NY: Routledge.

Lewis, A., Newton, H., & Vials, S. (2008). Realising child voice: The development of cue cards. *Support for Learning, 23*(1), 26–31.

Manning, B. H. (1991). *Cognitive self-instruction for classroom processes.* Albany, NY: State University of New York Press.

O'Donohue, W. T., & Fisher, J. E. (2009). *Cognitive behavior therapy: Applying empirically supported techniques in your practice* (2nd ed.). Hoboken, NJ: Wiley.

Pattillo, M. (2002). Assessing the gifts, talents, and skills of nursing home residents. *Geriatric Nursing, 23*(1), 48–50.

Sheafor, B. W., Horejsi, C. R. (1997). *Techniques and guidelines for social work practice* (6th ed., pp. 419–420). Toronto: Allyn & Bacon.

Weinter, C., & Cartwright, R. T. (1999). *Descripto-cards for adult aphasia.* New York: Psychological Corp.

Culturalgram

DESCRIPTION

This technique, which serves as both a diagnostic tool and an intervention, involves a process in which the social worker, along with the clients—be they individuals, a couple, or a family—prepares a written map of their cultural backgrounds that presents the clients' cultural base going back several generations.

ORIGINS

This technique was described by Dr. Elaine Congress of Fordham University. It is similar to the genogram and ecomap in that they are visually oriented techniques built on a systems-theory base.

The map technique emerged from the growing reality that an increasing number of the families we meet in practice are from mixed cultural, ethnic, and racial backgrounds. Accompanying this reality is the understanding that this component of the clients' familial relationships is a critically important part of their psychosocial identity, although this reality is not often fully understood and appreciated by the persons involved.

WHY THIS IS USEFUL TO SOCIAL WORK

The phenomenon of cultural diversity is not necessarily a problem-producing factor in the life of a family; it may well be a source of great strength and cohesion, often in ways they don't always recognize or overtly appreciate.

As with genograms, the purpose of the culturalgram is to assist clients in developing a visual picture of the components of their cultural identity. Such understanding can lead to an enriched awareness and appreciation of cultural identity in themselves and other members of the family. This includes the roles and functions that these factors play in their lives.

HOW THIS IS USEFUL TO SOCIAL WORK

In developing the culturalgram, the social worker collaborates with the family to address a series of factors that have been identified as important components of a person's cultural identity, and that influence an individual's psychosocial adjustment. Many of the ways in which cultures differ, both within themselves and versus other cultures, relate to critical value issues.

As mentioned, the technique stresses that these observed differences do not necessarily represent problems, but rather areas of actual and potential strength and a unique family identity. However, when the influence of some identified cultural factors are not recognized and understood, they can become areas of stress, problems, and difficulty.

The culturalgram can be used for families that are partly or all new arrivals from another country, and for those that are longtime residents. It is a way to help people understand how pervasive some cultural factors can be from generation to generation, and how these can be both strengths and strains on interpersonal relations. By improving the client's awareness of the cultural factors that influence relationships in this visual way, the social worker can open communications around these significant life areas.

A further positive side effect of visually focusing families on these cultural issues is the way it can help them discover or rediscover their cultural histories. It often opens up areas that have never been discussed because they were either forgotten or relegated to familial habits of thinking, perceiving, or acting without appreciating their origins and current significance.

RISK FACTORS

This is a low-risk technique.

REQUIRED SKILLS AND KNOWLEDGE

It is important that the social worker have a rich understanding of the range and complexity of cultural influences. It is not necessary—indeed, not possible—to understand the content of all cultural influences and how they interface. Rather, we need to understand the general areas of cultural content, and learn the details of each specific difference from the clients themselves.

The technique does not take a position that any one value or aspect of a cultural profile is better than another, but rather seeks to help clients understand how different life experiences in regard to their cultural identity can result in different perceptions of significant life situations within a family. It is in recognizing these perceptions, and how they often result in different viewpoints about such things as problem-solving methods, decision-making patterns, traditional practices, distribution of responsibilities, and variation in roles, that the technique helps the client.

Case Summary One

A father, mother, and their daughter recently started attending family therapy. The family immigrated to the United States from Mexico less than a year ago, and their daughter is having an especially hard time adjusting to her new living situation. The family is fluent in English and decided to start attending family therapy on the suggestion of a close family member who has lived in the United States for several decades.

SOCIAL WORKER: I would like to work on creating a culturalgram with you as a way to problem solve. A culturalgram focuses specifically on different aspects of your family culture. It will allow us to get a sense of what is important to you and discuss your areas of strength and support.

MOTHER: That sounds like a good activity for all of us to work together on.

SOCIAL WORKER: I will ask you some questions and we'll draw/write out the answers on this paper. First of all, what brought you here? What made you decide to leave Mexico?

FATHER: My sister moved here with her family about twenty-five years ago. She's been telling us about all of the great opportunities here. We made the decision to move after my father died and my mother came to live with my sister.

SOCIAL WORKER: How long have you lived in the United States?

MOTHER: We have been living here less than a year, about ten months now.

SOCIAL WORKER: You mentioned some family members living in the United States. Is there anyone else living close by that you can count on for support?

MOTHER: We have made good friends in the neighborhood that we live in. They help us out when we need it and we help them out when we can.

FATHER: My sister has many friends that we have gotten to know, and her husband's family lives here as well.

SOCIAL WORKER: Are there any significant others still living in Mexico?

DAUGHTER: Yes, my best friends and everyone I care about. Everything is so different here.

MOTHER: My family still lives in Mexico and our daughter was really close to my niece. They were inseparable.

The social worker and family continued to work on their culturalgram and discuss the issues involved in their move from Mexico to the United States.

The culturalgram works as a tool to empower the family. Creating a culturalgram provided a visual aid for the family to look at and actually see their sources of support and family strength. It also allowed the social worker to be more sensitive and aware of this family's unique situation and not generalize their challenges to stereotypes of families from a similar ethnic background.

Case Summary Two

The Allen family are immigrants from Jamaica. In Jamaica, the majority of people are Black. When they came to the United States, they experienced much racism because of the color of their skin and their accent. The Allens are naturalized citizens, but the family is having problems assimilating into American culture. They have three children, ages 14, 13, and 9. Mr. Allen had a respectable job in Jamaica and was an esteemed engineer there. They emigrated to the United States because of political conflict ensuing in their hometown. Mr. Allen's credentials are not recognized in the United States, so he had to settle for a job washing cars for a living. Mrs. Allen cannot read because she has dyslexia. The Allens were referred to therapy because their 14-year-old son was consistently performing poorly in school, and their 13-year-old son was sleeping in class. The clinical social worker assigned to this case completed a culturalgram to better understand the Allens' situation. He collected information about the Allens such as their legal standing in America, length of time spent in the country, preferred language, values, contact with community and religious organizations, health beliefs, and reason for relocating to the United States. The clinical social worker came to understand that Mr. Allen would not return to his country because he was apprehensive about the political climate in Jamaica.

Because the clinical social worker now understands the Allens' family history, he is better able to help them. He referred Mr. Allen to an employment agency in an effort to help him find a better job. Because dyslexia is considered a disability under the Americans With Disabilities Act, the social worker helped Mrs. Allen secure unemployment aid. The social worker spoke to a free after-school tutoring program to secure help for their 14-year-old. Last, he referred the 13-year-old to the school nurse, who spoke to him about the importance of nutrition in maintaining a high energy level. Thus the culturalgram was an essential tool in providing the "big picture" about the Allens. From the information documented in the culturalgram, the clinician was able to provide culturally competent services to this immigrant family.

REFERENCES AND ADDITIONAL SOURCES

Brownell, P. (1997). The application of the culturalgram in cross-cultural practice with elder abuse victims. *Journal of Elder Abuse and Neglect, 9*(2), 19–33.

Brownell, P., & Congress, E. P. (1998). Application of the culturagram to assess and empower culturally and ethnically diverse battered women. In A. R. Roberts (Ed.), *Battered women and their families: Intervention and treatment strategies* (pp. 387–404). New York, NY: Springer.

Coady, N., & Lehman, P. (2007). *Theoretical perspectives for direct social work practice: A generalist-eclectic approach.* New York, NY: Springer.

Congress, E. (1994). The use of culturalgram to assess and empower culturally diverse families. *Families in Society, 75*(9), 531–539.

Congress, E. (1997). Using the culturalgram to assess and empower culturally diverse families. In E. Congress (Ed.), *Multi-cultural perspectives in working with families* (pp. 3–16). New York: Springer.

Congress, E. P. (2004). Cultural and ethical issues in working with culturally diverse patients and their families: The use of the culturalgram to promote cultural competent practice in health care settings. *Social Work in Health Care, 39*(3–4), 249–262.

Congress, E. P. (2008). Individual and family development theory. In N. Coady & P. Lehmen, *Theoretical perspectives for direct social work practice: a generalist-eclectic approach* (2nd ed.), (pp 119–144). New York, NY: Springer Publishing Company.

Congress, E. P., & Brownell, P. (2007). The use of the culturalgram in understanding immigrant women affected by domestic violence. In A. R. Roberts (Ed.), *Battered women and their families: Intervention strategies and treatment programs* (3rd ed., pp. 491–508). New York, NY: Springer.

Congress, E. P., & González, M. J. (2005). *Multicultural perspectives in working with families* (2nd ed.). New York, NY: Springer.

Hardy, K. V., & Sasyloffy, T. A. (1995). The cultural genogram: Key to training culturally competent family social workers. *Journal of Marital and Family Therapy, 21*(3), 221–237.

Hunt, R. (2009). *Introduction to community-based nursing* (4th ed.). Philadelphia, PA: Wolters Kluwer/ Lippincott Williams & Wilkins.

Poon, V. H. K. (1996). The effects of immigration on family health for Hong Kong chinese emigrating to North America. *Hong Kong Practitioner, 18*(12), 647–654.

Roberts, A. R. (1998). *Battered women and their families: Intervention strategies and treatment programs* (2nd ed.). New York, NY: Springer.

Roberts, A. R,. & Watkins, J. M. (2009). *Social workers' desk reference* (2nd ed.). New York, NY: Oxford University Press.

Shellenberger, S., Dent, M. M., Davis-Smith, M., Seale, J. P., Weintraut, R., & Wright, T. (2007). Cultural genogram: A tool for teaching and practice. *Families, Systems & Health, 25*(4), 367–382.

Unger, R. K. (2001). *Handbook of the psychology of women and gender*. New York, NY: Wiley.

Degrees, Titles, and Awards

DESCRIPTION

This technique is based on a conviction that the physical surroundings in which we interview our clients are a strongly influential variable in the therapeutic process. From this perspective, one of the specific components of this influence that, in many instances, enhances the setting in a positive therapeutic manner is the display of our degrees and other relevant professional credentials.

ORIGINS

There is probably not a complete consensus in the profession as to the validity or origins of this technique. The argument in support of displaying our relevant degrees, licenses, and other professional credentials is based on our commitment to convey to our clients a sense of competence and security when they come to us. Our clients seek us out or are referred to us because of a societal perception that we are trustworthy and qualified persons. To reinforce this perception of competence, we need to do everything we can to convey these attributes.

WHY THIS IS USEFUL TO SOCIAL WORK

The majority of the people with whom we come in contact as clients or fellow professionals expect that we have been educated, trained, tested, and approved by some significant societal body as competent and qualified to practice. Clearly many clients will not know the varying importance of all our various degrees, titles, awards and licensing certificates issued by professional associations. Nevertheless they understand that these associations exist, and they expect to find some visible evidence of this in the form of certificates and degrees in our offices. Some professional bodies reinforce the importance of this technique by requiring us to display at least our membership in a professional association. This conveys a certain level of reassurance and security to those with whom we interact professionally. (When we think of how we use the skills of other professions and occupations for something personal in our own lives—whether it be our barber, auto mechanic, or dentist—we too feel a sense of security in seeing their credentials displayed in the setting where they practice.)

Awareness that we do have recognition, power, influence, and helping potential can be a client-empowering factor in their lives. Because one of our functions in contemporary practice is to empower clients, denying or minimizing the power we have harms our ability to perform this function. The question is not whether we have power or not. It is whether we can learn to use the power we have in an enabling way for the good of the client.

HOW THIS IS USEFUL TO SOCIAL WORK

Most social workers increasingly understand the general importance of this technique as a socio-cultural phenomenon expected of professional persons. Nevertheless some would argue that any such display of professionalism and status serves to create and reinforce the power barrier between us and the client. If this is true, we should avoid such manifestations of achievement.

It has been posited that a more effective way of interacting with clients is to ensure that the desired relationship should be one between equals. Thus we should avoid such things as using titles or displaying our accomplishments, which might convey to clients a sense of being on a lower level than we are. However, it can also be argued that when we attempt to present ourselves as being no different than our client, we can easily confuse them from the perspective of how we can be helpful, considering they have come to us because we are deemed to be experts, and thus (in this social system, at least) are different from them.

It may well be that the perception of this societal custom of displaying our credentials differs in some segments of our society or among various cultural groups. However, until evidence against the display of credentials in particular situations is revealed, there is sufficient support from a sociocultural perspective to continue this practice as a general, client-enabling technique in our practice.

RISK FACTORS

This is a low-risk technique. As mentioned, there are undoubtedly many cultural issues tied into this societal practice, and it may well be that we will meet clients who will find our display of credentials to be initially disconcerting. When this occurs, we need to take steps to minimize their discomfort. There is also the risk that displaying our degrees will instead be viewed as lording our differences over the client, and that our expertise ought to be taken for granted rather than having to remind the client of it.

REQUIRED SKILLS AND KNOWLEDGE

It is important to remember that clients do not come to us or get referred to us to seek a friend or a partner. They do so out of a perception that we have the knowledge, skills, and access to resources that can be of assistance to them in their psychosocial struggles. In some cases, of course, they have been ordered to see us by someone who also perceives us in some type of legitimized expert role. Thus we need to be conscious of the possibility, especially with new cases, that the client may wish to know who we are professionally, both in terms of training and competence, and we ought to do all we can to respond to this very legitimate wish for information.

Case Summary One

Aaron recently started attending therapy sessions. During this session, his social worker is trying to gather more information from him about why he is attending therapy.

SOCIAL WORKER: What led you to the decision to see a social worker?
AARON: I haven't been feeling like myself lately. I've talked to my friends for advice, but they don't know how to help me. When I spoke to my mom about it she suggested that I make an appointment to see a social worker.
SOCIAL WORKER: How do you feel about coming to see a social worker?
AARON: I feel good. I can see the degrees on your wall, I know you went to school for many years to be able to do this work. I'm sure you will be able to work with me in a way my friends and family can't.

Aaron decided to meet with a social worker when he noticed significant changes in his moods. Although he was a little nervous about going at first, seeing the social worker's degrees displayed prominently in the office made him feel better about the meeting. Being able to look at his social worker's degrees was a good reminder that the worker is an expert in his field and that Aaron can feel confident in his social worker's ability to work with him.

Case Summary Two

Mack is a 12-year-old male attending therapy sessions for issues with his self-esteem. At this point in treatment, Mack and his social worker are still building rapport and establishing trust in the counseling relationship. This is the first time in Mack's life that he has met with a social worker; before this, he wasn't sure exactly what a social worker was or what credentials they had to have.

MACK: Hey, I just noticed that you have more than one college degree on the wall in your office. I didn't even know that was possible.
SOCIAL WORKER: Yes, Mack, it is possible. A person has to have many years of education to become a social worker. In order to become a social worker you have to earn an undergraduate degree, also known as a bachelor's degree, and a graduate degree, also known as a master's degree.

MACK: Wow. You must really know what you're doing. That must be why I like talking to you. Do you think someone like me could possibly earn a graduate degree?

SOCIAL WORKER: I've met with many adolescents, very similar to you, who ended up earning multiple degrees and becoming successful professionals in their adult lives.

MACK: Really, that's so good to hear. Can you tell me more about how to earn college degrees?

SOCIAL WORKER: Of course. I can explain the process to you and then you can ask any questions that you might have.

The social worker's degrees provided an opportunity for Mack and his social worker to engage in conversation and learn more about each other. Mack had not discussed secondary education much before, so talking about his social worker's degrees was very beneficial to him. It opened up options to him that he was not aware of and made him feel more hopeful for the future. The social worker's degrees also allowed Mack to view him as a trustworthy and qualified expert in the field. Additionally, it increased Mack's confidence in his social worker's ability to help him.

REFERENCES AND ADDITIONAL SOURCES

Bloom, L. J., Weigel, R. G., & Trautt, G. M. (1977). "Therapeutic" factors in psychotherapy: Effects of office décor and subject, social worker sex pairing on the perception of credibility. *Journal of Consulting and Clinical Psychology, 45*(5), 867–873.

Davies, C., Guck, I. & Roscoe, I. (1979). The architectural design of a psychotherapeutic milieu. *Hospital Community Psychiatry, 30*, 453–460.

Hill, C. E. (1975). Sex of client and sex and experience level of counselor. *Journal of Counseling Psychology, 22*(1), 6–11.

Simon, W. E. (1973). Age, sex, and title of social worker as determinants of patient preferences and additional sources. *Journal of Psychology, 83*(1), 145–149.

Directives

DESCRIPTION

The technique of giving directives encompasses those actions where we communicate to the client that we wish them to do certain things that we deem helpful regarding some aspect of their lives.

ORIGINS

Telling the client what to do has long been considered inappropriate and unprofessional. Despite this tradition, we have probably always done so, and this technique does have a place in therapy.

This practice first seems to have been recognized in the writings and practices of Jay Haley in the field of family therapy. Haley (1976) formally legitimized the technique of giving directions during client interviews regarding things clients should do outside of the interview. Haley emphasized that the best kinds of tasks to assign to a family were those that focused on the family's presenting problem.

WHY THIS IS USEFUL TO SOCIAL WORK

This is a useful technique because we can often use our body of knowledge about human behavior, social systems, and the social environment to help clients avoid difficulties and dangers and achieve mastery over some component of their lives. It is also useful because it draws on the benevolent authority of the helping relationship, which can be employed from time to time to assist clients in their various life struggles.

Often, directing a client to try a certain modification to their accustomed pattern of functioning can bring them a sense of achievement, alleviate stress, or help them change a dysfunctional pattern. This in turn can lead to a sense of accomplishment and an enhanced self-image.

HOW THIS IS USEFUL TO SOCIAL WORK

The skill that makes directives useful and helpful stems from our understanding that areas of behavior in the client's lives outside treatment are producing stress and that timely changes are needed. We can then identify ways to modify this behavior that we consider the client to be capable of doing and that we believe would bring them immediate relief. We often use this technique in conjunction with rehearsal activities in the interview, which also requires us to focus on feedback, review, and support in subsequent interviews.

One other area where we need to be ready to use this technique is in situations where the client is engaged in activities that pose a risk to or endanger themselves or others. Of course, our acting in a directive manner will not always result in altered behavior in such situations. However, if the relationship is strong and positive, we can often draw on the superego aspects of the positive, parental figure component of the relationship to encourage behavior that is safer and less laden with risk.

RISK FACTORS

Giving clients a directive carries a high degree of risk, and requires skill, care, and awareness on the social worker's part. One area of risk comes from possible unrecognized needs on the practitioner's part to control and become a benign but authoritative parent figure. Such a possibility can create unnecessary and, indeed, unhealthy dependency patterns in the client.

A further risk in using this technique occurs when the client views the therapeutic process as one in which an expert gives advice, and we get drawn into this expected role. Often this shows itself when the client states a wish that we fix someone in their lives who is viewed as being a problem by telling them what they should or should not do.

REQUIRED SKILLS AND KNOWLEDGE

When we give a directive, it is very important that we be clear that we are doing this, so the client understands we want them to do something specific. Because of the traditionally casual quality of the technique, instead of direct language such as "Thou shalt …" or "I want you to do … ," we often use suggestions and questions as a way of giving directions. At times we seem to use such euphemisms as a way of denying to ourselves that in fact we were giving a direction.

This technique is built on the premise that although we may wish the process between us and the clients were a relationship of equals, it is not. There is a considerable imbalance of authority and power in the relationship. Our responsibility is to understand this, to assess it throughout the life of a case, and when appropriate to draw upon it when we anticipate it would be helpful to the client. It is a skill to be used sparingly and rarely, but when it is properly timed and assessed, it can have a dramatically positive impact on clients, often in critical areas of their lives.

Case Summary One

Margie reports that she has been experiencing an increased amount of stress lately. She is attending therapy to improve her moods. During this therapy session, Margie's social worker discovers that Margie has a habit of keeping her emotions bottled up.

MARGIE: I'm just so stressed out lately. It seems like I always feel tense or frustrated.

SOCIAL WORKER: How do you usually react when something upsets you?

MARGIE: I try so hard not to react. I don't want people to think I'm an emotional wreck or something. I just keep it all inside.

SOCIAL WORKER: Instead of keeping your emotions bottled up, I am going to direct you to try something different. As a way to let your emotions out, the next time something happens that upsets you or makes you feel sad I want you to write about how you're feeling. You can choose to write in a journal to keep or a piece of paper that you throw away. The important thing is that you express your emotions through your writing.

MARGIE: I think I can handle that.

[During the following session:]

SOCIAL WORKER: Last session, I directed you to modify a pattern of your behavior in the way you react when you feel upset or sad. How did that work for you?

MARGIE: I was a little hesitant at first, but I tried it anyway and it was great. I felt this sense of relief that I haven't felt in a long time. I was able to let my emotions out without feeling embarrassed.

Before her social worker's directive, Margie always tried to bury her emotions deep inside and not let anyone see her feel anything. After receiving the directive and writing about what she was feeling, Margie experienced an alleviation of the stress she felt so often. Completing the directive also provided Margie with a sense of accomplishment, which helped to improve her moods.

Case Summary Two

Fred is a 10-year-old boy engaging in destructive behavior at home. This behavior is not only having an impact on his life, but also the lives of his loved ones. Whenever Fred becomes angry he breaks objects that he finds around him, whether they belong to him or another family member. Paired with his destructive outbursts, Fred's angry feelings have strained his relationships with family members and friends.

SOCIAL WORKER: Fred, your mom has already told me that she would like you to learn new ways to express your angry feelings at home. Now, I would like to know what you would like to get out of coming to see me.

FRED: I would like to not get in trouble any more. Can you help me with that?

SOCIAL WORKER: I hope so. Tell me, what usually happens to get you in trouble?

FRED: Well, whenever I start feeling angry or I'm arguing with someone I break stuff and then I get punished. My mom says I could hurt myself or someone else, so I'm not allowed to do that. I just get so mad that I don't know what else to do.

SOCIAL WORKER: We definitely don't want you or anyone else to get hurt. We want you to be safe. From now on, when you start arguing with someone or you start to feel angry, I want you to tell the person you are with that you need a break. Then, I want you to walk out of the room for about five minutes to calm yourself down. You will calm yourself down by engaging in deep breathing and other techniques that I am going to teach you and we are going to practice during our sessions.

FRED: Okay, as long as you teach me what to do, I will try it.

In this example the social worker was able to communicate to Fred what he wanted him to do during certain situations in his life. The purpose of this directive is to help Fred avoid getting in trouble by modifying the way he expresses his anger. Fred's social worker was able to give him the directive because of his authority in this positive therapeutic relationship. The social worker's directive also provided Fred with replacement behaviors to engage in to keep him from hurting himself or someone else. It provided a positive impact on this problem area of his life and also alleviated some stress in the lives of those around Fred who were affected by his outbursts.

REFERENCES AND ADDITIONAL SOURCES

Ballou, M. B. (1995). *Psychological interventions: A guide to strategies.* Westport, CT: Praeger.

Frank, J. D., & Frank, J. B. (1993). *Persuasion and healing: A comparative study of psychotherapy* (3rd ed.). Baltimore, MD: Johns Hopkins University Press.

Gil, E. (1991). *The healing power of play: Working with abused children.* New York, NY: Guilford Press.

Gil, E. (1994). *Play in family therapy.* New York, NY: Guilford Press.

Grove, D. S. (2002). Strategic family therapy. In A. J. Roberts & G. J. Greene (Eds.), *Social workers' desk reference.* New York, NY: Oxford University Press.

Haley, J., & Richeport-Haley, M. (2007). *Directive family therapy.* Binghamton, NY: Haworth Press.

Norcross, J. C. (2002). *Psychotherapy relationships that work: Social worker contributions and responsiveness to patients.* New York, NY: Oxford University Press.

Norcross, J. C., & Goldfried, M. R. (2005). *Handbook of psychotherapy integration* (2nd ed.). New York, NY: Oxford University Press.

Payne, K. L., Prentice, D. S., & Allen, R. S. (2010). A comparison of two interventions to increase completion of advance directives. *Clinical Gerontologist, 33*(1), 49–61.

Seltzer, L. F. (1983). Influencing the "shape" of resistance: An experimental exploration of paradoxical directives and psychological reactance. *Basic and Applied Social Psychology, 4*(1), 47–71.

Umphress, E. E., Simmons, A. L., Boswell, W. R., & Triana, M. C. (2008). Managing discrimination in selection: The influence of directives from an authority and social dominance orientation. *Journal of Applied Psychology, 93*(5), 982–993.

Zeig, J. K. (1997). *The evolution of psychotherapy: The third conference.* New York, NY: Brunner/Mazel.

Dream Work

DESCRIPTION

This technique encompasses the deliberate use of a client's dream material by the social worker as a basis for understanding and helping the client understand something from their developmental history or current reality.

ORIGINS

The belief or conviction that dreams convey important understanding about ourselves and others has been a part of the cultural, religious, and healing literature of virtually every group going back thousands of years. Dreams are believed to perform many different roles, depending on one's beliefs about their function.

For some, dreams are seen as serving such functions as understanding our waking states, foretelling our future, understanding the present, solving our problems, and interpreting the past. Thus their use in treatment will depend very much on both the client's understanding of their significance and the social worker's views of their importance or relevance.

Legitimizing the use of dreams as a therapeutic technique was taken out of the realms of religion and magic, and became part of the diagnostic and interpretive armamentarium of many social workers, principally through the work of Freud and Jung. In contemporary practice, the range of interpretations of their significance in our nondreaming lives varies. For some, dreams continue to be seen as "the royal road to the unconscious," whereas others take the position that in fact they tell us nothing about a person. From this perspective they are said to be only random neurological activities—more related, as Scrooge maintained, to a piece of undigested meat than anything to do with one's early psychosexual development.

Nevertheless, we will meet many people in practice who think that, at least from time to time, dreams do have a level of significance. Their perceived significance can range from understanding ones problems or concerns, and unfinished developmental work from the past, to their struggles to made decisions about important aspects of their current lives.

WHY THIS IS USEFUL TO SOCIAL WORK

Even though we may only see dreams as a mildly useful way to understand someone's histories or problems, asking a client about their dreams and the importance they accord to them can be a very facilitating way of initiating client self-disclosure. For many of our clients, dreams do carry some level of significance. Discussing them can be a way of helping them focus on their inner conflicts and concerns. Opening this topic with clients can both legitimize and facilitate their ability to reflect upon their waking lives.

HOW THIS IS USEFUL TO SOCIAL WORK

Because a focus on dreams is a helpful way for some clients to examine issues from their past, having clients share them with us and then reflect with us on their possible significance does present a growth opportunity. Such dream work can serve several goals. Reflecting upon dreams can help clients complete some unfinished developmental work, make decisions about difficult issues, or assess conflicts in their lives. Interest in these issues on our part can open up many important areas for therapeutic focus. Of course, the focus of looking at dreams is always to help the client deal better with reality.

Some colleagues have reported that with seriously ill clients, for whom existential questions about life and death have come to the fore, having them talk about and reflect on dreams can be helpful in addressing such issues.

RISK FACTORS

One of the challenges in using dreams as a technique is that for some persons, all dreams are highly significant from a variety of perspectives. For some they foretell the future, for others they are a means of problem solving or the source of messages about what one should do or not do. Paying an undue interest to the dreams of a client who perceives them as having some magic or deterministic quality to predict the future could easily result in therapeutic complications.

Overall, because of this broad range of perceptions about the importance and significance of dreams, using this technique requires a high level of practitioner vigilance. For example, it is possible that being interested in or focusing on a client's dream life could lead us into material that serves as a way of avoiding reality rather than being helpful. Our interest could also reinforce problem-producing behavior. Because of the potential for client or social worker misunderstanding of the importance clients give to dreams, this technique has a moderate level of risk.

REQUIRED SKILLS AND KNOWLEDGE

In choosing to make use of dreams as a therapeutic technique, it is essential for the social worker to have a clear theoretical position and understanding of dreams. If this position will be formulated from classical psychoanalytic theory, the worker will require specialized training.

The worker must also have a clear understanding of the client's belief or understanding of the importance or unimportance of dreams, to assess whether exploring this material will be helpful or not.

Because most of us forget our dreams quickly once we have awakened, if the social worker is going to make use of dream material in a particular case, it is useful to have clients keep notes or records of dream material they consider significant for later discussion. We need to be careful in urging this, as this kind of record keeping can give the process and the dreams a greater level of significance than is needed or useful.

Case Summary One

Susie and Tom had been married for 4 years when they decided to attend therapy sessions together. They each felt resentment toward the other and blamed each other for their problems. They described their relationship as constant fighting. Their social worker introduced the idea of discussing their dreams as a way to gain better communication.

SOCIAL WORKER: Dreams can serve as guides to understanding our emotions. This can help us focus on problem-solving techniques and working through your marital concerns.

TOM: What if we can't remember everything that happened in our dreams?

SOCIAL WORKER: View your dreams as pictures. I want you to focus on the feelings in the dream, not necessarily the content of the dream. When you wake up each morning, write down everything you can remember and the way you felt, and we will discuss them during our sessions.

[During the next several therapy sessions, Susie and Tom discussed their dreams and any inner conflicts they might be having.]

SOCIAL WORKER: We've been discussing your dreams during therapy sessions for a while now. How do you two feel towards each other lately?

TOM: Discussing dreams during therapy has helped us to utilize our problem-solving skills and learn new ways to relate to each other.

SUSIE: I agree. I feel more emotionally connected to Tom now than I ever did. We are also more positive towards each other.

Dreams were a safe way for Susie and Tom to discuss their feelings without making their partner feel like an enemy. They were able to focus their attention on their own desires, needs, and feelings without blaming the other person for their problems. This activity of sharing dreams openly and honestly allowed the couple to feel more tolerant and closer to each other.

Case Summary Two

Jill is a young adult who has overcome a troubled childhood. She never knew her biological father and her mother was not around much. Jill admits that she was never able to count on her parents for anything, but states that it in no way bothered her and it doesn't matter to her.

SOCIAL WORKER: Jill, how have you been since our last session?

JILL: I've been okay, but slightly distressed lately. I keep having this recurring dream about my mother. The mornings after I've had the dream I wake up feeling upset. I know it must mean something, but I'm not sure what.

SOCIAL WORKER: That must make for some rough mornings. I'd like you to tell me more about your recurring dream if you feel comfortable.

JILL: In the dream I can see my mom, but we're separated by a clear glass wall or something. I call out to her over and over again, but she doesn't hear me. I don't think she even knows I'm there. It's really frustrating for me.

SOCIAL WORKER: Many times our dreams are a way to experience feelings that we won't let ourselves express in our everyday lives. I know when we talked about your family history you mentioned that your mother wasn't around too often. You said that it never really bothered you much, but I wonder if this recurring dream is a way of allowing you to let out some repressed feelings.

JILL: I think that really might be a possibility. The dream is very similar to how I grew up. My mom is there, but she doesn't see me or hear me. I feel like I'm being ignored and it really upsets me. I guess I just never let myself realize it before.

From their previous conversations, Jill's social worker knew that Jill believes that dreams are significant and always have some sort of meaning. Discussing her recent dreams with her social worker allowed Jill to reflect on her past and think about her feelings. It also helped her understand how her past is affecting her current reality.

REFERENCES AND ADDITIONAL SOURCES

Berube, L. (1999). Dream work: Demystifying dreams using a small group for personal growth. *Journal for Specialists in Group Work, 24*(1), 88–101.

Borenstein, L. (2003). The clinician as a dreamcatcher: Holding the dream. *Clinical Social Work Journal, 31*(30), 249–262.

Goelitz, A. (2001). Nurturing life with dreams: Therapeutic dream work with cancer patients. *Clinical Social Work Journal, 29*(4), 375–385.

Goellity, A. (2001). Dreaming their way into life: Group experience with oncology patients. A group experience with oncology patients. *Social Work With Groups, 24*(1), 53–68.

Hill, C. E. (2003). *Dream work in therapy: Facilitating exploration, insight, and action.* Washington, DC: American Psychological Association.

Kuelz, A. K., Stotz, U., Riemann, D., Schredl, M., & Voderholzer, U. (2010). Dream recall and dream content in obsessive-compulsive patients: Is there a change during exposure treatment? *Journal of Nervous and Mental Disease, 198*(8), 593–596.

Mahon, E. J. (1992). Dreams: A developmental and longitudinal perspective. *The Psychoanalytic Study of the Child, 47*, 49–65.

Muff, J. (1996). Images of life on the verge of death: Dreams and drawings of people with AIDS. *Perspectives in Psychiatric Care, 32*(3), 10–23.

Provost, J. A. (1999). A dream focus for short-term growth groups. *Journal for Specialists in Group Work, 24*(1), 74–87.

Schlachet, P. J. (1992). The dream in group therapy: A reappraisal of unconscious processes in groups. *Group, 16*(4), 195–209.

Schredl, M. (2010). Explaining the gender difference in dream recall frequency. *Dreaming, 20*(2), 96–106.

Schredl, M., & Sartorius, H. (2010). Dream recall and dream content in children with attention deficit/hyperactivity disorder. *Child Psychiatry and Human Development, 41*(2), 230–238.

Widen, H. A. (2000). Using dreams in brief therapy. *Psychoanalytic Social Work, 7*(2), 1–4.

Eco Map

DESCRIPTION

The eco map is an activity in which we engage with the client to prepare a map that visually represents the network of significant persons and systems of which the client is a part, or that appear to be playing a part in the client's life.

ORIGINS

This technique comes to us partly out of systems theory, but more directly from ecological theory as developed by Dr. Ann Hartman (Hartman, 1978). It is also strongly linked to the psychosocial tradition. It is a resource with both strong diagnostic and therapeutic potential.

WHY THIS IS USEFUL TO SOCIAL WORK

The strengths and utility of this type of map is that it helps the client get an overview of their lives and an appreciation of some of its ecological complexities in a visual form. It is particularly useful in helping clients pinpoint problem areas and how they are exacerbated, modified, or helped by various aspects of the eco map. The technique involves the client in a different manner than the traditional interview format.

HOW THIS IS USEFUL TO SOCIAL WORK

The map that is drawn usually takes the form of a series of ever-larger circles, with the client or the family in the center circle. The first surrounding circle includes significant others in the client's life, including family members and other important people. This is surrounded by a second circle, in which the client identifies systems that he or she interacts with, including individual professionals. Each person and each system is set out in the map in a separate, smaller circle.

In drawing the map, an effort is made to indicate the degree of involvement and importance of the persons or system by using different types of lines and arrows to show whether the designated person or system is a positive or negative factor in the client's life. Wherever possible, the intensity of the relationship is also indicated. Lines can also be used to show how various persons and systems are interconnected and whether they are linked in a positive, neutral, or negative way.

Rarely is it possible to complete the map in a single session. It is only as we get to know the client better, and as he or she continues to reflect on their lives and its significant systemic involvement, that all aspects of the map emerge.

This type of technique is also useful in helping clients identify areas where they are deficient in their ecosystems and consider ways of rectifying such deficits in a manner that will help their psychosocial reality.

Often our clients have never sat down and reviewed their lives in this way, and are astounded to see the complexity of their lives in a schematic format. This complexity itself is frequently what produces the client's problems.

This technique has shown itself to be useful both with individuals and families. One of the advantages of using it with a family is that it is an effective way for family members to see and hear how other members differentially view parts of the system and assess their positive and negative attributes.

A further way in which this technique can be therapeutic is to use it as a tool for evaluating change in a client or their system. Redrawing it some time after the original eco map has been completed facilitates the client's ability to see shifts that may have taken place in their system over time, and to plan for subsequent changes either as a part of ongoing therapy or as future tasks they set for themselves.

RISK FACTORS

Eco map use is low risk. Certainly some clients will not find this type of graphic activity useful. Others will not understand the concepts implied in the various linkages. In such instances little harm will be done, except perhaps to bore the client or to produce mild anxiety if they grow frustrated by not understanding what is required of them in the process or what it all means.

REQUIRED SKILLS AND KNOWLEDGE

The principal skill required to use this technique is to engage the client in a process that may seem to be of little value. We also need to know our client well and to be able to help them to identify, evaluate, and place the significant persons and systems in their lives.

The awareness and learning that occur as a result of successfully using an eco gram often will emerge without the aid of this type of visual picture of one reality. What this technique adds is a new way for the client to see themselves and their systemic reality, in a way that can lead them to identify areas where change would be beneficial. It also targets negative areas that can then can become the focus of subsequent therapeutic contacts.

Case Summary One

Charles presents with anxiety and panic attacks. He states that he is not sure what the source of his symptoms are. After several sessions with Charles, hearing his story, and building rapport, the social worker suggests drawing an eco map as a way to try and discover the origins of his symptoms.

SOCIAL WORKER: Today we are going to draw what is called an eco map. It will help us identify your relationship patterns and the type of influence significant others and your environment have in your life.

CHARLES: Okay. How do we do it?

SOCIAL WORKER: Well, we probably won't complete it during this session, but we can get a good start. We will begin by drawing a circle in the center of our paper. That circle represents you, so we will label it Charles. Next, we will draw circles of family members and others in your life that are important to you.

Charles and his social worker spent the remainder of the session completing what they could of his eco map. Drawing an eco map provided Charles with a visual representation of the people and relationships in his life. It allowed him to recognize positive supports, as well as sources of tension and stress.

Case Summary Two

The Suarez family has been attending therapy sessions as a way to improve their family relationships. Mrs. Suarez reports that the family doesn't talk that much anymore and the only way they communicate is through arguing. Mr. Suarez states that he feels disconnected from his daughter's life and wants the family to have a closer bond.

SOCIAL WORKER: Today I'd like the three of you to work on an activity as a family. We will all work together to draw an eco map. An eco map is a visual representation of the network of significant systems and persons in a family's life.

MRS. SUAREZ: What is an eco map for?

SOCIAL WORKER: Drawing out an eco map can help pinpoint problem areas in a family's life and how they can be helped or aggravated. While drawing the map you all will indicate the degree of involvement and importance of the persons or systems being represented. You will also indicate whether they are a positive or negative factor in the family's life.

MR. SUAREZ: And we're making one eco map for the three of us?

SOCIAL WORKER: Yes, the three of you are going to make one eco map. You will start by listing the three of you in a circle in the middle of the page. Then, you will work together to figure out which persons, groups, et cetera are most important to your family. Making one eco map together will allow each of you to see how other family members view relationships and influences in their lives.

The Suarez family and their social worker spent the majority of this session working on as much of the eco map as they could. Drawing an eco map provided the Suarez family and their social worker with a look at the clients' family life and the nature of the family's relationship with outside groups, associations, organizations, and other families and individuals. The process of drawing the eco map also allowed the family to increase their communication and understanding of one another.

REFERENCES AND ADDITIONAL SOURCES

Beauchesne, M., Kelley, B., & Gauthier, M. A. (1997). The genogram: A health assessment tool. *Nurse Educator, 22*(3), 9–16.

Brandell, J. R. (1997). *Theory and practice in clinical social work*. New York, NY: Free Press.

Carpenter-Aeby, T., Aeby, V. G., & Boyd, J. S. (2007). Ecomaps as visual tools for deconstructing reciprocal influences: Triage with disruptive students at an alternative school. *The School Community Journal, 17*(2), 45–72.

Coady, N., & Lehman, P. (2007). *Theoretical perspectives for direct social work practice: A generalist-eclectic approach*. New York, NY: Springer.

Connolly, C. M. (2005). Discovering "family" creatively: The self-created genogram. *Journal of Creativity in Mental Health, 1*(1), 81–105.

Frame, M. W. (2000). The spiritual genogram in family therapy. *Journal of Marital & Family Therapy, 26*(2), 211–216.

Feguson, D. (1999). Eco-maps: Facilitating insight in learning disabled sex-offenders. *British Journal of Nursing, 8*(18), 1224–1230.

Halevy, J. (1998). A genogram with an attitude. *Journal of Marital & Family Therapy, 24*(2), 233–242.

Hartman, A. (1978). Diagrammatic assessment of family relationships. *Social Casework, 59*(10), 465–478.

Helling, M. K., & Stovers, R. G. (2005). Genogram as a research tool. *Great Plains Sociologist, 17*(1), 78–85.

Hepworth, D. H., Rooney, R. J., & Larsen, J. A. (2009). *Direct social work practice: Theory and skills* (8th ed.). Pacific Grove, CA: Brooks/Cole.

Keiley, M. K., Dolbin, M., Hill, J., Karuppaswamy, N., Liu, T., Natrajan, R., …Robinson, P. (2002). The cultural genogram: Experiences from within a marriage and family therapy training program. *Journal of Marital & Family Therapy, 28*(2), 165–178.

Hodge, D. R. (2005). Spiritual ecograms: A new assessment instrument for identifying clients' spiritual strengths in space and across time. *Families in Society: The Journal of Contemporary Social Services, 86*(2), 287–296.

McGoldrick, M., Gerson, R., & Shellenberger, S. (1999). *Genograms: Assessment and intervention* (2nd ed.). New York, NY: Norton.

McGuinness, T. M., Noonan, P., & Dyer, J. G. (2005). Family history as a tool for psychiatric nurses. *Archives of Psychiatric Nursing, 19*(3), 116–124.

Milewski-Hertlein, K. (2001). The use of a socially constructed genogram in clinical practice. *The American Journal of Family Therapy, 29*(1), 23–38.

Olsen, S., Dudley-Brown, S., & McMullen, P. (2004). Case for blending pedigrees, genograms and eco-maps: Nursing's contribution to the "big picture." *Nursing and Health Sciences, 6*(4), 295–308.

Peluso, P. R. (2006). Expanding the use of the ethical genogram: Incorporating the ethical principles to help clarify counselors' ethical decision-making styles. *The Family Journal: Counseling and Therapy for Couples and Families, 14*(2), 158–163.

Petr, C. G. (2004). *Social work with children and their families: Pragmatic foundations* (2nd ed.). New York, NY: Oxford University Press.

Puskar, K., & Nerone, M. (1996). Genogram: A useful tool for nurse practitioners. *Journal of Psychiatric and Mental Health Nursing, 3*(1), 55–60.

Ray, R. A., & Street, A. F. (2005). Ecomapping: An innovative research tool for nurses. *Journal of Advanced Nursing, 50*(5), 545–552.

Rempel, G. R., Neufeld, A., & Kushner, K. E. (2007). Interactive use of genograms and ecomaps in family caregiving research. *Journal of Family Nursing, 13*(4), 403–419.

Sheafor, B. W., & Horejsi, C. R. (2003). *Techniques and guidelines for social work practice* (6th ed.). Boston, MA: Allyn & Bacon.

Thomas, A. J. (1998). Understanding culture and worldview in family systems: Use of the multicultural genogram. *The Family Journal: Counseling and Therapy for Couples and Families, 6*(1), 24–32.

Watts-Jones, D. (1997). Toward an African American genogram. *Family Process, 36*(4), 375–383.

Watts, C., & Shrader, E. (1998). The genogram: A new research tool to document patterns of decision-making, conflict and vulnerability within households. *Health Policy & Planning, 13*(4), 459–464.

Empowerment

DESCRIPTION

Although one of our implicit goals in practice is generally to seek to empower our clients, there are times when we address this goal by means of a specific technique. We do this by engaging in discrete efforts to expand the client's ability to assume, seize or find ways of taking charge or control of some component of their lives outside of the interview. It is in this way that empowerment is a technique.

ORIGINS

Empowerment theory has underscored for us the importance of leading clients to address ways in which they can free themselves, albeit in small ways, from some of the negative components of oppression in their lives. It is the general influence of this theory, and the broader understanding of the many ways in which clients can take a greater role in their autonomy, that has led us to understand how this can be one of our practice techniques.

WHY THIS IS USEFUL TO SOCIAL WORK

In recent decades we have expanded our understanding of the many forms of power that negatively impact our clients' lives. Likewise, in our work to enhance clients' psychosocial functioning, we have learned that a component of this objective is to help them to directly shape their own destinies—that we can help clients free themselves from the unhealthy controlling influence of others. By finding ways to minimize oppression or to address situations that inhibit their functioning, they, too can participate in the task of achieving their life goals. In an interesting way, this interest in empowering clients helps join the micro and macro dichotomy of our practice.

HOW THIS IS USEFUL TO SOCIAL WORK

In a general way, our overall use of the helping relationship in a manner that leads to enhanced self-autonomy and self-regard is a form of empowerment, especially when we focus on strengths and gains in treatment with the client and help them to see the extent to which they have become more autonomous. This happens in all treatment as it moves in a positive direction. Understanding the importance of empowerment, and its potential use in our practice, can lead us to add it to our treatment options.

That is not only do we help clients to seek greater development we can help them see that a component of this maturity is the responsibility and ability to bring about changes in their societal network. Empowerment is clearly a technique with a much stronger underlying value base than many other techniques, one strong enough to lead us to at least ask ourselves whether adding this technique to our intervention in particular cases will benefit certain clients.

As useful as this technique is for working with individuals, it can also be used with considerable effectiveness with groups interested in some external, problem-producing aspect of their lives and what can be done about it.

RISK FACTORS

Using empowerment entails a moderately high risk potential that needs to be kept in mind. The risk is that we might move beyond where the client is and where he or she is capable of going because of our commitment to this goal. Thus it is important to distinguish between a position that makes empowerment the goal of treatment, and one that uses empowerment techniques as one of many other techniques we will use to assist the client in moving forward further than they believed themselves capable of doing.

Although much of the teaching and encouragement role of building empowerment takes place in the interview, the test of its effectiveness in a particular case is what happens in a client's life. Is the client learning to make use of their newly acquired abilities in a manner that reflects both an understanding of and an ability to act differently in a positively empowered manner?

REQUIRED SKILLS AND KNOWLEDGE

The use of this technique entails a significant amount of teaching, encouragement, and reflection. The teaching includes both an assessment and understanding of how the client can make more effective use of themselves in situations that hold them back. It also aims to help them understand the extent to which tangible factors outside of themselves, whether in their past or continuing in the present, limit their ability to achieve the full flowering of their potential.

This teaching thus addresses ways in which persons can take an active role in changing their significant environments. We do this in a similar way to how we use consciousness-raising techniques. A further component of teaching is to help the client understand the strengths they have and the resources available to them to make more effective use of their abilities.

We also want to help the client reflect on ways they have minimized their potential or have let themselves get locked into nonproductive roles, functions, and perceptions that have interfered with ability to function in a more empowered way.

Case Summary One

Angie has been seeing her social worker for a few months. She disclosed to the social worker that about six months ago her husband left her after 10 years of marriage. During the marriage Angie did not work outside of the home. The divorce came as a shock to her; she did not see it coming. Angie had limited support at that time and felt like she was forced to apply for public assistance programs to make it on her own.

ANGIE: I feel like I have no control over my life anymore. I depend on public assistance just to make it day to day in my life.

SOCIAL WORKER: Tell me more about that. What is it that makes you feel that way?

ANGIE: Well, I never thought I would be on public assistance, let alone for this long. I went from having all my needs met all the time to struggling and not knowing if I would be able to pay the bills on time.

SOCIAL WORKER: It sounds like you're having a hard time with the transition to your new life situation. It must be very frustrating for you.

ANGIE: I feel like a failure. I don't know what to do. What should I do?

SOCIAL WORKER: What do you think you should do? What do you think would help you feel better about your situation?

ANGIE: Being able to support myself without public assistance would make a world of difference. I just have no idea what to do. Like I said, I feel like I have no control over my life.

SOCIAL WORKER: Let's figure out where you want to start. Only you have the power to change your circumstances. You said that being able to support yourself would help you feel better. What is the first step toward being able to support yourself?

ANGIE: I need to get a good-paying job.

SOCIAL WORKER: What is the first step in getting a good-paying job?

ANGIE: Well, first I need to update my resume and research available jobs.

In this case study, when Angie presented her issue the social worker did not tell her what she should do about it. He allowed her to determine what she wanted to do and to make her own decisions. Doing this provided Angie with a sense of control over her life and decreased her feeling of powerlessness. Angie started the conversation feeling hopeless about her situation and ended the conversation feeling motivated and empowered.

Case Summary Two

Darnell is a young adult attending therapy sessions for the first time in his life. He has been attending sessions for a few weeks now. Darnell grew up in an environment where he was talked to negatively the majority of the time, and he now feels that he is worthless and powerless. Darnell's social worker is using empowerment as a technique to improve his self-esteem and thereby increase his social interactions, assertiveness, and self-confidence.

SOCIAL WORKER: Darnell, tell me how you view yourself in relation to others.

DARNELL: Most of the time I just think I'm a stupid loser. I don't go out much because I'm afraid people won't like me. I'll never be anything without my family. I'll be stuck with them forever. I feel powerless.

SOCIAL WORKER: I remember you telling me that you have a full-time job. It sounds like a pretty good job, too. How did you end up working there?

DARNELL: I didn't do anything special. I just filled out the application and turned it in.

SOCIAL WORKER: Did you have to interview for the position?

DARNELL: Yes, I met with the person who is now my supervisor.

SOCIAL WORKER: So, let me make sure I understand the situation correctly. First, you found a place where you wanted to work. Then, you completed the application, which must have had some great accomplishments on it to get you an interview. Next, you engaged in an interview well enough for the supervisor to offer you a position with the company. Is that right?

DARNELL: Well, yes. I guess so.

SOCIAL WORKER: Was anybody there with you completing the application and interview for you to get the job?

DARNELL: No, I did everything by myself.

SOCIAL WORKER: It seems to me you have some pretty exceptional qualities to offer the world.

By using empowerment as a technique in this therapy session, Darnell's social worker was able to help free Darnell from the oppression of his family life. Through their conversations Darnell was able to reflect on times in his life when he was independent, and also to recognize the strengths and resources he has available to him. Feeling empowered will help Darnell achieve his life goals by addressing and changing situations that inhibit his functioning.

REFERENCES AND ADDITIONAL SOURCES

Anderson, J. (1996). Yes, but IS IT empowerment? Initiation, implementation and outcomes of community action. In B. Humphries (Ed.), *Critical perspectives on empowerment* (pp. 69–84). Birmingham: Venture Press.

Bernstein, E., Wallerstein, N., Braithwaite, R., Gutierrez, L., Labonte, R., & Zimmerman, M. A. (1994). Empowerment forum—A dialog between guest editorial-board members. *Health Education Quarterly, 21*(3), 281–294.

Boehm, A., & Staples, L. H. (2004). Empowerment: The point of view of consumers. *Families in Society: The Journal of Contemporary Social Services, 85*(2), 270–280.

Bolton, B., & Brookings, J. (1998). Development of a measure of intrapersonal empowerment. *Rehabilitation Psychology, 43*, 131–142. doi:10.1037/0090-5550.43.2.131

Braye S., & Preston-Shoot, M. (1995). *Empowering practice in social care.* Buckingham: Open University Press.

Cargo, M., Grams, G. D., Ottoson, J. M., Ward, P., & Green, L. W. (2004).Empowerment as fostering positive youth development and citizenship. *American Journal of Health Behavior, 27*(Suppl. 1), S66–S79.

Castro, R., Casique, I., & Brindis, C. D. (2008). Empowerment and physical violence throughout women's reproductive life in Mexico. *Violence Against Women, 14*(6), 655–677. doi:10.1177/1077801208319102

Cattaneo, L. B., & Chapman, A. R. (2010). The process of empowerment: A model for use in research and practice. *American Psychologist, 65*(7), 646–659.

Chinman, M. J., & Linney, J. A. (1998). Toward a model of adolescent empowerment: Theoretical and empirical evidence. *The Journal of Primary Prevention, 18*(4), 393–413.

Finfgeld, D. L. (2004). Empowerment of individuals with enduring mental health problems: Results from concept analyses and qualitative investigations. *Advances in Nursing Science, 27*(1), 44–52.

Fitzsimons, S., & Fuller, R. (2002). Empowerment and its implications for clinical practice in mental health: A review. *Journal of Mental Health, 11*(5), 481–499. doi:10.1080/09638230020023

Florin, P., & Wandersman, A. (1990). An introduction to citizen participation, voluntary organizations, and community development: Insights for empowerment through research. *American Journal of Community Psychology, 18*(1), 41–54.

Franzen, S., Morrel-Samuels, S., Reischl, T. M., & Zimmerman, M. A. (2009). Using process evaluation to strengthen intergenerational partnerships in the youth empowerment solutions program. *Journal of Prevention & Intervention in the Community, 37*(4), 289–301.

Foster-Fishman, P. G., Salem, D. A., Chibnall, S., Legler, R., & Yapchai, C. (1998). Empirical support for the critical assumptions of empowerment theory. *American Journal of Community Psychology, 26*(4), 507–536. doi:10.1023/A:1022188805083

Garcia-Ramirez, M., Martinez, M. F., Balcazar, F. E., Suarez-Balcazar, Y., Albar, M.-J., Domínguez, E., & Santolaya, F. J. (2005). Psychosocial empowerment and social support factors associated with the employment status of immigrant welfare recipients. *Journal of Community Psychology, 33*(6), 673–690. doi:10.1002/jcop.20072

Gillman, M. (1996). Empowering professionals in higher education. In B. Humphries (Ed.), *Critical perspectives on empowerment* (pp. 99–116). Birmingham: Venture Press.

Gibbs, J. T., & Fuery, D. (1994). Mental health and well-being of Black women: Toward strategies of empowerment. *American Journal of Community Psychology, 22*(4), 559–582.

Gutierrez, L. (1991). Empowering women of color: A feminist model. In M. B. Jenkins, N. R. Hooyman, & N. Gottlieb (Eds.), *Feminist social work practice in clinical settings* (pp. 199–214). Newbury Park, CA: Sage.

Gutierrez, L. M., Parson, R. J., & Cox, E.O. (1998). *Empowerment ins work practice: A Source-book.* Pacific Grove, CA: Brooks/Cole.

Hough, M., & Paisley, K. (2008). An empowerment theory approach to adventure programming for adults with disabilities. *Therapeutic Recreation Journal, 42*, 89–102.

Humphries, B. (Ed.). (1996). *Critical perspectives on empowerment.* Birmingham: Venture Press.

Hur, M. H. (2006). Empowerment in terms of theoretical perspectives: Exploring a typology of the process and components across disciplines. *Journal of Community Psychology, 34*(5), 523–540. doi:10.1002/ jcop.20113

Johnson, D. M., Worell, J., & Chandler, R. K. (2005). Assessing psychological health and empowerment in women: The Personal Progress Scale revised. *Women and Health, 41*(1), 109–129.

Jennings, L. B., Parra-Medina, D. M., Messias, D. K., & McLoughlin, K. (2006). Toward a critical social theory of youth empowerment. *Journal of Community Practice, 14*(1/2), 31–55.

Kar, S. B., Pascual, C. A., & Chickering, K. L. (1999). Empowerment of women for health promotion: A meta-analysis. *Social Science & Medicine, 49*(11), 1431–1460. doi:10.1016/S0277-9536(99)00200-2

Kasturirangan, A. (2008). Empowerment and programs designed to address domestic violence. *Violence Against Women, 14*(12), 1465–1475. doi:10.1177/1077801208325188

Kieffer, C. H. (1984). Citizen empowerment: A developmental perspective. *Prevention in Human Services, 3*(2), 9–36. doi:10.1300/ J293v03n02_03

Kim, S., Crutchfield, C., Williams, C., & Hepler, N. (1998). Toward a new paradigm in substance abuse and other problem behavior prevention for youth: Youth development and empowerment approach. *Journal of Drug Education, 28*(1), 1–17.

Kreisberg, S. (1992). *Transforming power: Domination, empowerment and education.* Albany, NY: State University of New York Press.

Kroeker, C. J. (1995). Individual, organizational, and societal empowerment: A study of the processes in a Nicaraguan agricultural cooperative. *American Journal of Community Psychology, 23*(5), 749–764. doi:10.1007/BF02506990

Laverack, G., & Wallerstein, N. (2001). Measuring community empowerment: A fresh look at organizational domains. *Health Promotion International, 16*(2), 179–185.

Lee, J. (1996). The empowerment approach to social work practice. In F. J. Turner (Ed.), *Social work treatment* (pp. 218–249). New York, NY: Free Press.

Lee., J. A. (2001). *The empowerment approach to social work practice* (2nd ed.). Chichester, England: Columbia University Press.

Leonardsen, D. (2007). Empowerment in social work: An individual vs. a relational perspective. *International Journal of Social Welfare, 16*(1), 3–11. doi:10.1111/j.1468-2397.2006.00449.x

Major, B., & O'Brien, L. T. (2005). The social psychology of stigma. *Annual Review of Psychology, 56*(1), 393–421. doi:10.1146/annurev-psych.56.091103.070137

Masterson, S., & Owen, S. (2006). Mental health service user's social and individual empowerment: Using theories of power to elucidate far reaching strategies. *Journal of Mental Health, 15*(1), 19–34. doi:10.1080/ 09638230500512714

Maly, R. C., Stein, J. A., Umezawa, Y., Leake, B., & Anglin, M. D. (2008). Racial/ethnic differences in breast cancer outcomes among older patients: Effects of physician communication and patient empowerment. *Health Psychology, 27*(6), 728–736. doi:10.1037/0278–6133.27.6.728

McWhirter, E. H. (1991). Empowerment in counseling. *Journal of Counseling & Development, 69*(3), 222–227.

McWhirter, E. H. (1998). An empowerment model of counsellor education. *Canadian Journal of Counselling, 32*(1), 12–26.

Novak, T. (1996). Empowerment and the politics of poverty. In B. Humphries (Ed.), *Critical perspectives on empowerment* (pp. 85–98). Birmingham: Venture Press.

Olin, S. S., Hoagwood, K. E., Rodriguez, J., Ramos, B., Burton, G., Penn, M., Crowe, M., Radigan, M., & Jensen, P. S. (2010). The application of behavior change theory to family-based services: Improving parent empowerment in children's mental health. *Journal of Child and Family Studies, 19*(4), 462–470.

Parsloe, P, (Ed.). (1996). *Pathways to empowerment.* Birmingham: Venture Press.

Parsons, R. J. (2002). Guidelines for empowerment-based social work practice. In A. R. Roberts & G. J. Greene (Eds.), *Social worker's desk reference* (pp. 396–401). Oxford, England: University of Oxford Press.

Peterson, N. A., Hamme, C. L., & Speer, P. W. (2002). Cognitive empowerment of African Americans and Caucasians: Differences in understandings of power, political functioning, and shaping ideology. *Journal of Black Studies, 32*(3), 336–351.

Peterson, N. A., & Hughey, J. (2004). Social cohesion and intrapersonal empowerment: Gender as moderator. *Health Education Research, 19*(5), 533–542. doi:10.1093/her/cyg057

Peterson, N. A., Lowe, J. B., Aquilino, M. L., & Schneider, J. E. (2005). Linking social cohesion and gender to intrapersonal and interactional empowerment: Support and new implications for theory. *Journal of Community Psychology, 33*(2), 233–244.

Peterson, N. A., Lowe, J. B., Hughey, J., Reid, R. J., Zimmerman, M. A., & Speer, P. W. (2006). Measuring the intrapersonal component of psychological empowerment: Confirmatory factor analysis of the Sociopolitical Control Scale. *American Journal of Community Psychology, 38*(3/4), 287–297. doi:10.1007/s10464–006–9070–3

Presser, H. B., & Sen, G. (Eds.). (2000). *Women's empowerment and demographic processes: Moving beyond Cairo.* New York, NY: Oxford University Press.

Price, R. H. (1990). Whither participation and empowerment? *American Journal of Community Psychology, 18*(1), 163–167.

Rappaport, J. (1981). In praise of paradox: A social policy of empowerment over prevention. *American Journal of Community Psychology, 9*(1), 1–25. doi:10.1007/BF00896357

Rappaport, J. (1987). Terms of empowerment/exemplars of prevention: Toward a theory for community psychology. *American Journal of Community Psychology, 15*(2), 121–148. doi:10.1007/BF00919275

Rappaport, J. (1995). Empowerment meets narrative: Listening to stories and creating settings. *American Journal of Community Psychology, 23*(5), 795–807. doi:10.1007/BF02506992

Riger, S. (1993). What's wrong with empowerment. *American Journal of Community Psychology, 21*(3), 279–292. doi:10.1007/BF00941504

Rocha, E. M. (1997). A ladder of empowerment. *Journal of Planning Research, 17*(1), 31–44.

Schulz, A. J., Israel, B. A., Zimmerman, M. A., & Checkoway, B. N. (1995). Empowerment as a multilevel construct: Perceived control at the individual, organizational and community levels. *Health Education Research, 10*(3), 309–327.

Simon, B. L. (1994). *Empowerment traditions: History of empowerment in social work.* New York, NY: Columbia University Press.

Solomon, B. B. (1987). Empowerment: Social work in oppressed communities. *Journal of Social Work Practice, 2*(4), 79–91. doi:10.1080/ 02650538708414984

Speer, P. W. (2000). Intrapersonal and interactional empowerment: Implications for theory. *Journal of Community Psychology, 28*(1), 51–61.

Speer, P. W., & Hughey, J. (1995). Community organizing: An ecological route to empowerment and power. *American Journal of Community Psychology, 23*(5), 729–748.

Speer, P. W., Jackson, C. B., & Peterson, N. A. (2001). The relationship between social cohesion and empowerment: Support and new implications for theory. *Health Education & Behavior, 28*(6), 716–732. doi:10.1177/109019810102800605

Tengland, P. (2008). Empowerment: A conceptual discussion. *Health Care Analysis, 16*(2), 77–96.

Treseder, P. (1997). *Empowering children & young people: Promoting involvement in decision-making.* London, England: Save the Children.

Trickett, E. J. (1991). *Living an idea: Empowerment and the evolution of an alternative high school.* Cambridge, MA: Brookline Books.

Wallerstein, N. (1992). Powerlessness, empowerment, and health: Implications for health promotion programs. *American Journal of Health Promotion, 6*(3), 197–205.

Wallerstein, N., & Bernstein, E. (1988). Empowerment education: Freire's ideas adapted to health-education. *Health Education Quarterly, 15*(4), 379–394.

Wood, T. E., Englander-Golden, P., Golden, D. E., & Pillai, V. K. (2010). Improving addictions treatment outcomes by empowering self and others. *International Journal of Mental Health Nursing, 19*(5), 363–368.

Wong, N. T., Zimmerman, M. A., & Parker, E. A. (2010). A typology of youth participation and empowerment for child and adolescent health promotion. *American Journal of Community Psychology, 46*(1–2), 100–114.

Worell, J., & Remer, P. (2003). *Feminist perspectives in therapy: Empowering diverse women* (2nd ed.). New York, NY: Wiley.

Wright, C. V., Perez, S., & Johnson, D. M. (2010). The mediating role of empowerment for African American women experiencing intimate partner violence. *Psychological Trauma: Theory, Research, Practice, and Policy*. Advance online publication. doi:10.1037/a0017470

Yoder, J. D., & Kahn, A. S. (1992). Toward a feminist understanding of women and power. *Psychology of Women Quarterly, 16*(2), 381–388. doi:10.1111/j.1471-6402.1992.tb00263.x

Zastrow, C. (2009). *Introduction to social work and social welfare: Empowering people.* (10th ed.). Belmont, CA: Brooks/Cole.

Zimmerman, M. A. (1995). Psychological empowerment: Issues and illustrations. *American Journal of Community Psychology, 23*(5), 581–599. doi:10.1007/BF02506983

Zimmerman, M. A. (2000). Empowerment theory: Psychological, organizational, and community levels of analysis. In J. Rappaport & E. Seidman (Eds.), *Handbook of community psychology* (pp. 43–63). New York, NY: Kluwer Academic/Plenum.

Zimmerman, M. A., & Rappaport, J. (1988). Citizen participation, perceived control, and psychological empowerment. *American Journal of Community Psychology, 16*(5), 725–750. doi:10.1007/BF00930023

Zimmerman, M. A., & Warschausky, S. (1998). Empowerment theory for rehabilitation research: Conceptual and methodological issues. *Rehabilitation Psychology, 43*(1), 3–16.

Empty Chair

DESCRIPTION

Although there are several variations in the use of this technique, in essence they are all similar. In its classical version the technique consists in setting out an empty chair in the interview setting and asking the client to imagine that some particular person in the client's past or present is present in that chair. The client is then asked to speak to the chair as if the person were actually there.

In most instances, we only have the client speak to the identified person in the chair, after which the material that was directed to the personified empty chair is discussed and reflected upon. In another variation, the client is asked to then move to the empty chair and, by assuming the role of the selected person, responds to the client.

ORIGINS

This technique has emerged principally from Gestalt therapy and the work of Fritz Perls. Gestalt therapy stresses the development of client self-awareness and personal responsibility. The empty chair technique is viewed as a way of aiding persons in understanding and experiencing some aspect of their relationship history. The chair provides a visible way for the client to focus on an identified relationship as a way of experiencing and later understanding feelings about this person more fully. The chair serves to highlight emotions and help a person get in touch with feelings in a targeted way.

WHY THIS IS USEFUL TO SOCIAL WORK

Because a great deal of our practice involves helping clients understand aspects of their lives and come to terms with various complex feelings—a very difficult task for many people—the empty chair technique provides a way of aiding this objective. It has a strong theoretical base and its effectiveness has been demonstrated. It is a highly utilitarian technique that is easily learned and, if it is congruent with a client's personality, it can be highly effective both diagnostically and therapeutically. It is also a technique that clients can easily understand. Last, this component of treatment can often result in very helpful, growth-enhancing awareness.

HOW THIS IS USEFUL TO SOCIAL WORK

Although it emerged from a particular thought system, the empty chair technique is readily adaptable to any theoretical body in which helping clients to grow through self-awareness is important. The material emerging from the client's dialogue with the personified chair can be of considerable assistance both to the social worker and, of course, to the client in understanding the dynamics of the identified relationship. The technique does requires the client to be comfortable in this type of "make believe" situation. Some persons are comfortable in speaking to a chair identified as a significant person in their lives, but are not able to assume the role of that person.

The technique is particularly useful in situations where the client seems to be unable to talk about some relationship aspect of their lives, or when there is some unfinished material from the past regarding a significant other about which the person needs to come to some closure.

It also proves to be most beneficial when used only sparingly in a case. On occasion it might be used over a series of interviews, but this would be somewhat unusual. Effective use requires that a client be able to assume the role of another person of significance in their lives. It also requires that a person be able to converse with someone who is only present symbolically.

Not only is this technique useful in helping clients to express and later reflect upon feelings, perceptions, and attitudes about a significant person in their lives, but it can also be helpful to the client (with the worker's assistance) in learning other useful means of self-expression.

RISK FACTOR

This technique has a low risk factor overall. Nevertheless, there are some caveats related to its use. Care needs to be taken that the use of the empty chair technique does not play into an unhealthy exhibitionistic feature of the client's ego structure. Such clients might use the opportunity to pretend to speak to the absent person represented by the chair in a manner that does not represent his or her true feelings. That is, the somewhat theatrical nature of the technique might encourage the venting of feelings and content that have little to do with the client's relationship with the absent person.

As with all techniques, it is important to assess whether a client is able to understand and participate in the process of talking to the chair. Either from undue shyness, a desire to please the worker, or from a sense of attempting it because their social worker wants them to, some people may find this process so distant from their perception of what would be helpful in their lives that the stress produced would outweigh any possible gain.

REQUISITE SKILLS AND KNOWLEDGE

Apart from the ever-present responsibility to assess the client's ability to involve themselves in this type of activity, and their acceptance of it as being potentially useful, no special skills are required for the use of this technique. It is understood that we need to be ready to deal with, and help the client deal with, the material that emerges from the person–chair interaction, and to ensure that we do not let the process continue in a manner that is harmful to the client.

There are no rules for when in the life of a case we would introduce this technique. Again, it is a judgment call based on where the process in going and when it appears that the client is both ready and able to make use of it. In some instances, we may realize we will need to provide support and encouragement to help the client attempt the technique and derive benefit from it.

Case Summary One

Sarah presented for therapy with unresolved family issues. She states that her biggest concern is her relationship with her father.

SOCIAL WORKER: Tell me about what your home life was like as a child.

SARAH: Well, everything seemed great for a while. Then, one night I woke up to the sound of my parents arguing. They yelled at each other for several minutes and then I just heard the slam of the front door. I never saw my father again after that.

SOCIAL WORKER: You said you never saw him again. Have you had any contact with him since he left that night?

SARAH: He sent a few letters. I couldn't even read them at first, I was so mad. Now, it's been so long and I don't even know where he is anymore. I feel like everything was left unresolved. I wish I could have told him how I felt.

SOCIAL WORKER: Go ahead and tell him how you felt. [moves chair into position] See your father sitting in this chair. Talk to him and tell him everything you want to. Tell him how it felt when he walked out and never came back.

SARAH: Dad, I felt like you abandoned me. How could you just leave like that with no good-bye or anything? It made me feel like I meant nothing to you.

[FOLLOWING THE TECHNIQUE:]

SOCIAL WORKER: How do you feel now?

SARAH: I actually feel much better now. I don't think I've ever let myself feel those emotions towards my father so fully.

At the time of this session, Sarah was unable to locate or even engage in conversation with her father. Using the empty chair technique allowed her to confront her feelings toward her father in an imaginative way. Sarah was able to express and reflect on those feelings as well. She is on her way toward achieving a sense of resolution about the issue.

Case Summary Two

John, a 72-year-old White male, self-referred for treatment following the loss of his wife after more than 50 years of marriage. He had become significantly depressed and isolated from family and friends, finding no pleasure in any of his usual activities. After 4 months he sought out treatment "to have someone to talk to" about his despair. His wife, age 70, had become significantly debilitated after a bout of pneumonia requiring hospitalization. On the recommendation of the hospital discharge planner, John and his wife had agreed that a brief stay at a skilled nursing rehabilitation facility would speed recovery. While at the facility, his wife contracted an infection and subsequently died. The sickness and death occurred quite suddenly and he was not able to be present at his wife's side when she died. John described his feelings of grief and responsibility for his wife's death. In session he explained how they had "never been apart" and how he "shouldn't have listened to the hospital." During sessions all attempts at helping the client see that what happened to his wife was not his fault proved unsuccessful, and his despair only worsened. Finally the social worker asked John if he would be willing to talk to his wife to tell her his feelings and perhaps come to understand hers as well. He agreed, and an empty chair was placed a few feet in front of him.

> **SOCIAL WORKER:** Now picture your wife sitting in the chair. You can close your eyes and try to imagine what she is wearing and how she looks. When you're ready, open your eyes and tell her what you want her to know.
>
> **JOHN:** I'm so sorry. You meant everything in the world to me. I'm sorry I let them put you in that place. I should have just taken you home. I could have taken care of you. Then nothing bad would have happened to you and we would still be together [voice breaking].
>
> **SOCIAL WORKER:** [softly] Now, John, I want you to try to listen to what Lily has to say about what you've told her. When you know, just say it out loud.
>
> **JOHN:** [closes his eyes] She says, John, you always took good care of all of us. But you still don't understand that even you can't fix everything all the time. [John hesitates, and then smiles and says:] Lily would remind me of something that she always said—I'd forgotten all about it.
>
> **SOCIAL WORKER:** What's that, John? What is Lily trying to remind you of?
>
> **JOHN:** [smiling] She says, didn't I always say that what's meant to be will be no matter what anyone does?
>
> **SOCIAL WORKER:** Is there anything else you want to tell Lily?
>
> **JOHN:** She already knows but I'll tell her again. I love you Lily, more than anything.

Following this exercise the client appeared calmer and was now able to address his feelings of sadness and loss without giving in to despair. John became more hopeful and, although still grieving, he returned to his relationships and activities.

Case Summary Three

Andrea, a 23-year-old White female was recommended for individual treatment following a crisis hospitalization due to depression, anxiety, and cutting behavior. She presented with a significant history of psychiatric symptoms and treatment. She was able to identify at least four Axis I diagnoses she had received since the age of 10, including bipolar disorder, borderline personality disorder, dissociative disorder, and psychotic disorder NOS. She clearly identified herself as a person with "lots of mental problems."

During treatment, Andrea was verbal and frequently used the psychiatric jargon she had learned throughout her life to explain her experiences. She had a very significant childhood history of sexual and physical abuse. She was bright and articulate, but the social worker noted that she appeared emotionally detached from her own experiences. The social worker determined that a more experiential approach to treatment was necessary to help Andrea move beyond her cognitive perception of herself as "sick" and "mental," as well as to help her reconnect emotionally with her own life experiences, thus allowing her to reintegrate these experiences, both positive and negative, into a holistic self-identity.

During a session in the middle phase of treatment, the social worker asked Andrea if she would be willing to "try something a little different today." Andrea asked what it was that the social worker was thinking of trying, and the social worker told her that she would like to create an opportunity for them to communicate with Andrea's childhood self. The parameters of safety were established with the social worker's assurance to Andrea that if the process became too anxiety provoking, they would stop immediately. Because a trusting therapeutic relationship had already been achieved, Andrea agreed with some trepidation to "give it a try."

An empty chair was set up in front of Andrea. The social worker sat next to her in order to provide a sense that both client and social worker would be entering this process together. The following is an excerpt of the intervention:

> SOCIAL WORKER: Okay. You can leave your eyes open or closed, whatever makes you feel more comfortable. [Andrea chooses to close her eyes.] Now let's take a few deep breaths in and out, just to relax. Breathe in through your nose, than out through your mouth. Breathe in a sense of relaxation and calm, and breathe out any stress or anxiety. And again.... Now, I'd like you to picture yourself as you were when you were five. See your five-year-old self sitting in that chair. What clothes were you wearing? How did your hair look? Are you holding anything in your hands? A favorite toy, something you loved to have with you?
>
> ANDREA: My blanket. I had a blue blanket when I was really little. It made me feel safe. Sometimes I put it over my head when there was lots of noise and yelling. When they took me away for the first time I ran back in the house screaming that I had to take my blanket with me. I had it for years, until I was in the hospital and it disappeared.
>
> SOCIAL WORKER: But now at five you have your blanket with you. I want you to feel the blanket in your hands. Does it feel soft? You can rub it on your cheek if you want. It's soft and warm and feels very safe.
>
> ANDREA: [smiles with her eyes closed and cups her hands to her cheek as if holding something there] I love my blanket. It makes me feel safe.

SOCIAL WORKER: [pauses before speaking to allow client to experience the sense of safety she has verbalized] Now, I want you to think about how little Andrea feels when she hears lots of noise and yelling, when she's by herself and she doesn't know what's about to happen. How does she feel inside? Can you describe that?

ANDREA: [speaks softly and in a childlike voice] She's real scared. She wants someone to come and get her and take her away before they hurt her again, but no one comes. She's all alone. She's scared.

SOCIAL WORKER: That is really scary. Can you talk to her and tell her that you're with her, that you're bigger now and that no one can hurt her now?

ANDREA: [hugs herself] I know you're scared. But I'm here now and I can protect you. I won't let anyone hurt you now.

SOCIAL WORKER: [notices that client seems to be holding back emotions] It's okay to feel sad for little Andrea. It is sad when a little girl feels scared and all alone. It's okay to hold her and tell her that you know how she feels. It's okay to let her know how you feel.

ANDREA: [begins to cry] I'm so sorry for everything that happened. I'm so sorry I couldn't protect you. But I'm here now. And everything will be okay. Really, we really will be okay.

Using an experiential technique that enabled the client to connect with the emotional content of her childhood abuse, while reducing her ability to rely on her verbal and intellectual skills to explain her experiences, helped the client to begin the process of reintegrating her emotions with her life experiences. This brought a new depth to the treatment. The reintegration of these previously split-off emotions also decreased the self-injurious cutting behaviors and increased the client's ability to self-regulate, thus reducing her need to require hospitalization and psychotropic medication. Andrea was able to grieve for her childhood self and to take back ownership of her own emotional responses.

REFERENCES AND ADDITIONAL SOURCES

Conoley, C. W., Conoley, J. C., McConnell, J. A., & Kimzey, C. E. (1983). The effect of the ABCs of rational emotive therapy and the empty-chair technique of Gestalt therapy on anger reduction. *Psychotherapy: Theory, Research & Practice, 20*(1), 112–117.

Fagan, J., & Shepherd, I. (1970). *Gestalt theory now: Theory, techniques, applications.* Ben Lomond, CA.: Science and Behavior Books.

Field, N. P., & Horowitz, M. J. (1998). Applying an empty-chair monologue paradigm to examine unresolved grief. *Psychiatry: Interpersonal and Biological Processes, 61*(4), 279–287.

Friedman, N. (1993). Fritz Perls's "layers" and the empty chair: A reconsideration. *Gestalt Journal, 16*(2), 95–119.

Greenberg, L. S., & Malcolm, W. (2002). Resolving unfinished business: Relating process to outcome. *Journal of Consulting & Clinical Psychology, 70*(2), 406–416.

Greenberg, L. S., Warwar, S. H., & Malcolm, W. M. (2008). Differential effects of emotion-focused therapy and psychoeducation in facilitating forgiveness and letting go of emotional injuries. *Journal of Counseling Psychology, 55*(2), 185–196.

Johnson, W. R., & Smith, E. W. L. (1997). Gestalt empty-chair dialogue versus systematic desensitization in the treatment of a phobia. *Gestalt Review, 1*(2), 150–162.

Norcross, J. C., & Goldfried, M. R. (2005). *Handbook of psychotherapy integration* (2nd ed.). New York, NY: Oxford University Press.

Paivo, S. C. (1995). Resolving "unfinished business": Efficacy of experiential therapy using empty-chair dialogue. *Journal of Consulting and Clinical Psychology, 63*(3), 419–425.

Sheafor, B. W., Horejsi, C. R., & Horejsi, G. A. (1997). *Techniques and guidelines for social work practice* (4th ed., pp. 478–479). Needham Heights, MA: Allyn & Bacon.

Turner, F. J. (1996). *Social work treatment: Interlocking theoretical approaches* (4th ed.). New York, NY: Free Press.

Wagner-Moore, L. E. (2004). Gestalt therapy: Past, present, theory, and research. *Psychotherapy: Theory, Research, Practice, Training, 41*(2), 180–189.

Examination of Alternatives

DESCRIPTION

In this technique, both the client and social worker engage in a process in which a range of possible alternatives for a particular situation are examined. It is not unlike the analysis of obstacles technique, and it has some characteristics of brainstorming, but it differs in that it is a much more cognitive activity. This technique is often a part of the problem solving technique.

ORIGINS

In many ways, looking with the client at alternatives in his or her life has always been something we have done. However, it has emerged as a specific technique as part of the general theoretical shift in therapy to a more general, problem-solving, cognitive, and task-oriented base that marks much of current practice. It has developed as a specific technique as we have come to realize that many of the clients we meet are not able to engage in examining alternatives except in a very nonproductive way.

WHY THIS IS USEFUL TO SOCIAL WORK

The facet of this technique that makes it most effective is the process of working toward a solution in which the joint cognitive and analytic abilities of worker and client are brought to the fore. Important as this process of working toward a desirable clarification of alternatives may be, conveying strength and ability to the client, and the respect and support for their ability to engage in an formal analytic process, can be helpful. It is a technique that enables us to be very helpful to many people we meet in practice.

HOW THIS IS USEFUL TO SOCIAL WORK

Clients often come to us in a highly anxious state because they have a problem or, more frequently, a cluster of problems that are so overwhelming that no clear course of action presents itself to them. Or it may be that they are faced with a decision for which the options are clear, but facing these options is the source of debilitating anxiety and confusion. In these situations the process of examining alternatives with the social worker can be very helpful in three ways.

First, the very process of examining alternatives within the security of the relationship may clarify what needs to be done. Second, the process may help to broaden the potential spheres of action by opening up possibilities not yet considered. And third, the very process of working with the social worker to identify and examine possible alternatives and decisions can, in itself, help calm the situation and bring the client to a position where they are once again thinking more clearly and able to act.

RISK FACTORS

Examination of alternatives has low risk. Important as this technique is, one of its inherent risks is that, in the process of considering alternatives, we begin to take on a role with the client where we are seen to be telling—and in fact might well be telling—the client what he or she should be doing.

This is especially possible if the client in an upset emotional state. In such situations, the client is often eager to have someone deemed to be an expert suggesting or even dictating what is best to do.

REQUIRED SKILLS AND KNOWLEDGE

Although the client may initially present as being in a state of ambivalence or even confusion, they often have already selected the optimum or desired alternative. The difficulty is that they are not able to bring themselves to act on it. That is, it is evident to the client what is to be done, but for any number of reasons they lack self-confidence, knowhow, or the desire to act. Much support and encouragement is therefore required.

Even though the technique is identified as a mutual process, the actual process that takes place in such a situation is one where the worker hears the client out as he or she goes through the various alternatives, which finally leads them to the chosen one. In such instances, our principal role is to convey our support of their decision with a commendation to them for their mature thinking.

Implied in this process is the possibility that we will always know what is best for the client. Obviously this will not always be the case; in fact we may not know. In such situations our task is to encourage the client to think through the alternatives and to use our knowledge and skills to help them to be as objective as possible in their own process of making choices. We also need to consider whether seeking advice from a more knowledgeable source might be helpful.

In some situations, of course, there may not be a best choice, or it might not be evident. This does not necessarily mean that we cannot be helpful. As we know from our own personal lives, frequently what we need in times of uncertainty in decision making is the opportunity to review the situation with a trusted other. We do this with the understanding that they will not necessarily have the answer, but also with the awareness that the very process of reviewing alternatives can be therapeutic and will lead us to the sought-after alternative, either now or in the future. So, too, with our clients.

This is one of our techniques in which we often will play a somewhat passive role, yet still be of great assistance to the client. The lives of many of our clients are highly complex and require a great deal of examination of and choice among alternatives. For such persons the opportunity to explore a range of possibilities with someone whom they respect can be of considerable assistance.

Case Summary One

Amanda is the single mother of a young boy. Recently, Amanda lost her job due to cutbacks. Amanda is a high school dropout and believes that there are few opportunities available to her. She thinks that she was lucky to have gotten her last job, and doesn't know what she'll do now to support herself and her son. During one of her therapy sessions, she discussed the situation with her social worker.

AMANDA: I lost my job and I don't have a high school diploma. How will I ever find another job that can support me and my son? The job market is so bad right now. My situation feels hopeless. I don't know what to do.

SOCIAL WORKER: I want you to think about your situation and try to look at some of your options. Do you have any money in your savings account?

AMANDA: Actually, yes, I was able to save quite a bit while I was working. Also, my mom did say she will help in whatever way she can. That will get us by for a little while, but what about finding another job?

SOCIAL WORKER: Have you thought about taking classes to earn your GED so you can have more job opportunities? I know of a place nearby that offers free classes.

AMANDA: Yes, but I've always been so busy with work and my son that it just got pushed to the side. That might actually work. I can afford to live off my savings for a few months while I get my GED and my mom is available to watch my son whenever I need her to.

SOCIAL WORKER: Wonderful, I think you've made a good choice for yourself.

Amanda doesn't need the social worker to tell her what to do or to decide for her, but she is so overwhelmed by her situation that she can't see past it. The social worker is able to offer different solutions that might work for her. It is helpful for her to be able to discuss her options in a therapeutic environment and really think them through and make a decision for herself.

Case Summary Two

Jerry is an adolescent male in his junior year of high school. He is attending therapy sessions to treat what he describes as symptoms of anxiety.

Social worker: Tell me what a typical day looks like for you.

Jerry: Well, I'm on the wrestling team at school, so I wake up really early in the morning to make sure I am able to exercise and train for any upcoming matches. Then, I shower, get dressed, eat breakfast, and head off to school. My time after school differs depending on the day. Some days I'm at football practice and other days I have math club. Then, there's always homework to be done and then I eat dinner and get ready for bed.

Social worker: What about the weekends? What are those usually like?

Jerry: On the weekends I work from 8:00 a.m. until 5:00 p.m. After that I have to find time to complete homework or school projects. Plus, sometimes I have practice for wrestling or football. I just don't want to continue feeling so anxious and overwhelmed all of the time.

Social worker: What do you think it is that makes you feel that way?

Jerry: It's all these activities I'm part of. I have school, work, math club, football, and wrestling. All together it's just too much, but my parents really push me to excel academically and in extracurricular activities. They say it will be good for my future and might even get me a scholarship for college. I never get any downtime. I'm just so busy every minute of every day. I don't know what to do.

Social worker: Your current situation is very upsetting to you. Let's try examining some alternatives and find a solution to your problem. Have you tried talking to your parents about how you're feeling?

Jerry: No, I'm afraid that they won't listen or that they'll think I'm weak because I can't handle everything on my own. I guess I could try it though.

Social worker: What else could be a possibility for you?

Jerry: My parents never told me that I had to get involved in multiple sports or have a job. Maybe I can cut back on a couple of activities to relieve some stress, but still excel in my other activities.

Jerry was feeling so overwhelmed by his situation that he was unable to work toward a solution to this problem on his own. Reflecting on the problem and examining the alternatives with his social worker assisted in calming the situation. That process brought Jerry to a point where he could begin thinking more clearly and determine possible solutions to his identified problem.

REFERENCES AND ADDITIONAL SOURCES

Doel, M., & Marsh, P. (1992). *Task-centered social work*. Hants, England: Ashgate.

Elder, R., Evans, K., & Nizette, D. (2008). *Psychiatric and mental health nursing* (2nd ed.). Chatswood, New South Wales: Elsevier.

Fleming, B., Freeman, A., Pretzer, J., & Simon, K. M. (2004). The treatment of depression. In *Clinical applications of cognitive therapy* (2nd ed., pp. 97–127). New York, NY: Kluwer Academic/Plenum.

James, R. K. (2008). *Crisis intervention strategies* (6th ed.). Belmont, CA: Brooks/Cole.

Reid, W. J. (1996). Task-centered social work. In F. Turner (Ed.), *Social work treatment* (4th ed., pp. 617–640). New York, NY: Free Press.

Tolson, E. R., Reid, W. J., & Garvin, C. D. (1994). *Generalist practice: A task-centered approach*. New York, NY: Columbia University Press.

Exploring

DESCRIPTION

The technique of exploring refers to those searching efforts of the social worker to clarify and assess both what the client has verbally shared with us and (equally important) what they have not.

ORIGINS

Exploring has always been one of the most important resources in the social worker's therapeutic set of tools. The technique is not associated with any one particular theoretical school. At one time in our history in the mental health field, social workers were seen as the gatherers of long and involved social histories, from which we formulated a treatment plan. In earlier days, various theories of practice, such as ego psychology and the psychosocial theory, emphasized the necessity of a thorough history as a part of the treatment process. In this way our skill at exploring was heavily stressed, so much so that we often had the negative reputation as "snoopers."

Nevertheless, understanding who the client is remains an important part of all practice theories. But we now understand that the process of exploration is a technique we often use right up to the end of a case.

WHY THIS IS USEFUL TO SOCIAL WORK

Exploring is an important technique for social work because a great deal of our work consists of listening to clients and seeking to assess their sources of problems, pain, and suffering as well as their strengths and resources.

Usually it is not difficult to engaging clients to talk to us from the very first contact. We then draw upon our exploring technique when we want to go beyond what the client has initially told us, either to ensure that we understand what is being said or, more often, to seek further elaboration of the issue or content of the communication, or to look at important life areas not yet covered.

It is a most important technique for us because we want to be sure that we are hearing a client at all important levels, and to test if we need to or should go deeper into what the client has originally told us.

HOW THIS IS USEFUL TO SOCIAL WORK

We make use of exploration to ensure that we understand what the client has shared with us. We also explore to test the possibility that there are other important layers in the client's reality that are of import and significance in our understanding and treatment strategies.

Initially, we explore to understand better, but just as often we explore to be certain that the client understands the importance of what he or she has told us. We also explore to look for and evaluate areas and resources of strength upon which to build. Last, we explore to understand areas of weakness or pain that may be relevant to the situation.

In more complex and less frequent situations, we may choose to explore to be sure that the client is not attempting to misinform us or delude themselves, either deliberately or by making use of an unrecognized ego defense.

It is a most important technique that, when used skillfully and sensitively, can lead clients to talk about and then reflect upon relevant material that may have been long hidden from themselves. More frequently, it is misunderstood material from their lives that affects their own identity and their relationship with others. It may also be material around which an incorrect interpretive myth has been woven, which the client does not want to touch.

We often encounter strong client resistance or ambivalence when we use this technique. Resistance arises because some of the material involved is sufficiently painful to the client that they find it difficult to talk about it, let alone reflect upon it. In the same way, we also frequently meet ambivalence, when the client wants us to help them with this material, but at the same time he or she is afraid we will and hopes we won't touch it, either due to its possible significance to them or, often, out of a fear that it will affect what we think of them.

We frequently forget that clients often view us as some sort of perfect humans without faults. This is especially true if they have developed positive transference feelings to us. In looking at themselves, their own negative feelings about themselves, or their own trauma-laden histories, they may fear that in no way can they measure up to our expectations of them. Thus, rather than looking at some difficult life areas, they prefer to keep them hidden and so protect their self image. Hence we must use this technique sensitively.

RISK FACTORS

Exploring has a moderate degree of risk, stemming from the possibility of our opening up material that is overwhelming to the client and not relevant to the presenting situation. There is also a risk that we will underexplore with a client because of our own fears that material will emerge that we ourselves are unable to or wish not to deal with. In such situations we sometimes enter into an implicit contract of silence with the client so that we do not explore when we should and when it would be of most benefit to the client.

Similarly, we often move too quickly or push too hard out of a conviction that there is more the client needs tell us. This can be intrusive to the client and frighten them away from what could have been a helpful process.

REQUIRED SKILLS AND KNOWLEDGE

Exploring is a technique requiring a high level of sensitivity, observation, and timing. It requires what Theodore Reik once called an ability to listen with a third ear. It requires sensitivity and timing because much of the material around which we seek to explore further may be emotionally charged for the client. Opening up a topic or pursuing it further can be highly upsetting to the client.

Because of the importance of exploring, and the risks of going too quickly or not deeply enough in our wish to be helpful, it is a technique that requires a strong sense of timing and a readiness and comfort in waiting. This also includes the ability to probe gently but assertively enough to be helpful.

Case Summary One

Harold presented with symptoms of depression, and his family was extremely worried about him. Harold got to the point where he could not get out of bed for days at a time. According to Harold, he feels empty and sad, and finds it hard to eat. After weeks of trying, Harold's family finally convinced him to see a social worker.

> **SOCIAL WORKER:** Harold, tell me what brings you to my office today.
> **HAROLD:** I haven't been feeling well lately.
> **SOCIAL WORKER:** How would you describe the way you've been feeling?
> **HAROLD:** I don't feel like myself, I'm sad all the time. I don't enjoy the things I used to.
> **SOCIAL WORKER:** When did you notice a change in the way you feel?
> **HAROLD:** A few weeks ago I started sleeping a lot more. I feel like I have no energy.
> **SOCIAL WORKER:** Is there anything you can think of that happened in the last month that could have triggered the change?
> **HAROLD:** Well, at the beginning of the month I found out that a close friend passed away. I had a really hard time dealing with it and I was unable to keep my job. I am still not over the loss of my friend and I feel like a failure because I'm not working.

Exploring allowed Harold's social worker to hear his complete story. If the social worker only took what Harold said at face value, he might not have revealed the events behind his depressive symptoms. Further exploration provided the social worker with the opportunity to work with Harold not only on improving his mood, but also to address his grief and concern over the loss of his job.

Case Summary Two

Jenny is a 7-year-old girl. She is attending therapy sessions with her parents, Kim and Mark, for issues of defiance. Her parents state that every morning it is a struggle to get her to go to school. Jenny presents as shy and spends most sessions sitting quietly clinging to her father.

SOCIAL WORKER: Tell me more about the defiant behaviors your daughter displays.

KIM: She constantly protests when we try to get her to go to school in the morning. Most days she tries to stay home from school by complaining of a headache or stomachache. When we tell her she has to go to school she throws herself on the floor and screams and cries.

SOCIAL WORKER: Has anything changed at her school recently that you believe would cause her to not want to go?

KIM: Nothing that I'm aware of. I've talked to her teacher and she said that nothing in the classroom environment is different. I asked Jenny what she hates about school so much and she can't give me an answer. She used to love school. I'm at my wit's end. I don't know why she is being so defiant suddenly.

SOCIAL WORKER: I've noticed throughout our sessions together that Jenny tends to sit quietly clinging to her father unless I directly ask her a question. Is that how she normally acts at home as well?

MARK: Actually, now that you mention it, she usually does do this at home. However, it hasn't always been like this. She just started clinging to me a few weeks ago, around the same time that she started complaining about attending school.

SOCIAL WORKER: I just want to make sure that I understand all of the information presented. Typically, Jenny loved school. Then, a few weeks ago Jenny became reluctant to attend school. She often tries to avoid going to school by throwing fits or faking an illness. Also, around the same time that she stopped wanting to go to school she began clinging to her father whenever he was around. Is that correct?

KIM AND MARK: Yes.

SOCIAL WORKER: Jenny, what do you think will happen to your dad while you are at school?

JENNY: He might get into a car accident and get hurt really bad like Michael's dad did while he was at school one day.

Assessing both what was shared verbally and nonverbally during the session by using exploring as a technique enabled the social worker to determine the true cause of Jenny's school refusal. The social worker's use of exploring unveiled other significant layers to the situation. What looked like defiant behaviors to her parents actually turned out to be Jenny's fear and anxiety about her dad expressed in an inappropriate way.

REFERENCES AND ADDITIONAL SOURCES

Hepworth, D. H., Rooney, R. H., & Larsen, J. (1997). *Direct social work practice* (pp. 205–209). New York, NY: Brooks/Cole.

Hill, C. E. (2005). Social worker techniques, client involvement, and the therapeutic relationship: Inextricably intertwined in the therapy process. *Psychotherapy: Theory, Research, Practice, Training, 42*(4), 431–442.

McQuade, S. (1999). Using psychodynamic, cognitive behavioral, and solution based questioning to co-construct a new narrative. *Clinical Social Work Journal, 24*(4), 339–353.

Woods, M., & Hollis, F. (2000). *Casework: A psychosocial therapy* (5th ed., pp. 144–146). New York, NY: Random House.

Eye Contact

DESCRIPTION

This activity refers to the use of eye contact with clients as an interviewing technique, as a way of showing interest and respect to facilitate their participation in the treatment process.

ORIGINS

There is no one theoretical origin of this technique, apart from a general conviction in much of North American Caucasian culture that this is a sign of respect and is one of the ways we can facilitate the process of connecting to another person.

WHY THIS IS USEFUL TO SOCIAL WORK

In many situations when interacting with our societal networks, maintaining eye contact with someone is indeed a sign of respect. It conveys to the person being interviewed that we are with them, we are interested, we are following and understanding what they are saying, we want to hear more, and we hope that we can be helpful. When appropriately done it is a way of putting a client at ease and of conveying to them our interest, desire, and capability of being helpful. Knowing of its potential as a helping technique, we will use it appropriately and sensitively.

HOW THIS IS USEFUL TO SOCIAL WORK

One of the most important ways in which this technique has been of use to us is in its teaching capacity. For many in society, eye contact in therapeutic interviews is a given. However, as we have become much more sensitive to the way such actions are culturally bound, we have become much more sensitive to the reality that other, similar activities such as handshakes, the use of names, and titles are also culturally bound and can be very powerful and significant both positively and negatively in a person's life. From this perspective we have learned that we must be aware of the potential significance of similar actions and ensure we use them as techniques, not as automatic responses to everyone with whom we are in contact.

RISK FACTORS

One of the challenges of learning to use this technique skillfully and thus effectively is that our own ways of relating to others in conversation have been so ingrained in us for so many years that it is difficult to develop other ways of using this very human activity in a different way. This is why eye contact needs to be seen as technique and not a question of a perceived social grace. Thus it needs to be viewed as having a moderate to high risk factor unless we are certain of its perceived significance for the client.

REQUIRED SKILLS AND KNOWLEDGE

Important as this technique of connecting with a client and seeking to put them at ease may be, life is just not that simple. The valuing of eye contact is very much a cultural habit and needs to be understood and utilized within a cultural framework.

Eye contact is a technique, not a rule of good interviewing. Thus as a technique it needs to be used differentially with understanding and skill. Even though in much of North America and similar parts of the world eye contact is a very important sign of respect and of politeness in conversation, we know that not everyone in the world views this process similarly.

There are people and cultures that find eye contact uncomfortable and who interpret it in a variety of ways, not always positively. For example, some people find eye contact rude and very off-putting. Others find it to be intrusive, verging on assault. Sometimes it is perceived as our trying to stare into their head to see what is going on.

As with so much of psychotherapeutic practice, the challenge is there are very few rules, and our skill and effectiveness as a social worker stems from our assessment and diagnostic acumen. Thus, like the rest of these techniques, we need to assess early in the contact whether eye contact is something with which the client is comfortable, whether it is taken for granted and is seen the expected behavior of a helping person, or whether it is something to which the client is not accustomed and finds very uncomfortable, or that they will misinterpret our wanting to help in other ways.

When we are not sure where a client stands in this regard, it is probably more sensitive to begin in a way that minimizes eye contact. As we assess how the client feels about this, we can move in the indicated direction. Often of course we just do not know the client's views on this culturally based habit and we need to ask. Seeking our clients' views on such an item can in itself be very facilitating and help us to learn about and understand their perceptions as they relate to this powerful human activity.

Case Summary One

Tim presented for therapy with issues related to low self-esteem. He has expressed to his social worker that he feels inferior and has low self-worth. Tim feels like he has no one to talk to and no support system.

> **TIM:** I feel like people don't listen to me. I wish I could open up to family members and friends.
>
> **SOCIAL WORKER:** [while maintaining eye contact with client] What would you say to those family members and friends?
>
> **TIM:** I would tell them how much I am hurting and how I need their support.
>
> **SOCIAL WORKER:** What keeps you from expressing yourself to them?
>
> **TIM:** I'm afraid they won't care what I have to say. I can't talk to them yet, but I feel comfortable talking to you about my concerns. When I talk to you, the way you look me directly in the eyes, I can tell you're paying attention and you seem interested in what I have to say.

During a time when Tim felt like he had no one to talk to or support him, he was able to connect with his social worker through the worker's use of eye contact. Tim's social worker made him feel important and conveyed a sense of interest in what Tim had to say, which helped validate Tim. This technique of eye contact and the feelings associated with it were a great first step in helping Tim improve his self-esteem.

Case Summary Two

Kelly is a young adult attending a university in her hometown. Kelly characterizes herself as a shy person. She states that she feels her shyness hinders her in many situations. She is attending therapy sessions to improve her social relationships with peers, family members, and professional contacts.

> **SOCIAL WORKER:** How have you been since our last session?
>
> **KELLY:** Overall, I've been well. I still find it hard to speak to new people. I think I make people around me feel uncomfortable because I'm so nervous when I try to start a conversation. I've realized something, though. I never understood how important eye contact can be. When I talk to people I am usually looking at the floor or my eyes are shifting around the room.
>
> **SOCIAL WORKER:** Tell me more about your realization about eye contact.
>
> **KELLY:** Whenever I am here in session and I'm talking to you, I notice that you always maintain eye contact with me. I don't usually look people in the eyes because I'm already so nervous to even be speaking to them. However, when you maintain eye contact with me while I'm speaking, it actually makes me feel like you respect me and are interested in what I have to say. Those feelings made me want to open up to you and speak to you more often.

SOCIAL WORKER: That's great. I'm glad you could see my interest and willingness to help through my eye contact with you. That is what I was trying to convey. Now that you have made this realization, what do you plan to do?

KELLY: I've starting maintaining eye contact with my family members and I have noticed a world of difference. They can tell that I want to understand and be involved in the conversation, and therefore they are more invested in the conversation.

In this situation, eye contact was used as a technique to help Kelly feel more at ease during therapy sessions, but it also helped her in her life outside of sessions. Knowing that eye contact during her therapy sessions helped her feel valued allowed Kelly to begin to use this technique in her conversations with others.

REFERENCES AND ADDITIONAL SOURCES

Abele, A. (1981). Acquaintance and visual behavior between two interactants: Their communicative function for the impression formation of an observer. *European Journal of Social Psychology, 11*(4), 409–425.

Argyle, M. (1972). Non-verbal communication in human social interaction. In R. A. Hinde (Ed.), *Nonverbal communication* (pp. 243–269). Cambridge, England: Cambridge University Press.

Argyle, M., & Cook, M. (1976). *Gaze and mutual gaze.* London, England: Cambridge University Press.

Argyle, M., & Dean, J. (1965). Eye contact, distance and affiliation. *Sociometry, 28*(3), 289–304.

Breed, G., & Porter, M. (1972). Eye contact, attitudes, and attitude change among males. *Journal of Social Psychology, 120,* 211–217.

Cary, M. S. (1978). The role of gaze in the initiation of conversation. *Social Psychology, 41*(3), 269–271.

Cherulnik, P. D., Neelv, W. T., Flanagan, M., & Zachau, M. (1978). Social skill and visual interaction. *Journal of Social Psychology, 104,* 263–270.

Cook, M., & Smith, M. C. (1975). The role of gaze in impression formation. *British Journal of Social and Clinical Psychology, 14*(1), 19–25.

Dhooper, S. S., & Moore, S. E. (2001). *Social work practice with culturally diverse people.* Thousand Oaks, CA: Sage.

Eisold, B. K. (2005). Notes on lifelong resilience: Perceptual and personality factors implicit in the creation of a particular adaptive style. *Psychoanalytic Psychology, 22*(3), 411–425.

Ellsworth, P. C., & Carlsmith. J. M. (1968). Effects of eye contact and verbal content on affective response to a dyadic interaction. *Journal of Personality and Social Psychology, 10*(1), 15–20.

Ellsworth, P. C., & Carlsmith, J. M. (1973). Eye contact and gaze aversion in an aggressive encounter. *Journal of Personality and Social Psychology, 28*(2), 280–292.

Fretz, B. R., Corn, R., Tuemmler, J. M., & Bellet, W. (1979). Counselor nonverbal behavior and client evaluation. *Journal of Counseling Psychology, 26*(4), 304–311.

Fromme, D. K., & Beam, D. C. (1974). Dominance and sex differences in nonverbal responses to differential eye contact. *Journal of Research in Personality, 8,* 76–87.

Grumet, G. W. (1983). Eye contact: The core of interpersonal relatedness. *Psychiatry, 46*(2), 172–180.

Jones, R. E., & Cooper, J. (1971). Mediation of experimenter effects. *Journal of Personality and Social Psychology, 20*(1), 70–74.

Kavanaugh, J. (2000). *Worldwide gestures.* Phoenix, AZ: Waterford.

Kelly, E. W. (1978). Effects of counselor's eye contact on student-clients' perceptions. *Perceptual and Motor Skills, 46*(2), 627–632.

Kelly, E. W., & True. J. H. (1980). Eye contact and communication of facilitation conditions. *Perceptual and Motor Skills, 51,* 815–820.

Kendon, A. (1967). Some functions of gaze-direction in social interaction. *Acta Psychologica, 26,* 22–63.

Kleck, R. E., & Nuessle, W. (1968). Congruence between indicative and communicative functions of eye contact in interpersonal relations. *British Journal of Social and Clinical Psychology, 7*(4), 241–246.

Kleck, R. E. (1968). Physical stigma and nonverbal cues emitted in face-to-face interactions. *Human Relations, 21,* 19–28.

Knapp, M. L., & Daly, J. A. (2002). *Handbook of interpersonal communication* (3rd ed.). Thousand Oaks, CA: Sage.

Leger, F. J., & Lazurus, A. A. (1998). *Behavioural biological and cognitive foundations of psychotherapy.* New York, NY: Haworth Press. Mozdzierz, G. J., Peluso, P. R., & Lisiecki, J. (2008). *Principles of counseling and psychotherapy: Learning the essential domains and nonlinear thinking of master practitioners.* New York, NY: Routledge.

Wieser, M. J., Pauli, P., Alpers, G. W., & Mühlberger, A. (2009). Is eye to eye contact really threatening and avoided in social anxiety?—An eye-tracking and psychophysiology study. *Journal of Anxiety Disorders. 23*(1), 93–103.

Word, C. O., Zanna, M. P., & Cooper, J. (1974). The nonverbal mediation of self-fulfilling prophecies in interracial interaction. *Journal of Experimental Social Psychology, 10*(2), 109–120.

Fees

DESCRIPTION

Charging fees for social work services is often part of a practice's administrative structure, with established scales paid by all clients. However, there are situations where the social worker has discretion over whether to charge fees or not and how much to charge. It is these latter situations, where paying fees is a variable with therapeutic implications, and in this way can be considered a technique, that are of interest in this chapter.

ORIGINS

For a long time in the development of clinical practice in social work, virtually all services were provided without a fee. The social workers providing these services were employed by a broad spectrum of public and private organizations. Fees were viewed as something that would deter persons from seeking services and be a confounding variable in the therapeutic relationship.

Even so, from the earliest days of the profession there were a few clinicians in private practice, especially in North America, who were paid by the client or some form of insurance. However, it was only as we began to understand the contractual components of the helping relationship that an awareness developed of the therapeutic attributes of fees as a part of treatment.

WHY THIS IS USEFUL TO SOCIAL WORK

There are several ways is which fees can facilitate the therapeutic process. From the client's perspective, the payment of a fee can give a value to the therapy that might not exist if there were no fee. For some people, it is very important that there be a payment for various therapeutic services. If not, they may perceive the services as having lesser value, and the client might not involve themselves fully in the therapeutic process.

This is very much a question of how one perceives the value of various societal benefits. Appreciating the value of something is often assessed on the basis of its monetary worth. For many, something obtained for free is often viewed as less important or useful than if they had paid for it.

HOW THIS IS USEFUL TO SOCIAL WORK

Because of the different perception of the worth of a given thing in relation to its cost, charging fees can be very much a way of meeting clients where they are, and thus more sensitively involve them in the helping process. In this way, paying a fee can indicate to the client or prospective client that this service is important, which can help the client make a more determined investment in the therapeutic process.

This emphasis upon the importance of treatment can be further reinforced if a formal contract is a part of the process. This contract can be something like, "You will provide the therapy, and I will commit myself to come for a certain number of times and pay an agreed upon amount."

A further factor related to fees is that such payments can reduce the client's perceived power imbalance in the relationship. Paying a fee can greatly neutralize this imbalance; the client might think, "I am paying for this, so I should make sure I get my money's worth."

Another facet of the question of whether to charge fees is seen when the therapy process doesn't require them, but at the point of termination the client wishes to make some kind of donation to the worker or the agency. This type of closing gesture can not only reflect the client's satisfaction with the process, but can also serve to reinforce the gains he or she has made, and to signify that from the client's perspective, the process is complete. Such a gift can also indicate the client's readiness to take control and responsibility for his or her life.

RISK FACTORS

An important risk in the matter of charging a fee as a part of treatment that may impinge on its use as a technique is when the social worker is uncomfortable with the idea of receiving fees from a client. If the worker doesn't recognize and deal with this discomfort, it could serve to complicate a relationship and lead the worker to miss an opportunity to use the fee in a therapeutic manner with the client.

There is also a risk that imposing a fee may be a deterrent for a client who expects the service to be free. Indeed, it may be that paying a fee would represent a severe hardship to them. This is a complex question in our society. Although from a value perspective many people would prefer to pay for services received, in many instances they believe their various contributions to such charities as the United Way, or to a church or synagogue, gives them access to such services—that is, in some way they have purchased insurance by means of their contributions.

Last, because charging a fee when doing so is at the social worker's discretion is a highly complex diagnostic challenge for us, which can also confront the client's value system, it is a technique with a moderate degree of risk.

REQUIRED SKILLS AND KNOWLEDGE

As with so many techniques, the most critical skill in the matter of fees is a diagnostic one, in two directions in this instance. First, it is critical that we understand our own value position on the worth of our services and on the usefulness of charging fees as a part of our intervention. Second, we need to understand the clients' views on money and the value they place on various required services. We also need to understand the client's financial situation and whether requiring a fee in situations where we have a choice will put more strain on the client than the good that charging a fee would achieve.

In summary, how various services are evaluated in our complex North American society, and perceptions of how they should be paid for, are multifaceted issues. We could avoid the question entirely by never charging fees, but in so doing we may miss opportunities to strengthen the investment of certain clients in the therapeutic alliance with us, and thus limit the extent to which we can help them.

Case Summary One

Jim is seeing his social worker for an initial intake appointment. The purpose of this visit is to review agency protocol, discuss what to expect in treatment, and complete the initial paperwork.

SOCIAL WORKER: I'm glad you could come in to see me today. We have finished most of the paperwork, there are just a few items left. This is the agency's fee agreement. Let's review the sliding fee scale together. According to the number of people living in your household and your income, your fee would be fifty dollars.

JIM: I think that I'm not going to be able to attend sessions very long if that's the fee.

SOCIAL WORKER: So fifty dollars isn't an amount you are able to pay. Well, we can complete this form, which is a request to adjust the fee for your services. How much do you think you can reasonably pay for each visit?

JIM: At this point in time I'm still trying to get back on my feet after the divorce, but attending therapy sessions is important to me. I believe I can afford to pay maybe fifteen dollars per visit.

SOCIAL WORKER: Okay, I will submit this request to my supervisor. From my past experience, I believe that amount will be approved. I am glad to hear that these services are important to you. I hope that means you will be attending sessions regularly.

JIM: Oh yes, I am paying for it so I will definitely be there.

SOCIAL WORKER: Great, let's finish the final few pieces of paperwork and we can schedule your permanent appointment day and time.

Associating a fee with Jim's therapeutic services reinforced the value and importance of therapy for him. Jim's commitment to receiving services can be seen in his willingness to pay an agreed-upon fee as required by the agency he is using. Jim stated that attending therapy sessions was important to him and therefore he was willing to pay an amount that was comfortable for him. The social worker's collaboration with Jim to adjust his fee also showed Jim that his social worker is invested in working with him.

Case Summary Two

Cameron recently started attending therapy sessions. It is important to discuss the fee that will be charged at the beginning of treatment. Cameron's social worker wants to make sure that she is ready to fully commit and invest in herself and the therapeutic process.

Social worker: Hi Cameron. How are you today?

Cameron: I am doing well.

Social worker: That's good to hear. During today's session we need to finalize some paperwork and come up with a fee arrangement. Time is an important resource. I know that my time is valuable and I'm sure yours is as well. To ensure that we do not waste each other's time, I would like for the two of us to come up with an agreement. By signing a fee agreement, it lets each of us know that we are both serious about working hard in therapy and attending sessions regularly.

Cameron: I appreciate the opportunity to discuss the fees to be paid and come to an agreement. Therapy is a valuable service, but if you charged too much I wouldn't be able to attend sessions.

Social worker: You are correct. Therapy is a valuable service and it's vital that we are on the same page in regards to the fees to be charged.

Fee Agreement with Cameron Smith   Date: January 12, 2011

As the client I agree to:

Pay the mutually determined amount of $30 per session.

Attend therapy sessions as scheduled. Furthermore, I understand that if I do not cancel a therapy appointment at least 24 hours in advance I will still be charged for the full amount of a therapy session.

*If the terms of this fee agreement are not upheld the client understands that treatment may be terminated for lack of compliance.

Client Signature: _____

Social Worker Signature: _____

From their previous conversations, the social worker was aware of Cameron's financial situation and knew her ability to pay for services. Charging fees in this situation reiterates that therapy sessions are a valuable service to the client. The use of a formal fee agreement further emphasizes the importance of treatment.

REFERENCES AND ADDITIONAL SOURCES

Barker, R. L. (1986). Fee splitting: A growing ethical problem. *Journal of Independent Social Work, 1*(2), 1–3.

Barth, F. D. (2005). Money as a tool for negotiating separateness and connectedness in the therapeutic relationship. In F. Turner (Ed.), *Social work diagnosis in contemporary practice* (pp. 701–710). New York, NY: Oxford University Press.

Berman, J. S., & Yoken, C. (1984). Does paying a fee for psychotherapy alter the effectiveness of treatment? *Journal of Consulting and Clinical Psychology, 52*(2), 254–260.

Bishop, D. R., & Eppolito, J. M. (1992). The clinical management of client dynamics and fees for psychotherapy: Implications for research and practice. *Psychotherapy: Theory, Research, Practice, Training, 29*(4), 545–553.

Bloch, M. H., & Rubenstein, H. (1986). Paying for service: What do clinical social workers believe? *Journal of Social Service Research, 9*(4), 21–35.

Borenzweig, H. (1981). Agency vs. private practice: Similarities and differences. *Social Work, 26,* 239–244.

Citron-Bagget, S., & Kempler, B. (1991). Fee setting: Dynamic issues for social workers in independent practice. *Psychotherapy in Private Practice, 9*(1), 45–60.

DeMuth, N., & Kamis, E. (1980). Fees and therapy: Clarification of the relationship of payment source to service utilization. *Journal of Consulting and Clinical Psychology, 48*(6), 793–795.

McMillan, B., & Callicutt, J. W. (1981). Fees for counseling services: Why charge them? *Administration in Mental Health, 9*(2), 100–122.

National Association of Social Workers. (1997). *Third-party reimbursement for clinical social work services.* Washington, DC: Author.

Newman, S. S. (2005). Considering fees in psychodynamic psychotherapy: Opportunities for residents. *Academic Psychiatry, 29*(1), 21–28.

Sax, P. R. (1978). An inquiry into fee setting and its determinants. *Clinical Social Work Journal, 6*(4), 305–312.

Schultz, K. (1988). Money as an issue in therapy. *Journal of Independent Social Work, 3*(1), 7–21.

Strom, K. (1992). Reimbursement demands and treatment decisions: A growing dilemma for social workers. *Social Work, 37*(5), 398–403.

Trachtman, R. (1999). The money taboo: Its effects in everyday life and in the practice of psychotherapy. *Clinical Social Work Journal, 27*(3), 275–288.

Twersky, R. K., & Cole, W. M. (1976). Social work fees in medical care. *Social Work in Health Care, 2*(1), 77–84.

Wolfson, E. R. (1999). The fee in social work: ethical dilemmas for practitioners. *Social Work, 44*(3), 269–273.

Films, DVDs, Videos

DESCRIPTION

The essential nature of this technique is to draw on the diverse and powerful ways that various types of audiovisual material can have a therapeutically positive impact.

It can be argued that each of the three forms of audiovisual presentations identified in the title is sufficiently different to be considered separate techniques, in that each has special characteristics. Nevertheless, it was decided that they had sufficient similarities from the perspective of a therapeutic resource to be considered parts of a single technique.

ORIGINS

These selected forms of informational and communications technology are societal resources that have come to play a important role in virtually everyone's lives. Although for the most part they were developed for business communication and entertainment, their utility in helping people learn about themselves and significant aspects of society has made them important resources for therapy. This is especially true as we have come to understand the many diverse components of our culture that can cause difficulty in people's interpersonal lives but that also can serve as very useful problem-solving tools.

WHY THIS IS USEFUL TO SOCIAL WORK

The power of these media as a therapeutic resource stems from two sources. The first is the emotional impact that they can have, which can evoke very intense feelings, conflicts, and memories in people. Such reactions can later become the substance of interview content. We know that, as with live theater, even when someone has seen a particular movie many times and knows each and every part, event, and line of dialogue, they may still have strong emotional experiences each time they see it.

Second, the emotional impact stemming from the content of a film can serve an educational function. For many people, a visual stimulus is much more powerful than the printed or spoken word. Hence many clients can derive considerable benefit from watching films that are relevant to them and their significant others.

HOW THIS IS USEFUL TO SOCIAL WORK

In this discussion, the term *film* is used as a generic description that includes any or all three of the mentioned formats. However, from the aspect of convenience, with their ever-increasing availability, simplicity, and affordability, videotapes and DVDs are much more available to a practitioner than filmstrips or movies. Nevertheless all three formats can have a powerful impact on individuals, families, and groups.

There are literally thousands of commercial films available whose purpose is not to entertain in the popular sense, but to inform and educate about some particular topic, issue, person, or event. Such films can be used with the goal of teaching clients about some topic or event of interest, import, or concern to them or significant others in their lives.

Films can also provide an opportunity for discussion, either on a one-to-one basis or as a group or family. Such discussions will often provide the chance to reinforce learning, correct misunderstandings, or to address personal material aroused by the film.

A different use of film as technique is where movies produced for general entertainment are watched as a way of helping clients meet and identify with some significant aspect of personal experience that facilitates their coming to terms with various stages of treatment. In this regard, one of our therapeutic challenges is to know a spectrum of films sufficiently well to select those that have the potential to be helpful. One way to solve this challenge is to let the client tell us about his or her most favorite or least favorite films, or about some film they have just seen that has had an impact on them, and to have them reflect upon why it had such an impact.

It may not always be necessary to actually view the film, if it is already known to the social worker and the client, so that their common knowledge is sufficient to use the film in a way that helps the client. In such instances the goal is to help the client identify, discuss, and cathect on some aspect of the film, or some person or incident in the film with which they particularly identify. Such reflection can be a way of helping a client come to closure on a significant event or person in their lives in a freeing and enabling way,

RISK FACTORS

This is a low-risk technique.

REQUIRED SKILLS AND KNOWLEDGE

If we are going to use these media in practice, it is essential that we know how to operate whatever technological format is being used. A further challenge in using film, in whatever format, is locating material on the particular topic of focus. Fortunately the current range of search engines makes this easier than ever. From a positive perspective, there are thousands, if not hundreds of thousands, of films with educational potential. Our challenge is to learn how to find just the right films for a client.

Unless we happen to be highly knowledgeable about the film world, at times it may be necessary to consult with experts to learn what general type or specific film might have the relevance that we seek. What is most important, however, is the impact of a film on the client, not what someone else thinks it might be.

A question of strategy in using films as part of therapy is whether the viewing should take place outside of the therapeutic process for later consideration, or whether we should watch the film with the client. One of the advantages of viewing part or all of a film with a client is the immediacy of the various emotional responses to particular aspects of it. Even those of us with minimal technology skills can learn to stop and start the film when we wish to review sections of it with a client.

Case Summary One

Steve and his parents are attending a family therapy session with Steve's social worker. Steve started attending therapy sessions on the suggestion of his teacher and guidance counselor. Recently, Steve was approached by a stranger at his school bus stop who intended to abduct him. Steve's school bus arrived and the stranger left the scene before he could harm or kidnap him. Since the incident, Steve has been afraid to take the bus to school and has started acting out in class.

Social worker: I have asked the three of you to come in for a family session this week because it is important for all of us to work together.

Mom: I agree. We are curious to know how the sessions have been going.

Social worker: Steve is making great progress. During today's family session we will watch a video.

Dad: What is the video about?

Social worker: The video is all about child safety. It helps teach children how to determine when they are in an unsafe situation and it suggests strategies for getting out of an unsafe situation.

[After watching the video:]

Social worker: Now that we have all watched the video together, let's discuss some additional strategies that might be helpful if Steve ever finds himself in another dangerous situation. Also, I would like for all of us to work together to develop a safety plan for Steve to help him better recognize and avoid potentially dangerous situations.

Having Steve and his parents watch a video in a family therapy session allowed the social worker to introduce the topic of child safety in a nonthreatening way. A good way to include a video in a therapy session is to use it as an educational tool, as in the above case study. The video acts as a supplement to what the social worker is already working on with the client and can normalize the situation. It also enables discussions that otherwise might not occur and provides some relative assurance that everyone is referring to the same information.

Case Summary Two

Jill is a high school student who comes from an economically disadvantaged socioeconomic status. Jill is seeing her school counselor for her depression and because she feels unmotivated. Her school counselor gave her a list of recommended movies to watch. Among them was an inspirational movie about urban youth coping with poverty, racial discrimination, and unemployment, yet who are able to have positive social lives and achieve academically regardless. The social worker assigned this movie to Jill for homework. They discussed the movie in the next session.

Social worker: Tell me Jill, did you watch the movie I assigned?

Jill: Yes, it was great! I really liked the ending!

Social worker: What did you think about the part where the main character was told she couldn't read, but persisted and achieved the highest reading level possible?

Jill: Yes, that was really amazing that she did that regardless of being poor. And in the end she got to go to college!

Social worker: Can you draw on any strengths from the movie?

Jill: Well, the main character signed up for a free tutoring program to get her grades up. I think I can see if our school offers free tutoring. I could really use some help on my homework. I guess I could use the main character as a role model.

Social worker: Great, you can use the next week to sign up for tutoring, and we will talk about it next time.

REFERENCES AND ADDITIONAL SOURCES

Arauzo, A. C., Watson, M., & Hulgus, J. (1994). The clinical uses of video therapy in the treatment of childhood sexual trauma survivors. *Journal of Child Sexual Abuse, 3*(4), 37–57.

Bigelow, K. M., & Lutzker, J. R. (1998). Using video to teach planned activities to parents reported for child abuse. *Child & Family Behavior Therapy, 20*(4), 1–14.

Carr, J. E., & Fox, E. J. (2009). Using video technology to disseminate behavioral procedures: A review of functional analysis: A guide for understanding challenging behavior (DVD). *Journal of Applied Behavior Analysis, 42*(4), 919–923.

Ceranoglu, T. A. (2010). Video games in psychotherapy. *Review of General Psychology, 14*(2), 141–146.

Corder, B. F., Whiteside, R., McNeill, M., Brown, T., & Corder, R. F. (1981). An experimental study of the effect of structured videotape feedback on adolescent group psychotherapy process. *Journal of Youth and Adolescence, 10*, 255–262.

Cox, E., & Lothstein, L. M. (1989). Video self-portraits: A novel approach to group psychotherapy with young adults. *International Journal of Group Psychotherapy, 39*(2), 237–253.

Fuat, U. (2003). *Movie therapy, moving therapy!* Victoria, British Columbia: Trafford.

Gallagher-Thompson, D., Wang, P., Liu, W., Cheung, V., Peng, R., China, D., & Thompson, L. W. (2010). Effectiveness of a psychoeducational skill training DVD program to reduce stress in Chinese American dementia caregivers. *Aging & Mental Health, 14*(3), 263–273.

Hajal, F. (1978). Using tape recorders in the treatment of latency-age children. *Social Casework, 59,* 371–374.

Hesley, J. W., & Hesley, J. G. (1998). *Rent two films and let's talk in the morning: Using popular movies in psychotherapy.* New York, NY: Wiley.

Higgins, W. H., Ivey, A. E., & Uhlemann, M. R. (1970). Media therapy: A programmed approach to teaching behavioral skills. *Journal of Counseling Psychology, 17*(1), 20–26.

Johnson, B. (2000). Using video vignettes to evaluate children's personal safety knowledge: Methodological and ethical issues. *Child Abuse and Neglect, 24*(6), 811–827.

Kingston, G., Gray, M. A., & Williams, G. (2010). A critical review of the evidence on the use of video-tapes or DVD to promote patient compliance with home programmes. *Disability and Rehabilitation: Assistive Technology, 5*(3), 153–163.

Mallery, B., & Navas, M. (1982). Engagement of preadolescent boys in group therapy: Videotape as a tool. *International Journal of Group Psychotherapy, 32*(4), 453–467.

Marziali, E., & Donahue, P. (2006). Caring for others: Internet video-conferencing group interven-tion for family caregivers of older adults with neurodegenerative disease. *The Gerontologist, 46*(3), 398–403.

Star, B. (1979). Expanding the boundaries of videotape self-confrontation. *Journal of Education for Social Work, 15*(1), 87–94.

Weber, L. A. (1980). The effect of videotape and playback on an in-patient adolescent group. *International Journal of Group Psychotherapy, 30,* 213–227.

Food

DESCRIPTION

Food is, of course, an essential component of our lives and those of our clients, not only in a physical sense, but also in emotional, symbolic, and cultural ways. Because of its multilayered importance in everybody's lives, and its relationship to our emotional development, food can and should be used as a deliberate part of our interventions.

ORIGINS

Of all the techniques that will be addressed in this book, food probably has the longest tradition as part of social work. Although variously used by people of different theoretical persuasions, it belongs to no one stream of the profession. In spite of its importance in the human odyssey, we have not given this technique high priority in our clinical work.

One of the early images of the social worker was that of "Lady Bountiful" with a basket of food on her arm. This once-common stereotypical societal image of the social worker is one we have sought to put behind us, even though the feeding role of social work continues today in such forms as the use of food vouchers, food stamps, food banks, and food baskets. Generally, however, we have tended not to see the direct provision of food as an important part of our clinical practice. It is a function not generally imagined as being in our range of techniques.

In striving to demystify the therapeutic relationship, feminist theory and existential theory have helped us to better understand the importance and utility of food as one of our techniques. Both of these theories have been much more open to the idea of meeting clients in much less structured ways than has been our tradition. However, the movement toward a more strategic use of food as a therapeutic tool, rather than viewing it as a detriment to the professional relationship, has emerged from the practice of skilled, sensitive colleagues rather than from any clearly formulated theoretical base.

WHY THIS IS USEFUL TO PRACTICE

Food can convey to the client a social worker's empathy and understanding. It can respond both symbolically and at times realistically to unmet basic needs of the client. It can show respect for some aspect of a client's ethnic, religious, or cultural identity. It can also be used to help a client celebrate an important life event. Food can enhance the professional bond between client and worker. In group situations, food can be a means of teaching group members about diversity topics in a way that brings understanding and respect for differences.

Food may be a regular part of the treatment process, or may be used to mark some significant event in the client's life. Furthermore, it may be used to celebrate an important part of the treatment process, such as a successful termination or the attainment of a planned goal. Food can also be used in very informal ways as a means of facilitating the intervention process, or in a highly ritualistic way to recognize some aspect of the client's life, such as a birthday, the birth of a child, and the like.

HOW THIS IS USEFUL TO PRACTICE

Food is such an essential and basic part of human needs, and a necessary yet mundane component of our daily routines, that over the years we seem to have overlooked or minimized its potential in therapy. Rather, we went in the opposite direction and frequently have been highly suspicious of the idea of sharing food with clients.

In addition to occasionally giving food to clients, we need to understand that there are times when it is important for the client to provide food to us. This might be a basket of fresh vegetables given by a rural family, something that was quite common in a hospital setting in which I practiced many years ago. Alternatively, clients might present us with some special dish that has a particular meaning to a client's ethnicity, provide a meal when we make a rural call to their homes, or share of a ritualistic glass of wine on a home visit, all of which have important and strong cultural significance.

RISK FACTORS

Because of the very complex ways in which food is viewed in society and hence by our clients, and because it is such a basic part of our lives, the use of food as a technique needs to be considered high risk. It is the very fact of its universality, as an essential human need replete with cultural, religious, geographic, economic, and biopsychosocial implications, that exacerbates the risk factor. However, the use of food as a component of treatment is such a powerful element of the human condition that we need to learn to tap its power in our therapeutic endeavors.

REQUIRED SKILLS AND KNOWLEDGE

Because of the diverse ways in which food is perceived, and because of the many ways of using it as a technique, we must be very careful to understand the different ways our clients might ascribe meaning to such an intervention.

As simple a thing as having a cup of coffee together can have a variety of meanings to different clients. For some clients this could be perceived as a seductive move on the part of the social worker, whereas for others the same gesture might convey that the worker understands the need for this sustenance at a particular time. For still others, this same cup of coffee might be viewed in a very neutral manner as an expected component of any professional relationship.

Thus there are two essential components of the knowledge required to make responsible and effective use of food as a treatment component. The first, of course, is our responsibility to understand the place of food in our own lives and culture, especially from its symbolic perspective. This will ensure that these meanings do not negatively impact our use of this technique. The second is to strive to understand the role of food in our clients' history, lives, and culture. Even discussing these matters with the client can be a rich source of understanding for this timeless component of their lives.

Case Summary One

Jason is a young adult attending weekly group sessions for anger management. While preparing for the next group session, his social worker realized that the date of the next session was also Jason's birthday. The social worker decided it would be nice to surprise Jason with a traditional birthday cake during the session.

> **SOCIAL WORKER:** Now that we are done with our group work for the day, I have one more activity before everyone leaves.
> [Social worker brings over a birthday cake for all members of the group.]
> **SOCIAL WORKER:** As we all know, today is Jason's birthday. Let's all sing and enjoy some cake together.
> [The presentation of the cake and everyone singing to him leads Jason to start sobbing.]
> **SOCIAL WORKER:** Are you okay, Jason?
> **JASON:** I'm fine, just a little embarrassed. This was a bit overwhelming for me. I've never had a birthday cake or birthday celebration in my entire life.

After the group enjoyed the birthday cake and left the session, Jason met with his group social worker alone to discuss some of his unhappy childhood experiences. The presentation of this food during session allowed Jason's social worker to learn new information about Jason, of which he had previously been unaware.

Case Summary Two

Julia has an eating disorder. Because Julia is severely bulimic, she has been hospitalized due to excessive bingeing and purging. She has a fear of gaining weight and abuses diet pills in an effort to control her weight. Part of Julia's recovery includes a long-term recovery plan. She will need to receive individual and group therapy to get her health problems under control. An effective treatment program for Julia involves working with her eating disorder support group, led by a clinical social worker. One of the topics the group discussed was healthy dieting; that is, eating healthfully, not just to lose weight. The group decided to focus on identifying nutritious food that will promote energy. The clinical social worker brought in some nutritious foods to demonstrate healthy serving sizes. For example, she brought in a medium-sized apple and a half-cup of yogurt to show what appropriate serving sizes of a healthy snacks look like. The group worked on planning out meals for the week using appropriate portion sizes. Furthermore, in this session, the clinical social worker taught the group to adhere to their eating disorder treatment plan and follow a routine filled with constructive activities, such as playing with a pet or taking a walk. The treatment program helped Julia have a more positive self-image and a healthier eating routine.

REFERENCES AND ADDITIONAL SOURCES

Craeynest, M., Crombez, G., De, H. J., Deforche, B., Tanghe, A., & De, B. I. (2005). Explicit and implicit attitudes towards food and physical activity in childhood obesity. *Behaviour Research and Therapy*, *43*(9), 1111–1120.

Franko, D. L. (1993). The use of a group meal in the brief group therapy of bulimia nervosa. *International Journal of Group Psychotherapy*, *43*(2), 237–242.

Kahn, S. R. (1993). Reflections upon the functions of food in a children's psychotherapy group. *Journal of Child and Adolescent Group Therapy*, *3*(3), 143–153. doi:10.1007/BF00999845

Kaslow, F. W., Magnavita, J. J., Massey, R. F., Patterson, T., Massey, S. D. (2002). *Comprehensive handbook of psychotherapy: Interpersonal/humanistic/existential*. New York, NY: Wiley.

Mishna, F., Muskat, B., & Shamess, G. (2002). Food for thought: The use of food in group therapy with children and adolescents. *International Journal for Group Psychotherapy*, *52*(1), 27–47.

Moldofsky, Z. (2000). Meals made easy: A group program at a food bank. *Social Work With Groups*, *23*(1), 83–96.

Rose, M. (1987). The function of food in residential treatment. *Journal of Adolescence*, *10*(2), 149–162.

Troester, J. D., & Darby, J. A. (1976). The role of the mini-meal in therapeutic play groups. *Social Casework*, *57*(2), 97–103.

Free Association

DESCRIPTION

In this technique, the client is encouraged to express to the social worker whatever content comes to mind regardless of how insignificant, bizarre, or unconnected it may appear to be. As much as possible, clients should not screen out any material. The social worker should not interrupt, lead the client, or comment on the material while the client is in this mode.

The goal is to eliminate as far as possible any interference, interruptions, or influence by the social worker so that material that has been suppressed or repressed can emerge. From this perspective, the classic client position for free association is on a couch, with the social worker out of sight at the head of the couch.

ORIGINS

Free association emerged from psychoanalytic theory and practice. The understanding in psychoanalytic theory is that this was a direct route to the client's unconscious life. It is believed that as the client becomes better able to carry out this process, superego screening will weaken and lesser amounts of relevant material will be filtered. This permits blocked material to come forward, which can then be examined by the social worker for patterns and hidden meanings. These in turn can be interpreted for the client, with a view to freeing him or her from issues that are inhibiting his or her functioning at an optimum level.

Social workers rarely use free association in its classic form, apart from those trained in some school of psychodynamic theory and practice. However, the idea that many persons do block out material in a manner that inhibits functioning, with which we can help them, is useful in some practice situations.

WHY THIS IS USEFUL TO SOCIAL WORK

The idea of helping people to become able to comfortably express blocked inner thoughts, feelings, and fantasies can be of great assistance in our practice. We know that we frequently meet clients who appear to have significant developmental and relationship material they avoid reviewing. They expend rather considerable psychic effort to keep such material out of their conscious minds. Helping them to become more comfortable in expressing it, and to understand how it has influenced their lives by drawing on the understanding and methods of free association, can thus be a useful technique.

HOW THIS IS USEFUL TO SOCIAL WORK

Frequently we meet clients who have very strict or even rigid personality structures who carefully screen their every thought and wish before allowing such material to enter their thought and speech. Drawing on a knowledge of free association, and the relief that comes when some things long held in are expressed to an understanding, nonjudgmental, sympathetic listener, can often be liberating to some clients.

In this way, we can help people become more comfortable with an open process of inner thinking and a much broader sense of what, in their view, are proper, acceptable, or factual mental materials. In many instances these unacceptable thoughts or interpretations are connected to early life experiences, the distortion of which markedly affects their day-to-day living.

As with other freeing-up techniques, even though the client may not be able to free-associate in the classical sense, just learning that it is all right to have an inner life, and that letting it emerge into our conscious minds is perfectly healthy and acceptable, can be very freeing to some clients. As clients become more comfortable with this process, they may keep less of a watch over what they dare to think about, imagine, or feel.

Understanding that some people can be made more comfortable with their inner lives, thoughts, and fantasies supports the occasional moderate or minimal use of free association with intact clients. In its classical use, it can be very helpful for some persons, presuming the social worker has a sufficiently strong theoretical base. In a more general sense, however, it is a way to assist persons to get in better touch with their inner lives in a manner that relieves stress and overly controlled behavior, thus permitting them to live a more objectively based life in their daily activities.

RISK FACTORS

Free association has a moderate to high risk, because there are persons for whom it could open up material that does not help them find relief, but rather becomes troubling or overwhelming. There is also the risk that material could emerge from a misuse of this technique that the social worker is not able to deal with or that would be of no help to the client.

One further risk of a misuse of this technique is the temptation to begin to interpret material the client expressed at a level beyond our competency.

REQUIRED SKILLS AND KNOWLEDGE

Free association requires both theoretical knowledge and—when more that a minimal use is being made of it—access to consultant or supervisory resources. It also requires an ability to judge whether the client is able to profit by the expression of sensitive and hidden psychic materials. The social worker must also be comfortable with the very bizarre and at times highly traumatic material that the client needs to share.

Case Summary One

Judy is currently seeing a social worker to help with her agoraphobia. Judy rarely leaves the house and never leaves it alone. When Judy does leave or even thinks about doing so, she feels intense anxiety and fear. Judy hates feeling this way and is not sure why she is afraid to leave the house. Judy's social worker has decided to try using free association to help understand the cause of her agoraphobia.

SOCIAL WORKER: We've been discussing your fear of leaving your house. With this in mind I want you to close your eyes and start talking.

JUDY: Start talking about what?

SOCIAL WORKER: Talk about anything that comes to mind. Don't censor yourself, don't pause between thoughts, just speak.

JUDY: Okay, I'll try. Blue skies turn dark outside. Heavy rains pour down as I walk. People staring and pointing and laughing at my expense. People talking and whispering when they see me. Joking and being mean because of my looks. Inside no one can see. Inside is where happiness lies. Outside is where shame and doubt live. Fear, humiliation, and embarrassment. Judy is a dork. Judy looks like a rat. No, I just want to play with my friends. Leave me alone. I'm going inside alone where you can't find me.

SOCIAL WORKER: Alright Judy, good job. Sometimes the reasons behind why our current problems exist can be hidden in our unconscious mind. The exercise that you just did allows bottled-up emotions and repressed memories to be expressed. Let's explore what was said.

Free association allows Judy to relay information to her social worker without carefully censoring what is shared. By using free association, Judy and her social worker can examine past events and the emotions associated with them. Once these underlying emotions and the reasons for her agoraphobia are examined, work to treat her symptoms can begin.

Case Summary Two

Angie is attending therapy sessions because she has been feeling down lately and she is hoping start feeling more positive about life again. She reports feeling strange for the past few weeks and not knowing why. She states that she just doesn't feel like herself lately and it's very upsetting to her. Her social worker decides to use free association as a technique to allow any suppressed or repressed material to surface that may be helpful in improving her mood.

> SOCIAL WORKER: How are you feeling this week?
>
> ANGIE: I've been feeling pretty much the same as last week. It's really perplexing to me. I don't even know how to describe it. I just don't feel like me lately and I don't know why or what to do to change it.
>
> SOCIAL WORKER: I'd like to try a free association exercise with you during today's session to see if we can uncover some hidden thoughts or feelings which might help you in your quest to improve your mood. To start, sit back and relax as best you can. When you feel comfortable, close your eyes.
>
> ANGIE: Okay, I feel relaxed and comfortable.
>
> SOCIAL WORKER: Now that you are comfortable and relaxed, I want you to clear your mind. Once your mind is clear, speak freely and openly about anything that happens to cross your mind.
>
> ANGIE: I wish it were a sunny day. I love to see the clouds in the sky. Fluffy, furry looking clouds make me smile. Where did the sun go? Where did the clouds go? Black cats run past so I chase them. They run into the dark alley, but I still follow. Why do I continue to follow them? I know this is going to be trouble. Stupid cats, stupid me. Why can't I make the right decisions? There's always hope, right? The clouds and sun can return, right? Where will I ever find them again?
>
> SOCIAL WORKER: Now that you are done, let's analyze the unconscious thoughts that were said.

Using free association as a technique in this case assisted Angie and her social worker in determining what was causing her gloomy moods. Once the cause was determined, Angie and her social worker could then work toward getting Angie to feel like herself again. The act of engaging in a free-association exercise also gave Angie an immediate sense of relief because it felt freeing and made her feel more in touch with her inner self.

REFERENCES AND ADDITIONAL SOURCES

Andreasen, N. C., O'Leary, D. S., Cizadlo, T., Arndt, S., Rezai, K., Watkins, L. G., Boles Ponto, L. L., & Hichwa, R. D. (1995). Remembering the past: Two facets of episodic memory explored with positron emission tomography. *American Journal of Psychiatry, 152*(11), 1576–1585.

Brakel, L. W. (1993). Shall drawing become part of free association? Proposal for a modification in psychoanalytic technique. *Journal of the American Psychoanalytic Association, 41*(2), 359–394.

Brandell, J. R. (2010). *Theory & practice in clinical social work.* Thousand Oaks, CA: Sage.

Corey, G. (2009). *Theory and practice of counseling and psychotherapy* (8th ed.). Belmont, CA: Brooks/Cole.

Hoffer, A. (2006). What does the analyst want? Free association in relation to the analyst's activity, ambition, and technical innovation. *American Journal of Psychoanalysis*, *66*(1), 1–23.

Hollis, F. (1964). *Social casework a psychosocial therapy* (pp. 137). New York, NY: Random House.

Kris, A. O. (1982). *Free association method and process*. New Haven, CT: Yale University Press.

Kris, A. O. (1992). Interpretation and the method of free association. *Psychoanalytic Inquiry*, *12*(2), 208–224.

Miller, P. H. (2002). *Theories of developmental psychology* (4th ed.). New York, NY: Worth.

Orcutt, B. A., Flowers, L. C., & Seinfeld, J. (1990). *Science and inquiry in social work practice*. New York, NY: Columbia University Press.

Pole, N., & Jones, E. E. (1998). The talking cure revisited: Content analyses of a two-year psychodynamic psychotherapy. *Psychotherapy Research*, *8*(2), 171–189.

Strean, H. (1979). *Psychoanalytic theory and social work practice* (pp. 66–70). New York, NY: Free Press.

Szalay, L. B., Carroll, J. F. X., & Tims, F. (1993). Rediscovering free associations for use in psychotherapy. *Psychotherapy: Theory, Research, Practice, Training*, *30*(2), 344–356.

Turner, F. J. (1996). *Social work treatment: interlocking theoretical approaches*. New York, NY: Free Press.

Genogram

DESCRIPTION

This technique consists of a process, usually introduced early in the relationship, used with an individual, couple, or family in which the history of the family for two or three generations is mapped out on a chart.

ORIGINS

The genogram technique emerged from the family therapy field as a diagnostic and therapeutic resource. As we have become more aware of how patterns of relationships, customs, and values repeat themselves in families over generations, and how useful it is for clients to begin to understand these patterns, this technique for uncovering them developed.

WHY THIS IS USEFUL TO SOCIAL WORK

The advantage of the genogram is that is presents a strong graphic depiction of a family and its interactional patterns. That is, it provides us and the client with a visual representation of the family's genealogy, which can help some clients get a much clearer understanding of their family and its background influences on their present functioning.

HOW THIS IS USEFUL TO SOCIAL WORK

The purpose of the genogram is to assist the social worker and clients in uncovering and examining possible patterns in the family history, especially areas of stress or strength, that may be contributing to the functioning of a person or family. It is still in a developmental mode as practitioners find various ways to use this method.

One of its strengths is that it can aid clients and the social worker to see patterns in the family history, or identify themes or myths that have been a part of the family culture, that are influencing present functioning. By identifying patterns in the family history from whatever focus is selected, clients can be helped to understand their family from a structural perspective. This in turn can help to normalize emotionally charged issues in their current situation.

Although the literature emphasizes the utility of this technique for helping to clarify and normalize a family's present functioning, it can also be useful to develop a graphic picture of how understanding a family's history can influence current individual history. It provides a clearer picture of the source of clients' current strengths and problems, and helps them avoid repeating these problem-producing patterns in future relationships.

Because of the potential power of the technique and the inherent utility of identifying problem patterns, computer programs are being developed that would permit the identification of many aspects of family history in a way that might underscore problems and interconnections between patterns not readily observed in the available data.

Although genograms are a powerful diagnostic resource, they are not always an effective therapeutic tool, because they presume a past-oriented value system and an interest in and ability to see the interconnections between past and present. Thus, it may not be effective with present- and future-oriented people.

RISK FACTORS

Genograms do not have a high level of risk, except that of confounding or disappointing clients who are more interested in focusing on the here and now in their lives. Likewise, it may not be helpful to clients with very traumatic family histories who prefer to put this behind them and get on with their lives.

REQUIRED SKILLS AND KNOWLEDGE

Using a series of easily learned codes (e.g., *M* for marriage and *D* for death), arrows, and lines, much of a family's history can be visually represented. One of the ways in which this technique can be most helpful is by not including too much in the charting process. Thus a genogram may focus only on one factor, such as the history of marriages, separations, divorces, education, or deaths. Other foci of the genogram may look at a family's health history over two or three generations. Similarly, one of the diagnostic skills required to make effective use of this technique is to select an area of family history that appears to be significantly operative in the present family functioning. Last, most practitioners suggest that attempting to go back more than three generations becomes too complex for most families.

Case Summary One

Amanda is a 42-year-old woman who is currently going through a difficult time in her life. She recently started seeing a social worker. She has a hard time opening up to others, but she is in need of the support and comfort of her loved ones. Amanda reports feeling overwhelmed with everything going on. She says that she often feels stressed and anxious in her day-to-day life.

SOCIAL WORKER: During today's session, I would like to complete your genogram.
AMANDA: Okay.
SOCIAL WORKER: A genogram is a visual representation of two or three generations of your family history. It allows both of us to get a clearer picture of sources of strength, problems, and patterns of behavior or values. I have you and your daughters already listed. Let's get started by writing out the names and ages of your parents and siblings.
AMANDA: My mom's name is Evelyn and she is 70 years old, and my dad is Andres and he is 71 years old. I have four siblings: Caroline is 44 years old, Edison is 41 years old, Roberto is 39 years old, and Kathy is 34 years old.
SOCIAL WORKER: Where does your family live?
AMANDA: Well, my parents, Caroline, Edison, and Kathy all live in another country. Roberto is the only one who lives in the same state as me.
SOCIAL WORKER: Okay, now that we have some basic information, let's start looking at the relationships and communication patterns within your family.

During this session, the genogram was used as a therapeutic resource to assess Amanda's support system, positive and negative familial relationships, and communication patterns, as well as behavior and value patterns that have repeated throughout the generations of the family. Using the genogram gave Amanda a visual representation of her family and a clearer understanding of her family and its functioning. The genogram also provided the opportunity for Amanda and her social worker to see ways in which her family influences her present functioning. Through the use of this genogram, Amanda was able to identify two siblings and a parent in whom she feels comfortable enough to confide and speak openly.

Case Summary Two

Jessie has been attending therapy sessions for a few weeks. He states that his life is very stressful right now. He says that he has noticed that he feels angry quite often lately and has been arguing more with his wife recently. Jessie would like to learn new ways to cope with the stress he feels. Jessie's social worker will use the genogram that they created to examine possible patterns in Jessie's family history that may be contributing to his current functioning.

SOCIAL WORKER: How have things been over the past week?

JESSIE: I just feel so much stress all the time and I don't know how to deal with it. It seems like I lash out at everyone around me and I don't want to be that person. It just happens so naturally, I don't know how to stop it.

SOCIAL WORKER: Let's look at the genogram we completed during our last session together. What do you notice in the area of emotional relationships?

JESSIE: I'm noticing that most of the members in my family have a distant and/or hostile relationship with at least one other family member.

SOCIAL WORKER: It seems as though the way you currently deal with stress, fighting with loved ones and pushing them away, might be a pretty common experience in your family.

JESSIE: You're right. I've learned to act this way from watching the way my other family members interact with each other all of these years.

SOCIAL WORKER: Now that we are aware of how your family history is affecting your current problem, we can start to work towards finding solutions to the problem.

In this example, the genogram is used as both an assessment tool for the social worker and as a learning tool for the client. Providing Jessie with a visual representation of his family history and the patterns of emotional relationships in his family really helped him understand what is currently going on in his own life. Identifying these family patterns will also help him avoid repeating the same patterns of behavior in the future.

REFERENCES AND ADDITIONAL SOURCES

Atshuler, S. J. (1999). Constructing genograms with children in care: Implications for casework practice. *Child Welfare, 78*(6), 777–790.

Bathgate, O. (2009). Review of "Genograms: Assessment and intervention." *Clinical Child Psychology and Psychiatry, 14*(3), 462–463.

Coupland, S. K., Serovich, J., & Glenn, J. E. (1995). Reliability in constructing genograms: A study among marriage and family therapy doctoral students. *Journal of Marital and Family Therapy, 21*(3), 251–264.

Davis, L., Geikie, G., & Schamess, G. (1988). The use of genograms in a group for latency age children. *International Journal of Group Psychotherapy, 38*, 189–210.

Estrada, A. U., & Haney, P. (1998). Genograms in multicultural perspective. *Journal of Family Psychotherapy, 9*(2), 55–62.

Frame, M. W. (2000). The spiritual genogram in family therapy. *Journal of Marital and Family Therapy, 26*(2), 211–216.

Gordon. E., & Hodge, D. R. (2010). Helping child welfare workers improve cultural competence by utilizing spiritual genograms with Native American families and children. *Children and Youth Services Review, 32*(2), 239–245.

Kosutic, I., Garcia, M., Graves, T., Barnett, F., Hall, J., Haley, E., … Kaiser, B. (2009).The critical genogram: A tool for promoting critical consciousness. *Journal of Feminist Family Therapy: An International Forum, 21*(3), 151–176.

Lim, S., & Nakamoto, T. (2008). Genograms: Use in therapy with Asian families with diverse cultural heritages. *Contemporary Family Therapy: An International Journal, 30*(4), 199–219.

McGoldrick, M., Gerson, R., & Shellenberger, S. (1999). *Genograms: Assessment and intervention* (2nd ed.). New York, NY: Norton.

Rait, D., & Glick, I. (2008). A model for reintegrating couples and family therapy training in psychiatric residency programs. *Academic Psychiatry, 32*(2), 81–86.

Rempel, G. R., Neufeld, A., & Kushner, K. E. (2007). Interactive use of genograms and ecomaps in family caregiving research. *Journal of Family Nursing, 4*(13), 403–419.

Rosenthal, H. G. (1998). *Favorite counseling and therapy techniques* (pp. 109–111). New York, NY and London, England: Brunner-Routledge.

Speraw, S. (2010). Book review of *Genograms: Assessment and intervention (3rd ed.)*. *Issues in Mental Health Nursing, 31*(8), 550.

Tavernier, D. L. (2009). The genogram: Enhancing student appreciation of family genetics. *Journal of Nursing Education, 48*(4), 222–225.

Willow, R. A., Tobin, D. J., & Toner, S. (2009). Assessment of the use of spiritual genograms in counselor education. *Counseling and Values, 53*(3), 214–223.

Gifts

DESCRIPTION

This technique addresses those situations when we present a gift to the client for some therapeutic goal.

ORIGINS

Although not often discussed in the literature, one of those "rules of good practice" that everyone seems to know but no one seems to have set out is that giving gifts to clients is not something we should do. In fact, it is usually viewed as unprofessional.

There does not appear to be a clear theoretical position that has opened up our understanding of and our increased comfort with using gifts as a part of practice. Certainly some of the thinking of feminist practice, which favors the demystification of the treatment relationship, has led us to be more comfortable with such things as gifts. From this perspective we are urged not to forget our humanness in our efforts to be professionally helpful.

WHY THIS IS USEFUL TO SOCIAL WORK

One of the ways in which we can foster our treatment relationship and reinforce therapeutic gains with our client is through the judicious use of gifts. Thus, an overly negative view of gift giving is overly simplistic, because gifts can be a powerful motivator for some clients. Because gifts can have such a powerful impact on a person, they can be used as an important component of a relationship. This is a complex topic because of the different role that gifts play in our multicultural societies.

HOW THIS IS USEFUL TO SOCIAL WORK

A gift can be a sign of respect for tradition, an indicator of interest in a person, a means of celebrating a life event or an achievement, a memento of a shared experience, a keepsake for a lapse of time, a joint celebration of a holiday or feast day, or a form of alternate payment for a service given, along with the many other ways that gifts are used in different societies. It is this broad range of the significance of gifts that presents a challenge to us in practice. However, this should not deter us from drawing on the potential of this technique.

There are many clients for whom a small gift to mark a special occasion can be especially significant, an act remembered long after the conclusion of our relationship with them. We often forget that many persons whom we will meet in practice have rarely received gifts, not even a birthday card. Thus our remembering an important event in their lives can have a very strong and positive meaning for them that may assist the therapeutic process.

When used appropriately, a gift can communicate to a client our respect for them, our interest in them, our appreciation of the work they have put into the treatment process, and our understanding of who they are, where they are, and where they have come from (i.e., a form of graduation). The skillful use of a gift can also be a learning experience for a client as to the role of gift giving in their life outside of treatment.

Gifts can also play a role in our practice with groups. Depending on the nature of the group, small gifts are often used to celebrate events in one member's life, the group's successful completion of therapy, or some cultural event of significance to all or part of the group.

Gifts can also play a role in work with families, from the same perspectives as our work with individuals. A particular aspect of family therapy as regards gift giving is to use it as an opportunity to help the family examine the role of gift giving within the family, a topic that for many families can be very complex.

RISK FACTORS

Gift giving is a high-risk technique and thus should be used very carefully and sparingly. It can have negative effects on the relationship. Certainly, if the transference aspects of the case are strong, a gift can be misinterpreted in a variety of ways. Thus, rather than facilitating the relationship, a gift may complicate it unnecessarily

We know that many of the clients we meet have a clear picture and expectation of what a professional relationship should entail and would be surprised, indeed embarrassed, if we presented them with a gift, even as some form of celebratory gesture. Only in the safety of a formal, almost impersonal, relationship are they prepared to risk sharing themselves for the sake of growth or solving problems. In such situations, gifts may operate against this perception and hinder rather than help the relationship.

Last, because of the very diverse and complex ways in which gifts function within and between cultures, we need to be very sure we understanding our clients before we make use of gifts as a part of our work with them.

REQUIRED SKILLS AND KNOWLEDGE

Because the use of gifts in practice can be so powerful, it requires a very accurate diagnostic understanding of the client, their history, and their identity and value systems in relation to gift giving and receiving.

Case Summary One

Joan has been meeting with her social worker for weekly sessions for several months. Now, her treatment goals have been met and it is time to terminate their therapeutic relationship.

SOCIAL WORKER: As we have previously discussed, today will be our final session. You have met all of your treatment goals and have made wonderful progress since our first meeting. How are you feeling about this being our last session?

JOAN: I feel okay about it. I just hope that I can keep up the good work once we stop meeting.

SOCIAL WORKER: In honor of our final session and your amazing progress during treatment, I have a gift I would like to give you. It's just a little something that you can keep with you or put out somewhere where you can look at it often. I hope it can serve as a reminder of how far you've come, how hard you've worked, and how much you have been able to achieve over the past several months.

JOAN: Thank you so much. It's great; I will definitely let it serve as a reminder of my growth.

This gift made Joan feel good about herself and motivated her to continue progressing by using the skills she learned in treatment in her everyday life. Receiving this gift showed the social worker's respect for her and that she appreciates Joan's hard work.

Case Summary Two

Johnny is an 8-year-old boy who has been attending therapy sessions for a few months. During the last therapy session Johnny spent a lot of time talking about how excited he was for his upcoming birthday. His social worker has decided to give him a small gift during today's session to celebrate his birthday and his success so far in therapy.

SOCIAL WORKER: Hi, Johnny. How are you doing this week?

JOHNNY: I'm doing well. I had a great time at my birthday party this weekend! It was my first time having a birthday party.

SOCIAL WORKER: What did you do?

JOHNNY: I had a party at the skating rink and a few of my cousins were there. It was so much fun!

> **SOCIAL WORKER:** I'm glad to hear that you had a great time at your party. Since it was your birthday this weekend and you've been doing so well in our sessions together, I would like to give you a gift.
>
> **JOHNNY:** You remembered that I love playing with race cars! This gift is awesome. Thank you!
>
> **SOCIAL WORKER:** You're welcome. I hope you had a happy birthday and I appreciate the great job you're doing in therapy.

Receiving a gift from his social worker helped Johnny to increase his self-esteem because it made him feel like his social worker really cares about him and wants him to do well. It also showed Johnny that his social worker truly listens to what he says and understands what's important to him. In addition, the gift is a motivation for Johnny to continue to work hard during therapy sessions.

REFERENCES AND ADDITIONAL SOURCES

Alley, J. R. The Gift: A narrative case study. *Reflections: A Journal for the Helping Professions, 8*(4), 32–36.

Goldberg, B. (2002). Unwrapping the secrets of the gift: Gift giving and psychotherapy. *Psychoanalysis & Contemporary Thought, 25*(4), 465–490.

Hahn, W. K. (1998). Gifts in psychotherapy: An intersubjective approach to patient gifts. *Psychotherapy: Theory/Research/Practice/Training, 35*(1), 78–86.

Hundert, E. M. (1998). Looking a gift horse in the mouth: The ethics of gift-giving in psychiatry. *Harvard Review of Psychiatry, 6*(2), 114–117.

Hundert, E. M., & Appelbaum, P. S. (1995). Boundaries in psychotherapy: Model guidelines. *Psychiatry, 58*(4), 345–356.

Knox, S. (2008). Gifts in psychotherapy: Practice review and recommendations. *Psychotherapy: Theory, Research, Practice, Training, 45*(1), 103–110.

Knox, S., Hess, S. A., Williams, E. N., & Hill, C. E. (2003). Here's a little something for you: How social workers respond to client gifts. *Journal of Counseling Psychology, 50*(2), 199–210.

Kritzberg, N. I. (1980). On patients' gift-giving. *Contemporary Psychoanalysis, 16*(1), 98–118.

Levin, S., & Wermer, H. (1966). The significance of giving gifts to children in therapy. *Journal of the Academy of Child Psychiatry, 5,* 630–652.

Ruth, J. A. (1996). It's the feeling that counts: Toward an understanding of emotion and its influence on gift exchange processes. In C. Otnes & R. F. Beltramini (Eds.), *Gift-giving: A research anthology* (pp. 195–214). Bowling Green, OH: Bowling Green State University Popular Press.

Smolar, A. I. (2002). Reflections on gifts in the therapeutic setting: The gift from patient to social worker. *American Journal of Psychotherapy, 56*(1), 27–45.

Spandler, H., Burman, E., Goldberg, G., Margison, F., & Amos, T. (2000). "A double-edged sword": Understanding gifts in psychotherapy. *European Journal of Psychotherapy, Counseling and Health, 3*(1), 77–101.

Stein, H. (1965). The gift in therapy. *American Journal of Psychotherapy, 19*(3), 480–486.

Sue, S., & Zane, N. (1897). The role of culture and cultural techniques in psychotherapy: A critique and reformulation. *American Psychologist, 42*(1), 37–45.

Talan, K. H. (1989). Gifts in psychoanalysis: Theoretical and technical issues. *Psychoanalytic Study of the Child, 44,* 149–163.

Home Visit

DESCRIPTION

A practice that has long been part of the social worker's repertoire has been to visit clients in their place of residence. Although we do this for several reasons, for this technique we focus on situations where we decide to make such visits for particular therapeutic reasons, such as to reinforce our relationship, to convey some information of import to the client, or to assess the extent to which the home is a positive or negative in the client's life.

ORIGINS

The practice of the home visit goes back to our earliest days. At one time a distinguishing mark of the social worker was that he or she was a person who made this type of visit, to the point that an early term for a social worker was, "The Friendly Visitor." Friendly or not, in some of these early practices the purpose of the home visit was exploratory and investigative to ensure that clients were so-called worthy recipients of help.

Even now, in fields of practice such as child welfare, geriatric work, and public assistance the home visit is a common social worker activity. Such visits are seen as a necessary, routine function, in some instances with an investigative quality rather than as a distinct technique emerging from a therapeutic decision.

WHY THIS IS USEFUL TO SOCIAL WORK

Even now, in our busy practices, there are undoubtedly times when we will make a home visit to a client for whom a trip to our office or agency is a major challenge due to expense, convenience, or physical ability. It is perfectly appropriate to do things on occasion that are more convenient for a client than for us, as they will greatly appreciate these gestures.

Because where a person lives is an essential part of their psychosocial reality, it is important that we understand its place and importance in our client's reality. Most of the time the client can convey sufficient information for us to understand this; at times, however, we may be uncertain about this and want to see it for ourselves.

Because where a person lives is important to them, clients may view our interest in seeing their home setting as a mark of respect and an opportunity for them to "show off" this component of their lives. Many clients might view having a professional person make a "house call" as an important event, reflecting the social worker's interest and concern to such an extent that it can take on the aura of a state visit.

HOW THIS IS USEFUL TO SOCIAL WORK

A home visit can be very useful to us diagnostically because it helps us understand to what extent the client's domicile contributes to the client's psychosocial reality. It can open up for us a part of the client's reality that we do not see in our in office contacts. Conversely, it can help us learn more directly about the how the home and its neighborhood produce stress in the client's life.

If a client has moved into a new setting, it may be very important for them to show this to us, especially if they see the move as a step upward. Equally important, it may help us to assess the extent to which the new setting is a resource or a stressor.

REQUIRED SKILLS AND KNOWLEDGE

We need to focus upon two important areas of knowledge when considering a home visit as a part of our intervention. The first is why we are doing it. Our reason for making use of this technique is frequently diagnostic. As mentioned earlier, however, it could also be out of curiosity, a wish to reward the client, or a sign of respect.

Because our homes are so essential to us, and also because of the many ways in which a home visit can be interpreted, it is very important that we be as clear as possible just what a home visit may mean to our client. For some people, the prospect of a home visit may be viewed as a social event that also requires them to prepare food and drink. In some cultures there may be particular customs that are a part of an outsider's first visit that, if possible, we should anticipate. Bringing a gift may be expected upon a first visit, or it may be a gesture that causes some discomfort to the client. The simple question of where we sit with the client may involve extensive adjustments for the family and cause us to commit complex faux pas.

Thus, what we see as a therapeutic goal, the client may see as a formal social visit requiring considerable preparation. This may include inviting others unbeknownst to us. There is also the possibility that some clients may see their home as a very private place, and may view our suggestion of a home visit as a form of intrusion.

One further factor to be kept in mind is how such a visit may be construed by friends, neighbors, and relatives. Although not as big an issue in larger communities, a social worker's visit to a home in a smaller community can be easily recognized. Our visit thus may be an almost public event, announcing that there is a problem in the home—the news of which will spread quickly.

RISK FACTORS

This technique has a moderate level of risk. First, there is the risk that the client will misunderstand the purpose and function of a home visit and expend an inordinate amount of time, effort, concern, and resources preparing for it. Second, there is the risk inherent in our not making it clear to the client why we are visiting. Third, as mentioned, there are very strong and complex cultural issues attached to the ceremony of a home visit that we need to understand and anticipate.

Included in the decision to make a home visit, of course, is the question of social worker safety. This may arise from a failure to understand how the client may perceive the visit, or from other factors such as the time of day and the nature of the surrounding neighborhood.

In summary, a planned visit to a client's home can help us understand the client and his or her situation in a richer way, while conveying to the client our interest and concern for him or her.

Case Summary One

A mother has been bringing her son, Trent, to weekly therapy sessions for about one month with complaints about Trent's behavior. Trent's mom reports that he has been acting out in inappropriate ways both at home and school. The social worker has been meeting with Trent in his office, but would like to conduct a home visit to be able to observe Trent's behavior.

SOCIAL WORKER: Next week, during our regularly scheduled appointment time, I would like to conduct a home visit.

MOM: Oh, okay.

SOCIAL WORKER: The purpose of this home visit is for me to be able to observe and interact with Trent in his home environment where your concerns for him are occurring. I believe it will be a helpful way for me to understand why these inappropriate behaviors are taking place, which will then allow us to work to modify these behaviors.

MOM: That sounds like a great idea. Then you can really see what I've been telling you about. Maybe it will help Trent feel more comfortable, too, and he will open up more and be receptive to what you are telling him.

SOCIAL WORKER: That's a very good point as well. I will call you earlier in the day to remind you of our home visit and to ensure that you will still be able to meet with me in your home.

MOM: Oh, I will make sure that I remember and that we are home. I appreciate your interest and concern for working with my son and our family.

Trent's home is an essential part of his psychosocial reality, and it is important that his social worker understand its place in Trent's reality. The home visit was a helpful way for the social worker to begin to understand how Trent's home environment is affecting his behavior. It was a way for his social worker to see aspects of his reality that he wouldn't be able to understand just from meeting in the social worker's office.

Case Summary Two

Jeremiah is a young male attending therapy sessions for the first time in his life. He has been meeting with his social worker for a few weeks now. Jeremiah reports feeling anxious and stressed out pretty much all day, every day. He has told his social worker that these negative feelings intensify when he is at home.

> **SOCIAL WORKER:** I'd like to start off by thanking you for allowing me into your home for this home visit. I think it will be an important aspect in fully understanding what is going on in your life right now.
>
> **JEREMIAH:** No problem. I appreciate you coming here so you can see what I've been talking about.
>
> **SOCIAL WORKER:** Tell me a little about your home.
>
> **JEREMIAH:** Well, as you can see it's pretty small. Normally that wouldn't be too much of an issue, but it just doesn't seem like there's enough room in here for me and my roommate. Anywhere you look in here you will see his stuff. Look around. To the left, to the right, he has stuff everywhere.
>
> **SOCIAL WORKER:** What is your roommate like?
>
> **JEREMIAH:** He is okay, I guess. We were introduced through mutual friends. I just don't like the fact that he comes in and out of the house all hours of the day and night. What if he forgets to lock the door or something? Plus, he's always bringing strangers to our house. I don't know these people. What if they want to hurt me or decide to rob the house? I feel like I'm constantly on edge because I don't know what to expect while I'm home.

Conducting a home visit allowed Jeremiah's social worker to see firsthand what Jeremiah described during his therapy sessions. It also gave his social worker the opportunity to assess exactly how much Jeremiah's home life was contributing to his anxious feelings. Through the use of the home visit as a technique, the social worker was able to gather more pertinent information and gain a clearer picture of Jeremiah's psychosocial reality.

REFERENCES AND ADDITIONAL SOURCES

Adams, J., & Maynard, P. (2000). Evaluating training needs for home-based family therapy: A focus group approach. *American Journal of Family Therapy, 28*(1), 41–52.

Allen, S. F., & Tracy, E. M. (2004). Revitalizing the role of home visiting by school social workers. *Children & Schools, 26*(4), 197–206.

Behrens, M., & Nathan, A. (1956). The home visit as an aid in family diagnosis and therapy. *Social Casework, 37*(1), 11–20.

Bloom, M. L. (1973). Usefulness of the home visit for diagnosis and treatment. *Social Casework, 54*(2), 67–75.

Cohen, S. N., & Egen, B. (1981). The social work home visit in a health care setting. *Social Work in Health Care, 6*(4), 55–67.

Ferguson, H. (2009). Performing child protection: Home visiting, movement and the struggle to reach the abused child. *Child & Family Social Work, 14*(4), 471–480.

Kapust, L. R., & Weintraub, S. (1988). The home visit: Field assessment of mental status impairment in the elderly. *The Gerontologist, 28*(1), 112–115.

Moraes, E., de Campos, G. M., Figlie, N. B., Ferraz, M. B., & Laranjeira, R. (2009). Home visits in the outpatient treatment of individuals dependent on alcohol: Randomized clinical trial. *Addictive Disorders & Their Treatment, 9*(1), 18–31.

Moynihan, S. K. (1974). Home visits for family treatment. *Social Casework, 55*(10), 612–616.

Morris, J. (2003). The home visit in family therapy. *Journal of Family Psychotherapy, 14*(3), 95–99.

Meyer, J. A., & Mann, M. B. (2006). Teachers' perceptions of the benefits of home visits for early elementary children. *Early Childhood Education Journal, 34*(1), 93–97.

Stover, C. S., Poole, G., & Marans, S. (2009). The domestic violence home-visit intervention: Impact on police-reported incidents of repeat violence over 12 months. *Violence & Victims, 24*(5), 591–606.

Wasik, B. (1990). *Home visiting: Procedures for helping families.* Newbury, CA: Sage.

Weiss, M. F. (1991). Using house calls in a psychotherapy practice. In P. A. Keller, & S. R. Heyman (Eds.), *Innovations in clinical practice* (Vol. 9, pp. 229–238). Sarasota, FL: Professional Resource Exchange.

Homework

DESCRIPTION

Using the homework technique, we build on the potential advantages of having the client engage in some planned activity outside the interview that is related to the overall treatment goals. Starting from our understanding of the client, we seek to identify with them aspects of their reality that could be improved by having them take responsibility for certain actions that are separate from those taken in the formal interview setting.

ORIGINS

This technique emerged from the practice of structural family theorists and the behaviorists. It also has similarities to the techniques used in other theories, such as task-centered and empowerment practice.

More generally than these very specific, latter approaches, homework builds on our efforts to capitalize upon the growing understanding of the therapeutic advantages of having clients take responsibility for certain actions to help enhance their autonomy. We do this by identifying with clients aspects of their reality that they could improve by performing some discrete activity we believe will help them take more responsibility for their lives. The emphasis is not on the task, but on the goal of increased autonomy.

WHY THIS IS USEFUL TO SOCIAL WORK

The advantage of this type of homework is that therapy-related actions such as these transfer to the client a level of responsibility for the therapeutic process. It expresses our confidence in them and their ability to take charge of their own lives. For some clients it serves to demystify the therapeutic process and help them experience a level of responsibility and control.

HOW THIS IS USEFUL TO SOCIAL WORK

Some homework assignments relate to highly specific behavioral actions in which the client practices some act; for example, in relation to some component of childcare or a significant other, such as, "I will try and ask my husband about his work five times in the next week," or "I will read to the children every evening at bedtime."

At other times, the agreed-upon homework will be designed around something focused upon in the interviews. For instance, we may have been working with parents on improving their behavior with one of their children in a specific way that conveys confidence and interest in the child. In such a situation, we will discuss with the parents how this might be carried out at home with a specific description of what they should do.

Another type of activity where the use of homework can be helpful is when we want the client take better care of themselves and learn to enhance and enjoy the benefit they obtain from various life situations. Perhaps we are dealing with a hard-driving person who finds it difficult to take pleasure in things or to let themselves enjoy some of the fruits of their labor. By giving them permission to do so, we help them move to a position where they learn to be able to do such things themselves, without direction or permission. This can be a powerful agent of change for many such people. To begin to deprogram them in a general way, the homework we assign may be as simple as assigning 15 minutes of pleasure reading or TV, or phoning a friend.

An additional type of client for whom this type of homework is useful would be those people for whom the general management of a range of life roles and responsibilities is problematic. By working on specific aspects of their life, we can bring the client to a less stressful level of social functioning in regard to their various day-to-day responsibilities, and in turn help them develop a more positive self-image. The kinds of people who would most profit from this technique appear to be present- or activity-oriented persons who wish to be in charge of their lives and destinies.

RISK FACTORS

Homework has a mild risk factor. Probably one of the biggest mistakes we make when using this technique is to overuse it and seek to move the client along too quickly as we begin to see results from very minor steps. We often underestimate the psychic payoff that a client receives from what appears to be very minor but successful gains as a result of some negotiated homework assignment, and then move the client to more challenging assignments too soon.

REQUIRED SKILLS AND KNOWLEDGE

When using this technique, we find that there is much in common with our client activities if we operate from a generally behavioral or task-centered approach. The difference here is that we are using a much less structured approach to the actions or homework tasks under consideration. In these instances, the homework projects we will consider are more generic ones that are much less structured than in behavioral and task-centered work. The payoff for the client is not in the specific task, but in improving their involvement in therapy and taking more control of one's life.

However, as in behavioral and task-oriented work we will seek client feedback and provide required levels of support and reinforcement, especially when the process does not go as planned, such as when the agreed-upon homework proves to be more difficult than first anticipated. It is a technique that requires imaginative planning with the client to find homework projects that will support the overall treatment goals.

Case Summary One

Rhonda started seeing a social worker on the advice of her mother due to issues with low self-esteem. Rhonda describes herself as worthless, stupid, unimportant, and a burden to those around her. Rhonda's fear of rejection has made her avoid most social contacts. She only has a few relationships with close friends and family members, and does not accept compliments or see any positive traits in herself.

After a few sessions, the social worker gave Rhonda a homework assignment.

SOCIAL WORKER: Rhonda, our first goal is to decrease your negative self-statements and increase your positive statements.

RHONDA: Okay.

SOCIAL WORKER: I want you to write down at least one positive statement about yourself daily in a journal. Then, bring the journal with you to sessions so we can review them. Also, together we will compile a list of some of your positive traits and talents that I want you to read three times a day. Do you already own a journal?

RHONDA: No, but I can get one on my way home.

[During the next session:]

SOCIAL WORKER: Do you have your journal with you?

RHONDA: Yes.

SOCIAL WORKER: Did you write in it and review it every day?

RHODA: Yes, I did. Some days I didn't want to do it or I couldn't think of anything positive right away, but I also knew I didn't want to let you down. I completed the homework each day so we could review it in session like you said.

Being assigned homework to complete and bring to sessions made Rhonda accountable and made her more likely to do it. Rhonda knew that if she did not complete the homework, the social worker would know when she came for her next session, and she didn't want to risk him being disappointed in her. Rhonda was willing to work at writing positive statements even though they didn't come naturally to her because she wasn't just doing it for herself; she was doing it and reporting back to someone else.

Case Summary Two

Jim is attending therapy sessions to try to improve his relationship with his wife. Jim is described as always working whether he is in the office or at home. He says his wife often calls him a workaholic, which makes him defensive and starts a fight.

> SOCIAL WORKER: Jim, what would you say is your overall goal for attending therapy sessions?
>
> JIM: I don't want to fight with my wife anymore. I want to have a better relationship her.
>
> SOCIAL WORKER: That's a great goal. As a way to try and achieve that goal, I have a homework assignment for you to complete. I'd like you to take thirty minutes at least three days this week to do an activity alone with your wife. The activity should be something that you both enjoy. The thirty minutes should be a time without disruption or focus on work. Does that sound like something you can do?
>
> JIM: Yeah, I can do that. I'll do whatever I need to for my marriage.
>
> [During the next session:]
>
> SOCIAL WORKER: What was it like for you to complete the homework assignment?
>
> JIM: It was a little strange at first, but after the first few days it felt great. I ended up spending more time with her than what you stated in the home work assignment.
>
> SOCIAL WORKER: That's wonderful. What did the two of you decide to do together?
>
> JIM: Mostly we just sat and talked. It was nice to have special time set aside to spend with each other. I didn't realize how buried I was in my work and how much I missed my wife.

Jim was used to having to work long hours for so many years that it just became a way of life for him and consumed other aspects of his life. Jim's social worker used homework as a technique to give Jim permission to take time away from his work and repair his relationship with his wife. The homework also gave Jim the ability to take more control over this aspect of his life and change in positive ways.

REFERENCES AND ADDITIONAL SOURCES

Broder, M. S. (2000). Making optimal use of homework to enhance your therapeutic effectiveness. *Journal of Rational-Emotive & Cognitive-Behavior Therapy, 18*(1), 3–18.

Burns, D. D., & Auerbach, A. H. (1992). Does homework compliance enhance recovery from depression? *Psychiatric Annals, 22*(9), 464–469.

Busch, A. M., Uebelacker, L. A., Kalibatseva, Z., & Miller, I. W. (2010). Measuring homework completion in behavioral activation. *Behavior Modification, 34*(4), 310–329.

Dattilio, F. M. (2002). Homework assignments in couple and family therapy. *Journal of Clinical Psychology, 58*(5), 535–547.

Dozois, D. J. (2010). Understanding and enhancing the effects of homework in cognitive-behavioral therapy. *Clinical Psychology: Science and Practice, 17*(2), 157–161.

Fehm, L., & Mrose, J. (2008). Patients' perspective on homework assignments in cognitive-behavioural therapy. *Clinical Psychology & Psychotherapy*, *15*(5), 320–328.

Freeman, A. (2007). The use of homework in cognitive behavior therapy: Working with complex anxiety and insomnia. *Cognitive and Behavioral Practice 14*(3), 261–267.

Hanson, W. E., Razzhavaikina, T. I., & Scheel, M. J. (2004). The process of recommending homework in psychotherapy: A review of social worker delivery methods, client acceptability, and factors that affect compliance. *Psychotherapy: Theory, Research, Practice, Training*, *41*(1), 38–55.

Harwood, T. M., Sulzner, J. M., & Beutier, L. E. (2006). *Handbook of homework assignments in psychotherapy*. New York, NY: Springer.

Houlding, C., Schmidt, F., & Walker, D. (2010). Youth social worker strategies to enhance client homework completion. *Child and Adolescent Mental Health*, *15*(2), 103–110.

Kazantzis, N., & Ronan, K. R. (2006). Can between-session (homework) activities be considered a common factor in psychotherapy? *Journal of Psychotherapy Integration*, *16*(2), 115–127.

Mausbach, B. T., Moore, R., Roesch, S., Cardenas, V., & Patterson, T. L. (2010). The relationship between homework compliance and therapy outcomes: An updated meta-analysis. *Cognitive Therapy and Research*, *34*(5), 429–438.

Sheafor, B. W., & Horejsi, C. R. (2003). *Techniques and guidelines for social work practice* (6th ed., pp. 402–403). Boston, MA: Pearson Education.

Shelton, J., & Levy, R. (1981). *Behavioral assignments and treatment compliance*. Champaign, IL: Research Press.

Hypnosis

DESCRIPTION

By hypnosis, we refer to the therapeutic use of the process described as "the phenomenon of being in a mental state of aroused concentration so intense that everything else in the subject's consciousness is ignored" (Barker, 2003, p. 205). Barker goes on to reinforce the fact that, despite popular opinion to the contrary, subjects cannot ordinarily be led to do things that are outside of their ethical systems.

ORIGINS

Of all the techniques discussed in this volume, hypnosis is probably the most controversial from the perspective of whether it is appropriate for social workers to use. As a therapeutic technique hypnosis itself is controversial because of its historical background, where it has been used as a way to help clients, a presumed method of controlling people, and as a form of entertainment. Because of its history of use by magicians and entertainers, many often see it as something more fitting for the stage than the clinical office. A further component of its somewhat shady reputation is the extent to which it has been inordinately popularized, distorted, and presented in nonprofessional literature, which has endowed it with powers and influences far beyond its actual potential.

The phenomenon of hypnosis was of interest to Freud in his earlier work. He concluded that it was a legitimate and useful tool for therapy, although he moved away from its use as he developed his theory of psychoanalysis, which relied more heavily on free association and dream interpretation. In spite of its baggage, it nevertheless has been carefully studied over the decades—indeed, over the centuries—and found to be a legitimate and useful form of help.

This technique is almost independent of any particular theoretical orientation because it has many sources of origin and has been put to so many different uses by persons with various theoretical bases. Because of its many-faceted origins, hypnosis has a range of explanations and, as with meditation, ways to best make use of it.

WHY THIS IS USEFUL TO SOCIAL WORK

Because the research base of hypnosis is sufficiently strong, and the necessary knowledge and skills are within the abilities of social workers with an adequate level of training in a recognized setting, it stands as a further technique for us and hence for our clients.

The number of social workers who make use of hypnosis is small. However, with a growing understanding of its potential and an equally growing appreciation of its limitations, as well as its demonstrated inability to lead persons to do inappropriate things, an increasing number of practitioners are implementing it as a further practice technique.

Dr. William Nugent, a social worker who has written about the use of hypnosis in the profession, focuses on a particular form of hypnosis conceptualized by Milton Erikson and Ernest Rossi called the *utilization model*. He sees this approach as a particularly useful model for social workers (Nugent, 1996, pp. 362–388).

HOW THIS IS USEFUL TO SOCIAL WORK

As a process, hypnosis has been found to be helpful for a variety of psychosocial disorders: for example, the control of pain or various behavioral problems and, collaboratively with physicians, for various medical problems. There is also evidence that hypnosis is useful for such things as weight loss, smoking, or other forms of addiction.

RISK FACTORS

Because of its reputation, the risk in misuse, and the special training and practice it requires, hypnosis is a high-risk technique. All of these factors indicate that anyone thinking about using hypnosis as a component of practice needs to ensure that they have received formal training in is use. This should include a component of initial supervision as one begins to use the training in practice.

Despite these inherent risks, we ought not to fear hypnosis because of its history, or adopt it simply because of its uniqueness. As with all techniques, we need to ensure that we have explained its various formats and made appropriate use of it in practice, assuming always we have received sufficient training and supervision.

REQUIRED SKILLS AND KNOWLEDGE

Due to the very checkered history of hypnotism, its mixed reputation in social work, and the evidence that it has considerable utility in clinical practice, it is a topic to which our profession needs to devote a considerable amount of research, to assess the various ways it can be of assistance to us.

Case Summary One

Magdalene has been in therapy for several months. She started attending therapy sessions after experiencing the trauma and devastation of a natural disaster while on vacation with her husband. Magdalene and her social worker have discussed the option of using clinical hypnosis as a way to ease her anxious feelings and put her intrusive, disturbing thoughts behind her.

SOCIAL WORKER: Over the past few sessions, we have discussed using clinical hypnosis during our therapy sessions. Are you ready to try hypnosis during today's session?

MAGDALENE: Yes, I would like to try it. I would really like to get rid of these disturbing images in my mind.

SOCIAL WORKER: Okay, great and I assure you that I will work to make this experience as comfortable and gentle as possible.

During this session and for several sessions that followed, Magdalene engaged in hypnosis. She reported leaving her sessions feeling powerful and ready to face life's challenges. Through the use of hypnosis, Magdalene was able to change the way she experienced her life. She was able to ease her feelings of anxiety and replace the intrusive, disturbing thoughts of her traumatic event with more pleasant ones.

Case Summary Two

Julian reports feeling overwhelmed practically all day, every day. He states that the pressure of his job, coupled with the responsibilities associated with being a husband and father, are becoming too much for him.

JULIAN: I feel like I'm on edge all of the time. I'm willing to do anything to change this constant feeling of being overwhelmed.

SOCIAL WORKER: We've discussed the use of hypnosis during our therapy sessions as a way to enhance your mental, physical, and emotional well-being. Are you comfortable with having a hypnosis session today?

JULIAN: I've been thinking about it. It definitely sounds like something I'd like to try. Let's start today.

SOCIAL WORKER: First, I'd like you to sit and relax in this comfortable chair and then we'll start the hypnosis process.

[After hypnosis:]

SOCIAL WORKER: How do you feel following our hypnosis session?

JULIAN: I actually feel very relaxed. I also have a feeling of clarity now. This is great.

Julian was feeling so overwhelmed and stressed in his everyday life that he couldn't think clearly. Hypnosis was used as a technique during this session to create a deeply relaxed state, which was then used to reduce Julian's mental stress and bodily tension. Eventually, the social worker will be able to lead Julian on a path of greater understanding, which will help to alleviate the overwhelming, stressful feelings in his life.

REFERENCES AND ADDITIONAL SOURCES

Barker, R. (2003). *The social work dictionary* (5th ed.). Washington, DC: NASW Press.

Erikson, M., & Rossi, E. (1981). *Experiencing hypnosis: Therapeutic approaches to altered states.* New York, NY: Irvington.

Gafner, G. (2005). *Clinical applications of hypnosis.* New York, NY: Norton Professional Books.

Nugent, W. (1996). The use of hypnosis in social work practice. In F. Turner (Ed.) *Social work treatment* (pp. 362–388). New York, NY: Free Press.

Rhue, J. W., Lynn, S. J., & Kirsch, I. (Eds.). (1993). *Handbook of clinical hypnosis.* Washington, DC: American Psychological Association.

Ruysschaert, N. (2009). (Self) hypnosis in the prevention of burnout and compassion fatigue for caregivers: Theory and induction. *Contemporary Hypnosis, 26*(3), 159–172.

Interpretation

DESCRIPTION

Interpretation is the technique of feeding back to the client our perceptions and understanding of various aspects of their personality, history, and behavior. The general goal of this technique is to help the client gain a richer and deeper comprehension of their difficulty and its historical and dynamic origins, so he or she can achieve a more healthy and satisfying level of functioning.

ORIGINS

The initial origins of this technique come from early psychoanalytic practice, in which interpretation was considered the essence of treatment. At that time, treatment sought to deal exclusively with the unconscious components of the client's psyche. Because of its perceived importance, it was viewed within the professional culture from a status perspective. The more a client's unconscious came to the fore and laid itself open to interpretation, the more important the treatment was seen as being.

Over the years, the very existence of unconscious material was questioned as more theories and therapies gained prominence. It has became more common to believe that if there is an unconscious part of our personalities, it was not nearly as important as once thought.

WHY THIS IS USEFUL TO SOCIAL WORK

It was eventually better understood that not all successful treatment involves dealing with the clients' unconscious. In fact, most social workers did not deal with as much unconscious material as was first considered necessary. Rather, much of what was dealt with in therapy focused on problems of daily living, some of which did of course involve reflection upon material from clients' early history.

Nevertheless, many clients do view the need to understand their pasts as important, indeed as essential, and this is the reason they seek or come to treatment. Such clients expect that they will need to talk about their pasts. In so doing, they also expect to receive opinions, suggestions, and feedback from the social worker of an interpretive nature that will help them move along in their maturational course.

HOW THIS IS USEFUL TO SOCIAL WORK

Regardless of one's theoretical base, few would deny that all of us bring to our present functioning something of our earlier history. Overall, there is general consensus that by talking about and coming to understand our earlier histories with the help of a supportive and knowledgeable social worker, we can put many of these influences behind us, especially those that have hindered or limited our functioning. Such understanding of our past can then help us to develop a more positive and productive self-image and bring a heightened level of self-acceptance and self worth.

Although the technique of interpretation usually applies to material from one's earlier life, there is a broader understanding of the term's meaning as used in contemporary parlance. In this sense, *interpretation* refers to any activity on our part where we are seeking to help a client better understand any aspect of their lives and behaviors. Viewed this way, it is a technique closer to that of clarification.

RISK FACTORS

Dealing with a client's deep-seated and trouble-laden material from the past through interpretation can be of great assistance to them in a highly dramatic and long-lasting way. However, it has a significant level of risk, as it can result in high levels of transference, which, if not appropriately understood and managed, can cause considerable confusion and anger in the client. Thus, interpretation needs to be used in a careful, parsimonious, and prudent fashion.

REQUIRED SKILLS AND KNOWLEDGE

In deciding to use interpretation as a part of our technique repertoire in a particular case, we first must decide if the client wishes us to interpret their early life. If so, we need to assess if it is something that seems necessary or useful from the perspective of their present situation. We also need to assess if they are capable of doing and dealing with the kind of work that is required.

As we get to know clients as intensely as we often do, we begin to understand much about them that they clearly do not understand about themselves. In using such material judiciously, we can be of considerable help by interpreting some of the things they say, do, or plan to do in a way that will help them to expand their own knowledge about themselves and their history, and to begin to find other ways of functioning in their interpersonal spheres. Often this kind of interpretive assistance leads them to understand the things they need to do in their life or to make highly important and mature decisions that alter their psychosocial journey.

Many people who turn to us need to work out some of their baggage from the past and are ready and able to do the work involved. Much of this work requires us to interpret some of the material they present to us. This can be very intense, and we need to be certain that we are prepared to do the work this entails, that we are sufficiently theoretically competent to understand what may come to the fore, and that we understand how intense the relationship can and frequently does become. Thus it is important that we have consultative resources available to us to ensure that we are being as helpful to the clients as possible.

Case Summary One

Kayla started seeing her social worker due to problems she was having maintaining quality interpersonal relationships. Kayla has been meeting with her social worker for a few months and he is well informed of her familial history. Kayla describes her mother as a clingy, way too dependent drain on her friends and family. According to Kayla, her mother has always been demanding to everyone she knew, but never helped anyone. During the current session, Kayla's social worker believes he has enough information to provide interpretive feedback.

SOCIAL WORKER: Tell me more about your concerns related to your relationships.

KAYLA: I don't know why I am having so much difficulty maintaining relationships. I'm a great friend. I'm independent, I never ask anyone for anything, but somehow all I attract are these difficult and demanding people.

SOCIAL WORKER: After getting to know you the past few months and learning your family history, I believe you don't ask for any help now because you are afraid of being seen as a needy, overwhelming person like you view your mother as being. In addition, when anyone comes to you for help you decide they are just like your mother and will only drag you down, so you end the relationship. It's important to find the right give-and-take balance in every relationship.

KAYLA: Yes, yes, I believe that's it. I've never even considered that before, but I think you're right.

Having this realization as a result of the social worker's interpretation brought Kayla a feeling of relief. Being provided with an explanation for her situation has provided her with a new perspective for why she acts the way she does. Kayla is now able to evaluate her conduct and begin to change it, which will open her up to other ways of functioning in relationships.

Case Summary Two

Laine has been attending therapy sessions for about 2 months now. Her father passed away 6 months ago. Laine still feels very angry about her father's passing and frequently states that she didn't get to spend enough time with him. During previous sessions, Laine reported that she has good relationships with and is close to all of her siblings.

LAINE: If they sell my father's house I'm going to make their lives miserable! They are so inconsiderate. I can't believe they would do something like this.

SOCIAL WORKER: Tell me more about how you're feeling.

LAINE: I'm so mad at my brother and sister-in-law. They lived near my dad and were able to visit him anytime they wanted to. They know how important that house was to him. Now they want to get rid of it like it's junk. They are just awful people and I can't believe I'm related to them. If they sell his house I will make sure they feel as bad as I do. It's so unfair.

SOCIAL WORKER: From what I'm hearing you say now and what you've told me in the past, I don't think you're really mad at your brother and sister-in-law. You're more upset at the thought of losing another part of your dad.

LAINE: Yes, I am. That house is all I have left of my dad. If they sell it I'll have nothing, he'll be completely gone. I guess I understand why they have to do it. I just don't like it.

SOCIAL WORKER: Now that we understand what is really going on, we can work together to help you make better choices.

In this example the social worker used interpretation as a technique to help Laine better understand her behavior. By interpreting what Laine was saying and planning on doing, the social worker was able to expand Laine's knowledge about herself and help her to find other, more positive ways of functioning.

REFERENCES AND ADDITIONAL SOURCES

Claiborn, C. D. (1982). Interpretation and change in counseling. *Journal of Counseling Psychology, 26,* 378–383.

Clark, A. J. (1995). An examination of the technique of interpretation in counseling. *Journal of Counseling and Development, 73*(5), 483–490.

Devereaux, G. (1951). Some criteria for the timing of confrontations and interpretations. *International Journal of Psychoanalysis, 32,* 19–24.

Ellis, A. (1968). Rational therapy: A rational approach to interpretation. In E. F. Hammer (Ed.), *Use of interpretation in treatment: Technique and art* (pp. 232–239). New York, NY: Grune & Stratton.

Gambrill, E. (1997). *Social work practice* (pp. 309–310). New York, NY: Oxford University Press.

Gazzola, N., & Stalikas, A. (1997). An investigation of counselor interpretations in client centered therapy. *Journal of Psychotherapy Integration, 7*(4), 313–327.

Gazzola, N., & Stalikas, A. (2004). Social worker interpretations and client processes in three therapeutic modalities: Implications for psychotherapy integration. *Journal of Psychotherapy Integration*, *14*(4), 397–418.

Hammer, E. F. (1968). Interpretation: What is it? In E. F. Hammer (Ed.), *Use of interpretation in treatment: Technique and art* (pp. 1–4). New York, NY: Grune & Stratton.

Hill, C. E., Thompson, B. J., & Mahalik, J. R. (1989). Social worker interpretation. In C. E. Hill (Ed.), *Social worker techniques and client outcomes: Eight cases of brief psychotherapy* (pp. 284–310). Newbury Park, CA: Sage.

Lowenstein, R. (1951). The problem of interpretation. *Psychoanalytic Quarterly*, *20*, 1–14.

Lowenstein, R. (1957). Some thoughts on interpretation in the theory and practice of psychoanalysis. *The Psychoanalytic Study of the Child*, *12*, 127–150.

Northen, H. (1995). *Clinical social work knowledge and skills* (2nd ed.). New York, NY: Columbia University Press.

O'Conner, K. (2002). The value and use of interpretation in play therapy. *Professional Psychology: Research and Practice*, *33*(6), 523–528.

Schut, A. J., Castonguay, L. G., Flanagan, K. M., Yamasaki, A. S., Barber, J. P., Bedics, J. D. (2005). Social worker interpretation, patient-social worker interpersonal process, and outcome in psychodynamic psychotherapy for avoidant personality disorder. *Psychotherapy: Theory, Research, Practice, Training. Special Issue: The Interplay of Techniques and the Therapeutic Relationship in Psychotherapy*, *42*(4), 494–511.

Strean, H. (1996). Psychoanalytic theory and social work treatment. In F. Turner (Ed.). *Social work treatment* (4th ed., pp. 544–546). New York: Free Press.

Tosone, C. A. (1993). *Impact of the level of patient functioning on the content and frequency of therapist interpretation* (Unpublished thesis, New York University, School of Social Work).

Interpreter

DESCRIPTION

In viewing the use of a language interpreter as a technique, we focus on situations where the skills of a professional language interpreter are used to facilitate the client's involvement in a therapeutic relationship.

ORIGINS

From its very beginnings, social work in North America has dealt with clients from all parts of the world. In so doing most practitioners have frequently made use of an interpreter's assistance to facilitate communications with clients who lacked fluency in a language we speak. Very little has been written in our professional literature about this process, especially in earlier years of the profession, when it was clear that we had to depend on the assistance of bilingual or partially bilingual persons for the most basic communications with people from other countries.

In particular there has been very little written about our working with professional interpreters. There seem to have been three reasons for this. The first is the strongly held position that newcomers to a country should learn its primary language, and the belief that having an interpreter would delay this process. Second, the perception that the use of an interpreter did not fit our understanding of the therapeutic relationship as being a dyadic one. Adding a third person was thus seen as contravening our commitment to confidentiality. Last, there has been a failure to recognize that interpreting is a highly skilled and demanding profession that holds many of the same values as we do about the importance of people, their right to be fully understood, and the necessity of confidentiality. Our failure to appreciate the skills of the professional interpreter has led us to a make-do practice, in which we made use of whoever was available when we needed interpreting assistance. Most of us have had the experience of attempting to make use of someone in an interpretive role who was neither trained as an interpreter nor fully competent in one or both of the languages involved. Often these experiences have been fraught with difficulties and misinterpretations.

In many ways, the existence of the United Nations has helped us to appreciate the skills of the professional interpreter. This body, like other international groups, has been able to deal with the most delicate of international questions involving the lives of millions through the medium of skilled interpreting. To successfully carry out this duty requires people with a very thorough understanding of the languages involved and all of their nuances. As we begin to appreciate the importance of this role and the skills involved, we are now beginning to appreciate the potential of this resource and the importance of using a skilled interpreter when needed.

WHY THIS IS USEFUL TO SOCIAL WORK

Certainly as our practice becomes more and more culturally diverse from the perspective of language skill, we meet many people who are not sufficiently fluent in a language we speak to function well in an intensive interview. Providing interpretive services can make it possible for the communication to take place in a comfortable, secure, and effective manner.

Working in conjunction with a professional interpreter when there is a language barrier can bring a level of confidence and comfort to a client that would not be present when either no interpreter or an inadequate one is used in an interview. Many clients have lived for years in an environment where they have had to function in a second language that they only partially understand and speak, and have had to make do with unskilled interpretation, often in relation to highly sensitive material. Providing competent interpretive assistance can be a very enabling experience that brings clients a long-sought sense of security that they are finally being understood.

HOW THIS IS USEFUL TO SOCIAL WORK

A competent interpreter can put both the interviewer and interviewee at ease with the assurance that each participant in the interview will be understood and will understand the verbal content of the interview. Once some clients realize that they are now being understood, they will be ready to deal with material they have never been able to process, often for years.

Providing an interpreter reflects a level of respect to our clients, a factor that may assist considerably in our ability to work with and assist them. This is especially important for clients who have been traumatized by unskilled or inappropriate people serving in this role.

In our era of massive and often sudden population shifts, many people will need the services of skilled interpreters. Much of our work in this area will involve contacts with colleagues in other countries. Often in such situations we expect our colleagues to function in English. This may detract significantly from the richness of information available if it could be fully understood and expressed by both parties.

Many persons who experience the ease of communication that comes with this technique, often for the first time in years, find they are able to involve themselves more deeply in the complex dynamics of a helping relationship. This often permits them to deal with highly sensitive issues.

RISK FACTORS

Several issues can create a moderate degree of risk in using this technique. An important one is to ensure that we understand the role of the interpreter, and that before therapy begins we agree with the interpreter what this role will entail. Otherwise we can readily create confusion and uncertainty in the client's mind.

We need also to ensure that the person serving in the interpreter role is acceptable to the client. By not doing so, we can make serious errors. For instance, our lack of sensitivity to historic and ethnic issues can become a problem. Such things as the interpreter's name, accent, gender, or country/region of origin can make that person totally unacceptable to the client, regardless of his or her language skill and training.

There is also the risk that, because the client has had a long history of bad experiences with inadequate interpretation, he or she will find it difficult to move easily into a comfortable relationship that involves an interpreter. This issue may be the one that needs to be addressed first.

REQUIRED SKILLS AND KNOWLEDGE

It is essential that we understand the role of the interpreter as being a voice conduit, rather than a third person in the relationship. Hence the question arises of whether the interpreter should be physically present or elsewhere and connected by some form of technology. However, even when present in the interview, a skilled interpreter is able to quickly ensure that what appears to be a triadic interview situation will quickly become and remains dyadic .

One further challenge is the question of cost. As professionals, interpreters' services are expensive, and our access to the resources to pay for these services is often very limited. The temptation is to compromise and make do with whatever is available, even if it is inadequate. This is a complex ethical question and an equally complex policy issue, but it needs to be addressed; when an interpreter is available to us, we can provide high levels of help to people whose language deficits might otherwise cut them off from the services of a skilled social worker.

Case Summary One

A few months ago, Maria's mother Linda moved from Mexico and is currently living with her in the United States. She does not speak English. Maria has noticed that her mother has been really quiet lately and is not engaging in activities that used to bring her joy. Maria is afraid that Linda is becoming increasingly isolated, and she wants to make her transition to the United States a pleasant one. Maria decided to meet with a social worker to see if she can get help for her mom.

Maria brings her mother to the social worker's office; she speaks to the social worker while her mom sits nervously and silently.

MARIA: My mother, Linda, recently moved here from Mexico and is in need of help. I don't know what else to do.

SOCIAL WORKER: Well coming in to talk was a good first step. [Addressing Linda] Are you open to meeting with me?

MARIA: Yes, I explained to her that you are here to help. She is just very nervous right now.

SOCIAL WORKER: Does she speak any English?

MARIA: She is familiar with English, but definitely does not speak it fluently. Even though she doesn't speak it fluently she still wants therapy. She might be able to have short conversations with you in English.

SOCIAL WORKER: That won't be necessary. We have trained interpreters on staff that will attend sessions and make sure that your mother fully understands what I am saying and vice versa.

MARIA: That will be wonderful. I think she will be a lot more comfortable talking to someone who is fluent in her native language.

SOCIAL WORKER: Let's bring in the interpreter to make introductions and schedule our first appointment.

MARIA: Okay, that sounds great. I will let her know what is going on.

Linda was so nervous with the English-speaking social worker that she just sat silently and allowed her daughter to do all of the talking for her. Having an interpreter in the room during therapy sessions will help Linda feel more at ease and may encourage her to express herself more deeply. Having an interpreter will also make sure that both Linda and the social worker fully understand what each other is saying so there are no errors in communication. The interpreter must have a full understanding of the ethics of confidentiality and the communication nuances specific to each language.

Case Summary Two

Joe is a young man who has been attending therapy sessions to deal with family issues he is having with his parents. He has told his brother, Tom, how helpful the sessions have been, and his brother has decided that he would also like to attend therapy sessions. Joe has discussed the possibility of bringing Tom into a session with his social worker. Joe and his social worker have agreed to have a family session today.

JOE: I brought my brother, Tom, to join me for session today. He would also like to attend therapy sessions individually, but there's a problem.

SOCIAL WORKER: What's the problem?

JOE: He is deaf and only understands sign language. I can sign for him, but he told me he is too embarrassed to have me in his individual sessions with him. Also, he is worried that I might not express exactly what he wants me to.

SOCIAL WORKER: No worries there. We have a large range of language interpreters available at our agency. If Tom would like to attend therapy sessions we can have a sign language interpreter attend sessions with your brother. The interpreter is a skilled professional and will also maintain your brother's confidentiality.

JOE: That's so great. He's been dealing with these issues by himself for so long because he didn't think he would be able to find a social worker that could understand him. He's very relieved to have the opportunity to attend therapy sessions.

SOCIAL WORKER: I'm glad to hear that. We can even bring an interpreter into our session today so that Tom can meet him and he can start being a voice conduit for him.

The use of a sign language interpreter will ensure that Tom is fully understood during his therapy sessions. It will also provide Tom with the confidence and sense of comfort he needs to fully engage in the therapeutic relationship.

REFERENCES AND ADDITIONAL SOURCES

Amodeo, M., Grigg, S. D., & Robb, N. (1997). Working with foreign language interpreters: Guidelines for substance abuse clinicians and human service practitioners. *Treatment Quarterly, 15*(4) 75–87.

Brunson, J. G., & Lawrence, P. S. (2002). Impact of sign language interpreter and social worker moods on deaf recipient mood. *Professional Psychology: Research and Practice, 33*(6), 576–580.

Caruth, M., Lopez, D., Martell, Z. L., Miller, K. E., & Pazdirek, L. (2005). The role of interpreters in psychotherapy with refugees: An exploratory study. *American Journal of Orthopsychiatry, 75*(1), 27–39.

Freed, A. (1988). Interviewing through an interpreter. *Social Work, 33*(4), 315–319.

Glasser, I. (1983). Guidelines for using an interpreter in social work. *Child Welfare, 57*, 468–470.

Jacobs, E. A., Chen, A. H., Karliner, L. S., Agger-Gupta, N., & Mutha, S. (2006). The need for more research on language barriers in health care: A systematic review and proposed research agenda. *Milbank Quarterly, 84*(1), 111–133.

Karliner, L. S., Jacobs, E. A., Chen, A. H., & Mutha, S. (2007). Do professional interpreters improve clinical care for patients with limited English proficiency? A systematic review of the literature. *Health Services Research, 42*(2), 727–754.

Kaufert, J. M., & Putsch, R. W. (1997). Communication through interpreters in health care: Ethical dilemmas arising from difference in class, culture, language and power. *Journal of Clinical Ethics, 8*(1), 71–87.

Marcos, L. R. (1979). Effects of interpreters on the evaluation of psychopathology in non-English-speaking patients. *American Journal of Psychiatry, 136*(2), 171–174.

Miller, K., Martel, Z., Pazdirek, L., Caruth, M., & Lopez, D. (2005). The role of interpreters in psychotherapy with refugees: An exploratory study. *American Journal of Orthopsychiatry, 75*(1), 27–39.

Padilla, A. M., & Salgado de Snyder, V. N. (1992). Hispanics: What the culturally informed evaluator needs to know. In M. A. Orlandi, R. Weston, & L. G. Epstein (Eds.), *Cultural competence for evaluators: A guide for alcohol and other drug abuse prevention practitioners working with ethnic/racial communities* (pp. 117–146). Rockville, MD: U.S. Department of Health and Human Services, Substance Abuse and Mental Health Services Administration, Office for Substance Abuse Prevention.

Putsch, R. W. (1985). Cross-cultural communication: The special case of interpreters in health care. *Journal of the American Medical Association, 254*(23), 3344–3348.

Searight, H. R., & Searight, B. K. (2009). Working with foreign language interpreters: Recommendations for psychological practice. *Professional Psychology: Research and Practice, 40*(5), 444–451.

Turner, F. J. (2002). The role of interpreters in contemporary practice. In F. Turner (Ed.), *Social work practice* (2nd ed., pp. 545–552). Scarborough, Ontario: Prentice Hall, Allyn & Bacon.

Vasquez, C., & Javier, R. A. (1991). The problem with interpreters: Communicating with Spanish-speaking patients. *Hospital and Community Psychiatry, 42*(2), 163–165.

Yakushko, O. (2010). Clinical work with limited English proficiency clients: A phenomenological exploration. *Professional Psychology: Research and Practice, 41*(5), 449–455.

Journal Writing

DESCRIPTION

Having a person maintain a journal as a specific form of therapeutic homework can be an effective way to help a client involve themselves in the therapeutic process.

ORIGINS

Journal keeping has long been used by social scientists to ensure an ongoing record of their observations. More recently, it has been used as a tool in qualitative research.

This technique does not appear to have emerged from any one theoretical orientation. Rather, all theories see the advantages of having some clients focus on the matter discussed during interviews in this structured, concrete way. Some Gestalt practitioners would certainly recognize the advantage of having clients record some of their thoughts and feelings about treatment. It is also considered useful in psychoanalytic tradition for clients to record their dreams when they awaken. Other theories consider it beneficial for the client to use a journal to reflect upon material discussed in therapy, or as a way of keeping track of some behavioral pattern that has become a focus in treatment.

There has of course been a long tradition in social work for us to record the therapy process, focusing on our perceptions, observations, and reactions to the client. This experience has inspired us to encourage our clients to record their own reactions to therapy.

WHY THIS IS USEFUL TO SOCIAL WORK

The reflection involved in this kind of record-keeping activity can influence the client to take a further level of responsibility for and ownership of the treatment experience.

Furthermore, a journal can help a client who is seeking to understand themselves better to come to terms with components of their earlier history. In these instances, keeping a journal may ensure for the client, and thus for the social worker, that the ideas, memories, or feelings that come to mind about the matter under consideration will not be forgotten. This includes having having the client record dreams that may touch upon the relevant phase of life.

HOW THIS IS USEFUL TO SOCIAL WORK

Over the years, practitioners have found that many clients do reflect on many aspects of the treatment process and their own reactions to it outside of the formal interview process. Likewise, they often reflect on relevant things about themselves that emerge from the relationship. Having a formal structure such as journal keeping to capture these ideas, feelings, questions, and memories between interviews can greatly strengthen the therapeutic process.

RISK FACTORS

The risk of this technique is minimal. It is understood that we must ensure sure that the client is capable of the type of writing required to keep a journal, so the process does not become unduly stressful for him or her. (In our enthusiasm for the technique, we can overlook the possibility that the client lacks the ability to write this way.)

A further diagnostic consideration that could create risk if ignored is to ensure that this process does not play into any of a client's possible obsessive characteristics, so the record-keeping process becomes all encompassing. (The reverse side of this point, however, is the potential for journal-keeping activity to help very scattered persons bring a needed bit of order to their lives.)

Yet another risk factor is the question of confidentiality. How sure can the client be that the material they write will be safe from others who may use the content in a mischievous or negative manner?

REQUIRED SKILLS AND KNOWLEDGE

This technique requires no particular skills on the social worker's part, but it does require an understanding that there are a variety of formats a journal could take. At times, we will have the client use the journal to reflect on the treatment process itself. This serves two functions. First, it can help the client to better understand his or her views, reactions, and feelings about the treatment. In this way, the journal can serve to keep the treatment in focus. Second, it can help the social worker adjust the content and process of the treatment, especially if it seems to have shifted from its primary intent. Just as we keep notes about the progress of a case as a form of *aide-mémoire*, the client can benefit from a like process.

The client can also keep a journal to focus on other aspects of their life. This is especially useful if he or she is struggling with an important life decision, a difficult relationship, or seeking to alter some aspect of their life in a particular direction.

When using this technique, both client and social worker need to be clear with each other over whether the material is to become a part of the record, left with the client, or be destroyed (and if so, when and by whom).

Case Summary One

Melinda has been attending therapy sessions following a traumatic car accident she was in about one month ago. The accident and her subsequent feelings of anxiety are interfering in her daily life.

MELINDA: I have such trouble traveling now. Any time I get into a car I feel tense, nervous, and sick to my stomach.

SOCIAL WORKER: I can understand how big of a problem that will be for you. I know from our previous sessions that when you go back to work, you will be required to drive several times per day.

MELINDA: That's correct. I don't know what I'm going to do.

SOCIAL WORKER: Some people use journal writing to help recognize and better understand their anxious feelings and their causes. Would you like to try that?

MELINDA: Sure, if it will help.

SOCIAL WORKER: Here is a notebook. I want you to keep a journal of your feelings. Write in the journal any time you have an anxious feeling. I want you to write what the feeling was, what happened right before you became anxious, where you were, and what you were doing. I also want you to write what you did after you started feeling anxious. Do you think you can do that?

MELINDA: Yes, I can do that.

SOCIAL WORKER: Bring your journal to each session and we can review what you wrote.

Journal writing is a useful technique in this case because it can help ensure that Melinda remembers the what, when, where, and why of her anxious feelings. It will also help her reflect on her feelings when she is alone, as well as in therapy sessions. Writing in her journal and sharing it with the social worker will help Melinda recognize her feelings of anxiety and better understand what triggers them. She and her social worker can then explore ways to cope with them.

Case Summary Two

Audrey is a young adult attending therapy sessions. She reports that she is going through a rough time right now with her long-term boyfriend, and she is trying to decide whether or not she should continue the relationship.

SOCIAL WORKER: How are things going this week?

AUDREY: It's been a difficult week. Some days we get along so well and others we just seem to hate each other. I don't know what to do. I feel so torn and confused. I'm starting to lose sleep over it.

SOCIAL WORKER: I understand that this is very difficult for you to go through. When a person has to make a difficult decision it can be helpful to write in a journal. Journal writing would allow you to get all of your thoughts and feelings out. It would also provide the opportunity for you to access the information later either by yourself or by bringing it to session for us to discuss. I'd like you to start writing in a journal at least three times over the next week.

AUDREY: I think that's a good idea. I'm willing to try it.

[The following week:]

SOCIAL WORKER: Has journal writing been helpful for you?

AUDREY: Yes, I've written in my journal several times over the past week and it has helped me to realize a few things about my relationship. I was able to sort out all my thoughts and feelings. I also found the act of taking the time to be by myself and write in my journal to be very calming and relaxing.

Journal writing was used as a technique in this case to help Audrey while she was struggling with a difficult decision about her relationship. Writing in her journal allowed Audrey to express all of her thoughts and feelings and reflect upon them as much as she needed. Journal writing brought more organization to her thoughts, which helped her feel better able to make a difficult decision.

REFERENCES AND ADDITIONAL SOURCES

Bell-Pringle, V. J., Jurkovic, G. J., & Pate, J. L. (2004). Writing about upsetting family events: A therapy analog study. *Journal of Contemporary Psychotherapy, 34*(4), 341–349.

Canada, E. R. (1989). Therapeutic use of writing and other media with Southeast Asian refugees. *Journal of Independent Social Work, 4*(2), 47–60.

Furman, R., Coyne, A., & Negi, N. J. (2008). An international experience for social work students: Self-reflection through poetry and journal writing exercises. *Journal of Teaching in Social Work, 28*(1/2), 71–85.

Greenhalgh, T. (1999). Writing as therapy. *British Medical Journal, 319*, 270–271.

Largo-Marsh, L., & Spates, C. R. (2002). The effects of writing therapy in comparison to EMD/R on traumatic stress: The relationship between hypnotizability and client expectancy to outcome. *Professional Psychology: Research & Practice, 33*(6), 581–586.

Lepore, S. (1997). Expressive writing moderates the relation between intrusive thoughts and depressive symptoms. *Journal of Personality and Social Psychology, 73*(5), 1030–1037.

Nye, E. F. (1997). Writing as healing. *Qualitative Inquiry, 3*(4), 439–452.

O'Callaghan, C. (2005). Qualitative data-mining through reflexive journal analysis: Implications for music therapy practice development. *Journal of Social Work Research and Evaluation, 6*(2), 217–229.

Oppawsky, J. (2001). Client writing. An important psychotherapy tool when working with adults and children. *Journal of Clinical Activities, Assignments and Handouts in Psychotherapy Practice, 1*(4), 29–40.

Pennebaker, J. (1993). Putting stress into words: Health, linguistic, and therapeutic implications. *Behavior Research and Therapy, 31*(6), 539–548.

Smyth, J. (1998). Written emotional expression, effect sizes, outcome types, and moderating variables. *Journal of Consulting and Clinical Psychology, 66*(1), 174–184.

Smyth, J. M., Stone, A. A., Hurewitz, A., & Kaell, A. (1999). Effects of writing about stressful experiences on symptom reduction in patients with asthma or rheumatoid arthritis: A randomized trial. *Journal of the American Medical Association, 281*(14), 130–149.

Talerico, C. J. (1986). The expressive arts and creativity as a form of therapeutic experience in the field of mental health. *The Journal of Creative Behavior, 20*(4) 229–247.

Torres, L., & Ong, A. D. (2010). A daily diary investigation of Latino ethnic identity, discrimination, and depression. *Cultural Diversity and Ethnic Minority Psychology, 16*(4), 561–568.

Van der Oord, S., Lucassen, S., Van Emmerik, A. A. P., & Emmelkamp, P. M. G. (2010). Treatment of post-traumatic stress disorder in children using cognitive behavioural writing therapy. *Clinical Psychology & Psychotherapy, 17*(3), 240–249.

Letter Writing by Client

DESCRIPTION

This technique focuses on situations where we support or encourage a client to write a letter to a significant other in their lives, whether living or dead. It is a therapeutic activity that can be of considerable benefit in several ways.

ORIGINS

Although letter writing as a societal practice is not as common as it once was, writing a letter can be an important way for clients to organize their thoughts and express their feelings quite differently than they would using the more technological resources through which much interpersonal communication takes place in today's world.

As a technique, it emerges from the thinking of Gestalt practitioners, who have helped us to understand the importance and utility of helping clients find different ways of expressing and communicating their feelings to themselves and others.

WHY THIS IS USEFUL TO SOCIAL WORK

In this era of telecommunications, especially with the prevalence of e-mail and cell phones, it seems a bit out of fashion to think of letter writing as a therapeutic technique. However, in our culture and in most cultures of the world a letter still has an important role.

A letter is a way to express feelings, provide or seek information, or foster or repair a relationship. A letter can open communications, maintain contact, or come to closure on some important interpersonal issue. A letter can also serve as a significant gift that the recipient will long cherish.

One of the things that makes a letter different from other forms of communications—and a factor that enhances its potential as a therapeutic tool—is that the process of letter writing requires a level of cognitive input, planning, and deliberation that is not as necessary for a phone call or an e-mail. Even with this cognitive element, it is still possible to express the deepest of human emotions with exactly the nuance one wishes to convey, often in a way that is not possible via more technologically advanced modes of communication.

A further important quality of the written word is its permanence. A letter is frequently kept for long periods of time, and can be reread, providing an opportunity to reflect on the content, to plan a response, or to experience the emotional tenor of the contents again. Also, the very fact that a letter is handwritten adds a further personal and intimate quality that comes from the distinctive style of writing each of us has.

HOW THIS IS USEFUL TO SOCIAL WORK

In the current age of technological sophistication, there are probably many who have never or rarely written the type of personal letter being considered here. Helping them learn how to make use of this communication medium can expand their modes of expressing themselves in a broader sphere than the ongoing work of therapy.

In addition to having clients write letters as a task to be completed outside of an interview as a form of therapeutic homework, we should also consider its use as a technique within the interview. For example, there are times in a case where it might prove beneficial during a session to have the client write a letter that never gets sent. Thus a client might write a letter to someone who is deceased to complete some unfinished emotional work, to express feelings, or to talk about something that was never fully expressed while the person was alive.

Depending on its content, such a letter may be destroyed in the interview or kept by the person as an important memento of this period of growth. For some people, this can also be a way of dealing with guilt and a need to confess to someone in a formal way.

A letter that the client intends to destroy or never to send does not have to be directed to someone who is dead. Before a client expresses their feelings and concerns in written form, it may be important to him or her to state that it will never be sent. The client may need to express their feelings about someone in this formal fashion, but with the understanding that it remain within the confines of the therapeutic relationship.

The reason for not sending it may vary. It just may not be prudent to send such a letter even though it may be very useful for the client to express words, feelings, or ideas related to the target of the letter in this semistructured way. Writing it in this fashion has a concrete quality that may be sufficient for the client's growth.

An act of destroying a letter the client never intends to mail can have a strong symbolic impact, and how it is destroyed also may be important. For some, burning the letter can be strongly meaningful, and thus can be a useful way to bring this facet of the client's life to closure. It also may be something that the client presents to the worker for destruction; that is, the presentation serves as a "good-bye" to the letter's content.

RISK FACTORS

This is a low-risk technique, presuming as always an accurate diagnostic judgment that the person is capable of writing a letter, and that its contents will not cause more harm than good. If the letter is to be sent, a useful procedure is to agree to have the client let you see it before it is sent.

REQUIRED SKILLS AND KNOWLEDGE

The principal skill for use of this technique is to find the line between being helpful to a client for whom this process is something quite novel in their lives, and in letting this urge to help overly influencing the letter's content. It is also important that we have accurately gauged the potential benefits for the client in pursuing this route and, again, that it doesn't unduly reflect our interest in the process. Last, because many people with whom we use this technique may have had little experience in letter writing, it is important that we do not unduly influence the process and the content in our desire to be helpful.

Case Summary One

Michelle started seeing a social worker following the death of her brother. Her brother committed suicide, and it was an unexpected shock to everyone in her family. Michelle is upset that she did not get to say good-bye to her brother, and has unresolved emotions bottled up inside of her. Michelle is hoping that therapy will allow her to work through her grief and understand her emotions better.

> SOCIAL WORKER: Michelle, you've said that your brother's death was unexpected and you feel as though you didn't get to say good-bye to him. Is that correct?
>
> MICHELLE: Yes. I had no idea he was going to kill himself. I feel cheated.
>
> SOCIAL WORKER: I'd like to try an exercise with you. I want you to write a letter to your brother telling him everything you didn't get to say. After you write it, we can discuss how you feel about what you wrote. Do you think you're up to it?
>
> MICHELLE: Yes, I can do that. I believe it will help.
>
> SOCIAL WORKER: I really want you to take your time and make sure you write down everything that you want to say to your brother. Why don't you write it at home when you have adequate time to be alone, and we will discuss it when you come for your next session?
>
> MICHELLE: That sounds good. It will give me time to collect my thoughts and figure out exactly what I want to say.

Because Michelle's brother committed suicide and died so suddenly, she has a lot of unresolved issues surrounding his death. Michelle is not able to talk to her brother directly, so writing a letter will allow her to express her feelings and say good-bye to him. Even though she can't mail the letter to her brother, just the act of writing her thoughts and feelings down is a big help. Having her emotions on paper will help Michelle and her social worker process her feelings and work through her grief.

Case Summary Two

Cathy is attending therapy sessions due to problems she is having at work. She reports feeling anxious and stressed recently even at the thought of attending work. According to Cathy, she feels tremendous pressure from the responsibilities and deadlines associated with her job. This has been made worse by the negativity she feels radiates from some of her coworkers.

SOCIAL WORKER: How have things been at work over the past week?

CATHY: They have been about the same. There is so much to do and not enough time to get everything done. Then, on top of all that I have to hear people talking negatively about me. I feel so conflicted. I thought this was my dream job. Now, it makes me feel sick. I'm angry and I'm hurt. I thought I was doing a good job and now I'm questioning myself.

SOCIAL WORKER: During today's session, I'd like you to try an activity. Take this time to write a letter to one of your coworkers who you feel has wronged you. This is your opportunity to express all of your thoughts and feelings related to this situation. After writing the letter you can choose to share it with me, fold it up and keep it to reflect on later, or rip it to shreds. You can do whatever you choose with it.

Dear Mary,

I don't appreciate your comments about me at work yesterday. I felt they were unfair and they were not true. I wish you would have approached me directly instead of badmouthing me to coworkers. I'm so upset right now that it makes my stomach hurt. I work hard and try my best at work each and every day. I wish you could appreciate my efforts. It's just so frustrating. I don't talk negatively about you and I hate hearing you slander me. Stop it! Stop it now!

Frustrated,
Cathy

CATHY: I'm finished writing my letter now.

SOCIAL WORKER: How do you feel after writing your letter?

CATHY: I actually do feel a little better now. It was nice to get all of that out on paper.

Writing a letter during her therapy session provided Cathy with an opportunity to organize her thoughts and express emotions hidden deep inside of her. After sharing the contents of her letter with the social worker, Cathy was able to destroy the letter in a way that allowed her to let even more of her frustration out.

REFERENCES AND ADDITIONAL SOURCES

Bacigalupe, G. (1996). Writing in therapy: A participatory approach. *Journal of Family Therapy, 18*(4), 361–373.

Berger, A. A. (1993). *Improving writing skills: Memos, letters reports and proposals.* Newbury Park, CA: Sage.

Davidson, H., & Birmingham, C. L. (2001). Letter writing as a therapeutic tool. *Eating and Weight Disorders, 6*(1), 40–44.

Epston, D. (2009). The legacy of letter writing as a clinical practice: Introduction to the special issue on therapeutic letters. *Journal of Family Nursing, 15*(1), 3–5.

Epston, D., & White, M. (1989). *Literate means to therapeutic ends*. Adelaide: Dulwich Centre Publications.

Goldberg, D. (2000). "Emplotment": Letter writing with troubled adolescents and their families. *Clinical Child Psychology and Psychiatry, 5*(1), 63–76.

Lown, N., & Britton, B. (1991). Engaging families through the letter writing technique. *Journal of Strategic and Systemic Therapies, 10*(2), 43–48.

Nau, D. S. (1997). Andy writes to his amputated leg: Utilizing letter writing as an interventive technique in brief family therapy. *Journal of Family Psychotherapy, 8*(1), 1–12.

Pennebaker, J. W. (1990). *Opening up: The healing power of expressing emotions*. New York, NY: Guilford.

Pyle, N. R. (2009). Therapeutic letters as relationally responsive practice. *Journal of Family Nursing, 15*(1), 65–82.

Rodgers, N. (2009). Therapeutic letters: A challenge to conventional notions of boundary. *Journal of Family Nursing, 15*(1), 50–64.

Rasmusen, P., & Tomm, K. (1992). Guided letter-writing: A long brief therapy method. *Journal of Strategic and Systemic Therapies, 11*(4), 1–18.

Strong, T. (2002). Poetic possibilities in conversations about suffering. *Contemporary Family Therapy, 24*(3), 457–473.

Tubman, J. G., Montgomery, M. J., & Wagner, E. F. (2001). Letter writing as a tool to increase client motivation to change: Application to an inpatient crisis unit. *Journal of Mental Health Counseling, 23*(4), 295–311.

White, V. E., & Murray, M. A. (2002). Passing notes: The use of therapeutic letter writing in counseling adolescents. *Journal of Mental Health Counseling, 24*(2), 166–176.

Letter Writing by Social Worker

DESCRIPTION

The previous technique spoke to the usefulness of having the client write letters on their own behalf. Here we consider a technique whereby, as a part of our overall intervention, we write letters on behalf of the clients.

ORIGINS

Even in our era of high technology, much of the formal business of day-to-day living is still carried out through the medium of letters written back and forth between two parties to deal with various matters. The import of many of these letters can be critical in our clients' lives. In such instances, the outcome of the matter under consideration frequently depends upon the quality of the exchange of correspondence, be it in the form of paper letters or e-mail. Over the decades, we have learned that being skilled at the formal systematic exchanges of letters with our clients can be very helpful.

WHY THIS IS USEFUL TO SOCIAL WORK

Because so many of our client's difficulties arise from unsatisfactory interactions with various social systems, and because much of the formal interaction between these systems occurs via formal correspondence, our basis of practice supports a strong use of skilled letter writing on clients' behalf.

HOW THIS IS USEFUL TO SOCIAL WORK

Formal letters are written to provide information that may be important to and for a client. Letters seek information. They can be used to seek aid of various kinds, clarify issues where differences may exist, or examine or negotiate differences of viewpoint. Letters can also convey information about problem areas that may be influencing a client or interfering with some aspect of his or her functioning.

A further use of letter writing as a technique is when we write to the client rather than for the client. This can be done to note some specific event or achievement in their lives. Alternatively, it may be that we have been separated from the client for a period of time, and we use letters to maintain a contact we deem to be useful and important.

For some clients, a letter from their social worker might well be the only letters of a personal kind they have ever received. Thus, in addition to fostering and maintaining a significant relationship, a letter can serve as a gift to be saved and treasured.

A further use of the letter on behalf of a client is that of the "letter to the editor." In virtually all newspapers there is a section that publishes viewpoints on a particular issue of the day. This is clearly a potentially powerful tool, one frequently used in the social advocacy field. We may occasionally use this technique to write to an editor on behalf of a particular client or group of clients. For instance, we might be looking for a specific resource that these clients need, or we may want to bring that need before the public eye, such as a gap in social policy or failure to make resources available to which a client is eligible. One of the advantages of this strategy is that so many of the issues our clients face also relate to or are identical to those that many or all people also might be facing. In this way, readers can identify easily with the issue for which we are seeking assistance.

RISK FACTORS

Although this technique has only moderate risk, there are several areas where we need to be on our guard. The first is that of taking over an area in a client's life where he or she is competent because we believe we can do what is necessary better than the client. We may be well able to write a better letter than the client in some particular situation, but the client may be able to do so themselves, and in this way enhance their autonomy.

Another risk is that we might harm a client. For example, in our efforts to assist a client, we might reinforce his or her dependency needs in a way that is not necessary or indeed helpful. The line between doing *with* the client and doing *for* the client is a delicate one that we need to keep in the foreground when planning with them.

It is also possible that, when seeking to improve things for the client by writing on their behalf, we can hurt the client in the process through, for instance, lack of sensitivity or a disregard of confidential materials in a manner over which we have no control.

REQUIRED SKILLS AND KNOWLEDGE

Whenever we write on behalf of a client, it is essential that the client be involved in the decision. We also need to keep communications confidential as needed. In all such instances, it is critical that the client as well as ourselves understand all the possible ramifications of writing on behalf of a client.

When it comes to the impact your letter will have, the quality of the writing is as important as the content. Thus it is important that we carefully heed such matters as syntax, style, and form. Just as its important information will endure, so too will spelling and grammatical errors. "The written word remains."

Although it is possible of course to dash off an emotionally charged letter on a client's behalf, we must be careful not to do so. Rather, we need to give careful attention to what it is we want to say and how to say it.

Letters of this kind have a quality of formality about them that renders them important to both the sender and the receiver. They also have a quality of permanence that may be important in ensuring that the letter will be kept. This is especially crucial for letters exchanged between or within bureaucratic systems.

Case Summary One

Ned is in therapy to work on improving himself and his life. Ned wanted to improve his self-image and his self-esteem. He has been seeing his social worker for several months now and is really starting to achieve his goals. Ned's social worker has decided to write him a letter to summarize his progress, praise his efforts, and reinforce the work that he has done.

Dear Ned,

Our session today left me thinking about the progress that you have made. The first time I met with you it was so hard for you to think of even one positive statement you could make about yourself. Now, you have an entire journal full of positive self-statements. It has been a process, but those little steps you take add up to amazing results. I am really impressed by your reduction in negative thoughts each day. You are doing great and each day you are closer to achieving all of your goals. I look forward to our upcoming sessions and to hear more about the improvement you are seeing in your life.

Keep up the good work,

Dr. Hall

Through this letter, Ned receives praise and reinforcement from his social worker, but because it is in a letter, Ned is also able to read it as often as necessary to give himself a boost. Having this letter from his social worker gives Ned the opportunity to remind himself of the hard work he has put into achieving his goals. It also gives Ned a way to remember that he is not alone in his efforts and he has someone encouraging him to succeed. The physicality of the letter serves as a pat on the back from the social worker anytime Ned feels he needs it.

Case Summary Two

Dylan is an 8-year-old boy meeting with a social worker weekly. Dylan's parents have been divorced for several years and used to have shared custody of him. About a month ago, Dylan's mom, Dana, found out that Dylan was being emotionally abused by his father. Dylan also witnessed domestic violence during that time between his father and his father's girlfriend. Dana has filed for a temporary restraining order against Dylan's father and is keeping Dylan full time, but she has to go to court soon so the judge can determine whether or not to grant a permanent restraining order.

> DANA: I'm hoping you can write a letter for me that I can show to the judge when I go to court in a few days.
> SOCIAL WORKER: What type of letter are you looking for?
> DANA: During session, I would like you to ask Dylan how he would feel if he had to see or be around his father again. Then, I'd like you to write his response in a letter that I can show to the judge. I'm trying to do everything I can to keep my son safe. I really want the judge to understand that it would be detrimental for my ex-husband and me to continue to have shared custody of Dylan.
> SOCIAL WORKER: Okay, I will discuss the matter with Dylan during our session today and get his reaction. Then, I will write a letter to you with his response and you can pick it up from my office tomorrow. At that point in time the letter will be yours to do what you wish with it and show it to whomever you feel necessary.

In this example, the social worker is writing a letter on Dylan and Dana's behalf to try to help promote their safety and well-being. Through this letter, the social worker is able to communicate the thoughts and feelings that Dylan expressed while in the safe and comfortable therapeutic environment. Without this letter, Dylan would not be able to express himself in the courtroom. It also has the ability to serve as a formal means of correspondence to convey information to any other agency or professional Dana feels needs to see it.

REFERENCES AND ADDITIONAL SOURCES

Bacigalupe, G. (1996). Writing letters in therapy: A participatory approach. *Journal of Family Therapy,* *18*(4), 361–373.

Berger, A. A. (1993). *Improving writing skills: Memos, letters reports and proposals.* Newbury Park, CA: Sage.

Blanton, P. G. (2006). Introducing letter writing into Christian psychotherapy. *Journal of Psychology and Christianity,* *25*(1), 77–86.

Couper, J., & Harari, E. (2004). Use of the psychiatric consultation letter as a therapeutic tool. *Australasian Psychiatry,* *12*(4), 365–368.

Epston, D. (2009). The legacy of letter writing as a clinical practice: Introduction to the special issue on therapeutic letters. *Journal of Family Nursing,* *15*(1), 3–5.

Epston, D., & White, M. (1989). *Literate means to therapeutic ends*. Adelaide, South Australia: Dulwich Centre.

Goldberg, D. (2000). "Emplotment": Letter writing with troubled adolescents and their families. *Clinical Child Psychology and Psychiatry, 5*(1), 63–76.

Lown, N., & Britton, B. (1991). Engaging families through the letter writing technique. *Journal of Strategic and Systemic Therapies, 10*(2), 43–48.

Marner, T. (2000). *Letters to children in family therapy: A narrative approach*. London, England: Jessica Kingsley.

Mason, J., & Rice, D. (2008). Does a business-like letter written for a general practitioner meet the standards for patients? *Psychiatric Bulletin, 32*(7), 259–262.

Nau, D. S. (1997). Andy writes to his amputated leg: Utilizing letter writing as an interventive technique in brief family therapy. *Journal of Family Psychotherapy, 8*(1), 1–12.

Restifo, S. (2009). Writing a letter to patients. *Australasian Psychiatry, 17*(2), 123–125.

Rombach, M. (2003). An invitation to therapeutic letter writing. *Journal of Systemic Therapies, 22*(1), 15–32.

Steinburg, D. (2000). *Letters from the clinic: Letter writing in clinical practice for mental health professionals*. London, England: Routledge.

Vidgen, A., & Williams, R. (2001). Letter-writing practices in a child and family service. *Journal of Family Therapy, 23*(3), 317–326. doi:10.1111/1467–6427.00186

Listening

DESCRIPTION

Regardless of one's field of practice, learning to listen is essential. Hence, as social workers one of our very basic and universal techniques is that of listening. It is a powerful technique, one in which we become skilled early in our careers.

In viewing listening as a technique, we refer to those skills we develop and draw upon to ensure that we are hearing and, as far as possible, understanding all the client is telling us. Of equal importance is to be aware of what they are not or only partly telling us. Listening also includes our ability to convey to the client that we are indeed listening to them in a concerned, interested manner.

ORIGINS

The idea that a member of the various helping professions is someone who can and will listen to us has always been a key component of their role. However, it was principally through the development of psychoanalytic thinking that we began to understand that what a person was conveying to us in their verbal exchanges during therapy was usually much more complex and multilayered than their words might at first make it seem. As we learned the full complexity of what a client says to us during various stages of an interview, we also learned that listening is a technique that requires a range of skills and activities, and is far more complicated than just ensuring that we hear the client's words at a rational and logical level.

WHY THIS IS USEFUL TO SOCIAL WORK

There are several reasons why this technique is important to our practice. For instance, many of the clients we meet in our various roles have not had, for various reasons, the experience of being heard and listened to during much of their lives. It may go back to their early family histories, when their ideas and thoughts were not considered important or were even dispar-aged. A pattern of not being listened to when a person is young can manifest in later life as problems in many different areas.

Alternatively, a person may not be listened to because the client does not speak the language in which a particular situation is being enacted. A person with a handicap that involves an inability to easily express oneself verbally can also lead to a pattern of not being understood or, at times, an expectation that one will not be understood.

The experience of being listened to in a therapeutic interview can be very enabling and highly therapeutic. Because much of our therapeutic input with clients involves verbal interaction, it is essential that we listen to our clients and ensure that we are hearing what it is they are conveying to us in our verbal exchanges. This ensures that we remain sensitive to areas that reveal strengths upon which we can build, as well as those that appear to be difficult for the client or that they are unable to express in words.

If used skillfully, listening can convey to the client our acceptance, respect, and understand-ing—qualities often absent in their day-to-day lives. Often it is our ability to convey to our client that we are listening to them in an understanding, supportive, and respectful manner that emerges as the essence of our intervention. Most of us have experienced situations where a client has worked out complex life situations in a single interview just by being heard and encouraged to talk things through, even to the point where we may not fully understand the importance and significance of what the client has told us. The helping factor is that they have been listened to, and out of this a new sense of confidence and self-respect can emerge.

RISK FACTORS

This is a technique with minimal risk. One thing to be careful about is to not stop listening once we think we can anticipate where the client is going. This can lead us to push them too quickly. In a different way, there is also the risk of listening so passively that we encourage them to speak more than we do, rather than taking a more active part in the exchange so they take necessary actions in their lives.

A further risk for us when making use of this technique is to perceive it almost as a nontech-nique, from the misconception that everyone knows how to listen—you just sit there and let the client talk and attend to what they are saying.

SKILLS AND KNOWLEDGE

The first and most important requisite for the successful use of this technique is to understand that one must study and practice this skill in a deliberate, planned way to make most effective use of it. It is far from a passive technique; it requires a high level of attention on our part as we seek to understand what the client is telling us.

An important component of the requisite skill set is that of body language. That is, not only do we need to listen to the client, but we have to be perceived by the client as listening. This is an area where our idiosyncratic mannerisms can interfere. For example, at times when many of us want to concentrate on what the client is saying, we will close our eyes and frown or tap our fingers as we attempt to focus accurately on what is being said.

There are any number of other mannerisms that we draw upon when we are involved in the listening role, mannerisms that can be disquieting to the client and, rather than helping, can create discomfort or a sense of not being heard. For example, many people in our culture seek to maintain eye contact with a person who is speaking, who will view this as a sign of interest. But for those in other cultures, such eye contact is disquieting or even rude. Providing some sort of summary feedback to the client will indicate that what we have heard is useful, as will using gestures that indicate we want to hear more.

This is a complex issue. There are of course no set of rules about our body language, our posture, or how we encourage the client to go further. The important thing is for us to assess as quickly as possible in our early contacts with a person what appears to make them comfortable in expressing themselves, and in the way we communicate to them that we are listening and appreciate the importance of what they are telling us. In a more general way, it is important that we be aware of the ways in which we convey our interest in listening and ensure that they are congruent with where the client is in the therapeutic process.

Case Summary One

Caleb is a young, single undergraduate student who presented himself at his university's counseling service to ask for advice on a career choice. He spoke easily about himself and his dilemma, and the social worker had no difficulty engaging him in the interview.

SOCIAL WORKER: What brings you to my office today?

CALEB: I am confused as to what I should do with the rest of my life. I need someone to help me figure it out.

SOCIAL WORKER: Tell me more.

CALEB: Well, I am about to graduate with my bachelor's degree, but I haven't figured out exactly what I want to do after graduation yet. I mean, I could continue working at the same job that got me through school or I could start searching for a long-term career. I've always imagined myself with more education; maybe I can start graduate school next semester.

SOCIAL WORKER: It sounds like you have much to think about and many options to choose from. It is important to think about each option and determine which one will work best for you and your life.

Throughout their conversation it became clear to the social worker that Caleb had made a choice, but needed support for his decision from a parent-like person, which he received from the social worker. Following this session, Caleb thanked his social worker for listening and "hearing him out." Being listened to in this therapeutic environment was very empowering for Caleb and gave him the confidence he needed to make a decision for his life.

Case Summary Two

Yasmin is a young adult who has been meeting with a social worker for several weeks. She started seeing a social worker when coworkers and friends mentioned being concerned with the way she was acting. While growing up, any time Yasmin started to show emotion or express feeling sad or upset, her parents would dismiss her feelings and refuse to hear what she had to say. Due to her upbringing Yasmin learned to bottle up her feelings, which led her to express her frustration in inappropriate ways.

> **SOCIAL WORKER:** Tell me how things have been going at work since we've started meeting.
> **YASMIN:** Things have actually gotten better recently. My friends have stopped telling me that they think I have an anger management problem.
> **SOCIAL WORKER:** I'm glad to hear that.
> **YASMIN:** It feels so good to be able to talk and have someone really listen to me. I've kept my feelings bottled up inside for so long because of the way my parents were. It's nice to be able to finally express myself. It used to feel like there was a volcano ready to erupt inside of me most of the time. When I talk to you I can tell that you are truly listening to what I'm saying and you are interested and concerned about me.
> **SOCIAL WORKER:** From what you've told me it sounds like your friends can and are willing to be a good source of strength and support for you, too. They cared enough about you to suggest that you seek counseling when they were concerned with your behavior.
> **YASMIN:** Yes, I think you're right. I've actually been thinking about opening up to some of my close friends more. I'm beginning to understand that not everyone thinks the way my parents do.

Through the social worker's listening technique, Yasmin has started to feel understood, supported, and respected. Now that Yasmin has recognized that she is being listened to she has started to develop a new sense of confidence and self-respect. This will lead Yasmin to improved behavior and the ability to express her feelings in appropriate ways.

REFERENCES AND ADDITIONAL SOURCES

Adler, S., & Carrara, D. A. (1977). The therapeutic impact of listening. *Long Term Care & Health Services Administration Quarterly, 1*(1), 52–57.

Barish, S. (1975). Lend me your ear: An exploration of clinical listening. *Clinical Social Work Journal, 3*(2), 75–84.

Brenneis, C. B. (1994). Observation and psychoanalytic listening. *Psychoanalytic Quarterly, 63*(1), 29–53.

Cummins, L., Sevel, J., & Pedrick, L. (2006). *Social work skills demonstrated* (2nd ed.). Boston, MA: Allyn & Bacon.

Fitzgerald, P., & Leudar, I. (2010). On active listening in person-centered, solution-focused psychotherapy. *Journal of Pragmatics, 42*(12), 3188–3198.

Hibel, J., & Polanco, M. (2010). Tuning the ear: Listening in narrative therapy. *Journal of Systemic Therapies, 29*(1), 51–66.

Huerta-Wong, J. E., & Schoech, R. (2010). Experiential learning and learning environments: The case of active listening skills. *Journal of Social Work Education, 46*(1), 85–102.

Ivey, A., Gluckstern, N., & Ivey, M. B. (1993). *Basic attending skills.* Amherst, MA: Microtraining Associates

Lee, B. R., Munson, M. R., Ware, N. C., Ollie, M. T., Scott, L. D., & McMillen, J. C. (2006). Experiences of and attitudes toward mental health services among older youths in foster care. *Psychiatric Services, 57*(4), 487–492.

Meissner, W. W. (2000). On analytic listening. *The Psychoanalytic Quarterly, 69*(2), 317–367.

Myers, S. (2000). Empathic listening: Reports on the experience of being heard. *Journal of Humanistic Psychology, 40*(2), 148–173.

Nugent, W. R. (1995). Testing the effects of active listening. *Research on Social Work Practice, 5*(2), 152–175. doi:10.1177/104973159500500202

Reik, T. (1948). *Listening with the third ear.* New York, NY: Grove.

Welch, I. D. (1998). *The path of psychotherapy. Matters of the heart* (pp. 33–38). New York, NY: Brooks/Cole.

Wood, M. R. (2010). What makes for successful speaker-listener technique? Two case studies. *The Family Journal, 18*(1), 50–54.

Loci of Interviewing

DESCRIPTION

This technique is based on the assumption that the physical place where we conduct our interviews can greatly affect the process, and when these differential effects are considered specific therapeutic goals can be achieved.

ORIGINS

We have all learned in our practice that, for any number of reasons, we sometimes find it necessary to carry out interviews in settings not of our choice, for reasons that include convenience, opportunity, time, and emergencies. For a long time we have viewed these situations as second or third best from our own conception of where we felt it was it best to interview.

However, what we have done out of expediency has taught us much. We have learned that each different interview locus has its own particular set of attributes, not necessarily all bad, that influence the interview's quality and effectiveness. In particular, we have learned that some of these loci have special positive features. These can be tapped in a way that enhances the interview and makes it more productive.

WHY THIS IS USEFUL TO SOCIAL WORK

Because we are a profession based on a commitment to understand all components of the reality of a person's situation, it behooves us to view the locale of an interview as a situation that can have specific influences on the process. If it can be demonstrated that, by altering the place of an interview, we can enhance the climate for relationship building we seek and the fostering of a therapeutic process, then the locale of an interview is a variable we can manipulate to enhance our therapeutic activities. Thus, rather than always seeing an out-of-office situation as a less-than-desirable situation, we will instead make a conscious effort to consider the possibility of changing our locus to achieve a particular therapeutic goal.

HOW THIS IS USEFUL TO SOCIAL WORK

There are several possibilities when selecting a particular place to interview. We have already discussed the home visit as a separate technique because of its special place in the culture of social work. Another possibility is to meet the client in a neutral setting such as a restaurant. Apart from the obvious confidentiality-related disadvantages of a restaurant setting, there is the very strong factor of sharing food with the client and of the intimacy that can be a component of this, even if it is only a coffee or a Big Mac.

Another possibility in choice of locale is that of interviewing in a car. This strategy has several advantages. From a systems perspective, a car is very nearly a closed system, a situation that can facilitate feelings of trust and the sharing of confidences and troubles. It has been suggested that having two people in a side-by-side position as in a car or plane lends itself to feelings of confidence and openness.

Similar to the car from the perspective of privacy, yet for some a much less threatening setting, is the "walk in the park" form of interview. It is a type of situation that permits strong confidentiality and a high degree of emotional safety for the client. Meeting a client in a neutral setting such as a park is a factor that, for some clients, is important in equalizing the power balance of the relationship.

A different type of out-of-office setting is to build the interview around some type of social activity, such as a visit to the museum, gallery, or zoo. This kind of shared activity can makes it possible for some clients to engage in therapeutic work in a manner that may feel much safer or less intimidating than our more traditional office setting.

We can envision other situations outside the office, each with its positives and negatives from the perception of a given client. Our challenge is to assess the potential strengths or limitations of each for our clients and ourselves.

RISK FACTOR

Each setting brings with it different risk factors; thus, there is an overall moderate level of risk in using them. Careful assessment of the client and situation is essential before we use one.

For example, the matter of interviewing over food in a public place is not a choice that we make lightly. Powerful and significant as this strategy can be, it can also be problematic in many ways and needs to be considered very carefully. It is essential that we know who and where the client is, from the perspective of their psychosocial situation, so we do not find ourselves, for instance, in the middle of a coffee shop dealing with highly charged material and a very upset client. Another important diagnostic and intervention component of sharing a meal that we should clarify in advance is the question of who pays, as well as the relationship implications of all three possibilities (social worker pays, client pays, or sharing the cost).

Using a car for an interview can raise the issue of intimacy and all the mixed messages such a process can give, which may contraindicate this technique. Likewise, using a walk in the park or museum visit may make the interview more of a social event than a therapeutic one.

REQUIRED SKILLS AND KNOWLEDGE

One of the realities of social work treatment is that the most powerful technique for a given situation often makes use of everyday realities in all of our lives. In this way, a shared meal in a restaurant to celebrate a client's birthday may be one of the most important events in their lives and may help them get on with life's challenges.

This strategy of selecting a different locale is not as dramatic a technique as the high-tech equipment that serves as the basis of practice in other professions, but it is just as important. Our task is to analyze the component features of each of the various interview locales available to us, and to learn to tap their potential while taking appropriate steps to neutralize any negative factors. Because the power of these forms of human interaction is immense, we have a responsibility to harness this potential in a facilitating way.

In summary, all of the possible locations for an interview are the kind we use in our own lives to deal with our own personal psychosocial realities, joys, sorrows, and problems. We know how we personally view their relative importance in various situations. In our therapeutic roles we need to learn to harness the different potential of each type of locus and tap its potential for enhancing our treatment goals.

Case Summary One

Tommy is a 14-year-old male meeting with a social worker due to behavior concerns observed in school and at home as a result of his parent's divorce. The first few sessions were conducted in his social worker's office with minimal information gathered. For the current session, Tommy's social worker has decided to try something different.

SOCIAL WORKER: Tommy, I know that you are very active on your school's baseball team and you enjoy the outdoors. How would you like to have today's session outside?
TOMMY: That's fine with me.
SOCIAL WORKER: Great. Let's go down to the park at the end of the block where we can walk and talk.
TOMMY: Okay.
[During the session in the park, the social worker was able to obtain much more information from Tommy than in previous sessions held in the office.]
SOCIAL WORKER: What did you think about our session today?
TOMMY: I think it was good. It was cool to actually do something. It was a lot better than sitting still and talking for an hour.

Conducting the session while walking in the park created a neutral and less threatening environment for Tommy to open up to and connect with his social worker. Walking gave Tommy something else to focus on other than the fact that he was "spilling his guts" to his social worker. It allowed him to relax and talk without feeling overwhelmingly vulnerable. Having the session outside also provided an opportunity for Tommy to release some of his energy and boost his mood through the exercise of walking.

Case Summary Two

Connie is a woman in middle adulthood who has been attending therapy sessions for several weeks. Connie has had issues with low self-esteem and a lack of confidence throughout her entire life. Recently, Connie was asked by her supervisor to facilitate training for her office peers. Connie has expressed to her social worker that she feels extremely anxious anytime she thinks about the training. She reports feeling scared that she will present horribly and end up getting fired. Connie and her social worker usually meet in the social worker's office. However, for a future session Connie's social worker has decided to change the location as a way to enhance their therapeutic activities.

SOCIAL WORKER: Connie, for our next therapy session I would like to meet at the museum downtown. They have a wonderful Salvador Dalí exhibit, which I know from previous discussions that you are very knowledgeable about.

CONNIE: Yes, I love Salvador Dalí.

SOCIAL WORKER: As we walk through the exhibit, I would love for you to teach me more about the artwork and the artist. I think it will be a good opportunity for you to practice and become more comfortable with teaching others.

[At the end of their session at the museum:]

SOCIAL WORKER: Connie, I appreciate all of the information you were able to so eloquently relay to me about the artist and the artwork. How was this session experience for you?

CONNIE: It was great, actually. I was a little nervous at first, but I really knew the information, so after my nerves calmed down the information flowed quite easily.

SOCIAL WORKER: What about the topic you are supposed to train your coworkers on? I'm guessing you must be knowledgeable in that area as well if your supervisor has asked you to facilitate a training.

CONNIE: Yes, I really do know a lot about the subject I will be teaching at work. After today I'm feeling less nervous about it. I have a better idea of how I will facilitate the training. If I can teach my social worker something, I'm sure I can help my coworkers learn a thing or two.

For this therapy session Connie and her social worker went to a different location as a way to help achieve one of Connie's therapeutic goals. A museum can be an appropriate location for a session because it can be a quiet place and offer the opportunity for confidentiality. Going to the museum allowed Connie to teach her social worker about the artist as a way to build her confidence and allow her to practice facilitating a training. Meeting in the museum helped Connie feel more comfortable, was less intimidating, and led to a very effective and productive therapy session.

REFERENCES AND ADDITIONAL SOURCES

Ammerman, R. T., Hersen, M., & Fishman, C. A. (1995). Handbook of child behavior therapy in the psychiatric setting. *Child & Family Behavior Therapy, 17*(4), 23–33.

Emile, V. (2009). Outdoor therapy. Retrieved from http://www.vanessaemile.co.uk/counselling/outdoor.html

Franklin, C., Moore, K., & Hopson, L. (2008). Effectiveness of solution-focused brief therapy in a school setting. *Children & Schools, 30*(1), 15–26.

Kadushin, A., & Kadushin, G. (1997). *The social work interview* (4th ed.). New York, NY: Columbia University Press.

Media (*The Wall Street Journal*). (2012). [Walk&Talk website]. Retrieved from http://www.walkandtalk.com/media.html#twsj

Pepper, R. S. (2003). Be it ever so humble: The controversial issue of psychotherapy groups in the home office setting. *Group, 27*(1), 41–52.

Phillips, B. (1999). Reformulating dispute narratives through active listening. *Mediation Quarterly, 17*(2), 161–180.

Russell, K. C. (2000). Exploring how the wilderness therapy process relates to outcomes. *The Journal of Experiential Education, 23*(3), 170–176.

Sauer, R. J. (1984). Family therapy in a partial hospitalization setting. *Family Therapy, 11*(3), 211–215.

Weiss, Y. (1993). Teaching bedside interviewing skills in a social work training programme. *Social Work in Health Care, 18*(314), 201–219.

Woods, L. J. (1988). Home-based family therapy. *Social Work, 33*(3), 211–214.

Mediation

DESCRIPTION

This technique addresses the use of the general method of mediation in therapy as a way of helping clients deal with areas of conflict that are outside of but inhibiting the therapeutic process.

ORIGINS

It has long been known to social scientists that all of us, throughout all of our lives, engage in the process of mediation. In our profession, however, it appears that William Schwartz first identified it as a formal process in group functioning that provides a way to help people manage tensions between individuals and societal rules. Larry Shulman (Fusco, 2002) also addressed this same function of formally helping people resolve differences through mediation.

In recent years, this very human aspect of interpersonal interaction has become a specialized methodology and a service that several professions offer, including social work. People involved in this practice have identified what makes a mediation successful, what does not help it, and the kinds of factors that interfere with the process.

Mediation initially emerged as a separate methodology in social work practice. However, its processes can also be used as a technique called upon to deal with conflictual issues that arise from time to time in the therapeutic process that can derail it or slow it down.

WHY THIS IS USEFUL TO SOCIAL WORK

Mediation occurs when we have a difference of opinion with someone with whom we are interacting. Often these are very minor issues, but they can also involve major life decisions. To ensure that we are not constantly living in a situation of strife, we often employ, almost without being aware of it, a mediation process, as does the other person. That is, by discussion,

271

suggestion, and weighing alternatives, we seek to find a solution for dealing with the issue that is acceptable to the parties involved.

However, it also happens on occasion that we become involved in situations where our accustomed mediation strategies are insufficient. At such times we find it necessary to seek someone else's help. Such a person, depending on their skills and perspicacity, can be helpful in finding a solution. But if it happens to be someone who does not understand the required process, it can make the outcome worse.

HOW THIS IS USEFUL TO SOCIAL WORK

As a practice methodology, mediation needs to be seen as a separate process from therapy, in that the function of the mediator is not primarily therapeutic. This is true even though, if the mediation process is successful, there are frequently therapeutic gains to be accrued from it.

From time to time, however, situations arise in treatment that are not an essential part of the agreed-upon goals of the process, in which differences of opinion arise about some life situation that needs to be resolved before the therapeutic process can continue. These may involve such things as a disagreement between two clients over a convenient time for a joint interview, or where the interviews should take place, or any number of areas where differences can arise that are not essential to the planned intervention strategy but may be getting in the way of it.

Mediation is a useful therapeutic technique in clinical work when used sparingly. Not only is it a process that can help deal with the clients' issues outside therapy, but it can also help the disputants acquire or strengthen skills that will stand them in good stead in other life situations.

RISK FACTORS

Using the mediation technique as part of the general therapeutic process is risky, as it is often difficult to be sure that the topic for which mediation is being used is really something that both sides are prepared to mediate, rather than having it become yet another topic for a problem-solving approach as part of the overall treatment goal. It is a practice technique that has a high risk factor, in that it is easy for us to have our own preferred solution, which can easily lead us to take sides.

REQUIRED SKILLS AND KNOWLEDGE

For mediation to be an effective process, the situation being mediated must be one about which the social worker is neutral. We cannot pick a side in the dispute. Our goal in instituting a mediation technique is to help the two sides find a win-win situation; that is, one to which both are prepared to commit themselves and work toward for the therapeutic process to continue.

When using mediation, we strive to have both sides fully involved in seeking a solution. We help the process through questions and suggestions and by pointing out difficulties in proposed solutions. Its goal is always to get the process of treatment back on track. It is appropriate for us to raise alternative solutions that they have not considered, but we do this to help them think about possibilities, rather than trying to persuade them to choose a particular solution.

Case Summary One

A husband and wife have been meeting separately with their social worker for a few months, and they are now ready to begin meeting together. However, they are having trouble agreeing on a time when they will both be available to meet for couple's sessions. Their social worker is going to use mediation as a way for them to come to an agreement to facilitate couple's sessions.

SOCIAL WORKER: Okay, we are here today to mediate the issue of finding a regular meeting time for your couple's sessions. What is the conflict you two are encountering?

MARISSA: Well, I feel like Turner isn't willing to compromise at all to allow us to determine a day and time that we can meet.

TURNER: I am willing to compromise; it just seems like it's impossible to please Marissa. No matter what I suggest it doesn't work for her schedule.

SOCIAL WORKER: Tell me about some of the days and times you have discussed.

MARISSA: We started by looking over the list you gave us of your available days and times to meet with us. Most of the times that are available I cannot meet because I am still at work at that time.

TURNER: Yes, but you could always leave work a little early one day a week or every other week. I can't meet any of the other times because I have my kickboxing class. I really look forward to going; it helps me stay in shape, stay healthy, and relieve stress.

Marissa and Turner were progressing nicely in their separate therapy sessions. However, their conflict of not being able to agree on a day and time to meet for couple's sessions was beginning to slow down the therapeutic process. Going through mediation provided the two with an opportunity to find a solution to their dilemma with the guidance of a neutral third party. After the mediation, Turner realized that he could change his kickboxing class on the day of the sessions to the morning instead of the evening, so that way he can attend the couple's sessions without missing out on something he enjoys doing.

Case Summary Two

A mother, Amy, and her teenage son, Rob, have been attending concurrent therapy sessions for several weeks. Rob's parents have been divorced for a few years and the family has a history of domestic violence. Amy recently discovered that Rob was physically abused by his father when he was younger. For today's session, Rob and Amy are meeting together for a family session. However, during the session Rob and Amy began bickering regarding Rob's class schedule in high school next year.

SOCIAL WORKER: How have things been going lately?

ROB: My mother is being so unfair.

AMY: I'm not being unfair. I am your mother and I only want what's best for you.

SOCIAL WORKER: Rob, please tell me about the situation you are referring to.

ROB: Students are able to determine which elective classes they want to take next year. I want to take drama and my mom wants me to take journalism. That doesn't even seem like it would be an elective. I might as well take all academic courses.

AMY: That's the point. I'm trying to help you reach your full potential in life. I want you to be challenged.

ROB: I want to be able to take at least one class about something I enjoy and I think that I'm good at.

SOCIAL WORKER: Let's see if we can resolve this difference of opinion during our time together today. First, we can start by having each of you list the pros and cons you see associated with each class. Then, we can compare the lists, discuss some options, and see if we can come up with a solution that both of you are happy with.

Rob and Amy's argument about Rob's class schedule was hindering their ability to work towards achieving their therapeutic goal during the session. Through the social worker's unbiased mediation, they were able to come up with a win-win situation that they both felt comfortable with and to get the therapy session back on track.

REFERENCES AND ADDITIONAL SOURCES

Bannick, F. P. (2007). Solution-focused mediation: The future with a difference. *Conflict Resolution Quarterly, 25*(2), 163–183.

Barry, T. D., Dunlap, S. T., Lochman, J. E., & Wells, K. C. (2009). Inconsistent discipline as a mediator between maternal distress and aggression in boys. *Child & Family Behavior Therapy, 31*(1), 1–19.

Barsky, M. (1984). Strategies and techniques of divorce mediation. *Social Casework, 65*(2), 102–108.

Cohen, O. (2009). Listening to clients: Facilitating factors, difficulties, impediments, and turning points in divorce mediation. *Family Therapy, 36*(2), 63–82.

Favaloror, G. J. (1998). Mediation: A family therapy technique? *Australian and New Zealand Journal of Family Therapy, 19*(1), 11–14.

Fusco, L. (2002). Mediation in social work practice. In F. J. Turner (Ed.), *Social work practice: A Canadian perspective* (pp. 230–240). Toronto, Ontario: Pearson.

Hadas-Lidor, N., Naveh, E., & Weiss, P. (2006). From social worker to teacher: Development of professional identity and the issue of mediation. *Journal of Cognitive Education and Psychology, 6*(1), 100–114.

Hahn, R. A., & Kleist, D. M. (2000). Divorce mediation: Research and implications for family and couples counseling. *The Family Journal, 8*(2), 165–171.

Holmes, S. (2006). Becoming "the best possible" family counselor or family mediator: What expertise research has to say. *Journal of Family Studies, 12*(1), 113–122.

Hyden, M. (2001). For the child's sake: Parents and social workers discuss conflict-filled parental relations after divorce. *Child & Family Social Work, 6*(2), 115–128.

Kirst-Ashman, K. K., & Hull, G. H (1993). *Understanding generalist practice* (pp. 8–89). Chicago, IL: Nelson-Hall.

Kressel, K. (1987). Clinical implications of existing research on divorce mediation. *American Journal of Family Therapy, 15*(1), 69–74.

Kurtz, S., Stone, J. L., & Holbrook, T. (2002). Clinically sensitive peer-assisted mediation in mental health settings. *Health and Social Work, 27*(2), 155–159.

Perez-de-Albeniz, A., & Holmes, J. (2000). Meditation: Concepts, effects and uses in therapy. *International Journal of Psychotherapy, 5*(1), 49–58.

Schuman, E. (2004). Family therapy and family mediation. *Psychology and Education: An Interdisciplinary Journal, 41*(2), 38–39.

Meditation

DESCRIPTION

This technique draws upon thousands of years of mediation tradition by applying some of its values, skills, and processes as therapeutic resources that can benefit many of our clients.

ORIGINS

The origins of meditation as a form of helping are of course ancient. Its use can be found in all of the world's major religions and cultures. In all its forms, and at all levels, its purposes are to lead to greater inner peace and harmony with self and nature and to develop inner and outer self-control. In its most advanced forms, it becomes an entire lifestyle. To reach such a level, where one has achieved mastery of its more complex philosophy and techniques, can require years of training.

As a result of recent research findings into its efficacy and ability to bring about measurable change in neurological functioning, it has attracted great interest from the helping professions, both as an adjunct to and as an actual form of therapy. Some practitioners have studied this phenomenon intensely, have undergone formal training in meditation and its instruction, and use it as a practice technique. In these situations, meditation becomes the theoretical basis of practice rather than being used as a specific technique along with other techniques.

WHY THIS IS USEFUL TO SOCIAL WORK

It is not possible, of course, to reduce this millennia-old process to merely another social work technique; this would be presumptuous. Rather, we suggest that some of the basic thinking and skills of meditation can be adapted to our practice as a technique.

In our contemporary practice, we meet many hard-driving people whose very intensity leads to problems in physical and psychosocial functioning, as well as in their relationships with others in their various significant social systems. Many clients like this can be helped by teaching them some of the basic concepts and practices of meditation. Much of the current interest in various forms of relaxation come directly or indirectly from some of the basic premises and practices of meditation.

HOW THIS IS USEFUL TO SOCIAL WORK

There are several ways in which social workers have found the use of meditation to be a resource in their spectrum of techniques. At a very basic level, it is useful to be aware of its potency as a method and, hence, a resource we can call upon or introduce to clients whom we deem could benefit from some formal exposure to it. We also meet clients who are interested in a more self-reflective and introspective form of treatment who find that basic meditation practices can be most helpful in learning to turn inward.

Still other social workers have used formal periods of meditation together with the client as a precursor to an interview. This has been particularly effective in working in some group therapy, where the meditation process becomes a part of the group's traditions.

Although other social workers do not directly teach their clients to meditate, they support their clients' efforts to seek such training. Then, during regular interviews, they can use the experience of their meditation practice as a way to focus more intently on some of the life areas that have been sources of stress or difficulty.

Some colleagues who don't use meditation directly in interviews have drawn upon its conceptual views on the effect of a setting on human interaction, involving such things as temperature, furniture, lighting, and clothing, to develop a more therapeutic and welcoming practice environment.

On another level, we have colleagues who do not use meditation directly in practice, but through training have become sufficiently skilled in the process to make it a part of their own self-development. Colleagues who have moved in this direction report that once they have learned to meditate, they are much more able to connect to clients and stay with them, especially for clients with poor relationship skills or whose communication patterns are highly scattered.

RISK FACTORS

In general, this is not a technique with a high risk factor, in that much of the value base and many of its goals (i.e., looking inwards and getting in better touch with others and their environment) fit the overall goals we have for our clients. The risk comes in moving too quickly into introducing meditation procedures in our treatment without adequate training. There is also the risk of seeing meditation as a useful technique for all clients out of our own enthusiasm for its potential, forgetting that this is not a suitable technique for all people both from ability and value perspectives.

REQUIRED SKILLS AND KNOWLEDGE

Because of its demonstrated ability to help, and because meditation is a highly important component of many of the cultures with whom we come in contact in our population of ever-increasing diversity, it is important that we know something of its potential and basic premises, even if we do not use it directly ourselves. Even a preliminary knowledge of the goals and methods of meditation can provide us with a basis for developing procedures to help people relax, slow down, and learn to look inward in a manner very different from the hectic lifestyles many of our clients follow.

Case Summary

Lindsey is a survivor of domestic violence who initially presented for therapy with difficulty concentrating, nervousness, and other anxiety symptoms. Lindsey attends therapy sessions weekly and recently began utilizing meditation as a way to cope with her anxiety symptoms during sessions as well as outside of therapy.

> **SOCIAL WORKER:** What do you think about the use of meditation for coping with anxiety? Has it been helpful to you?
>
> **LINDSEY:** Oh yes, it's been extremely helpful. I think it's a great way for me to relax and clear my mind. I am able to reflect on my life and all the positive things I have in my life when I meditate.
>
> **SOCIAL WORKER:** When do you meditate?
>
> **LINDSEY:** I meditate whenever I feel like I need to. If I am at home and I start feeling overwhelmed or stressed out with life, I stop what I'm doing, take a deep breath, and begin meditating.
>
> **SOCIAL WORKER:** How have you been feeling overall since you started meditating?
>
> **LINDSEY:** I have been feeling wonderful. I feel a new sense of peace about my life. After I meditate I have this feeling of tranquility towards myself and the world around me. I feel I am more in control of myself when I meditate.

Meditation is a technique that Lindsey is able to use during sessions when she needs to, but is also one that she has the ability to perform anytime she feels it is necessary. Time during meditation provides Lindsey with an opportunity that she may not otherwise have to be self-reflective and introspective. It also allows her to feel a sense of calm and tranquility in her life that she had not previously experienced.

Case Summary Two

Jeremy is a 40-year-old man attending therapy sessions because he is unhappy with his life. He reports that about a year ago, his mother and brother convinced him to move with them to a new city. Ever since the move, Jeremy has felt increasingly isolated and angry about his life circumstances.

JEREMY: I don't know why my life is so crummy. I've been dealt a bad hand, I guess.

SOCIAL WORKER: Tell me more about that.

JEREMY: Everyone around me bothers me. I get so frustrated sometimes. I can't stand being around my family. They forced me to move here and I should've never done it. I don't have anything or anyone out here. My entire body gets tense just thinking about it.

SOCIAL WORKER: I can definitely hear the frustration in your voice as you speak. In my experience I've known many people who have benefited from learning the basic concepts and skills of meditation. Meditation can be helpful for relaxation, but also to assist people in looking inward and being more reflective. What do you think about the idea of seeking training in meditation?

JEREMY: I'm open to it. It actually sounds kind of interesting. At this point I'm willing to try anything to feel differently.

[After Jeremy has learned meditation concepts and skills:]

SOCIAL WORKER: How have things been in your life since you started meditating?

JEREMY: Meditating has really given me the time and opportunity to reflect on my life. I've been able to focus on areas of my life that were sources of difficulty for me, and determine what truly caused them and how to avoid them in the future.

SOCIAL WORKER: Let's use the experience of your meditation to focus on these difficult areas you have identified and discuss them further.

Jeremy was having problems in his physical and psychosocial functioning, as well as his personal relationships. Using meditation as a technique in this example led Jeremy to a better development of inner and outer self-control. It provided him with a basis to relax, slow down, and learn to look inward in a manner very different from what he was used to. Additionally, it provided Jeremy and his social worker with a starting point for meaningful therapeutic discussions.

REFERENCES AND ADDITIONAL SOURCES

Baer, R. A. (2003). Mindfulness training as a clinical intervention: A conceptual and empirical review. *Clinical Psychology: Science and Practice, 10*(2), 125–143.

Beauchemin, J., Hutchins, T. L., & Patterson, F. (2008). Mindfulness meditation may lessen anxiety, promote social skills, and improve academic performance among adolescents with learning disabilities. *Complementary Health Practice Review, 13*(1), 34–45.

Bell, L. (2009). Mindful psychotherapy. *Journal of Spirituality in Mental Health, 11*(1–2), 126–144.

Brown, K. W., & Ryan, R. M. (2003). The benefits of being present: Mindfulness and its role in psychological well-being. *Journal of Personality and Social Psychology, 84*(4), 822–848.

Carlson, B. E., & Larkin, H. (2009). Meditation as a coping intervention for treatment of addiction. *Journal of Religion & Spirituality in Social Work, 28*(4), 379–392.

Dreskill, J. G. (1989). Meditation as a therapeutic technique. *Pastoral Psychology, 38*(2), 83–103.

Dezerotes, D. (2000). Evaluation of yoga and meditation training with adolescent sex offenders. *Child and Adolescent Social Work Journal, 17*(2), 97–113.

Fredrickson, B. L., Cohn, M. A., Coffey, K. A., Pek, J., & Finkel, S. M. (2008). Open hearts build lives: Positive emotions, induced through loving-kindness meditation, build consequential personal resources. *Journal of Personality & Social Psychology, 95*(5), 1045–1062.

Kabat-Zinn, J. (2005). *Coming to our senses: Healing ourselves and the world through mindfulness.* New York, NY: Hyperion.

Keefe, T. (1996). Meditation and social work treatment. In F. J. Turner (Ed.), *Social work treatment* (pp. 434–460). New York, NY: Free Press.

Miller, J., Fletcher, K., & Kabat-Zinn, J. (1995).Three year follow-up and clinical implications of a mindfulness meditation-based stress reduction intervention in the treatment of anxiety disorders. *General Hospital Psychiatry, 17*(3), 192–200.

Shapiro, S. L., & Walsh, R. (2003). An analysis of recent meditation research and suggestions for future directions. *Humanistic Psychologist, 31*(2–3), 86–114.

Wolf, D., & Abbell, N. (2003). Examining the effects of meditation techniques on psychosocial functioning. *Research on Social Work Practice, 13*(1), 27–42.

Zamparo, J. (2005). Meditation. In F. Turner (Ed.), *Encyclopedia of Canadian social work* (pp. 233–234). Waterloo, Ontario: Wilfrid Laurier University Press.

48

Meeting Skills

DESCRIPTION

The technique being considered here is one where we can achieve specific therapeutic goals for our client through our adeptness in participating in or chairing meetings held in our client's interest.

ORIGINS

From the earliest days of the profession, our psychosocial base has led us to be involved in many societal systems that are a part of our clients' lives. Because of the nature of our service network and of society's bureaucratic structure, we frequently deal with client issues through the medium of meetings.

Over our history, however, there has been an unfortunate tendency to divide practice into micro and macro interests. One of the outcomes of this division is that useful intervention techniques also get dichotomized. In this way, meeting skills are often seen more as an administrative function than one that can directly influence the achievement of designated psychosocial goals.

Therefore, many clinicians do not view their participation in meetings as a technique that requires specific knowledge and skills to ensure they are getting the most out of them for their client. Colleagues whose practice is directed more toward macro issues well understand the necessity of meeting skills as a necessary part of their spectrum of techniques.

The impact of systems theory on the profession has helped clinicians to understand the importance of meetings as systems that do in fact have an impact upon the lives of our clients, and the need to view these systems as a component of our therapeutic activities. Thus, skill in the technique of managing meetings needs to be recognized as a useful therapeutic technique.

WHY THIS IS USEFUL TO SOCIAL WORK

Meeting skills are important in our practice because much of our clients' lives is influenced by the many societal systems that impinge on their psychosocial functioning. Amid this complexity, many critical decisions are made, resources allotted or denied, and critical child-welfare choices agreed upon within the medium of meetings.

Because of the socially oriented nature of our theories and practice, much of our work involves an understanding of the person's social reality, even when the principal focus is on individual therapy. The implication is we need to understand the many and complex interactions among our clients' societal systems. In so doing, we need to be alert to the possibility of finding assistance in these same social networks.

This inevitably requires us both to understand a person's network as well as the available sources of assistance outside that network, and, when appropriate, to become involved in them in an interpersonal way. Often this takes place in the format of a meeting. Hence, we need to develop the skill to function within the setting and dynamics of a meeting structure.

HOW THIS IS USEFUL TO SOCIAL WORK

The psychosocial base of social work clinical practice implies involvement in the client's life beyond the interviewing room in many ways, including attending various meetings on their behalf. In such instances, we may be present as a member of a committee, sometimes as chair and other times as an outsider. How successfully we function in these instances, and how we present the issues that involve our client, will depend to a great extent on our understanding of the nature and function of meetings.

We may meet with an agency to obtain support for a specific resource or to formally consult with colleagues about some aspect of the case. Similarly, we may consult with another resource for some form of resource or assistance. A meeting may involve several agencies or community bodies who have been involved or whom we hope to involve in a case. A meeting may also involve such aspects as finding the best way to work together with other resources, or to clarify some aspect of a particular service; or it may be a situation where we lobby on behalf of a particular client or group of clients with whom we are working.

RISK FACTORS

The level of risk to the client or worker is low. The exception to this arises in situations where our lack of knowledge about correct procedures, or our inability to perceive the meeting's dynamics, results in failure to achieve the goal we are seeking. In such situations, decisions that are detrimental to the client are often made.

REQUIRED SKILLS AND KNOWLEDGE

Several formal sets of rules and procedures for conducting meetings have emerged over the years to facilitate committees' work. *Robert's Rules of Order* is probably the best known such set in this part of the world.

It is not necessary that we know every rule for conducting meetings. Rather, it is more important to have a general knowledge of the way a meeting is to be run, to ensure that all the matters relating to our client are clearly presented, heard, and understood, and that there is no inappropriate control of particular agenda items. However, we will greatly improve our chances of achieving our goals for the client by knowing the rules and how to use the procedures associated with them. Useful as such procedures in helping meetings achieve their goal, such procedures can also be used in a way to ensure that a meeting does not achieve its ends. Even though we as social workers spend a great deal of time in various kinds of meetings, being competent in their conduct is something we often take for granted. Most of us have been involved in meetings that were poorly conducted, or where the presenter of a particular issue was either unprepared or presented it poorly, often to a client's detriment.

It is not only knowledge of the rules of procedure that assist in making this technique useful in our practice. We also need also to be sensitive to group dynamics. In addition, we need to assess and tap the positives of the group's growth and development as a group.

The mistake most frequently made from the perspective of this technique is to overlook or be unaware of the overall group dynamic in a particular situation, so that rules of order get used in a manner that interferes with the group's overall functioning.

Case Summary One

Jessica is a stay-at-home mom of two children and has been married for 5 years. Over the last year, Jessica's husband has increasingly abused her physically. Jessica has finally made the decision to leave her husband, and has asked her social worker for help with her situation. Jessica will need a place to live, employment, child care, and legal assistance to obtain a divorce. The social worker suggested having a team meeting that will include family members, friends, and community members who can become her support system. Jessica invited her mom, Vicky, and her sister, Natalie, because they are the only family members who still live nearby, and her friend, Stacey, who lives in the same town and is also a stay-at-home mom. The social worker also invited a few community members who could possibly provide resources or services for Jessica and her children.

SOCIAL WORKER: Thank you all for attending this meeting. We are here to discuss Jessica's current needs and resources that can be provided. Based on the information that you have given me regarding your needs, I have invited Mr. Smith from the community center that provides assistance in situations of domestic violence, and Mrs. Davis from the local women's shelter. Jessica, what would you say is your most immediate need?

JESSICA: The first thing that I need is a place for me and my children to live.

SOCIAL WORKER: Mrs. Davis, would you like to tell Jessica about the shelter?

MRS. DAVIS: Sure, we are a shelter specifically for women and children. It is a safe environment and we currently have space available to accommodate you and your children.

VICKY: I also have room for you and the children at my house, but I work full time so I won't be able to help with child care once you start working.

STACEY: I could probably help with that. I'm home with my son during the day. It would be no problem to watch your children, too.

SOCIAL WORKER: Jessica, what do you think about that?

JESSICA: That sounds great. I need help finding a job, though.

SOCIAL WORKER: Mr. Smith, could you tell Jessica about your program at the community center, please?

MR. SMITH: Of course. We work with individuals who have been a victim of domestic violence, and part of our services includes GED courses and job training, if needed. We also help prepare resumes and practice interviewing skills. In addition, our program can provide legal services for our clients.

Meeting skills were a very important contribution to this situation. Using these skills made it possible for the social worker to bring each potential source of support for Jessica together at one time. By meeting them in a group, Jessica was able to hear about all of her options for resources at the same time. Having everyone come together to help Jessica also allowed her to realize that she was not alone in her situation, and empowered her to do what she needed to do to meet her goals of safety and self-sufficiency.

Case Summary Two

Ryan is a 12-year-old boy attending therapy sessions to reduce the verbally and physically aggressive behavior he displays at home and school and in the community. Ryan's teachers and coaches have told his mom that his behavior is starting to escalate, and they are concerned that if he keeps going along this path, he is going to end up getting multiple suspensions and possibly get expelled from school. Ryan's social worker, Mr. Smith, is attending a meeting at Ryan's school to determine how everyone involved can best support Ryan and help him be successful in school.

TEACHER: Thank you for attending this meeting, Mr. Smith. We have some concerns about Ryan's behavior at school that we wanted to make sure you were aware of. It seems Ryan has become increasingly agitated with his peers at school. We are trying to intervene now before something happens that would require a suspension.

SOCIAL WORKER: I am happy to attend this meeting for Ryan. We have been meeting weekly for therapy sessions for a few weeks now. During the past few sessions we have been building rapport, getting to know each other better, and formulating our therapeutic goals. We are beginning to work on decreasing the verbally and physically aggressive behavior that is being seen. Can you give me some examples of what you see at school?

TEACHER: Often he is getting into verbal arguments with peers, which lately have been on the verge of becoming physical. Also, he seems to be more and more frustrated at school and has had a few episodes of throwing items in the classroom. We have some ideas we'd like to share and we would love to hear any thoughts that you have.

SOCIAL WORKER: As Ryan and I are meeting weekly to work towards achieving Ryan's therapeutic goals, I think it would be extremely beneficial for Ryan to have additional support while he is in school. Perhaps he could spend some time each week with the guidance counselor and school social worker outside of the classroom.

SCHOOL SOCIAL WORKER: That's what we were thinking also. I would like to start meeting with Ryan as needed during the school week to talk and problem solve.

GUIDANCE COUNSELOR: I would like to meet with Ryan for a few minutes each morning before school starts just to check in and remind him to make good choices throughout the school day.

The meeting continued and the school staff, Ryan's parents, and Ryan's social worker collaborated to determine the best interventions to help Ryan be successful in school. By attending and appropriately functioning in Ryan's school meeting, his social worker was better able to understand Ryan's interactions within the school system. It also provided Ryan's social worker with the opportunity to gain assistance in supporting Ryan while he works to achieve his therapeutic goals.

REFERENCES AND ADDITIONAL SOURCES

Barretta-Herman, A. (1990). The effective social service staff meeting. In F. Slegio (Ed.), *Business communication: New Zealand perspectives* (pp. 136–147). Auckland, New Zealand: Software Technology.

Dimeff, L. A., Koerner, K., & Linehan, M. M. (2007). *Dialectical behavior therapy in clinical practice: Applications across disorders and settings*. New York, NY: Guilford.

Frey, A. (2002). Enhancing children's social skills through classroom meetings. *School Social Work Journal, 26*(2), 46–57.

Nelson, E. C., Batalden, P. B., & Godfrey, M. M. (Eds.). (2007). *Quality by design: A clinical microsystems approach* (pp. 243–257, 321–330). San Francisco, CA: Jossey-Bass.

Robert, H. E. (1990). *Robert's rules of order* (9th ed.). Glenview, IL: Scott, Foresman.

Miracle Question

DESCRIPTION

In this technique, the client is asked during the interview to imagine that a miracle has taken place at some point in his or her current life—for example, while asleep. The make-believe miracle is that, while they were asleep, their most serious problem has been solved. Having identified the problem that was solved, the client is then asked to focus on and talk about how their life would be different if such a miracle had in fact taken place. The client is asked not to focus upon why their life would be different, but rather upon how it would be different: what aspects of their life situation would change, and how such changes would affect them and others around them. They are then asked to think about steps they can start taking to bring about the changes that stem from the miracle.

ORIGINS

This technique originally emerged from the solution-focused therapy literature. Much of its conceptual base also reflects the thinking of task-centered therapy. This type of technique focuses on the client's cognitive and behavioral abilities. In and of itself, the miracle question technique does not lead to expanded awareness, at least initially, but rather helps the client identify things they can do in their lives that will bring about change in a manner beneficial to them.

The miracle question technique reflects an understanding that many clients in a variety of situations are, with help, able to take charge of certain areas of their lives. This is done by tapping their ability to solve problems by finding solutions that are within their abilities and resources. It therefore builds on the client's own abilities and skills.

WHY THIS IS USEFUL TO PRACTICE

The miracle question fits well into much of the current thinking about therapy. It builds on the understanding that many of the psychosocial problems our clients face can be addressed by having the client build upon their resources and abilities. Much of our work in this sort of cognitive, task-focused approach builds clients' strengths with the aim of helping them see ways to break large problems in their lives into smaller ones, which they can then manage themselves. It is a type of technique that leads the client to focus on things they are able to do to bring about desired change. It is not an approach that leads to enhanced self-awareness of things related to one's developmental history. Rather, it emphasizes a future-looking approach to reality, with a focus on what clients can do to bring about the kinds of change in their life they seek.

HOW THIS IS USEFUL TO PRACTICE

Not everyone will benefit from the miracle question technique. It can be of great assistance to those who are functioning well overall and have good cognitive skills who need assistance in getting their lives in order. As some order begins to emerge in how they understand their lives, a new process of strategy building and objective setting takes place. Often clients can move on to take greater responsibility for themselves in identifying and seeking realistic solutions to their psychosocial realities.

This technique reflects a positive, goal-oriented approach to clients' particular situations. Its orientation toward the future stresses that problems and their solutions are frequently based on an understanding of the present and in identifying what realistically can be done about them to enhance the future. It has a high expectation of client involvement in setting and carrying out identified objectives.

The miracle question technique leads clients to focus on solutions rather than problems, and to begin to see ways in which some of the sought-after solutions might be achieved. It is only used occasionally in particular cases where the client seems to be stuck while trying to sort out their lives.

RISK FACTORS

The miracle question technique has a minimal degree of risk. Certainly, it is not a technique that will be understood by or appeal to all clients, and perhaps in extreme situations could be so unacceptable to a client seeking a different form of help that they would withdraw from treatment. Some view this technique as having an off-putting fringe or theatrical quality to it. It can also move a client too quickly toward potential behavioral changes for which they are not ready. It is also the type of technique about which we can get enthusiastic but often does not fit the client's value set or expectations for therapy.

SKILLS AND KNOWLEDGE

As with so many other techniques, the decision to use the miracle question technique requires two important assessments. First, we need to be sure that it will fit the client's value set and perceived manner of approaching problems. Second, we must ensure that the type of problems or difficulties the client faces do lend themselves to this type of approach. For example, it may well be that the client still needs to do a great deal of work on past material before he or she is ready to approach their reality in this form of problem-solving strategy.

Case Summary One

Buddy is a college student who started attending therapy sessions because he was worried about what his peers thought of him. Buddy and his social worker have previously discussed this problem of worry. He reports having trouble sleeping and difficulty concentrating on his studies because he is so nervous and worried that others might not like him. During this session, after reviewing what Buddy identified as his problem, Buddy's social worker decided to ask him the miracle question.

SOCIAL WORKER: Suppose while you are sleeping tonight, a miracle happens and the problem that brought you here is solved. However, because you were sleeping you did not know that this miracle occurred. When you wake up the next morning, how will your life be different so that you know the miracle occurred and the problem that brought you here is gone?

BUDDY: I would know that the problem was solved and a miracle occurred because I would feel happy, I would fall asleep easily and sleep eight hours a night, and I would enjoy time with my friends without feeling awkward.

SOCIAL WORKER: Now, let's think about this wonderful miracle. Let's identify a small piece of this miracle which will be a sure sign that things are moving in the right direction.

BUDDY: Well, I guess my first small miracle would be falling asleep easily at night.

SOCIAL WORKER: What are some steps that you think you can take to fall asleep easily?

BUDDY: I can try lying in my bed feeling relaxed and counting backwards from one hundred. Also, I can turn off my television a little earlier than usual to see if that helps.

SOCIAL WORKER: Those are great ideas, Buddy. Over the next week, I would like you to note those nights that you find yourself able to fall asleep easily and we will discuss your small miracles during the next session.

In this example, Buddy and his social worker are working together to achieve Buddy's proposed solution to his self-identified problem. Using the miracle question allowed Buddy to take control over his life instead of feeling like his problem is controlling him. The miracle question provided Buddy with an opportunity to visualize a range of problem-solving possibilities. Using the miracle question as a technique will allow Buddy to establish small steps toward achieving the changes necessary to bring about his solution.

Case Summary Two

Carissa has met with her social worker only a few times. Carissa describes herself as a generally negative and pessimistic person. She states that she is easily frustrated and snaps at anyone and everyone who annoys her. Carissa even told her social worker that some days she just tries to avoid people all together so that she doesn't have to feel angry or upset those around her. During today's session her social worker has decided to use the miracle question as a technique to focus on positive solutions rather than her current problems.

SOCIAL WORKER: Imagine that you go home tonight and while you are asleep, a miracle occurs. The miracle is that the problem you brought here is gone. However, since this miracle happened while you were asleep you didn't know that the miracle occurred. When you woke up the next morning, how would you know that the miracle happened and your problem was gone?

CARISSA: I wouldn't feel angry and negative all day long.

SOCIAL WORKER: What else would tell you that things were different or better?

CARISSA: I would enjoy being around others. I would feel glad when someone started a conversation with me.

SOCIAL WORKER: What would others notice about you that would tell them that the miracle occurred?

CARISSA: My parents would probably notice a smile on my face more often. My friends would probably notice that I was going out more and talking about life in a more positive manner.

SOCIAL WORKER: What do you think can be done right now to start talking about life in a more positive manner?

CARISSA: I tend to complain about things a lot. I guess it would be helpful to focus on the things I am thankful for and the aspects of life that I truly enjoy more often.

Using the miracle question as a technique in this example helped Carissa to identify things she can do in her life that will bring about beneficial changes. This technique provided Carissa with an opportunity to find solutions to her problem by building on her strengths and abilities through problem solving. It assisted her in breaking her large problem into smaller chunks so it was easier to take charge and make changes in her life. By gradually increasing these positive changes, she will slowly decrease the frequency of her negative situations.

REFERENCES AND ADDITIONAL SOURCES

Berg, I. K., & Miller, S. D. (1992). *Working with the problem drinker: A solution-focused approach*. New York, NY: Norton.

Christensen, D. N., Todahl, J., & Barrett, W. C. (1999). *Solution-based casework: An introduction to clinical and case management skills in casework practice*. New York, NY: Aldine De Gruyter.

Corcoran, J. (2002). An integrative framework for solution-focused and cognitive-behavioral therapy: A case application of adolescent depression and suicide. In A. R. Roberts & G. J. Greene (Eds.), *Social workers' desk reference* (pp. 591–598). Oxford, England: Oxford University Press.

De, J. P. (1995). How to interview for client strengths. *Social Work, 40*(6), 729–736.

Ferraz, H., & Wellman, N. (2009). Fostering a culture of engagement: An evaluation of a 2-day training in solution-focused brief therapy for mental health workers. *Journal of Psychiatric & Mental Health Nursing, 16*(4), 326–334.

Gingerich, W. J., & Eisengart, S. (2000). Solution-focused brief therapy: A review of the outcome research. *Family Process, 39*(4), 477–498.

Greene, G. J., Lee, M., Mentzer, R. A., Pinnell, S. R., & Niles, D. (1998). Miracles, dreams, and empowerment: A brief therapy practice note. *Families in Society, 79*(4), 395–399.

Hollingsworth, L. D., Allen-Meares, P., Shanks, T. R., & Gant, L. M. (2009). Using the miracle question in community engagement and planning. *Families in Society, 90*(3), 332–335.

Hurn, R. (2003). Butterflies in possibility land: An example of the miracle question when counselling briefly. *Counselling Psychology Review, 18*(4), 17–27.

Lethem, J. (2002). Brief solution focused therapy. *Child and Adolescent Mental Health, 7*(4), 189–192.

Nickerson, P. R. (1995). Solution-focused group therapy. *Social Work, 40*(1), 132–133.

Rosenberg, B. (2000). Mandated clients and solution focused therapy: "It's not my miracle." *Journal of Systemic Therapies, 19*(1), 90–99.

Santa Rita, E. J. (1998). What do you do after asking the miracle question in solution-focused therapy? *Family Therapy, 25*(3), 189–195.

Shilts, L., & Gordon, A. B. (1996). What to do after the miracle occurs. *Journal of Family Psychotherapy, 7*(1), 15–22.

Strong, T., & Pyle, N. R. (2009). Constructing a conversational "miracle": Examining the "miracle question" as it is used in therapeutic dialogue. *Journal of Constructivist Psychology, 22*(4), 328–353.

Money

DESCRIPTION

Giving money to a client can be viewed both as a goal of the service being provided to a client, and as a specific action to facilitate a particular therapeutic goal. It is in this latter use that we consider it here as a technique.

ORIGINS

Providing money to clients was one of the first services of our social work colleagues before the profession was formally established. In those days, a charity worker's principal function was to collect and pass on to clients deemed to be "worthy" the funds they needed for their physical requirements. This giving was usually accompanied by some form of moral suasion. As mentioned in the food technique (Chapter 32), the 19th-century social worker thus had a popular image as "Lady Bountiful," a disperser of funds provided by others. In those times, giving money was the service being provided, not a clinical technique as we understand it today.

Over the decades, giving money to clients as a component of clinical practice was seen as something to be avoided. It was perceived that such giving would create unhealthy dependency and seriously jeopardize the professional relationship. Social workers viewed this dependency as being associated with the transference issues thought to be a part of all professional relationships.

WHY THIS IS USEFUL TO SOCIAL WORK

As we became more sophisticated in our theoretical perspectives, and much more open and sensitive to the range of factors that can help people grow and develop, we became much more comfortable with the idea that there were some goals a social worker could achieve through the judicious use of money. In many ways, systems theory, with its insights into the principles of multifinality and equifinality, has greatly helped us to understand that sought-after changes in therapy could be achieved in various ways.

HOW THIS IS USEFUL TO SOCIAL WORK

One of the most important factors in using money as a therapeutic tool is the need to understand just how the client perceives money. This is a very complex question that relates to the client's history and cultural identity, as well as the roles money has played in the significant relationships in the client's life. Some will view money as a symbol of power, others as a way of purchasing affection, and still others as a reminder of deprivation of early basic needs. Some will also view money or the lack of it as a symbol of success or failure.

More generally, money has different implications for clients from cultural, ethnic, and historical origins different from our own. Thus for some clients, the idea of money having any role in a therapeutic relationship would be totally unacceptable, whereas for others it is an expected and available resource.

In spite of the potential complications around the use of money in treatment, there are times in therapeutic situations where providing funds for a specific purpose can be a powerfully influential technique. Money can be used to provide a treat for a person who has never or rarely had such a thing happen to them. It can be a concrete indicator to the client of the worker's caring, concern, and understanding. Money can be a tremendous stress reliever for a person unable to meet some particular need. It can permit a client to take an important step forward in their developmental journey that might not be possible at that particular time in their life. Recently, there have been news reports about using money successfully being used as a reward for those attempting to stop smoking or break a drug habit.

RISK FACTORS

The use of money as a technique is a high-risk undertaking, requiring considerable diagnostic skill. As suggested for the gift technique (Chapter 35), using money this way carries the risk of creating inappropriate dependencies in clients, which could damage the therapeutic relationship and hinder the social worker's goals and objectives of the situation. Crossing the line from the professional to the personal is one of the biggest risks inherent in this technique. The source of the money also needs to be addressed. This is a particular challenge for a social worker in private practice, where the division between one's personal and professional resources is much less clear. Additionally, we need to understand our own perceptions and history in relation to money to ensure that, by providing money to a client, we are not seeking to meet our own needs.

Even though it is risky, it is a technique that needs to be considered because of its positive potential in our practice.

REQUIRED SKILLS AND KNOWLEDGE

As mentioned, the most important skill required in using this technique is to understand our own values, attitudes, and behavior in regard to money, as well as the client's. In dispensing whatever funds we decide to give, we must be clear with the client regarding any overt or implied expectations of repayment. For some clients it will be very important that the money be returned; for others this may not be an issue. What is important is that there be a clear understanding about this matter.

Case Summary One

Denise is a wife and mother who reports that she is so caught up in her family life that she never has time for herself. She states that she is always taking care of others and constantly putting their needs first. As part of her treatment goals, she would like to learn how to take time for herself.

SOCIAL WORKER: Denise, you have expressed a desire to take time for yourself, which is very important when you are taking care of a family. You must be able to take care of yourself to be able to adequately care for your family members.

DENISE: I completely agree. Sometimes I feel so burned out that I get angry and resentful. I love my family so much. I just want to do what is best for all of us.

SOCIAL WORKER: Before I give you your homework assignment, I am curious. How often do you spend money on yourself compared to others?

DENISE: I can't even remember the last time I bought something for myself. It seems like there is always someone else the money needs to be spent on.

SOCIAL WORKER: As part of your homework assignment this week, I am going to give you ten dollars on behalf of my agency. Your job is to schedule time this week that is designated just for you to do something that you enjoy. During this time you are to spend this ten dollars only on you. You can choose to spend it any way you'd like, whether it is buying a latte while hanging out at the coffee shop with a friend, or purchasing a book you've been looking forward to reading. What do you think about that?

DENISE: It is definitely not something I'm used to, but it sounds exciting. I can't wait to report back on what I decide to do.

In this case, money is being used as a way to facilitate Denise's goal of making time for herself as a way to take care of her needs, so she can take better care of her family. This gesture also showed Denise that her social worker understood her dilemma and cared about her and her well-being, which made her want to take care of herself even more. Additionally, the fact that the money was given to her by the social worker's agency and was part of a homework assignment eased her sense of guilt in telling her family that she would be unavailable to them for a designated period of time.

Case Summary Two

Jared is a young adult who has been attending therapy sessions for a couple of months. He recently moved to a new state to attend the university. This is his first time living on his own and so far away from his family, and he is having difficulty with the transition. Jared is attending therapy sessions to ease his anxieties and decrease his overwhelming feelings.

JARED: I haven't been able to do much in regards to our therapeutic work, because I've been so worried about my water getting turned off.

SOCIAL WORKER: What's been going on that's led to your water being in jeopardy of getting turned off?

JARED: My hours were reduced at work, so I haven't been taking home as much money as I am used to. I am working on finding a part-time job to make up for the time I'm losing at my current job. In the meantime I'm having trouble paying all of my bills.

SOCIAL WORKER: My agency has certain funds that are available for situations like these. How would you feel if my agency provided you with the money to keep your water from getting shut off?

JARED: That would be fine with me. It would be great actually. That would relieve a lot of the stress and worry that I have right now.

SOCIAL WORKER: I'm glad to hear that. This will be a one-time payment for your current water bill. This money is being given to you by the agency and it does not have to get paid back.

JARED: Wow, thank you so much. I'm really struggling right now and this will help so much. Plus, I won't have to worry about my water getting shut off so I can focus more time and energy on our therapeutic work.

Money as a technique was used in this example to help Jared pay his water bill. Providing for Jared's basic needs relieves a stressor in his life and allows him to focus on other aspects of his life including his treatment. Having the money to pay his water bill before it was shut off helped him to feel empowered and cared for. It permitted him to take an important step toward his treatment goal that otherwise would not have happened.

REFERENCES AND ADDITIONAL SOURCES

Allen, A. (1971). The fee as a therapeutic tool. *Psychoanalytic Quarterly, 40,* 132–140.

Barth, F. D. (2001). Money as a tool for negotiating separateness and connectedness in the therapeutic relationship. *Clinical Social Work Journal, 29*(1), 79–94.

Borneman, E. (1976). *The psychoanalysis of money.* New York, NY: Urizen.

Burnside, M., & Krueger, D. (Eds.). (1986). Fee practices of male and female social workers. In *The fast taboo: Money as symbol and reality in psychotherapy and psychoanalysis* (pp. 48–54). New York, NY: Brunner/Mazel.

Herron, W., & Welt, S. (1992). *Money matters: The fee in psychotherapy and psychoanalysis.* New York, NY: Guilford.

Klebenow, S. (1991). Power, gender, and money. In S. Klebanow & E. L. Lowenkopf (Eds.), *Money and minds* (pp. 3–14). New York, NY: Plenum.

Needleman, J. (1991). *Money and the meaning of life.* New York, NY: Doubleday.

Sitkowski, S., & Herron, W. G. (1991). Attitudes of social workers and their patients toward money. *Psychotherapy in Private Practice, 8*(4), 27–37.

Tracktman, R. (1999). The money taboo. Its effects in everyday life and in the practice of psychotherapy. *Clinical Social Work Journal, 27*(3), 275–288.

Warner, S. L. (1989). Sigmund Freud and money. *Journal of the American Academy of Psychoanalysis, 17*(4), 609–622.

Office Setting

DESCRIPTION

As a technique, paying attention to the office setting in which we interview is based on the premise that the physical qualities of our offices are important, and when these are sensitively addressed they can strongly affect the client's comfort, sense of security, perception of professional competence, and, to some extent, the degree to which he or she participates in the therapeutic process.

ORIGINS

We view the general topic of the office setting as a technique in that it is something that is a part of treatment and is observable, replicable, and (within limits) variable. Because it is a part of our client's significant environment, we thus consider it a part of treatment. Social workers previously have not paid a great deal of attention to this topic, except to recognize the general importance of such things as comfort and privacy. For some complex sociocultural reasons we seem to have assumed that our interviewing skills were sufficient, and any attention to other factors was not necessary or might even smack of needless luxury that our client could indeed find offensive.

WHY THIS IS USEFUL TO SOCIAL WORK

As members of a profession with a strong psychosocial orientation, we know that many factors in a client's environments affect their degree of comfort and their ability to function in various settings. Hence, if we are able to shape a setting in a manner that contributes to a client's sense of well-being, security, and readiness to be helped by attending to our physical environment, then we can facilitate the therapeutic process.

HOW THIS IS USEFUL TO SOCIAL WORK

We will make some general observations about the office setting, and then mention a few specific factors about which colleagues have spoken. There are many components that go into making an office an optimal therapeutic setting, including the color of the walls; the nature and placement of furniture; the use and type of pictures; the kind of flooring; the critical factors of lighting, temperature, and humidity; the use or nonuse of the accoutrements of our profession such as degrees, books, and honors we have received; the type of equipment we need to have in the office according to the nature of our practice; and the degree of flexibility in regard to seating. All these variables go into creating a sense of comfort, security, and confidentiality for the client, and also ensure our own security.

RISK FACTORS

Apart from the often overlooked question of confidentiality and the more modern issue of worker safety, there are no serious risks in the general techniques related to our basic office facilities. Rather, it seems to be more a question of a lack of sensitivity on our part, by failing to appreciate how important these factors are and how addressing them can bring our clients an expanded sense of comfort.

REQUIRED SKILLS AND KNOWLEDGE

One of the important challenges in regard to this cluster of techniques relates to our growing understanding that clients have large and differential perceptions about what conveys the professional and helping qualities that we wish to offer. Even such things as how close to sit to a client, where to sit, and whether to interview from behind a desk or not are all important variables to clients.

Therefore, one of the initial qualities we desire for our interviewing space is a convenient and high degree of flexibility. We know the importance of environmental variables in our personal lives, but we do not seem to consider them important in our practice, even though there are large bodies of knowledge, expertise, and skill in the area of office design. Although most social work theories do not speak in much detail about the physical settings in which we interview, such things as comfort and security for both the social worker and the client are taken for granted as necessary attributes.

In working to achieve these essential qualities, one of the most important of course is clients' privacy. This privacy not only has to be present but also must appear to be present. The concept of privacy has several dimensions. For instance, not only do we want to ensure that sound inside the room doesn't go beyond its walls, but also that the client cannot hear sounds from outside them. These are distracting and can lessen the client's assurance that what goes on in the office is private. Although it should go without saying, interruptions, either by people or phone calls, should be prohibited (apart from emergencies, as sometimes happens).

Office furniture is also an important factor. There should be sufficient furniture to permit some choice to the client as to where to sit and on what. The furniture also should be of good quality, both from the perspective of comfort and appearance, for clients as well as ourselves.

Although some colleagues suggest that a desk is a deterrent to fostering a relationship, because the client views it as a sign of power and a distancing mechanism, a desk or table can be very useful. It should be placed in a manner that reduces the barrier effect, but still permits some distance when needed.

The desk is not always a deterrent for clients; it may also serve as an important perceived source of protection. This may be very important for them, especially in the early phases of contact, until the treatment process has been tested and is under way, at which time the client might become comfortable with a less formal arrangement.

The colors in the room should convey calm and professionalism. Considerable attention needs to be given to lighting. Lamps are much better than overhead lighting, especially the fluorescent lights so common in many North American offices.

Clean and easily accessible washrooms are important, with the assurance that the client knows where they are and has access to them without others knowing they are being used.

The temperature of the room should be subject to control and adjusted to suit the client. Also, any materials we may need, such as forms or referral slips, testing materials, and the like need to be close at hand, as well as materials such as directories of information about frequently used services. No other clients' records are to be visible!

There should be a phone at hand in the event the client or social worker needs to use it. Obviously, it needs to be one that can be set not to ring during the interview. There should also be a visible clock and writing materials for both parties, and a mirror somewhere near the exit, for people to check their appearance before leaving, especially after emotionally laden interviews.

We need to remember that we can quickly get accustomed to various physical features of our lives and cease to appreciate the possible limitations or deficits in our interview rooms. In general, we know that these things can powerfully influence human behavior, and are thus topics that should be given more than minimal attention. Hence, we need to continuously assess the varying impact of our offices on particular clients, and ensure that we can incorporate the necessary level of flexibility.

Although we have not ordinarily considered the physical setting of our interviews as a technique, because our offices are a component of the clients' environment that we can control, and because the characteristics of our offices can impact clients differently, our ability to modify these factors to suit individual clients and influence our interviews makes them techniques.

Case Summary One

Mary has started seeing a social worker. This is her second visit to his office. During this session, Mary's social worker is continuing to gather psychosocial information and is trying to gain a sense of what Mary's childhood and family life were like growing up.

SOCIAL WORKER: Mary, I would like to gather some background information from you so that I may get to know you a little better. Tell me, what your family was like growing up?

MARY: I have two brothers and my parents divorced when I was five. The three of us spent most of our childhood being shuttled back and forth from my mom's house or dad's house. I don't have many happy childhood memories.

SOCIAL WORKER: Tell me more about that.

MARY: You know, I usually feel tense and nervous when I start talking about my family history. Your office is just such a nonthreatening environment that I feel comfortable enough to open up to you.

SOCIAL WORKER: I'm glad my office helps you feel at ease enough to talk to me. What do you like about it?

MARY: The paint color in here makes the space seem so warm and inviting. Also, these chairs are so comfortable, they help me feel relaxed, which helps to relieve the stress I normally feel.

SOCIAL WORKER: Are you able to continue talking to me about your family?

MARY: Sure, what would you like to know?

Mary becomes very nervous when she starts talking about her childhood. She usually finds it hard to get her story out. However, her social worker's consideration of his office space has produced an environment that helps Mary feel calm and comfortable enough to speak to him.

Case Summary Two

Kenny is a 7-year-old boy who has been meeting with a social worker for several weeks. For the first few sessions, Kenny and his social worker have been engaging in play therapy. During the play therapy sessions, the social worker kept the office bright using overhead lighting so the two could better participate in therapeutic games and play. However, for today's session the social worker wants to teach Kenny coping and relaxation skills. The social worker has prepared his office for the session by turning off the overhead lighting and turning on a desk lamp and a floor lamp to light the room.

KENNY: Hey, something is different. It's usually brighter than this in here.

SOCIAL WORKER: Yes, Kenny, you are correct. The lighting is a little different today because we are going to do some different activities than we usually do.

KENNY: What are we going to do?

SOCIAL WORKER: We are going to learn and practice different ways to keep our bodies calm and relaxed. What do you think about that?

KENNY: That sounds good. This is definitely the right lighting to keep a person calm and relaxed.

In this example, the social worker used his office setting as a technique to facilitate feelings of calm and relaxation in Kenny. Whereas Kenny was used to the bright lights and high-energy playtime of the office space, the dimmer lighting set the tone for him to feel calm and behave in a similar manner. The social worker was able to modify the setting of his office to a style that helped Kenny achieve an aspect of his therapy.

REFERENCES AND ADDITIONAL SOURCES

Brookes, M. J., & Kaplan, A. (1972). The office environment: Space planning and affective behavior. *Human Factors, 14*(5), 373–391.

Dhillon, A. M., & Davis, H. (1985). Socialization, locus of control, and dogmatism as related to counsellors' office settings. *Psychological Reports, 56*(1), 328–330.

Elsbach, K. D. (2004). Interpreting workplace identities: The role of office décor. *Journal of Organizational Behavior, 25*(1), 99–128. doi:10.1002/job.233

Knez, I., & Enmarker, I. (1998). Effects of office lighting on mood and cognitive performance and a gender effect in work-related judgment. *Environment and Behavior, 30*(4), 553–567.

Lambe, L. (1995). Gardening a multisensory experience. In J. Hogg & J. Court (Eds.), *Making leisure provision for people with profound learning and multiple disabilities* (pp. 160–177). London, England: Chapman & Hall.

Mandel, D. R., Baron, R. M., & Fisher, J. D. (1980). Room utilization and dimensions of density: Effects of height and view. *Environment and Behavior, 12*(3), 308–319.

Manning, P. (1965). *Office design: A study of environment.* Liverpool, England: University of Liverpool.

Perry, C. W. (2002). *Basic counselling technique: A beginning social worker's toolkit.* Bloomington, IN: First Books Library.

Pliska, S. (2005, November-December). Helping to heal: Therapeutic garden design. *Interscope Magazine,* 16–22.

Spreckelmeyer, K. F. (1993). Office relocation and environmental change: A case study. *Environment and Behavior, 25*(2), 181–204.

Paradox

DESCRIPTION

The use of paradox, sometimes called paradoxical directives, is a technique in which we ask the client to think about or even do things that appear to contradict the overall goals of our intervention.

ORIGINS

Credit is given to Victor Frankl, the existentialist, for its development as a technique. It is a technique that in itself appears to be a paradox from the perspective of what we are attempting to accomplish in treatment. Although emerging from a discrete body of theory, it is best viewed atheoretically.

WHY THIS IS USEFUL TO SOCIAL WORK

Helping clients to do the very opposite of some symptom or behavior that they are trying to eliminate—that is, to have them focusing on the symptom rather than trying to avoid it—can often lead to a better understanding of the role that the particular behavior is playing in their lives. It is also useful in helping people struggling with existential issues to consider some of life's paradoxes in order to come to terms with these uncertainties.

HOW THIS IS USEFUL TO SOCIAL WORK

Colleagues who have used this type of paradoxical intervention describe it as a powerful technique when used appropriately. At this point, however, there is not a strong body of research-based literature to help us fully understand its different uses.

By helping the client to focus on a contrary or opposite belief or action, we can help them better understand the importance to them of their first position or to become more comfortable with the polarities of life and faith with which they are confronted in their daily lives. We know from our own lives that in situations where we are uncertain about what to do, or when we are worried about some aspect of our behavior, that focusing on the opposite of what we think we want, and even exaggerating the opposite position or behavior, often gives us a clearer picture of this aspect of our makeup. This in turn can give us the strength to give it up and find certainty and security in the behavior or value to which we had originally aspired.

RISK FACTORS

The paradox technique has a high risk factor. Primarily there is the risk of causing harm in situations where the exaggeration of a symptom would result in the client being put in a worse position than before. There is also the risk of losing a client who would find this type of focusing to be unacceptable to a point where they would withdraw from treatment just when they could start benefiting from it.

REQUIRED SKILLS AND KNOWLEDGE

In using this technique, we begin by asking ourselves as social workers whether this client is a person who would benefit from focusing on opposites in their psychological makeup. We help them do this by having them attempt to exaggerate the very behavior or attitude they are seeking to expunge. We need to know our client well enough to use this process, and from our own perspective we must guard against this technique becoming a fad.

Before using it in a case, we must devote careful attention to the timing of its introduction and to the personality and value constructs of the client. It is clearly not a technique that would or could be used frequently in a case. Also, some clients will find it totally unacceptable as a concept and unwilling to attempt this behavior.

Case Summary One

Marcie is attending therapy to improve her anger management skills and to learn to express herself appropriately. She reports that she feels like she is constantly fighting with everyone around her. According to Marcie, she just wants attention from them and doesn't know how else to get it. During this session, Marcie's social worker decides to use a paradoxical directive.

SOCIAL WORKER: What are you currently doing to express your anger?
MARCIE: I yell, jump up and down, throw things, break items that I find near me, and just generally have a bad attitude towards anyone that talks to me. I do it a lot and I never know when it is going to happen.

SOCIAL WORKER: This might seem a little strange to you, but I'm going to encourage you to continue expressing your anger the way you usually do. Choose a twenty-minute time period each day to do nothing but express your anger.

MARCIE: Okay, I guess I can try that.

SOCIAL WORKER: I want you to get as mad as you want and let everything out that you had bottled up all day. During your designated twenty-minute anger time, do the same things you would usually do when you're angry.

Marcie followed her social worker's instructions and, after some time, discovered that she was sick and tired of the way she was acting. She decided that the way she was expressing herself was not appropriate and she found it hard to purposely engage in that behavior. As a result of her social worker's paradoxical directive, Marcie started learning proper communication skills and healthier ways of expressing her anger.

Case Summary Two

Darryl is attending therapy sessions to try to decrease the anxiety he feels on a daily basis. Darryl describes himself as an excessive worrier. His anxiety symptoms are impairing his everyday functioning. Darryl reports that he finds it difficult to go to work or meet up with friends because he automatically becomes nervous about what could go wrong as soon as he even thinks of going out.

SOCIAL WORKER: Tell me more about how you are feeling.

DARRYL: Worrying is getting in the way of my everyday life. I find it hard to do anything because of my intense feelings of anxiety. It seems like I'm too nervous to do anything lately. The worry gets so bad sometimes that it makes my stomach hurt. I just don't know what I can do. I feel like I've tried everything already. What should I do?

SOCIAL WORKER: My recommendation is that you continue to worry about all the things that make you feel anxious each day.

DARRYL: What? That seems rather odd.

SOCIAL WORKER: I know my directive may come as a surprise to you, but I suggest that you follow it. While you are at home in the morning, after you prepare for your day, but before you leave for work, take fifteen minutes to worry about everything that could happen during the day. Worry as much as you can during those fifteen minutes and then go on with your day. [During the next session:]

SOCIAL WORKER: What was it like following my recommendation over the past week?

DARRYL: I followed your directive for a while, but then I got sick of it. I just couldn't do it anymore. I realized that worrying wasn't helping anything. All it was doing was making me feel sick. Nothing that bad has happened to me. The things I was worrying about didn't make any sense.

As Darryl followed his social worker's paradoxical directive, he gained a sense of control over his anxious feelings. This sense of control resulted in Darryl changing his behaviors. Knowing that he had a specified time that he was allowed and even expected to worry, led Darryl to feel less worried on a day to day basis.

REFERENCES AND ADDITIONAL SOURCES

Betts, G. R., & Remer, R. (1993). The impact of paradoxical interventions on perceptions of the social worker and ratings of treatment acceptability. *Professional Psychology: Research and Practice, 24*(2), 164–170.

Brown, J. E., & Slee, P. T. (1986). Paradoxical strategies: The ethics of intervention. *Professional Psychology: Research and Practice, 17*(6), 487–491.

Cade, B. (1984). Paradoxical techniques in therapy. *Journal of Child Psychology and Psychiatry, 25*(4), 509–516.

Cavell, T. A., Frentz, C. E., & Kelley, M. L. (1986). Acceptability of paradoxical interventions: Some non-paradoxical findings. *Professional Psychology: Research and Practice, 17*(6), 519–523.

Conoley, C. W., & Beard, M. (1984). The effects of a paradoxical intervention on therapeutic relationship measures. *Psychotherapy, 21*, 273–277.

Dell, P. F. (1986). Why do we still call them "paradoxes"? *Family Process, 25*(2), 223–234.

Dowd, E. T., & Milne, C. R. (1986). Paradoxical interventions in counseling psychology. *The Counseling Psychologist, 14*(2), 237–282.

Haley, J. (1976). *Problem solving therapy*. San Francisco, CA: Jossey-Bass.

Hill, K. A. (1987). Meta-analysis of paradoxical interventions. *Psychotherapy, 24*(2), 266–270.

Hunsley, J. (1988). Conceptions and misconceptions about the context of paradoxical therapy. *Professional Psychology: Research and Practice, 19*(5), 553–559.

Johnson, M. (1986). Paradoxical interventions: From repugnance to cautious curiosity. *The Counseling Psychologist, 14*(2), 297–302.

Kolko, D. J., & Milan, M. A. (1983). Reframing and paradoxical instruction to overcome "resistance" in the treatment of delinquent youths: A multiple baseline analysis. *Journal of Consulting and Clinical Psychology, 51*(5), 655–660.

Kolko, D. J., & Milan, M. A. (1986). Acceptability of paradoxical interventions: Some paradoxes of psychotherapy research. *Professional Psychology: Research and Practice, 17*(6), 524–527.

Van Deurzen, A. (1998) *Paradox and passion in psychotherapy*. New York, NY: Wiley.

Weeks, G., & L'Abate, L. (1978). A bibliography of paradoxical methods in psychotherapy of family systems. *Family process, 17*(1), 95–98.

Partializing

DESCRIPTION

This technique describes the process we all use when confronted by multidimensional problems. Over the course of our daily lives, we have learned that, for the most part, we cannot and do not solve life's challenges in their entirety. Rather, we know that these challenges can only be addressed effectively by breaking them up into manageable parts. Helping clients to do this is a useful technique in our practice.

ORIGINS

This term was originally brought into our professional vocabulary through the problem-solving writings of Helen Perlman (Perlman, 1957). Much of the theory behind task-centered practice makes use of this concept.

WHY THIS IS USEFUL TO SOCIAL WORK

Partializing can be very useful in many of the situations our clients bring to us. It is particularly useful to our practice because it is universal to life. That is, it is a process that is a part of all adult living. When this is understood and utilized, its power can be harnessed along with and on behalf of a client in a very effective way.

We often meet clients whose principal problem is that they are facing such a cluster of problems and difficulties that they begin to lose control of their lives. It is not that they lack the personal and material resources to deal with these problems. Rather, it is just that they have become so overwhelmed by the whole picture that they have lost the ability to draw on their resources in a manner that leads them to regain control.

The need to divide the situations that life presents into workable pieces may result from the nature of a particular problem; that is, something has occurred that, by its very nature, can only be handled on a piece-by-piece basis. Alternatively, the situation may be time sensitive, so partializing will help some parts of therapy to be done immediately.

It may also mean that partializing is required from the perspective of available resources, which forces us to go a step at a time until we are in a position to deal with other parts of the situation when the resources needed do become available. A component of these resources may be a renewal of our psychic energy.

Although this process of partializing may be long and complex, drawing on the strengths of the therapeutic relationship, it is often something we do for and with the client in a first or second interview. That is, in concert with the client, we identify problems, look at possible and available solutions, place them in priority order, and strategize an approach.

HOW THIS IS USEFUL TO SOCIAL WORK

Partializing is such a part of our daily lives that for a long time it was not recognized as a distinct technique, that when appropriately used, can be of tremendous help to a client. It is a technique that builds clients' strengths; thus, it is useful not only in the treatment process, but also, when the client learns it, as a very useful tool for daily living.

RISK FACTORS

Overall partializing is not a high-risk technique. One risk in making use of partializing is that it can begin to take on an overly cognitive and logical flavor as the process moves to planning strategy. In so doing, we can easily overlook the emotional factor that is a part of the process. Thus we need to know how the person really feels about particular problems and their ability to handle them. What may be evident to us as the most useful and potentially helpful way of dividing a problem into workable parts may not be seen in the same way by the client. Likewise, what we may see as a rather easy and obvious next step in approaching a situation may be perceived and felt by the client as a major roadblock. Here the focus of our help becomes working with the client to address the roadblock rather than moving to a next step that seems obvious to us.

A related risk in the overuse or misuse of partialization is that the agenda that emerges in the partialization strategy becomes ours rather than the client's. However, this is what needs to occur in some cases. That is, we will meet persons who are so overwhelmed with problems that the solution is for us to take over for a period of time. Here we are making use of the authority of the relationship to do the needed partialization for them in a manner that will eventually allow them to take over their lives again. In such instances, we will be functioning as a benign expert. In so doing, we need to assist the client in resuming control over their lives as soon as possible and in a manner that fosters improved and more mature functioning.

REQUIRED SKILLS AND KNOWLEDGE

In using the partializing technique, our task is to help clients sort out what is manageable from the perspective of the problem or problems they face, as well as their order of urgency. We also need to consider what will bring the optimum level of relief. This requires a high level of assessment skill on the worker's part, both to help the client work their way through this process and to assess the client's ability to follow through on the decisions reached through the partializing process.

Case Summary One

Julie is a young adult attending therapy sessions while she is working toward moving out of her parent's house to live on her own. She is nervous about the impending transition, but also very excited, and she can't wait for it to happen. During the first few sessions, Julie and her social worker discuss Julie's goals for their sessions.

SOCIAL WORKER: What is your overall goal for our time together?
JULIE: I would like to be self-sufficient and not have to rely on my parents for everything.
SOCIAL WORKER: Okay, now let's partialize your goal and break it down into smaller, more manageable parts. What would be the first step to achieving your goal?
JULIE: Well, I need to be financially stable, so my first step would be to get a job.
SOCIAL WORKER: Next, let's partialize the task of getting a job. What are the steps that need to be taken for you to obtain a job?
JULIE: First, I need to develop my resume. Then, look for companies that are hiring. Next, complete applications, submit my resume, and schedule interviews.

This case study provides an example of partializing Julie's goal for therapy sessions. When a goal is too broad it can seem overwhelming and unattainable. Partializing the goal is a great way to make the individual tasks manageable. Also, Julie will be able to feel a sense of accomplishment sooner as she completes her partialized tasks on her way to achieving her larger goal.

Case Summary Two

Jonathan is a young adult in his late twenties. He has been meeting with a social worker for a few weeks following a rough breakup with his girlfriend of 3 years. Jonathan and his girlfriend, Jill, had been living together for the past 2 years and the breakup came as a shock to him. Jonathan reports being in a depressed mood most days and feeling overwhelmed because of everything that's happened.

JONATHAN: I've been so down and low energy lately that I've let most of the housework and domestic duties pile up. Jill used to handle all of that stuff. She was so good at it. It seemed to come so naturally to her.

SOCIAL WORKER: What exactly do you feel needs to get done around the house?

JONATHAN: The house is a mess in general. I'm also almost out of food. I'm going to have to go grocery shopping soon and probably learn how to cook more than just macaroni and cheese. Just thinking about everything that has to get done makes me feel completely overwhelmed.

SOCIAL WORKER: I can understand how that might feel overwhelming to you. Let's think for a few minutes about your problem and discuss ways that we can partialize it into smaller tasks. What is your biggest concern at this point in time?

JONATHAN: I guess the most important thing that needs to get done would be to clean up and sanitize the living areas of my house. I'm not even sure I know how to properly clean a bathroom or a kitchen, though.

SOCIAL WORKER: I know you've mentioned before that you have family and friends who live close to you. Is there a family member or close friend who you think might be willing to help you?

JONATHAN: Yes, I didn't even think of that. My mom lives a few blocks away. I'm sure she would be okay with coming over to help me out. She always did try to teach me how to cook and clean growing up.

In this example Jonathan had become so overwhelmed by the whole picture of his problem that he lost the ability to draw on his strengths and resources. Jonathan was more effectively able to address his seemingly overwhelming challenge by using partializing as a technique to break it up into more manageable pieces.

REFERENCES AND ADDITIONAL SOURCES

Brandell, J. R. (2004). *Psychodynamic social work*. New York, NY: Columbia University Press.

Davidson, K. W., & Clarke, S. S. (1989). *Social work in health care: A handbook for practice* (Vol. 1). Binghamton, NY: Haworth.

Elaine, M. B., & Vayda, E. J. (1998). *The practice of field instruction in social work: Theory and process* (2nd ed.). New York, NY: Columbia University Press.

Fusco, L. (2002). The techniques of intervention. In F. Turner (Ed.), *Social work practice* (p. 236). Toronto, Ontario: Prentice Hall.

Gitterman, A., & Germain, C. B. (2008). *The life model of social work practice: Advances in theory and practice*. Chichester, England: Columbia University Press.

Hull, G. H., & Mather, J. H. (2005). *Understanding generalist practice with families*. Belmont, CA: Thomson Brooks/Cole.

Middleman, R. R., & Wood, G. G., (1990). *Skills for direct practice in social work*. New York, NY: Columbia University Press.

Perlman, H. H. (1957). *Social casework: A problem solving process* (pp. 147–149). Chicago, IL: University of Chicago Press.

Turner, F. J. (1996). *Social work treatment: Interlocking theoretical approaches*. New York, NY: Free Press.

Walsh, J. (2010). *Theories for direct social work practice* (2nd ed.). Belmont, CA: Wadsworth.

Pets

DESCRIPTION

This technique encompasses the use of animals to assist clients with various personal needs, to serve as a solution to some of their limitations, and to provide a range of emotional supports.

ORIGINS

Anthropologists tell us that pets have been a part of our evolutionary history for thousands of years. Over these millennia, animals have performed a variety of functions for our ancestors. They have served and continue to serve as companions, providers of labor, protectors, and as a substitute for lost or impaired bodily functions. In various combinations of these roles, they have played complex and important social and emotional roles in the lives of many people. It is our appreciation and understanding of their function as companions and sources of security that has helped us appreciate the important roles they can play in providing many psychosocial needs for our clients.

WHY THIS IS USEFUL TO SOCIAL WORK

We know how close many people (perhaps even ourselves) have become to pets at various times in their lives. Those who have experienced such a long-term relationship appreciate the intensity of feelings they can generate and the comfort, security, companionship, and entertainment they can provide to us for long periods of our lives. We can sense and understand the intensity of these relationships when we or a friend loses a pet; our feelings of loss can sometimes be extreme enough to require professional assistance.

Pets are very much a part of contemporary society, are reasonably easy to obtain, and can be quite inexpensive to purchase, although they can be expensive to maintain.

HOW THIS IS USEFUL TO SOCIAL WORK

Apart from the extent to which a pet can help meet many psychosocial needs, many people realize a secondary advantage to having a pet, one that is often overlooked. Not only do pets help fill certain people's emotional needs, but so too does the community of people with whom the pet owner frequently interacts as a result of having and caring for a pet. For a dog owner, this includes such things as meeting others during their daily walk and becoming a part of the network of people involved in its training and care. This aspect of pet ownership can greatly expand some people's personal networks.

A further role of pets is that of providing realistic physical security, a very important issue for many in our society. Dogs are particularly well-suited to this role, one that can greatly reduce an owner's anxiety. It is understandable, therefore, for us to consider the possibility of a pet for some clients when thinking of ways to help them grow and develop or to satisfy some realistic need.

RISK FACTORS

This technique has moderate risk. It stems from the many implications for a person who takes on the responsibility of a pet. Often these are minimized by someone for whom this is a first-time experience. Thus, we need to be sure that we have helped the client examine them carefully. If such assessment and diagnostic care have been appropriately carried out, helping clients to introduce a pet into their lives potentially can be a powerfully positive technique.

REQUIRED SKILLS AND KNOWLEDGE

As with all techniques involving the provision of resources, it is important that all possible positive and negative effects of a pet on the client's life be assessed in the diagnostic process. We need to be sure that our own enthusiasm does not lead us to attempt to move a client in this direction who is not interested in or unable to accommodate the risks involved in such an addition to their social network. Likewise, it is important that we ensure that the client is given the opportunity (through our own assistance or by recruiting others) to learn and asses what will be involved in pet ownership, including the expense. This is an area where volunteer assistance can be of great benefit. One of the advantages of helping a client connect to someone well-experienced with pets is the possibility that this will further expand the client's circle of human resources.

It is important, of course, that if we ourselves know little about life with an animal, including their care and feeding, we should help find the necessary assistance to fully assess the ramifications of such a move in particular cases, and we should assist in the early days of the client's life with the new family member.

Case Summary One

Maria is a 10-year-old girl diagnosed with posttraumatic stress disorder and a history of physical and sexual abuse. According to her mother, she lied, stole, has been hyperactive and aggressive, and has acted out sexually. A certified pet therapy dog was introduced to improve some of Maria's problematic behaviors because she viewed meeting the dog as a reward.

> SOCIAL WORKER: Maria, would you like to meet my dog friend, Rex?
>
> MARIA: Yes, I love dogs. Dogs are my favorite animals.
>
> SOCIAL WORKER: First, I am going to explain the rules of interacting with Rex [the pet therapy dog]. The rules are: allow him to sniff you, stay calm and still, do not get loud and rough, always be gentle, and pet him only on his head and back. Do you agree to obey these rules?
>
> MARIA: Yes, I will obey all of the rules for playing with Rex.
>
> SOCIAL WORKER: Allow me to introduce you to Rex. Rex is four years old and enjoys playing with children. Are you ready to stay relaxed and pet Rex?
>
> MARIA: Yes, I am ready. I like his soft fur, he feels cuddly.

During Maria's sessions with Rex, she was able to sit quietly, follow rules, share thoughts and feelings, and disclose memories of her abuse. Maria's mother reported improved behavior at home and school and a reduction in Maria's anxiety.

Case Summary Two

Laura is a widowed mother in her fifties. Recently, the last of her three children moved out of the house. Laura reports conflicting feelings of happiness and sorrow about the situation. She misses the noise and activity in her house, and she would also like to feel a sense of companionship again.

> LAURA: I'm happy for my children, but at the same time I miss them so much. They were all I had left after my husband died. The house is just too quiet now.
>
> SOCIAL WORKER: The loss of the full-time parenting role can be stressful, especially for single mothers. Have you ever considered the possibility of owning a pet?
>
> LAURA: I have actually considered that, but I wasn't sure if it would be a good idea. I'd like to get a dog. I've always loved dogs, but haven't owned one since my childhood because my husband and daughter were allergic. I sure do miss having someone to take care of.
>
> SOCIAL WORKER: Owning a dog is a wonderful idea if you have the desire and ability to care for it properly. A pet can provide a sense of security, emotional support, comfort, and entertainment, among other things. Let's take some time to discuss all of the possible positive and negative aspects of owning a pet, and then you can decide what will be best for you.

In this example Laura was looking to fulfill her need for companionship as well as her desire to care for others. Not only will having a pet provide Laura with companionship at home, but it will also increase her social network and resources through pet activities such as walks and dog parks. Laura's pet will play an important and complex social and emotional role in her life.

REFERENCES AND ADDITIONAL SOURCES

Dadds, M. R., Whiting, C., & Hawes, D. J. (2006). Associations among cruelty to animals, family conflict, and psychopathic traits in childhood. *Journal of Interpersonal Violence, 21*(3), 411–429.

Dembicki, D., & Anderson, J. (1996). Pet ownership may be a factor in improved health of the elderly. *Journal of Nutrition for the Elderly, 15*(3), 15–31.

Duncan, S. L., & Men, K. (2000). Service animals and their role in enhancing independence, quality of life and employment for people with disabilities. In A. Fine (Ed.), *Handbook of animal-assisted therapy* (pp. 303–323). San Diego, CA: Academic.

Ebenstein, H., & Wortham, J. (2005). The value of pets in geriatric practice: A program example. In F. Turner (Ed.), *Social work diagnosis in contemporary practice* (pp. 719–728). New York, NY: Oxford University Press.

Friedmann, E., Katcher A. H., Thomas S. A., Lynch, J. J., & Messent, P. R. (1983). Social interaction and blood pressure. Influence of animal companions. *Journal of Nervous and Mental Disorder, 171*(8), 461–465.

Filan, S. L., & Llewellyn-Jones, R. H. (2006). Animal-assisted therapy for dementia: A review of the literature. *International Psychogeriatrics, 18*(4), 597–611.

Levinson, B. (1972). *Pets and human development* Springfield, IL: Charles C. Thomas.

Levinson, B. M., & Mallon, G. P. (1997). *Pet oriented child psychotherapy* (2nd ed.). Springfield, IL: Charles C. Thomas.

Martin, F., & Farnum, J. (2002). Animal-assisted therapy for children with pervasive developmental disorders. *Journal of Nursing Research, 24*(6), 657–670.

Muschel, I. (1984). Pet therapy with terminal cancer patients. *Social Casework, 65*(8), 451–458.

Risley-Curtiss, C. (2010). Social work practitioners and the human-companion animal bond: A national study. *Social Work, 55*(1), 38–46.

Robin, M., ten Bensel, R. W., Quigley, J., & Anderson, R. K. (1984). Abused children and their pets. In R. K. Anderson, B. L. Hart, & L. A. Hart (Eds.), *The pet connection* (pp.111–130). Minneapolis: University of Minnesota.

Sellers, D. M. (2006). The evaluation of an animal assisted therapy intervention for elders with dementia in long-term care. *Activities, Adaptation & Aging, 30*(1), 61–77.

Sable, P. (1995). Pets, attachment and well-being across the life cycle. *Social Work, 40*(3), 334–341.

Wilkes, J. K. (2009). *The role of companion animals in counseling and psychology: Discovering their use in the therapeutic process.* Springfield, IL: Charles C. Thomas.

Photos

DESCRIPTION

This technique focuses on helping clients address various components of their histories and relationships with significant persons in their lives through the use of available personal photographs.

ORIGINS

There does not appear to be any particular, identifiable theoretical or historical route that has led to an awareness of the potential of this technique. Perhaps it has been the growing availability of photos in our culture, along with a realization of the significance they often play in many people's lives. We know from our own lives the importance that particular photos can have for someone, such as when a person has carried a significant photo with them for years.

WHY THIS IS USEFUL TO SOCIAL WORK

Because photos can be an important component of a person's life, being aware of such possible significance can help us to understand a client in a therapeutic situation. Appreciation of this phenomenon gives us a way to learn about a person in a nonthreatening manner as we reflect with them on a particular photo or set of photos, or a person in a photo of import to them.

Not only can we learn about our clients by reflecting upon their photos, but this is often a useful way to help them deal with various relationships and aspects of their history. In many ways, photographs can play the same role in treatment as do some projective instruments, in that they can trigger specific emotions and memories.

HOW THIS IS USEFUL TO SOCIAL WORK

An old family photo album can be used as a technique in several ways. From an assessment perspective, reviewing these resources with the client can help us get a picture of family structure, roles, and history, factors that, not unlike the genogram technique, may not be understood or recognized by the client as significant.

Having clients talk about photos can tap into significant emotional material that may not be forthcoming in a more verbally focused interview. Not only can pictures evoke memories of past events, or of people and their role in the family history, but they can also can conjure memories of physical, historical, and socioeconomic aspects of a client's life and origins in a way that can help us better understand their history,

One particular facet of using family photos is the way that this process can help us understand tradition and its place in a client's history. Photos, especially those taken over the last 8 to 10 decades, usually tell us a great deal about the traditions in a family and what things, events, and people were considered important. Such factors may not appear significant to the client today. Although such factors may not appear significant to the client today, learning about these traditions can help explain some of their current views, concerns, and values.

The strength of the photo technique stems from the same roots as some projective tests, in that they can serve as both positive and negative stimuli about many aspects of a client's life. Even the process of having a client identify which pictures they view as important and why not only tells us much about the client, but also can serve as a powerful emotional stimulus from a therapeutic perspective.

The use of photos with groups and especially families can serve the same goals of reviewing history and reflecting on cultural issues. This can be particularly useful as we observe how different persons who are interconnected with one another in some way can remember a person or event differentially. Identifying such differences can help clients recognize where and why they differ.

RISK FACTORS

This technique does not have significant risk. However, in using it we need to be aware that, for some clients, the reality of an event portrayed in a picture and the meaning the client attributes to it may be quite different. The photo may represent a distortion of the real event and serve as a means of cloaking the real situation and its meaning to the client. However, hearing these differential descriptions of the photos' meaning can be a very useful source of understanding for us and open up areas for therapeutic attention.

REQUIRED SKILLS AND KNOWLEDGE

Although our discussions regarding the use of photos implies that we are more interested in older, historic pictures of the family, this should not be overly stressed. Many families and people do not have photos from the past. However, in this part of the world, in the last few years virtually every moment of many clients' lives have been captured digitally or on film. For some clients, this prevalence seems to take away the powerful meaning they attribute to older pictures. Nevertheless, having clients use these contemporary photos as stimuli for telling us about themselves, their significant others, and events, either from the present or past, can be still therapeutically productive.

Case Summary One

Bernice is an older adult feeling depressed because she has "lost her youth." Bernice explains that many of her family and friends have passed away. She feels it's only a matter of time before she dies, too, and she is discouraged about life.

> SOCIAL WORKER: Last session, we spoke about you bringing in some photos that are significant to you in some way. Were you able to do that?
> BERNICE: Yes. I have a stack with me. Here you go.
> SOCIAL WORKER: Tell me about them.
> BERNICE: The first one is my husband and me when we got married. That was a wonderful time in my life. He was an extraordinary man. He passed away a few years ago.
> SOCIAL WORKER: Who is in this next picture?
> BERNICE: This is my daughter and her two children. They live in another state; I don't get to see them often.

Looking at the photos that Bernice brought in gave the social worker some insight into Bernice's background and life history. It provided Bernice a nonthreatening way to talk to her social worker about people and things that are significant to her. Photos are also a good way for Bernice to bring out her emotions naturally without feeling forced. The social worker must learn about Bernice and understand what is important to her in order to be most effective while working with her.

Case Summary Two

Chad is a teenager attending therapy sessions following a traumatic accident. He has met with his social worker a few times. Chad's social worker has noticed that Chad feels uneasy when he talks about his life during therapy sessions. The social worker has asked Chad to bring in photos as a way to facilitate open communication in the therapeutic relationship in a nonthreatening manner.

> SOCIAL WORKER: During our last therapy session, I asked you to bring in some photographs of happy times in your life. Were you able to find some pictures and bring them in?
> CHAD: Yes, I have several photos with me.

SOCIAL WORKER: Let's discuss them. What is going on in the first picture?

CHAD: This is from my most recent birthday party. It was a few months before my accident. I had a blast that day.

SOCIAL WORKER: It looks like everyone in this picture is very happy and having fun. Tell me about the other pictures you have. When were they taken?

CHAD: This photo is from a vacation with my family last summer. We went to the beach for a week. We all had an amazing time. The next one is me with my friends during the homecoming dance from the beginning of the school year. That was a great night.

SOCIAL WORKER: What wonderful pictures you have. Are they all from before your accident?

CHAD: Yes. I can't really think of many happy times that have occurred in the past few months since my accident.

Being able to hear Chad's descriptions of his photos allowed Chad's social worker to learn more about Chad and open up areas of therapeutic communication. Also, just seeing which photos Chad chose to bring in, whether they were from before the accident, after the accident, or both, provided the social worker with useful assessment information. Having the pictures as a reference point for discussions during the therapy session helped Chad feel more comfortable when sharing details of his life with the social worker. He was able to talk about emotionally charged material that he might not otherwise speak about.

REFERENCES AND ADDITIONAL SOURCES

Clarke, G. (1997). *The photograph*. Oxford, England: Oxford University Press.

Kaslow, F. W., & Friedman, J. (1977). Utilization of family photos and movies in family therapy. *Journal of Marital and Family Therapy*, 3(1), 19–25. doi:10.1111/j.1752-0606.1977.tb00441.x

Kozloff, M. (1978). *Photography and fascination*. New York, NY: Addison House.

Scharf, A. (1968). *Art & photography*. London, England: Allen Lane/The Penguin Press.

Sontag, S. (1977/1980). *On photography*. New York, NY: Dell.

Stewart, D. (1979). Photo therapy: Theory & practice. *Art Psychotherapy*, 6(1), 41–46.

Weiser, J. (1990). More than meets the eye: Using ordinary snapshots as tools for therapy. In: Laidlaw, T., Malmo, C., & Associates (Eds.), *Healing voices: Feminist approaches to therapy with women* (pp. 83–117). San Francisco: Jossey-Bass.

Weiser, J. (2001). Phototherapy techniques: Using clients' personal snapshots and family photos as counseling and therapy tools. *The Journal of Media Arts and Cultural Criticism*, 29(3), 10–15.

Weiser, J. (2003). A picture is worth a thousand words: Using phototherapy techniques in counselling practice. *Bulletin of the Private Practitioners Chapter Newsletter (Canadian Counselling Association)*, 3(2), 3–4.

Weiser, J. (2004). Phototherapy techniques in counseling and therapy: Using ordinary snapshots and photo-interactions to help clients heal their lives. *The Canadian Art Therapy Association Journal*, 17(2), 23–53.

Zayfert, C., & Becker, C. B. (2007). *Cognitive-behavioral therapy for PTSD: A case formulation approach*. New York, NY: Guilford.

Poetry

DESCRIPTION

Being aware of how some poetry can touch us emotionally in very significant ways provides us with an understanding of how to make use of this phenomenon in a therapeutic manner.

ORIGINS

To an increasing extent, we have come to appreciate that there are many aspects of persons' lives that can assist us in our therapeutic endeavors. Because many of these do not appear to be the essence of therapy, their potential as therapeutic resources has long been overlooked. However, as we have come to appreciate their potential, we have become more comfortable in drawing on them in a direct manner.

WHY THIS IS USEFUL TO SOCIAL WORK

We are all aware of the ability of a poem to touch us in very profound ways. We know that a poem can evoke emotional responses and memories. Poems can sooth and excite us or trouble and arouse us. Such responses can be strong on occasion, and can also relate to our clients' day-to-day lives, thus giving us a further opportunity to connect to them.

HOW THIS IS USEFUL TO SOCIAL WORK

Although poetry is not a frequently utilized technique, there are several ways in which we can use this resource in a facilitative manner. For example, we can encourage clients to read poetry as an easily accessible and inexpensive form of relaxation and enjoyment. This is especially relevant for persons whose lifestyle allows little time for stress-free or peaceful activities.

Clients also may be encouraged to read specific poems as a way of experiencing emotions vicariously, to help them get more in touch with their own emotional life and to make this form of stimulation the content of interviews. This can help us better understand the client diagnostically while assisting the client in understanding themselves. In a similar way, we can read some relevant selected poetry together with the client and make use of his or her emotional response as a way of enhancing self-awareness.

Poetry can also be used to prepare a client for an interview; its soothing power can help the client relax and ready themselves for the process. In such instances, the poetry selected is not aimed at striking a particular emotional tone. Rather, as with music or meditation, it should aim to give pleasure and aid the person in distancing themselves from the reality of their hectic lifestyle.

A further use of poetry as a treatment technique involves encouraging clients to write their own poetry. We might do this to help a person express some of their inner thoughts or emotions. Such experiences could be those that bring joy and satisfaction, but the poem may instead be a way for the client to touch on repressed or suppressed emotional content. Just as some people are able to reach and express aspects of their inner lives though media such as music or art, others can do so through poetry. Obviously, however, not all clients would understand this purpose or be able to create their own poems.

Another use of poetry comes from our work in diversity. It may well be that our client is well versed in the poetry of his or her cultural background, often in their native language. Even though we ourselves do not understand the language in which it is written, we can still make use of this material by having the client tell us about it and its meaning and impact upon them. Here we are letting the client teach us in a manner that can be useful to them.

RISK FACTORS

Using poetry is not a technique with a high risk factor, but it is one we can overuse out of our enthusiasm for it to the point that it becomes an end in itself rather than an adjunct. Rather than helping, poetry can also become a diversion from the real situation to which we and the client should be attending.

REQUIRED SKILLS AND KNOWLEDGE

Making effective use of the various aspects of this technique requires specific knowledge on the part of the social worker. As with all techniques, it is essential that we understand the client, in this case their ability to read, understand, and connect to whatever poetry has been selected or recommended. It is not necessary for clients to understand what the poet had in mind. Rather, we seek a degree of understanding that lets clients open themselves to being touched by the perceived themes of the poem as they experience it.

Effective use of this technique understandably requires a rich knowledge base about poetry, its range, variation, and content, and its overall ability to touch people in particular ways. It may well require the social worker to seek outside consultation.

Poetry is not a technique for all clients and all social workers. Clearly it is a technique with which one must proceed very slowly, so we can assess clients' ability and interest in making use of this medium and progressively assess its positive and possibly negative impact on the therapeutic process.

Case Summary One

Allie is an adolescent female attending therapy sessions to learn how to cope with difficult emotions, including anger and anxiety. Allie has described herself to the social worker as being a creative person and having a love for reading and writing. During one of their sessions, Allie and her social worker discussed several relaxation and coping techniques that Allie could employ during times of distress. One technique they discussed that Allie thought would be extremely beneficial for her was reading and writing poetry.

> SOCIAL WORKER: Anytime you start to feel frustrated, overwhelmed, or stressed out about something, write about it. Channel your energy and emotions into writing poetry. If you are not in the mood to write, then try reading poems that lead to positive feelings and a sense of peace. Find poems that can put you in a good mood no matter what you're going through.
>
> ALLIE: I really think that will be helpful for me. I enjoy reading poetry, and thinking back, I do believe it has improved my mood in the past.
>
> [During the next session:]
>
> SOCIAL WORKER: Were you able to read and write poetry as a way to relax over the past week?
>
> ALLIE: Yes, and it was a wonderful way to calm myself down when I was feeling angry. I felt good about myself every time I wrote a poem. I felt a sense of accomplishment instead of feeling out of control.

Allie's enjoyment of reading and writing made poetry a useful relaxation and coping technique for her when she is feeling stressed or angry. Writing and reading poetry was a wonderful method for Allie to express her emotions in an appropriate manner and bring a feeling of peace. Completing a poem also provides Allie with a sense of accomplishment and increased self-esteem.

Case Summary Two

Leslie is an adult who has been attending therapy sessions for several weeks. Leslie reports that she finds it hard to express her emotions appropriately and tends to keep them bottled up inside. According to Leslie this has caused problems in her personal relationships over the years. She has come to therapy to learn how to appropriately talk about and express her feelings as a way to improve her relationships.

> SOCIAL WORKER: Leslie, during a previous session you mentioned how much you enjoy reading poetry. I have a poem with me today that I would like you to read.

LESLIE: Okay, that sounds great. I never get tired of reading poetry.

SOCIAL WORKER: I'm glad to hear that. I would like for you to read the poem aloud and then we can discuss it after.

[AFTER READING AND DISCUSSING THE POEM:]

SOCIAL WORKER: What did you think of that experience?

LESLIE: It was really neat. Discussing what the author of the poem was feeling and trying to express really caused me to think. It helped me start to look at feelings and feelings expression from a different perspective.

SOCIAL WORKER: The written word is a powerful thing. I think it has given us some good, thought-provoking discussion points to elaborate on.

In this example, the social worker used poetry to evoke emotional responses in Leslie. During the session, Leslie was able to vicariously experience the emotions of the provided poem. This also opened up therapeutic communication about expressing feelings. Through this experience, Leslie was able to begin to get in touch with her own emotions and gain better insight.

REFERENCES AND ADDITIONAL SOURCES

Alschuler, M. (2000). Healing from addictions through poetry therapy. *Journal of Poetry Therapy, 13*(3), 165–173.

Coulehan, J. (2010). Poetry therapy. *Patient Education and Counseling, 81*(2), 257–258.

Daniel O., & Halfacre, D. (1994). Poetry therapy with the sexually abused adolescent: A case study. *The Arts in Psychotherapy, 21*(1), 11–16.

Furman, R. (2003). Using poetry as a tool for self-reflection in social work education. *Arete-Columbia South Carolina, 27*(2), 65–70.

Furman, R., Downey, E. P., Jackson, R. L., & Bender, K. (2002). Poetry therapy as a tool for strengths-based practice. *Advances in Social Work, 3*(2), 146–157.

Goldstein, H. (2001). Poetry and practice. *Families in Society, 81*(3), 235–237.

Goldstein, M. (1989). Poetry and therapeutic factors in group therapy. *Journal of Poetry Therapy, 2*(4), 231–241.

Gustavan, C. B. (2000). In-versing your life: Using poetry as therapy. *Families in Society, 81*(3), 328–331.

Kissman, K. (1989). Poetry and feminist social work. *Journal of Poetry Therapy, 2*(4), 221–230.

Maddalena, C. J. (2009). The resolution of internal conflict through performing poetry. *The Arts in Psychotherapy, 36*(4), 222–230.

Mazza, N. (1996). Poetry therapy: A framework and synthesis of techniques for family social work. *Journal of Family Social Work, 1*(3), 3–18.

Mazza, N. (1999). The poetic in family social work. *Journal of Family Social Work, 3*(3), 69–73.

McLoughlin, D. (2000). Transition, transformation and the art of losing: Some uses of poetry in hospice care for the terminally ill. *Psychodynamic Counselling, 6*(2), 215–234.

Rossiter, C. (2001). Long ago and far away: On the use of classical Chinese poetry in poetry therapy. *Journal of Poetry Therapy, 15*(1), 37–39.

Smith, M. A. (2000). The use of poetry therapy in the treatment of an adolescent with borderline personality disorder: A case study. *Journal of Poetry Therapy, 14*(1), 3–14.

Power

DESCRIPTION

In addition to the power that is inherent in certain formal societally recognized roles, there are also other, less formal types of power in the therapeutic relationship. These grant the social worker the ability to wield influence in a manner that can be of considerable assistance to a client. Usually these various sources of power are much more subtle than formally granted authority, but they still can be used for the good of the client.

ORIGINS

The social worker's power in the therapeutic relationship arises from several sources. It comes from having the status of a professional person, from the understanding that we have access to societal and professional resources, and from the perception that we have special skills. Power also comes from the status that we may have as an individual member of the profession, as well as from the overall reputation of the profession.

WHY THIS IS USEFUL TO SOCIAL WORK

Practitioners have long viewed power in a negative sense because of the harm done by its misuse. Thus they have not commonly thought about it in a positive sense; that is, as a way of helping clients. This is true even though, in recent decades, we have talked frequently about empowering clients—or rather, helping clients to empower themselves—while forgetting that we usually achieve this goal by drawing on our own sources of power.

Whether or not we like this or believe that it is true, there is a considerable amount of sociological power inherent in the clinical role. As clinicians we need to be aware of this power, both real and what clients attribute to us. We also need to learn to tap it as a very influential technique.

Clearly, however, this power has limitations, and one of our tasks is to be able to assess its scope in individual circumstances.

Another area where we often seem reluctant to make use of our inherent power is when we pull back when we are in a position to do something positive for some aspect of a client's external reality. We have all had moments in our practice when we could be of tremendous help to our clients by using our power in this way—of course, with their permission and due regard for confidentiality.

HOW THIS IS USEFUL TO SOCIAL WORK

In practice, as simple a thing as asking a client if they have considered a certain action or decision, stemming from our wish to explore some possibility with them, can be readily viewed by some clients as a directive to do something. This also can occur when we ask exploratory questions to learn the possible significance of something a client has mentioned. A client can easily take such questions as an interpretation or explanation, based on their perception of professional power.

RISK FACTORS

As a technique, power has a high degree of inherent risk, especially if its existence and influence are not recognized. This occurs when we are uncomfortable with the realization of power and fearful of subjecting our clients to a further abuse of power. This, in turn, reinforces power's negative influence.

One other serious mistake we can make in the use of power as a technique is to overestimate it and seek to draw on it when we lack sufficient authority upon which to act. In so doing, we may seek to do something with or for the client that is not successful due to our overestimation of this technique. A further risk comes from situations where we lead the client to do something they are not ready to do, or that is inappropriate, even though we think it will be for their own good.

REQUIRED SKILLS AND KNOWLEDGE

It is very important for us to continually assess the power influences in our various relationships and the extent to which we draw upon our professional power, even when we think we aren't doing so. For example, at times we will suggest a possible course of action to a client in the form of a question, when in fact what we are attempting to do is to have the client carry it out. Clients often see through this, and what we present as a question or possibility will be viewed correctly as our wish or strong suggestion that they take that particular action.

On the other hand, there are times when we do wish the clients to take some action that would bring about changes in their lives, sometimes in areas of considerable importance. Hence it is quite appropriate, and at times necessary, for us to draw on the power aspects of the relationship to suggest a particular course of action, or to help them to understand the importance of some material they have shared with us.

As far as possible in the life of a case, we need to be constantly aware of the levels and intensity of power with which the client has endowed us, and, when necessary, minimize it—just as, at other times, we need to be ready to draw upon it to steer the client in a particular direction when needed. What we need to avoid is pretending to ourselves and the client that we are power neutral and thus hesitate giving an opinion, venturing an explanation, or encouraging a particular action when it is critical that this be done.

In summary, because of its potency as a technique, we need to be ready to draw upon power as a way of influencing clients in a helpful, growth-enhancing manner when this is needed, wanted, or indicated. However, we must always remain cognizant of our responsibility to be aware of our own needs, and ensure these do not get in the way of the therapeutic process.

Case Summary One

Miles is a high school senior who has told his social worker that he wants to be a successful businessman. During one of his therapy sessions Miles reported that he is upset because he was not accepted to the university he applied to.

> **MILES:** I can't believe that the university denied my acceptance. What should I do?
> **SOCIAL WORKER:** Have you heard from any other universities?
> **MILES:** No, I only applied to that one because they provided us with the applications at my high school.
> **SOCIAL WORKER:** Are you willing to attend another university?
> **MILES:** Yes, but I don't know if any other universities will be giving us applications.
> **SOCIAL WORKER:** Miles, you don't become successful in life by waiting around and doing nothing. It takes work to get what you want. It is important for you to take the initiative to research universities you would like to attend and download their applications from the university website.
> **MILES:** Yeah, I can do that. It doesn't sound as scary as I thought it would be to apply for college.

In this case example, Miles's social worker empowered Miles and influenced his future course of action. Telling Miles about the importance of taking initiative and being proactive will help facilitate Miles's growth and bring positive change to his life.

Case Summary Two

Tula is a woman in middle adulthood attending therapy sessions following a rough divorce from her husband of 15 years. She has been separated from her husband for the past 6 months, and the divorce was just finalized about a month ago. Tula has started feeling pessimistic and powerless at the thought of living life without her husband.

Tula: I can't do anything now. I'm nothing without my husband by my side.

Social worker: Tell me more about how you feel about the situation.

Tula: I've never been on my own before. I went straight from my parent's house to living with my husband after we got married. I don't know how to live on my own. Maybe I should try to get my ex-husband to take me back. Maybe I should move back in with my parents for a while.

Social worker: Tula, I just want to remind you that not knowing how to do something and not being able to do something are two completely different things. Do you agree with my statement?

Tula: Yes, I guess so.

Social worker: You may think that you don't know how to live on your own, but you have shown that you are completely capable of living on your own and taking care of yourself. Haven't you been living in your own apartment for the past three months? Haven't you paid all of your bills on time and kept yourself fed and healthy?

Tula: Well, yes. I've done all of that with a little help from family and friends of course.

Social worker: That's wonderful. It's okay to accept help in times of need. That doesn't mean that you are not able or willing to take care of yourself. In fact that is part of taking care of yourself. I am confident in your ability to make it on your own.

Tula: I never looked at it like that before. What you're saying makes sense though. I guess I am a little better off than I thought. Maybe I can do it on my own.

In this example, the social worker used his inherent power in the therapeutic relationship to give Tula the power to move on with her life. Through previous assessments and interviews with Tula, her social worker knew that she was ready and able to be led toward self-sufficiency. The social worker's power was used as a technique to influence Tula in a helpful and needed growth-enhancing manner.

REFERENCES AND ADDITIONAL SOURCES

Bagarozzi, D. A. (1990). Marital power discrepancies and symptom development in spouses: An empirical investigation. *American Journal of Family Therapy, 18*(1), 51–64.

French, J. R., & Raven, B. (1959). The bases of social power. In D. Cartwright (Ed.), *Studies in social power* (pp. 150–167). Ann Arbor, MI: Institute for Social Research.

Gannon, L. (1982). The role of power in psychotherapy. *Women & Therapy, 1*(2), 3–11.

Holloway, E. L., Freund, R. D., Gardner, S. L., Nelson, M. L., & Walker, B. R. (1989). Relation of power and involvement to theoretical orientation in supervision: An analysis of discourse. *Journal of Counseling Psychology, 36*(1), 88–102.

Kirst-Ashman, K. K., & Hull, G. H. (1993). *Understanding generalist practice* (pp. 376–377). Chicago, IL: Nelson-Hall.

Lowery, C. T., & Mattaini, M. A. (2001). Shared power in social work: A Native American perspective of change. In H. Briggs & K. Corcoran (Eds.), *Social work practice* (pp. 109–124). Chicago, IL: Lyceum.

Murphy, M. J., & Wright, D. W. (2005). Supervisees' perspectives of power use in supervision. *Journal of Marital and Family Therapy, 31*(3), 283–295.

Parker, L. (1997). Unraveling power issues in couples therapy. *Journal of Feminist Family Therapy, 9*(2), 3–18.

Parker, L. (2009). Disrupting power and privilege in couples therapy. *Clinical Social Work Journal, 37*(3), 248–255.

Reandeau, S. G., & Wampold, B. E. (1991). Relationship of power and involvement to working alliance: A multiple-case sequential analysis of brief therapy. *Journal of Counseling Psychology, 38*(2), 107–114.

Simon, J. (1990). The single parent: Power and the integrity of parenting. *The American Journal of Psychoanalysis, 50*(2), 187–198.

Weiss-Gal, I., & Welbourne, P. (2008). The professionalization of social work: A cross-national exploration. *International Journal of Social Welfare, 17*(4), 281–290.

Whisman, M. A., & Jacobson, N. S. (1990). Power, marital satisfaction, and response to marital therapy. *Journal of Family Psychology, 4*(2), 202–212.

58

Prayer

DESCRIPTION

For many people, prayer is a significant and important component of their daily lives. This can be an area of strength for clients, one we can build upon as we assist and support their search for enhanced development and functioning.

ORIGINS

Only recently has the topic of prayer been viewed as one of significance in our practice. For a long time, clients' spiritual lives were an aspect of their lives that we generally kept at arm's length from the clinical process. Indeed, although we have not always acknowledged this, we rarely touched upon prayer in our assessments and knew little about this area of our clients' lives. When we did treat clients for whom spiritual life and prayer was highly important, we often viewed such material as less than healthy for them.

In the last few years, however, social workers have devoted considerable interest to this part of our clients' lives. In so doing, we are becoming increasingly aware that a client's spiritual life is frequently important to their lives and often a source of considerable strength. There is no one clear reason that explains our growing interest. Undoubtedly, our growing understanding of the myriad systems upon which a person may draw during therapy (as systems theory has taught us), as well as our growing appreciation of the power in practices such as meditation and existential treatment, have expanded our growing sensitivity to prayer's role.

WHY THIS IS USEFUL TO SOCIAL WORK

As mentioned, prayer is an essential part of many clients' lives, a highly personal resource that they call upon in many situations. For some it is part of their daily routine, in the form of morning or evening prayers, prayers before meals, or at other times of the day. Some cultures have very clearly specified times for prayers, and adherence to these customs is an important component of such clients' reality.

HOW THIS IS USEFUL TO SOCIAL WORK

Some would question the idea of attempting to transform prayer into a therapeutic technique because it is a different order of reality. However, if it is an area that we and the client are comfortable exploring, and if it is something we can call upon to aid in our intervention with clients, then prayer can be an appropriate technique. Our sensitivity to the place of prayer in a client's life can ensure that we will pay attention to this factor as a part of the case's focus.

Thus, for clients who include prayer as part of their daily ritual, saying a brief prayer before and/or after an interview can highlight for the client the importance and seriousness of the treatment process while strongly benefiting the therapy. This practice can be useful for individual clients, but can also serve as a strengthening bond in group and family settings.

RISK FACTORS

This technique has little risk. We need to be sure, of course, that as social workers we are clear where we stand on this topic so we don't convey a misleading message to the client. Do we view a client's prayer life as a strength or an area of immaturity or pathology? An ethical challenge can emerge when the social worker does not consider prayer to be an appropriate matter for therapy, but the client clearly considers it to be important.

REQUIRED SKILLS AND KNOWLEDGE

Because of the very private and personal ways some people view their religious lives, prayer is an area of practice that requires great sensitivity on our part. Also, if prayer emerges as an area of focus with potential for therapeutic gains, we must ensure that we have sufficient knowledge of the nature and format of the client's prayer practice and, when necessary, have resources at our disposal that we can consult. But when there is mutual comfort and understanding between client and social worker about this significant part of the client's social system, then prayer can be a component of our focus and a means to facilitate growth.

Case Summary One

Jill is an alcoholic who lost her job and most of her meaningful relationships due to her drinking. Jill was a very spiritual person and felt prayer was an important part of her daily life. When her husband died unexpectedly, Jill started drinking heavily and stopped engaging in her spiritual

---

activities. After losing almost everything that was important to her, Jill decided to seek help and regain her spirituality.

SOCIAL WORKER: Would you like to start our session with a prayer?

JILL: Yes, that would be nice.

SOCIAL WORKER: Dear Lord, please bless this therapy session and provide Jill with the support and strength she needs.

JILL: Thank you, Lord, for leading me to therapy and giving me the determination to overcome my problems. Amen.

SOCIAL WORKER: During our sessions it's important to stay focused on God and believe that He has already provided what you need.

JILL: I agree. When I pray at home I gain a sense of calmness and I feel better able to overcome my drinking problem. Praying helps me feel more in control of my life and my choices.

SOCIAL WORKER: That's great. What do you pray for?

JILL: I pray for healing, for God to surround me with supportive people, and I thank Him for His love, mercy, and for helping to keep me sober.

For Jill, being able to pray during therapy sessions allowed her to gain insight, feel inner peace, and imagine a better way of life while being guided by a professional. Prayer also helped Jill to feel safe and speak more honestly with her social worker. Prayer and spirituality were such an important part of Jill's life that it was imperative to include it in her sessions for maximum therapeutic benefit.

Case Summary Two

Elisa is a 30-year-old Caucasian female presenting with difficulty focusing on tasks and high levels of stress. Elisa is a single mother of three young children. All three attend elementary school. Elisa came to therapy because she was having difficulties balancing her work requirements and the responsibilities that come with being a single parent. Every day Elisa must rise early to wake the children up for school, feed them, and take them to school. She must then go to work, where she receives an average salary. In the late afternoon, she must pick up her children from their afterschool programs, take them home, make their dinner, and put them to bed. Elisa has a family history of anxiety and depression. She has presented with depressive symptoms in the past but has not received medical treatment. Elisa came to therapy because she was experiencing moderate depressive and anxious symptoms. These did not warrant medication, however, so she was referred to a social worker who specializes in cognitive behavioral therapy (CBT) and yoga and meditation practices. Her social worker assigned her CBT homework in order to deal with the negative thoughts she was having behind her anxiety. Her social worker also taught her proper breathing techniques to use in times of high stress. Most notably, the social worker used her prayer schedule as a means of therapy.

Elisa is a practicing Muslim, so she is required to pray five times a day. Her prayers often go neglected due to her hectic work and family schedule. Because her social worker wanted to use her prayer schedule as a means of therapy, he taught her a few things. He suggested that she set aside a clean, quiet place to pray; for example, a corner in a room or a in a spare bedroom. He taught Elisa to use her prayer rug as a constant reminder for her prayers, and that she keep her favorite rug in her prayer area so that she can remind herself of her prayer times. He also suggested that she use the movements in her prayer as a means of therapy. She can go through the motions of rising and prostrating herself slowly and rhythmically while breathing deeply and deliberately. He told her to recite her prayer verses slowly, rhythmically, and thoughtfully while breathing. Notably, he taught her how to keep a written schedule so that her she can keep track of her five daily prayers and make sure that she performs them on time.

This alleviated a lot of Elisa's stress, because she reported that the five prayers gave her structure away from her stressful work and family life. She reported that she liked physically seeing her prayer rug in her corner, because it was a constant reminder that she needed to pray. She reported that she felt less guilt because she was satisfying her religious requirements. She reported that the time alone that she had with God gave her a sense of belonging. She reports that she can now use prayer as a special time to escape the hassles of daily life and connect with God. Last, she reports that her children have seen her praying, and consequently they will sometimes join her in group prayers. She reports that this helps her connect with them. Often they will perform their evening prayers together, and she says this helps the family to form a bond and connect with a higher being. Overall she reports positive satisfaction with the intervention.

REFERENCES AND ADDITIONAL SOURCES

Abamowitz, L. (1993). Prayer as therapy among the frail Jewish elderly. *Journal of Gerontological Social Work, 19*(3/4), 69–75.

Belcher, J. R., & Casey, T. (2001). Social work and deliverance practice: The Pentecostal experience. *Families in Society, 82*(1), 61–68.

Dossey, L. (1993). *Healing words: The power of prayer and the practice of medicine.* San Francisco, CA: Harper.

Dusek, J. A., Astin, J. A., Hibberd, P. L., & Krucoff, M. W. (2003). Healing prayer outcomes studies: Consensus recommendations. *Alt Therapies, 9*(3), A44–A53.

Gilbert, M. C. (2000). Spirituality in social work groups: Practitioners speak out. *Social Work With Groups, 22*(4), 67–84.

Hodge, D. R. (2005). Spiritual lifemaps: A client centered pictorial instrument for spiritual assessment, planning and intervention. *Social Work, 50*(1), 77–87.

Hover-Krame, M. D. (1996). *Healing touch: A resource for health care professionals.* Albany, NY: Delmar.

Koenig, H. (1997). *Is religion good for your health? The effects of religion on physical and mental health.* New York, NY: Haworth.

Koenig, H. G., Meador, K., & Parkerson, G. (1997). Religion index for psychiatric research: A 5-item measure for use in health outcome studies. *American Journal of Psychiatry, 154*(6), 885–886.

Levin, J. S. (1994). Religion and health: Is there an association, is it valid, and is it causal? *Social Science & Medicine, 38*(11), 1475–1482.

Northcut, T. B. (2000). Constructing a place for religion and spirituality in psychodynamic practice. *Clinical Social Work Journal, 28*(2), 155–169.

O'Connor, P. J., Pronk, N. P., Tan, A., & Whitebird, R. R. (2005). Characteristics of adults who use prayer as an alternative therapy. *American Journal of Health Promotion, 19*(5), 369–375.

Sloan, R. P., Bagiella, E., & Powell, T. (1999). Religion, spirituality, and medicine. *Lancet, 353*(9153), 664–667.

Tan, S. Y. (2007). Use of prayer and scripture in cognitive-behavioral therapy. *Journal of Psychology and Christianity, 26*(2), 101–111.

Washington, O., & Moxley, D. (2001). The use of prayer in group work with African American women recovering from chemical dependency. *Families in Society, 82*(1), 49–59.

Prescription

DESCRIPTION

By prescription, we refer to those situations in practice where we tell the client that we want them to carry out some very specific action that we believe will help them and for which we take responsibility.

ORIGINS

A long-held belief in social work practice has been that we did not and ought not to prescribe activities or resources for our clients. However, as we became more comfortable with a greater diversity of theories, more skilled in using our knowledge, and more aware through research that clients did expect us to prescribe, we concluded that there is a legitimate place in our practice for giving prescriptions to clients.

WHY THIS IS USEFUL TO SOCIAL WORK

We know that prescribed behavior implies power and authority in our client relationships. We also know that, overall, we believe it is better for clients to take full charge of their own lives without anyone telling them what they should be doing, including us.

However, we also know that we need to become more comfortable with the reality that clients do appropriately endow us with much knowledge and influence that we can use to help them. Clients expect that we will make use of our knowledge and experience to inform them of things they might do in their lives that we view to be important, to help them move toward the goals they have for themselves.

We understand that they expect us to use our knowledge in the ways most helpful to them; when appropriate, they do want us to prescribe actions for them. Thus, we need to be ready to do this when we judge it to be necessary.

HOW THIS IS USEFUL TO SOCIAL WORK

We prescribe in a variety of ways. We might tell clients to keep written track of some behavior, or we might ask them to try some particular way of relating to someone of significance in their lives. We might instruct clients to read some specific material for discussion at the next interview. We might also direct a client with assurance to practice some new approaches to his boss. We might quite comfortably inform a client about some aspect of child care and suggest that they make use of it. We might tell a client that we want them to come back on a specific date and time. We also might be direct in telling a client that they must see a physician or other professional in relation to something they have shared with us.

RISK FACTORS

Of course, we are all well aware of the perils of telling persons what they should or should not do. Thus, using prescriptive techniques needs to be viewed as a high-risk technique. We also need to be aware, however, of the risks of not prescribing when this is needed. It is important for us to understand that, at times, we can and must prescribe things for clients that will help them move forward and avoid situations and behaviors that are deleterious to them or others around them.

If we feel uncomfortable giving our clients prescriptions, we may evade the issue by giving them a so-called pseudoprescription, in which we couch our expectations of the client in nonprescriptive terms. The difficulty with this is that it often sends conflicting messages to the client—that we expect him or her to do something, but we are not telling him or her to do so. To avoid putting the client in a position of uncertainty, we must be clear to him or her, and in our own minds, when we are actually prescribing something.

REQUIRED SKILLS AND KNOWLEDGE

There is much that we know from our practice, and there is much we can do to help clients advance as they seek a more growth-enhancing pattern of living. For the most part, we will achieve this by striving to help them find their own ways to use our less directive advice and the resources available in their own lives to move forward. But there are times in our practice when our judicious use of prescription can facilitate their progress and help them avoid situations and behaviors that are producing or may soon produce problems for themselves or others in their lives

This technique has much in common with the advice and authority techniques. However, the degree of specificity our prescriptions carry makes this practice distinct enough to consider it a separate technique.

Case Summary One

Tanya is an adolescent female who has been attending therapy for a few weeks. She started attending therapy sessions following her parents' divorce. Tanya's mom reports that she is worried about Tanya because recently there has been a decline in their relationship and she finds it hard to talk to Tanya.

> **SOCIAL WORKER:** What would you say your relationship with your mom is like?
>
> **TANYA:** Our relationship is decent, I guess. It seems like we fight a lot, though.
>
> **SOCIAL WORKER:** Tell me more about that.
>
> **TANYA:** Well, it just seems like every time we talk to each other we end up in an argument. Looking back it seems like it's usually some kind of miscommunication. She takes the things I say the wrong way and then gets mad about it.
>
> **SOCIAL WORKER:** When you say that she takes things you say the wrong way, what do you mean by that?
>
> **TANYA:** I might say something innocently or ask something, and she thinks I'm trying to insult her or she gets offended and starts fighting with me.
>
> **SOCIAL WORKER:** Okay, the next time you speak to your mom I would like you to try something different. The first thing I want you to do is to make sure you think about what you want to say in your head, wait a few seconds, and then say it out loud if you still think it's a good idea. I would also like you to be aware of the tone of voice you use when you speak. Sometimes it's not what we say, it's how we say it. Do this every time you have a conversation with your mom and I'm sure you will see an improvement in communication.
>
> **TANYA:** That sounds like something I can do. I will start trying it tonight.

Tanya felt like she was constantly fighting with her mom, but she wasn't sure how to stop it. After meeting with Tanya for several weeks, her social worker was able to gather enough information to prescribe an action for Tanya to improve her communication and help her avoid fighting with her mom.

Case Summary Two

Irwin is an older adult client who is a recent war veteran. Irwin is attending therapy because he has posttraumatic stress disorder (PTSD) following an evaluation and diagnosis by his psychiatrist. Irwin's psychiatrist recommends that he attend therapy in order to talk about his PTSD with a social worker in conjunction with receiving medication for his treatment.

The social worker focuses on the client's presenting issue: Irwin refuses to fall asleep in his home because he does not feel safe there.

SOCIAL WORKER: How is your sleep, Irwin? Do you get enough rest?

IRWIN: My sleep is not very good. I don't allow myself to fall asleep. I guess. I am too alert and scared to fall asleep in my home. I keep thinking someone is trying to enter my home and kill me.

SOCIAL WORKER: Tell me more about that.

IRWIN: Well, it just seems that if I fall asleep, then someone will break into my home and harm me.

SOCIAL WORKER: I hear you say that you are too frightened to fall asleep. Did you think about getting an alarm set up in your house? That way if there is an intruder, you will know.

IRWIN: No that idea did not occur to me. I think installing an alarm will help me feel safer at night.

SOCIAL WORKER: Great. Another thing that can be beneficial for you is practicing good sleep hygiene.

IRWIN: What is sleep hygiene? I've never heard of that before.

SOCIAL WORKER: Sleep hygiene involves applying good sleep practices. For example, setting up a safe place for you to fall asleep in your home can help you to get more sleep. Let's read this sheet on sleep hygiene together. Then you can take a copy of this sheet home to practice.

After discussing his sleeping problems with his social worker, the social worker prescribed sleep hygiene for Irwin to practice at home. Following several weeks of meeting with his social worker, Irwin's quality of sleep improved.

REFERENCES AND ADDITIONAL SOURCES

Barkham, M., Shapiro, D. A., & Firth-Cozens, J. (1989). Personal questionnaire changes in prescriptive vs. exploratory psychotherapy. *British Journal of Clinical Psychology*, *28*(2), 97–107.

Beutler, L. E., Consoli, A. J., & Lane, G. (2005). Systematic treatment selection and prescriptive psychotherapy: An integrative eclectic approach. In J. C. Norcross & M. R. Goldfried (Eds.), *Handbook of psychotherapy integration (pp. 121–143)*. New York, NY: Oxford University Press.

Beutler, L. E., & Harwood, T. M. (1995). Prescriptive psychotherapies. *Applied and Preventive Psychology*, *4*, 89–100.

Beutler, L. E., & Harwood, M. T. (2000). *Prescriptive psychotherapy*. New York, NY: Oxford University Press.

Hardy, G. E., & Shapiro, D. A. (1985). Social worker response modes in prescriptive vs. exploratory psychotherapy. *British Journal of Clinical Psychology*, *24*(4), 235–245.

Jacobs, J. T. (2005). Treatment of depressive disorders in split versus integrated therapy and comparisons of prescriptive practices of psychiatrists and advanced practice registered nurses. *Archives of Psychiatric Nursing*, *19*(6), 256–263.

Llewelyn, S. P., Elliott, R., Shapiro, D. A., Hardy, G., & Firth] Cozens, J. (2011). Client perceptions of significant events in prescriptive and exploratory periods of individual therapy. *British Journal of Clinical Psychology*, *27*(2), 105–114.

Moreira, P., Beutler, L. E., Gonçalves, Óscar, F. (2008). Narrative change in psychotherapy: Differences between good and bad outcome cases in cognitive, narrative, and prescriptive therapies. *Journal of Clinical Psychology, 64*(10), 1181–1194.

Norcross, J. C., & Beutler, L. E. (2000). A prescriptive eclectic approach to psychotherapy training. *Journal of Psychotherapy Integration, 10*(3), 247–261. doi:10.1023/A:1009444912173

Startup, M., & Shapiro, D. A. (1993). Social worker treatment fidelity in prescriptive vs. exploratory psychotherapy. *British Journal of Clinical Psychology, 32*(4), 443–456.

Steinmetz, H. C. (2006). Directive psychotherapy: Freeing from the dilemma. *Journal of Clinical Psychology, 3*(3), 288–293.

Stricker, G., & Gold, J. R. (1993). *Comprehensive handbook of psychotherapy integration.* New York, NY: Plenum.

Thorne, F. C. (1948). Theoretical foundations of directive psychotherapy. *Annals of the New York Academy of Sciences, 49*(6), 869–877.

Problem Solving

DESCRIPTION

Regardless of our theoretical orientation, there are frequent occasions in practice when, as part of the general intervention process, a specific problem or set of problems in the client's life emerges that we elect to focus on with him or her. The problem-solving technique can thus permit or help the broader therapeutic process to move ahead or facilitate some aspect of the client's life.

ORIGINS

For many practitioners, problem solving is the essence of social work intervention. Indeed, one of the major theoretical bases of practice is that developed by Helen Harris Perlman, the problem-solving approach (Perlman, 1957). In addition, generalist and solution-based social work practice are based on problem solving. In addition to viewing problem solving as the overall goal of treatment, it can also be seen as a discrete technique.

WHY THIS IS USEFUL TO SOCIAL WORK

This is a most useful technique because, in many situations, we are meeting the client where they are. That is, the very hectic and complex circumstances in which many people live are precisely what leads them to turn to a social worker for help in solving the problem or problems these situations create.

At times, solving a particular problem in an overt way can appropriately lead to the termination of treatment; this is all the client was looking for. At other times, the solution is not the goal of the situation, as it permits a broader therapeutic process to begin or continue.

HOW THIS IS USEFUL TO SOCIAL WORK

Problem solving is useful to our practice because so many clients come to us laden with problems. In such situations we help both by addressing the particular problem or problems that emerge, and—perhaps of equal if not greater importance—by helping them to learn problem-solving skills that can stand them in good stead in their posttreatment lives.

RISK FACTORS

Although this is not a technique with a strong risk factor, problems can stem from our enthusiasm for the technique. We may therefore be tempted to implement a plan based on our perception of what the solutions to the identified problem are, and on our wish to get on with the problem-solving process, before the client is ready, even though we are convinced that this is for the good of the client. This is especially difficult if we are a future- and activity-oriented person and our client a more present-oriented person.

REQUIRED SKILLS AND KNOWLEDGE

In using this technique as a visible and distinct component of treatment, the following process is usually followed. The social worker and/or the client identifies a specific problem, whose dimensions they jointly analyze. Next, they work out a possible set of strategies and develop a plan for how they both will proceed toward the solution. Last, they implement the plan, and make any required modifications that may become necessary.

In this process, the worker is deeply involved in such things as helping the client identify and analyze the issue and selecting possible outcomes and repercussions. In addition to the cognitive components of this process, the client may require much support, and their progress may need ongoing review.

In most cases, we will draw upon many other techniques as well as the formal type of problem solving being considered here. What is important is that we need to focus not only on the process of how we believe problems should be solved, but also on the different ways clients solve problems. In this way, we look at a specific problem with them while focusing on their overall strategy. We often need to reflect with them on how useful these strategies are in their lives, and to consider whether it is the clients' approach to problem solving that needs to be reviewed, or the specific problem itself.

The most important component in the use of this technique is that it is an overt process in which both the client and the social worker are involved. Other processes and techniques do assist and achieve the goals of the intervention, with problem solving as an adjunct. Here we are focusing on using problem-solving as the main process in a manner recognized by both worker and client working together on it.

Case Summary One

Julian is a freshman in college who has been attending therapy sessions to cope with his anxiety symptoms. During this session, Julian wants his social worker to help him with a problem he is having with school.

SOCIAL WORKER: What would you like to work on today?

JULIAN: I've been having trouble when it comes to completing class assignments. The problem seems to be getting worse.

SOCIAL WORKER: Tell me more about the problem. What happens when you try to complete your class assignments?

JULIAN: Knowing that a deadline is approaching makes me so nervous that I freeze up. Then, when I start working on the assignment I feel really tense. While I'm working on it I think about all the other classes I'm taking and assignments that are going to be due soon, which makes me feel overwhelmed. These feelings become so intense that I can't work on the assignment anymore.

SOCIAL WORKER: Do your assignments get turned in?

JULIAN: Usually, they get turned in on time. However, I am not proud of the quality of the work that I end up with, and I don't want to affect my grade point average. There have also been a few times that I had to turn in an assignment late for a grade reduction.

SOCIAL WORKER: When do you usually start working on your assignments?

JULIAN: Most of the time I am rushing to complete assignments at the last minute. I might start working on it a few hours or a day before it's due.

SOCIAL WORKER: Let's work together to think of some ways we can problem-solve this issue. What do you think you could do to reduce the anxious feelings that occur when you are close to an assignment deadline?

JULIAN: Well, when I start to feel overwhelmed and tense, I can do one of the relaxation techniques we discussed to try and calm down.

SOCIAL WORKER: That's a great idea. Is it also a possibility to start working on assignments sooner so that you are not feeling anxious about the impending deadline?

JULIAN: Yes, I can try to do that. Typically, I just forget that I have an assignment due until right before I'm supposed to turn it in.

SOCIAL WORKER: What can you do to remember assignment due dates better to start on assignments earlier?

JULIAN: I can start actually using the planner that my mom gave me and write down all of my assignment due dates, as well as the date I want to start working on the assignment. That way I am sure to start working on it well in advance.

To use this technique, Julian's social worker had to make sure that he completely understood the problem as Julian viewed it. Once Julian and his social worker were on the same page, they could start the problem-solving process and develop a plan. Focusing on ways to solve this problem was an important aspect in facilitating overall success in treatment. Also, going through this problem-solving process during a therapy session was a learning experience for Julian that will be helpful when he encounters problems in the future.

Case Summary Two

Marcel is a high school dropout and former substance abuser and drug addict. Marcel is out of rehabilitation and is presently living with his brother. He wants therapy in order to attain legitimate employment so he can move out on his own.

SOCIAL WORKER: What brings you here today, Marcel?

MARCEL: Well, as you know I have been sober and clean for two years. Since I left rehab I have been living with my brother.

SOCIAL WORKER: Well, I want to applaud you for being sober and clean for that period of time. Good for you! That takes initiative and persistence!

MARCEL: I know that living the life of drugs and alcohol is not a healthy way to live. Since I left rehab my brother has been kind to me and has treated me well, but I don't expect for him to take care of me and my living expenses forever. I have to stand on my own two feet.

SOCIAL WORKER: Okay so I understand from you that housing is an issue?

MARCEL: I can't wait to get a legal job, move out on my own, and start my life again.

SOCIAL WORKER: Let's work together to think of some ways we can problem-solve this issue. Have you had a job in the past? Did you finish high school?

MARCEL: I dropped out of school before I could finish high school. In high school my neighbors used to pay me to wash their cars. But that's pretty much it, because I started to sell drugs for a living.

SOCIAL WORKER: So, what I hear from you, housing and a job are an issue. First, I need you to know that this may take some time to achieve. However, I do believe that with time and persistence, you can achieve anything you set out to do.

MARCEL: I understand and I am willing to do what it takes to live my life the way I am supposed to again.

SOCIAL WORKER: First, I want you to attend a training program. Here is a flier containing their website where you can register. Once you've completed your training, they will help you work on your resume and fill out job applications. Then I want you to come back in two weeks and we will go from there.

Marcel's social worker had to make sure that he completely understood Marcel's problem from Marcel's standpoint. Once Marcel and his social worker were on the same page they could start the problem solving process and develop a treatment plan. Focusing on ways to solve this problem is an important aspect in facilitating overall treatment success. Also, going through this problem solving process during a therapy session was a learning experience for Marcel and will be helpful for when he encounters problems in the future. Thus the social worker uses problem solving as a technique to achieve constructive change for the client.

REFERENCES AND ADDITIONAL SOURCES

Areán, P., Hegel, M., Vannoy, S., Fan, M., & Unuzter, J. (2008). Effectiveness of problem-solving therapy for older, primary care patients with depression: Results from the IMPACT project. *The Gerontologist, 48*(3), 311–323.

Areán, P. A., Perri, M. G., Nezu, A. M., Schein, R. L., Christopher, F., & Joseph, T. X. (1993). Comparative effectiveness of social problem-solving therapy and reminiscence therapy as treatment for depression in older adults. *Journal of Consulting and Clinical Psychology, 61*(6), 1003–1010.

Ayalon, L., Bornfeld, H., Gum, A. M., & Areán, P. A. (2009). The use of problem-solving therapy and restraint-free environment for the management of depression and agitation in long-term care. *Clinical Gerontologist: The Journal of Aging and Mental Health, 32*(1), 77–90.

Bannan, N. (2010). Group-based problem-solving therapy in self-poisoning females: A pilot study. *Counselling & Psychotherapy Research, 10*(3), 201–213.

Black, D. W., Allen, J., St. John, D., Pfohl, B., McCormick, B., & Blum, N. (2009). Predictors of response to systems training for emotional predictability and problem solving (STEPPS) for borderline personality disorder: An exploratory study. *Acta Psychiatrica Scandinavica, 120*(1), 53–61.

Dixon, W. A. (2000). Problem-solving appraisal and depression: Evidence for a recovery model. *Journal of Counseling & Development, 78*(1), 87–91.

Dowrick, C., Dunn, G., Ayuso-Mateos, J. L., Dalgard, O. S., Page, H., Lehtinen, V., … & Wilkinson, G. (2000). Problem solving treatment and group psychoeducation for depression: multicentre randomised controlled trial. *British Medical Journal, 321*(7274), 1450–1454.

D'Zurilla, T. J., & Goldfried, M. R. (1971). Problem solving and behavior modification. *Journal of Abnormal Psychology, 78*(1), 107–126.

D'Zurilla, T. J., & Nezu, A. M. (2007). *Problem-solving therapy: A positive approach to clinical intervention* (3rd ed.). New York, NY: Springer.

Egan, G. (2002). *The skilled helper: A problem-management and opportunity-development approach to helping* (6th ed.). Pacific Grove, CA, Brooks/Cole.

Eskin, M., Ertekin, K., & Demir, H. (2008). Efficacy of a problem-solving therapy for depression and suicide potential in adolescents and young adults. *Cognitive Therapy & Research, 32*(2), 227–245.

Gellis, Z. D., & Bruce, M. L. (2010). Problem-solving therapy for subthreshold depression in home healthcare patients with cardiovascular disease. *The American Journal of Geriatric Psychiatry, 18*(6), 464–474.

Haley, J. (1976). *Problem-solving therapy*. San Franicisco, CA: Jossey-Bass.

Perlman, H. (1957). *Social casework: A problem-solving process*. Chicago, IL: University of Chicago Press.

Turner, J., & Rose-Marie, J. (1996). Problem-solving theory and social work treatment. In F. J. Turner (Ed.), *Social work treatment* (4th ed., pp. 503–522). New York, NY: Free Press.

Wade, S. L., Walz, N. C., Carey, J. C. P., & Williams, K. M. (2008). Preliminary efficacy of a web-based family problem-solving treatment program for adolescents with traumatic brain injury. *Journal of Head Trauma Rehabilitation. Focus on Clinical Research and Practice, Part 2, 23*(6), 369–377.

Public Speaking

DESCRIPTION

A technique that is so much a part of our daily practice lives that we take it for granted is that of speaking on a client's behalf. This may include such activities as a presentation to a committee of colleagues, an appearance in court, a referral to an agency, a case discussion, or a request to some level of officialdom. Here we are focusing on those situations where we make a presentation to a body, whether professional or not, regarding some aspect of our client to obtain goods, service, or assistance we judge will be useful.

ORIGINS

Although we recognize that public speaking is a highly necessary skill for our macro practicing colleagues, we rarely consider it to be a clinical technique. However, if our practice is based on a clinical psychosocial orientation, there will be many occasions when it is important for us to act on behalf of the client by using our public speaking abilities to seek something for them or inform third parties about them.

The concept of public speaking as a technique does not come from any particular theoretical position, except perhaps communication theory. More often it is our awareness of our limitations in this area, or our experience of seeing colleagues perform ineptly, to the detriment of their client, that we become aware of its importance to our practice.

WHY THIS IS USEFUL TO SOCIAL WORK

Public speaking is critical to our practice because much of our clinical work that involves difficulties clients are having with some systemic component of their lives requires the interventions of someone skilled in understanding and involving themselves in particular systems. Speaking for a client at an appropriate time or place is a powerful way to bring about specific changes for a client and to develop skills in this area, and can thus be an important resource in our arma-mentarium of techniques.

HOW THIS IS USEFUL TO SOCIAL WORK

As mentioned, clients' areas of difficulty often arise from a lack of knowledge or understanding regarding a particular system in their lives. Being able to speak for the client and convey information in a way that enhances mutual understandings can be of considerable help to them.

In addition to the primary potential of public speaking, to aid an individual or group of clients in a particular manner, it can have an important secondary effect related to social work's public image. A well-prepared and well-presented report can speak favorably of us all, just as a poorly prepared report, or one presented with insufficient skill, can have negative repercussions.

RISK FACTORS

There are few risks in using this technique, apart from those emerging from our possible ineptitude. Rather than assisting the client for whom we are speaking, our lack of skill can make a situation more complex or fail to accomplish the goal we are seeking.

Because this component of practice is insufficiently recognized as a clinical technique, we often do not give it the attention that it deserves. One reason may be that we don't take advantage of its potential in a situation when a well-prepared oral presentation may be of considerable assistance to the client. Another may be that we fail to recognize that we are not skilled in this area, and make a presentation that serves the client poorly due to our ineptness. We may also avoid public speaking because it makes us very uncomfortable, and, by not using what might be an important source of assistance, we fail our clients.

REQUIRED SKILLS AND KNOWLEDGE

Preparation and practice are two of the requisites for any public presentation. Most of us are reasonably skilled in this technique, or view ourselves to be so. However, there are many for whom the necessity of speaking before a group causes great anxiety; thus, when they need to do so, they don't tap its potential for their clients.

Case Summary One

Jamie was arrested for fighting in a local bar. After being released on bail, his lawyer suggested that he see a social worker for an evaluation. Jamie had an evaluation done and continued to see his social worker weekly until his court date for sentencing. Jamie's social worker attended his hearing to speak on his behalf and contribute his findings from the therapy sessions.

LAWYER: Your Honor, we would now like you to hear from the defendant's social worker.

JUDGE: Okay, proceed. First, tell me how long you've known the client and in what capacity.

SOCIAL WORKER: Jamie came to my office a couple of months ago for an evaluation, and we have been meeting weekly for therapy sessions ever since.

LAWYER: Please tell us the results of your evaluation of the defendant.

SOCIAL WORKER: After completing my evaluation and assessment, it was determined that Jamie has a dual diagnosis of substance abuse issues along with depression and anxiety. The night that Jamie had the altercation in the bar, he had been drinking heavily and was not in his right state of mind.

LAWYER: What would be your recommendation for your client?

SOCIAL WORKER: In my opinion, jail is not going to give Jamie the help he needs. I think Jamie would benefit more from a substance abuse treatment program and continued therapy. Jamie understands that his actions were wrong and recognizes his need for treatment.

Without the input of his social worker, Jamie probably would have been sentenced to jail and missed out on receiving the assistance that would be most beneficial to him. Having the social worker speak on his behalf provided a credible source and a professional, therapeutic opinion for the judge to take into consideration. Public speaking in an open court can be intimidating at first; we recommend that a social worker observe a few cases in advance to get a sense of what it can be like.

Case Summary Two

Nolan is in a liberal arts program for his undergraduate studies. Nolan really wants to be a lawyer and he knows that public speaking is an essential component in practicing law. Nolan possesses a fear of public speaking that he has had since he was a child. For that reason, Nolan decides to seek help for his fear.

NOLAN: Well, I know that as a lawyer I will be required talk publicly, and I don't know if I can get the better of my fear of public speaking.

SOCIAL WORKER: Well, the fact that you are in therapy today shows that you are taking strong initiative to learn how to overcome your anxiety with public speaking.

NOLAN: What would be your recommendation for me?

SOCIAL WORKER: In my opinion, not pursuing what you love to do for fear of the public speaking is not the right answer. I think you would benefit from therapy. We can work together so that you can overcome your fear of public speaking. Conquering public speaking can lead you to a great and rewarding career as a lawyer.

Nolan understands that in order to be able to pursue a career as an attorney, he must overcome his great fear of speaking publicly. He recognizes his need for treatment and is willing to work with this social worker. With the social worker's input, Nolan will learn how to relax, make eye contact, pay attention to his body language, get out of his comfort zone, prepare and practice, and get to know his audience when making a public speech to allow his voice to be heard.

Without the input of his social worker, Jamie probably would have given up his dream of having a legal career. Public speaking can be intimidating at first, but with practice this fear can be overcome. This will lead the client to have great leadership skills and a rewarding career.

REFERENCES AND ADDITIONAL SOURCES

Botella, C., Gallego, M. J., Garcia-Palacios, A., Baños, R. M., Quero, S., & Alcañiz, M. (2009). The acceptability of an internet-based self-help treatment for fear of public speaking. *British Journal of Guidance & Counselling, 37*(3), 297–311.

Botella, C., Guillén, V., Banos, R. M., Garcia-Palacios, A., Gallego, M. J., & Alcañiz, M. (2007). Telepsychology and self-help: The treatment of fear of public speaking. *Cognitive and Behavioural Practice, 14*(1), 46–57.

Botella, C., Hofmann, S. G., & Moscovitz, D. A. (2004). A self-applied internet-based intervention for fear of public speaking. *Journal of Clinical Psychology, 60,* 1–10.

Carlbring, P., Bohman, S., Brunt, S., Buhrman, M., Westling, B., Ekselius, L., & Andersson, G. (2006). Remote treatment of panic disorder: A randomized trial of Internet-based cognitive behavior therapy supplemented with telephone calls. *American Journal of Psychiatry, 163*(12), 2119–2125.

Frank, S. (2000). *Public speaking.* Holbrook, MA: Adams Media.

Heimberg, R. G. (2002). Cognitive-behavioral therapy for social anxiety disorder: Current status and future directions. *Biological Psychiatry, 51*(1), 101–108.

Hofmann, S. G., & DiBartolo, P. M. (2000). An instrument to assess self-statements during public speaking: Scale development and preliminary psychometric properties. *Behaviour Therapy, 31*(3), 499–515.

Hope, D. A., Heimberg, R. G., & Turk, C. L. (2010). *Managing social anxiety: A cognitive-behavioral therapy approach: Social worker guide* (2nd ed.). New York, NY: Oxford University Press.

Lucas, S. E. (2005). *The art of public speaking.* New York, NY: McGraw-Hill.

Osborn, M., & Osborn, S. (1991). *Public speaking* (2nd ed.). Boston, MA: Houghton Mifflin.

Rodebaugh, T. L., Holaway, R. M., & Heimberg, R. G. (2004). The treatment of social anxiety disorder. *Clinical Psychology Review, 24*(7), 883–908.

Tannous, C. (2000). Social workers as advocates for their clients with disabilities: A conflict of roles? *Australian Occupational Therapy Journal, 47*(1), 41–46.

Trexler, L. D., & Karst, T. O. (1972). Rational-emotive therapy, placebo, and no-treatment effects on public-speaking anxiety. *Journal of Abnormal Psychology, 79*(1), 60–67.

Wallach, H. S., Safir, M. P., & Bar-Zvi, M. (2009). Virtual reality cognitive behavior therapy for public speaking anxiety: A randomized clinical trial. *Behavior Modification, 33*(3), 314–338.

Questions

DESCRIPTION

We discussed the use of a specific type of question, the miracle question, as a particular technique earlier in this book. Here we are focusing on the more general use of questions as a therapeutic technique.

ORIGINS

In our overall interviewing activities, we are seeking to understand the client in many areas of their lives. We do this to formulate as clear a psychosocial picture of the client as possible, and, as needed, to be of assistance to them in a responsible way. Although much of this material comes spontaneously through the judicious use of many techniques, much is obtained by asking questions. Although our general interview strategy over the years minimized this method, we have learned that the skillful and timely use of questions can be a powerful source of information.

WHY THIS IS USEFUL TO SOCIAL WORK

The essence of our therapeutic activities is to help our clients in an accountable, responsible manner. To do so requires that we know, in as much detail as possible, who the client is from the perspective of their psychosocial reality. We know that this reality covers a broad, multidimensional spectrum, and that in many situations it is only the client who can tell us who they are and what elements constitute their reality, at least as they see it. Posing questions can help them present their reality to us.

HOW THIS IS USEFUL TO SOCIAL WORK

We use questions in a variety of ways:

- to obtain necessary factual information about the client that only he or she knows;
- to clarify material that a client shares with us and to seek further depth;
- to ensure we have understood what a client has told us;
- to open up material or topics that have not been mentioned by the client, whether deliberately, out of anxiety or fear, or perhaps from a lack of awareness that the material might be significant, relevant, or important;
- to lead a client to reflect when we encourage them to consider some aspect of what we have been told more deeply, or to look further at some topic that may be emerging; and
- to help persons to recognize and come to appreciate their inner strengths and abilities, as well as other resources they haven't recognized or are not using in an ego-enhancing way.

RISK FACTORS

This is not a technique with a high degree of risk, apart from that of overusing it in a challenging or intrusive manner, which can be frightening to clients. Often in our practice, our awareness that questions can upset or frighten clients requires us to settle for obtaining a minimal amount of knowledge. Also, out of a professional curiosity that surpasses the needs of the situation, we sometimes question clients because we wish to learn more or to test a diagnostic formulation we are considering.

REQUIRED SKILLS AND KNOWLEDGE

Gathering information through questions is not something we necessarily do at the beginning of a case, of course, but is a process that may continue through its entire life. Indeed, sometimes it is only at the end of a case when we ask a question that elicits information of help to us and the client.

Probably the most important skill for using of questions is timing. We can frequently sense or observe that a client is not yet ready to move into a particular area, and even though we may want to obtain the information we seek, we need to wait until the time is right.

Some topics for questioning may be as seemingly innocuous as providing a name and address, material that the client may wish to withhold until he or she sizes us up and assesses the process to decide just how intensely he or she may wish to invest in it. How we ask questions is a highly developed skill, ranging from posing them very directly to a friendly frown or period of silence. Throughout the process, we need to avoid letting the interview become a question-and-answer process, bordering on a form of interrogation.

Much of our work with clients consists of leading them to make use of their ego strengths and cognitive abilities by helping them to develop the behavior patterns that best fit their abilities and values. To do this, we often use questions to help them move toward considering an alternate understanding or significance of some aspect of their lives. We also use questions to help them expand their thinking, perception, and behavior in a more growth-enhancing direction. The content of our questions is shaped by the ongoing process of assessment and diagnostic work as we seek to organize our thoughts, impressions, and judgments about how we can be helpful.

Although this is not always the case, we probably use questions more often in the earlier stages of a relationship, when the social worker and client are trying to find the best fit with each other.

Case Summary One

Bobby is an adolescent male presenting with anger concerns. His parents became worried when he appeared to become isolated from his friends, and his angry outbursts at home escalated. According to Bobby, he has become increasingly angry over the past few months and is not sure why.

BOBBY: I just don't know why I'm in such a bad mood all the time. It seems like I'm always frustrated.

SOCIAL WORKER: What has upset you recently?

BOBBY: I'm mad at my best friend. He keeps blowing me off after school and we haven't spoken lately. I hate him now.

SOCIAL WORKER: What happens when you come home after school?

BOBBY: First, I go into my room and just stay by myself for a while. Later in the evening, my parents usually start bugging me. They are so irritating.

SOCIAL WORKER: How do you react when they start irritating you?

BOBBY: I scream at them and tell them to get out of my face.

SOCIAL WORKER: How does that work for you?

BOBBY: They yell back at me and punish me for disrespecting them.

Bobby's social worker asked specific questions to get Bobby to start thinking about his angry feelings and behavior, as well as their consequences. The social worker posed certain questions to elicit detailed information from Bobby. Through this questioning, Bobby will be able to expand his thinking further and enhance his growth to achieve his goal of decreasing his anger.

Case Summary Two

Kenneth is an adolescent male. According to his parents, Kenneth is engaging in risky behaviors such as drinking and stealing, and is doing poorly in school. At home, Kenneth fights with his siblings. According to him, he is not sure why he is engaging in these behaviors.

KENNETH: I don't know why I act out in school and at home. It seems like I am always getting into trouble. I make bad grades in school. I don't think I will ever have a future.

SOCIAL WORKER: In this session, I am going to ask you some questions in order to help you.

KENNETH: Okay.

SOCIAL WORKER: Can you recall a time in your life when you were successful? How did you feel?

KENNETH: In the first grade I got an award for doing well in my music class. I felt good, like I had accomplished something.

SOCIAL WORKER: Can you describe to me in five words specifically how you felt at that time?

KENNETH: Well, I felt proud, confident, worthy, energetic, and excited.

SOCIAL WORKER: Now I want you to remember a time when you had failed at something. How did you feel?

KENNETH: I remember when I failed at my first-grade Christmas play. I forgot all my lines. I felt awful.

SOCIAL WORKER: Can you list five words telling me how that felt to you at the time?

KENNETH: I felt embarrassed, nervous, angry, sad, and humiliated when I forgot my lines that day at the school play.

The social worker uses a solution-focused approach to ask Kenneth questions that will eventually help him realize his specific strengths and help him discover some of his own solutions to his problems. By using specific questions, the social worker is able to demonstrate to the client that he does have control over his own behavior.

REFERENCES AND ADDITIONAL SOURCES

Armstrong, L. (1999). The well-built clinical question: The key to finding the best evidence efficiently. *Wisconsin Medical Journal, 98*(2), 25–28.

Berg, I. K., & de Shazer, S. (1993). Making numbers talk: Language in therapy. In S. Friedman (Ed.), *The new language of change* (pp. 5–24). New York, NY: Guilford.

Dillon, J. T. (1990). *The practice of questioning.* New York, NY: Routledge.

Furman, B., & Ahola, T. (1992). *Solution talk: Hosting therapeutic conversations.* New York, NY: Norton.

Gambrill, E. (1997). *Social work practice* (pp. 302–306). New York, NY: Oxford University Press.

Guilfoyle, M. (2003). Dialogue and power: A critical analysis of power in dialogical therapy. *Family Process, 42*(3), 331–343.

McNamee, S., & Gergen, S. (Eds.). (1992). *Therapy as social construction.* Newbury Park, CA: Sage.

Miller, G. (1997). *Becoming miracle workers: Language and meaning in brief therapy.* New York, NY: Aldine de Gruyter.

O'Hanlon, W. H., & Weiner-Davis, M. (1989). *In search of solutions: A new direction in psychotherapy.* New York, NY: Norton.

Strong, T., Pyle, N. R., & Sutherland, O. (2009). Scaling questions: Asking and answering them in counselling. *Counselling Psychology Quarterly, 22*(2), 171–185.

Watzlawick, P., Bavelas, J. B., & Jackson, D. (1967). *Pragmatics of human communication: A study of interactional patterns, pathologies, and paradoxes.* New York, NY: Norton.

Weingarten, K. (1992). A consideration of intimate and non-intimate interactions in therapy. *Family Process, 31*(1), 45–59.

White, M., & Epston, D. (1990). *Narrative means to therapeutic ends.* New York: Norton.

Wolpe, J. (1973). *Practice of behavior therapy* (2nd ed.). New York, NY: Pergamon.

Reading

DESCRIPTION

There are several ways in which we can use the printed word for specific therapeutic goals. Although not everyone we meet in practice is capable of learning from the act and art of reading, we do know that there are many who can be profoundly influenced by written material, and that such an influence can often be used in a growth-enhancing way.

ORIGINS

Like many other techniques in our profession, we are learning that many of the methods we influence people therapeutically draw on their day-to-day activities. When properly understood, we can draw upon them in a helpful manner. Reading is one of these.

WHY THIS IS USEFUL TO SOCIAL WORK

Our awareness of the powerful and differential effects of the printed word on most people has led to the development of a whole new approach to therapy known as *bibliotherapy*. Here, however, we are focusing on specific ways of making use of this life component as a technique in therapy rather than a whole intervention modality.

HOW THIS IS USEFUL TO SOCIAL WORK

There are several ways to use the printed word for specific therapeutic goals. We know that by reading, people can learn about themselves, others in their lives, and events and significant social issues that affect them. This can help clients change their self-image, knowledge, and behavior.

The use of the written word for self-development has a broad scope of applicability. These sources of growth range in scale from informative pamphlets about some particular resource or problem, to a vast collection of nonfiction books. The range of these resources is virtually limitless, and many people can learn a great deal from this type of material. They also have the advantage of being available whenever concrete information is needed.

In addition to making therapeutic use of nonfiction material, we can also use fictional material in practice. From our own experience, we know we can be dramatically moved by a well-written novel. We often identify with the book's events or characters in a way that can bring self-understanding or give us the opportunity to share in a significant and sometimes powerful emotional experience. So, too, can our clients.

A further use of the printed word is simply to help a client learn the great pleasure and satisfaction that can come from reading. Many of us assume that most people can and do read for pleasure; however, this is not so. Thus, introducing clients to the world of reading, or seeing that they find their way into it, can be a very helpful, inexpensive, and satisfying thing for many of them, beyond the primary focus of our treatment. This is especially true for isolated persons of all ages, who can benefit from reading not only from the perspective of learning about themselves, but also just to enjoy the pleasure to be derived from reading.

Although we often view this type of therapy from a one-to-one perspective, it of course has equally powerful utility for couples and group situations. The advantage of the group setting is that looking at a particular piece of writing from the group's viewpoint permits a broad range of perceptions around a particular issue or experience that the characters have, allowing clients to identify with those features and experience positive change without having to talk about themselves directly.

RISK FACTORS

Reading can be a most effective and long-lasting way to influence clients in a helpful manner that entails very little risk. There are, however, two low-level risks in using this technique. The first is that we overestimate the client's ability to read. Illiteracy in varying degrees is common in our society, and in some instances, rather than leading the person to read, we will first need to help them find a way to learn to read.

The other risk is one of values. Many persons in our society do not view reading as pleasant, and we need to be careful not to let our interest in reading be projected insensitively upon the client.

REQUIRED SKILLS AND KNOWLEDGE

Two important requisite skills for using reading material as a form of therapy are to be able to assess the sources and accuracy of self-help material, and the ability to match the right material to the client.

Finding useful fiction material to help our clients in a specific way is a discrete skill, and requires a rich knowledge of literature, both modern and classical. Thus, unless this is a particular talent of ours, we will want to make use of a social worker with a literary background or a librarian to help us locate material with specific foci and at the appropriate level of comprehension.

Case Summary One

Carrie is a 15-year-old female attending therapy following her mother's discovery that she was having a relationship with a 40-year-old man. Carrie disclosed that she had the relationship with him for 2 months and had sex with him once. She stated that the sex was consensual and doesn't believe that there is anything wrong with the nature of the relationship she had with the older man. However, she does say that she can understand her mother's position. During one session she also reported that she is confused about her feelings.

> **CARRIE:** I feel all mixed up about my feelings for him. One day I think he is a creep and he tricked me. Other days I just think that he is a nice guy. My feelings fluctuate from day to day.
>
> **SOCIAL WORKER:** Sometimes older individuals know how to manipulate younger individuals and they know exactly what to say to them to get what they want. I have some information here on emotional grooming that might be helpful. Let's read it together and then discuss what we've read.

In this case study, reading is used as an educational tool and a way to facilitate discussion. It is important to have printed documentation to back up what the social worker is explaining so that Carrie does not have to take just the social worker's word for it. It was also helpful that the book on emotional grooming included information written by teenagers who have been through similar situations as Carrie.

Case Summary Two

Demi is in therapy due to domestic violence in which her husband physically, emotionally, and domestically abused her. She reports having trouble sleeping, feeling numb, and experiencing paranoia and phobia about leaving her home, even to go to the grocery store. Demi is disabled and must walk on crutches. She worries her husband might come after her or try to kill her, so consequently she does not let herself fall asleep.

During the first counseling session, the social worker and Demi talk about forming a safety plan. The social worker makes sure that Demi is as safe as possible. For example, Demi reports that all the locks on her doors have been changed. The social worker gives Demi a safety plan worksheet for her to look over at home in order to get a few more ideas on how she can keep safe.

> **DEMI:** I don't know how I did this to myself. I attracted the wrong person. I am in a real bind this time. I met him online and he was so nice at first. I don't know how I let myself get into something like this.
>
> **SOCIAL WORKER:** Sometimes it is not evident going into a relationship that the person will turn out to be abusive. Don't be so hard on yourself.

DEMI: That's true; there was no way for me to know in the beginning that things would turn out this way. I just can't sleep at night. I haven't slept in three days. All I can think of is what will happen if he finds me. I leave on all the lights and televisions on in my apartment all the time so that I don't feel alone. Whenever I start to doze off I wake myself back up.

SOCIAL WORKER: I have some information here on sleep hygiene that might be helpful. Let's read it together and then discuss what we've read.

Here, reading is used as an educational tool and a way to facilitate dialogue. It is important to have printed material to back up what the social worker is explaining so that Demi can have the information to refer to later. It was also helpful that the book on sleep hygiene included information used by women who have experienced the same situation.

REFERENCES AND ADDITIONAL SOURCES

Ayres, J. (1986). Perceptions of speaking ability: An explanation for stage fright. *Communication Education, 35*(3), 275–287.

Ayres, J. (1988). Coping with speech anxiety: The power of positive thinking. *Communication Education, 37*(4), 289–296.

Ayres, J., & Hopf, T. (1993). *Coping with speech anxiety.* Norwood, NJ: Ablex.

Behnke, R. R., & Sawyer, C. R. (2001). Patterns of psychological state anxiety in public speaking as a function of anxiety sensitivity. *Communication Quarterly, 49*, 84–94.

Bodie, G. D. (2010). A racing heart, rattling knees, and ruminative thoughts: Defining, explaining, and treating public speaking anxiety. *Communication Education, 59*(1), 70–105.

Burns, G. L., & Kondrick, P. A. (1998). Psychological behaviorism's reading therapy program: Parents as reading social workers for their children's reading disability. *Journal of Learning Disabilities, 31*(3), 278–285.

Chung, Y., & Kwon, J. (2008). The efficacy of bibliotherapy for social phobia. *Brief Treatment & Crisis Intervention, 8*(4), 390–401.

Doherty, D., & Mccoll, M. A. (2003). Illness stories: Themes emerging through narrative. *Sound Work in Heath Care, 37*(1), 19–39.

Garcia, C. L. (1986). Extending reading tradition: An educational therapy approach. *Reading Psychology, 7*(4), 305–311.

Gardiner, J. C., Furois, M., Tansley, D. P., & Morgan, B. (2000). Music therapy and reading as intervention strategies for disruptive behavior in dementia. *Clinical Gerontologist: The Journal of Aging and Mental Health, 22*(1), 31–46.

MacInnis, C. C., Mackinnon, S. P., & MacIntyre, P. D. (2010). The illusion of transparency and normative beliefs about anxiety during public speaking. *Research in Social Psychology, 15*, 42–52.

Pardeck, J. T., & Musich, J. A. (2005). Recommended children's books on disabilities. *Journal of Social Work and Rehabilitation, 1*(2), 53–72.

Tussing, H. L., & Valentine, D. P. (2001). Helping adolescents cope with the mental illness of a parent through bibliotherapy. *Child & Adolescent Social Work Journal, 18*(6), 455–469.

Venberg, B., & Schum, M. J. (2002). Internet bibliotherapy: A narrative analysis of a reading simulated support group. *Journal of Social Work and Disability and Rehabilitation, 1*(1), 81–97.

Wu, C., & Honig, A. S. (2010). Taiwanese mothers' beliefs about reading aloud with preschoolers: Findings from the Parent Reading Belief Inventory. *Early Child Development and Care, 180*(5), 647–669.

Referral

DESCRIPTION

One of a social worker's most important functions is to help clients connect to the network of resources and people that make up the complex structure of human services. In fact, so much of our practice in some settings involves referral, that it is sometimes said quite cynically that the first rule of good social work practice is to refer the case.

ORIGINS

In its origins, social work was a phenomenon that principally took place in the urban areas of various countries. Most cities in this era featured a complex network of variously sponsored and multifunctional helping services. Thus from our earliest days, an important function of social work was to help clients find their way though this highly uncoordinated service maze.

WHY THIS IS USEFUL TO SOCIAL WORK

One of the difficulties of this aspect of our practice is that it is frequently viewed as simply an administrative function, thus minimizing the therapeutic components of the process. This is a serious misunderstanding of the importance and complexities of this crucial part of our practice, as well as a failure to appreciate the skills involved. It also underestimates its potential for assistance when this technique is used effectively.

HOW THIS IS USEFUL TO SOCIAL WORK

The social services structure of our contemporary world remains highly complex, as are the many needs of our clients. Skill in knowing this structure and learning how to use it in a helpful, individualized way is thus an important and requisite skill for all practitioners.

On the plus side, it is gratifying to know that in many situations we can be of great assistance to clients by understanding them well enough to connect them to the resources that can be most helpful to them. On the minus side, the reality remains that the available helping network is often overly complex. Thus rather than being of assistance to our clients, the process becomes one of frustration and anxiety for them, requiring us to draw upon other techniques and a further search for resources.

RISK FACTORS

This is not a technique with a high risk factor. However, there are areas where we need to be very careful. An essential point is to ensure that there is clarity among all concerned as to the dimensions of each referral.

For example, does the referral imply that contact with the worker doing the referral is deemed to have been terminated? Or is the referral built on the understanding that some type of coordinated service or therapy will now continue? This latter point is most important to avoid situations where the client inappropriately remains in contact with the original worker in a manner that could interfere with beginning the process in the new setting.

In these situations, it is also important to establish what kind of information, if any, is to be shared between the two settings, how much of it, and by what method; and to ensure that the client is involved in this agreement.

REQUIRED SKILLS AND KNOWLEDGE

There are several components to this technique:

- The first is the essential responsibility to understand the client and his or her needs, desires, and capabilities.
- The second is to ensure that we understand just what resources exist that do or do not fit where the client is and what the client needs.
- The third factor is to ensure that we are knowledgeable about the policies and procedures of the service to which we are referring the client.
- The fourth component of this technique is the need to know the idiosyncrasies of the resources we are considering. This, of course, is much more complex than looking up the sought-after services in an agency directory or running a search on the Internet. We all know from our practice that what a service might state it can do, and what it actually does, may not always coincide. It is also important that we understand matters such as fees, hours of service, eligibility requirements, waiting periods, intake procedures, general reputation, and accessibility (including parking and bus service). We must try to avoid

having clients be handed from one service to another in a series of referrals, each of which may require a complete intake and assessment procedure. This can be highly anxiety-provoking and frustrating for clients.

- A further component of using this technique effectively is our skill in facilitating the referral by dealing sensitively with the client's questions, possible ambivalence, and anxieties about the referral. Such concerns are frequently very strong and may not be verbalized. This process of preparing a client for a planned referral may itself be time consuming, requiring a range of other techniques (e.g., sustaining and brokering) to be called into play.

Case Summary

Tracy has been meeting with her social worker for several months now. She has a job and steady income, but a few unexpected expenses left her short on her rent payments for the past few months. Falling behind on rent has made her worry that she is going to be evicted from her apartment.

> **TRACY:** I feel like I'm practically homeless. I don't know what I'm going to do. I can't lose my apartment.
>
> **SOCIAL WORKER:** From what you have told me, it sounds like you earn a good amount of money, but just need a little help to play catch-up. Is that correct?
>
> **TRACY:** Yes. I've never had a problem paying my bills before, but after the car repairs I had to pay for unexpectedly, it's been difficult. I can pay my utilities, but then I don't have enough to pay the full amount for my rent.
>
> **SOCIAL WORKER:** So what I hear you saying is that if you didn't have to pay all of your utilities, you would be able to pay the full amount of your rent. Is that right?
>
> **TRACY:** That is exactly right, but I don't want to get my water or electricity shut off either, so I pay those first.
>
> **SOCIAL WORKER:** I'm going to give you a referral to one of our local agencies. They will pay your utilities for one month, allowing you to catch up on your rent payments. You just have to arrive at their office tomorrow morning at 8:00 a.m. with the referral from me. Also, make sure you bring your utility bills, your identification, and proof that you are employed, because that is one of the eligibility requirements.
>
> **TRACY:** Thank you so much. I didn't even know a program like that existed. It is just what I need to relieve my financial stress.

Because Tracy's social worker knew her needs and capabilities, and was aware of the available resources, he was able to provide her with an appropriate referral. Her social worker was also able to answer questions Tracy had with regard to the referral, and provide her with detailed information about the process involved in obtaining services, which eased Tracy's frustrations and anxieties about her situation.

Case Summary Two

Kristina and her 6-year old son, José, are in therapy since her son witnessed his mother being physically abused. Kristina and José are safe, and José is getting therapy so that he can receive psychoeducation and relaxation skills to use when he is in a situation where he feels tense or angry. Kristina also states that her son has been having trouble in school with disruption and acting out.

SOCIAL WORKER: What grade is José in and how is he doing in school?

KRISTINA: José is in the first grade. He is not doing well in school at all. He is constantly bossing the other kids and yelling at the teacher and causing classroom disruptions. I am worried that he will be dismissed from school.

SOCIAL WORKER: So what I hear you say is that you are worried that Jose is going to get expelled from school because of his uncontrollable behavior.

KRISTINA: Yes that is correct. He just doesn't get along with anyone.

SOCIAL WORKER: I am going to refer you to a child specialist who works within our agency. We often refer clients who have conduct issues or disruptive acting-out behaviors to her. She is a child psychologist who specializes in parent–child interaction therapy. She will provide services to José and teach you to reinforce José's positive behavior and ignore his negative behavior.

KRISTINA: That sounds helpful, but it also sounds rather expensive.

SOCIAL WORKER: Since the psychologist works with our agency, she can provide you with services on a reduced, sliding fee scale depending on your income.

KRISTINA: Thank you so much. I didn't even know a program like that existed. It is just what I need to get help for José and not have to pay a fortune.

Because José's social worker knew that José's problem requires the services of a practitioner who specializes in handling childhood acting-out behaviors, she was able to suit José's needs and capabilities to the available resources that she knew about and provide a helpful referral. Kristina's social worker was also able to provide her with detailed information about the process of obtaining services, which eased her frustrations and apprehension about the situation.

REFERENCES AND ADDITIONAL SOURCES

Adeyemi, J. D., Olonade, P. O., & Amira, C. O. (2002). Attitude to psychiatric referral: A study of primary care physicians. *Nigerian Postgraduate Medical Journal, 9*(2), 53–58.

Ashworth, M., Clement, S., Sandu, J., Farley, N., Ramsey, R., & Davies, T. (2002). Psychiatric referral rates and the influence of on-site mental health workers in general practice. *British Journal of General Practice, 52*(474), 39–41.

Bentley, K. J., Walsh, J., & Farmer, R. (2005). Referring clients for psychiatric medication: Best practices for social workers. *Best Practices in Mental Health, 1*(1), 59–71.

Franz, C. E., Barker, J. C., Kim, K., Flores, Y., Jenkins, C., Kravitz, R. L., & Hinton, L. (2010). When help becomes a hindrance: Mental health referral systems as barriers to care for primary care physicians treating patients with Alzheimer's disease. *The American Journal of Geriatric Psychiatry, 18*(7), 576–585.

Hardiman, E. R. (2007). Referral to consumer-run programs by mental health providers: A national survey. *Community Mental Health Journal, 43*(3), 197–210.

Johnson, L. C. (1986). *Social work practice: A generalist approach* (2nd ed., pp. 312–314). Toronto, Ontario: Allyn & Bacon.

Leigh, A. (1998). *Referral and termination issues for counselors.* London, England: Sage.

Livingston, P. M., White, V. M., Hayman, J., Maunsell, E., Dunn, S. M., & Hill, D. (2010). The psychological impact of a specialist referral and telephone intervention on male cancer patients: A randomised controlled trial. *Psycho-Oncology, 19*(6), 617–625.

Matthews, M., Fawcett, S., & Stephen, B. (1981). *Referral for psychological testing. Matching clients and services: Information and referral.* Beverly Hills, CA: Sage.

Montoya, L. A., Giardino, A. P., & Leventhal, J. M. (2010). Mental health referral and services for maltreated children and child protection evaluations of children with special needs: A national survey of hospital- and community-based medically oriented teams. *Child Abuse & Neglect, 34*(8), 593–601.

Ramirez, A., Ekselius, L., & Ramklint, M. (2009). Mental disorders among young adults self-referred and referred by professionals to specialty mental health care. *Psychiatric Services, 60*(12), 1649–1655.

Rees, L., & Clark, S. S. (2006). Can collaboration between education and health professionals improve the identification and referral of young people with eating disorders in schools? A pilot study. *Journal of Adolescence, 29*(1), 137–151.

Sheafor, B. W., & Horejsi, C. R. (2003). *Techniques and guidelines for social work practice* (6th ed., pp. 313–315). New York, NY: Allyn & Bacon.

Walrath, C., dosReis, S., Miech, R., Liao, Q., Holden, E. W., De Carolis, G., … & Leaf, P. (2001). Referral source differences in functional impairment levels for children served in the comprehensive community mental health services for children and their families program. *Journal of Child and Family Studies, 10*(3), 385–397.

Wolock, I., Sherman, P., Feldman, L. H., & Metzger, B. (2001). Child abuse and neglect referral patterns: A longitudinal study. *Children and Youth Services Review, 23*(1), 21–47.

Reflective Thinking

DESCRIPTION

Reflective thinking describes those efforts we make to have clients look at something they have said, some event that has been a part of their past or present lives, or some plan of action they have set out for themselves in an analytic cognitive manner.

ORIGINS

Reflective thinking is so much a part of our practice repertoire of practice that we frequently fail to see it as a separate technique. Although it has long been used in social work practice, it has not always been designated as a technique. An examination of what practitioners actually do in interviews shows that much of the help clients receive in the therapeutic process stems from a skilful and timely use of reflective techniques.

WHY THIS IS USEFUL TO SOCIAL WORK

For many clients, especially those whose behavioral patterns are spontaneous and impulsive, reflection is a new way of dealing with reality. It is a technique that aims at having the client do the therapeutic work. It is not the same as interpretation or explanation, which come from the social worker. Rather, we use our persuasion and permission-giving skills to lead the client to think and ponder.

The ability to draw upon one's cognitive abilities to consider explanations, alternatives, and solutions is one of our most powerful abilities, one that we all use in our day-to-day lives. Yet it is one that many persons we meet in practice have not learned to use constructively, either in their own lives or in the process of treatment.

HOW THIS IS USEFUL TO SOCIAL WORK

Using this technique leads the client to draw upon their cognitive skills within the security, comfort, and safety of the therapeutic relationship, and to look at some particular aspect of their lives in a thinking, analytic manner. We do this to help them see if there are other ways of viewing a situation, other possibilities they have not considered, or alternative actions, explanations, or interpretations, all with the goal of leading the client to change.

Our aim is to help the client expand their understanding of themselves, others, and situations in their lives to find more effective ways of dealing with them. We also want them to expand their ability to look at situations from a thinking, planning perspective. As with many other techniques, there is an element of teaching underlying this intervention.

Many clients we meet in our practice live a very hectic lifestyle that affords them little or no time to engage sufficiently in this kind of reflection. We can help these people to use the security of the interview to draw upon their reflective abilities.

For some clients, much of the content of our work with them will be this type of reflective thinking. Many clients we meet have never learned to do this; thus, the principal benefit of treatment is learning how to reflect. Others may not need to learn reflection, but do need to practice it.

Reflective thinking can be very useful in couples work, especially when the clients are ready and able to look at explanations and alternatives in their lives. In such situations, we frequently find ourselves needing to be more active in the interview to keep the reflective process on track.

This technique can also be important in group therapy, especially when the focus of the group is understanding and considering different life strategies. Here, as with couples, we usually have to actively keep the group's focus on reflection, and ensure that everyone is heard and has an opportunity to present ideas, explanations, and differing perceptions.

RISK FACTORS

Reflective thinking has minimal risk, presuming we are careful not to overestimate clients' ability to engage in this type of activity. We also need to ensure that we are not attempting to lead the client to our chosen solution or interpretations of the topic at hand.

REQUIRED SKILLS AND KNOWLEDGE

In using this technique, we frequently make use of comments such as, "What else could you have done?," "What else might this mean?," "What other reason might there be for his acting in this way?," "What would happen if you … ?," and so forth.

In some situations, once the client has become comfortable with a reflective stance we find ourselves doing and saying less in the interview, apart from indicating that we are listening and conveying our interest and support for the reflective work in which they are engaged. At times, as the client struggles with themselves to clarify some significant aspect of their lives, it almost seems that they are interviewing themselves while they wrestle with alternatives and consider possible outcomes. Here we can be very helpful by conveying encouragement and reinforcing conclusions they have reached, or by gently encouraging them to pursue the topic further if this seems to be needed.

Case Summary One

Ryan started attending therapy sessions because he felt unhappy at work. He states that he has bad feelings anytime he thinks of work, and that this has been going on for a long time. While attending therapy sessions, Ryan reports that he has been having a conflict with a coworker.

RYAN: I just can't stand going into work anymore. I lie in bed each morning debating whether or not I should go into work or just quit.

SOCIAL WORKER: Tell me more about this. What is it about work that makes you dread going?

RYAN: There's this guy, Ned, he's a coworker in my office. He's just so gloomy all the time. Anytime he opens his mouth it's nothing but negativity. I can't live my life hearing that day after day. I used to love my job and I hate that I don't look forward to going to work anymore.

SOCIAL WORKER: What might be some reasons why your coworker is acting this way?

RYAN: I don't know. He's just a nasty human being.

SOCIAL WORKER: Think about it a little more. What else could it be?

RYAN: I guess he could be unhappy with his life and he takes it out on everyone that he comes in contact with.

SOCIAL WORKER: That is a possibility. So, what can you do in the future when encounter your coworker?

RYAN: Hmm … I suppose I can try to remember that he is probably going through something in his personal life and not take in what he has to say.

Ryan's social worker helped him use the technique of reflective thinking. It allowed Ryan to see beyond his immediate dilemma and come up with alternatives for dealing with it. Going through this process helped him feel more in control of his situation.

Case Summary Two

Ezra is getting help from a social worker in conjunction with seeing a psychiatrist for depression and anxiety. He states that he is depressed for most of the day and can't stand being around his wife and children. Ezra also states that he has been having conflicts with his friends and coworkers.

EZRA: I feel so depressed and anxious for most of the day. I can't seem to stand anyone. My psychiatrist said it would help if I spoke to someone about my depression.

SOCIAL WORKER: Explain that. What do you think is making you unhappy?

EZRA: Well, nothing good ever happens to me. They always happen to other people. I am always going to feel dreadful.

SOCIAL WORKER: Can you identify any reasons as to why you might be feeling so low lately?

EZRA: I'm not sure. I just don't think I'll ever feel good.

SOCIAL WORKER: Try to think a little further. Can you think of something that could be making you upset?

EZRA: Well, I recently experienced a death in my family. I haven't felt the same since I found out my beloved uncle died of cancer.

SOCIAL WORKER: That is a possibility. It sounds like it is hard to appreciate things since your uncle died. This sounds like a tough situation to be in.

EZRA: I guess. Going through that experience has been rough. Maybe that is why I have been feeling down lately.

SOCIAL WORKER: Perhaps. Can you think of another situation lately where something good has happened to you?

EZRA: Let me see. Well, last week my daughter did well in her ballet rehearsal. I was pleased when she won.

Ezra's social worker helped him challenge his distorted thinking through the process of reflective thinking. Reflective thinking helped Ezra to change the all-or-nothing maladaptive thinking pattern that was contributing to his depression. Engaging in reflective thinking helped Ezra find a middle ground in his situation; as a result, he feels more in control.

REFERENCES AND ADDITIONAL SOURCES

Badger, J. (2010). Assessing reflective thinking: Pre-service teachers' and professors' perceptions of an oral examination. *Assessment in Education: Principles, Policy & Practice, 17*(1), 77–89.

Cormier, W. H., & Cormier, L. S. (1991). *Interviewing strategies for helpers: Fundamental skills and cognitive behavioral interventions* (3rd ed.). Monterey, CA: Brooks/Cole.

Dewey, J. (1933). *How we think: A restatement of the relation of reflective thinking to the educative process.* Boston, MA: D.C. Health.

Kember, D., Leung, D. Y., Jones, A., Loke, A. Y., McKay, J., Sinclair, K., … & Yeung, E. (2000). Development of a questionnaire to measure the level of reflective thinking. *Assessment & evaluation in higher education, 25*(4), 381–395.

Kossly, S. M. (2005). Reflective thinking and mental imagery: A perspective on the development of post-traumatic stress disorder. *Development and Psychopathology, 17*(3), 851–863.

Lietz, C. A. (2010). Critical thinking in child welfare supervision. *Administration in Social Work, 34*(1), 68–78.

Northen, H. (1995). *Clinical social work knowledge and skills* (2nd ed., p. 154). New York, NY: Columbia University Press.

Phan, H. P. (2009). Reflective thinking, effort, persistence, disorganization, and academic performance: A mediational approach. *Journal of Research in Educational Psychology, 7*(3), 927–952.

Phan. H. P. (2009). Exploring students' reflective thinking practice, deep processing strategies, effort, and achievement goal orientations. *Educational Psychology, 29*(3), 297–313.

Woods, M. E., & Hollis, F. (1990). *Casework: A psychosocial therapy* (4th ed., pp. 135–146). New York, NY: McGraw-Hill.

66

Reframing

DESCRIPTION

Reframing, sometimes called relabeling, is a technique in which the client is helped to rename or relabel some aspect of their behavior, that of some significant person in their lives, or some facet of their reality. The general goal is to help the client get a different perspective on the identified behavior, either to better understand and modify their own behavior, or that of someone with whom they interact.

ORIGINS

Reframing entered the social work literature and practice out of family theory and practice, transactional analysis, and learning theory.

WHY THIS IS USEFUL TO SOCIAL WORK

There is a strong cognitive aspect to reframing. It calls upon the client's ability to focus on a particular aspect of their reality in a manner that leads to a new perception of themselves or others. It is based on the everyday reality that what we call something very much affects how we evaluate it and respond to it.

HOW THIS IS USEFUL TO SOCIAL WORK

Being able to put a new and different label or descriptor on a symptom or pattern that the client is considering often allows him or her to alter the response to it. This new perspective can affect their understanding of themselves, others, or actions in their lives; it can also result in changes in other people.

Another facet of this technique is to have the client focus on some particular behavioral component. Rather than looking for or considering only one alternative suggestion or label, we help the client think of several explanations or interpretations for the behavior and assign labels to them. We can then use this plurality of options as the basis to examine alternate interpretations of the matter under discussion. This, in turn, can open up a number of possible ways of responding to other people, or to change the ways they respond to the client. The very fact that there may well be a cluster of possible alternatives can serve to weaken an existing reflexive response and to open up the possibility of a less fixed pattern of behavior, despite the fact that we never find the precise cause of every type of response.

Although much of the discussion of reframing looks at aspects of significant persons in a client's life it is also a useful technique in helping individuals look at themselves to find alternate descriptors for some behavioral or attitudinal patterns in their own functioning that can be altered by a reframing process. This technique will be ineffective with clients who are not able to understand the concept and process of labeling, and the freight with which such labels are often loaded.

RISK FACTORS

Reframing is not a technique with a high risk factor. However, employing these techniques carries the risk that accompanies all forms of labeling: that a new perception of behavior can result in an altered pattern that is just as dysfunctional as the one that we were seeking to change, along with the reinforcement that the social worker's influence gives this new perception a stamp of approval.

Clearly we need to be very careful that we do not let our own view of causality dominate. As well we need to be careful that we do not fall into the pattern of worker and client(s) becoming a team that focuses on analyzing the behavior of persons not present in a way that leads the client to avoid looking at themselves and the need to reframe some of their own self-perceptions.

REQUIRED SKILLS AND KNOWLEDGE

The power of the technique stems from an understanding that how we label things—that is, what we call them—can greatly affect how we respond to them. Thus, for example, I can be much more positively responsive to my partner if I can begin to understand that a particular facet of the other person's behavior is caused by a depressive component of their personality, rather than a strategy to irritate me. If I can then label such situations differently, I can be much more positive to that person.

Reframing does not ordinarily result in immediate behavioral changes, although at times just coming to an awareness of another perspective does bring about change. Usually a degree of reinforcement and interpretation on the social worker's part is necessary. Clearly it is a technique that requires the social worker to deeply understand the client and his or her differential perspective of behaviors, either the client's own or others'.

Case Summary One

Carl is attending therapy sessions following a recent breakup with his long-term girlfriend. Carl is not used to being single and feels like he failed in the relationship.

CARL: I don't have a girlfriend because I am unlovable. I want someone to share my life with, someone who will love me unconditionally. If I don't have a girlfriend I feel like I am a failure.

SOCIAL WORKER: Let's try reframing your situation and looking at it a little differently.

CARL: Okay, I'm willing to try.

SOCIAL WORKER: Instead of looking at not having a girlfriend as a failure, let's view it as an opportunity.

CARL: An opportunity for what?

SOCIAL WORKER: We will discuss that together. If you don't have a girlfriend, could that be an opportunity to focus on yourself and do something good for you without having to worry about another person?

CARL: I suppose. I guess it would give me an opportunity to travel where I want to go without having to worry about what someone else wants to do. It will save me some money, too.

SOCIAL WORKER: That's great. What else could it be an opportunity for?

Reframing was helpful for Carl in this situation because it allowed him to see his situation in a new perspective. Carl viewed not having a significant other as being horrible and that it indicated he was a failure. After reframing what it meant to not have a girlfriend, he was able to look at it more positively and be excited about his future, which improved his chances of forming a relationship.

Case Summary Two

Mr. and Mrs. Diaz have decided to seek marital therapy because they are having problems.

MRS. DIAZ: My husband complains that I am stubborn. For example, one time I wanted to go the movies when everyone else wanted to go play pool. I stuck to my guns and said I wouldn't go anywhere unless we went to the movies, and we went to the movies.

MR. DIAZ: See! She always does only what she wants, she never cares about what I want; she only wants to please herself! If I say playing pool is better, then it is better!

SOCIAL WORKER: I can see you are both very opinionated people, Mr. Diaz. Mr. Diaz, can you think of a time when your wife put her mind to something and helped you accomplish something?

MR. DIAZ: Well, there was that one time when I told her several times not to cook for dinner and she did anyways and it ended up being amazing. She has a real talent for baking!

SOCIAL WORKER: Can you see how your wife's stubbornness helped her accomplish something?

MR. DIAZ: Yeah, I guess, I mean that meal was pretty good. Maybe she is stubborn sometimes because she wants to protect herself or accomplish something.

MRS. DIAZ: I guess sometimes I feel that people don't want to listen to me or treat me like a rug. I have to be stubborn so I don't get treated like a doormat.

After the therapy session, Mr. Diaz was able to see the value in his wife's stubborn personality. He saw the unwanted quality in a different context where it would be valuable. The reframing session helped the Diazes see things in a new light.

REFERENCES AND ADDITIONAL SOURCES

Amoako, E., Skelly, A. H., & Rossen, E. K. (2008). Outcomes of an intervention to reduce uncertainty among African American women with diabetes. *Western Journal of Nursing Research, 30*(8), 928–942.

Bagwell-Reese, M. K., & Brack, G. (1997). The therapeutic use of reframing and worldview in mental health counseling. *Journal of Mental Health Counseling, 19*(1), 78–86.

Ballou, M. B. (1995). *Psychological interventions: A guide to strategies*. Westport, CT: Praeger.

Brack, G., Brack, C., & Hartson, D. (1991). When a reframe fails: Explorations into students' ecosystems. *Journal of College Student Psychotherapy, 6*(2), 103–118.

Coyne, J. C. (1985). Toward a theory of frames and reframing: The social nature of frames. *Journal of Marital and Family Therapy, 11*(4), 337–344.

Fusco, L. (2002). The techniques of interviewing. In F. Turner (Ed.), *Social work practice: A Canadian perspective* (pp. 232–234). Toronto, Ontario: Pearson.

Ivings, K., & Khardaji, S. (2007). Cognitive reframing of positive beliefs about smoking: A pilot study. *Behavioural and Cognitive Psychotherapy, 35*(1), 117–120.

Jessee, E. H., Jurkovic, G. J., Wilkie, J., & Chiglinsky, M. (1982). Positive reframing with children: Conceptual and clinical considerations. *American Journal of Orthopsychiatry, 52*(2), 314–322.

Kirst-Ashman, K. K. (1993). *Understanding generalist practice* (pp. 354). Chicago, IL: Nelson-Hall.

LaClave, L. J., & Brack, G. (1989). Reframing to deal with patient resistance: Practical application. *American Journal of Psychotherapy, 43*(1), 68–76.

Nugent, W. (2001). Mediation techniques for persons in dispute. In H. Briggs & K. Corcoran (Eds.), *Structuring change* (pp. 311–323). Chicago, IL: Lyceum Books.

Reiff, H. B. (2004). Reframing the learning disabilities experience redux. *Learning Disabilities Research & Practice, 19*(3), 185–198.

Renk, K. P. D., Roddenberry, A. B. S., & Oliveros, A. B. A. (2004). A cognitive reframing of ghosts in the nursery. *Journal of Child & Family Studies, 13*(4), 377–384.

Swoboda, J. S., Dowd, E. T., & Wise, S. L. (1990). Reframing and restraining directives in the treatment of clinical depression. *Journal of Counseling Psychology, 37*(3), 254–260.

Watzlawick, P., Weakland, J., & Fisch, R. (1974). *Change: Principles of problem resolution*. New York, NY: Norton.

Rehearsal

DESCRIPTION

Sometimes called role rehearsal, this technique is aimed at assisting clients to prepare for various future, real-world situations in their lives outside therapy, in which they are going to have to carry out a particular function.

ORIGINS

Much of the understanding of how useful this technique can be in practice emerged in the development of task-centered therapy. In this practice, an important part of the intervention consists of helping clients develop a specific plan of action for various future events or situations, and then reviewing with the social worker what needs to be done to implement the identified tasks.

WHY THIS IS USEFUL TO SOCIAL WORK

There are many facets of our daily living that we handle well as a result of some level of preparation. This may be as simple as thinking while on the way to meet a friend about the kinds of things we want to talk about, to a more formal preparation where we work at acquiring a necessary skill or information to prepare for some task we have to perform.

Rehearsal is a function that most human beings make use in many different life situations. For some people, however, the idea of engaging in some form of practice or review regarding how they are going to carry out a particular function, or what they are going to say, or how they will deal with a particular contingency, is not an accustomed component of their day-to-day psychosocial functioning.

HOW THIS IS USEFUL TO SOCIAL WORK

Important as this type of intervention can be regarding some special issue in the client's life, in many instances there is a much longer payoff, because the client learns to develop patterns for dealing with future daily life issues in a more resourceful manner. Acquiring this skill can help clients to reduce levels of impetuosity that may have been creating problems in their past.

RISK FACTORS

Rehearsal is a low-risk technique. Although it can be of great assistance to a client, we do, however, need to be especially careful that our wish for the client to do something specific is not ahead of where the client is. Thus, we need to be assured that the action being rehearsed is something that the client wants to do, is capable of doing, and is ready to do. We also need to be ready to plan alternate strategies with the client as needed, when we both have a better understanding of the situation and what is required to change it.

REQUIRED SKILLS AND KNOWLEDGE

Rehearsal is a technique in which the social worker takes a very active role, doing things such as coaching, practicing, anticipating, encouraging, and demonstrating the identified future action for the client. Other activities in which we may get involved are rehearsing answers to possible questions, identifying potential scenarios, and planning strategies to deal with them.

As we have learned from task-centered therapy, often a client will need further rehearsal in subsequent interviews when he or she was not able to carry out the planned activity or ran into unexpected challenges. Support is particularly needed here, as this kind of experience frequently represents yet another failure in their lives. Such failures set them back rather than helping them. In such situations, the process may need to be reviewed and rehearsed again, with the social worker's continuing encouragement and support.

Case Summary One

Phil recently graduated with his bachelor's degree and is currently looking for a job. Phil has had problems gaining employment in the past, and he is worried that he will never get hired. He is not sure what has gone wrong, but he has told his social worker that he has trouble getting beyond the first interview.

> **PHIL:** I'm so nervous about going on interviews. I get so flustered that I forget everything I want to say.
> **SOCIAL WORKER:** Phil, do you think it would be helpful for you if we practiced some skills that might be helpful for you to use in your interview?

PHIL: Yes, I think that would help me feel less tense.

SOCIAL WORKER: We can rehearse an interview and think about answers to possible questions from your potential employer.

PHIL: That sounds great. Maybe if I'm more prepared I won't get so mixed up about what I want to say.

SOCIAL WORKER: Let's get started. If the interviewer asks you why you are interested in working for their company, what could you say?

PHIL: I could tell the interviewer that I have researched their company, and after reading their mission statement I feel it is in line with my career goals.

SOCIAL WORKER: That's a good start. What else could you say?

Phil has stated that he gets very nervous and stressed when he meets with a potential employer for an interview. Rehearsing an interview with his social worker was a way for Phil to decrease his anxiety about the situation. It also gives him the opportunity to think about what he would like to say to an interviewer and work through different scenarios that could occur.

Case Summary Two

Tommie is a 22-year old college junior who has a history of abusing drugs and alcohol. Tommie has had difficulties in the past resisting alcoholic beverages, and he is concerned that he will relapse and start drinking again. He tells his social worker that he has an upcoming event sponsored by his fraternity that he would like to attend, but he is not sure if he can resist the tempting alcoholic beverages that are likely to be served.

TOMMIE: I'm so apprehensive about going to this event. I get so drawn when I see alcohol or wine. I have been sober for a year now. The very sight of alcohol is tempting to me. I don't know if I can resist having a drink if offered.

SOCIAL WORKER: Tommie, would you like to practice some skills that might be helpful for you to use when you are presented with alcohol at the event?

TOMMIE: I think that might be helpful.

SOCIAL WORKER: We can rehearse a situation where you are being offered a drink by a friend, and I want you to practice saying "no" and to think about answers to questions you might get.

TOMMIE: That sounds great. Maybe if I practice saying "no" I won't be tempted to have a drink.

SOCIAL WORKER: Let's get started with the following scenario. You are at a party and are conversing with friends. You see alcohol being served at the table in the opposite corner of the room. A friend comes up to you and says, "Would you like a drink?" What do you say?

TOMMIE: No thanks, I don't drink.

SOCIAL WORKER: That's a good start. What else could you say?

TOMMIE: I could say that I can have a Coke instead if that is okay.

Tommie has stated that he gets tempted and drawn in when he attends parties where alcohol is being served. Rehearsing an instance where Tommie could say no to alcohol with his social worker is a way for Tommie to decrease his anxiety about the situation. It also gives him the opportunity to think about what he would like to say to friends and work situations where these scenarios could occur.

REFERENCES AND ADDITIONAL SOURCES

Alvord, M. K., & Grados, J. J. (2005). Enhancing resilience in children: A proactive approach. *Professional Psychology—Research & Practice, 36*(3), 238–245.

Germain, A., & Nielsen, T. (2003). Impact of imagery rehearsal treatment on distressing dreams, psychological distress, and sleep parameters in nightmare patients. *Behavioral Sleep Medicine, 1*(3), 140–154.

Gittleman, M. (1965). Behavior rehearsal as a technique in child treatment. *Journal of Child Psychology and Psychiatry, 6*(3–4), 251–255.

Goldfried, M. R., & Davison, G. C. (1994). *Clinical behavior therapy*. New York, NY: Wiley.

Krakow, B., Hollifield, M., Johnston, L., Koss, M., Schrader, R., Warner, T. D., … & Prince, H. (2001). Imagery rehearsal therapy for chronic nightmares in sexual assault survivors with posttraumatic stress disorder. *JAMA: the journal of the American Medical Association, 286*(5), 537–545.

Krakow, B., Kellner, R., Neidhart, J., Pathak, D., & Lambert, L. (1993). Imagery rehearsal treatment of chronic nightmares: With a thirty month follow-up. *Journal of Behavior Therapy and Experimental Psychiatry, 24*(4), 325–330.

Krakow, B., & Zadra, A. (2006). Clinical management of chronic nightmares: Imagery rehearsal therapy. *Behavioral Sleep Medicine, 4*(1), 45–70.

Lazarus, A. A. (1966). Behaviour rehearsal vs. non-directive therapy vs. advice in effecting behaviour change. *Behaviour Research and Therapy, 4*(3), 209–212.

McFall, R. M., & Marston, A. R. (1970). An expert-mental investigation of behavior rehearsal in assertive training. *Journal of Abnormal Psychology, 76*(2), 295–303.

Peeks, A. L. (1999). Conducting a social skills group with Latina adolescents. *Journal of Child and Adolescent Group Therapy, 9*(3), 139–153.

Souchay, C., Moulin, C. J. A., Isingrini, M., & Conway, M. A. (2008). Rehearsal strategy use in Alzheimer's disease. *Cognitive Neuropsychology, 25*(6), 783–797.

Spence, S. H. (2003). Social skills training with children and young people: Theory, evidence and practice. *Child & Adolescent Mental Health, 8*(2), 84–96.

Starr, A. (1977). *Rehearsal for living: Psychodrama: Illustrated therapeutic techniques*. Chicago, IL: Nelson-Hall.

St-Onge, M., Mercier, P., & De Koninck, J. (2009). Imagery rehearsal therapy for frequent nightmares in children. *Behavioral Sleep Medicine, 7*(2), 81–98.

Ward, G., Woodward, G., Stevens, A., & Stinson, C. (2003). Using overt rehearsals to explain word frequency effects in free recall. *Journal of Experimental Psychology: Learning, Memory, and Cognition, 29*(2), 186–210.

Relaxation

DESCRIPTION

As a technique, relaxation refers to our efforts to help clients learn to introduce specific calming factors in one's life to enhance the impact of treatment. It does not encompass situations where the overall goal of treatment is to help a client achieve a more relaxed method of dealing with reality.

ORIGINS

From a behavioral perspective, we have learned that, at times, our overall treatment goal for the client is to use the skills being taught to treatment to help him or her achieve a generally less stressful pattern of life. In our experience with these types of cases, we have also learned that relaxation techniques can be used as a part of our treatment. Relaxation is a means to an end in these situations. Along with behavioral practice, our interest in meditation and aspects of feminist thinking have also helped us to see relaxation as a useful treatment technique.

WHY THIS IS USEFUL TO SOCIAL WORK

As a specific therapeutic technique, relaxation begins from the understanding that many people whom we meet in today's practice are high strung or uptight. Many can better address the challenges of psychosocial therapy by being helped to relax, at least to a point where they can engage the challenge of their own situations for which they are seeking assistance.

HOW THIS IS USEFUL TO SOCIAL WORK

One of the strategies we use with some of our more more intense clients is to give them permission to relax. This dynamic of treatment can be quite complex, often drawing upon the authority of the relationship. As a person learns that it is possible, permissible, and helpful to learn to relax in a particular therapeutic process, they may also learn that this attitude and skill is something they can carry over usefully to other situations.

Once an interested client finds that the ability to relax is an acceptable practice, it can be introduced as a formal component of the interview reality. As mentioned in the meditation chapter, some practitioners engage in a few moments of relaxation exercises with the client prior to the beginning of an interview. The goal is to help the client turn away from their everyday pressures so they can more easily look inward and involve themselves thoughtfully and correctively in the therapeutic relationship.

RISK FACTORS

There is little risk in making use of easily learned relaxation skills, unless a client gets themselves into a situation where they create more stress by attempting to relax in an aggressive way, thus doing more harm than good.

REQUIRED SKILLS AND KNOWLEDGE

Our skill in using relaxation as a technique stems from our ability to assess a client's needs and ability to engage in the activities that lead to relaxation. These can range from the simple existential dictum of "learning to smell the roses" to highly programmed physical activities that can bring relaxation. For these more demanding and complex programs, it is important for the client to clear these activities with a physician, and for the social worker to have sufficient training to ensure the suitability of the relaxation methods introduced.

In situations where our goal is to help a client develop a more relaxed lifestyle, we will teach our clients bodily and breathing exercises to aid relaxation. If we are not sufficiently knowledgeable about these, we need to find appropriate resources or consultation before building these homework activities into our overall treatment.

Although it is useful for us to learn some of the basic physical techniques for relaxation, our most important contribution in this area is our ability to assess the client's own ability to relax and the factors that prohibit them from doing so. Focusing on the methods a client uses to relax is thus an approach that can be of considerable benefit. As we know from our own lives and those of our friends, the ways that we use to relax are varied.

A useful way to start introducing a relaxing overall quality to our practice is by attending to the place where we usually see our clients, as described under the office setting technique (Chapter 51). There is abundant evidence that, when properly designed and equipped, our office can introduce an evident and functional climate of relaxation into our practice.

In this regard, aspects such as the furniture, lighting, the color of the walls, plants, the type of floor covering, the pictures we display, and so forth all create a mood. When carefully planned, these factors can contribute greatly to an atmosphere that will be highly conducive to establishing and maintaining a relaxed therapeutic setting.

Most of us are not experts in designing an office that can enhance clients' relaxation, safety, and security, so we should therefore consult a professional. It is surprising just how little attention we have given to these very influential facets of human existence.

Case Summary One

Lawrence recently started attending therapy sessions because he is going through a difficult divorce. He has never seen a social worker before and is very nervous. Lawrence is not sure how he is going to handle everything he is facing.

> **SOCIAL WORKER:** We'll start our session today as usual with a guided-imagery exercise to help with relaxation.
> **LAWRENCE:** Sounds good. It has really been helpful for me.
> **SOCIAL WORKER:** Sit back comfortably and close your eyes. Imagine yourself in a favorite, peaceful place. Imagine that you are experiencing all of the sights, smells, and sounds of this place.
> **SOCIAL WORKER:** [after a few seconds] How do you feel?
> **LAWRENCE:** I feel better. I don't feel as overwhelmed as I usually do. I'm not as tense as I was when I first arrived.
> **SOCIAL WORKER:** That's great. That is the purpose of the exercise. Now we can continue with the session and work towards your therapy goals.

Lawrence was so nervous about seeing the social worker and weighed down with everything he is trying to handle in his personal life, that he wouldn't have been able to participate in the session very well if he didn't take a few moments to relax. Starting the session off with a relaxation technique will ensure that Lawrence will be calm and focused as he engages in the session. Being relaxed helps Lawrence to think clearly and handle his challenges in a more effective manner. Because the social worker is the one initiating the relaxation technique, the worker is encouraging and therefore reinforcing the importance of being relaxed. Lawrence will also be able to use this technique in his everyday life outside of therapy sessions to relax in stressful situations.

Case Summary Two

Nia has been in therapy for a few months for her experience of physical violence not too long ago. She is doing well in therapy, but has moments outside of therapy where she engages in risky behavior. Nia's social worker's treatment goals are to increase Nia's self-worth and teach her how to be more assertive. The social worker finds out from Nia's caseworker that she has an upcoming court date where she will confront her abuser.

NIA: I have to go to court next week to testify against my abuser. I am very nervous.

SOCIAL WORKER: Okay. We'll start our session today with a relaxation exercise to help you to learn how to calm your nerves if you begin to feel anxious. You can use this technique next week if you start to feel overwhelmed.

NIA: Sounds good.

SOCIAL WORKER: I want you to sit back on the couch as comfortably as you can and close your eyes. Pretend that you are in a serene and restful place. Visualize that you are resting in this place and that you are at peace. No one or nothing can disturb you.

[AFTER THE RELAXATION EXERCISE IS COMPLETE THE SOCIAL WORKER ASKS NIA HOW SHE FEELS:]

NIA: I feel more peaceful. I am not as nervous as I was when I first arrived here.

SOCIAL WORKER: That's great. That is the purpose of the exercise. Now we can continue with the session and work towards your therapy goals.

Nia was nervous about the upcoming court date. The social worker felt that Nia could use the relaxation technique to reduce her stress when she is feeling angry, scared, or anxious. Through relaxation Nia is able to think more clearly and handle her challenges more efficiently. Nia can use this technique anytime she has a stressful situation in her daily life.

REFERENCES AND ADDITIONAL SOURCES

Benson, H. (1974). *The relaxation response*. New York, NY: Avon.

Bernstein, D. A., Borkovec, T. D., & Hazlett-Stevens, H. (2000). *New directions in progressive relaxation training: A guidebook for helping professionals*. New York, NY: Praeger.

Borkovec, T. D., & Costello, E. (1993). Efficacy of applied relaxation and cognitive-behavioral therapy in the treatment of generalized anxiety disorder. *Journal of Consulting and Clinical Psychology, 61*(4), 611–619.

Chang, J. (1991). Using relaxation strategies in child and youth care practice. *Child and Youth Care Forum, 20,* 155–169.

Clark, D. M., Ehlers, A., Hackmann, A., McManus, F., Fennell, M., Grey, N., Waddington, L., & Wild, J. (2006). Cognitive therapy versus exposure and applied relaxation in social phobia: A randomized controlled trial. *Journal of Consulting and Clinical Psychology, 74*(3), 568–578.

Cohen, M., & Fried, G. (2007). Comparing relaxation training and cognitive-behavioral group therapy for women with breast cancer. *Research on Social Work Practice, 17*(3), 313–323.

Dugas, M. J., Brillon, P., Savard, P., Turcotte, J., Gaudet, A., Ladouceur, R., Leblanc, R., & Gervais, N. J. (2010). A randomized clinical trial of cognitive-behavioral therapy and applied relaxation for adults with generalized anxiety disorder. *Behavior Therapy, 41*(1), 46–58.

Manzoni, G. M., Pagnini, F., Castelnuovo, G., & Molinari, E. (2008). Relaxation training for anxiety: A ten-years systematic review with meta-analysis. *BMC Psychiatry, 8*(1), 41. doi:10.1186/1471-244X

Matsumoto, M., & Smith, J. C. (2001). Progressive muscle relaxation, breathing exercises, and ABC relaxation theory. *Journal of Clinical Psychology, 57*(12), 1551–1557.

McComb, J. J. R., & Clopton, J. R. (2003). The effects of movement, relaxation, and education on the stress levels of women with subclinical levels of bulimia. *Eating Behaviors, 4*(1), 79–88.

Nakaya, N., Kumano, H., Minoda, K., Koguchi, T., Tanouchi, K., Kanazawa, M., & Fukudo, S. (2004). Preliminary study: Psychological effects of muscle relaxation on juvenile delinquents. *International Journal of Behavioral Medicine, 11*(3), 176–180.

Ost, L. G., Westling, B., & Hellström, K. (1993). Applied relaxation, exposure in-vivo, and cognitive methods in the treatment of panic disorder with agoraphobia. *Behaviour Research and Therapy, 31*(4), 383–394.

Safren, S. A., Sprich, S., Mimiaga, M. J., Surman, C., Knouse, L., Groves, M., & Otto, M. W. (2010). Cognitive behavioral therapy vs relaxation therapy with educational support for medication-treated adults with ADHD and persistent symptoms: A randomized controlled trial. *Journal of the American Medical Association, 304*(8), 875–880.

Schade, M., Hruza, T., Washburne, A., & Carns, M. (2006). Relaxation as an adjunct to psychotherapy. *Journal of Clinical Psychology, 8*, 338–346.

Yu, D. S. F., Lee, D. T. F., & Woo, J. (2010). Improving health-related quality of life of patients with chronic heart failure: Effects of relaxation therapy. *Journal of Advanced Nursing, 66*(2), 392–403.

Resource Location

DESCRIPTION

The essence of this technique is to locate and help connect the client to an appropriate helping resource or resources as a part of the therapeutic process.

ORIGINS

From the earliest days of the profession, an important role of the social worker has been that of resources location. However, as the profession's clinical component developed with an emphasis on a psychotherapeutic base, this aspect of practice tended to be seen as a second-level type of technique.

This perception was further reinforced by a division of the conceptual base of practice into what was called direct and indirect practice. The latter, encompassing the location of resources that were seen as assisting the client's life, was viewed as being clearly of a lower priority when compared to the more intrapsychic activities and techniques of direct practice. This dichotomy is no longer relevant, and the social worker's role in locating and connecting the client to other resources (e.g., referrals) is now taken for granted, almost to the point where the skills are minimized.

WHY THIS IS USEFUL TO SOCIAL WORK

One of the exciting aspects of our times is the number, richness, and variety of organizations and systems that can provide assistance in our communities, across our land, and in many parts of the world. However one of the highly complex challenges of this reality is the skill required to locate such resources and to understand what is involved in accessing them. This is a most important technique for us, one that should not be overlooked.

HOW THIS IS USEFUL TO SOCIAL WORK

The utility of this technique flows from the rich diversity of resources available, both formal and informal. We meet very few situations in practice for which there isn't some group in society—privately or publicly funded, volunteer based, national or international, local or regional—that can provide assistance. Our challenge is to find these resources when needed, to ensure they indeed will be helpful to a client, and how best to begin the process.

RISK FACTORS

Resource location is a low-risk technique. The area where there is possibly some minimal risk is getting the client ensnared in complex bureaucratic systems that become almost immobilizing without adequate support, leaving them in a vulnerable situation. Another risk arises when we fail to clarify various eligibility requirements and involve our client in an elaborate referral process, when we could have learned from the beginning that they were ineligible.

REQUIRED SKILLS AND KNOWLEDGE

Although resource location is very similar to referral, there is a difference: the skill of locating services that often are not in the mainstream helping network. To use this technique effectively, the practitioner needs to know six things:

1. what resources the client needs, wants, and is prepared and capable of using;
2. what resources exist;
3. where to locate them, if they are not readily available through the usual network;
4. what is required to make the necessary connections;
5. what must be done to create the required package of resources; and
6. what must the client do to make use of the resources.

One of the challenges in using resource location effectively stems from the wide variation in services that exist in most communities that may be of assistance to a client. The list of available services in many areas can seem larger than the community's phonebook. As well, more and more computer-search procedures exist to facilitate the location of particular patterns of service for various client types and requirements.

Another challenge in using this technique emerges when it is necessary to seek a resource in another community or even another country, in which case contact with various international organizations is required. Even in these instances, much of the information needed is available online.

Experienced practitioners know that locating a resource and involving them in the interest of the client are only a part of the process. Often our most intensive clinical skills are required to help the client understand and be ready to take the requisite risks to make use of the resources they need. Furthermore, the process of working one's way through the bureaucratic structure of complex service systems requires a high degree of interpersonal skill, knowledge, and at times advocacy.

For the most part, social workers become so highly skilled in using this technique that it becomes almost second nature to them. However, with the growing complexities of our world, when this highly demanding technique is used appropriately and skillfully, it can be of great assistance to many of people who turn to us or are referred to us for help.

Case Summary One

During Miranda's previous session, she reported being worried about the development of her son, Jordan. Her social worker listened to her concerns and took time before the next session to find a resource appropriate to her needs.

SOCIAL WORKER: During the last session you mentioned that you are concerned about your son, Jordan's development.

MIRANDA: Yes, and I don't have the money to take him to a specialist to have all kinds of evaluations done.

SOCIAL WORKER: Well, I've done some research and I found a resource that will be helpful to you.

MIRANDA: How exciting. What is it, what do I have to do?

SOCIAL WORKER: I have found a resource that provides children up to age five with a free developmental screening. The purpose of this program is to identify children who may be at risk of developmental delays and connect them with early intervention programs for appropriate services. They will screen Jordan in the areas of vision, hearing, speech/language, cognitive, motor, and behavior and the services that they link him with will be free or low cost.

MIRANDA: What does "screening" mean?

SOCIAL WORKER: Sorry. It is a term we use that means testing and evaluation.

MIRANDA: A free screening, that's wonderful. Plus, they check so many different areas of development. This resource is more than I could have hoped for. How do I get my son screened?

SOCIAL WORKER: Here is the phone number to call. A program staff member will interview you over the phone to make sure you meet the eligibility requirements, and then they will schedule an appointment. You will meet the eligibility requirements because Jordan is four years old and you live in this county.

MIRANDA: That's great. Where and when are the screenings?

SOCIAL WORKER: There is a screening once a month in various sites around the county so that parents can choose the site that is most convenient for them.

Miranda was worried about Jordan's development, but thought she was unable to have him tested due to financial restrictions. Her social worker's knowledge of resources in the area provided Miranda with an answer to her needs and relief for the stress she felt.

Case Summary Two

Thirty-nine-year-old Anna, and her 5-year old son, Lee, are victims of domestic abuse who see a counselor for therapy. During the first therapy session, the social worker talks with Anna about the domestic violence incident.

SOCIAL WORKER: What brings you here today?

ANNA: Well, a few months ago, my husband physically abused me. One night when I was asleep, he physically assaulted Lee. The next day I saw the bruises on Lee and I left my husband and went to my sister's. Since then my husband has been in jail.

SOCIAL WORKER: I see you've been through a lot. So are you and Lee safe now?

ANNA: Yes, we are safe. I live with my sister. My husband is in jail, so I am not worried about him attacking us.

SOCIAL WORKER: That's great that you have a safe place to remain. Tell me, what do you do for work?

ANNA: I work two part-time jobs. But my work doesn't provide insurance.

SOCIAL WORKER: I wanted to let you know that our agency has a resource book that we can use to help refer our clients.

ANNA: Well, I would like to have a more stable full-time job so that my son and I can live on our own.

SOCIAL WORKER: Certainly. I can help you locate some resources in the community. There are a few employment agencies that I can contact to set you up for an appointment so that you can speak to them. They have located jobs for our clients in the past.

ANNA: That sounds really helpful. What about medical services? Can you help me locate a doctor that my son and I can go to? I don't have any insurance so I am not able to pay.

SOCIAL WORKER: In our resource manual we have the phone numbers of a few free clinics in the area that offer services such as free dental and medical care. I can make a list of contact information for free clinics and give that information to you next time.

After establishing some initial rapport, the social worker is able to ask Anna if she is safe and has a place to live. Anna tells the social worker that she lives with her sister and works two part-time jobs to support Lee and herself. Anna tells the social worker that she would like to find a steadier full-time job so that she can live on her own with her son. The social worker uses resource location as a technique to help Anna secure a more stable future for herself and her son.

REFERENCES AND ADDITIONAL SOURCES

Buelow, S. A., Lyddon, W. J., & Johnson, J. T. (2002). Client attachment and coping resources. *Counselling Psychology Quarterly, 15*(2), 145–152.

Byrd, M. E. (2006). Social exchange as a framework for client-nurse interaction during public health nursing maternal-child home visits. *Public Health Nursing, 23*(3), 271–276.

Connaway, R. S., & Gentry, M. E. (1988). *Social work practice,* Englewood Cliffs, NJ: Prentice Hall.

Echevarria, D. S. (2001). Resource-based reflective consultation: Accessing client resources through interviews and dialogue. *Journal of Marital and Family Therapy, 27*(2), 201–212.

Edgar, L., Remmer, J., Rosberger, Z., & Fournier, M. A. (2000). Resource use in women completing treatment for breast cancer. *Psycho-Oncology, 9*(5), 428–438.

Fishman, H. C., Andes, F., & Knowlton, R. (2001). Enhancing family therapy: The addition of a community resource specialist. *Journal of Marital and Family Therapy, 27*(1), 111–116.

Hokkanen, H., Häggman-Laitila, A., & Eriksson, E. (2006). Resources and support of home-dwelling elderly people—Literature review. *Gerontologia, 20*, 12–21.

Kirst-Ashman, K. K., & Grafton, H. H. (1993). *Understanding generalist practice* (pp. 495–505). Chicago, IL: Nelson-Hall.

Miller, A. A. (1961). Diagnostic evaluation for determining the use of psychiatric resources or family casework resources. *American Journal of Orthopsychiatry, 31*, 598–611.

Rotering, L. H. (1994). *A comparison of professional disciplines' utilization of self-help groups as client resources*. Albany, NY: State University of New York Press.

Tourse, R., & Mooney J. F. (Eds.). (1999). *Collaborative practice*. Westport, CT: Praeger.

Ritual

DESCRIPTION

Although we often think of ritual only in a formal religious, ceremonial, or celebratory way, the concept has a much broader meaning that enables us to consider it as a therapeutic technique. In this sense, we are referring to repetitive patterns of behavior that are a part of the therapeutic process. Such behaviors are observable, repeated around a particular component of therapy, and viewed by the participants as having some significance.

ORIGINS

There is no clear history of the development of ritual as a technique. Certainly, group and family social workers have long understood that in significant human interactions, repeated actions quickly develop that tend to give shape to continuing relationships. Later social workers began to appreciate that these same ritualistic patterns existed in one-to-one and couples therapy and could be built upon as a part of the therapeutic strategy.

Usually such rituals develop in treatment in an unplanned fashion instead of through a deliberate plan, as they do in our social lives. A particular act gets repeated in regard to some aspect of treatment, and the people involved begin to view it as something important that needs to be continued. This may be as simple a thing as always starting an interview in exactly the same way (e.g., a handshake), repeating the same opening or closing words, or pouring a cup of coffee. They are often only recognized as rituals when omitted for some reason or another and someone involved in the process reacts to the omission.

Some rituals develop very quickly in a treatment situation. These include such things as where a client sits, how an interview begins and ends, what topics are acceptable for consideration and which are not, what the social worker and client call each other, whether food and drink are a part of the process, and so on through the many rituals that develop in the course of establishing, maintaining, and facilitating a therapeutic process.

WHY THIS IS USEFUL TO SOCIAL WORK

Positive and supportive rituals can be a source of comfort to clients. They can foster a sense of security, contribute to a sense of ownership and participation in the treatment process, and help them develop an identity. Rituals can minimize fear and uncertainty about the treatment process and a constricting sense of the unknown.

Some rituals can be very informal and are scarcely recognized by those involved as a ritual. Others that we might draw upon are more formal, such as a minute of meditation before starting, a brief prayer or reading, or some other highly structured way of beginning or ending the interview. Either way, because of their potential for developing security and comfort in an interview, we can build them into the treatment process in a facilitating way.

HOW THIS IS USEFUL TO SOCIAL WORK

Rituals are such an important component of our lives that, if we can build on their strength, we can add another useful resource to our therapeutic endeavors. The development of rituals in the treatment process also opens up the possibility of using them to help clients examine how rituals do or do not assist in their day-to-day living, especially with regard to their interactions with significant others.

Often when we focus upon rituals, beginning with an examination of the place of ritual in the treatment situation can lead to an examination of rituals in clients' lives. These may be unrecognized sources of strain, which can be substituted by developing rituals that are more mutually supportive.

RISK FACTORS

This is a low-risk technique, presuming we maintain a sufficient degree of self-awareness so we do not allow our therapeutic style to become locked into a ritualistic pattern that may not be helpful to all clients. We also need to recognize when our client has similarly gotten locked into an unhelpful pattern of therapeutic behavior.

REQUIRED SKILLS AND KNOWLEDGE

We need to recognize when rituals are developing and what role they are playing in treatment. This is important because rituals can lead a treatment situation to a place where little is happening except the repetition of the same material and the same cycle of activities.

Ritual is of course a part of all cultures. Often we only recognize rituals in cultures other than our own. We need to be aware that we all surround ourselves with a curtain of rituals that mark many aspects of our lives, including our practice. Our therapeutic challenge is to observe ourselves to see how we tend to ritualize components of our treatment, and to determine when, how, and where this is helpful or a hindrance. Most important, we need to learn how to draw on these patterned human behaviors as a further building block in our instruments of intervention.

Case Summary One

Ray sought counseling to deal with his emotional issues, which were being masked by his substance abuse. Each therapy session began with meditation. The purpose of meditation was to provide Ray with a heightened awareness, to concentrate on his breathing, and to allow the thoughts and sensations that arise to appear and pass away while bringing a sense of calm.

SOCIAL WORKER: What do you think of the meditation during our sessions?

RAY: It's great. Meditation has become a daily practice for me. While concentrating on my breath, I attempt to quiet the chatter of my mind. I await insight into myself and all things.

SOCIAL WORKER: Do you think you have become more insightful?

RAY: During meditation I am able to become more aware by observing the thoughts that come to my mind and then letting them go.

SOCIAL WORKER: How do you feel after meditating?

RAY: When I meditate regularly I find that I am more at ease with myself and the world. For the first time in my life, I am actually experiencing a feeling of serenity.

SOCIAL WORKER: Do you still feel like you need drugs to survive?

RAY: I still struggle with sadness and emotional pain, but meditation as a daily ritual is one tool that seems to help me find my way through.

SOCIAL WORKER: You have definitely confronted your addiction; do you feel like you have the power to overcome it?

RAY: Through meditation it became clear to me that the path I desired was in the complete opposite direction of my substance abuse.

Ray's daily ritual of meditation allowed him to gain insight and realize that he was trying to erase his pain by taking drugs. Meditation let Ray realize some of his past hurt and tell his story, grieve for what he lost in his life, and feel hopeful for the future. Ray was able to start the healing process and regain a sense of power and control in his life.

Case Summary Two

Julie is brought in by her foster parents to see a counselor for therapy because she was physically abused as an infant by her biological parents. Julie is 8 years old, and her social worker recommends that she receive psychoeducation on the topic of personal safety. Her social worker also believes that Julie needs to be taught relaxation techniques she can implement when she is feeling angry or scared.

SOCIAL WORKER: Hi, Julie. It's nice to see you today. We can go work today in the playroom if that's okay with you.

JULIE: Okay.

[The social worker and Julie meet in the playroom for the first session. Julie enters the playroom and the social worker tells her that they are going to work on a feelings game for the day's session. Halfway through the game, Julie is tired of the feelings game.]

JULIE: I want to play with the dolls and I want to color and I want to paint.

[The social worker wants Julie to focus on one task. She explains to Julie a ritual to help keep her on task.]

SOCIAL WORKER: I am going to explain a system that we are going to follow.

JULIE: Okay.

SOCIAL WORKER: If you work hard and finish the feelings game with me, we can go to the treasure chest and you can pick a toy to take home with you. Every time you come here to work with me and you finish the task I assign you, I will take you to the treasure chest to pick out your favorite prize.

JULIE: So every time I come here, if I am good and finish the work that you tell me to do, I can get a toy from the treasure chest?

SOCIAL WORKER: Exactly.

JULIE: Okay. We can finish the feelings game so that we can go to the treasure chest.

Julie's daily ritual of visiting the treasure chest allowed her the chance to earn a prize if she focused on the task her social worker assigns for the session. Julie realizes that if she completes the activity of the day successfully, she can enjoy taking a toy home. This gives her something to look forward to the end of each therapy session.

REFERENCES AND ADDITIONAL SOURCES

Bennett, L. A., Wolin, S. J., & McAvity, K. J. (1988). Family identity, ritual, and myth: A cultural perspective on life cycle transitions. In C. J. Falicov (Ed.), *Family transitions: Continuity and change over the life cycle* (pp. 211–232). New York, NY: Guilford.

Bossard, J. H. S., & Boll, E. S. (1949). Ritual in family living. *American Sociological Review, 14*(4), 463–469.

Goldsmith, M. (2001). When words are no longer necessary: The gift of ritual. *Journal of Religious Gerontology, 12*(3/4), 139–150.

Gutheil, I. A. (1993). Rituals and termination procedures. *Smith College Studies in Social Work, 63*(2), 163–176.

Imber-Black, E. (1991). Rituals and the healing process. In F. Walsh & M. McGoldrick (Eds.), *Living beyond loss: Death in the family* (pp. 207–223). New York, NY: Norton.

Imber-Black, E., & Roberts, J. (1992). *Rituals for our times: Celebrating, healing, and changing our lives and our relationships.* New York, NY: HarperCollins.

Imber-Black, E., Roberts, J., & Whiting, R. (Eds.). (1988). *Rituals in families and family therapy.* New York, NY: Norton.

Kobak, R. R., & Waters, D. B. (1984). Family therapy as a rite of passage: Play's the thing. *Family Process, 23*(1), 89–100.

Laird, J. (1984). Sorcerers, shamans, and social workers—The use of ritual in social work practice. *Social Work, 29*(2), 123–129.

Laird, J. (1988). Women and rituals in family therapy. In E. Imber-Black, J. Roberts, & R. A. Whiting (Eds.), *Rituals in families and family therapy* (pp. 331–362). New York, NY: Norton.

Olson, F. (1993). The development and impact of ritual in couple counseling. *Counseling and Values, 38*, 12–21.

Selvini-Pazzololi, M. S., Boscolo, L., Cecchin, G. F., & Prata, G. (1977). Family rituals: A powerful tool in family therapy. *Family Process, 16*, 445–453.

Wolin, S. J., & Bennett, L. A. (1984). Family rituals. *Family Process, 23*(3), 401–420.

Wolin, S. J., Bennett, L. A., Noonan, D. L., & Teitelbaum, M. A. (1980). Disrupted family rituals: A factor in the intergenerational transmission of alcoholism. *Journal of Studies on Alcohol, 41*(3), 199–214.

Role Playing

DESCRIPTION

Role playing is a treatment technique in which either the client or the social worker overtly assumes the role of another person, usually someone significant in the clients life, for a short period of time. This procedure is done openly with the client and with his or her agreement. This is distinct from situations where either the client or worker chooses unilaterally to function as if they were someone else in the client's life, whether consciously or unconsciously.

ORIGINS

The technique has come into social work practice from several sources. Elements of it were first discussed in the literature of the profession and in the practice of psychodrama in the 1950s. Proponents of this approach built their practice from the observation that many people who assume the role of someone else, as in a play, are able to safely express feelings, perceptions, and reactions to significant people in their lives through the presumed protection of the role.

One would expect this technique to be an important component of role theory, but it does not appear to have been a spinoff of this theory. Two other bodies of theory, however, do make overt use of this technique: Gestalt theory and task-centered theory. Both of these theories have helped us to understand various ways of helping people to look at themselves or others of significance in their lives by having them step out of their accustomed self-perception and take the role of someone else.

WHY THIS IS USEFUL TO SOCIAL WORK

The opportunity to step out from one's daily or accustomed role permits people to express their views about themselves and how they perceive and feel about others. This is done in a safe and protected manner that permits later reflection and thought about others and their reactions to them.

HOW THIS IS USEFUL TO SOCIAL WORK

The objective of role playing is to permit the client or worker to assume the perceived characteristics, actions, and speech of the person whose role is being assumed in the safety of the treatment relationship. This allows them to examine both the aspects of the person being imitated and the client's perception of and response to the person. The process allows the client to express feelings, examine attitudes, and review perceptions of significant others or events in their lives.

Another form of role playing is designed to help the client prepare for some future situation in their lives, such as how they might address someone with whom they are going to interact in the future (e.g., confronting a significant other or preparing for a job interview).

Role playing is used in a variety of other modalities besides one-to-one interviews. It is also used in couple therapy, in which one of the dyad assumes the role of someone significant in the couple's life as a way of better understanding the relationship and some of its difficulties.

It has also been found to be useful in groups, where one member of the group is asked to assume the role of another member to understand some of the group's dynamics. It is also useful in assisting members of the group to rehearse some proposed action. In so doing, the group can comment on the assumed role to help the member alter his or her functioning in a more constructive and satisfying way.

RISK FACTORS

Overall there is a low degree of risk in using role playing. For some clients, this type of activity would be unduly uncomfortable, or indeed in some situations would be viewed as unacceptable. Thus we need to be sure that our own enthusiasm for this procedure does not lead us to use it inappropriately or too much. Last, it is obviously a technique only to be used with intact people.

REQUIRED SKILLS AND KNOWLEDGE

Special skills are not required to use role playing, assuming a basic level of practitioner diagnostic and treatment competence. The procedure does assume that the client or clients are able to step outside of themselves to some degree and play aspects of the the other person's role. Clearly some clients will need some assistance to do this so they understand its potential as a helping process.

Case Summary

Stewie is seeing a social worker because he characterizes himself as the least assertive person on earth. He claims that people walk all over him and he is sick of it. His biggest concern is that he feels his brother tries to take advantage of him every chance he gets. Stewie would like to talk to his brother about the way he feels, but he is terrified.

STEWIE: I don't even know how to begin to approach him about the subject.

SOCIAL WORKER: What do you think would happen if you let your brother know how you feel?

STEWIE: I fear that he will laugh in my face and disregard everything I say to him.

SOCIAL WORKER: I hear that you are very nervous about confronting your brother. I would like to try role playing the situation with you. What do you think about that?

STEWIE: That sounds good. I think I'll feel better about it if I have some practice first.

SOCIAL WORKER: This is a safe space for you to think through what you want to say to your brother and how you want to approach the subject with him. We can role-play several different scenarios depicting all the different ways your brother might react.

Stewie has wanted to confront his brother about the way he acts toward him for a long time, but his nerves always held him back. Role playing during his therapy session gave Stewie the opportunity to practice what he wanted to say and feel more comfortable with his future encounter with his brother. The role play also provided an opportunity for the social worker to give Stewie some constructive alternatives for what he is planning to do.

Case Summary Two

Role playing is being used to teach a child who has a diagnosis of moderate mental retardation appropriate social skills. The 7-year old client, Todd, has a social phobia with speaking out loud and doing a class presentation. As a treatment goal, the social worker helps the client to role-play the situation by assuming the role of educator during a counseling session.

SOCIAL WORKER: We are going to do an activity today. It is called role playing, and we will be role playing in order to help you practice how to speak out loud during class time and when you are doing speeches and presentations.

TODD: Sounds like fun!

SOCIAL WORKER: Great. I will play the role of your classroom teacher and you will practice speaking out loud. Did you bring in your essay that I asked you to bring with you the last time we met?

TODD: Yes. I picked a paper that I wrote about jungle animals that I really liked.

SOCIAL WORKER: You can use the essay that you wrote that I asked you to bring in last time as a script. Try teaching me about the topic of your essay. You can read from your essay. Pretend you are in front of the class and say your speech as loud as you can.

Todd begins his speech in a barely audible voice, but as he works and practices with the social worker over a few sessions, he is able to bring his voice up to the appropriate intensity of volume needed for delivering a speech in class. Todd can use this mock situation with his social worker in real-life situations where he is asked to speak loudly or deliver a speech. Through role playing with his social worker, Todd is allowed to confront his fear of communicating out loud, which will greatly reduce that fear.

REFERENCES AND ADDITIONAL SOURCES

Avrahami, E. (2003). Cognitive-behavioral approach in psychodrama: Discussion and example from addiction treatment. *The Arts in Psychotherapy, 30*(4), 209–216.

Ballou, M. B. (1995). *Psychological interventions: A guide to strategies.* Westport, CT: Praeger.

Bohart, A. C. (1977). Role playing and interpersonal conflict resolution. *Journal of Counseling Psychology, 24*(1), 15–24.

Boies, K. G. (1972). Role playing as a behavior change technique: Review of the empirical literature. *Psychotherapy: Theory, Research and Practice, 9*(2), 185–192.

Hepworth, D. H., Rooney, R. H., & Larsen, J. (1997). *Direct social work practice* (pp. 424–426). Toronto, Ontario: Nelson Canada.

Kipper, D. A. (1988). The differential effect of role-playing conditions on the accuracy of self-evaluation. *Group Psychotherapy, Psychodrama and Sociometry, 41,* 30–35.

Levenson, R. L., & Herman, J. (1991). The use of role playing as a technique in the psychotherapy of children. *Psychotherapy: Theory, Research, Practice, Training, 28*(4), 660–666.

Perlman, H. H. (1968). *Persona: Social role and personality* (pp. 193–227). Chicago, IL: University of Chicago Press.

Shearer, R., & Davidhizar, R. (2003). Using role play to develop cultural competence. *Journal of Nursing Education, 42*(6), 273–276.

Teevan, K. G., & Gabel, H. (1978). Evaluation of modeling—role-playing and lecture—discussion training techniques for college student mental health paraprofessionals. *Journal of Counseling Psychology, 25*(2), 169–171.

Role Reversal

DESCRIPTION

Role reversal is a technique in which the social worker and the client, or two clients, assume each other's role and attempt to think and speak as if they were that person. It differs from role playing in that only two persons are involved, each attempting to assume the role of the other.

ORIGINS

The theoretical origins of role reversal are not fully clear. It appears to have several roots. Clearly there are elements of the work of Moreno and his use of psychodrama in the 1950s. Gestalt practitioners and task-centered social workers have also highlighted the use of the technique.

WHY THIS IS USEFUL TO SOCIAL WORK

It is a technique with a touch of the theatrical to it. It draws on some people's ability to imitate the verbalizations and mannerisms of someone else, especially someone close to them. Unlike role playing, which is a more generalized assumption of roles, in this technique only two persons participate in the role enactments, and each assumes or attempts to assume the other's role.

The strength of the technique lies in the observation that, unless one is a professional actress or actor, it is very difficult if not impossible for someone to assume another's role without eventually projecting one's views, feelings, and wishes of how the other person either should act or is perceived to act. These perceptions may be totally different from how the person whose role has been taken sees himself or herself. The process of role reversal helps to bring out these differing perceptions and provides material for further discussions and interactions between the pair or in the group or family situation.

HOW THIS IS USEFUL TO SOCIAL WORK

Role reversal is often used in couple or dyadic work, but can also be used in groups or family work by having two members exchange roles.

The theory underlying this technique is that the reversal situation gives both parties involved an opportunity to act out how one is perceived by the other, but in a reverse manner. Thus, if a wife assumes the role of the her husband and he takes the role of the wife, each can see how they perceive each other and how they hope the other persons might or should behave with the other.

The technique is also useful to help clarify some real-life situations where some type of role reversal has in fact taken place in a manner that causes strain. For example, in a family it can happen that the oldest girl has begun to take on the role of the wife, and the wife in turn has assumed the role of one of the children. This reality is not the technique, but by making use of the technique, the situation can sometimes be acted out in a way that brings a new level of understanding.

RISK FACTORS

Role reversal does not have a high risk factor overall, apart from the possibility that the social worker's enthusiasm for the potential of the technique might overshadow the client's actual progress in treatment, to the detriment of the ongoing therapeutic process. There is also a risk that one of the pair will be more interested and able to engage in a role-reversal situation than the other, so the process creates anxiety instead of helping both members.

REQUIRED SKILLS AND KNOWLEDGE

In general, role reversal is strongly akin to role playing, but with sufficient differences to consider it a separate entity. It will not be useful for everyone. Some clients find it a much too theatrical process, one that does not fit their perception of what therapy should be like. Others are much too uncomfortable in attempting this kind of reversal, not unlike a person who cannot bring themselves to speak in public. Still others are not able to understand the concept at all and find themselves unable to be the other person, even for a short time. Likewise, there are probably some would-be thespians who would relish the opportunity to enact the perceived role of someone else, especially someone significant in their lives, but be unable to benefit from the self-revelatory facets of the technique.

In addition to having two clients in a role-reversal situation, there is the possibility of the worker assuming the role of the client and vice versa. This gives the client the opportunity to be an authority figure or an expert in a way that can be helpful in shaping alternate behaviors or dealing with some aspect of the treatment relationship.

This technique is best used sparingly and on a short-term, episodic basis. Its purpose is to give the client an opportunity to view a situation in a different way, and for the worker to help the client reflect upon the different perceptions that emerge.

Case Summary One

Megan and her daughter, Briley, have been attending family therapy sessions to improve their communication. The two of them have been working together to make changes in their relationship. During this session, their social worker has decided to introduce the technique of role reversal as a way to help them reach their treatment goal.

> SOCIAL WORKER: So how has everything been this past week? I notice some tension.
>
> MEGAN: Do you want to start or should I start?
>
> BRILEY: You tell her.
>
> MEGAN: Well, we had an argument this afternoon. I asked one question and Briley just went off the deep end. She took it as an opportunity to say as many hurtful things to me as she could think of.
>
> SOCIAL WORKER: Tell me what happened. How did the argument begin?
>
> MEGAN: Last week Briley told me that she wasn't talking to her friend Sam anymore because he hasn't been a good friend to her and he is a bad influence on her. All I did was ask Briley if she spoke to Sam recently.
>
> SOCIAL WORKER: Briley, how did you feel when your mom asked you that question?
>
> BRILEY: I felt accused. I was wondering why she would ask me something like that after I told her I wasn't speaking to him anymore.
>
> SOCIAL WORKER: I would like the two of you to try a role reversal. Briley, I want you to play the role of your mom, and Megan, I want you to play the role of Briley. The two of you will re-enact the conversation you had this afternoon, only this time I want you to say what the other person could have said, or what you would have liked to hear from the other person, to avoid feeling angry.

Engaging in a role reversal was a good way for Megan and Briley to open up the lines of communication and begin to understand what the other wants a little better, while discussing alternate outcomes for future conversations. The process of role reversal helped to bring out their differing perceptions and provided material for further discussions and interactions between Megan and her daughter.

Case Summary Two

Lenny works in an auto supply company where his father-in-law, David, is his immediate supervisor. Lenny has become increasingly frustrated, feeling that he is a hard worker but that he never seems to satisfy his father-in-law. He has attempted to speak with his wife about his frustrations, but he is concerned that she either will take sides or, worse, speak to her father and embarrass him.

LENNY: I go to work feeling good and energetic, but by the end of the day my father-in-law's criticisms have me worn down to a point where I want to call in sick the next day. Maybe I should find another job.

SOCIAL WORKER: Have you spoken with your father-in-law to let him know how you feel?

LENNY: No, I think that would just make matters worse.

SOCIAL WORKER: Let's try an experiment. Think about what it is like to be your father-in-law and have your daughter's husband working directly for you. What might be your thoughts and concerns?

LENNY: Well, I know my daughter looks up to you, and maybe I am a little jealous about that. I know you are a hard worker and I like to have a good relationship with my employees. I think what I'm most concerned about at work is that the other guys will think I'm playing favorites and not respect me.

SOCIAL WORKER: Perhaps, Lenny, you can share this understanding with both your wife and your father-in-law and explore new ways to communicate.

Role reversal can be helpful for becoming more understanding of another person's position or beliefs and for reevaluating their intentions. In this situation, it can provide an opportunity for more open communication between Lenny and his father-in-law, as well as his wife.

REFERENCES AND ADDITIONAL SOURCES

Alexander, P. (2003). Parent-child role reversal: Development of a measure and test of an attachment theory model. *Journal of Systemic Therapies, 22,* 31–44.

Bratter, T. (1967). Dynamics of role reversal. *Group Psychotherapy, 20,* 88–94.

Brewer, U. (1993). Using the role-reversal technique in an industrial setting. *Journal of Group Psychotherapy, Psychodrama and Sociometry, 46*(2), 73–74.

Greenberg, I. A. (1974). *Psychodrama: theory and therapy.* New York, NY: Behavioral Publications.

Jarvik, L. F. (1990). Role reversal: Implications for therapeutic intervention. *Journal of Gerontological Social Work, 15*(1/2), 23–34.

Kreider, D. G., & Motto, J. A. (1970). Parent-child role reversal and suicidal states in adolescence. *Adolescence, 9*(35), 365–370.

Macfie, J., Toth, S. L., Rogosch, F. A., Robinson, J., Emde, R. N., & Cicchetti, D. (1999). Effect of maltreatment on preschoolers' narrative representations of responses to relieve distress and of role reversal. *Developmental Psychology, 35*(2), 460–465.

Mayseless, O., Bartholomew, K., Henderson, A., & Trinke, S. (2004). I was more her mom than she was mine. Role reversal in a community sample. *Family Relations, 53,* 78–86.

Oznobishin, O., & Kurman, J. (2009). Parent-child role reversal and psychological adjustment among immigrant youth in Israel. *Journal of Family Psychology, 23*(3), 405–415.

Richeson, J., A., & Ambady, N. (2001). When roles reverse: Stigma, status, and self-evaluation. *Journal of Applied Social Psychology, 31*(7), 1350–1378.

Sculpting

DESCRIPTION

Sculpting is a technique that provides an opportunity for members of a family or group to sculpt their views of the family as it functions on a day-to-day basis or where they were at some relevant time in their lives. This is done by having the chosen sculptor physically arrange the participants (including themselves) and their perceived place in the family by setting them in particular positions and stances in relation to one another.

ORIGINS

Sculpting emerged from the family therapy field in general. In working with families, many social workers became aware of the extent to which family members' body language, and where and how they positioned themselves in interviews, could tell us a great deal about family dynamics. By focusing on these differential body-language messages, we can help family members come to perceive and understand some of the nuances of their family life.

WHY THIS IS USEFUL TO SOCIAL WORK

Sculpting is useful for therapy because it builds on the specific structure of a family or group in a manner that can be easily observed and understood by those involved. It helps the entire family or group identify different perceptions of the physical family structure. Once these have been identified, they can then examine such differences and consider whether they can be changed for the overall good of the family.

HOW THIS IS USEFUL TO SOCIAL WORK

The overall purpose of this technique is to provide a stimulus that can open group or family discussions of the members' self-perceptions and their interaction within and outside their primary group or family setting, either with regard to some particular pattern within the group or family, or an event. Although most frequently used in family therapy, it also has been used with groups and on occasion in one-to-one treatment, where cards are used to represent the other persons in the family or group.

RISK FACTORS

Sculpting is not a high-risk technique, but practitioners differ over its effectiveness and appropriateness, with some seeing it as too theatrical and not of great utility.

At times, the family or group, or some members of it, will be unable to bring themselves to participate in a manner that facilitates the useful forum of dialogue that the social worker seeks. Other families may see it as a therapeutically irrelevant or puzzling technique or even consider it totally unacceptable.

There is always the risk that, when there is a high level of dissent among the persons involved in the sculptor's perception, this will get carried over into interactions outside the interview. Such dissent can produce large amounts of stress. Thus it is presumed that, when introducing this technique, the worker is sufficiently comfortable with its goals and procedures to help clients participate in it.

REQUIRED SKILLS AND KNOWLEDGE

Sculpting often requires considerable coaching and encouragement by the social worker to engage the family in this activity and to get someone to volunteer to be the sculptor. If possible, the sculptor should try to have the individual members pose in a manner that reflects his or her view of their place in the family and their relationships to one another.

The term *sculpt* is used to reflect that, as far as possible, the family or group member doing the sculpting should refrain from speaking to the other members during the process, but should only use position, poise, and location to indicate the family situation.

Sculpting should take place with the cooperation of all members present. It does not mean that each individual needs to agree with the sculptor's placement of them or others, or the interpretation the sculptor makes of some significant family event.

This technique permits a considerable amount of variation. There is no formal set of rules apart from the overall strategy. For example some practitioners do permit the "director/sculptor" to talk, in the form of giving directions for how and where he or she wants members of the family to place themselves in the emerging sculpture. Others suggest that there should be no talking until the sculpture is finished. Once a sculpture has been completed to the satisfaction of the selected sculptor, all parties, including the sculptor, share their perceptions of the final sculpture, whether they agree or not with the depictions in the sculpture, and why.

Case Summary One

A mother, father, daughter, and son are attending family therapy sessions to improve their communication.

SOCIAL WORKER: Today we are going to engage in a sculpting exercise. One of you will sculpt, or position, the other family members the way you view them to be on a day-to-day basis. Who would like to be the sculptor?

MADISON [DAUGHTER]: I can do it.

SOCIAL WORKER: All right, go ahead and stand up and start positioning your family members.

[Madison moves her family members into the positions that she perceives they should be in.]

SOCIAL WORKER: Madison, tell me about the positions you placed your family members in and why.

MADISON: I had my dad stand up because he is the head of our family. Dad is the one in charge. My mom is positioned next to my dad because she is his partner and helps him run the family. I sat my brother in the chair because he has to do what my parents tell him to until he turns eighteen and can move out on his own. I sat down on the floor next my brother because I am the youngest member of the family and have no say in anything.

SOCIAL WORKER: Does anyone have anything to change or add to what Madison said?

GLORIA [MOTHER]: I would have to disagree with her last comment. I don't believe she has no say in anything.

MADISON: Well, maybe I have a say in some stuff. I just meant I'm definitely not in charge.

All family members continued to discuss the way the family was sculpted and expressed their point of view regarding their roles.

Engaging in this technique helped facilitate several conversations between family members regarding the familial hierarchy and respect. They were also able to begin to understand the differing perceptions among them. Discussing these perceptions and roles in the family allowed the members to determine whether or not anything within the family unit needed to change.

Case Summary Two

Holly and Roger were divorced during the past two years. Holly has remarried hastily to an individual named Larry and they have moved in together. Roger is single and lives with their 13-year-old teenage son named Brent. Brent has had some referrals in school for misconduct and skipping school. He has been referred to his school social worker by his teacher for individual and family counseling. Brent has told his social worker that he feels like he doesn't have a family and that no one cares about him. The social worker decides that it would be helpful for the family to engage in a sculpting technique during a family session. During the session, the social worker explains the sculpting activity to the family.

> SOCIAL WORKER: Thank you all for being here today. We are going to partake in an activity known as sculpting. Brent, I am going to ask you to stand in the middle of the room and place your mom and her husband and your dad around this room in terms of how you perceive them on a daily basis.
> [The social worker positions the teenage son in the middle of the room. He uses his direction to place the other family individuals nearby him in terms of relative emotional nearness and detachment. The social worker asks Brent to explain why he placed his family the way he did.]
> BRENT: I placed my mom and her husband standing next to the far wall because I feel the most distant to her. Since she married Larry, I only get to see her on the weekends. It seems that he is all that she cares about. I placed my dad on the chair next to me because he takes care of me and I see him every day, but he is so busy that he is always working in his office. Most of the time I feel all alone.

Through the use of the sculpting technique in family therapy, the social worker is able to help the family members express their mental representation of each other to one another, thus helping the family communicate and grow better. The family is able to perceive how they are now and how they would like to be in the future with everybody's input.

REFERENCES AND ADDITIONAL SOURCES

Bobes, T., & Rothman, B. (2002). *Doing couple therapy: Integrating theory with practice*. New York, NY: Norton.

Costa, L. (1991). Family sculpting in the training of marriage and family counselors. *Counselor Education and Supervision, 31*(2), 121–131.

Duhl, F. S., Kantor, D., & Duhl, B. S. (1973). Learning space and action in family therapy: A primer of sculpting. In D. Bloch (Ed.), *Techniques of family psychotherapy: A primer (47–63)*. New York, NY: Grune & Stratton.

Jefferson, C. (1978). Some notes on the use of family sculpture in therapy. *Family Process, 17*(1), 69–76.

Kirst-Ashman, K. K., & Hull, G. (1993). *Understanding generalist practice* (p. 355). Chicago, IL: Nelson-Hall.

Laitila, A., & Aaltonen, J. (1998). Application of the assimilation model in the context of family therapy: A case study. *Contemporary Family Therapy, 20*(3), 277–290.

Lawson, D. M. (1988). Using family sculpting and choreography in a student growth group. *Journal of Counseling & Development, 66*(5), 246–247.

Marchetti-Mercer, M. C., & Cleaver, G. (2000). Genograms and family sculpting: An aid to cross-cultural understanding in the training of psychology students in South Africa. *The Counseling Psychologist, 28*(1), 61–80.

McMahon, M. O'Neil. (1996). *The general perspective* (3rd ed., pp. 217–218). Boston, MA: Allyn & Bacon.

Papp, P., Silverstein, O., & Carter, E. (1973). Family sculpting in preventative work with well families. *Family Process, 12*(2), 197–212.

Robbins, A., & Erismann, M. (1992). Developing therapeutic artistry: A joint countertransference supervisory seminar/stone sculpting workshop. *The Arts in Psychotherapy, 19*(5), 367–377.

Venter, C. A. (1993). Graphic family sculpting as a technique in family therapy. *Social Worker-Research-Practitioner, 6*(2), 12–15.

Self-Disclosure

DESCRIPTION

Self-disclosure is a technique in which the social worker chooses to share some personal material with the client as a way of helping the client make more effective use of the therapeutic process.

ORIGINS

Certainly one of the dicta that was a part of our teaching in earlier days was that we kept ourselves and our lives outside of client relationships. It was considered unprofessional to share anything of ourselves with our clients apart from our name. However, as we have become much more theoretically pluralistic and diversely oriented, we have found that this position is a culturally bound perception—one that, in some instances, is not only unhelpful but indeed could be detrimental to the therapeutic relationship.

WHY USEFUL TO SOCIAL WORK

Because our therapy in its various formats is based on an understanding of the human person not only as a psychological entity but also as an individual with values and a specific cultural setting, we have learned that for many clients it is very important that they know something about us as people while forming a trusting relationship with us. Thus, in some of our client relationships there will be occasions where we deliberately choose to share something of ourselves as a way of conveying understanding and instilling trust and confidence.

HOW THIS IS USEFUL TO SOCIAL WORK

At times a client will need to know such things as our marital status, our cultural and ethnic origins, our level and type of training, our theoretical orientation, and so forth. Telling clients about ourselves can give our lives a level of reality, and clients a sense of security as to who we are.

There are also times when it is helpful for the client to know that we have been through similar life experiences to their own, in regard to such things as divorce, suffering a loss, death, separation, assault, or disease. By sharing these with a client, we can convey to them that we are human, while helping them see that our perceptions of what they are going through can be trusted. By building on common life experiences or significant points in our own histories, we can impart to the client a level of awareness of their own situation built on some component of our own life history.

RISK FACTORS

Self-disclosure has moderate risk. One possible source comes from having an attitude that minimizes the potential harm of self-revelation. What we think could be helpful to the client may have the opposite effect. We may think, for example, that a client who is in the process of a divorce may be helped if we talk about our own divorce. This may affect their confidence in the social worker's ability to be objective or helpful. For many clients, our more traditional practice of keeping ourselves out of the relationship may be the very factor that permits them to share their most intimate material with us.

REQUIRED SKILL AND KNOWLEDGE

Here we are talking about this use of ourselves as a targeted technique, not as something to be done with all clients out of some ideological perspective. That is, we are focusing on the conscious and deliberate use of some component or facet of our lives with the goal of influencing the client in a manner deemed to assist in achieving some aspect of the therapeutic intent. What we tell the client about ourselves, either when they ask or when we choose to do so, is done from our perspective of using this sharing as a technique.

The decision about what will be shared and when should be viewed on the basis of our judgment as to what will be most helpful to the client. Thus, we need to make a conscious decision to use some personal matter to achieve a particular therapeutic goal. That is, based on our knowledge of the client, we decide that our sharing some aspect of our own life history will be helpful to the client in some particular way.

The range of what kinds of personal things would be helpful is vast. Undoubtedly as we gather more data on this topic, patterns will emerge indicating when, what, and how we should share, depending on such factors as age, culture (ethnic, religious, and historic), and gender factors.

What we do know is that for some clients, knowing some things about who we are beyond being their social workers can help them be more secure, more comfortable in sharing, more able to examine themselves, more understanding of their own and others' situations, and more able to invest in the therapeutic process.

Case Summary One

Kelsey is an adolescent girl attending therapy after she was abused by her mother's boyfriend. Kelsey told her social worker that she feels sad, scared, and embarrassed anytime she thinks or speaks about the abuse. Her social worker has noticed that Kelsey often has difficulty talking about herself during sessions. Kelsey also has not been able to discuss the abuse that occurred yet.

> SOCIAL WORKER: Kelsey, today we are going to play a game so that I can get to know you a little better. How does that sound to you?
>
> KELSEY: That's fine.
>
> SOCIAL WORKER: Okay, great. Here's how you play. This ball has several different questions on it. I will toss the ball to you and then you will answer whichever question you see. Do you have any questions about how to play?
>
> KELSEY: No, I understand. The question says: "If you could change one thing in your life what would it be?" Umm … I don't know. I can't think of anything.
>
> SOCIAL WORKER: Well, before we move on, I want you to think about it a little bit more. I'll answer the question first. I had a close family member that passed away about a year ago. If I could change one thing I would make it so that he did not pass away.
>
> KELSEY: If I could change one thing I would make it so that what happened to me did not happen.

Knowing that Kelsey was hesitant to reveal personal information, her social worker decided it would be beneficial to self-disclose a small amount about herself during the session. Initially, Kelsey had a hard time opening up, but hearing her social worker share a bit of personal information made Kelsey feel more at ease. Knowing that her social worker has been through something that she wished she hadn't helped Kelsey realize that her social worker can understand how she is feeling. It also facilitated a trusting relationship between Kelsey and her social worker and led Kelsey to talk about herself more.

Case Summary Two

Carla is a freshman in college seeking help from a college counselor for her career because she is confused about which career path to pursue. In her first year of college, she thought she would like to become a veterinarian. She changed her major to "undecided" because she was not making good grades in the veterinary medicine track. Carla saw posters for career counseling at her student resource center, so she decided it might be helpful to talk to someone who would be able to help her decide on a major and a career.

Carla feels awful that this is happening to her, and she is slightly depressed because she thought veterinary medicine was the field for her. She feels alone and thinks that she is the only one going through a situation like this. She speaks to a social worker who helps her explore her interests and career options. Her social worker discloses to Carla that she went through a similar situation when she was in college exploring her own career options:

CARLA: I really want to decide on a major and a career that is right for me. I feel like a loser! I worked so hard to get into college and I really thought being a veterinarian was what I wanted! Now I feel lost and I am so frustrated. Sometimes I think will I ever find a career? I don't know what is right for me. I need to decide so that I can get a move on with my coursework.

SOCIAL WORKER: You sound unsure and frustrated. But I want to let you know that you are not alone. Lots of freshmen and even upper-class students experience changing majors and careers. Let me tell you a personal story. For a long time, I was an undecided major for three years before I decided to do social work. At first I thought I wanted to be a teacher, but then I realized that I wanted to work outside of the classroom. So I know how you feel when you say that you're scared and frustrated because you are ready to move on, declare a major, and get started on your career.

By using self-disclosure, the social worker helped the client to realize that she is not alone with her problem. The client was able to relax because she knows that someone understands what she is going through and can empathize with her situation. Carla feels much calmer knowing that someone else experienced a career crisis but persevered and succeeded. This has given her a push to further explore her career options and interests through her career resource center, where she can read books, watch videos, and do research about different careers in order to choose the right career.

REFERENCES AND ADDITIONAL SOURCES

Anderson, S. L., & Mandell, D. L. (1989). The use of self-disclosure by professional social workers. *Social Casework, 70*(6), 259–267.

Audet, C. T., & Everall, R. D. (2010). Social worker self-disclosure and the therapeutic relationship: A phenomenological study from the client perspective. *British Journal of Guidance & Counselling, 38*(3), 327–342.

Carew, L. (2009). Does theoretical background influence social workers' attitudes to social worker self-disclosure? A qualitative study. *Counselling & Psychotherapy Research, 9*(4), 266–272.

Cormier, S., & Hackney, H. (1999). *Counseling strategies and interventions* (5th ed., pp. 29–30). Boston, MA: Allyn & Bacon.

Edwards, C., & Murdock, N. (1994). Characteristics of social worker self-disclosure in the counseling process. *Journal of Counseling and Development, 72*(4), 384–389.

Hanson, J. (2005). Should your lips be zipped? How social worker self-disclosure and non-disclosure affects clients. *Counselling & Psychotherapy Research, 5*(2), 96–104.

Hill, C. E., Mahalik, J. R., & Thompson, B. J. (1989). Social worker self-disclosure. *Psychotherapy, 26*(3), 290–295.

Miller, M. (2002). How much should psychosocial workers tell about themselves? *Harvard Mental Health Letter, 19*(4), 3–6.

Myers, D., & Hayes, J. A. (2006). Effects of social worker general self-disclosure and countertransference disclosure on ratings of the social worker and session. *Psychotherapy: Theory, Research, Practice, Training, 43*(2), 173–185.

Peterson, Z. D. (2002). More than a mirror: The ethics of social worker self-disclosure. *Psychotherapy: Theory, Research, Practice, Training, 39*(1), 21–31.

Separation

DESCRIPTION

Separation is a technique through which we encourage, enable, or assist a client in separating themselves from someone or some situation for a period of time, with a view toward enhancing some aspect of their psychosocial reality we are dealing with. (Here we are not considering the types of placements that social workers become involved with as a part of our childcare or disability work; or when, in situations of danger and harm, the separation sought becomes the goal of the intervention, not the technique.)

ORIGINS

From the early days of the profession, social workers have been involved in the precarious function of physically separating people from each other and from certain situations. This is seen most clearly in the child welfare field.

From these experiences, and from our knowledge of environments and systems, we have learned that on occasion in our voluntary practice, there are times when a client struggling with various issues can benefit from a period of separation from some significant person or situation to achieve or permit some therapeutic goal. As mentioned, this is done as a treatment technique, not its entire goal.

WHY THIS IS USEFUL TO SOCIAL WORK

In experiencing this type of structured distancing from some person or some system of significance in their lives, clients will frequently be much more able to think about and work through other components of the therapeutic relationship that are being addressed.

HOW THIS IS USEFUL TO SOCIAL WORK

A separation could be from someone in the client's life who is a source of problems of some kind, or it may be a home difficulty where the situation has reached a point where a short-term separation, a form of time-out, might be useful. It also may be a relationship situation that is proving to be deleterious to the client's ongoing development and growth.

In addition to relationship situations, there may be factors outside of the home, such as a work situation that is proving to be unduly stressful, that can indicate a separation. The actual separation need not be long or distant. It might well be something like a short vacation, a visit to a friend, or even a weekend—any kind of formal process to effect a physical separation from the relevant people or situation.

For some young people, it may be important for them to distance themselves from a home life that is troubled enough to greatly impair their ability to function. Often such clients need both our permission and help to make the proposed move. Some such moves may only be symbolic, yet they can be of tremendous import, such as a few days with a friend. Other moves may need to be much more structured and long term, such as going to school or starting a job.

All such moves are not necessarily done for negative reasons. Instead, the goal may be to give someone a needed opportunity to try their wings in a new situation.

RISK FACTORS

Separation is clearly a technique with a high risk factor, because of the seriousness of the proposed action for the client and the potential outcomes of the situation. This decision of course needs to have the full support of the client and, when needed, of any parents and guardians. Clearly we need to be careful that we are not overly influencing the client toward a move for which they are not ready or to which they are not fully committed.

REQUIRED SKILLS AND KNOWLEDGE

It is crucial that, if the separation is geographically distant, the person moving is connected to and has access to therapeutic help if needed. In all such situations, efforts need to be made to ensure that there is agreement on all sides and that this planned separation is understood and supported by all involved. This of course may not be achievable, as the separation may be planned to help the client free themselves from a situation or person who is not healthy to their growth and development.

Case Summary One

Rosemary has been attending therapy sessions and was making adequate progress in treatment, but has recently hit a roadblock.

> SOCIAL WORKER: Rosemary, tell me about what's going on lately.
>
> ROSEMARY: I have been feeling so sluggish recently. Work has become so stressful that I can't seem to function lately. It feels like I can't concentrate on anything other than what is going on at work.
>
> SOCIAL WORKER: Sometimes separating ourselves from a stressful situation can help give us a little perspective and time to think more clearly. Have you thought about using some vacation time?
>
> ROSEMARY: Actually, I do have quite a bit of vacation time accumulated. I haven't used it in a while. I don't know where I would want to go, though.
>
> SOCIAL WORKER: Even if you don't go anywhere far away and you just stay home for a few days it can be helpful. Also, staying at a close friend's house for a few days can be an inexpensive way to go on a mini-vacation and leave behind the stressful situation of your work atmosphere.
>
> ROSEMARY: Well, I haven't seen my friend Alicia in a long time and she's been asking me to visit. I could probably stay with her for several days. I believe that would really take my mind off the stress of work and help me to feel rejuvenated.
>
> SOCIAL WORKER: I agree. The short separation from your stressful work situation will be a wonderful way to clear your mind and be able to continue working towards your treatment goals.

Rosemary was so stressed out by her work situation that she couldn't function in any other area of her life. Her social worker's encouragement to separate herself from her job allowed her to enhance her functioning in all areas of her life. Putting distance between herself and her job also gave Rosemary the chance to think of ways to cope with the stress she feels on a daily basis.

Case Summary Two

Tia is going through some disputes with her husband Alex. Alex and Tia have been married for approximately five years, and they describe their relationship as being ideal at first. Both were emotionally vested in the relationship, everything was going as planned, and they got married after dating for a short 6 months.

Although Tia and Alex don't have kids together, Tia did have one miscarriage. Soon after the miscarriage she began to discover that Alex has been having a relationship with a woman outside of their marriage. Alex has admitted to having had an affair, but he still wants to be with Tia because he still loves her. Tia says that she still loves her husband, and had considered staying together with him, but she is infuriated due to his infidelity and wants a divorce.

Social worker: It seems that you were both vested in the relationship in the beginning. You both still love each other. One of you wants a divorce and the other wants to work things out.

Tia: We still love each other. But he cheated on me and I find that extremely hard to forgive. I don't want to give him up, but what he did seriously hurt me. Part of me wants to stay together and part of me wants a divorce. I don't know what to do.

Alex: I am sorry that I had the affair. I still love Tia and I want to fix this relationship and move on with our lives.

Social worker: It seems that you both still possess feelings for each other and you both expressed an interest in trying to fix things. My recommendation to you is that you separate from one another for at least a few months until you have had a chance to think about the relationship and whether or not you want to stay together. Does this sound like a reasonable thing to do?

As one can see, the social worker employed the use of separation as a technique to counsel two individuals who are considering a divorce but who are undecided if that is the solution for them. Using separation will allow the couple to to take a break from each other and reflect on whether or not they want to continue their marriage together.

REFERENCES AND ADDITIONAL SOURCES

Chrzastowski, S. (2007). Comparison of separation patterns between parents and offspring in psychiatric and nonclinical families. *Psychological Reports, 101*(1), 171–176.

Cowal, K., Shinn, M., Weitzman, B. C., Stojanovic, D., & Labay, L. (2002). Mother-child separations among homeless and housed families receiving public assistance in New York City. *American Journal of Community Psychology, 30*(5), 711–730.

Michalshi, J. H., Mishna, F., Worthington, C., & Cummings, R. A. (2003). Multi-method impact evaluation of a therapeutic summer camp program. *Child and Adolescent Social Work Journal, 20*(1), 53–76.

Mishna, F., Michalshi, J., & Cummings, R. (2001). Camps as social work intervention: Returning to our roots. *Social Work With Groups, 24*(3/4), 153.

Saintonge, S., Achille, P. A., & Lachance, L. (1998). The influence of Big Brothers on the separation–individuation of adolescents from single-parent families. *Adolescence, 33*(130), 343–353.

Suárez-Orozco, C., Todorova, I. L., & Louie, J. (2004). Making up for lost time: The experience of separation and reunification among immigrant families. *Family Process, 41*(4), 625–643.

Silence

DESCRIPTION

Although not always thought of as a technique, the skillful use of silence in an interview is a treatment tool with potentially strong and effective impact. Although the word *silence* might suggest that it is simply the absence of speech, and thus requires little skill, it is an observable reality that we choose to introduce or minimize in an interview. Thus, although it is passive in appearance, choosing to be silent or encouraging the client to do so requires a deliberate action on our part.

ORIGINS

Silence did not emerge from any specific theoretical orientation. Rather, its importance has arisen from the awareness of skilled interviewers of all orientations that, silence plays an important role in many human interactions. This reality needs to be understood in order to use silence skillfully.

We know from our own nontherapeutic interactions with significant others in our lives that the frequency and extent of silence varies depends on many things, such as the person, his or her habits, the situation, and its importance. In some conversations, silences can be a minimal occurrence, whereas in others, we can sit for long periods of time without a word being spoken, in both cases understanding that these silences are mutually understood, effective, respected, appreciated, and enabling.

WHY THIS IS USEFUL TO SOCIAL WORK

This technique is important for our practice because it reflects an important component of many (if not most) of our significant human interactions. It is a reality that, when properly understood and utilized, can be a highly effective way of conveying our interest, concern, understanding, and respect to our clients.

HOW THIS IS USEFUL TO SOCIAL WORK

There are two components to the therapeutic use of silence: the one where we allow the client to be silent and not interject into this silence; and the other, where we choose to remain silent to facilitate a reflective process in the client, or to allow a client to regain his or her composure after a difficult part of an interview.

At times clients are ready to focus on some significant aspect of their lives, and in the interview will talk about it virtually nonstop. It can seem like much of the whole interview consists of the client's venting or reflecting upon some critical area. We remain silent in such instances, but we do so in a way that assures the client we are listening, supportive, and encouraging. Using such things as our body language, facial expressions, physical position, or gestures, we can maintain an active silence.

There are some clients who find silences in an interaction to be uncomfortable, and will want to interrupt these silences just to keep a verbal process going. At other times, we will permit a client's silence to continue while remaining silent ourselves. We can do this for several reasons, such as allowing clients to think about some topic of import, to consider alternatives, or to deal internally with some issue that has emerged in the interview. We can also use silence in a ritualistic way to allow a client to pay respect to a lost significant other.

On occasion we will deliberately and overtly introduce periods of silence into our interviews, perhaps to allow a period of cooling off after a process that may have become overly intense, to ponder some important issue, or to let the client regain his or her composure following some highly charged topic or issue. Just as we have found in our own lives that having a friend with us during some difficult time where little or nothing is said can be highly supportive and facilitating, so too can we be helpful to many of our clients by the skillful use of silence.

Silence also has an important role in multiple-client situations. There are times in these modes of interviewing when we will remain silent to permit or encourage further interactions or dialogue among the group to continue.

RISK FACTORS

Silence is a low-risk technique.

REQUIRED SKILLS AND KNOWLEDGE

An important aspect of silence that needs to be understood is that its use and significance varies considerably among people, events, groups, and cultures. Many people view an overly rapid rate of response in conversation as rude. Silence in these instances conveys that the matter under discussion is important and worthy of a period of inner reflection on our part.

If we misunderstand some of our clients' periods of silence, and do not view such events as possible signs of politeness and indication of respect for what is being discussed, we can mistakenly think that the person has not heard us, and either repeat a comment or ask if they have understood what we have said. This is especially true if our own style of verbal exchange is rapid, often cutting a person off before a sentence is finished, not as a sign of impatience but to show them we understand where they are and that we wish to get on with the important business being discussed.

Thus it is important that we remain aware of how we use silence in our own lives to understand how we use it in contact with our clients. We also need to attempt to understand how our client uses silence in either a positive or negative manner. Addressing this question directly with the client can also be a component of our intervention. That is, helping our clients reflect on their feelings and patterns of silence in their everyday interactions can be a source of learning for them. In this way they can begin to use silence in a more creative and positive way.

Although this is apparently a technique that requires no skill other than saying nothing, in reality it is filled with subtleties. It can have a highly positive and sustained impact on our clients when understood and skillfully used, but it can also create puzzlement, uncertainty, irritation, and discomfort when not understood.

Case Summary One

Jack is attending grief counseling following the unexpected death of his cousin. During one of his sessions, Jack is explaining the nature of his relationship to his cousin and how close they were. Suddenly, Jack begins to speak very rapidly and then starts crying uncontrollably.

JACK: I just don't know what to say. I can't believe this happened. It's not fair.
SOCIAL WORKER: Why don't we take a few moments to be silent? Try closing your eyes and collecting your thoughts. Once you've calmed down and you're ready, finish telling me about your cousin.
[The social worker and Jack sit together in silence while Jack contemplates the message he is trying to convey. After several minutes, Jack finishes sobbing and begins to speak.]
JACK: I am so frustrated with this entire situation, that while I was speaking about it, it just overtook me and I couldn't get a grip. I felt like I was starting to spin out of control. I'm calmer now.

Jack was becoming extremely overwhelmed while speaking about the cousin he lost. Stopping to be silent allowed him to focus, calm down, and breathe more steadily. He was able to come back to the here and now of the therapy session and feel the emotion he was trying to express. The social worker's silence also facilitated Jack's ability to do this.

Case Summary Two

Betty is getting counseling because she has been physically abused by her husband. She speaks to Cassie, who is a trauma counselor at the counseling center. Betty tells Cassie that her husband verbally and physically assaulted her for a long time throughout their marriage.

> **BETTY:** One night I went to a friend's house. When I came home around nine o'clock in the evening, my husband had been upset that I didn't tell him where I was. He beat me brutally and threatened to end my life, so I called the police. The police arrested my husband and I moved in with my friend.
>
> **CASSIE:** I see. Tell me more about that.
>
> **BETTY:** At the time, I felt disoriented and confused and for a while I couldn't remember the story. But lately I am starting to remember parts of the story and I can now recall the traumatic event in its entirety.

As Betty recalls the story to Cassie she starts to choke up and eventually starts to cry. Cassie decides to allow some silence and give Betty some time to let loose her emotions before proceeding with talking.

By permitting silence, the social worker respects the client's needs and permits feelings of sensitivity and understanding to the client. More important, the social worker conveys to the client feelings of safety when permitting silence appropriately in a therapy session. Since her husband's arrest Betty has been feeling depressed and suicidal. She will continue to work with her social worker through counseling and medication until she has fully recovered from the abuse. Betty hopes to one day regain control of her life and be an active member of society.

REFERENCES AND ADDITIONAL SOURCES

Blanton, G. P. (2007). Adding silence to stories: Narrative therapy and contemplation. *Contemporary Family Therapy: An International Journal, 29*(4), 211–221.

Brown, G. R. (1987). Therapeutic effect of silence: Application to a case of borderline personality. *Psychoanalytic Technique, 4,*123–130.

Cook, J. J. (1964). Silence in psychotherapy. *Journal of Counseling Psychology, 11*(1), 42–46.

Elson, M. (2001). Silence, its use and abuse: A view from self-psychology. *Clinical Social Work Journal, 79*(4), 351–360.

Hackney, H., & Cormier, L. S. (1979). *Counselling strategies and objectives.* Englewood Cliffs, NJ: Prentice Hall.

Hill, C. E., Thompson, B. J., & Ladany, N. (2003). Social worker use of silence in therapy. *Journal of Clinical Psychology, 59*(4), 513–524.

Kadushin, A. (1990). *The social work interview.* New York, NY: Columbia University Press.

Ladany, N., Hill, C. E., Thompson, B. J., & O'Brien, K. M. (2004). Social worker perspectives on using silence in therapy: A qualitative study. *Counselling & Psychotherapy Research, 4*(1), 80–89.

Rajski, P. (2003). Finding God in the silence: Contemplative prayer and therapy. *Journal of Religion & Health, 42*(3), 181–190.

Slavson, S. R. (1966). The phenomenology and dynamics of silence in psychotherapy groups. *International Journal of Group Psychotherapy, 16*(4), 395–404.

Zeligs, M. A. (1961). The psychology of silence: Its role in transference, counter-transference and the psychoanalytic process. *Journal of the American Psychoanalytic Association, 9*(1), 7–43.

Storytelling

DESCRIPTION

This technique encompasses our telling stories to clients or having the client tell us stories for therapeutic purposes.

ORIGINS

Throughout human history, one of the important ways in which cultural history and its inherent values have been transmitted from generation to generation and person to person has been through the process of storytelling. Much of the moral socialization of children in all parts of the world takes place this way. Apart from our understanding of the role telling stories plays for children, we often view this as something that happens only in other cultures. However, it is a facet of all cultures for people of all ages. What differs is the way it is done, by whom, and when.

WHY THIS IS USEFUL TO SOCIAL WORK

Stories are an important way of helping persons learn about themselves—their origins, beliefs, histories, values, and customs—and thus can serve as a powerful therapeutic resource. Effective as the impact of the printed word may be, a story told to us by a significant person in our lives leaves a different kind of impression. We often can remember such stories many years after we have first heard them. Many of these stories are couched in a fable-like "once upon a time" format. Others are pieces of family or cultural history delivered in a storylike fashion. History and the fiction are frequently mixed together as they get passed on from generation to generation, with the essence of the story being that it carries some value or moral message.

Having the client tell us stories can be a rich and effective way of helping us to understand them and their histories. It also can help them understand their own life journey. In this way, the client is given an active role in the helping process, as well an opportunity to better understand who they are, their worldview, their values, and their perception of how they function outside therapy.

For some people, couching a certain point in story form can help incorporate its meaning and significance into their own lives. This happens because telling and listening to a story are not highly cognitive or cerebral processes. Stories touch the imagination; hence, for some clients they can be readily understood and appreciated, and are the best way to address some component of a value set.

The storytelling technique is not well known or often discussed in our profession's traditions and history. However, it may well have more therapeutic potential than we have accorded it up to now.

HOW THIS IS USEFUL TO SOCIAL WORK

At times, we will be the storyteller, but the process can be reversed to have the client tell us stories that have been important to them throughout their lives. Often it is this latter role with which we are more comfortable.

When the client is the storyteller, in addition to having him or her tell the story we will have the client reflect with us upon its meaning and significance in their lives. It is often through sharing stories, and subsequently pondering their messages and place in personal or family tradition, that both the client and social worker can learn much about the teller's family, culture, values, ethics, and worldview.

A particular role of stories in many of our own lives and those of our clients is to develop a sense of morality and our place in history. This is why the childhood nursery stories on which many of us were raised often carry a theme of good and bad behavior. These early-life stories do not easily translate into the context of a more mature technique; however, stories such as parables from various religious writings, some of which are almost universally known, can be the topic for reflection with some clients. These stories are important because often they play or once played a role in helping people develop a sense of history, as well as shaping their sense of identity, values, and place in the family.

RISK FACTORS

This is a low-risk technique.

REQUIRED SKILLS AND KNOWLEDGE

To effectively tap this very useful way of helping people learn about their origins, beliefs, histories, values, and customs requires a level of cultural legitimization between the teller and the listener. At times this already exists between the client and the social worker, but in our increasingly multicultural society this is rarely the situation. Thus, one required skill is often to find someone who carries the needed legitimacy to function in this role.

When we have the client tell us stories of importance to them, the cultural similarity between us is not as important. In fact, differences in cultural identity that may interfere with the therapeutic process can often be minimized through storytelling. This gives the client an opportunity to teach the social worker and to provide information that can expand the basis of the therapeutic process.

Although we do not frequently view social workers as storytellers, there are people who do see themselves and function in society as storytellers. Usually the primary purpose of their stories is to entertain. Many people, however, view the storyteller's role as much more than entertainment; they see it as a way to help people get to know themselves and their cultural origins better. Often there is a religious component in the stories. The point is that even though we ourselves may not be competent in a storytelling role, we may choose to collaborate with such a person as a way of helping clients get in better touch with their histories and values.

Case Summary One

Joslyn is going through a difficult time in her life, so she decided to start attending therapy sessions. She views herself as being at a crossroads and says she can't decide what path to take. She feels stuck and doesn't know how to proceed with her life.

JOSLYN: I don't know what to do with myself. I'm beginning to question everything in my life.

SOCIAL WORKER: Tell me more about how you're feeling.

JOSLYN: I'm very confused and overwhelmed. I feel like I've lost my way and lost my identity. I don't know what to do.

SOCIAL WORKER: Sometimes stories can help us learn a great deal about ourselves and others. Tell me a story from your life, one that is important to you or has special meaning to you.

[After hearing Joslyn's story:]

SOCIAL WORKER: Now, let's think about and discuss the significance of this story and reflect on its meaning as it relates to you and your life.

Hearing Joslyn's story gave her social worker the opportunity to learn more about her and understand her history. Telling the story also helped Joslyn understand her own life's journey and the direction she would like to take for her future. It provided her with the chance to make sense of her world and her role in it.

Case Summary Two

Ten-year-old Carl was brought to treatment by his mother on the recommendation of his school guidance counselor. Carl and his mother recently moved out of the maternal grandparents' home and relocated to a city about 1 hour away. Carl's mother took a new job that requires her to work longer hours. This required Carl to begin attending an afterschool program until 7:00 in the evening. Carl began getting into fights at his new school in which he was the aggressor. One day he left the afterschool program and was found by a staff member walking on a busy highway. He refused to say where he was going. Carl's mother reports that he has generally been a quiet, well-behaved child who was "very close to his grandmother." She notes that Carl is "not happy that we moved" and that he "misses his grandparents, especially my mom." During the course of treatment, the social worker decides to engage Carl in mutual storytelling to help him process his feelings about the changes in his family life.

The social worker suggested that, during sessions, they would work together on creating their own storybook. She asked Carl what his favorite animal was, and he told her it was a brown puppy with white spots. They decided to write a story about Larry the Lonesome Puppy. The social worker provided a variety of crayons and colored pencils for drawing, stamps, stickers, shapes, glue, and other art supplies that Carl could use to illustrate the unfolding story. As a part of each individual session, Carl would work on the storybook.

SOCIAL WORKER: Carl, today we can begin to write the storybook. Would you like to draw some of the pictures for the book first? You can use any of the art supplies here.

CARL: I can just start drawing what I want?

SOCIAL WORKER: Yes. And while you draw you can tell me what's happening with Larry and I'll write down what you're telling me. And this will become the story. How does that sound?

CARL: Will you be able to write down everything I say?

SOCIAL WORKER: I'll try my best. If I miss something, is it okay if I ask you to tell me again?

CARL: Sure, I'll help you remember.

SOCIAL WORKER: Then we'll make a good team.

The following excerpt paraphrases the beginning of Carl's work on the storybook.

Carl began to draw an elaborate picture of a brown dog with white spots sitting on a rug. After a while he began to tell the story of how Larry had been out exploring near his home when a "nice lady" thought that he was a stray dog and put him in her car taking him far away from his home. At first Larry thought he was just going for a ride "with the nice lady" and that she would take him back home later. But when night came, and Larry was sleepy and wanted to go back home to his own bed, the lady gave him a rug to sleep on and told him that this was his new home. But he didn't know where he was, and the rug was scratchy and the room was strange. Sometimes Larry didn't sleep at all because there were strange noises in this new place that didn't sound the same as the noises from his old house. Sometimes he cried, but because he was a dog no one knew what he was crying about. After a while Larry was so frustrated that he started biting people who came near him. Sometimes thinking about biting people made him forget about being so sad and lonely, and about how much he missed his family.

Carl and the social worker continued to work on the storybook during sessions. Carl put great effort into illustrating the pages, and he would read over the social worker's transcriptions to make certain she was writing the story "correctly." He even complimented her for "doing a great job of listening."

During the creation of the story, Carl and the social worker were able to talk about Larry's feelings and experiences. Although Carl was typically reserved when it came to discussing his own thoughts and feelings, he was quite open to discussing those of Larry. When Larry would get upset and bite someone in the story, the social worker would ask questions about what would happen to Larry when he bit someone, or what else Larry could have done instead of biting. As the story unfolded, Carl noted that sometimes Larry felt like biting but chose to do something else instead. Finally, the social worker invited Carl to read the story to his mother in a session. The social worker had coached mother to respond with praise to the great effort that Carl had put into the storyline and illustrations. She was urged to ask questions about the characters and story rather than making her questions directly about Carl. This process went well, with the mother pointing to a page and asking about how Larry was feeling, or why the lady with the rug looked angry. Carl and mother were able to have a productive therapeutic conversation that revealed much about what Carl was experiencing within the context of talking about Carl's storybook characters.

REFERENCES AND ADDITIONAL SOURCES

Doherty, D., & Mccoll, M. A. (2003). Illness stories: Themes emerging through narrative. *Sound Work in Heath Care, 37*(10), 19–39.

Friedberg, R. D. (1994). Storytelling and cognitive therapy with children. *Journal of Cognitive Psychotherapy, 8*(3), 209–217.

Grafanaki, S., & McLeod, J. (1999). Narrative processes in the construction of helpful and hindering events in experiential psychotherapy. *Psychotherapy Research, 9*(3), 289–303.

Kestenbaum, C. J. (1985). The creative process in child psychotherapy. *American Journal of Psychotherapy, 39*(4), 479–489.

Krietemeyer, B. C., & Heiney, S. P. (1992). Storytelling as a therapeutic technique in a group for school-aged oncology patients. *Children's Health Care, 21*(1), 14–20.

Rappaport, J. (1995). Empowerment meets narrative: Listening to stories and creating setting. *American Journal of Community Psychology, 23*(5), 795–807.

Robertson, M., & Barford, F. (1970). Story-making in psychotherapy with a chronically ill child. *Psychotherapy Theory, Research and Practice, 7*(2), 104–107.

Rosenthal, H. G. (1998). *Favorite counseling and therapy techniques* (pp. 95–97). New York: Brunner-Routledge.

Salvatore, G., Dimaggio, G., & Semerari, A. (2004). A model of narrative development: Implications for understanding psychopathology and guiding therapy. *Psychology & Psychotherapy: Theory, Research & Practice, 77*(2), 231–254.

Smith, G. G., & Celano, M. (2000). Revenge of the mutant cockroach: Culturally adapted storytelling in the treatment of a low-income African American boy. *Cultural Diversity and Ethnic Minority Psychology, 6*(2), 220–227.

Stirtzinger, R. M. (1983). Story telling: A creative therapeutic technique. *The Canadian Journal of Psychiatry/La Revue canadienne de psychiatrie, 28*(7), 561–565.

Sustaining and Supporting

DESCRIPTION

Using this technique, we convey to the client our understanding and confidence in their strengths and effort when they are struggling with the pain, frustration, and confusion of life's challenges.

ORIGINS

Sustaining and supporting is perhaps one of our most powerful and effective techniques, and has always been a part of our interventions. It fits well with the values of social work, is viewed as essential in virtually all social work theories, and is a part of all of our clinical methods. Few clients do not benefit from some degree of support from the social worker. This component of practice becomes almost second nature to most experienced practitioners, to the extent that it is often scarcely recognized as a technique.

WHY THIS IS USEFUL TO SOCIAL WORK

Its importance and effectiveness stem from a realization that many of the people we meet in practice have had little support, understanding, encouragement, or recognition of their abilities and talents, or of the weight and impact of their problems. To receive understanding and support from someone of influence can be very enabling and, at times, highly empowering. Often when the client is in a high-stress situation, the social worker may be the only person in the client's life who functions as a source of support.

We know from our own lives how uplifting and effective a sustaining comment or gesture from a friend or colleague can be in times of difficulty. Remembering this can help us appreciate the potential of sustaining and supporting as a technique in our practice.

HOW THIS IS USEFUL TO SOCIAL WORK

By using this technique, we are attempting to make our clients feel understood and helped. This in turn will help them make use of their potential and available resources to deal realistically with whatever life situations they are confronting.

RISK FACTORS

This is a low-risk technique. However, it is certainly a technique that can be misused by using it too often. That is, it is possible to so overwhelm the client with our support that they are insufficiently challenged to take charge of their own destiny, or to confront issues and tasks in an autonomous way that would enhance their psychosocial lives.

Overuse of sustaining and support can result in clients' developing excessive dependence upon the worker or other significant people in their lives. Usually it is a combination of sustaining and challenge that facilitates the client being able to take a more assertive or self- directed role.

REQUIRED SKILLS AND KNOWLEDGE

In using this technique, we attempt to help our clients to feel understood and assisted, so they can make better use of their potential and available resources to deal realistically with whatever life situations they are confronting.

There is no script to follow in making correct use of this technique. Probably the majority of our use will be done overtly through the use of such comments as, "You are doing very well," "You must have suffered a great deal," "I am pleased you were able to do this," and "This must have been very difficult," among others. Our overall demeanor and body language while working with clients, as well as our office setting, will convey an enabling sense of respect and recognition and an overall air of support.

Case Summary

Jason has been attending therapy sessions for several months and is making good progress in his treatment. Recently, Jason has noticed that his company has been laying off quite a few employees. Jason is starting to worry that he might be next.

Social worker: Jason, tell me about the concerns you are having with your job.
Jason: Well, over the past few weeks I have noticed that several employees at my job have been laid off. I'm afraid that I could be the next one to have to leave. I don't know what I would do if I lost my job.

SOCIAL WORKER: It sounds like these layoffs are very troubling to you. You are doing very well in treatment. I'm sure you have many talents and abilities that you bring to your job. Let's list some of those attributes that make you an asset to your employer.

JASON: I am always on time. I don't stroll in thirty minutes late like some of my other colleagues. Oh, and I do what I'm asked and meet all my deadlines.

SOCIAL WORKER: Well, those sound like some wonderful reasons for employer to keep you around. Now, I would also like to look at the other side. If for some unfortunate reason your employer had to let you go, what could you do?

JASON: I am really good with computers and I know how to use many different software programs. Hopefully, I would be able to find another job with the qualifications that I have. I would definitely start sending out resumes right away. If all else fails, I could always go back to school and boost up my resume that way.

SOCIAL WORKER: That all sounds great. I'm proud that you were able to look at the situation that was troubling you and think of positive outcomes for it.

Jason was going through a high-stress situation and needed his social worker to be a source of support for him. Jason's social worker was able to sustain his progress in treatment and support him during this time by encouraging him and helping him recognize his talents and abilities. The support of his social worker enabled and empowered Jason to look past his worries and think about his options for the future.

Case Summary Two

Jen is a clinical social worker who has been seeing Damien, a 19-year-old client, because he is feeling depressed and has feelings of worthlessness and diminished hope for the future. Damien admits that he is a survivor of a childhood domestic-violence trauma, and that he currently lives with his foster parents while he attends college. In one particular session, Jen decided to employ sustaining to help Damien by making a deliberate attempt to have the client center his attention on envisioning a desirable future. She instilled feelings of worth in Damien, so he would realize that he is a valuable individual. In order to help construct a future Damien would seek, Jen assisted Damien in discovering small steps that he could take in order to attain the desired future.

JEN: Do you see that how you talk to yourself is important? When you talk to yourself problematically, it distracts you from forming solutions. Do you agree with me that you are a precious person?

DAMIEN: Yes. I think I am a valuable individual.

JEN: So you see, you are a valuable person. You are worth the future you set out for yourself.

Thus, in this session, Jen was able to sustain Damien through language and envisioning a brighter future. The result was that Damien felt that he was a sustained and worthy individual capable of having a bright future and achieving the goals that he sets out to accomplish.

REFERENCES AND ADDITIONAL SOURCES

Fusco, L. C. (1997). The techniques of intervention. In F. J. Turner (Ed.), *Social work practice: A Canadian perspective* (pp. 203–231). Toronto, Ontario: Prentice Hall.

Johnson, L. C. (1997). *Social work practice* (6th ed., pp. 335–337). Toronto, Ontario: Allyn & Bacon.

Munford, R., & Sanders, J. (2007). Drawing out strengths and building capacity in social work with troubled young women. *Child & Family Social Work, 13*(1), 2–11.

Smith, J. C., Cumming, A., & Xeros-Constantinides, S. (2010). A decade of parent and infant relationship support group therapy programs. *International Journal of Group Psychotherapy, 60*(1), 59–90.

Woods, M. E., & Hollis, F. (2000). *Casework: A psychosocial therapy* (5th ed., pp. 133–138). New York, NY: McGraw-Hill.

Task

DESCRIPTION

Task as a technique refers to those times in a case when we work toward having the client carry out some specific action outside of the interview situation, with a goal of achieving and enhancing a sense of control, autonomy, or empowerment.

ORIGINS

The importance of task in therapy was underscored in the development of task-centered therapy, a theoretical approach to practice developed by Dr. William Read. The importance and benefit of having clients take responsibility for specific, identified actions emerged from a study of short-term cases. These studies identified that having clients perform actions on their own outside of the interview situation often led to significant improvements in their situation.

WHY THIS IS USEFUL TO SOCIAL WORK

Having clients take responsibility for various tasks can enhance a sense of independence and empowerment, which is a general goal of many of our interventions. Such gains on the part of the client can lead them to take greater charge of various areas of their lives. This, in turn, can empower them to take further steps toward independence.

HOW THIS IS USEFUL TO SOCIAL WORK

Many of the situations that we face in practice consist of various kinds of problems in the clients' day-to-day lives. Addressing these directly and in a manner that builds on and reinforces client autonomy can be a most useful technique.

Having the client carry out a particular act may only be—and often is—only one very small part of the treatment process. At times, however, this type of mutually planned, out-of-interview action does become the overall modality of treatment.

This technique has utility beyond one-to-one intervention. Couples can benefit from the technique, as can families and groups. In these multiclient systems, not only is there the primary benefit of the achieved goal, but also the secondary benefit of the necessary negotiations within the client group of having to learn or relearn ways of working together to achieve a common goal.

RISK FACTORS

Using tasks as a technique has minimal to moderate risk. The greatest risk is to ensure that our own enthusiasm and that of the client to see progress or to resolve a problem through specific tasks do not get in the way and cause one or both parties to take on a task or action that is not within the client's abilities.

REQUIRED SKILLS AND KNOWLEDGE

Things do not always go well in this use of a client-implemented task. What appeared to be something the client saw themselves as able to do may in fact prove to be too difficult, for any number of reasons. Sometimes they stem from the client's inability to bring themselves to carry out the agreed-upon act. At other times, the problem may be due to unanticipated difficulties or challenges that are out of the client's control. The challenge in this case for the social worker is to provide the necessary level of support and encouragement, and to review what had been planned, to ensure that the worker and the client have not overestimated either the client's ability or the level of difficulty of the challenge.

It is also very important to assess what will be required of the client in taking on this challenge, and to have a clear understanding of what is involved in the task in the multisystemic life of the client. When things do go well, it is also important that we provide encouragement and reinforcement to the client and that we acknowledge their enhanced level of functioning.

In using this technique, it is important that we understand that the therapeutic payoff does not rest in the nature of the client-instigated action outside of the interview, but in the significance of this act for them and their family and friends. Thus, what might appear to many to be a very minor gain for the client may in fact be something of considerable importance for the major sources of stress in their lives.

The task can be a single significant move in the client's life, whereas in other situations it can be the first of what becomes a series of gradual steps. In these latter instances, the skill required by the worker is to establish a sequence of steps that each lead the client to assume an increasing level of autonomy.

Case Summary One

Mark is a man in middle adulthood. He started attending therapy sessions while going through a transition in his life. Mark entered the workforce directly after he graduated high school, but he is now contemplating furthering his education.

MARK: I'm miserable in my current employment. I'd like to go to school to pursue a career in something I'm really excited about and interested in, but I don't know if I can do it.

SOCIAL WORKER: What makes you say that?

MARK: First of all, I don't think I would even get accepted. Second, I'm not sure if I can afford to attend school right now.

SOCIAL WORKER: Before our next session, I'd like you to visit the admissions office at the school you would like to attend and find out their admissions requirements, as well as options for financial assistance.

[During the next session:]

SOCIAL WORKER: How was your visit to the university?

MARK: It wasn't as difficult as I thought it would be. I was able to speak to an admissions counselor and even start the application process. I also obtained information from the financial aid office while I was there and found out that I have many options to pay for my education.

SOCIAL WORKER: It sounds like you were very productive in your trip to the university. Congratulations on your accomplishment. You are on your way to achieving your goal of furthering your education.

Before attending therapy sessions, Mark was full of doubts and was not sure that he could accomplish what he wanted to. Completing the task of visiting the university led Mark to feel empowered and gave him a sense of control. Completing research about the admissions process and speaking to the necessary staff at the school provided Mark with a boost to his self-confidence.

Case Summary Two

Sara, Tim, and their 9-year-old child, Betty, are attending family therapy because Betty has been acting out in school and received a suspension for conduct disorder. Sara and Tim are considering a divorce because Sara complains that Tim is too busy at work and puts it ahead of his family. Tim complains that Sara is self-absorbed and spends too much time shopping. They sought family therapy in order to help the family stay together.

The social worker spent the first couple of sessions working to counsel Sara and Tim on their issues. She employed the use of goal setting to help Betty get on track with her homework and conduct.

Social worker: Sara, Tim, and Betty, now that we have had a few sessions working on some of your individual issues, I would like to try giving you a task to work on as a family. I would like for you to all get together for a family dinner at home every day. I want you to have no distractions during dinnertime. Focus on talking to each other and having quality family time. Research shows that children who eat meals with their families at dinner have healthier eating habits. Further, children and parents communicate more when they eat dinner together. What do you think?

Tim: Well, it would be nice to get together without any distractions once during the day. I am willing to do this task.

Sara: This sounds like a good idea. Especially if research shows that it works! I am prepared to try it out!

Through the use of assigning a task to the family, the social worker was able to bring the family together for a meal where they could bond. After the session, the family reported positive results in terms of getting along more healthily and being more involved in one another's lives.

REFERENCES AND ADDITIONAL SOURCES

Bateman, N. (2000). *Advocacy skills for health and social care professionals*. Philadelphia, PA: Jessica Kingsley.

Colvin, J., Lee, M., Magnano, J., & Smith, V. (2008). The partners in prevention program: Further development of the task-centered case management model. *Research on Social Work Practice*, *18*(6), 586–595, 607–615.

Dorfman, R. A. (1996). *Clinical social work: Definition, practice, and vision*. New York, NY: Brunner/Mazel.

Hepworth, D. H., Rooney, R. H., & Larsen, J. (1997). *Direct social work practice* (pp. 371–389). New York, NY: Brooks/Cole.

Kanter, J. S. (1983). Reevaluation of task-centered social work practice. *Clinical Social Work Journal*, *11*(3), 228–244.

Reid, W. J. (1996). Task-centered social work. In F. J. Turner (Ed.), *Social work treatment* (pp. 617–640). New York, NY: Free Press.

Tolson, E. R., Reid, W. J., & Garvin, C. D. (1994). *Generalist practice: A task-centered approach*. New York, NY: Columbia University Press.

Task Analysis

DESCRIPTION

Task analysis is a technique in which the client and worker mutually examine within the interview setting a proposed task for the client to carry out. The examination process ensures that as far as possible, all facets of the task will be considered (including alternative tasks) to guarantee the action's desired outcome will be attained.

ORIGINS

As mentioned in the task chapter, this joint activity with the client is one of several task-related techniques that have come into social work practice through the conceptual base of task-centered therapy. This theory emerged principally through the work of Dr. William Read and his colleague, Dr. Laura Epstein. Read was originally interested in short-term interventions. In his research, he observed that many clients made considerable progress in short-term contacts even though the prevailing model of treatment at the time (the mid- to late 1960s) was still long-term intervention. Read also observed that clients frequently began to make progress when they were engaged in doing something active in the therapeutic setting, such as task planning.

Task analysis is one of the techniques that have developed out of this theory. It is a deliberate activity in which clients are helped to think through a particular task they are considering.

WHY THIS IS USEFUL TO SOCIAL WORK

Even though task analysis emerged from, and is closely identified with, task-centered therapy, it can be used quite separately from this theory.

It is a highly educational technique with a strong pedagogical quality. In addition to helping the client deal with his or her current reality, the technique has secondary effects. For example, as the client experiences the satisfaction of learning to take charge of some aspect of his or her life, this can spread into other life situations and serve as a useful tool for them in dealing with new challenges. This in turn can bring an enhanced sense of self-control.

HOW THIS IS USEFUL TO SOCIAL WORK

Task analysis is especially useful with clients for whom this type of structured planning is not a part of their problem-solving behavioral pattern. It is particularly helpful in dealing with people whose life, or some aspects of it, are disorganized to the point of creating problems for the client.

The strength of this technique lies in the process of helping a goal the client has set become something more feasible. A further advantage lies in helping clients to learn to analyze actions they have planned and to identify their components—a process that is quite alien to many clients.

RISK FACTORS

Task analysis has moderate risk. The greatest risk in using it stems from a social worker or client's excess enthusiasm, which can lead the client to attempt an unrealistic task, or unrealistic components of a task. A secondary risk comes from the social worker's possible failure to anticipate difficulties or aspects of a task that could have and should have been foreseen that lead the client to frustration, failure, or even harm.

REQUIRED SKILLS AND KNOWLEDGE

The skills a social worker requires are to help steer the client through a cognitive process that divides a particular planned strategy into manageable parts, and to help the client move to implement a plan of action.

Directing the interviews should not be done with a heavy hand. Rather, effective use of the technique requires the worker to keep the client focused on the identified task, and to clarify and prioritize the various activities that have to be done, and how and when they are to be done, to achieve the identified goal. Considerable support and encouragement by the worker will be necessary for this technique.

An important component of using task analysis effectively is the social worker's skill in anticipating with the client what difficulties could emerge, and helping the client develop appropriate strategies of dealing with them. Obviously not all aspects of a task can be anticipated. The worker's skill in this technique is reflected in their ability to understand the meaning of a particular task for the client and the realistic components of the task the client must face. One of the possible outcomes of a task analysis process is that the client and the social worker come to a decision that nothing can be done in a given situation; in this case, the therapeutic process should look at ways of living with the identified difficulty.

Case Summary One

Sherry describes her life as hectic, stressful, and disorganized. As a coping mechanism for her stressful life, Sherry smokes cigarettes. Recently, Sherry told her social worker that she would like to quit smoking and find a healthier coping habit.

SHERRY: I want to stop smoking, but how will I ever be able to do that? Everything just seems so overwhelming.

SOCIAL WORKER: Let's look at quitting smoking as a task to be achieved. Together we will come up with a plan to accomplish your goal. What do you think would be a good first task for you to quit smoking?

SHERRY: The first task for me would be cutting down on the number of cigarettes I smoke each day, because I don't think it would be a good idea for me to quit cold turkey.

SOCIAL WORKER: That sounds like a very smart idea. How many cigarettes are you currently smoking each day?

SHERRY: I've been so stressed out lately that currently I am smoking a pack a day.

SOCIAL WORKER: To start, how much would you like to cut back on your smoking?

SHERRY: I'd like to start by going from smoking a full pack to half a pack a day. I think I can handle that.

SOCIAL WORKER: The next task would be to determine your triggers for smoking. Are you comfortable with keeping a log?

SHERRY: Yeah, I can do that. How often should I write in the log?

SOCIAL WORKER: Every time that you smoke a cigarette, I want you to write down what happened right before you started smoking. I also want you to write down how you felt before smoking, while you were smoking, and after smoking the cigarette.

Sherry and her social worker continued to look at her task of smoking cessation and all the aspects it comprises, including any difficulties or setbacks that may arise.

Sherry has wanted to quit smoking for a long time, but felt too overwhelmed and disorganized. She stated that she didn't know where to start, so she never did. Task analysis allowed Sherry to take charge of her situation and work toward achieving her goal. The technique made Sherry's goal seem much more attainable than it did before, and will also be useful in the future when she faces other challenges.

Case Summary Two

Fred has been referred to a counselor by his employer because Fred has an anger management problem, as evidenced by acting-out behavior that includes aggression toward his peers and anger eruptions in the workplace. Fred admits to having a problem, and he wants to work with his social worker to gain control over his behavior and to learn to better manage and control his anger.

Fred tells his social worker that he uses anger as a way to vent his feelings of frustration and as a coping mechanism because he is frustrated at work. Fred and his social worker collaborate to address why Fred is unhappy at work, and they look at the possibility of Fred changing careers or jobs. Nonetheless, the social worker wants Fred to focus on analyzing the task of learning to manage his anger and remain calm regardless of whatever situation he is in.

FRED: I want to manage my anger. But it just seems like an enormous task and I don't know where to begin!

SOCIAL WORKER: We will begin by making anger management our goal for the next few sessions. We will come up with a practical plan to help you feel more in control over your anger. Our first goal will be for you to complete a cognitive behavior therapy workbook that will teach you to reframe some negative thoughts. You can complete chapters one to three for next time, and we can discuss it. How does that sound?

FRED: That sounds fair. But is that all that I need to do to manage my anger?

SOCIAL WORKER: We will also need to go over some relaxation and breathing techniques so that you can practice relaxing and breathing in stressful situations.

FRED: Sounds okay.

SOCIAL WORKER: I will also want you to keep a log documenting how you feel throughout the course of therapy. Every time you feel overwhelmed or angry I want you to write about it.

Thus through the use of task analysis, the social worker and the client are able to take a huge goal and break it down into parts that were achievable for the client. Task analysis makes the process of teaching a client to manage their anger attainable through identifiable goals.

REFERENCES AND ADDITIONAL SOURCES

Aubin, G., Chapparo, C., Gelinas, I., Stip, E., & Rainville, C. (2009). Use of the perceive, recall, plan and perform system of task analysis for persons with schizophrenia: A preliminary study. *Australian Occupational Therapy Journal, 56*(3), 189–199.

Clarke, K. (1989). Creation of meaning: An emotional processing task in psychotherapy. *Psychotherapy, 26*, 139–148.

Fortune, A. E. (Ed.). (1985). *Task centered practice with families and groups.* New York, NY: Springer.

Gambrill, E. (1997). *Social work practice* (pp. 391–392). New York, NY: Oxford University Press.

Greenberg, L. S. (1983). Toward a task analysis of conflict resolution in Gestalt therapy. *Psychotherapy, 20*, 190–201.

Greenberg, L. S. (1984). Task analysis: The general approach. In L. N. Rice & L. S. Greenberg (Eds.), *Patterns of change* (pp. 124–148). New York, NY: Guilford.

Heatherington, L., & Friedlander, M. L. (1990). Applying task analysis to structural family therapy. *Journal of Family Psychology, 4*(1), 36–48.

Kitayama, S., Park, H., Sevincer, T. A., Karasawa, M., & Uskul, A. K. (2009). A cultural task analysis of implicit independence: Comparing North America, Western Europe, and East Asia. *Journal of Personality & Social Psychology, 97*(2), 236–255.

Reid, W. J. (1996). Task-centered social work. In F. J Turner (Ed.) *Social work treatment* (pp. 617–640). New York, NY: Free Press.

Rice, L. N., & Saperia, E. P. (1984). Task analysis of the resolution of problematic reactions. In L. N. Rice & L. S. Greenberg (Eds.), *Patterns of change* (pp. 29–66). New York, NY: Guilford.

Teaching

DESCRIPTION

Teaching is a technique we use to deliberately try to convey knowledge, attitudes, and skills to a client in an open, pedagogical manner. We sometimes do this quite consciously and openly; however, because we have not always recognized this function as a useful component of treatment, we sometimes enter a teaching mode with our clients without realizing it.

ORIGINS

For a long time, teaching was not seen as a therapy technique, because we strove to keep the lines between the professions clear: Teaching was not therapy and therapy was not teaching. However, the influence of behavioral and cognitive theories, among others, has helped us to recognize that we frequently use instructional strategies with our clients, and in turn that pedagogy can be a highly effective technique.

WHY THIS IS USEFUL TO SOCIAL WORK

Because most of us can think of teachers in our lives who profoundly influenced us, we understand the impact that supportive, challenging teaching can have. Our task as clinicians is to be aware of the power that the methods and strategies of this function can have, and in turn to use them in the therapeutic relationship when appropriate.

HOW THIS IS USEFUL TO SOCIAL WORK

We need not apologize for the deliberate use of this technique, for we have much to teach clients, including:

- how to act in particular situations;
- about systems in which they are involved, and how they can best function within them;
- the dynamics of various ages and stages in human development, information that can be very helpful to them in their lives;
- ways of coping with various situations;
- ways in which their histories have shaped them;
- basic health matters; and
- how to perform in particular roles.

For the most part, the kinds of situations where we use the technique of formal teaching in our practice relate to the daily aspects of the client's life. It is not a technique that aims to make up for major knowledge or skill deficits in the client's psychosocial reality. In such situations, an extension of the use of teaching as a technique would be to collaborate with someone else to fulfill the teaching role in an identified necessary life area. Examples of this might be a client who wants or needs to learn to read, improve their language skills, or get a driver's license.

RISK FACTORS

Teaching is a low-risk technique; however, it does require us to ensure that we do not become so enamored with our presumed pedagogical skills that we overuse this potentially powerful technique.

Of course, it is not always helpful to teach clients in the formal sense we have described here. For many clients, it is preferable that, like a good parent, we let them learn for themselves, even to the point of having to learn through failure. Our task in such situations is to confront them with what has occurred and help them to learn from it. (This is also a form of teaching.)

REQUIRED SKILLS AND KNOWLEDGE

The skill involved in this technique is that we know when we enter a teaching mode with the client and to be sure we want to do so. For example it might be very important for the client to learn some specific activity related to an application for a job. The client may be deficient in the social skills needed to carry out this function, and may require knowledge, demonstration, practice, and encouragement in the safe and helpful setting of the therapy relationship. In such an instance, we can build on the medium of the relationship to teach these needed skills.

At other times, the client may be going into a new life situation for which he or she has had little or no life training or experience. Here the social worker's knowhow can be conveyed directly in a manner that reduces anxiety while helping the client get a running start in a new situation. Other frequently needed skills are related to helping the client imagine "What do I do if …" kinds of realities.

Sometimes our teaching will consist of imparting of some form of information that can be of help to the client. On other occasions, we will deliberately move into a formal teaching role, in which not only verbally, but also through such resources as charts, pamphlets, video, and the like, we seek to convey information sought by the client or deemed by us as useful to them.

In addition to the formal mode of teaching that can occur in the therapeutic process, it is important for us to be aware that we teach our clients other things that we are not always fully aware of unless we attend to them. Aspects such as how we dress, talk, ask questions, deal with others in a group, or respond to a family crisis may all be learning experiences for clients that they acquire through our influence. It is very important that we try to stay conscious of these influences, as some may be unintended and indeed counterproductive for the client.

Case Summary One

Malory is a young adult who has been attending therapy sessions for a few months and who recently found out that she is pregnant. She is feeling very overwhelmed and unsure of herself. Malory states that she did not have good parental figures growing up and does not know how to be a parent.

> MALORY: I haven't even been to the doctor yet. I couldn't get an appointment until next week, but I need answers now. I am very excited about my pregnancy, but I don't know the first thing about raising children. What am I going to do?
>
> SOCIAL WORKER: Well, we can take time during your sessions to talk about child rearing if you would like.
>
> MALORY: Yes. I have no idea what I'm supposed do or what is going to happen.
>
> SOCIAL WORKER: We can start with the basics of what to expect during your pregnancy. Then later we can discuss child development and the dynamics of various ages and stages. What do you think about that?
>
> MALORY: That sounds great. Can we get started today?
>
> SOCIAL WORKER: Sure. I can begin by teaching you the different stages of your pregnancy.

During this therapy session, Malory's social worker used teaching as a way to educate Malory about a subject of concern to her, but also used it as a way to ease her fears of the unknown. Not only will her social worker teach her verbally, but also through educational resources and materials. The information the social worker offers will be helpful to Malory throughout her life.

Case Summary Two

Mark is a 15-year-old adolescent male trauma survivor. Although Mark is very intelligent, he lacks many social skills. Roy is a social worker who specializes in working with trauma survivors and who works with Mark to teach him social skills. Social skills therapy may entail group activities (usually games and conversation), sharing, and conversations with children who have survived trauma and their peers. Today Roy is teaching Mark how to stand straight and maintain eye contact during a conversation.

> ROY: Today I am going to teach you how to stand tall and make eye contact with people when having conversations.
> MARK: Okay.
> ROY: When someone is talking to you, you want to stand straight with your shoulders back.
> MARK: Okay. What about my arms?
> ROY: Well you want your arms to be relaxed at your side. Try not to fidget. Focus on the person and the conversation.
> MARK: Okay.
> ROY: When you talk to someone, look them in the eyes and say what you need to tell them. Don't look down when you are talking. Try to maintain eye contact throughout the conversation.
> MARK: Okay. It sounds easy!

As one can see, through the use of teaching, Roy is able to give Mark some important conversation skills.

REFERENCES AND ADDITIONAL SOURCES

Blunt, K. (2007). Social work education: Achieving transformative learning through a cultural competence model for transformative education. *Journal of Teaching in Social Work, 27*(3/4), 93–114.

Lange, R. (1994). *Empowered psychotherapy: Teaching self processing.* London: Karnac.

Sheafor, B. W., Horejsi, C. R., & Horejsi, G. A. (1997). *Techniques and guidelines for social work practice* (4th ed., pp. 60–61). Toronto, Ontario: Allyn & Bacon.

Tharp, R. G. (1999). Social worker as teacher. *Human Development, 42,* 18–25.

Walters, K., Buszewicz, M., Russell, J., & Humphrey, C. (2003). Teaching as therapy: Cross sectional and qualitative evaluation of patients' experiences of undergraduate psychiatry teaching in the community. *British Medical Journal, 326*(7392), 740.

Telephone

DESCRIPTION

Although the telephone has many uses in our everyday communication, here we focus on its use as a resource we can call upon to help ourselves and our clients achieve identified therapeutic objectives.

WHY THIS IS USEFUL TO SOCIAL WORK

The telephone is such a prevalent component of our daily lives and those of virtually everyone we meet that it is often not readily seen as a therapeutic resource, but rather a highly useful administrative resource. Likewise, a walk down any busy street, with many of the passersby talking on their cell phones, demonstrates the phone's ubiquity. Thus, we often fail to appreciate its therapeutic utility.

Its importance stems from its declining cost and virtually universal availability. This universality permits clients and social workers to be in contact at any time and in any place (presuming that this is something we desire in particular cases). Availability of this kind can strongly boost clients' confidence and security, when desired.

Another important way a phone can aid therapy is by making multiple connections using conference calls. In this way, we can facilitate communications by conducting family or group interviews when the participants are in different locations. Aside from their convenience, conference calls can also keep group members separated while participating when this is necessary.

A further reason why the phone can function as an important therapeutic technique relates to its potential to empower the client: He or she can always hang up, thus reducing the power imbalance when they view this as helpful. By contrast, it can be much more difficult for them simply to walk out of an interview.

Another therapeutically powerful aspect of the phone is its potential for intimacy. From our personal lives, we know that some of the most private conversations we have with our significant others are by telephone, even with people we see on a regular basis. It is certainly more than just the factor of availability that fosters this; rather, it is the phone's quality of intimacy. If this is true in our own lives, so too with our clients'.

HOW THIS IS USEFUL TO SOCIAL WORK

Because of the potential to give the client control over the setting from which they call, the length of calls, and the sense of security and intimacy that a call can provide, some clients will share highly sensitive material with us and deal with important life issues over the phone. This spares them having to deal with the complex roles and behaviors required in a face-to-face interview. One further possibility that can enhance client security is that the caller can have someone with him or her for support or coaching without our being aware of it.

The rising availability of phones that allow callers to see each other takes away some of the advantages of an audio-only conversation. Not seeing the person to whom we are speaking may well be a strength and an asset for clients who prefer this further level of privacy. However for other clients this may be a plus in some situations, and we should view this as a further resource.

From extensive research into crisis hotlines, we know that in these instances the phone becomes the basis of the case; some are resolved entirely via phone contact. Many such cases have had very positive outcomes, some even with life-saving implications. The availability of the phone, and a skilled person on the answering end, provide the necessary help resources.

A recent advance in phone technology that may also affect its therapeutic potential is the increased ability to determine the source of a phone call, either through Caller ID or geographic location. At one time this was a very complex and expensive process, thus allowing persons to remain anonymous if they chose. This ability to totally hide one's identity provided a level of power and control to some clients, which thus enabled them to tap into needed therapeutic resources. Anonymity is becoming less voluntary, and even if we are not able to easily trace the source of a call, the client may think we can and thus become more reticent.

Having a phone also lets people seek out and connect to a community's network of resources. An important part of this is maintaining contact with friends and acquaintances, a function that is very important for those with limited mobility. Some of our most intense therapy can be done by telephone, and it is in this way that this one of the most mundane of our technological resources can become one of our most powerful therapeutic tools.

RISK FACTORS

Telephone use in therapy is a low-risk technique. There is, of course, the possibility that by depending on phone interviews, rather than working face to face, we may miss material and data that might be most important in properly assessing a case. There is also the chance that, in using the phone to unite family members, for example, we may aid in keeping them apart by using the phone as a means of separation. Last, there is the risk of letting some clients become inappropriately dependent upon us by our being too readily available.

SKILLS AND KNOWLEDGE

As we continue to examine the potential of the phone as a therapeutic instrument, we must keep up to date on technological developments to ensure that we understand their potential and limitations. We should also work at developing and enhancing our phone-interviewing skills.

When engaging in a phone interview, we need to ensure we are hearing all of what is being said and seeking to understand its relevance for a case. Last, we need to be sure that we do not become so enamored with the phone's potential that we treat clients by phone who would benefit more from office interviews.

In summary, the telephone is one of the most powerful technological therapeutic instruments; if properly used, it can be a strongly positive technique.

Case Summary One

Tammy has been meeting with her social worker weekly for a few months. Recently her social worker learned that she will need to be out of town for several weeks to take care of a family matter. Tammy has been progressing well in therapy, but was nervous at the thought of not seeing her social worker for several weeks in a row.

> SOCIAL WORKER: Due to some unforeseen circumstances, I have to be away from the office for several weeks.
> TAMMY: Oh, okay.
> SOCIAL WORKER: However, while I am away I will keep in phone contact with you weekly to check in and see how things are going. Also, if anything comes up in the meantime you are more than welcome to call me on my cell phone. How does that sound to you?
> TAMMY: That is fine with me. I was a little nervous when you first said that you were going to be out of town, I don't want any setbacks in my treatment. However, I feel much better now that I know I will be able to reach you if I need to.

The potential for Tammy and her social worker to be in contact with each other at any time and in any place provides Tammy with a sense of confidence and security. It is also a way for her social worker to be supportive even when they are not in close proximity. Naturally, normal boundaries and protocol must be clarified so this option is not misused.

Case Summary Two

Terry works in her local crisis center on the suicide hotline. Terry coaches callers on talking about their crisis condition and working to make the best of their situation. In one instance, a client named Paul called because he was feeling suicidal. Terry sought to allow Paul to vent and reduce his isolation. By using the telephone, she was able to calm Paul down and identify the cause behind his suicidal feelings, which was that Paul had lost his job. After calming Paul down, Terry was able to speak to him, form an assessment, and make a safety plan.

> **TERRY:** Do you need financial resources to help you? I think I can speak to an agency which offers help to individuals who have recently lost their jobs to help pay rent.
> **PAUL:** Yes. That would be very helpful to me in this time of crisis. This will give me time to look for another job.

After doing some further counseling, Terry got Paul to talk about his alcohol and drug use, which he was using to calm his worried feelings. She sought to address this by referring him to substance abuse counseling. As can be seen, by using the telephone, the social worker was able to counsel a suicidal individual as well as help him locate tangible resources.

REFERENCES AND ADDITIONAL SOURCES

Bobevski, I., Holgate, A. M., & McLennan, J. (1997). Characteristics of effective telephone counselling skills. *British Journal of Guidance & Counselling, 25*(2), 239–249.

Bombardier, C. H., Bell, K. R., Temkin, N. R., Fann, J. R., Hoffman, J., & Dikmen, S. (2009). The efficacy of a scheduled telephone intervention for ameliorating depressive symptoms during the first year after traumatic brain injury. *Journal of Head Trauma Rehabilitation, 24*(4), 230–238.

Davies, P. G. K. (1982). The functioning of British counselling hotlines: A pilot study. *British Journal of Guidance and Counselling, 10*(2), 195–199.

France, K. (1975). Evaluation of lay volunteer crisis telephone workers. *American Journal of Community Psychology, 3*, 197–217.

Hornblow, A. R. (1986). Does telephone counselling have preventive value? *Australian and New Zealand Journal of Psychiatry, 20*(1), 23–28.

Hornblow, A. R., & Sloane, H. R. (1980). Evaluating the effectiveness of telephone counselling services. *British Journal of Psychiatry, 137*, 377–378.

Hunt, P. A. (1993). Relateline: An evaluation of a telephone helpline counselling service for marital problems. *British Journal of Guidance and Counselling, 21*(3), 277–289.

Kashyn, M., (1999). Telephone group work: Challenges for practice. *Social Work With Groups, 22*(1), 63–77.

King, G. D. (1977). An evaluation of the effectiveness of a telephone counselling centre. *American Journal of Community Psychology, 5*(1), 75–83.

Ligon, J. (2002). Fundamentals of brief treatment: Principals and practices. In A. R. Roberts & G. J. Greene (Eds.), *Social workers' desk reference* (pp. 96–100). Oxford, England: Oxford University Press.

Ludman, E. J., Simon, G. E., Tutty, S., & Von Korff, M. (2007). A randomized trial of telephone psychotherapy and pharmacotherapy for depression: Continuation and durability of effects. *Journal of Consulting & Clinical Psychology, 75*(2), 257–266.

Mclennan, J., Culkin, K. & Courtney, P. (1994). Telephone counsellors' conceptualising abilities and counselling skills. *British Journal of Guidance and Counselling, 22*(2), 183–195.

Miscall, B. K., & Sorter, D. (2008). Voice and cure: The significance of voice in repairing early patterns of disregulation. *Clinical Social Work Journal, 36*(1), 31–39.

Rosenthal, H. G. (1998). *Favorite counseling and therapy techniques* (pp. 189–190). New: Brunner-Routledge.

Waters, J. A., & Finn, E. (1995). Handling client crises effectively on the telephone. In A. R. Roberts (Ed.), *Crisis intervention and time-limited cognitive treatment* (pp. 251–289). Thousand Oaks, CA: Sage.

Television

DESCRIPTION

Although not often thought of as a therapeutic technique, but rather as a medium of escape, entertainment, or information, there are several facets of television that make it a useful tool in treatment.

ORIGINS

As we have broadened our scope of what we can use to connect with people more effectively, we have begun to appreciate that the broad range of enhanced communication resources available to us offers opportunities to better achieve this goal. One of these resources is television in its various forms.

Because the essence of our therapeutic work with clients involves communications of various types, and television is a powerful medium of communication available to almost everyone, its potential presents us with a way to connect with clients in many ways that can be useful in treatment.

WHY THIS IS USEFUL TO SOCIAL WORK

The potential that video recording has to easily capture human interaction permits the client and social worker to review material in a manner that can greatly benefit the client. With relatively inexpensive equipment and very little technical knowledge, either parties can record material to replay and review as a part of the therapeutic process.

HOW THIS IS USEFUL TO SOCIAL WORK

With readily available resources, it is possible to record a one-on-one interview, which can permit the client and social worker to view, examine, and reflect upon significant material. In the same way, a recording can be made of a group or family, permitting all involved to see themselves and their behavior and to observe some of their important interactions. This can lead to altered behavior and enhanced understanding. A couple could make a record of various aspects of their day-to-day relationship, which they could then review and reflect upon during an interview.

Regardless of format, a video recording permits us to easily review sections of a process in a way that lets us go back and forth between examples of significant material or behavior in a way that expands understanding and effects behavioral change.

A further way in which videos of material can be used therapeutically is historically, when a client or clients compare content of early interviews with later ones, helping them to see areas of progress and growth. More generally, we can help a client see their behavioral changes in such very basic areas as how they dress, express themselves verbally and through body language, and other behavioral factors. Sharing such recordings can help the social worker reinforce client progress.

From the perspective of commercial television, there is not a great deal that can be said for its utility in treatment, apart from accessing some of the excellent educational programs that might be available on some specific topic of relevance to the client. For example, sharing some historic material with the client that he or she might identify with in a retrospective or reflective manner could prove useful.

RISK FACTORS

Television has a low risk factor, apart from possibly catering to a client's histrionic qualities so they play to the camera rather then being themselves. Other clients may find the process of being filmed a threatening experience that causes them to become reticent rather than more open. Also, for some people, just seeing and hearing themselves on television can be an upsetting experience and might be detrimental to the treatment process instead of facilitating it.

REQUIRED SKILLS AND KNOWLEDGE

This technique requires only minimal technical knowledge to tap its usefulness. Nevertheless, it is important that we understand and can easily use the equipment. It is also important that whatever technical resource we use be as unobtrusive as possible in the interview setting.

Additionally, it is vital that clients agree to the use of this medium, and that at any time they can ask to have the recording stopped. The client and social worker also need to discuss who will keep the tape, disk, or storage medium at the conclusion of the treatment, and if the worker keeps it, how will it be used. On occasion a client will want to keep the recording, both as a memento of a positive therapeutic experience and/or as a behavioral reinforcement of some particular facet of the process.

Case Summary One

Brianna is an adolescent girl. Her mother is taking her to see a social worker because she is worried about Brianna's behavior lately. She believes that Brianna is having sex, but doesn't want to talk to her about it. Brianna's mother wants to make sure that her daughter is educated and informed when it comes to sex and her sexuality. She is scared that Brianna may end up with an unintended pregnancy or contract a sexually transmitted disease.

After gathering Brianna's psychosocial information and building rapport with her during the first few sessions, her social worker decides to use television viewing as a way to start their conversation about sex.

> **SOCIAL WORKER:** During our last session I asked you about the type of television shows you like to watch. You told me that you enjoy watching family sitcoms, as well as teen dramas.
> **BRIANNA:** Yes.
> **SOCIAL WORKER:** Today we are going to view a television show and then discuss what we saw. How does that sound?
> **BRIANNA:** That's fine. It sounds interesting.
> [After watching the television show:]
> **SOCIAL WORKER:** What are your thoughts about the interactions between the two characters?
> **BRIANNA:** I thought they really seemed to care about each other. It was nice to see them have an open conversation without being embarrassed.

Watching a television show that Brianna could be engaged in provided a wonderful opportunity to start some meaningful conversations and a connection with her social worker. Her social worker was able to find a show that Brianna could enjoy, but that was also relevant to her situation. Allowing Brianna to talk about the television show and characters instead of her life gives her the opportunity to discuss features that are important to her or to ask questions about her circumstances without feeling embarrassed.

Case Summary Two

Scott is a college senior at his local university. He is pursuing a career in accounting and needs to search for jobs, because he will be graduating with a bachelor's degree the following semester, and he will need to support himself and pay off his student loans. Scott feels confident about the steps involved in a job search. He knows he must write a resume, find job openings, complete applications, attend interviews, and make a final decision on a job. However, he is anxious and nervous about going to job interviews.

To alleviate his anxiety, he decides to attend career counseling at his university counseling center. After talking with Scott, his social worker decides to use television as an aid in teaching Scott interviewing techniques, to help Scott reduce his feelings of anxiety when interviewing. During the counseling sessions, Scott and his counselor view videotapes showing interview techniques. They review a particular technique every week, practice it, and then talk about how to use it effectively. After a few counseling sessions, Scott reports that he feels more confident about the interview process.

REFERENCES AND ADDITIONAL SOURCES

Barak, A., & Grohol, J. M. (2011). Current and future trends in Internet-supported mental health interventions. *Journal of Technology in Human Services, 29*(3), 155–196.

Dunstan, D. A., & Tooth, S. M. (2012). Treatment via videoconferencing: A pilot study of delivery by clinical psychology trainees. *Australian Journal of Rural Health, 20*(2), 88–94.

Glueckauf, R. L., Fritz, S. P., Eckland, J., Eric, P., Liss, H. J., & Dages, P. (2002). Videoconferencing-based counseling for rural teenagers with epilepsy: Phase 1 findings. *Rehabilitation Psychology, 47*(1), 49–72.

Glueckauf, R. L., & Noel, L. (2011). Telehealth and family caregiving: Developments in research, education, policy, and practice. *Education and Support Programs for Caregivers*, 85–105.

Inagaki, T. (2004). When the seal was revealed: The process that TV games mediated between the social worker and the client. *Psychiatry and Clinical Neuroscience, 58*(5), 533–534.

Jerome, L. W., DeLeon, P. H., James, L. C., Folen, R., Earles, J., & Gedney, J. J. (2000). The coming of age of telecommunications in psychological research and practice. *American Psychologist, 51*, 407–421.

Jerome, L. W., & Zaylor, C. (2000). Cyberspace: Creating a therapeutic environment for telehealth applications. *Professional Psychology: Research and Practice, 31*(5), 478–483.

Kilgussk, A. F. (1977). Therapeutic use of a soap opera discussion group with psychiatric in-patients. *Clinical Social Work Journal, 5*(1), 58–65.

Mair, F., & Whitten, P. (2000). Systematic review of studies of patient satisfaction with telemedicine. *British Medical Journal, 320*, 1517–1520.

Rees, C. S., & Haythornthwaite, S. C. (2004). Telepsychology and videoconferencing: Issues, opportunities, and guidelines for psychologists. *Australian Psychologist, 39*(3), 212–220.

Rogers, C. R. (1951). *Client-centered therapy*. London: Constable.

Rubin, L., & Livesay, H. (2006). Look, up in the sky!! Using superheroes in play therapy. *International Journal of Play Therapy, 15*(1), 117–133.

Schopp, L., Johnstone, B., & Merrell, D. (2000). Telehealth and neuropsychological assessment: New opportunities for psychologists. *Professional Psychology: Research and Practice, 31*, 179–183.

Tower, K. D. (2000). Fashionably late? Social work and television. *Journal of Technology in Human Services, 16*(2/3), 175–192.

VandenBos, G. R., & Williams, S. (2000). The Internet versus the telephone: What is telehealth, anyway? *Professional Psychology: Research and Practice, 31*(5), 490–492.

Time

DESCRIPTION

Time is a variable that we often view only as the administrative medium in which we practice rather than as an important therapeutic technique. As a technique, time is a treatment tool that, when skillfully used, can have an important impact on a client's life.

ORIGINS

Time is not a technique that belongs to any one theoretical orientation. Rather, it has emerged as an important technique in a wide range of theories where, as experience has taught us, there are several ways for us to use time in our treatment activities.

WHY THIS IS USEFUL TO SOCIAL WORK

Although we cannot control time, we can control the different ways that we use it in treatment. In fact, it is one of our most important variables. It is a useful technique because it is a resource that is always available to us, even though it constantly seems to be in short supply.

HOW THIS IS USEFUL TO SOCIAL WORK

We first encounter time as a variable at the point of our first contact with a new client. Within the limits of our schedule, letting the client select the time for this interview conveys a sense of respect that can begin to empower our client.

The length of an interview, a factor that we rarely consider as influencing the process of a case, is also a variable involving time. At least here in North America, we easily fall into the administrative reality of planning our interviews according to some kind of set limit, usually an hour. This is a factor over which the client has little if any say. We just follow this rather than considering clients' perspective of time, their ability to engage in the process or stay focused, or their physiological comfort. By being sensitive to this, we might instead use a series of short interviews for some clients, and much longer interviews with others, than our traditional one-hour unit.

The time of the day when we see a client may also be an important variable. This is a factor in our clients' lives that may be affected by such things as working hours, family responsibilities, or medication use. Often we are not aware that we are dealing with someone who sees himself or herself, and indeed really is, a morning or evening person regarding their ability to function and focus.

Time can also be used as a technique with regard to the frequency of interviews. For example, for some identified diagnostic reason we may elect to see a client on a daily basis, whereas for another client we leave it to them to contact us on an as-needed basis.

Another use of time as a technique is inherent in the very structure of an interview. This relates to the rhythm of interviews, the slowness and deliberateness or rapidity at which the interchange takes place.

Time is also a factor in deciding how long we will keep a case open, an important issue in these days of brief therapy. This practice has undoubtedly led to the premature closing of cases, just as in earlier days we no doubt kept some cases open too long. Instead of viewing each case as having a designated beginning, middle, and ending, we should realize there are some clients for whom the clinical use of time should be open ended. For many persons to continue to function in a satisfactory or growth-directed manner, they need to be assured that there is an ongoing source of help available when required.

Time can also be used as a way to help a client gradually take back control over their lives by increasing the time between interviews, so that the client is left more and more on their own. This can be done in an open manner with the client, or it can be built into the structure of interview scheduling.

RISK FACTORS

Apart from highly critical situations where our use or misuse of time could have drastic outcomes for the client, as in veiled cries for help, this is a low-risk technique. In situations that aren't crises, it is quite easy to presume that our personal orientation to time is the correct one and that everyone perceives time in the same way. In so doing we can create unrecognized strains in the therapeutic relationship.

REQUIRED SKILLS AND KNOWLEDGE

In our practice, it is important to understand time as a value orientation in the client's life. By failing to do this, we can let our own perspective of how to use time take precedence in a way that puts us out of step with a client. For example, we may be a future-oriented person whose perception of practice focuses upon helping clients look ahead, dealing with present situations as preparation for the future. However, our client might be past oriented and need instead to focus upon historical factors in his or her life's odyssey.

The important thing is to be as aware of how our clients perceive and use time as we are of the ways we use it. Indeed, time and its place in a client's life may well be the focus of our intervention, and we can address it by using time as a technique.

The passage of time in the pace of conversations frequently has cultural roots. It requires skill on our part to adjust to the rhythm and speed of conversation in a way that is comfortable for the client, even if it is not for us. Even though we may differ with the client from the perspective of time, it does not mean that we will not challenge this value at times, when we observe that their time orientation is creating problems for them.

As a reality present in every case, time is a powerful technique that needs to be assessed for its potential use with each client. It is much better to use time as a conscious technique for the client's benefit, rather than as a variable that suits our realities.

Case Summary One

Harold has been meeting with his social worker for several months and is working steadily toward achieving his treatment goals. He was recently offered a new position in his company and now needs to change the time of his therapy sessions.

SOCIAL WORKER: During the last session, you told me that you might be moving into a new position at your workplace. How did your interview go?

HAROLD: It went extremely well, and they offered me the new position on the spot.

SOCIAL WORKER: Will this new position change the time that you are able to meet for sessions?

HAROLD: Actually, it will. I will be working longer hours, so I will need to meet in the evening instead of the afternoon. Is that okay or will we have to stop meeting? I know I value my time, and I'm sure you do too.

SOCIAL WORKER: Well, off the top of my head I'm pretty sure I have time available to change your appointment. I'll look at my schedule now so together we can choose a day and time that will work for both of us. Also, if you think you may have a hard time meeting every week due to your increased work hours, we can discuss starting to meet every other week.

HAROLD: Okay, that could be helpful, especially in the beginning when I am learning my new position.

The social worker's flexibility allowed Harold to continue treatment even when his circumstances changed and he needed to adjust his appointment time. Having the option to change his session time also gave Harold a sense of control and empowerment over his treatment and his life. The social worker's comment about the possibility of spacing out the sessions a little further apart told Harold that his social worker thought treatment was progressing well enough that he didn't have to be in session every week. The spacing of the sessions will also help keep Harold from becoming overwhelmed about his decrease in personal time.

Case Summary Two

Mary is a licensed clinical social worker at an elementary school. She addresses problems in her school such as student misbehaviors, and advises teachers on how to cope with difficulties in their student population. In one instance, a 6-year-old named Chris presented with problematic classroom behavior, which consisted of temper tantrums during class. To reduce the problem's occurrence, Mary decided to approach it by using a disciplinary method known as the time-out method over the course of a 3-month span of time. Mary knew that in order to counsel Chris, she would need a fixed amount of time to effectively discipline Chris's aberrant behavior. In addition, Mary used praise to reinforce Chris's positive prosocial behavior. She hypothesized that time-outs, along with the use of praise over a reasonable period of time, would result in positive change.

Every day for approximately 3 months, when Chris displayed a disruptive behavior, Mary placed him in time-out, for no more than a few minutes each time. In the beginning, she had to place him in time-out very frequently. Over the course of the next couple of weeks, however, the amount of time Chris spent there decreased significantly. Chris's teacher reports that his classroom learning has improved, and his interactions with his peers have gotten much better. Thus, Mary employed the use of the time-series design over a 3-month time span to help Chris reduce the disruptive behavior. The result is an observable progress in Chris's behavior due to a consistent intervention over an appropriate amount of time.

REFERENCES AND ADDITIONAL SOURCES

Box, G. E. P., & Jenkins, G. M. (1970). *Time-series analysis: Forecasting and control*. San Francisco, CA: Holden-Day.

Brillinger, D. R. (1981). *Time series: Data analysis and theory*. San Francisco, CA: Holden-Day.

Chatfield, C. (1984). *The analysis of time series: An introduction*. London: Chapman & Hall.

Dattalo, P. (1998). Time series analysis: Concepts and techniques for community practitioners. *Journal of Community Practice, 5*(4), 67–85.

Gelso, C. J., Kivlighan, D. M., Wine, B., Jones, A., & Friedman, S. C. (1997). Transference, insight, and the course of time-limited therapy. *Journal of Counseling Psychology, 44*(2), 209–217.

Gottman, J. M. (1981). *Time-series analysis: A comprehensive introduction for social scientists*. New York, NY: Cambridge University Press.

Gyorky, Z. K., Royalty, G. M., & Johnson, D. H. (1994). Time-limited therapy in university counseling centers: Do time-limited and time-unlimited centers differ? *Professional Psychology—Research & Practice, 25*(1), 50–54.

Jones, E. J., Ghannam, J., Nigg, J. T, & Dyer, J. F. P. (1993). A paradigm for single-case research: The time-series study of a long-term psychotherapy for depression. *Journal of Consulting and Clinical Psychology, 61*(3), 381–394.

Laken, A. (1973). *How to get control of your time and your life*. New York, NY: New American Library.

Lemon, E. C., & Goldstein, S. (1978). The use of time limits in planned brief casework. *Social Casework, 59*(10), 588–596.

Paat, E. R., Shadden, E. B., & Miller, E. C. (1988). Time therapy technique: The use of time as a catalyst for treatment. *Hospital & Community Psychiatry, 39*(2), 177–185.

Turner, F. J. (2002). Psychosocial therapy. In R. A. Roberts & G. J. Greene (Eds.), *Social work desk reference* (p. 111). New York, NY: Oxford University Press.

Touch

DESCRIPTION

By the identification of touch as a technique, we are focusing on the social worker's deliberate use of physical contact to convey some positive aspect of the relationship or some appropriate emotion deemed to be helpful at a particular time in the therapeutic process.

ORIGINS

We know that touch is one of the oldest facets of human interaction. From the first instant of life and throughout our whole existence, touch is an essential component of our human experience. It is an important way in many interpersonal situations for us to show our interest and concern for others.

Our understanding of how important and natural various forms of touch can be in particular situations is accepted as so fitting, expected, and proper, that our use of touch is often totally spontaneous and virtually automatic. This sometimes makes it difficult to view them as techniques that we consciously use or avoid in a therapeutic, planned way.

Certainly in earlier days, much of our practice was based on a very stereotyped view of the formal therapeutic relationship. Part of this was the custom of avoiding revealing anything personal about ourselves, and certainly avoiding any physical contact with the client. With the help of theories such as existentialism, Gestalt, and feminism, as well as dialogue with colleagues from other parts of the world, and a growing understanding of the richness of diversity, we began to understand that such stereotypical relationships were not of the greatest help to many of the clients we met in our practices.

WHY THIS IS USEFUL TO SOCIAL WORK

The reason we use physical touch in therapy is, of course, their power. We know that there are occasions with people in our practice when a gesture, a pat on the back, a hand around the shoulders, an embrace, or holding the client's hand are not only appropriate but can be of tremendous import. Such gestures can help a client understand and experience our interest and confidence in them, our concern or compassion for them, or our pride in them. These are all good reasons to make use of touch.

HOW THIS IS USEFUL TO SOCIAL WORK

If we think of our own lives, and how powerful and important even the simplest physical contact between two human beings can be, we can appreciate how this can be helpful with our clients. However, we also know that physical contact can be misunderstood by the recipient, especially in situations where the social worker and the client are from different backgrounds, where something in one person's culture is viewed much differently by the other. In light of these risks, it is undoubtedly better to err on the side of conservatism and avoid the use of touch unless we are certain that it will be viewed as a helping gesture.

Nevertheless, having considered the risks and the potential negatives, we feel there is still a place in practice for this powerful way to express our concern, compassion, and many other positive and enabling human emotions.

RISK FACTORS

In focusing on the potentially positive role of touch in our client relationships, we of course need to be aware of the risks. From this perspective, we know that just as touch is used to convey positive regard, it is also one of the ways in which we communicate our disrespect, dislike, and displeasure with someone. Also, at times during human interaction, what we view as a touch to convey interest and concern can be viewed by the recipient as a totally unacceptable negative gesture. For example, a tap on the back can be intended as a message of affection, but the recipient might view it as an assault, however mild its intent and force. A hug given as a gesture of welcome to convey interest and positive regard can likewise be viewed as an unwelcome sexual gesture.

The risk arises from the broad range of differences among various persons, groups, and cultures as to which gestures are viewed as positive and appropriate, which are not, and in what circumstances. This variability depends upon such things as occasion, sex, age, cultural identity, setting, the nature of the relationship, and many other factors, which can result in different perceptions of how significant various kinds of touch in this age of great diversity can be. For many of us, what appears to be as simple a thing as a handshake would not be viewed as acceptable or welcomed in some cultures. Yet we may view it as rude not to engage in such a gesture.

What makes this matter even riskier is that the rules and practices about touching are very much in a process of change within and among many groups. In American culture, for example, there is a growing comfort in many circles with touch as a sign of friendship and interest; at the same time, others are concerned about the possible existence of inappropriate touching, especially between persons in various helping roles and their clients or patients. This two-sided aspect of touch reminds us that, because of its power in human interaction, it is one of our techniques that is most fraught with risk for us.

REQUIRED SKILLS AND KNOWLEDGE

Evidently the skills and knowledge most required to use touch in our practice are our assessment skills, both regarding the place and use of touch in our own lives and those of our clients. It is both important and useful to understand how our clients regard touch, much of which we can learn from observation. However, it is equally important that we understand and assess how we ourselves regard touch, and ensure that we are aware of their potential impact on our relationship with clients. As mentioned above as apparently a simple and automatic a gesture as a hand shake can have a broad spectrum of meaning and comfort for different persons. As we become increasingly interested in this topic we find there is much to learn both about ourselves and those with whom we inter-act, knowledge that help us enhance our skills in making use of this powerful medium of human interaction.

Case Summary One

Clara was physically abused as a child and struggled with symptoms of anxiety for most of her life. She sought counseling while she was attending a university and noticed that some of her behaviors were holding her back from enjoying the "college experience." Clara was not like the other students in her classes; she could not walk freely about the campus without a care in the world, as she perceived they did. Clara wanted a change and decided to see a social worker.

During one particular therapy session Clara lost herself in the past and was staring off into space.

SOCIAL WORKER: [as he holds Clara's hand] Clara, you were talking and you trailed off. Let's focus on ways to improve your daily life. Would you like that?
CLARA: Yes, I am ready to engage in activities on campus without this nagging fear that plagues me each day.
SOCIAL WORKER: Why don't you tell me what behaviors are troubling you most and when these behaviors started?
CLARA: Do you mind if we continue to hold hands while I speak? I find it soothing and it helps to comfort me while I'm telling my story.
SOCIAL WORKER: No problem, Clara. Take your time and let me know at any time if you want me to stop holding your hand.

Clara was so used to negative touching through the physical abuse of her childhood that she did not know what it felt like to engage in positive touching. Receiving touch by holding her social worker's hand allowed Clara to talk about and relive her past abuse while feeling safe and reassured. After another two sessions, Clara no longer felt the need to hold her social worker's hand.

Case Summary Two

Sarah attended counseling with her college counselor for her diagnosis of clinical depression. Sarah is an international student pursuing her graduate degree in epidemiology. Because she grew up in a country beset by war, Sarah has trouble with anxiety and depression symptoms and feels she needs to be in control all the time. She has seen her social worker for over eight sessions to discuss what was going on in her life, and has reported overall satisfaction with her therapy. At the end of her session, Sarah tells her social worker, "I have had such a good experience talking with you. I really felt better after attending therapy with you."

SOCIAL WORKER: You were really brave to attend therapy.
SARAH: I am really going to miss our conversations together. I felt like you really empathized with me. Thank you for that. Would it be okay if I gave you a hug? I am really going to miss you now that our sessions are over!
SOCIAL WORKER: I will miss you as well. Good for you for attending therapy.

Through the use of appropriate touch, the social worker and client were able to acknowledge their feelings of friendship. The hug gave the social worker and client a way to end their sessions on a friendly note.

REFERENCES AND ADDITIONAL SOURCES

Borenzwig, H. (1983). Touching in clinical social work. *Social Casework, 64*(4), 238–242.

Field, T., Lasko, D., Mundy, P., Henteleff, T., Kabat, S., Talpins, S., & Dowling, M. (1997). Brief report: autistic children's attentiveness and responsivity improve after touch therapy. *Journal of Autism and Developmental Disorders, 27*(3), 333–338.

Halbrook, B., & Duplechin, R. (1994). Rethinking touch in psychotherapy: Guidelines for practitioners. *Psychotherapy in Private Practice, 13*(3), 43–53.

Kramer, B. J., & Gibson, J. W. (1991). The cognitively impaired elderly's response to touch: A naturalistic study. *Journal of Gerontological Social Work, 18*(1/2), 175–193.

Major, B. (1981). Gender patterns in touching behavior. In C. Mayo & N. M. Henley (Eds.), *Gender and nonverbal behavior* (pp.15–37). New York, NY: Springer-Verlag.

Major, B., Schmidlin, A. M., & Williams, L. (1990). Gender patterns in social touch: The impact of setting and age. *Journal of Personality and Social Psychology, 58*(4), 634–643.

Pinson, B. M. (2002). Touch in therapy: An effort to make the unknown known. *Journal of Contemporary Psychotherapy, 32*(2–3), 179–196.

Sakiyama, Y., & Koch, N. (2003). Touch in dance therapy in Japan. *American Journal of Dance Therapy, 25*(2), 79–95.

Wilson, J. M. (1982). The value of touch in psychotherapy. *American Journal of Orthopsychiatry, 52*(1), 65–72.

Woods, M. (1964). *Casework: A psychosocial therapy* (4th ed., p. 409). New York, NY: McGraw-Hill.

Toys

DESCRIPTION

This technique builds on the role that toys play and have played in the lives of our clients in times of stress and anxiety, and how they can provide comfort and security during the interview process.

ORIGINS

One of the very important things we all learn about children in the very early months of life is the importance of toys in their emotional and personal development. We often see how a plain, battered, but much-loved rag doll can virtually become a part of the child, something that needs to be kept close and clutched through all of life's situations, especially scary ones.

Although many of us would deny it, toys continue to play a role in our own psychological and emotional lives through our various ages and stages, and thus can be an aid in times of stress and difficulty.

WHY THIS IS USEFUL TO SOCIAL WORK

Throughout our lives, many things emerge as our toys—that is, the physical things we need or like to have near us in situations of stress and strain. Such objects are usually very well disguised both to ourselves and others: a favorite chair, pillow, or blanket; a trinket on our desk, such as a picture or lucky stone, shell, or souvenir; and so forth, throughout the many objects that assume a comforting role.

We realize the emotional component of such objects most clearly when they are not available to us when we are upset or under stress. Our understanding of this role physical objects play in our lives makes them a reality that can be addressed as a useful component of therapy.

Toylike objects play the same role in practice as do some uses of food; for example, a bowl of candy or some type of snack food available to clients during interviews. Clearly for some clients, these types of resources can be important in helping to deal with the emotions that can and do emerge during the interviewing experience.

HOW THIS IS USEFUL TO SOCIAL WORK

Many of our client interviews open up and focus upon areas of great sensitivity to them. These often comprise material that is highly emotionally laden. Hence a useful technique in our practice is to ensure that we have various toy-like objects close at hand in our interviewing space. (It may be that we already have some of our own personal toys in our offices without being conscious of their potential in this regard.)

It is probably rare that we would we inquire or know about the specific things that serve as toys to our clients, but we can provide substitute objects in our offices that are readily available to the client. In the absence of these, we have often noted that clients play or toy with objects in the office, or on the desk or coffee table, in a childlike manner.

One other aspect of toys as a component of treatment is using a client's toy history as a way to understand them better. What roles did toys play in their developmental history? What are the important toys in their present lives, and what role do they play? For some clients, this is an important part of who they are, whereas others would be surprised that we are interested.

RISK FACTORS

As a general technique, using toys as a part of our overall interviewing strategy is very low risk.

REQUIRED SKILLS AND KNOWLEDGE

As a practice technique, we will typically not introduce toys at a particular time or point in an interview as we might other techniques. Rather, it is a technique of a general type, in that we consider it an available resource to clients. Thus we want to ensure there are toy-like objects in the interview setting that they can easily touch or handle as they so desire.

Case Summary One

A social worker is conducting an initial interview with Nancy. Nancy is a young adult attending a university several states away from her hometown. This is the first time Nancy has lived without her parents. She has never seen a social worker before and is very nervous.

SOCIAL WORKER: Hi, Nancy, welcome to my office. You can take a seat wherever you'd like. On the back of each chair you will find a blanket. My office tends to get cold, so feel free to use the blanket at any time. Also, I have a few items on the table next to you that you can use if you wish.

NANCY: Okay, thanks.

SOCIAL WORKER: So, Nancy, what brings you to my office?

NANCY: I really don't know why I'm here. I feel silly. I'm just having a little difficulty adjusting to my new life away from home.

SOCIAL WORKER: Tell me more about that.

NANCY: Well, I was so excited to move out on my own and go to college, but it's not what I thought it would be. [Nancy squeezes a stress relief ball she found on the table as she speaks.] Everything seems so much harder here. I'm worried I won't be able to make it to graduation.

Nancy was extremely nervous about seeing a social worker and felt a little hesitant regarding what she should say. Having an object to play with gave Nancy something else to focus on while she was speaking to the social worker. It allowed her to ease the discomfort she was feeling and talk more openly.

Case Summary Two

Mrs. Smith brought her 6-year-old daughter, Alia, into therapy because Alia was diagnosed with oppositional defiant disorder. Alia consistently displays defiant and disobedient behaviors toward authority figures. Through parent–child interaction therapy (PCIT), the social worker will work on changing the interaction patterns between mother and child. This will form a nurturing relationship between Mrs. Smith and Alia, decrease negative behavior, and increase prosocial behavior.

The social worker gives Mrs. Smith an earplug through which she will receive instruction on how to set limits for Alia. The social worker coaches Mrs. Smith through a one-way mirror. The PCIT therapy playroom is equipped with many interesting toys. In the first session, Alia chooses to play Legos with Mrs. Smith. With help from the social worker, Mrs. Smith will learn to use positive reinforcement to praise Alia for her good behaviors.

ALIA: Mom, we can play with the Legos together!

MRS. SMITH: [with help from the social worker through earpiece] Thank you for including me in your playtime, Alia. I really enjoy playing Legos with you!

SOCIAL WORKER: Nice going, Mrs. Smith! Good use of positive reinforcement to show Alia that you are interested in playing Legos with her!

Through the use of toys in therapy, Mrs. Smith and Alia can be coached by a social worker on fostering cooperation and developing constructive behaviors. Through these positive reinforcement techniques, Alia will have a more healthy relationship with her mother and other authority figures.

REFERENCES AND ADDITIONAL SOURCES

Beckman, P. J., & Kohl, F. L. (1984). The effects of social and isolate toys on the interactions and play of integrated and nonintegrated groups of preschoolers. *Education and Training of the Mentally Retarded, 19*(3), 169–174.

Carter, M., & O'Gorman Hughes, C. (2001). Toys and materials as setting events on the social interaction of preschool children. *Australasian Journal of Special Education, 25*(1 & 2), 49–66.

Cowden, J. E., & Torrey, C. C. (1990). A comparison of isolate and social toys on play behaviors of handicapped preschoolers. *Adapted Physical Activity Quarterly, 7*, 170–182.

Halperin, D. (2001). The play's the thing: How social group work and theatre transformed a group into a community. *Social Work With Groups. 24*(2), 27–46.

Ivory, J. J., & McCollum, J. A. (1999). Effects of social and isolate toys on social play in an inclusive setting. *The Journal of Special Education, 32*(4), 238–243.

Johnson, J. E., Christie, J. F., & Yawkey, T. D. (1987). *Play and early childhood development.* New York, NY: HarperCollins.

Johnson, J. E., & Ershler, J. L. (1985). Social and cognitive play forms and toy use by nonhandicapped and handicapped preschoolers. *Topics in Early Childhood Special Education, 5*(3), 69–82.

O'Connor, K. (2000). *The play therapy primer.* New York, NY: Wiley.

Shohet, C., & Klein, P. S. (2010). Effects of variations in toy presentation on social behaviour of infants and toddlers in childcare. *Early Child Development and Care, 180*(6), 823–834.

St, Herzka, H. (1969). The significance of toys in the child's maturation. *International Child Welfare Review*, 3–7.

Vail, C. O., & Elmore, S. R. (2011). Tips for teachers selecting toys to facilitate social interaction. *NHSA Dialog: A Research-to-Practice Journal for the Early Childhood Field, 14*(1), 37–40.

Transference

DESCRIPTION

The term *transference* describes those facets of the therapeutic relationship in which the client reacts emotionally to the social worker as if he or she were someone significant from their past, usually a parental figure. As a specific technique, it is based on an understanding and acceptance of the fact that some components of many of our clients' relationships with us carry aspects of their parental figures' real or wished-for qualities. These components, if skillfully tapped, can influence the process and outcome of therapy.

ORIGINS

Transference is a phenomenon first discussed by Freud and used by him and his colleagues as a critical component of treatment. Barker (2003) gives a very succinct definition of this phenomenon: "A concept, originating in psychoanalytic theory that refers to emotional reactions that are assigned to current relationships but originated in earlier, often unresolved and unconscious experiences" (p. 439).

It is a highly controversial concept in contemporary clinical social work practice from two perspectives. For some social workers transference is an essential component of treatment, a powerful phenomenon that exists in all helping relationships as a part of a normal human response to any relationship. Others, however, deny its existence and view it as a concept that has little or nothing to do with treatment. In general, most contemporary social workers do not view it as a major factor.

WHY THIS IS USEFUL TO SOCIAL WORK

Here we assume that transference is a part of many therapeutic relationships that, when properly addressed, can be a technique of great utility in treatment. Because the essence of our therapy is the concept of a caregiving relationship's power, whether we view it from a transference perspective or not, we do know that many clients endow us with real or wished-for parent-like attributes. When this occurs, we can draw on the positive elements of such earlier relationships to assist clients as they look at their lives, struggle with decisions, or deal with difficult or crisis-laden realities.

HOW THIS IS USEFUL TO SOCIAL WORK

This technique can help in situations where it is clear that the client views us and is relating to us in a positive parental manner. When this occurs, we can use this technique by responding as a caring, loving, and challenging parent. In this way we can help the client look at things they could be doing differently in their lives to enhance their functioning. We can then give them the courage and support they need to make difficult life decisions. We also can use this positive component of the helping relationship to offer needed support to clients in times of difficulty or loss.

Even if we begin our interventions from a theoretical base that does not view transference as a concept of great import, understanding it provides us with a technique upon which we can draw from time to time. That is, at times we will knowingly accept or indeed foster the role of the all-caring parent to assist a client in taking a needed step toward maturity, or to put aside some unnecessary baggage from the past. As Lucille Austin (1948) used to say, "A touch of corrective positive transference never hurt anyone."

RISK FACTORS

Of the many techniques available to us as social workers, this is probably the one that carries the greatest risk. The major part of the risk comes from the fact that, in addition to the positive aspects of transference, there can also be facets of the carryover from the past that are negative, often strongly so. Few persons have only positive feelings about their parents. Therefore, strong negative factors can often be intermixed with a client's positive responses to a parent-like social worker. These can be directed toward the social worker in a manner that can be upsetting to the client and disastrous to the relationship if not correctly assessed.

One additional risk in using transference as a technique is that we can find ourselves enjoying the adulation of the loving, needy child and begin to misuse this therapeutic power. In such situations, rather than creating independence and growth, we foster the maintenance or development of regression, and our needs are being met rather than the client's.

REQUIRED SKILLS AND KNOWLEDGE

To deliberately develop a transference relationship and make effective use of it as a technique to help the client in a particular way requires us to have a thorough knowledge of this phenomenon and its theoretical base. This includes both its positive and negative components as well as the related concept of countertransference. Also, if we decide to build a major part of our intervention on the basis of transference, it is essential that we have access to outside consultation and supervision.

Case Summary One

Jessie is a young mother of three children. She frequently left her children home alone and beat them when she thought they misbehaved. She attended family therapy sessions to allow her children to remain in her custody after a child welfare investigation. Jessie needed someone who would challenge her and who could also command her attention and respect. She attended the first two family sessions as scheduled, but did not show up for the third appointment. After missing the appointment, the social worker called Jessie to discuss this.

SOCIAL WORKER: Why didn't you come to the appointment today?

JESSIE: I forgot about it.

SOCIAL WORKER: Let's reschedule the appointment for Thursday. I take this seriously and I cannot help you if you do not come for appointments. I will only help you if you're willing to work and attend your sessions as scheduled.

JESSIE: I understand and I will be at the next appointment.

[During one therapy session, Jessie told the social worker about her son's disruptive behavior at school and his chances of retention. The social worker explained how school failure could possibly lead to delinquency. Several sessions later, Jessie reported a positive change in her son's behavior.]

SOCIAL WORKER: What happened to change his behavior?

JESSIE: I had a talk with him. I spoke to him the same way you spoke to me.

Throughout Jessie's therapy sessions, she continuously tested her social worker's limits, the way a child would a parent's. The social worker responded in an appropriate parental way. The relationship between Jessie and her social worker allowed her to have an appropriate parental relationship with her children. She was able to provide discipline in a positive way, not as abuse.

Case Summary Two

Chris is a young adult attending therapy sessions to improve his self-esteem. He grew up with a demanding and domineering father. Chris remembers feeling angry at or fearful of his father for most of his life. Chris is searching for the loving, caring father figure that he did not have. Throughout the therapeutic relationship, Chris has endowed his social worker with the parental attributes that he wished his father had had. During today's therapy session, Chris works with his social worker through a major life decision.

Chris: I have this wonderful job opportunity, but I'm afraid to take it.

Social worker: I would love to hear more about this job opportunity.

Chris: I'm very excited at the possibility of this new position within my company. It is more responsibility and an increase in pay. However, I would have to transfer to another state.

Social worker: I understand how that could pose some challenges. Please tell me more.

Chris: Well, the travel and housing expenses would be paid for so I know that will be okay. On the other hand, I'm afraid I won't be able to make it on my own in another state. What if I'm not good enough? I'm excited about the opportunity and I want to take the position, but I'm scared.

Social worker: From the time I've spent with you I know that you are smart, determined, and a hard worker. I believe that you can achieve any goal you make for yourself.

Chris: Do you really think so? Sometimes I think I might be able to make it on my own, but then I start to doubt myself.

Chris and his social worker continued to discuss the pros and cons of taking this new job position. Through the use of transference as a technique, the social worker was able to respond to Chris as a caring, loving parent and assist him through this major life decision. Having his social worker in the role of the all-caring parent allowed Chris to receive the support and encouragement he desired.

REFERENCES AND ADDITIONAL SOURCES

Austin, L. (1948). Trends in differential treatment in social casework. *Journal of Social Casework, 29,* 203–211.

Barker, R. (Ed.). (2003). *The social work dictionary.* Washington, DC: NASW Press.

Butler, S. R., Flasher, L. V., & Strupp, H. H. (1993). Countertransference and qualities of the social worker. In N. Miller, L. Luborsky, J. Barber, & J. Docherty (Eds.), *Psychoanalytic treatment research: A handbook for clinical practice* (pp. 342–360). New York, NY: Basic Books.

Epstein, L., & Feiner, A. H. (1988). Countertransference: The social worker's contribution to treatment. In B. Wolstein (Ed.), *Essential papers on countertransference* (pp. 282–303). New York, NY: New York University Press.

Gelso, C. J., Hill, C. E., & Kivlighan, D. M. (1991). Transference, insight, and the counselor's intentions during a counseling hour. *Journal of Counseling and Development, 69*(5), 428–433.

Gelso, C. J., Hill, C. E., Mohr, J. J., Rochlen, A. B., & Zack, J. (1999). Describing the face of transference: Psychodynamic social workers' recollections about transference in cases of successful long-term therapy. *Journal of Counseling Psychology, 46*(2), 257–267.

Gelso, C. J., Kivlighan, D. M., Wine, B., Jones, A., & Friedman, S. C. (1997). Transference, insight, and the course of time limited therapy. *Journal of Counseling Psychology, 44*(2), 209–217.

Graff, H., & Luborsky, L. L. (1977). Long-term trends in transference and resistance: A report on a quantitative-analytic method applied to four psychoanalyses. *Journal of the American Psychoanalytic Association, 25*(2), 471–490.

Hayes, J. A., McCracken, J. E., McClanahan, M. K., Hill, C. E., Harp, J. S., & Carozzoni, P. (1998). Social worker perspectives on countertransference: Qualitative data in search of a theory. *Journal of Counseling Psychology, 45*(4), 468–482.

Multon, K. D., Patton, M. J., & Kivlighan, D. M. (1996). Development of the Missouri Identifying Transference Scale. *Journal of Counseling Psychology, 43*, 243–252.

Rhoads, J. M., & Feather, B. F. (1972). Transference and resistance observed in behavior therapy. *Journal of Medical Psychology, 45*(2), 99–103.

Robbins, S. B., & Jolkovski, M. P. (1987). Managing countertransference feelings: An interactional model using awareness of feeling and theoretical framework. *Journal of Counseling Psychology, 34*(3), 276–282.

Ryan, V. L., & Gizynski, M. N. (1971). Behavior therapy in retrospect: Patients' feelings about their behavior therapy. *Journal of Consulting and Clinical Psychology, 37*, 1–9.

Schafer, R. (1983). *The analytic attitude.* New York, NY: Basic Books.

Strean, H. S. (1996). Psychoanalytic theory and social work treatment. In F. J. Turner (Ed.), *Social work treatment* (4th ed., pp. 523–554). New York, NY: Free Press.

Woods, M. E., & Hollis, F. (2000). *Casework: A psychosocial therapy* (pp. 238–239, 258, 429–432). New York, NY: McGraw-Hill.

Working With Others

DESCRIPTION

One of our most important techniques involves our working directly with people of significance to our clients in addition to our direct work with the client. We do this to access their strengths or minimize their negative influence and the role they play in our clients' lives.

ORIGINS

This technique has no clear theoretical roots. It clearly has some connection to psychosocial thinking, with its emphasis on what the literature calls indirect work. In a more general way, it has its origins in the longstanding tradition of understanding that our overall focus in social work treatment is driven by an understanding of person in situation.

WHY THIS IS USEFUL TO SOCIAL WORK

The rationale for this technique comes from our awareness that all of us are greatly influenced by a broad range of persons in many aspects of our realities. Sometimes these relationships can become and remain highly significant for us, such as our relationship with a teacher, friend, boss, coach, an elder, and so forth. When such relationships are drawn upon appropriately, they can be of great assistance to the client in regard to specific issues they are facing in treatment.

HOW THIS IS USEFUL TO SOCIAL WORK

Often our clients' relationship with various significant others are and remain much stronger and more important than the client's relationship with us. These relationships can be of such a strength and significance that, by our working directly with these people, we can help our client more effectively than through our direct contacts.

RISK FACTORS

In using this technique, it is important that we do not let the significant other whom we decide to involve become a client themselves, or somehow make them into one. It is also important that we do not make or permit the person to become some kind of co–social worker. Rather, what we want to achieve is a situation where we build on the strengths and resources of the other person and their importance in the client's life in a manner that assists the client in achieving the type of change he or she seeks. A moderate element of risk in using this technique stems from the possibility of our wrongly assessing the relationship between the client and the chosen significant other, or having overly high expectations of that person.

REQUIRED SKILLS AND KNOWLEDGE

A distinction needs be made regarding this technique between working with someone important to the client on his or her behalf, and other techniques such as conjoint therapy, collaboration with a colleague from another profession, or collaborating with one of our own colleagues. There are also important ethical issues to be considered, especially confidentiality and assurances that consent has been fully understood and obtained for sharing knowledge. Furthermore, we want to be sure that we clearly understand the role the significant other plays in the client's life.

From the perspective of this technique, we are focusing on situations where, with the client's agreement, we work with someone in their lives who can provide some targeted assistance to help a client deal with problematic challenges of limited scope. This arrangement is usually only for the short term.

Working with others is similar to but separate from important programs and services such as Big Brother or Big Sister, where the relationship is aimed at filling a gap in the client's life and can continue on for several years. Similarly, long-term foster care and permanent adoption are ways to use others in a client's life to provide missing resources. These types of structured services are modes of service, rather than the highly individualized role of significant others under consideration here.

In considering the use of the technique, it is important that we understand the client's cultural profile, as there may be significant people in a client's life that ordinarily we might not recognize. This could include an elder, a spiritual leader, or another person whose role, once recognized and understood, may well emerge as a powerful treatment resource.

Although we tend only to think of this as a technique to call upon when working with young people, we know from such groups as Alcoholics Anonymous that having a designated and available friend as a community contact known to others can be a tremendous source of support and reassurance in trying situations for persons of all ages.

Case Summary One

Cara presented for therapy with problems in coping with stress. When Cara becomes stressed she tends to engage in risky sexual behaviors to release her tension. With Cara's knowledge and consent, her social worker started working with Amy, a trusted friend of Cara's.

The social worker had a conversation with Amy on Cara's behalf as a way to help Cara overcome her challenge and learn to cope with stress in an appropriate way.

SOCIAL WORKER: As you know, when Cara begins feeling stressed out she immediately tries to relieve the tension she feels. Currently, she is relieving that tension by meeting random guys in bars and having sex with them. As part of her treatment plan, Cara is working on replacing this stress relief behavior with a healthy one.

AMY: Okay. Cara is my best friend and I want to help keep her healthy and safe. What can I do?

SOCIAL WORKER: Would you be willing to be available to Cara when she is distressed?

AMY: Yes, of course.

SOCIAL WORKER: Great. When Cara starts to feel like she needs to relieve her tension, I want her to be able to call you so that the two of you can meet and engage in some type of safe activity that Cara enjoys doing.

AMY: That sounds like a wonderful idea. I can definitely do that.

By working with Amy, Cara's social worker was able to provide Cara with a positive outlet that she can use when she is feeling overwhelmed. Amy will be a powerful resource and source of strength for Cara while she is working toward achieving the change that she desires.

Case Summary Two

Dan is an affluent 30-year-old single male. He is healthy and has had no past history of mental health problems. Dan is seeking help from a social worker because he recently went through a divorce and is feeling depressed. He has feelings of sadness, irritability, hopelessness, and loneliness. After speaking with Dan over a few sessions, his counselor decides that Dan could benefit from volunteering. He decides to volunteer his time in his community providing help to those in need.

Dan chooses to volunteer his time in a local community center, working with others as a literacy volunteer. He provides his services to elder individuals who never learned how to read. This offers Dan the opportunity to give back to the community in a positive way. Working with others helps Dan provide understanding, support, and encouragement to other individuals who are facing stress. He also grew personally from his volunteer work; he says his stress is lower and he has an improved sense of well-being while working in the community. Through his volunteer work, Dan is also able to network and form important contacts that he can use in the future. Volunteering has given Dan a sense of inclusion, and as a result he feels less lonely and more involved as a citizen in his community.

REFERENCES AND ADDITIONAL SOURCES

Cossom, J. (1999). Working with informal helpers. In F. J. Turner (Ed.), *Social work practice: A Canadian perspective* (pp. 410–426). Scarborough, Ontario: Prentice Hall, Allyn & Bacon Canada.

De Bruin, M. (2011). *Help seeking of adolescents when faced with a psychological problem* (Unpublished master's thesis). Hamilton, New Zealand: University of Waikato.

Kurtz, L. F. (1997). *Self-help and support groups: A handbook for practitioners.* Thousand Oaks, CA: Sage.

Kurtz, P. D., Lindsey, E. W., Jarvis, S., & Nackerud, L. (2000). How runaway and homeless youth navigate troubled waters: The role of formal and informal helpers. *Child and Adolescent Social Work Journal, 17*(5), 381–402.

Miller, P. A. (1985). Professional use of lay resources. *Social Work, 30*(5), 409–416.

Shechtman, Z., Vurembrand, N., & Hertz-Lazarowitz, R. (1994). A dyadic and gender-specific analysis of close friendships of preadolescents receiving group psychotherapy. *Journal of Social and Personal Relationships, 11*(3), 443–448.

Sullivan, K., Marshall, S. K., & Schonert-Reichl, K. A. (2002). Do expectancies influence choice of help-giver? Adolescents' criteria for selecting an informal helper. *Journal of Adolescent Research, 17*(5), 509–531.

Write a Self-History

DESCRIPTION

A technique that is probably infrequently used, but that potentially can have a strongly positive impact, is to have the client write his or her life history.

ORIGINS

This technique comes principally from narrative therapy, in which the power of having a person reflect upon their histories has been recognized and developed into a theoretical basis of treatment. Over the decades, however, many therapeutic practices from a range of theoretical orientations have been based on having clients think about, talk about, and reflect upon part or all of their life histories with the social worker. The specific technique being considered here is to have the client prepare a written history as a form of homework, which he or she then brings into sessions and uses as a basis of discussion and reflection.

WHY THIS IS USEFUL TO SOCIAL WORK

There are several reasons why we might elect to have a client embark on this exercise. As with the culturalgram and genogram techniques (Chapters 20 and 34, respectively), one reason is because this process can help both the client and social worker to see patterns or events previously unrecognized as important or not fully understood. Such patterns may have contributed to the strength of the person's life journey or may have been the source of repeated problems detrimental to his or her development.

HOW THIS IS USEFUL TO SOCIAL WORK

Apart from those who prepare their autobiographies for commercial audiences, people rarely write out their history. However, this process can be of great benefit for some of our clients who struggle to better understand themselves—their origins and histories—and put their lives in order. Such an exercise can also be of considerable use to us in understanding a client's self-perception and what they view as significant or unimportant in their lives.

Writing a self-history may also be an important way for someone to work out unfinished issues from their past and come to closure. In this way, they can actually and symbolically close the book on some aspect of their lives and move on.

Another reason a client may find it useful and helpful to do this might be a wish to leave a legacy to their family, to help them understand some aspect of the family's history that may not be known, understood, or appreciated. Some of the older clients with whom we work have lived through some of the most exciting, dramatic, and horrendous experiences in human history, but have not shared these experiences with family members. Writing about them can be both cathartic for the writer and a teaching and learning experience for the family, while leaving a legacy of potential societal import. Some families will view a project such as this as a very precious family treasure.

Social workers have long been experts in eliciting and preparing the psychosocial histories of our client. We have prepared these against our own professional template of what we considered important and essential. Here, we are suggesting a technique in which the client has full control over what is important and in what order one's history is to be presented. The process can be of considerable assistance to the client and ourselves as we engage in the process of helping the client find the therapeutic goals to which they aspire.

RISK FACTORS

Writing a self-history is a low-risk technique. The social worker would need to be careful, however, that when the client uses this technique, they don't unnecessarily open highly sensitive and emotionally laden material they have dealt with and put away and that has little if any reason to be revisited.

REQUIRED SKILLS AND KNOWLEDGE

Obviously, this is not a technique that everyone is capable of using, for several reasons. It may be that a client knows their history all too well and attempting to set it in tangible, written form would unnecessarily stir up material with which the client has long since been finished. It may also be that the issues for which the client is seeking help are very much centered in the present, so that a history-writing exercise would not only be less than useful, but detract greatly from a more productive present- and future-oriented therapeutic journey. Furthermore, such an exercise can be very taxing and difficult, beyond some people's ability, or at least more difficult and demanding than its potential payoff in therapy.

At times we will have clients for whom this technique appears to have potential, but to use it the client needs some assistance in getting the process started and in giving it shape and direction. In such situations, we need to be careful that our own perception of which topics from a client's history are significant does not lead us to over direct or over influence the process. Short-term community-based courses available for persons interested in this kind of history writing can assist the client in this case.

Last, although we describe this technique here as "writing" one's history, we know that there are many available technologies that can facilitate the process.

Case Summary One

Anabelle is a divorced woman in middle adulthood. After her divorce she felt like she had nothing good left in her life. It took Anabelle a long time to grieve the loss of her in-laws and the friends they acquired as a couple. Now she feels ready to close that chapter in her life and is hoping to gain new perspective.

SOCIAL WORKER: As a homework assignment this week, I would like you to write a self-history. It will be an opportunity for you to look back over your life and share your experiences with me.

ANABELLE: Which parts of my life do you want me to write about?

SOCIAL WORKER: You have complete control over this homework assignment. You decide what is an important aspect of your life history and what isn't.

ANABELLE: That sounds good to me.

SOCIAL WORKER: Take some time to reflect on your life and decide which events you consider to be significant. Then, write your self-history in your journal and bring it to our next therapy session so we can review it and discuss it.

[During the next session:]

SOCIAL WORKER: How did you feel while writing your self history?

ANABELLE: It was truly a freeing experience. I felt more in control of my life and it helped me realize that I actually have more positive people and events in my life than I thought.

SOCIAL WORKER: Great. I'm glad to hear that. Let's look at what you wrote.

Writing a self-history gave Anabelle a great sense of empowerment in her life and provides Anabelle with something to refer to when she is feeling down. She can look at it to see sources of support in her life and focus on what she feels is important. It also helps Anabelle's social worker to be more aware of what is important to her.

Case Summary Two

Pam is a 28-year-old female seeking therapy because she is battling depression and social anxiety. As part of her therapy, Pam's counselor assigns her a task to write about her life story. The point of this exercise is to get Pam to think about her life and to realize that the stressors that she experienced in her life were a normal part of her sociopolitical environment.

PAM: I am so depressed. I feel like I am abnormal and that I am the only one who has problems. I am such an abnormal person!

SOCIAL WORKER: You are no different from anyone else. This exercise will help you to look back and reevaluate your life.

PAM: Sure. I will give it a shot. Can I write about everything that happened to me in my life?

SOCIAL WORKER: You are allowed to write about whatever you like. In other words, this is your personal "life story," to use another word.

[Pam used the following week to write about all the events in her life. The following week she discussed her autobiographical memoir with her social worker.]

PAM: I really learned a lot when I wrote this self-history. I especially learned a lot when I wrote about the part of my life when I was bullied as a child. At the time I thought I was just an anomaly because I was chubby, but now I realize that a large portion of the U.S. population faces obesity because of unhealthy eating habits and lack of physical exercise. Another thing I realized is that those kids were mean to bully me about my weight. I think bullying is a huge problem our society faces these days.

Through the use of using self-history, Pam was able to see past her anxiety and reevaluate her life in a new light. She is now able to form new, supportive friendships and reports decreased depression and anxiety in her life.

REFERENCES AND ADDITIONAL SOURCES

Alschuler, M. (1997). Life stories—Biography and autobiography as healing tools for adults with mental illness. *Journal of Poetry Therapy, 11*(2), 113–117.

Barsalou, L. W. (1988). The content and organisation of autobiographical memories. In U. Neisser & E. Winograd (Eds.), *Remembering reconsidered: Ecological and traditional approaches to the study of memory* (pp. 193–243). New York, NY: Cambridge University Press.

Bayer, A. M., Gilman, R. H., Tsui, A. O., & Hindin, M. J. (2010). What is adolescence? Adolescents narrate their lives in Lima, Peru. *Journal of Adolescence, 33*(4), 509–520.

Bluck, S. (2001). Autobiographical memories: A building block of life narratives. In G. M. Kenyon, P. G. Clark, & B. de Vries (Eds.), *Narrative gerontology: Theory, research, and practice* (pp. 67–89). New York, NY: Springer.

Bluck, S. (2003). Autobiographical memory: Exploring its functions in everyday life. *Memory, 11*(2), 113–123.

Bluck, S., & Alea, N. (2002). Exploring the functions of autobiographical memory: Why do I remember the autumn? In J. D. Webster & B. K. Haight (Eds.), *Critical advances in reminiscence: From theory to application* (pp. 61–75). New York, NY: Springer.

Bluck, S., Alea, N., Habermas, T., & Rubin, D. R. (2005). A tale of three functions: The self-reported uses of autobiographical memory. *Social Cognition, 23*(1), 91–117.

Bluck, S., & Habermas, T. (2000). The life story schema. *Motivation and Emotion, 24*(2), 121–147.

Brewer, W. F. (1986). What is autobiographical memory? In D. C. Rubin (Ed.), *Autobiographical memory (p. 25–49).* Cambridge, England: Cambridge University Press.

Burt, C. D. B., Kemp, S., & Conway, M. A. (2003). Themes, events, and episodes in autobiographical memory. *Memory & Cognition, 31*(2), 317–325.

Conway, M. A. (2005). Memory and the self. *Journal of Memory and Language, 53*(4), 594–628.

Hunt, C. (2000). *The therapeutic dimensions of autobiography in creative writing.* London, England: Jessica Kingsley.

Kellett, U., Moyle, W., McAllister, M., King, C., & Gallagher, F. (2010). Life stories and biography: A means of connecting family and staff to people with dementia. *Journal of Clinical Nursing, 19*(11–12), 1707–1715.

Schauer, M., Neuner, F. & Elbert, T. (2005). *Narrative exposure therapy (NET).* Cambridge, MA: Hogrefe and Huber.

Thomsen, D. K. (2009). There is more to life stories than memories. *Memory, 17*(4), 445–457.

Westerhof, G. J., & Bohlmeijer, E. T. (2012). Life stories and mental health: The role of identification processes in theory and interventions. *Narrative Works Issues, Investigations, & Interventions, 2*(1), 106–128.

GENERIC TECHNIQUES

Behavioral Techniques

Dr. Alex Polgar is a senior consultant, clinician in Hamilton, Ontario, Canada.

DESCRIPTION

Behavioral techniques that employed direct reinforcement, aversive therapy, and counterconditioning have evolved into cognitive behavioral strategies that include focus on thoughts as a person's conditioned or learned responses in interaction with the environment (Beck, Rush, Shaw, & Emery, 1979; Jacobson et al., 1996). More recently, dialectical behavioral therapy has expanded the focus to include the intense emotional suffering that people seek to escape or avoid, often through substance use and abuse (Marra, 2005). Nevertheless, in spite of the evolution behavioral techniques have undergone since learning principles were first applied to helping people better manage their lives (Wolpe, 1958), the basis of this therapeutic intervention essentially remains the same.

In all learning there are three basic elements, starting with a stimulus, followed by a response, and then a consequence to the response, which may be either rewarding or aversive. Responses that are rewarded have a greater probability of being repeated; those that produce an aversive consequence have a greater probability of not being repeated. It is critically important to recognize that what constitutes rewarding and aversive consequences ranges across a broad spectrum and invariably is subjectively defined. Considerable clinical skills are sometimes required to determine what is or is not rewarding to a particular client.

All behavioral techniques are derived from two broad types of learning situations. Much of what behavioral techniques morphed into is based upon principles of operant conditioning, first described by B. F. Skinner (1938). However, in certain clinical settings (e.g., chronic pain clinics), the principles of classical conditioning first described by I. Pavlov (1927) are also relevant. A response such as involuntary muscle contraction, the cause of chronic pain, becomes conditioned not because it is rewarding but because of the repeated pairings of this reflexive reaction with pain originally caused by a physical injury.

Behavioral techniques based on operant conditioning principles have as their primary goal the extinction of an undesired response by increasing the frequency of the exact opposite or incompatible response. The task is to define a desired response that cannot exist simultaneously with the undesired response. To modify behaviors, emotions, and thoughts by applying operant conditioning principles requires identifying what a particular client considers to be a positive consequence and then designing the most effective reinforcement schedule. It is equally important to establish a therapeutic alliance with a client to achieve optimal compliance with the application of the behavioral technique.

Behavioral techniques based on classical conditioning principles also have as their primary goal the extinction of a conditioned behavior by having the client learn a totally incompatible response. As the frequency of the incompatible desired response increases, the frequency of the negative conditioned response decreases proportionately. Extinction of the undesired conditioned response occurs when the newly learned incompatible conditioned response totally replaces it. To modify behaviors, emotions, and thoughts by applying classical conditioning principles includes accurately defining the hierarchy of conditioned responses to a stimulus, teaching an incompatible desired response, often employing very specific techniques, and doing everything in a time-efficient manner, knowing when to progress from in vitro to in vivo application.

ORIGINS

Behavior modification as a clinical intervention technique emerged out of the investigations conducted by B. F. Skinner (1938). Initially, he studied the behaviors of nonhuman mammals, most notably rats, in his "Skinner box." He described operant conditioning as spontaneous behaviors that become conditioned because of positive consequences. In contrast, classical conditioning was described by the pioneer Ivan Pavlov (1927) as reflexive responses elicited by a stimulus. In classical conditioning the responses are involuntary reflexive actions, as, for example, muscle contraction to protect the site of a physical injury.

Current publications hardly, if ever, reference the work of pioneer learning investigators such as Skinner, Wolpe, and Pavlov. The clinical application of their work has gradually morphed into many new methodologies that rightfully focus not only on behavior but also on the emotional and cognitive processes in which human beings engage. The belief that only the behavior of clients matters no longer prevails. Although individuals' emotional suffering was always acknowledged, initially it was attributed to their maladaptive behaviors. As such, it was believed that the sooner these behaviors could be modified, the sooner an individual's emotional suffering could be alleviated.

This clinical thinking about human suffering has been greatly transformed by evolving knowledge about how humans interact with their environment. For example, failed attachment is now recognized to produce myriad negative later-life consequences and situational trauma (Meichenbaum & Gilmore, 1984), constituting such painful emotional reactions as to precipitate an intense drive to escape the emotional suffering through behaviors such as substance abuse. Moreover, the thinking that people do about their emotional suffering has also gained prominence (Jacobson et al. 1996), the view being that especially negative emotions are likely to cause certain maladaptive thoughts or explanations. Together, the early behavior modification techniques and current factors have greatly influenced how behaviorism is now applied as a clinical technique.

WHY THIS IS USEFUL TO SOCIAL WORK

The singularly distinguishing feature of social work, regardless of the area of practice, clinical or not, is the psychosocial perspective the profession applies to the study and understanding of the human condition. Specifically, the human condition is always viewed in its historical and current context, whereby the emphasis is on the person in interaction with the physical and social environment. All behavioral techniques, past and current, are based on the reality that functionality and dysfunctionality are environmentally induced. As such, behavioral techniques are optimally compatible with how social work views the human condition. Presenting problems are analyzed in the context of past and current environmental factors, the former mostly as precipitating events and the latter mostly as perpetuating factors in disturbances in mood, thinking, and behavior. Behavioral techniques therefore represent the practical application of the psychosocial perspective specific to social work.

HOW THIS IS USEFUL TO SOCIAL WORK

Since all behavioral techniques ideally fully invoke a psychosocial approach, attention to history and current environmental conditions serves to validate the client as the sum total of all of life's experiences. The focus is not only on the presenting problem but on the total person. The client's strengths in this approach are simultaneously identified and immediately engaged in the therapeutic alliance, the purpose of which is to employ specific strategies designed to increase the frequency of occurrence of emotions, cognitions, and behaviors that are incompatible with or are the antithesis of the presenting problem.

All behavioral techniques are also consistent with the value social work places on collaborative effort with a fully informed client. When using a behavioral technique, everything must make sense for a client to be optimally compliant. This is especially important because behavioral techniques invariably require practice and/or application outside of the office.

RISK FACTORS

The current popularity of behavioral techniques, such as cognitive behavior therapy or dialectical behavior therapy, is largely attributable to the vast empirical evidence supporting their effectiveness. This positive reality also establishes its risk factor. Specifically, the risk is that the technique will be applied immediately without first ruling out possible alternate explanations of a presenting problem, such as organic conditions that can cause disturbances in mood and behavior, which then precipitates faulty thinking by a client in distress. Whereas it is always sound clinical practice to rule out possible organic causes, as, for example, hypothyroidism associated with intellectual impairment, change in personality, or the onset of psychosis, immediately addressing the presenting problem with a behavioral technique could have fatal consequences. Even if the consequences are not fatal, the failure to benefit from a technique that is not relevant to addressing a presenting problem can further exacerbate a client's distress. There also is the potential in such situations that clients will blame themselves for not benefitting from what was initially perceived to be a perfectly reasonable approach to addressing their problem.

At the opposite end of the continuum of client engagement, the risk factor in using behavioral techniques is a singular focus on the technique, at a cost of establishing a therapeutic alliance with the client. Unfortunately, this risk is increased by the fact that pioneers in the use of this intervention methodology seldom referenced the importance of establishing such a relationship. Most assuredly, however, they were masterful at it, as evidenced by their reported successes.

REQUIRED SKILLS AND KNOWLEDGE

Perhaps because all behavioral techniques require the client's active participation in the process, especially outside of the social worker's office, establishing a therapeutic relationship or alliance is especially important when using this intervention methodology. The interventions and the rationale for using them have to be explained in ways to which the client can relate. Trust is also crucially important for the client to persevere and be compliant with the application of the behavioral techniques, especially during inevitable spontaneous recovery of the presenting problem. This usually occurs when positive expectations are at their highest during the last phases of the extinction process. Without trust, it is difficult for clients to maintain their commitment to the behavioral program when spontaneous recovery occurs. With trust, when the predicted relapse occurs, it will be recognized to be of short duration, as long as the behavioral technique continues to be applied. After a spontaneous recovery, total extinction of the presenting problem almost always follows shortly after.

Techniques that address emotional, cognitive, and behavioral dysfunctionalities require knowledge and skills specific to various phases in the intervention process. Specific assessment knowledge and skills are required to generate an operational definition of a presenting problem, sometimes using monitoring techniques to produce baseline measures. Because clients are fully active participants in the therapeutic process, considerable knowledge and skills are required to impart information and to teach concomitant skills to be used to address a presenting problem. Often teaching new skills is combined with activating dormant coping skills already in the client's repertoire.

The array of cognitive and emotional coping skills that may need to be either taught or activated include, but are not limited to, meaning making, mindfulness, emotional regulation, and distress tolerance. The array of behavioral coping skills that may need to be either taught or activated include, but are not limited to, interpersonal effectiveness skills, strategic behavioral skills, and relaxation skills as incompatible responses to stimuli that precipitate a negative response.

The greatest knowledge and skills required when using behavioral techniques therefore, is balancing psychotherapy, which requires a therapist to follow the client's lead, with knowledge and skills teaching, which requires a client to follow a well-defined behavioral agenda and protocol (Marra, 2005).

Case Summary

One case study will serve to illustrate the clinical application of operant learning and classical conditioning behavioral techniques to address three different but related presenting problems. The example is drawn from the field of rehabilitation following a physical injury, because social workers are almost always integral members of multidisciplinary teams in this area of practice.

Franco, a robust-appearing man in his mid-40s physically hardened by years of manual labor, was rapidly losing functionality after an industrial injury that required surgical fusion of two of his vertebrae. After discharge from an acute care hospital, Franco's major presenting problems were identified on a follow-up home visit by the rehabilitation-team social worker to be chronic pain, rapidly declining physical conditioning, and escalating despondency about his circumstances.

The pain was said to be at the site of the vertebrae fusion, and because of Franco's illness his family stopped making demands on him. He was becoming virtually immobile, rapidly losing his physical conditioning, and was in constant pain. Furthermore, he was becoming increasingly more despondent and believed his life to be over.

After a comprehensive review of events with Franco and his family, and consultation with the rehabilitation team, an assessment was made by the social worker that Franco's chronic pain was attributable to a conditioned muscle contraction that was originally a natural protective response to his two cracked vertebrae. The social worker also assessed his rapidly declining physical fitness as attributable to learned illness behavior, reinforced by the absence of expectations by Franco's family. Inadvertently, they were reinforcing his inactivity by completely catering to his needs.

Franco's natural emotional despondence, in reaction to his circumstance, was made worse by his ill-informed explanation or thinking about his circumstance. His explanations of why the industrial accident occurred and his lost capabilities were irrational and superstitious. He explained that he was being punished and could see no hope for the future. This explanation of course increased his emotional despondence. Furthermore, the more Franco's overall illness behavior increased, the more his family catered to him. Being almost totally inactive also served to increase his chronic pain. Franco was in a vicious cycle from which he and his family could see no escape.

BEHAVIORAL TECHNIQUE ONE (90)

The first task of the social worker was to invoke cognitive behavior therapy, essentially to modify Franco's thinking or explanation of his circumstance. This was considered to be a prerequisite task to forming a therapeutic alliance with him to address his chronic pain and declining physical fitness. To modify Franco's explanation of his circumstance, it was necessary to validate his emotional and physical suffering and to explore alternate explanations for his circumstance. It was especially useful to explore with him past negative experiences and the coping strategies he used to successfully overcome the adversity at the time. Cognitive coping strategies, already in his repertoire, were thus reawakened and applied to his current situation to stop the downward spiraling of his overall condition.

An integral part of the cognitive restructuring intervention, when Franco was ready, was to explain the cause of the chronic pain and rapidly declining physical fitness in a manner to which he and his family could relate. Knowledge of Franco's family history, culture, beliefs, and values, among a number of other psychosocial factors, were invaluable in achieving this objective.

BEHAVIORAL TECHNIQUE TWO (91)

The second task for the social worker was to address Franco's conditioned behavioral problems simultaneously—specifically, his chronic pain and rapidly declining physical fitness. To do so, the social worker relied on lessons learned from operant and classical conditioning principles.

Franco's physical fitness was addressed using operant conditioning principles. A time-targeted activation plan was developed with Franco and his family using observable and measurable objectives. Key elements of the intervention were using behavior-shaping strategies that relied on Franco's family rewarding healthy behaviors that approximated his pre-injury activities. With each positive gain in activation there was an equal extinction in the magnitude and occurrence of Franco's illness behaviors.

BEHAVIORAL TECHNIQUE THREE (92)

Franco's chronic pain was addressed using classical conditioning principles. First it was necessary to rule out organic causes. Once it was established that the pain was attributable to conditioned muscle contractions, which originally were natural responses to his cracked (and now completely healed) vertebrae, the use of behavioral techniques was introduced. These included the use of biofeedback technology to teach Franco muscle relaxation and scheduled practice sessions at home, which the team social worker assisted and facilitated.

The three behavioral techniques, greatly augmented by the social worker's psychosocial perspective, which was invaluable in optimally engaging both Franco and his family, produced predictably timely results. Franco learned adaptive ways of explaining his circumstance. He then unlearned the conditioned muscle contractions that were the cause of his chronic pain. Franco's family learned to reinforce his wellness/healthy behaviors and as he became more active his physical conditioning, concomitantly improved. In short order, Franco and his family were functioning as they did before his industrial accident, if not better.

REREFERENCES AND ADDITIONAL SOURCES

Beck, A. T., Rush, A. J., Shaw, F. F., & Emery, G. (1979). *Cognitive therapy of depression*. New York, NY: Guilford Press.

Jacobson, N. S., Dobson, K. S., Truax, P. A., Addis, M. E., Koerner, K., Gollan, J. K., ... & Prince, S. E. (1996). A component analysis of cognitive-behavioral treatment for depression. *Journal of Consulting and Clinical Psychology, 64*(2), 295.

Marra, T. (2005). *Dialectical behavior therapy: A practical and comprehensive guide*. Oakland, CA: New Harbinger.

Meichenbaum, D., & Gilmore, J. B. (1984). The nature of unconscious processes: A cognitive-behavioral perspective. In K. Bowers & D. Meichenbaum (Eds.), *The unconscious reconsidered (pp. 273–298)*. New York: Wiley.

Pavlov, I. P. (1927). *Conditioned reflexes*. New York, NY: Oxford University Press.

Skinner, B. F. (1938). *The behavior of organisms*. New York: Appleton-Century-Crofts.

Wolpe, J. (1958). *Psychotherapy by reciprocal inhibition*. Stanford, CA: Stanford University Press.

Music-Based Intervention

Dr. Mark Ragg is a faculty member of the School of Social Work at Eastern Michigan University. He has written and practiced extensively in the use of music in therapy.

DESCRIPTION

Music-based intervention involves using music to help the client access internal resources or experiences that can help resolve personal situations. Music allows for the symbolic expression of emotion and life problems (Craig, 2007). Through symbolically expressing unresolved conflicts and emotions, they become available for resolution, leading to decreased symptoms and distress (Holmes, 2007). Concurrently, music resonates and calms clients, allowing them to integrate therapeutic messages and information that they might otherwise resist (Hilliard, 2007).

ORIGINS

The healing power of music extends to prehistoric times. Shamans used rhythmic chanting as one of their magical techniques. Throughout history, music has been used as a powerful method for accessing the spiritual and mental world of patients. All major civilizations including ancient Egypt, Greece, and Rome used music as part of healing rituals (MacKinnon, 2006).

Although the mood-altering influence of music was well noted, it wasn't until the late 1800s that formal helping professions explored its healing power in a scientific manner. Initially, professionals thought the healing capacity of music was due to distraction (McKinnon, 2006). Clinical observation and research expanded the knowledge base, finding that music can influence bodily rhythms such as heart rate, gait, and agitation (Schauer & Mauritz, 2003: Schneider, Schönle, Altenmüller, & Münte, 2007). Music-based intervention began to be used to help ease the distress of physically and mentally ill patients (Gfeller, 2002; McKinnon, 2006).

In the early 20th century, music-based treatment became formalized as social workers used music to help soldiers with posttraumatic stress disorder (MacKinnon, 2006). The focus and scope of music therapy expanded as specializations in using music as a therapeutic medium emerged. Although specialized music social workers are now common, social workers and other helping professionals have incorporated music as part of their generalist and clinical practice.

WHY THIS IS USEFUL TO SOCIAL WORK

Music-based intervention is a powerful technique that can be easily integrated into social work practice. It enhances other interventions and can improve the efficacy of interventions such as cognitive-behavioral programming (Dingle, Gleadhill, & Baker, 2008). These enhancements are due to the universal appeal of music. Workers can select music to appeal to cultures, age groups, gender, and specific experiences. Workers can also use music to sidestep the pitfalls of verbal language by using expressive rhythms, chants, and musical activities. Such activities can facilitate positive engagement and emotional responsiveness (Dingle et al., 2008).

The power of music-based interventions may be associated with the brain's lateral specialization, where logical and verbal activity originates in the dominant hemisphere. Musical expression, however, operates in the nondominant side of the brain. As such, music can create experiences that are unfiltered by the logic and client resistances associated with the verbal and logical brain functions. The direct access to the brain without filtering may explain music's ability to shape emotion. Workers can combine words, rhythm, and movement to create experiences that involve both logical and holistic brain functions.

There is some evidence demonstrating the efficacy of musical interventions. Although much of the research is focused on musical therapy, there is some indication that music is a strong adjunctive intervention that can supplement other treatment protocols. Given the universal appeal of music and the great diversity common in social work practice, including music-based intervention as part of a professional skill set may be a wise expansion.

HOW IS MUSIC-BASED INTERVENTION USEFUL IN SOCIAL WORK?

There are two common approaches to music-based intervention: expressive and receptive intervention. *Expressive intervention* refers to activities in which the clients are actively generating music. As the client creates rhythm and sound, the music is a symbolic expression of their internal state. *Receptive intervention* is when a client listens to music. In such interventions, the music evokes emotions and internal responses that can be used as part of treatment.

Often, expressive musical interventions involve clients using instruments, noisemakers, or vocalizations to produce music. As the music is expressed, symptoms, conflicts, and emotions are symbolically expressed in the music (Hilliard, 2007). The act of expression is the main mechanism of healing (McClary, 2007). Expressive musical interventions are associated with a decrease in psychological symptoms and emotional distress (Gold, Wigram, & Voracek, 2007; Hilliard, 2007).

During sessions, expressive interventions often involve improvisation with the social worker playing one instrument and the client playing a second instrument. This method has demonstrated improvements in social skills, relationship enhancements, and decreased emotional symptoms (Oldfield, 2006; Solli, 2008). The expressive use of music has also been expanded to enhance engagement in treatment groups with populations historically resistant to treatment (Dingle et al., 2008).

Some expressive social workers include musical interaction as an aspect of the music intervention, requiring clients to cooperate or respond to each other as an element of the music-based intervention (Boso, Emanuele, Minazzi, Abbamonte, & Politi, 2007). Such interventions are associated with improved social (Boso et al., 2007; Goodman, 2007), language, and motor skills (Kim & Tomaino, 2008). Interactive expressive interventions are now becoming common in marriage and family relationship interventions (Botello & Krout, 2008; Nicholson, Berthelsen, Abad, Williams, & Bradley, 2008).

In group intervention, expressive social workers have combined the use of music and written expression by having group members write songs (Nesbitt & Tabatt-Haussmann, 2008). Song writing allows clients to symbolically express their conflicts musically while concurrently working to resolve issues using language. This approach involves more brain functions and allows for an integration of thinking and emotion (O'Callaghan, 1997).

A second common approach to music-based intervention involves clients listening to the music from a receptive rather than a creative position (Grocke & Wigram, 2007). This approach is more evocative as the client is often in a relaxed state while listening and responding to the music. Some social workers have coupled imagery with receptive music, allowing for increased direction and focus (Aksnes & Ruud, 2008). Receptive music interventions have been used to manage pain (Whitehead-Pleaux, Zebrowski, Baryza, & Sheridan, 2007) and decrease psychological symptoms (Chlan, 2009; Choi, Lee, Cheong, & Lee, 2009).

With receptive musical interventions designed to evoke emotional responses, this technique is becoming common with trauma patients. Social workers can use specific musical passages associated with the time of the trauma to trigger trauma-related memories (Clements-Cortes, 2008). Social workers can also craft lyrics with specific messages to trigger discussions (Mandel, Hanser, Secic, & Davis, 2007). The combination of music and words can engage both sides of the brain, stimulating thinking and emotional experiences.

Often the receptive use of musical intervention seeks to promote discussion through introducing both content and emotional experience. Many workers shape the lyrics or select songs carefully, knowing that the music facilitates the delivery of verbal content. This power of receptive music is also being used in psychoeducational group interventions with disabled populations. In such interventions, the lyrics become an important element as the music becomes the delivery mechanism.

RISK FACTORS

The expressive use of music is a low-risk technique because clients are typically producing the sounds and rhythms and have control over their internal process. However, when music is used to evoke emotion, there may be some risk, depending on the population. The unfiltered elements of music can produce powerful emotional reactions. If working with clients who suffer from PTSD or emotional fragility, feelings may be overwhelming for the client. The following three precautions may help mitigate any potential risks.

1. Discuss the potential for evoking powerful emotions before beginning the musical activity.
2. Develop a cueing system with your client so they can identify emotional amplification and end the exercise.
3. Be prepared to help the client debrief old memories and events.

REQUIRED SKILLS AND KNOWLEDGE

Skill requirements are fairly high for expressive intervention strategies. Workers should possess moderate skill on several instruments to ensure the ability to improvise and engage in interactive exercises. Concurrently, workers should know basic music theory so they can construct songs. This is more important if you are planning to use music as the main intervention method; if you are using music as an adjunctive technique, moderate skills should be sufficient.

It is possible to incorporate some expressive music activities in groups or family practice by engaging clients together in musical activities. This would require more worker skill in providing directives than in producing music. Similarly, engaging clients in writing songs or rapping involves more facilitative than musical skill unless you are providing musical accompaniment. Ideally, some instruments such as drums can be made available to promote the use of music.

The receptive use of music requires very few musical skills. Some activities such as playing a song on a stereo require no skill aside from selecting an appropriate song. With the receptive use of music it is more important that you have a plan for the exercise. These skills are really no different than those required for planning group or other intervention activities.

MUSIC TECHNIQUE 1 (93)

Case Summary One—Passive Use of Music With a Group of Developmentally Disabled Clients

A sheltered workshop serving adults diagnosed with developmental disabilities implemented sexuality programming for clients with IQ scores above 45, but had no programming for clients diagnosed with severe and profound levels of disability. Many of the severely disabled clients were living in group homes and were vulnerable because they possessed little understanding of their body rights.

Group leaders mandated to develop such programming were immediately challenged by the lack of expressive language skills. They noticed that music was a reward for many of the clients in the workshop program. Consequently, a music-based approach to sexuality training was selected. This began by identifying specific areas of programming. Eventually two core programming areas were identified: body rights and appropriate sexual behavior. Songs were developed for each area.

A group program was developed where four clients, two men and two women, meet twice per week in a group. The group lasted 30 minutes and consisted of singing about six to eight songs per session. All of the songs were short and allowed for the use of visual aids to illustrate the points. For example, a body rights song included the lyrics, "You can touch me here, here, here" (touching the hand), "you can touch me here, here, here" (touching the arm), "but if you touch me here, here, here" (gesturing to the chest), "I will tell a staff" (pointing to a staff member).

Only one group member had an expressive vocabulary, which was limited to about ten words. All other members had some receptive vocabulary but could not verbally communicate.

After about 4 weeks, a group member approached the staff member who was used for illustration and communicated that another resident had been touching her inappropriately. The situation was investigated and the offending client, who was much higher functioning, was moved.

In assessing the program, feedback was collected from workshop staff and a visually based pretest and posttest (pointing to pictures) was used to assess outcomes. The staff noticed that the group members appeared motivated and would begin walking to the group room as soon as the leaders entered the workshop. Concurrently, gains in body rights and appropriate behavior were noted for all members in the posttest results. It was concluded that using music as a vehicle for transmitting sexual information was effective for low-verbal clients.

MUSIC TECHNIQUE 2 (94)

Case Summary Two—Expressive Use of Music With a Group of Foster Youth

In a weekend group workshop for adolescent foster youth, workers wanted to help them share and hopefully resolve some of their negative experiences in foster care. However, the youth were resistant to opening up about their experiences. Most of the youth were living near "street level" and tended to respond with one-word answers when workers attempted to help them open up. Several of the youth had openly stated that they didn't like talking to workers because they couldn't be trusted.

The workers noticed that the youth all related well to rap music and paid very close attention to the words. The workers consequently decided to use music to help the youth express some of their experiences. The workers split the group into two equally sized subgroups and challenged each group to write a rap song that captured the essence of "growing up in foster care." The subgroups each worked together for about 40 minutes, discussing their experiences and writing phrases that captured the experience. The subgroups then performed their raps for the larger group.

After the performances, the members discussed how the rap songs captured different elements of the foster care experience. They began sharing experiences openly and were able to enthusiastically respond to one another's experiences. When the workshop was evaluated, many of the youth identified writing the rap song as one of the most helpful elements in the weekend.

MUSIC TECHNIQUE 3 (95)

Case Study Three—Active Use of Drumming With an Uncommunicative Adolescent

A worker in a children's mental health center was working with a 14-year-old boy diagnosed as depressed. The assessment indicated several situational contributors to the depression, including reactions to parental divorce, his mother's recent cohabitation with a new boyfriend (with daughters), and exposure to domestic violence perpetrated by the new boyfriend. The young man also had a speech impediment that made it very difficult for him to speak, especially when experiencing intense emotion.

The worker had used many cognitive-behavioral techniques to help the young man understand and cope with the family transitions and violence. These were helpful in providing frameworks for understanding family events. However, the young man remained very angry about the intrusion of the boyfriend and his own inability to protect his mother. In one session, he was talking about the boyfriend and his speech impediment caused him to stutter. In frustration he pounded the arm of the chair in a rhythmic manner.

Upon observing the pounding, the worker went to the bookshelves and handed the young man a drum, instructing him to close his eyes and share his feelings about the boyfriend by tapping on the drum. The young man began pounding on the drum as hard as possible. The worker then began asking questions about some of the recent transitions. With each question the rhythm and inflection would change; some transitions resulted in slow drumming and others would increase the intensity. Conversation about the meaning of the drumming changes allowed the young man to discuss his situation without feeling overwhelmed.

Drumming became a staple in the sessions, as the young man would immediately go to the shelves and take the drum as he proceeded to his chair. He would then perform a drum solo indicating the events of his week followed by integrated talking and drumming. He became comfortable speaking about family events, and his depressive symptoms decreased.

DISCUSSION

The case examples show different uses of music to facilitate communication. The passive use of music helped information to integrate even with a client population with clear communication challenges. Similar results were achieved with the expressive use of music. With the foster youth, the lyrics were a very important element in expressing experiences, whereas with the individual adolescent the rhythm carried his emotion. None of these practice situations were formal music therapy. Rather, music became an adjunctive technique easily integrated with traditional intervention approaches.

REFERENCES AND ADDITIONAL SOURCES

Aksnes, H., & Ruud, E. (2008). Body-based schemata in receptive music therapy. *Musicae Scientiae, 12,* 49–74.

Boso, M., Emanuele, E., Minazzi, V., Abbamonte, M., & Politi, P. (2007). Effect of long-term interactive music therapy on behavior profile and musical skills in young adults with severe autism. *The Journal of Alternative and Complementary Medicine, 13*(7), 709–712.

Botello, R. K., & Krout, R.E. (2008). Music therapy assessment of automatic thoughts: Developing a cognitive behavioral application of improvisation to assess couple communication. *Music Therapy Perspectives, 26,* 51–55.

Chlan, L. (2009). A review of the evidence for music intervention to manage anxiety in critically ill patients receiving ventilatory support. *Archives of Psychiatric Nursing, 23,* 177–179.

Choi, A-N., Lee, M. S., Cheong, K. J., & Lee, J. S. (2009). Effects of group music intervention on behavioral and psychological symptoms in patients with dementia: A pilot-controlled trial. *International Journal of Neuroscience, 119*(4), 471–481.

Clements-Cortes, A. (2008). Music to shatter the silence: A case study on music therapy, trauma, and the Holocaust. *Canadian Journal of Music Therapy, 14,* 9–21.

Craig, D. G. (2007). An exploratory study of the concept of meaningfulness in music. *Nordic Journal of Music Therapy, 16,* 3–13.

Dingle, G. A., Gleadhill, L., & Baker, F. A. (2008). Can music therapy engage patients in group cognitive behaviour therapy for substance abuse treatment? *Drug and Alcohol Review, 27*(2), 190–196.

Gfeller, K. E. (2002). Music as therapeutic agent: Historical and sociocultural perspectives. In R. G. Unkefer & M. H. Thaut (Eds.), *Music therapy in the treatment of adults with mental disorders: Theoretical bases and clinical interventions* (2nd ed., pp. 60–67). St. Louis, MO: MMB Music.

Gold, C., Wigram, T., & Voracek, M. (2007). Predictors of change in music therapy with children and adolescents: The role of therapeutic techniques. *Psychology and Psychotherapy: Theory, Research and Practice, 80,* 577–589.

Goodman, K. D. (2007). *Music therapy groupwork with special needs children: The evolving process.* Springfield, IL: Charles C. Thomas.

Grocke, D., & Wigram, T. (2007). *Receptive methods in music therapy: Techniques and clinical applications for music therapy clinicians, educators, and students.* London, England: Jessica Kingsley.

Hilliard, R. E. (2007). The effects of Orff-based music therapy and social work groups on childhood grief symptoms and behaviors. *Journal of Music Therapy, 44,* 123–138.

Holmes, E. (2007). Sound and song as hypnotherapy: A holistic approach for transformation through the use of sound and song. *Australian Journal of Clinical Hypnotherapy and Hypnosis, 28,* 12–18.

Kim, M., & Tomaino, C. M. (2008). Protocol evaluation for effective music therapy for persons with nonfluent aphasia. *Topics in Stroke Rehabilitation, 15,* 555–569.

Mandel, S. E., Hanser, S. B., Secic, M., & Davis, B. A. (2007). Effects of music therapy on health-related outcomes in cardiac rehabilitation: A randomized controlled trial. *Journal of Music Therapy, 44,* 176–197.

McClary, R. (2007). Healing the psyche through music, myth, and ritual. *Psychology of Aesthetics, Creativity, and the Arts, 1,* 155–159.

MacKinnon, D., (2006). Music, madness and the body: Symptom and cure. *History of Psychiatry, 17,* 9–21.

Nesbitt, L. L., & Tabatt-Haussmann, K. (2008). The role of the creative arts therapies in the treatment of pediatric hematology and oncology patients. *Primary Psychiatry, 15,* 56–62.

Nicholson, J. M., Berthelsen, D., Abad, V., Williams, K., & Bradley, J. (2008). Impact of music therapy to promote positive parenting and child development. *Journal of Health Psychology, 13,* 226–238.

O'Callaghan, C. C. (1997). Therapeutic opportunities associated with the music when using song writing in palliative care. *Music Therapy Perspectives, 15*, 32–38.

Oldfield, A. (2006). *Interactive music therapy in child and family psychiatry: Clinical practice, research and teaching.* London, England: Jessica Kinglsey.

Schauer, M., & Mauritz, K. H. (2003). Musical motor feedback (MMF) in walking hemiparetic stroke patients: Randomized trials of gait improvement. *Clinical Rehabilitation, 17* (7), 713–722.

Schneider, S., Schönle, P. W., Altenmüller, E., & Münte, T. F. (2007). Using musical instruments to improve motor skill recovery following a stroke. *Journal of Neurology, 254,* 1339–1346.

Solli, H. P. (2008). "Shut up and play!" Improvisational use of popular music for a man with schizophrenia. *Nordic Journal of Music Therapy, 17,* 67–77.

Whitehead-Pleaux, A. M., Zebrowski, N., Baryza, M. J., & Sheridan, R. L., (2007). Exploring the effects of music therapy on pediatric pain: Phase 1. *Journal of Music Therapy, 47,* 217–241.

Play Therapy as Theory and Technique

Dr. Nancy Riedel Bowers is a member of the Faculty of Social Work at Wilfrid Laurier University, a social practitioner and supervisor in play therapy.,

Anna Lee Bowers is a psychology student at the University of Waterloo in Waterloo, Ontario.

DESCRIPTION

Play therapy, a term often used loosely by many child social workers who employ play as a technique for healing, is "the systematic use of a theoretical model to establish an interpersonal process where play social workers use the therapeutic powers of play to help clients prevent or resolve psychosocial difficulties and achieve optimal growth and development" (American Play Therapy Association, 2012). There are approximately 14 models (O'Connor & Braverman, 1997) of play therapy, all embedded in research and originating from established theories such as psychoanalysis; attachment and developmental theories; client-centered, filial, cognitive, and behavioral theories, systems and structural models; Gestalt theory; Adlerian, Jungian, and Ericksonian models; and the ecosystemic and narrative paradigms. When applied to the play therapy process, these theories are often differentiated by their so-called directive and nondirective thrusts (Gil, 1991).

Those registered as play social workers (American Play Therapy Association, 2009) may use a prescriptive approach, applying models of intervention specific to the needs of the child, whether short or longer term therapy, relationship based, strengths focused, or family based. Although research has recently had an efficacy-based focus, there remains an interest in and need for better descriptions of the intervention process of play therapy. Thus, both quantitative and qualitative play therapy research are to be found in peer-reviewed, published journals such as the *International Journal of Play Therapy,* as well as in the ubiquitous technique-based publications.

HISTORY AND ORIGINS

The historical background of play therapy has been one of a slow progression, but it has led to a solid theoretical foundation supporting the intervention model of play therapy. In 1909 Sigmund Freud wrote about the use of play in his work with Hans and his father as a way to uncover the fears and concerns of clients. It was not until the 1920s that play was more formally used by Hermine Von Hug-Hellmuth (1921) in the treatment of children. Over the last century, concepts have been expanded upon and established models have been introduced. Four key methods of play therapy that have evolved include psychoanalytic play therapy, structured play therapy, relationship play therapy and nondirective play therapy.

In 1930, Anna Freud and Melanie Klein introduced psychoanalytic play therapy, which continues to be a very prominent form of child therapy. This model is based on the notion that play is a way to build strong relationships between the child and social worker, is a substitute for talking, and is a way for the child to work through difficulties while the social worker gains insight through interpretation (Gil, 1991).

In the late 1930s, a goal-oriented model known as structured play therapy was formulated. New ideas took hold, such as the social worker determining the direction of the therapy, using Levy's release therapy by recreating the traumatic experience, letting the child play freely to express emotions at his or her own speed, and focusing on the nature of the child's relationships. These evolving methods using play paved the way for relationship-focused play therapy models that form the basis of play therapy as we know it today.

Relationship play therapy, a more passive form of play therapy, was introduced in the 1930s and 1940s. This model suggests that individuals have the ability to solve their own problems, thereby promoting acceptance of the child as they are and stressing their relationship with the social worker (Gil, 1991). An emphasis on the social worker observing and participating while the child increasingly works out difficulties at his or her own pace became prevalent.

In the 1950s, nondirective play therapy starting becoming prominent. Similar to previous forms of play therapy, this child-centred approach stressed human values, the full acceptance of the child, and the therapeutic relationship (Axline, 1950; Rogers & Meador, 1980). Behavior was understood by letting the child decide the nature and direction of the path toward change and freedom of experience, whereas the playroom was thought to be a key variable for change. Two influential nondirective-play social workers are Moustakas and Axline, who postulate that the child is capable of self-realization, self-awareness, and self-direction. They suggest that a child, through the discovery of the play therapy environment, can develop a clearer sense of self through insight and mastery.

The therapeutic relationship has played a key role throughout the history of play therapy and has become the basis for other play therapy models and techniques.

WHY AND HOW THIS IS USEFUL
TO SOCIAL WORK

Historically, social work has been a profession that contributes to the healing of children and their families. The lifecycle of birth to adulthood is observed in the healing process, beginning with the assessment and leading to the choice of the appropriate intervention model. As play is widely accepted the natural medium of expression for a child (Axline, 1950), the implementation of the various models of play therapy has evolved as social work has evolved as a profession. In fact, both social work and the therapy that uses play embrace the same theoretical thrusts. Consequently, the play therapy profession has developed with and alongside that of social work.

In an effort to provide a healing option for children, play provides a voice (Riedel Bowers, 2001, 2009) with which the child can be heard, often within the family context. The provision of puppetry, long used in history to allow children to have a mode of expression, or sandplay, for instance, provide children with an opportunity to express their emotions, to understand and develop insight into their worlds, and develop choice and a sense of empowerment to express themselves within the context of the family.

RISK FACTORS

The risk of any entity that offers choice (Saleebey, 2006) is that the correct one must be applied. In the area of mental health for children, the risks of applying a play therapy model are that it needs to be carefully understood and chosen for its applicability to the child's needs, and that the professional has been trained in the model. Consequently, registered bodies have been set up to offer proper training and supervision requirements and to ensure ongoing professional advancement to lessen the risk of harm.

REQUIRED SKILLS AND KNOWLEDGE

Around the world there are organizations that provide training as play social workers, usually requiring a master's degree with specific course requirements and detailed and monitored supervision. The American Play Therapy Association is one such organization; it has links with most countries in the world and registered play social workers and supervisors representing all corners of five continents.

PLAY TECHNIQUE 1 (96)

Case Summary One

Presenting Problem: Jenny, a 4-year-old girl of Spanish and Caucasian-diverse background, was recently moved to her third foster home in 18 months and was presenting detached reactions to other children in the foster home and at preschool. She was otherwise in good physical health, but was not eating and sleeping properly in the new foster home setting. Plans for adoption were imminent, but the child protection social worker was reticent about placement before the child's mild depression had lifted.

Historical Background: Jenny is the third and youngest child of a Spanish mother, sharing a common father with one other sibling. All three children were apprehended when Jenny was 18 months, with all three children being placed in different foster homes. The mother was the attachment figure in the early months of Jenny's life, but apprehension took place after the mother indicated an inability to care for the children and asked that they be placed for adoption. The children were witness to verbal abuse between their natural mother and her partners but did not observe physical violence. There has been some effort to have the siblings visit one another bimonthly while in foster home, and to have Jenny and her 1-year-older sister be placed together for adoption.

The treatment planning involved the choice of an attachment-based, long-term (30 weekly sessions), client-centered play therapy model that allowed Jenny to safely develop a relationship of trust and security. With this in place, she was able to play out in a repetitive way many narratives of her life events that had previously caused her to be fixated and stuck. In the final phase of treatment, Jenny had developed a new insight into what her attachments have been like and how she can develop a sense of mastery and empowerment over future choices. Through this process, the recognition of a "new attachment" was seen as a major healing aspect of the play therapy process.

PLAY TECHNIQUE 2 (97)

Case Summary Two

Presenting Problem: Lucas, a 15-year-old, was diagnosed with mild Asperger's syndrome as a young child. He has difficulty forming and maintaining social interactions because it is challenging for him to relate to others. Lucas instead finds great comfort and self-satisfaction in Lego. He spends hours in his room attempting various projects, and gets fixated and frustrated when he encounters a barrier in the building process. Lego takes precedence over the other people in Lucas's life, and playing Lego has become part of a repetitive pattern that Lucas has formed after school and on the weekends. When Lucas becomes anxious and uncomfortable (most commonly in social situations), he retreats to Lego as an escape.

Historical Background: Lucas is the middle child, with two brothers ages 12 and 17. Lucas had difficulty adjusting when his younger brother was born and distanced himself instead of attempting to form an attachment.

His parents divorced when he was 5 years old. Lucas and his brothers now live with their father, visiting their mother once a month. Lucas's father has recently begun to disapprove of Lucas's playing with Lego, believing he should be spending more time doing homework and playing outside with kids his age, thus indicating a lack of comprehension concerning Lucas's disability. At the age of 3, Lucas was diagnosed with Asperger's because he had not yet begun relating to others. Lucas has undergone therapy in the past with little success. Lucas excels in school as a result of concentration and careful attention to detail. While his language and cognitive development are consistent with those of his classmates, his ability to socially interact is in need of attention and improvement.

The treatment planning focused on Lucas gaining a sense of mastery in many aspects. Building on the idea that Lucas is already a master of Lego, collaborative goals and strategies were created with his family that would lead to acceptance and celebration of Lucas' mastery in relationships with others and in daily social interaction through Lego. Lego was used as a metaphor for gradual improvement and the process from start to finish of a task. Problem-solving strategies also needed to be addressed to find alternatives to Lucas's reacting with frustration and his sense of defeat when Lego building and social interactions become challenging.

PLAY TECHNIQUE 3 (98)

Case Summary Three

Presenting Problem and Historical Background: Sonya, a 9-year-old girl of mixed European background, attends grade school in an inner-city setting. She has been living in a family that has engaged in escalating domestic violence, and over the summer she witnessed the abuse of her mother. She has presented at the beginning of the school year with aggression toward friends and classmates not seen in previous school years.

While entering play therapy with a client-centered model in place, Sonya quickly chose her comfort play (Riedel Bowers, 2009) as the sandbox, in which she shared the narrative of her recent life of escalating abuse and, through the deconstruction of this story, asked to reconstruct a happier ending. In doing so, the cognitive play therapy model was incorporated into this healing process. With Sonya's wish to start "feeling happier than I used to," goals were placed in a Narrative Book, along with an ongoing storytelling section that provided for drawings of feelings and expressions of emotions on a basis that Sonya could plan. The book, acting as a transitional object (Winnicott, 1971) between therapy and home, empowered this child to carry away a new relationship/attachment, thereby validating her sense of self. Consequently, she felt ready to confront the challenges and choices in the ensuing family therapy that followed in the subsequent year.

REFERENCES AND ADDITIONAL SOURCES

American Play Therapy Association. (2012). Play therapy makes a difference! Retrieved from www.a4pt. org

Axline, V. (1950). Entering the child's world via play experiences. *Progressive Education, 27*, 68–75.

Gil, E. (1991). *The healing power of play*. New York: Guilford.

O'Connor, K., & Braverman, L. (Eds.). (1997). *Play therapy theory and practice—A comparative presentation*. New York, NY: Wiley.

Riedel Bowers, N. (2001). *A journey within a journey: A naturalistic inquiry of the early relationship development process of non-directive play therapy*. (Unpublished doctoral dissertation). Wilfrid Laurier University, Waterloo, Ontario.

Riedel Bowers, N. (2009). A naturalistic inquiry of the early relationship development process of non-directive play therapy. *International Journal of Play Therapy, 18*(3), 176.

Saleebey, D. (1996). The strengths perspective in social work practice: Extensions and cautions. Social work, 41(3), 296–305.

Von Hug-Helllmuth, H. (1921). On the technique of child-analysis. *International Journal of Psychoanalysis, 2*, 286–305.

Winnicott, D. (1971). *Playing and reality*. London, England: Routledge.

Standardized Instruments

Dr. Alex Polgar is a senior consultant and clinician in Hamilton, Ontario, Canada.

This section reviews measurement with standardized instruments and the competence with which a therapeutic approach is applied; the effectiveness of the approach to facilitating an agreed-upon outcome; and using standardized instruments to inform clinical assessment formulations.

DESCRIPTION

A standardized instrument is a particular type of clinical technique that provides objective, quantifiable information about a specific behavior. Behaviors, to name just a few, generally can include how one responds to a set of questions, or more specifically can pertain to intelligence, aptitude, personality, emotional state, and how one perceives an interpersonal relationship. There are hundreds of standardized instruments, some better than others, some more sophisticated and able to provide more information than others, and most developed for a singular research purpose forever archived in some thesis or doctoral dissertation.

An increasing number of social workers are conducting forensic assessments to assist the courts in matters such as parenting plans and parenting capacity related to child welfare (Polgar 2005). A significant focus in such assessments is the personality structure of parents as determined by the sum total of their life experiences. Consistent with the psychosocial perspective that social work brings to such assessments is the identification of experience-induced strengths and weaknesses in parents' personality structures. Raymond Cattell's standardized instrument, the Sixteen Personality Factor Questionnaire (Cattell, Eber, & Tatsuoka, 1988), is ideally suited to augmenting clinical formulations in this respect. It has a long, auspicious history and thereby much credibility. The instrument is based on the premise that traits are the essential component of personality and that the inordinate number of adjectives that describe personality can be honed down to 16 primary factors. Each factor is evaluated on a continuum that ranges from being a strength to being a hindrance to adaptive functioning in a specific context. As the profession of social work increasingly moves to embrace empirical practice, this and similar standardized instruments are invaluable assessment techniques to support both the clinical formulations and the concomitant recommendations of a social worker acting in the role of an expert witness in court.

ORIGINS

Unfortunately, many social workers have forgotten—or no longer consider it important—that the first social reformers, the precursors to professional social workers, were primarily economists. They were the first to introduce objectivity and empirical methods to the study of the charitable treatment of dependency. This was the genesis of social diagnosis distinctly characterized as a thorough investigation.

Initially a thorough investigation was narrowly focused and limited to people's economic circumstances. In short order, however, the scope of investigation broadened to viewing people in the context of their history and current circumstance (psychosocial perspective). Consistent with the use of objective methods to inform the charitable treatment of dependency, Mary Richmond was the first to admonish the profession of social work not to base its perceived social relevance simply on good intentions. In her seminal work, *Social Diagnosis*, Richmond (1917) advocated that professional social work activities be subjected to critical analysis: measuring effectiveness by the best standards available at the time. By so advocating as early as the turn of the 20th century, Richmond also was distinguishing between competence and the relevance of applying a competence to a particular presenting problem. Regardless of competence in a particular modality, if the approach is not relevant to addressing a problem, effectiveness (outcome) will be seriously compromised. A significant method of avoiding this is the technique of repeated measures using standardized instruments.

For the most part, standardized instruments have been developed by psychologists to investigate the structure of personality, specific behaviors, and effectiveness of educational programs. As a result, standardized instruments are mistakenly referred to as psychological tests. This is a misnomer that has produced an unintended negative result: namely, the belief that only psychologists can and are allowed to use standardized instruments as one way of objectively measuring a sample of behavior.

In reality, there is much overlap in the social sciences with less exclusivity than generally has been assumed. For example, with respect to the technique of using standardized instruments, there is specific reference in *The Code of Ethics and Standards of Practice* of the Ontario College of Social Workers and Social Service Workers (2000) to the use of clinical tools such as questionnaires, diagnostic assessment measures, and rating scales. In other words, there is an explicit expectation that social workers will use standardized instruments to augment clinical formulations.

WHY THIS IS USEFUL TO SOCIAL WORK

Of all mental health service providers internationally, the discipline of social work comprises the greatest number. Social workers are the primary practitioners of psychotherapy. Moreover, there is unequivocal massed empirical evidence that psychotherapy is effective in helping people with their problems (Duncan & Miller, 2000). There also is ample evidence that the type of psychotherapy practiced is not the major determining factor of outcome. In fact, the various methods of intervention reportedly produce more or less the same outcomes (Luborsky, Singer, & Luborsky 1975). This finding has not been challenged since it was first published. The type of psychotherapy used has been found to represent only 15% of the outcome determining factor, superseded by the client factor (40%), followed by the client perception of the therapeutic relationship (30%), and the client's hopes and expectations of the process (Tallman & Bohart, 1999). These are rather compelling findings that diminish neither the importance of the type of psychotherapy nor the techniques used to enhance competence and effectiveness. On the contrary, the findings serve to firmly establish the importance of incorporating in all psychotherapeutic modalities the technique of measuring outcomes—not just at the end of treatment, but throughout the process, so optimal results will be obtained from the 15% determining factor attributed to modality and technique.

Using a technique or measuring with standardized instruments to inform clinical social work practice and assessment is a continuing response to Mary Richmond's admonishment not to rely simply on good intentions, but to demonstrate empirically the effectiveness of what social work does.

HOW THIS IS USEFUL TO SOCIAL WORK

It seems that there has never been a time of adequate economic support for social services. To say, therefore, that any period of time is one of financial constraints for social services is tantamount to saying the obvious. Moreover, to relate the need to empirically demonstrate the effectiveness of social work intervention and assessment to financial issues arguably is inconsistent with both the profession's history and its fundamental value to *do good*. Implicit in this value is that the good being done can be empirically demonstrated, and that this is done regardless of prevailing economic conditions.

Although slow to be used uniformly by all clinical social workers, there is a markedly discernable movement to incorporate the technique of using standardized instruments. Social workers Corcoran and Fischer (1987), with a significantly complimentary introduction to their work by the psychologist Barlow, produced and continue to update a compendium of standardized instruments ideally suited to measuring clinical practice and informing assessment formulations rapidly and with ease. In their volumes, required knowledge about the use of standardized instruments is delineated, as well as information about the sources through which they can be purchased.

As social work practice is enhanced by the technique of using standardized instruments, so also the clients that social workers serve benefit. Not the least of the benefits accrued is the client's active participation in providing, interpreting, and constructively using objective data.

RISK FACTORS

The greatest risk to employing the technique of using standardized instruments is to become clinically deferential to the results any or all such tools produce. The better the tool, the more comprehensive the information the tool can produce, the greater the risk of second-guessing or completely discounting other sources of information, especially when conducting an assessment. Good clinical practice—indeed, a sound clinical formulation—demands, however, that multiple sources of relevant information be marshalled as evidence to support it. The broader the supportive information and the greater the internal logic of the supportive information, the higher will be the confidence level with which a clinical formulation and concomitant recommendation can be made. No standardized instrument can be used as the sole source of information on which to draw a conclusion or make a formulation.

There also is an inherent risk to using any tool, including standardized instruments. If the user is not fully knowledgeable and skilled in the use of a tool, serious harm could result. In the use of standardized instruments, the harm may be to the client as well as the social worker, who has a professional responsibility to practice within existing competencies. As tempting as it may be to start using or expand on the use of standardized instruments, it is incumbent on the social worker first to understand the knowledge and skills required for the competent use of each and every tool. This is usually made explicit by the publisher and/or distributor of the standardized instrument. Second, it is incumbent on the social worker to acquire the necessary training (or supervision), if required, to learn the competent use of certain standardized instruments, especially those pertaining to personality. There are no short cuts, and taking one can be a risky journey to embark upon.

REQUIRED SKILLS AND KNOWLEDGE

Fischer and Corcoran (1994), in their much-expanded list of rapid assessment instruments, continue to include sections containing the knowledge and skills required to competently use the tools they describe. Theirs is an entry-level, prerequisite instruction that must be augmented with the instruction-manual information that accompanies each tool. Practitioners always are advised to fully familiarize themselves with the standardized methods used to administer, score, and interpret even the least sophisticated tool.

More sophisticated standardized instruments—those that tap into personality, psychopathology, or intellectual functioning—have more stringent requirements to purchase and use. Publishers of such instruments clearly specify requirements, classifying purchasers into three categories of purpose: decision making, research, and library reference. Users in the first category are required to have successfully completed a minimum of two university courses in test and measurement. Appropriately qualified equivalent courses also are acceptable requirements to purchase first-category standardized instruments. To use some instruments, a specific period of supervision is also required.

Both the publishers and suppliers of standardized instruments make disclaimers specifically that it is ultimately the user's responsibility to know his or her own qualifications and how well they match the qualifications required to use specific instruments. Therefore, the responsibility to employ appropriately any standardized instrument is clearly articulated to rest with the user. The categories of requirements essentially are intended to protect the public.

Consistent with the origins of social work, the discipline has always considered itself and has always been perceived to be a social science. Social work has, and continues to teach and use, scientific methods to advance its knowledge and skill base, as well as the competencies of its practitioners. Many undergraduate and graduate social work programs have as a core requirement the successful completion of courses such as empirical practice or single-case research design that incorporate the basic principles of test and measurement. In most cases, these and similar courses meet the user qualification requirement that the publishers and distributors of standardized instruments impose.

Three commonly encountered presenting problems by social workers can illustrate the integral measuring technique regardless of the intervention modality or approach used by a clinician.

STANDARDIZED INSTRUMENTS TECHNIQUE ONE (99)

The first example concerns working with a depressed client. The Beck Depression Inventory (BDI; Beck, 1967) is one of many rapid assessment instruments (RAI) available that measures the severity of a condition. It is a 21-item scale that quantifies the affective, cognitive, motivational, vegetative, and psychomotor components of depression. Each item relates to a particular symptom of depression, and respondents indicate on a 3-point scale the current severity of each. The technique of using this instrument provides objective data to aid the development of an operationally defined statement of a presenting problem. Of equal importance, the relative ease with which the instrument can be administered, scored, and interpreted affords the clinical social worker the ability to track, from one session to the next, changes in the severity of each symptom. Invoking the repeated-measures technique also serves to identify when resolution has been achieved as evidenced by the empirically established criterion scores provided.

Case Summary

At intake, Mr. Jones reported that lately he has been having performance problems at work and that he has been progressively feeling disconnected from his spouse and children. During the interview, he elaborated that at work he does not complete in a timely fashion what he used to be capable of doing, and that what he does do is below the standards he easily met before. He described himself as similarly listless at home and as having no interest in doing things he enjoyed previously.

As an afterthought, Mr. Jones reported that his father died over a year ago, stating, however, that he was not adversely affected by his father's death because he never had much of a relationship with him throughout his life.

Based on this information and other indicators, the working hypothesis is that Mr. Jones is suffering from reactive depression exacerbated by lifelong unresolved relationship issues with his deceased father. The mourning for his father has been unconsciously obstructed, because to feel the loss would signify that in spite of their estrangement, Mr. Jones' father had significance in his life.

It is explained to Mr. Jones that part of the intake and intervention process involves the use of questionnaires (standardized instruments) to assist with problem formulation, goal setting, and decision making about how to achieve the best results from intervention.

Among other tools, Mr. Jones is administered the BDI. Affective, cognitive, motivational, vegetative, and psychomotor components of depression are all above the clinical cutoff scores that define severity.

During the session following intake, clinical formulations based on the various findings are discussed with Mr. Jones. The working hypothesis of reactive depression is confirmed by a number of indicators, including the BDI. This gave cause to discuss the fundamental dynamics of reactive depression. Faced with the overwhelming evidence, especially the objective data, Mr. Jones reluctantly acknowledged that probably he has been more negatively affected by the death of his father than he believed he could have been.

Based on his new level of awareness, Mr. Jones agreed to the goal of intervention to work through the mourning process and to increase his activity level through a cognitive behavioral intervention approach. Recognizing the value of the BDI in helping to formulate a statement of his presenting problem, Mr. Jones agreed to complete the standardized instrument after every session to monitor his progress and emotional state. He also agreed to self-monitor specific behaviors throughout each day.

When the scores on the BDI fell two standard deviations below the clinical criteria levels of severity, his performance at work was returning to previous levels of competence and punctuality, and his interpersonal relationships (especially with significant others) were considered subjectively to be improving, Mr. Jones agreed that the goal and related objectives of psychotherapy had been achieved.

STANDARDIZED INSTRUMENTS TECHNIQUE TWO (100)

The second example concerns a married couple. One standardized instrument that has significant potential to inform social workers' practice methods positively in these cases is the Index of Marital Satisfaction scale (IMS; Hudson, 1982). This is a 25-item instrument designed to measure the degree, severity, or magnitude of a problem one spouse or partner has in a relationship. The instrument does not characterize the relationship. Instead, the focus is on the extent to which one partner perceives problems in the relationship. Comparing the partners' perspectives can be extremely informative with respect to arriving at an operationally stated problem definition, as well as defining what would constitute a resolution. The instrument has a cutoff score above which there is a clinically significant problem and below which no such problem exists. Repeated measures also can be obtained from the use of this instrument to objectively track progress in therapy.

Case Summary

The request for marriage counseling was initiated by one partner who stated that the other was willing to attend, albeit reluctantly. During the intake session, it became evident that the initiator's expectations of the process were that the other would be "fixed." The reluctant participant's expectation was that the social work professional would confirm that indeed there is nothing wrong in the relationship.

These observations were shared during the intake session and used as objective information that indeed there was something amiss in the relationship. Both agreed that if nothing else there was a marked difference of perception that was troubling to each. They also agreed that it would be beneficial to explore further the nature of their respective different perceptions of the relationship. They agreed to complete the IMS to assist in this process of exploration.

As predicted by the couples' clinical presentation during the intake interview, the results of the standardized instrument confirmed their different evaluation/perceptions of the relationship. The results of one exceeded the cutoff score of 30 but did not reach the score of 70, which is indicative of severe discord or dissatisfaction with a possibility that some type of violence could be used to deal with problems.

The reluctant participant, faced with the professional social worker's feedback and the markedly different scores they each produced on the scale, acknowledged the inappropriateness and hurtfulness of disregarding the other's discontent with their relationship. With focused effort, in short order, the marked variance between the individual's perceptions of the relationship was confirmed and quantified.

Consequently, both agreed to address their relationship problem by reviewing their respective responses to each of the 25 items that make up the IMS. Each learned a great deal about the other's needs (e.g., for affection) and how to respond to the needs in ways that would be accepted as relevant and meaningful.

Repeated administration of the scale confirmed success on the various scale items allowing for systematic and rational progression in the therapeutic process. When all scale items were addressed to the satisfaction of each, the quantified results served as the predetermined criteria to terminate the social worker's involvement with the couple.

STANDARDIZED INSTRUMENTS TECHNIQUE THREE (101)

The third example of a clinically useful standardized instrument is for social workers who counsel families. The Family Adaptability and Cohesion Evaluation Scale (FACES; Olson, Portner, & Lavee, 1985) has 20 items that measure the two main dimensions of family functioning. This standardized instrument taps into how family members see their family (perceived) and how they would like it to be (ideal). This standardized instrument also readily lends itself to repeated-measures application and is a useful technique to evaluate the competence with which an intervention modality is applied, as well as the relevance (effectiveness) of the modality to bringing about an agreed-upon resolution to a presenting family problem.

Case Summary

The Smith family was referred for counseling by the local Family Court Clinic. The referral was precipitated by the violent, assaultive behavior of their 15-year-old daughter against another youth. Court proceedings were stayed until the benefits of counseling could be ascertained. If counseling was deemed to be successful, the Court was amenable to an unconditional discharge. The family—or at least the parents—were therefore highly motivated to address and resolve the problems that may have caused the daughter's acting out.

By definition, *acting out* is the behavioral manifestation of unlabeled and often unconscious but intense negative emotional states. Violence is almost always indicative of anger, frustration and/or fear. The question therefore is: about what?

The family, both parents, a 10-year-old son, and the 15-year-old daughter, presented as essentially bewildered about their circumstance, both over what had happened and how to fix it. Trouble of this magnitude was new to them, but at a lesser intensity it was a familiar occurrence.

Accepting that separation and individuation is a life task that begins almost immediately when a child is born, and based on the parents' protestation that they are extremely responsible caregivers who structure every moment of their children's' lives, a hypothesis was made of rigid family dynamics and growing alienation.

To test the hypothesis and to engage the family in the process of defining and solving the problem, the FACES instrument was introduced to them.

Consistent with the clinical formulations, the scale results characterized the family dynamics as rigid on the Adaptability dimension and as disengaged on the Cohesion dimension. The parents' well-intentioned but misinformed responses to the children's natural separation and individuation developmental cycle inadvertently precipitated the acting out against the rigid controls imposed on them. The acting out was anger based and indiscriminately directed at others.

The results of the scale and the professional social worker's clinical formulations were discussed with the family. The fact that all family members indicated on the scale a desire to change their family dynamics also was discussed and used to arrive at a consensus about how to solve their two-pronged problem. As the parents and children became less rigid and oppositional about their respective needs (control vs. independence), they also reported verbally and through repeated administration of the scale greater emotional cohesion among themselves. The children's acting out virtually ceased. This was reported to the Court, and the charges against the daughter were dispensed with by means of an unconditional discharge.

REFERENCES AND ADDITIONAL SOURCES

Beck, A. T. (1967). *Depression: Clinical, experimental and theoretical aspects.* New York, NY: Harper & Row.

Cattell, R. B., Eber, H. W., & Tatsuoka, M. M. (1988) *Handbook for the Sixteen Personality Factor Questionnaire (16PF).* Champaign, Illinois: Institute for Personality and Ability Testing.

Corcoran, K., & Fischer, J. (1987). *Measures for clinical practice: A source book*. New York, NY: Free Press.

Duncan, B. L., & Miller, S.D. (2000). *The heroic client: Doing client-directed outcome-informed therapy*. San Francisco, CA: Jossey-Bass.

Fischer, J., & Corcoran, K. (1994). *Measures for clinical practice: A source book* (2nd ed., Vols. 1 & 2). New York, NY: Free Press.

Hudson, W. W. (1982). *The clinical measurement package: A field manual*. Chicago, IL: Dorsey. (Instrument available through The Dorsey Press, 224 South Michigan Avenue, Suite 440, Chicago, IL 60604.)

Luborsky, L., Singer, B., & Luborsky, L. (1975) Comparative studies of psychotherapies: Is it true that "everyone has won and all must have prizes"? *Archives of General Psychiatry*, *32*, 995–1008.

Olson, D. D., Portner, J., & Lavee, Y. (1985). FACES-III. St. Paul, MN: Family Social Science, University of Minnesota. (Instrument available through Dr. David H. Olson, Family Social Science, University of Minnesota, 290 McNicol Hall, 1985 Buford Avenue, St. Paul, MN 55108.)

Ontario College of Social Workers and Social Service Workers. (2000). *Code of ethics and standards of practice*. Toronto, Ontario: Author.

Polgar, A. T. (2005). *Conducting parenting capacity assessments: A manual for mental health practitioners*. Hamilton, Ontario: Sandrian.

Richmond, M. (1917). *Social diagnosis*. Philadelphia, PA: The Russell Sage Foundation.

Tallman, K., & Bohart, A. C. (1999). The client as a common factor: Clients as self-healers. In M. A. Hubble, B. L. Duncan, & S. D. Miller (Eds.), *The heart and soul of change: What works in therapy* (pp. 91–131). Washington, DC: American Psychological Association.

PART THREE

THE WAY AHEAD

We began this book with a sixfold purpose: (a) to contribute to the clarification of the meaning and use of the term *technique* in the vocabulary of our profession; (b) to urge that the concept be given a much higher status in the profession's lexicon than it has at present; (c) to present a collection of techniques already identified as being a part of our practice; (d) to provide brief case examples for each technique; (e) to help expand for students and practitioners the roster of techniques used in practice; and most important, (f) to urge a profession-wide process of encouraging the development, specification, evaluation, and expanded use of our range of techniques for the betterment of the clients we serve.

Implied in these goals is the expectation that the process of developing new techniques and assessing old ones will be an ongoing one as the profession expands its theoretical and methodological base, and as we learn from each other within the reality of an excitingly complex and diverse profession and clientele.

These goals all stem from our general commitment to evidence-based practice. As we move in this direction, it is essential that our evidence must be based both on the specific things we do in our interventions and our ability to identify them and assess their differential impacts.

To achieve these goals, several interlinking and interfacing processes would be required:

1. *Enhanced literary precision:* We hope that our profession's increasingly competent and highly productive group of authors use the term *technique* in a much more precise way than it has to the present. This requires that the term be kept distinct from the many terms with which it is often identified, as discussed in Part I, "Techniques in Social Work Practice: An Overview."

2. *Identification.* We need to keep reminding ourselves, as did Dr. Joel Fischer (Fischer, 1978) some years ago, that all of our practice is composed of a set of actions we take on behalf of clients. Together these actions comprise the range of techniques of which our practice is constructed. Because everything we do with a client is a group of techniques, we need to be able to specify the techniques we are using in particular cases. Otherwise we are practicing mystery or magic, or drawing on some diffuse perception of the power of the therapeutic relationship.

3. *Confidence:* We must not be uncomfortable with the word *technique* as has been the case over the years with other concepts, such as *treatment* and *diagnosis*. When we are tentative about a concept, we become imprecise. In so doing we deprive our clients of a quality of specificity that is essential to a practice such as ours.

4. *Research:* As we become more specific and precise in our use of the term *technique,* we will be in a much better position to assess the differential use of various techniques and their effects. As long as the concept remains imprecise, our inability to accurately assess the differential uses of each will continue.

   There are many questions about technique that we need to address in our research. We need more data on factors such as when various techniques are effective, when they are not, and with whom. We also need to explore the kinds of risks involved in the use of various techniques, including when particular techniques have the potential of being harmful and with what types of client. It is these kinds of research that will help us alter and adjust various techniques to make them more differentially effective, and, when necessary, to reduce their potential negative components in particular situations while ensuring that each is ethical and theoretically grounded.

Another research challenge is to continue to work on an agreed-upon definition of *technique,* so that when we discuss the concept we do so in a manner that ensures precision.

Stressing the need to measure the impact of various techniques does not, and will not, take away any aspect of our humanity, or our concern for, interest in, worry about, respect for, or admiration of our clients. Rather, it will expand it. It will mean that we will still be driven by our traditional value set, but this drive will be more effective as we learn to more consciously and skillfully apply these techniques of human interaction in a way that will enhance our effectiveness.

5. *Awards:* If we do implement the idea of giving technique greater focus, then it would be worthwhile to find ways to award colleagues for important, imaginative, useful, and tested new techniques. Identifying and recognizing new techniques or new uses of existing techniques would serve as a way of enriching practice on a broad basis, and would encourage and recognize ways in which theory can be applied in more effective and diverse ways.

6. *Diversity Awareness:* Further studies of technique would also help us better understand possible regional, cultural, and diversity issues that may be involved in the development, utility, sanctioning, and use of various techniques. We know in a general way what might be acceptable and even desirable with some clients, or what may not be acceptable to or efficacious for others. We now need to bring more precision to this area.

7. *Process of legitimization:* This is a more sensitive area. It has a twofold component. On one hand, we need to find ways to encourage the development, testing, and importance of technique. But on the other, we need to find a way of legitimizing technique.

We therefore need a range of ways in which new techniques and their testing are encouraged. But there also needs to be some process of professional gatekeeping to ensure that nothing potentially harmful to clients or the reputation of the profession becomes incorporated into its mores.

This is a complex and difficult road to travel, and we need to steer carefully between the Scylla of overenthusiastic and untested development of new techniques and the Charybdis of an overly stringent, limiting professional structure of approval. We need always to balance risks and advantages.

8. *Personal Preferences and Additional Sources:* There is nothing wrong, of course, with each of us having some favorite techniques. Just as we have favorite methods and theories that best fit our values, knowledge, worldview, human personality, and practice orientation, so too do we have preferred techniques. However, we need to be sure that we do not impose them on clients indiscriminately.

Each of us has a set of values and principles that influence not only our lifestyle in general, but also our professional practice and the spectrum of techniques to which we are drawn and that we avoid. Thus we need to be sure that our cadre of techniques are responsive to who the client is and what might best fit him or her. If necessary, we need to be ready to move toward those to which the client will be more responsive, even if they are not those that we prefer.

Even though techniques for the most part emerge from theory and method, we need to start to think about them as discrete entities separate from theory and method.

We need to get to know them in their own uniqueness and then connect or reconnect them to theories.

9. *Facilitating Development:* We want to be sure that we incorporate a watchdog functions in the profession to encourage responsible and effective creativity and novelty worldwide.

   We have long held that our practice is a combination of art and science. We are in a historic period that fosters development. Within the profession there is a greatly expanded view of practice, based on a multimethod and multitheoretical approach. This thrust, combined with the exciting new ways we have for gathering and sharing information, provides us with great opportunity. There has never been a better time in our profession to enhance our effectiveness through the study and expansion of our body of techniques than in the current climate. Let us seize this opportunity. Carpe diem!

10. *Process:* We need to encourage a process in ourselves and our colleagues that develops a habitual practice of asking what techniques come to mind, what techniques should we think about, or what techniques we should draw upon in a given situation. Our choice of techniques should be just as important as our choice of theory or method. Techniques should be chosen separately from theory and method, but always should be built upon the ongoing processes of assessment, diagnosis, and planned intervention.

11. *Technique's Identity:* Only when we give technique a life, specificity, and identity of its own will we learn to optimize its potential. By doing this, we will be able to identify its strengths, limitations, and risks. We will also be much more able to select a cluster of specific techniques for different purposes and different clients.

    It is quite all right, of course, and indeed desirable, that some colleagues become expert in some techniques or group of techniques, and use them almost exclusively, just as it possible to practice from a specific theoretical base. It helps the profession to have experts with various identified and specialized quality skills.

12. *An International Perspective:* A further strategy that may prove highly beneficial in our search to identify our cadre of techniques is to emphasize an international perspective. It is critically important to remember that all new ideas need not come from one part of the world. Rather, as we all begin to appreciate how much there is to learn about aspects of differentiation, this education will include the many ways in which humans have developed to assist each other on an interpersonal basis. Many of these ways have already been adopted into practice in different parts of the world. Our whole profession could learn much by identifying and sharing these techniques.

13. *"Show and Tell":* As we begin to emphasize technique, it is also important that we make more of an effort to share with each other those techniques with which we are experimenting and our findings as to their utility and limitations. We need to let others know what we are doing and to hear what others are doing as a way of expanding not only our own repertoire of techniques, but that of the profession. This sharing includes our comfort about discussing things that did not work when we tried them. It is by comparing and discussing our successes as well as our failures that we will advance our knowledge. This is turn will help us identify new areas of challenge and targets for research.

CONCLUSION

It is important to remind ourselves of the need for prudence and caution. Our techniques all must eventually be grounded into one or more theoretical bodies, even if they first emerge from other sources. This keeps open the possibility that a new theory or theoretical understanding will emerge from the development of new techniques.

If we move in this direction, there is the real and frightening risk of part or all of the profession becoming overly technique oriented. As with all professions, there are styles, fashions, and trends that come and go. There is a strong wish to be at the leading edge of practice, and we strive to get there. Certainly out of these trends and efforts new knowledge emerges, but sometimes not before harm has been done. Thus as we become more technique oriented, we must remain conscious of our responsibility to ensure that, in our commitment to be helpful, we pledge, as Hippocrates did many years ago, to "abstain from all intentional wrongdoing and harm." (*Bartlett's Familiar Quotations*). Throughout this process of making our spectrum of techniques more visible and operational, it is important that we continually connect technique to theory. Otherwise we are just functioning as technicians. Only when we can give a theoretical base or bases to such techniques can we use them to their optimum benefit. The importance of a technique is not its complexity or mystique, the degree of difficulty required to learn it, its remoteness from daily living, or its technological sophistication. Rather, its importance is in its potential and actual impact on the persons and systems with whom we interact professionally.

In the process of preparing this manuscript, we have been struck by the reality of how rich our practice is. There are just so many ways we have learned to connect to influence and help others. We need to reinforce awareness of this richness with each other, especially with our students, and foster an excitement about what we are doing.

We are well aware that there are many other techniques that we have not mentioned in this book, for several reasons. For one, we were not aware of them, or we were not sure if they were techniques. Also, in limiting the number of techniques addressed, we wanted to indicate there were many others. But this book is a start, and we will continue to struggle with this critical aspect of practice.

It may well be that identifying our entire range of techniques is similar to the challenge faced by astronomers to identify all of the galaxies in the universe. It was once believed they were few in number, but we now believe they may number in the hundreds of billions. So too it may be that there are not just these 101 techniques that we use in our practice, but indeed many, many hundreds. If so, we need to continue to try and identify them all.

During the process of developing this book, we met a colleague from a country far from here where kite flying is an important and common cultural and spiritual event. We learned how she was tapping this custom as a way of helping clients deal with troubled material from the past. Now that we have come to the end of this work, we hope it will serve to expand the range of human activities upon which we can draw to find even more effective ways of helping individuals, couples, families, groups, and societal systems achieve a better level of psychosocial functioning. In so doing, we will examine, analyze, and research even such activities as kite flying and any others that might emerge in such a way that will help us make more effective use of them for the sake of our clients.

Thus, as we get to know more about the therapeutic efficacy of kite flying—realistically and symbolically—we may judge it to be of equal importance to techniques developed by professionals in other disciplines seeking more efficient ways to facilitate space travel. Thus, telling a client to "go fly a kite" may lose its popular pejorative meaning in our culture, or its potential as a *Wheel of Fortune* clue, and be listed as an important, powerful, and widely used technique in clinical social work practice.

Bibliography

Abamowitz, L. (1993). Prayer as therapy among the frail Jewish elderly. *Journal of Gerontological Social Work, 19*(3/4), 69–75.

Abele, A. (1981). Acquaintance and visual behavior between two interactants: Their communicative function for the impression formation of an observer. *European Journal of Social Psychology, 11*(4), 409–425.

Abell, M. L., & Galinsky, M. J. (2002). Introducing students to computer-based group work. *Journal of Social Work Education, 38*(1), 39–54.

Adams, J., & Maynard, P. (2000). Evaluating training needs for home-based family therapy: A focus group approach. *American Journal of Family Therapy, 28*(1), 41–52.

Adeyemi, J. D., Olonade, P. O., & Amira, C. O. (2002). Attitude to psychiatric referral: A study of primary care physicians. *Nigerian Postgraduate Medical Journal, 9*(2), 53–58.

Adler, S., & Carrara, D. A. (1977). The therapeutic impact of listening. *Long Term Care & Health Services Administration Quarterly, 1*(1), 52–57.

Adolph, M. (1983). The all-women's consciousness raising group as a component of treatment for mental illness. *Social Work With Groups, 6*, 117–132.

Aiken, L. R. (1996). *Rating scales and checklists: Evaluating behavior, personality, and attitude.* New York, NY: Wiley.

Aksnes, H., & Ruud, E. (2008). Body-based schemata in receptive music therapy. *Musicae Scientiae, 12*, 49–74.

Aldridge, D. (1994). Single-case research designs for the creative art social worker. *The Arts in Psychotherapy, 21*(5), 333–342.

Alexander, P. (2003). Parent-child role reversal: Development of a measure and test of an attachment theory model. *Journal of Systemic Therapies, 22*, 31–44.

Allen, A. (1971). The fee as a therapeutic tool. *Psychoanalytic Quarterly, 40*, 132–140.

Allen, S. F., & Tracy, E. M. (2004). Revitalizing the role of home visiting by school social workers. *Children & Schools, 26*(4), 197–206.

Allery, J. R. The Gift, a narrative case study. *Reflections, 8*(4), 32–36.

Alschuler, M. (1997). Life stories—Biography and autobiography as healing tools for adults with mental illness. *Journal of Poetry Therapy, 11*(2), 113–117.

Alschuler, M. (2000). Healing from addictions through poetry therapy. *Journal of Poetry Therapy, 13*(3), 165–173.

Altshuler, S. J. (2003). From barriers to successful collaboration: Public schools and child welfare working together. *Social Work, 8*(1), 52–63.

Alvord, M. K., & Grados, J. J. (2005). Enhancing resilience in children: A proactive approach. *Professional Psychology—Research & Practice, 36*(3), 238–245.

Ammerman, R. T., Hersen, M., & Fishman, C. A. (1995). Handbook of child behavior therapy in the psychiatric setting. *Child & Family Behavior Therapy, 17*(4), 23–33.

Amoako, E., Skelly, A. H., & Rossen, E. K. (2008). Outcomes of an intervention to reduce uncertainty among African American women with diabetes. *Western Journal of Nursing Research, 30*(8), 928–942.

Amodeo, M., Grigg, S. D., & Robb, N. (1997). Working with foreign language interpreters: Guidelines for substance abuse clinicians and human service practitioners. *Treatment Quarterly, 15*(4) 75–87.

Anderson, F. (2001). Benefits of conducting research. *Art Therapy: Journal of the American Art Therapy Association, 18*(3), 134–141.

Anderson, H. (2001). Postmodern collaborative and person-centred therapies: What would Carl Rogers say? *Journal of Family Therapy, 23,* 339.

Anderson, J. (1996). Yes, but IS IT empowerment? Initiation, implementation and outcomes of community action. In B. Humphries (Ed.), *Critical perspectives on empowerment* (pp. 69–84). Birmingham: Venture Press.

Anderson, S. L., & Mandell, D. L. (1989). The use of self-disclosure by professional social workers. *Social Casework, 70*(6), 259–267.

Andreasen, N. C., O'Leary, D. S., Cizadlo, T., Arndt, S., Rezai, K., Watkins, L. G., Boles Ponto, L. L., & Hichwa, R. D. (1995). Remembering the past: Two facets of episodic memory explored with positron emission tomography. *American Journal of Psychiatry, 152*(11), 1576–1585.

Andsell, G., & Pavlicevic, M. (2001). *Beginning research in the arts therapies.* London: Jessica Kingsley Publishers.

Arauzo, A. C., Watson, M., & Hulgus, J. (1994). The clinical uses of video therapy in the treatment of childhood sexual trauma survivors. *Journal of Child Sexual Abuse, 3*(4), 37–57.

Areán, P., Hegel, M., Vannoy, S., Fan, M., & Unuzter, J. (2008). Effectiveness of problem-solving therapy for older, primary care patients with depression: Results from the IMPACT project. *The Gerontologist, 48*(3), 311–323.

Areán, P. A., Perri, M. G., Nezu, A. M., Schein, R. L., Christopher, F., & Joseph, T. X. (1993). Comparative effectiveness of social problem-solving therapy and reminiscence therapy as treatment for depression in older adults. *Journal of Consulting and Clinical Psychology, 61*(6), 1003–1010.

Argyle, M. (1972). Non-verbal communication in human social interaction. In R. A. Hinde (Ed.), *Non-verbal communication* (pp. 243–269). Cambridge, England: Cambridge University Press.

Argyle, M., & Cook, M. (1976). *Gaze and mutual gaze.* London: Cambridge University Press.

Argyle, M., & Dean, J. (1965). Eye contact, distance and affiliation. *Sociometry, 28*(3), 289–304.

Armstrong, L. (1999). The well-built clinical question: The key to finding the best evidence efficiently. *Wisconsin Medical Journal, 98*(2), 25–28.

Ashworth, M., Clement, S., Sandu, J., Farley, N., Ramsey, R., & Davies, T. (2002). Psychiatric referral rates and the influence of on-site mental health workers in general practice. *British Journal of General Practice, 52*(474), 39–41.

Atshuler, S. J. (1999). Constructing genograms with children in care: Implications for casework practice. *Child Welfare, 78*(6), 777–790.

Aubin, G., Chapparo, C., Gelinas, I., Stip, E., & Rainville, C. (2009). Use of the perceive, recall, plan and perform system of task analysis for persons with schizophrenia: A preliminary study. *Australian Occupational Therapy Journal, 56*(3), 189–199.

Audet, C. T., & Everall, R. D. (2010). Social worker self-disclosure and the therapeutic relationship: A phenomenological study from the client perspective. *British Journal of Guidance & Counselling, 38*(3), 327–342.

Austin, L. (1948). Trends in differential treatment in social casework. *Journal of Social Casework, 29*, 203–211.

Avrahami, E. (2003). Cognitive-behavioral approach in psychodrama: Discussion and example from addiction treatment. *The Arts in Psychotherapy, 30*(4), 209–216.

Axline, V. (1950). Entering the child's world via play experiences. *Progressive Education, 27*, 68–75.

Ayalon, L., Bornfeld, H., Gum, A. M., & Areán, P. A. (2009). The use of problem-solving therapy and restraint-free environment for the management of depression and agitation in long-term care. *Clinical Gerontologist: The Journal of Aging and Mental Health, 32*(1), 77–90.

Ayres, J. (1986). Perceptions of speaking ability: An explanation for stage fright. *Communication Education, 35*(3), 275–287.

Ayres, J. (1988). Coping with speech anxiety: The power of positive thinking. *Communication Education, 37*(4), 289–296.

Ayres, J., & Hopf, T. (1993). *Coping with speech anxiety.* Norwood, NJ: Ablex.

Bacigalupe, G. (1996). Writing letters in therapy: A participatory approach. *Journal of Family Therapy, 18*(4), 361–373.

Badger, J. (2010). Assessing reflective thinking: Pre-service teachers' and professors' perceptions of an oral examination. *Assessment in Education: Principles, Policy & Practice, 17*(1), 77–89.

Baer, R. A. (2003). Mindfulness training as a clinical intervention: A conceptual and empirical review. *Clinical Psychology: Science and Practice, 10*(2), 125–143.

Bagarozzi, D. A. (1990). Marital power discrepancies and symptom development in spouses: An empirical investigation. *American Journal of Family Therapy, 18*(1), 51–64.

Bagwell-Reese, M. K., & Brack, G. (1997). The therapeutic use of reframing and worldview in mental health counseling. *Journal of Mental Health Counseling, 19*(1), 78–86.

Ballou, M. B. (1995). *Psychological interventions: A guide to strategies.* Westport, CT: Praeger.

Bannan, N. (2010). Group-based problem-solving therapy in self-poisoning females: A pilot study. *Counselling & Psychotherapy Research, 10*(3), 201–213.

Bannick, F. P. (2007). Solution-focused mediation: The future with a difference. *Conflict Resolution Quarterly, 25*(2), 163–183.

Barish, S. (1975). Lend me your ear: An exploration of clinical listening. *Clinical Social Work Journal, 3*(2), 75–84.

Barker, R. (Ed.). (2003). *The social work dictionary* (5th ed.). Washington, DC: NASW Press.

Barker, R. L. (1986). Fee splitting: A growing ethical problem. *Journal of Independent Social Work, 1*(2), 1–3.

Barkham, M., Shapiro, D. A., & Firth-Cozens, J. (1989). Personal questionnaire changes in prescriptive vs. exploratory psychotherapy. *British Journal of Clinical Psychology, 28*(2), 97–107.

Barretta-Herman, A. (1990). The effective social service staff meeting. In F. Slegio (Ed.), *Business communication: New Zealand perspectives* (pp. 136–147). Auckland, New Zealand: Software Technology.

Barry, T. D., Dunlap, S. T., Lochman, J. E., & Wells, K. C. (2009). Inconsistent discipline as a mediator between maternal distress and aggression in boys. *Child & Family Behavior Therapy, 31*(1), 1–19.

Barsalou, L. W. (1988). The content and organisation of autobiographical memories. In U. Neisser & E. Winograd (Eds.), *Remembering reconsidered: Ecological and traditional approaches to the study of memory* (pp. 193–243). New York, NY: Cambridge University Press.

Barsky, M. (1984). Strategies and techniques of divorce mediation. *Social Casework, 65*(2), 102–108.

Barth, F. D. (2001). Money as a tool for negotiating separateness and connectedness in the therapeutic relationship. *Clinical Social Work Journal, 29*(1), 79–94.

Barth, F. D. (2005). Money as a tool for negotiating separateness and connectedness in the therapeutic relationship. In F. Turner (Ed.), *Social work diagnosis in contemporary practice* (pp. 701–710). New York, NY: Oxford University Press.

Bateman, N. (2000). *Advocacy skills for health and social care professionals.* Philadelphia, PA: Jessica Kingsley.

Bathgate, O. (2009). Review of "Genograms: Assessment and intervention." *Clinical Child Psychology and Psychiatry, 14*(3), 462–463.

Bayer, A. M., Gilman, R. H., Tsui, A. O., & Hindin, M. J. (2010). What is adolescence? Adolescents narrate their lives in Lima, Peru. *Journal of Adolescence, 33*(4), 509–520.

Beauchemin, J., Hutchins, T. L., & Patterson, F. (2008). Mindfulness meditation may lessen anxiety, promote social skills, and improve academic performance among adolescents with learning disabilities. *Complementary Health Practice Review, 13*(1), 34–45.

Beauchesne, M., Kelley, B., & Gauthier, M. A. (1997). The genogram: A health assessment tool. *Nurse Educator, 22*(3), 9–16.

Beaulieu, E. M. (2002). *A guide for nursing home social workers.* New York, NY: Springer.

Beck, A.T. (1967). *Depression: Clinical, experimental and theoretical aspects.* New York, NY: Harper & Row.

Beck, A. T. (1995). *Cognitive therapy: Basics and beyond.* New York, NY: Guilford Press.

Beck, A. T., Rush, A. J., Shaw, F. F., & Emery, G. (1979). *Cognitive therapy of depression.* New York, NY: Guilford Press.

Beckman, P. J., & Kohl, F. L. (1984). The effects of social and isolate toys on the interactions and play of integrated and nonintegrated groups of preschoolers. *Education and Training of the Mentally Retarded, 19*(3), 169–174.

Behnke, R. R., & Sawyer, C. R. (2001). Patterns of psychological state anxiety in public speaking as a function of anxiety sensitivity. *Communication Quarterly, 49*, 84–94.

Behrens, M., & Nathan, A. (1956). The home visit as an aid in family diagnosis and therapy. *Social Casework, 37*(1), 11–20.

Belcher, J. R., & Casey, T. (2001). Social work and deliverance practice: The Pentecostal experience. *Families in Society, 82*(1), 61–68.

Bell, L. (2009). Mindful psychotherapy. *Journal of Spirituality in Mental Health, 11*(1–2), 126–144.

Bell-Pringle, V. J., Jurkovic, G. J., & Pate, J. L. (2004). Writing about upsetting family events: A therapy analog study. *Journal of Contemporary Psychotherapy, 34*(4), 341–349.

Bennett, L. A., Wolin, S. J., & McAvity, K. J. (1988). Family identity, ritual, and myth: A cultural perspective on life cycle transitions. In C. J. Falicov (Ed.), *Family transitions: Continuity and change over the life cycle* (pp. 211–232). New York, NY: Guilford Press.

Benson, H. (1974). *The relaxation response.* New York, NY: Avon Books.

Bentley, K. J., & Walsh, J. (2001). *The social worker and psychotropic medication: Toward effective collaboration with mental health clients families and providers* (2nd ed.). Belmont, CA: Wadsworth.

Bentley, K. J., Walsh, J., & Farmer, R. (2005). Referring clients for psychiatric medication: Best practices for social workers. *Best Practices in Mental Health, 1*(1), 59–71.

Berg, I. K., & de Shazer, S. (1993). Making numbers talk: Language in therapy. In S. Friedman (Ed.), *The new language of change* (pp. 5–24). New York, NY: Guilford Press.

Berg, I. K., & Miller, S. D. (1992). *Working with the problem drinker: A solution-focused approach.* New York, NY: Norton.

Berger, A. A. (1993). *Improving writing skills: Memos, letters reports and proposals.* Newbury Park, CA: Sage.

Berkman, B., & D'Ambruoso, S. (2006). *Handbook of social work in health and aging.* New York, NY: Oxford University Press.

Berman, J. S., & Yoken, C. (1984). Does paying a fee for psychotherapy alter the effectiveness of treatment? *Journal of Consulting and Clinical Psychology, 52*(2), 254–260.

Bernstein, D. A., Borkovec, T. D., & Hazlett-Stevens, H. (2000). *New directions in progressive relaxation training: A guidebook for helping professionals.* New York, NY: Praeger.

Bernstein, E., Wallerstein, N., Braithwaite, R., Gutierrez, L., Labonte, R., & Zimmerman, M. A. (1994). Empowerment forum—A dialog between guest editorial-board members. *Health Education Quarterly, 21*(3), 281–294.

Berube, L. (1999). Dream work: Demystifying dreams using a small group for personal growth. *Journal for Specialists in Group Work, 24*(1), 88–101.

Betts, D. J. (2003). *Creative arts therapies approaches in adoption and foster care: Contemporary strategies for working with individuals and families.* Springfield, IL: Charles C. Thomas.

Betts, D. J., & Laloge, L. (2000). Art social workers and research: A survey conducted by the Potomac Art Therapy Association. *Art Therapy: Journal of the American Art Therapy Association, 17*(4), 291–295.

Betts, G. R., & Remer, R. (1993). The impact of paradoxical interventions on perceptions of the social worker and ratings of treatment acceptability. *Professional Psychology—Research & Practice, 24*(2), 164–170.

Beutler, L. E., & Harwood, M. T. (2000). *Prescriptive psychotherapy.* New York, NY: Oxford University Press.

Beutler, L. E., & Harwood, T. M. (1995). Prescriptive psychotherapies. *Applied and Preventive Psychology, 4*, 89–100.

Beutler, L. E., Consoli, A. J., & Lane, G. (2005). Systematic treatment selection and prescriptive psychotherapy: An integrative eclectic approach. In J. C. Norcross & M. R. Goldfried (Eds.), *Handbook of psychotherapy integration* (pp. 121–143). New York, NY: Oxford University Press.

Beyer, M. (1986). Overcoming emotional obstacles to independence. *Children Today, 15*(5), 8–12.

Bigelow, K. M., & Lutzker, J. R. (1998). Using video to teach planned activities to parents reported for child abuse. *Child & Family Behavior Therapy, 20*(4), 1–14.

Bishop, D. R., & Eppolito, J. M. (1992). The clinical management of client dynamics and fees for psychotherapy: Implications for research and practice. *Psychotherapy: Theory, Research, Practice, Training, 29*(4), 545–553.

Black, D. W., Allen, J., St. John, D., Pfohl, B., McCormick, B., & Blum, N. (2009). Predictors of response to systems training for emotional predictability and problem solving (STEPPS) for borderline personality disorder: An exploratory study. *Acta Psychiatrica Scandinavica, 120*(1), 53–61.

Blanton, P. G. (2007). Adding silence to stories: Narrative therapy and contemplation. *Contemporary Family Therapy: An International Journal, 29*(4), 211–221.

Blanton, P. G. (2006). Introducing letter writing into Christian psychotherapy. *Journal of Psychology and Christianity, 25*(1), 77–86.

Bloch, M. H., & Rubenstein, H. (1986). Paying for service: What do clinical social workers believe? *Journal of Social Service Research, 9*(4), 21–35.

Bloom, L. J., Weigel, R. G., & Trautt, G. M. (1977). "Therapeutic" factors in psychotherapy: Effects of office décor and subject, social worker sex pairing on the perception of credibility. *Journal of Consulting and Clinical Psychology, 45*(5), 867–873.

Bloom, M. L. (1973). Usefulness of the home visit for diagnosis and treatment. *Social Casework, 54*(2), 67–75.

Bloomgarden. J., & Netzer, D. (1998). Validating art social workers' tacit knowing: The heuristic experience. *Art Therapy: Journal of the American Art Therapy Association, 15*(1), 51–54.

Blot, K. J., Zarate, M. A., & Paulus, P. B. (2003). Code-switching across brainstorming sessions: Implications for the revised hierarchical model of bilingual language processing. *Experimental Psychology, 50*(3), 171–183.

Bluck, S. (2001). Autobiographical memories: A building block of life narratives. In G. M. Kenyon, P. G. Clark, & B. de Vries (Eds.), *Narrative gerontology: Theory, research, and practice* (pp. 67–89). New York, NY: Springer.

Bluck, S. (2003). Autobiographical memory: Exploring its functions in everyday life. *Memory, 11*(2), 113–123.

Bluck, S., & Alea, N. (2002). Exploring the functions of autobiographical memory: Why do I remember the autumn? In J. D. Webster & B. K. Haight (Eds.), *Critical advances in reminiscence: From theory to application* (pp. 61–75). New York, NY: Springer.

Bluck, S., Alea, N., Habermas, T., & Rubin, D. R. (2005). A tale of three functions: The self-reported uses of autobiographical memory. *Social Cognition, 23*(1), 91–117.

Bluck, S., & Habermas, T. (2000). The life story schema. *Motivation and Emotion, 24*(2), 121–147.

Blunt, K. (2007). Social work education: Achieving transformative learning through a cultural competence model for transformative education. *Journal of Teaching in Social Work, 27*(3/4), 93–114.

Bobes, T., & Rothman, B. (2002). *Doing couple therapy: Integrating theory with practice.* New York, NY: Norton.

Bobevski, I., Holgate, A. M., & McLennan, J. (1997). Characteristics of effective telephone counselling skills. *British Journal of Guidance & Counselling, 25*(2), 239–249.

Bodie, G. D. (2010). A racing heart, rattling knees, and ruminative thoughts: Defining, explaining, and treating public speaking anxiety. *Communication Education, 59*(1), 70–105.

Boehm, A., & Staples, L. H. (2004). Empowerment: The point of view of consumers. *Families in Society: The Journal of Contemporary Social Services, 85*(2), 270–280.

Bogolub, E. B. (1986). Tape recorders in clinical sessions: Deliberate and fortuitous effects. *Youth and Adolescence, 10*, 255–262.

Bohart, A. C. (1977). Role playing and interpersonal conflict resolution. *Journal of Counseling Psychology, 24*(1), 15–24.

Boies, K. G. (1972). Role playing as a behavior change technique: Review of the empirical literature. *Psychotherapy: Theory, Research and Practice, 9*(2), 185–192.

Bolton, B., & Brookings, J. (1998). Development of a measure of intrapersonal empowerment. *Rehabilitation Psychology, 43*, 131–142. doi: 10.1037/0090-5550.43.2.131

Bombardier, C. H., Bell, K. R., Temkin, N. R., Fann, J. R., Hoffman, J., & Dikmen, S. (2009). The efficacy of a scheduled telephone intervention for ameliorating depressive symptoms during the first year after traumatic brain injury. *Journal of Head Trauma Rehabilitation, 24*(4), 230–238.

Borenstein, L. (2003). The clinician as a dreamcatcher: Holding the dream. *Clinical Social Work Journal, 31*(30), 249–262.

Borenzweig, H. (1981). Agency vs. private practice: Similarities and differences. *Social Work, 26*, 239–244.

Borenzwig, H. (1983). Touching in clinical social work. *Social Casework*, *64*(4), 238–242.

Borkovec, T. D., & Costello, E. (1993). Efficacy of applied relaxation and cognitive-behavioral therapy in the treatment of generalized anxiety disorder. *Journal of Consulting and Clinical Psychology*, *61*(4), 611–619.

Borneman, E. (1976). *The psychoanalysis of money*. New York, NY: Urizen Books.

Boso, M., Emanuele, E., Minazzi, V., Abbamonte, M., & Politi, P. (2007). Effect of long-term interactive music therapy on behavior profile and musical skills in young adults with severe autism. *The Journal of Alternative and Complementary Medicine*, *13*(7), 709–712.

Bossard, J. H. S., & Boll, E. S. (1949). Ritual in family living. *American Sociological Review*, *14*(4), 463–469.

Botella, C., Gallego, M. J., Garcia-Palacios, A., Baños, R. M., Quero, S., Alcañiz, M. (2009). The acceptability of an internet-based self-help treatment for fear of public speaking. *British Journal of Guidance & Counselling*, *37*(3), 297–311.

Botella, C., Guillén, V., Banos, R. M., Garcia-Palacios, A., Gallego, M. J., & Alcañiz, M. (2007). Telepsychology and self-help: The treatment of fear of public speaking. *Cognitive and Behavioural Practice*, *14*(1), 46–57.

Botella, C., Hofmann, S. G., & Moscovitz, D. A. (2004). A self-applied internet-based intervention for fear of public speaking. *Journal of Clinical Psychology*, *60*, 1–10.

Botello, R. K., & Krout, R. E. (2008). Music therapy assessment of automatic thoughts: Developing a cognitive behavioral application of improvisation to assess couple communication. *Music Therapy Perspectives*, *26*, 51–55.

Bowen, C. J., & Howie, P. M. (2002). Context and cue cards in young children's testimony: A comparison of brief narrative elaboration and context reinstatement. *Journal of Applied Psychology*, *87*(6), 1077–1085.

Bowes, A., & Sim, D. (2006). Advocacy for black and minority ethnic communities: Understandings and expectations. *British Journal of Social Work*, *36*, 1209–1225.

Box, G. E. P., & Jenkins, G. M. (1970). *Time-series analysis: Forecasting and control*. San Francisco, CA: Holden-Day.

Brack, G., Brack, C., & Hartson, D. (1991). When a reframe fails: Explorations into students' ecosystems. *Journal of College Student Psychotherapy*, *6*(2), 103–118.

Brakel, L. W. (1993). Shall drawing become part of free association? Proposal for a modification in psychoanalytic technique. *Journal of the American Psychoanalytic Association*, *41*(2), 359–394.

Brandell, J. R. (1997). *Theory and practice in clinical social work*. New York, NY: Free Press.

Brandell, J. R. (2004). *Psychodynamic social work*. New York, NY: Columbia University Press.

Brandell, J. R. (2010). *Theory & practice in clinical social work*. (2nd ed.). Thousand Oaks, CA: Sage.

Bransford, C. L. (2005). Conceptions of authority within contemporary social work practice in managed mental health care organizations. *American Journal of Orthopsychiatry*, *75*(3), 409–420.

Bratter, T. (1967). Dynamics of role reversal. *Group Psychotherapy*, *20*, 88–94.

Braye S., & Preston-Shoot, M. (1995). *Empowering practice in social care*. Buckingham: Open University Press.

Breed, G., & Porter, M. (1972). Eye contact, attitudes, and attitude change among males. *Journal of Social Psychology*, *120*, 211–217.

Brennan, L., Giovannetti, T., Libon, D. J., Bettcher, B. M., & Duey, K. (2009). The impact of goal cues on everyday action performance in dementia. *Neuropsychological Rehabilitation*, *19*(4), 562–582.

Brennan, P. F., Moore, S. M., & Smyth, K. A. (1992). Alzheimer's disease caregivers' uses of a computer network. *Western Journal of Nursing Research*, *14*, 662–673.

Brenneis, C. B. (1994). Observation and psychoanalytic listening. *Psychoanalytic Quarterly*, *63*(1), 29–53.

Brewer, U. (1993). Using the role-reversal technique in an industrial setting. *Journal of Group Psychotherapy, Psychodrama and Sociometry*, *46*(2), 73–74.

Brewer, W. F. (1986). What is autobiographical memory? In D. C. Rubin (Ed.), *Autobiographical memory*. Cambridge, England: Cambridge University Press.

Bricker-Jenkins, M. (2002). Feminist issues and practices in social work. In A. R. Brillinger (Ed.), *Time series: Data analysis and theory*. San Francisco, CA: Holden-Day.

Broder, M. S. (2000). Making optimal use of homework to enhance your therapeutic effectiveness. *Journal of Rational-Emotive & Cognitive-Behavior Therapy*, *18*(1), 3–18.

Brookes, M. J., & Kaplan, A. (1972). The office environment: Space planning and affective behavior. *Human Factors*, *14*(5), 373–391.

Brown, G. R. (1987). Therapeutic effect of silence: Application to a case of borderline personality. *Psychoanalytic Technique*, *4*,123–130.

Brown, J. E., & Slee, P. T. (1986). Paradoxical strategies: The ethics of intervention. *Professional Psychology: Research and Practice*, *17*(6), 487–491.

Brown, K. W., & Ryan, R. M. (2003). The benefits of being present: Mindfulness and its role in psychological well-being. *Journal of Personality and Social Psychology*, *84*(4), 822–848.

Brown, V. R., & Paulus, P. B. (2002). Making group brainstorming more effective: Recommendations from an associative memory perspective. *Current Directions in Psychological Science*, *11*(6), 208–212.

Brownell, P. (1997). The application of the culturalgram in cross-cultural practice with elder abuse victims. *Journal of Elder Abuse and Neglect*, *9*(2), 19–33.

Brownell, P., & Congress, E. P. (1998). Application of the culturagram to assess and empower culturally and ethnically diverse battered women. In A. R. Roberts (Ed.), *Battered women and their families: Intervention and treatment strategies* (pp. 387–404). New York, NY: Springer.

Brunson, J. G., & Lawrence, P. S. (2002). Impact of sign language interpreter and social worker moods on deaf recipient mood. *Professional Psychology: Research and Practice*, *33*(6), 576–580.

Brydon, K. (2010). Social work advocacy in Singapore: Some reflections on the constraints and opportunities. *Asian Social Work and Policy Review*, *4*(3), 119–133.

Budgen, D., Turner, M., Kotsiopoulos, I., Zhu, F., Russell, M., Rigby, M., … Layzell, P. (2003). *Managing health care information: The role of the broker. In From grid to health grid: Proceedings of health GRID* (pp. 3–16). Oxford, England: IOS Press.

Buelow, S. A., Lyddon, W. J., & Johnson, J. T. (2002). Client attachment and coping resources. *Counselling Psychology Quarterly*, *15*(2), 145–152.

Burns, D. D., & Auerbach, A. H. (1992). Does homework compliance enhance recovery from depression? *Psychiatric Annals*, *22*(9), 464–469.

Burns, G. L., & Kondrick, P. A. (1998). Psychological behaviorism's reading therapy program: Parents as reading social workers for their children's reading disability. *Journal of Learning Disabilities*, *31*(3), 278–285.

Burns, T., Fioritti, A., Holloway F., et al. (2001). Case management and assertive community treatment in Europe. *Psychiatric Services*, *52*, 631–636.

Burnside, M., & Krueger, D. (Eds.). (1986). *Fee practices of male and female social workers. In The fast taboo: Money as symbol and reality in psychotherapy and psychoanalysis* (pp. 48–54). New York, NY: Brunner/Mazel.

Burt, C. D. B., Kemp, S., & Conway, M. A. (2003). Themes, events, and episodes in autobiographical memory. *Memory & Cognition*, *31*(2), 317–325.

Busch, A. M., Uebelacker, L. A., Kalibatseva, Z., & Miller, I. W. (2010). Measuring homework completion in behavioral activation. *Behavior Modification, 34*(4), 310–329.

Butler, S. R, Flasher, L. V., & Strupp, H. H. (1993). Countertransference and qualities of the social worker. In N. Miller, L. Luborsky, J. Barber, & J. Docherty (Eds.), *Psychoanalytic treatment research: A handbook for clinical practice* (pp. 342–360). New York, NY: Basic Books.

Byrd, M. E. (2006). Social exchange as a framework for client-nurse interaction during public health nursing maternal-child home visits. *Public Health Nursing, 23*(3), 271–276.

Cade, B. (1984). Paradoxical techniques in therapy. *Journal of Child Psychology and Psychiatry, 25*(4), 509–516.

Canada, E. R. (1989). Therapeutic use of writing and other media with Southeast Asian refugees. *Journal of Independent Social Work, 4*(2), 47–60.

Caplan, G. (1970). *The theory and practice of mental health consultation.* New York, NY: Basic Books.

Carew, L. (2009). Does theoretical background influence social workers' attitudes to social worker self-disclosure? A qualitative study. *Counselling & Psychotherapy Research, 9*(4), 266–272.

Cargo, M., Grams, G. D., Ottoson, J. M., Ward, P., & Green, L. W. (2004). Empowerment as fostering positive youth development and citizenship. *American Journal of Health Behavior, 27*(Suppl. 1), S66–S79.

Carlbring, P., Bohman, S., Brunt, S., Buhrman, M., Westling, B., Ekselius, L., & Andersson, G. (2007). A randomized trial of Internet-based cognitive behavioural therapy supplemented with telephone calls. *American Journal of Psychiatry, 163*(12), 2119–2125.

Carlson, B. E., & Larkin, H. (2009). Meditation as a coping intervention for treatment of addiction. *Journal of Religion & Spirituality in Social Work, 28*(4), 379–392.

Carolan, R. (2001). Models and paradigms of art therapy research. *Art Therapy: Journal of the American Art Therapy Association, 18*(4), 190–206.

Carpenter-Aeby, T., Aeby, V. G., & Boyd, J. S. (2007). Ecomaps as visual tools for deconstructing reciprocal influences: Triage with disruptive students at an alternative school. *The School Community Journal, 17*(2), 45–72.

Carr, J. E., & Fox, E. J. (2009). Using video technology to disseminate behavioral procedures: A review of functional analysis: A guide for understanding challenging behavior (DVD). *Journal of Applied Behavior Analysis, 42*(4), 919–923.

Carter, M., & O'Gorman Hughes, C. (2001). Toys and materials as setting events on the social interaction of preschool children. *Australasian Journal of Special Education, 25*(1 & 2), 49–66.

Caruth, M., Lopez, D., Martell, Z. L., Miller, K. E., & Pazdirek, L. (2005). The role of interpreters in psychotherapy with refugees: An exploratory study. *American Journal of Orthopsychiatry, 75*(1), 27–39.

Cary, M. S. (1978). The role of gaze in the initiation of conversation. *Social Psychology, 41*(3), 269–271.

Castro, R., Casique, I., & Brindis, C. D. (2008). Empowerment and physical violence throughout women's reproductive life in Mexico. *Violence Against Women, 14*(6), 655–677. doi:10.1177/1077801208319102

Cattaneo, L. B., & Chapman, A. R. (2010). The process of empowerment: A model for use in research and practice. *American Psychologist, 65*(7), 646–659.

Cattell, R. B., Eber, H. W., & Tatsuoka, M. M. (1988). *Handbook for the Sixteen Personality Factor Questionnaire (IGPF).* Champaign, IL: Institute for Personality and Ability Testing.

Cavell, T. A., Frentz, C. E., & Kelley, M. L. (1986). Acceptability of paradoxical interventions: Some nonparadoxical findings. *Professional Psychology: Research and Practice, 17*(6), 519–523.

Ceranoglu, T. A. (2010). Video games in psychotherapy. *Review of General Psychology, 14*(2), 141–146.

Chang, J. (1991). Using relaxation strategies in child and youth care practice. *Child and Youth Care Forum, 20*, 155–169.

Charlop-Christy, M. H., & Kelso, S. E. (2003). Teaching children with autism conversational speech using a cue card/written script program. *Education and Treatment of Children, 26*(2), 108–127.

Chatfield, C. (1984). *The analysis of time series: An introduction*. London, England: Chapman & Hall.

Cherulnik, P. D., Neelv, W. T., Flanagan, M., & Zachau, M. (1978). Social skill and visual interaction. *Journal of Social Psychology, 104*, 263–270.

Chinman, M. J., & Linney, J. A. (1998). Toward a model of adolescent empowerment: Theoretical and empirical evidence. *The Journal of Primary Prevention, 18*(4), 393–413.

Chlan, L. (2009). A review of the evidence for music intervention to manage anxiety in critically ill patients receiving ventilatory support. *Archives of Psychiatric Nursing, 23*, 177–179.

Choi, A-N., Lee, M.S., Cheong, K-J., & Lee, J-S. (2009). Effects of group music intervention on behavioral and psychological symptoms in patients with dementia: A pilot-controlled trial. *International Journal of Neuroscience, 119*(4), 471–481.

Christensen, D. N., Todahl, J., & Barrett, W. C. (1999). *Solution-based casework: An introduction to clinical and case management skills in casework practice*. New York, NY: Aldine De Gruyter.

Chrzastowski, S. (2007). Comparison of separation patterns between parents and offspring in psychiatric and nonclinical families. *Psychological Reports, 101*(1), 171–176.

Chung, Y., & Kwon, J. (2008). The efficacy of bibliotherapy for social phobia. *Brief Treatment & Crisis Intervention, 8*(4), 390–401.

Cigno, K., & Gore, J. (1999). A seamless service: Meeting the needs of children with disabilities through a multi-agency approach. *Child and Family Social Work, 4*, 325–335.

Citron-Bagget, S., & Kempler, B. (1991). Fee setting: Dynamic issues for social workers in independent practice. *Psychotherapy in Private Practice, 9*(1), 45–60.

Claiborn, C. D. (1982). Interpretation and change in counseling. *Journal of Counseling Psychology, 26*, 378–383.

Clare, M. (1991). Supervision and consultation in social work: A manageable responsibility? *Australian Social Work, 44*(1), 3–10.

Clark, A. J. (1995). An examination of the technique of interpretation in counseling. *Journal of Counseling and Development, 73*(5), 483–490.

Clark, D. M., Ehlers, A., Hackmann, A., McManus, F., Fennell, M., Grey, N., Waddington, L., & Wild, J. (2006). Cognitive therapy versus exposure and applied relaxation in social phobia: A randomized controlled trial. *Journal of Consulting and Clinical Psychology, 74*(3), 568–578.

Clark, E. J. (2007). *Advocacy: Profession's cornerstone*. Washington, DC: NASW

Clark, J. J., Godlaski, T., & Leukefeld, C. (1999). Case management and behavioral contracting: Components of rural substance abuse treatment. *Journal of Substance Abuse Treatment, 17*(4), 293–304.

Clarke, G. (1997). *The photograph*. Oxford, England: Oxford University Press.

Clarke, K. (1989). Creation of meaning: An emotional processing task in psychotherapy. *Psychotherapy, 26*, 139–148.

Clements-Cortes, A. (2008). Music to shatter the silence: A case study on music therapy, trauma, and the Holocaust. *Canadian Journal of Music Therapy, 14*, 9–21.

Coady, N., & Lehman, P. (2007). *Theoretical perspectives for direct social work practice: A generalist-eclectic approach*. New York, NY: Springer.

Coady, N., & Lehman, P. (2008). (2nd ed.). *Theoretical perspectives for direct social work practice: A generalist-eclectic approach*. New York, NY: Springer.

Daniel O., & Halfacre, D. (1994). Poetry therapy with the sexually abused adolescent: A case study. *The Arts in Psychotherapy*, *21*(1), 11–16.

Dattalo, P. (1998). Time series analysis: Concepts and techniques for community practitioners. *Journal of Community Practice*, *5*(4), 67–85.

Dattilio, F. M. (2002). Homework assignments in couple and family therapy. *Journal of Clinical Psychology*, *58*(5), 535–547.

Davidson, H., & Birmingham, C. L. (2001). Letter writing as a therapeutic tool. *Eating and Weight Disorders*, *6*(1), 40–44.

Davidson, K. W., & Clarke, S. S. (1989). *Social work in health care: A handbook for practice* (Vol. 1). Binghamton, NY: Haworth Press.

Davies, C., Guck, I., & Roscoe, I. (1979). The architectural design of a psychotherapeutic milieu. *Hospital Community Psychiatry*, *30*, 453–460.

Davies, P. G. K. (1982). The functioning of British counselling hotlines: A pilot study. *British Journal of Guidance and Counselling*, *10*(2), 195–199.

Davis, C., Baldry, E., Milosevic, B., & Walsh, A. (2004). Defining the role of the hospital social worker in Australia. *International Social Work*, *47*(3), 346–358.

Davis, C., Milosevic, B., Baldry, E., & Walsh, A. (2005). Defining the role of the hospital social worker in Australia: Part 2. A qualitative approach. *International Social Work*, *48*(3), 289–299.

Davis, L., Geikie, G., & Schamess, G. (1988). The use of genograms in a group for latency age children. *International Journal of Group Psychotherapy*, *38*, 189–210.

De, J. P. (1995). How to interview for client strengths. *Social Work*, *40*(6), 729–736.

Deaver, S. P. (2002). What constitutes art therapy research? *Art Therapy: Journal of the American Art Therapy Association*, *19*(1), 23–27.

de Graaf, H. (1993). Computer use in social work: Pioneers and innovators. *International Journal of Sociology and Social Policy*, *10*(4/5/6), pp. 241–250.

Dell, P. F. (1986). Why do we still call them "paradoxes"? *Family Process*, *25*(2), 223–234.

Dembicki, D., & Anderson, J. (1996). Pet ownership may be a factor in improved health of the elderly. *Journal of Nutrition for the Elderly*, *15*(3), 15–31.

DeMuth, N., & Kamis, E. (1980). Fees and therapy: Clarification of the relationship of payment source to service utilization. *Journal of Consulting and Clinical Psychology*, *48*(6), 793–795.

Devereaux, G. (1951). Some criteria for the timing of confrontations and interpretations. *International Journal of Psychoanalysis*, *32*, 19–24.

Dewey, J. (1933). *How we think: A restatement of the relation of reflective thinking to the educative process*. Boston, MA: D. C. Health.

Dezerotes, D. (2000). Evaluation of yoga and meditation training with adolescent sex offenders. *Child and Adolescent Social Work Journal*, *17*(2), 97–113.

Dhillon, A. M., & Davis, H. (1985). Socialization, locus of control, and dogmatism as related to counsellors' office settings. *Psychological Reports*, *56*(1), 328–330.

Dhooper, S. S., & Moore, S. E. (2001). *Social work practice with culturally diverse people*. Thousand Oaks, CA: Sage.

Dillon, J. T. (1990). *The practice of questioning*. New York, NY: Routledge.

Dimeff, L. A., Koerner, K, & Linehan, M. M. (2007). *Dialectical behavior therapy in clinical practice: Applications across disorders and settings*. New York, NY: Guilford Press.

Dingle, G.A., Gleadhill, L., & Baker, F.A. (2008). Can music therapy engage patients in group cognitive behaviour therapy for substance abuse treatment? *Drug and Alcohol Review*, *27*(2), 190–196.

Dixon, W. A. (2000). Problem-solving appraisal and depression: Evidence for a recovery model. *Journal of Counseling & Development, 78*(1), 87–91.

Doel, M., & Marsh, P. (1992). *Task-centered social work*. Hants, England: Ashgate.

Doherty, D., & Mccoll, M. A. (2003). Illness stories: Themes emerging through narrative. *Sound Work in Heath Care, 37*(10), 19–39.

Donaldson, L. P. (2004). Toward validating the therapeutic benefits of empowerment-oriented social action groups. *Social Work With Groups, 27*(2/3), 159–175.

Dorfman, R. A. (1996). *Clinical social work: Definition, practice, and vision*. New York, NY: Brunner/Mazel.

Dossey, L. (1993). *Healing words: The power of prayer and the practice of medicine*. San Francisco, CA: Harper.

Dowd, E. T., & Milne, C. R. (1986). Paradoxical interventions in counseling psychology. *The Counseling Psychologist, 14*(2), 237–282.

Dowd, E. T., & Pace, T. M. (1989). The relativity of reality: Second order change in psychotherapy. In A. E. Freeman, K. M. Simon, L. Beutler, & H. Arkowitz (Eds.), *Comprehensive handbook of cognitive therapy*. New York, NY: Plenum Press.

Dowrick, C., Dunn, G., Ayuso-Mateos, J. L., Dalgard, O. S., Page, H., Lehtinen, V., et al. (2000). Problem solving treatment and group psychoeducation for depression: Multicentre randomized controlled trial. *British Medical Journal, 321*(7274), 1450–1454.

Dowson, S., & Greig, R. (2009). The emergence of the independent support broker role. *Journal of Integrated Care, 17*(4), 22–30.

Dozois, D. J. (2010). Understanding and enhancing the effects of homework in cognitive-behavioral therapy. *Clinical Psychology: Science and Practice, 17*(2), 157–161.

Dreskill, J. G. (1989). Meditation as a therapeutic technique. *Pastoral Psychology, 38*(2), 83–103.

Drisko, J. W. (1993). Special education teacher consultation: A student-focused, skill-defining approach. *Social Work in Education, 15*(1), 19–28.

Dugas, M. J., Brillon, P., Savard, P., Turcotte, J., Gaudet, A., Ladouceur, R., Leblanc, R., & Gervais, N. J. (2010). A randomized clinical trial of cognitive-behavioral therapy and applied relaxation for adults with generalized anxiety disorder. *Behavior Therapy, 41*(1), 46–58.

Duhl, F. S., Kantor, D., & Duhl, B. S. (1973). Learning space and action in family therapy: A primer of sculpting. In D. Bloch (Ed.), *Techniques of family psychotherapy: A primer*. New York, NY: Grune & Stratton.

Duncan, B. L., & Miller, S. D. (2000). *The heroic client: Doing client-directed outcome-informed therapy*. San Francisco, CA: Jossey-Bass.

Duncan, S. L., & Men, K. (2000). Service animals and their role in enhancing independence, quality of life and employment for people with disabilities. In A. Fine (Ed.), *Handbook of animal-assisted therapy* (pp. 303–323). San Diego, CA: Academic Press.

Dusek, J. A., Astin, J. A., Hibberd, P. L., & Krucoff, M. W. (2003). Healing prayer outcomes studies: Consensus recommendations. *Alt Therapies, 9*(3), A44–A53.

D'Zurilla, T. J., & Goldfried, M. R. (1971). Problem solving and behavior modification. *Journal of Abnormal Psychology, 78*(1), 107–126.

D'Zurilla, T. J., & Nezu, A. M. (2007). *Problem-solving therapy: A positive approach to clinical intervention* (3rd ed.). New York, NY: Springer.

Ebenstein, H., & Wortham, J. (2005). The value of pets in geriatric practice: A program example. In F. Turner (Ed.), *Social work diagnosis in contemporary practice* (pp. 719–728). New York, NY: Oxford University Press.

Echevarria, D. S. (2001). Resource-based reflective consultation: Accessing client resources through interviews and dialogue. *Journal of Marital and Family Therapy, 27*(2), 201–212.

Edgar, L., Remmer, J., Rosberger, Z., & Fournier, M. A. (2000). Resource use in women completing treatment for breast cancer. *Psycho-Oncology, 9*(5), 428–438.

Edwards, C., & Murdock, N. (1994). Characteristics of social worker self-disclosure in the counseling process. *Journal of Counseling and Development, 72*(4), 384–389.

Edwards, D. (1993). Why don't arts social workers do research? In H. Payne (Ed.), *Handbook of inquiry in the arts therapies: One river, many currents* (pp. 7–15). London: Jessica Kingsley.

Egan, G. (2002). *The skilled helper: A problem-management and opportunity-development approach to helping* (6th ed.). Pacific Grove, CA: Brooks/Cole.

Egan, G. (2007). *The skilled helper* (8th ed.). Belmont, CA: Thomson Brooks/Cole.

Eisold, B. K. (2005). Notes on lifelong resilience: Perceptual and personality factors implicit in the creation of a particular adaptive style. *Psychoanalytic Psychology, 22*(3), 411–425.

Elaine, M. B., & Vayda, E. J. (1998).*The practice of field instruction in social work: Theory and process* (2nd ed.). New York, NY: Columbia University Press.

Elder, R., Evans, K., & Nizette, D. (2008). *Psychiatric and mental health nursing* (2nd ed.). Chatswood, New South Wales: Elsevier.

Ellis, A. (1968). Rational therapy: A rational approach to interpretation. In E. F. Hammer (Ed.), *Use of interpretation in treatment: Technique and art* (pp. 232–239). New York, NY: Grune & Stratton.

Ellis, A. (2001). *Overcoming destructive beliefs, feelings, and behaviors.* Amherst, NY: Prometheus Books.

Ellis, A., & Dryden, W. (1997). *The practice of rational emotive behavior therapy* (2nd ed.). New York, NY: Springer.

Ellsworth, P. C., & Carlsmith. J. M. (1968). Effects of eye contact and verbal content on affective response to a dyadic interaction. *Journal of Personality and Social Psychology. 10*(1), 15–20.

Ellsworth, P. C., & Carlsmith, J. M. (1973). Eye contact and gaze aversion in an aggressive encounter. *Journal of Personality and Social Psychology, 28*(2), 280–292.

Elsbach, K. D. (2004). Interpreting workplace identities: The role of office décor. *Journal of Organizational Behavior, 25*(1), 99–128. doi: 10.1002/job.233

Elson, M. (2001). Silence, its use and abuse: A view from self-psychology. *Clinical Social Work Journal, 79*(4), 351–360.

Emile, V. (2009). *Outdoor therapy.* Retrieved from http://www.vanessaemile.co.uk/counselling/outdoor.html

Epstein, L., & Feiner, A. H. (1988). Countertransference: The social worker's contribution to treatment. In B. Wolstein (Ed.), *Essential papers on countertransference* (pp. 282–303). New York, NY: New York University Press.

Epston, D. (2009). The legacy of letter writing as a clinical practice: Introduction to the special issue on therapeutic letters. *Journal of Family Nursing, 15*(1), 3–5.

Epston, D., & White, M. (1989). *Literate means to therapeutic ends.* Adelaide, South Australia: Dulwich Centre.

Erdmann, Y., & Wilson, R. (2001). Managed care: A view from Europe. *Annual Review of Public Health, 22,* 273–291.

Erikson, M., & Rossi, E. (1981). *Experiencing hypnosis: Therapeutic approaches to altered states.* New York, NY: Irvington.

Eskin, M., Ertekin, K., & Demir, H. (2008). Efficacy of a problem-solving therapy for depression and suicide potential in adolescents and young adults. *Cognitive Therapy & Research, 32*(2), 227–245.

Estes, R. J., & Henry, S. (1976). The therapeutic contract in work with groups: A formal analysis. *Social Service Review, 50*(4), 611–622.

Estrada, A. U., & Haney, P. (1998). Genograms in multicultural perspective. *Journal of Family Psychotherapy, 9*(2), 55–62.

Fagan, J., & Shepherd, I. (1970). *Gestalt theory now: Theory, techniques, applications.* Ben Lomond, CA: Science and Behavior Books.

Farris-Dufrene, P. (1989). *Art therapy guidelines and practices.* Mundelein, IL: American Art Therapy Association.

Faust, J. R. (2008). Clinical social worker as patient advocate in a community mental health center. *Clinical Social Work Journal, 36*(3), 293–300.

Favaloror, G. J. (1998). Mediation: A family therapy technique? *Australian and New Zealand Journal of Family Therapy, 19*(1), 11–14.

Feder, B., & Feder, E. (1998). *The art and science of evaluation in the arts therapies.* Springfield, IL: Charles C. Thomas.

Feguson, D. (1999). Eco-maps: Facilitating insight in learning disabled sex-offenders. *British Journal of Nursing, 8*(18), 1224–1230.

Fehm, L., & Mrose, J. (2008). Patients' perspective on homework assignments in cognitive-behavioural therapy. *Clinical Psychology & Psychotherapy, 15*(5), 320–328.

Ferguson, H. (2009). Performing child protection: Home visiting, movement and the struggle to reach the abused child. *Child & Family Social Work, 14*(4), 471–480.

Ferraz, H., & Wellman, N. (2009). Fostering a culture of engagement: An evaluation of a 2-day training in solution-focused brief therapy for mental health workers. *Journal of Psychiatric & Mental Health Nursing, 16*(4), 326–334.

Field, N. P., & Horowitz, M. J. (1998). Applying an empty-chair monologue paradigm to examine unresolved grief. *Psychiatry: Interpersonal and Biological Processes, 61*(4), 279–287.

Field, T., Lasko, D., Mundy, P., Henteleff, T., Kabat, S., Talpins, S., et al. (1997). Brief report: Autistic children's attentiveness and responsivity improve after touch therapy. *Journal of Autism & Developmental Disorders, 27*(3), 333–338.

Filan, S. L., & Llewellyn-Jones, R. H. (2006). Animal-assisted therapy for dementia: A review of the literature. *International Psychogeriatrics, 18*(4), 597–611.

Finfgeld, D. L. (2004). Empowerment of individuals with enduring mental health problems: Results from concept analyses and qualitative investigations. *Advances in Nursing Science, 27*(1), 44–52.

Finn, J. (1995). Use of electronic mail to promote computer literacy in social work undergraduates. *Journal of Teaching in Social Work, 12*(1/2), 73–83.

Finn, J., & Lavitt, M. (1994). Computer-based self-help for survivors of sexual abuse. *Social Work With Groups, 17*(1), 21–46.

Fischer, J. (1978). *Effective casework practice: An eclectic approach.* New York, NY: McGraw-Hill.

Fischer, J. & Corcoran, K. (1994). *Measures for clinical practice: A source book* (2nd ed., Vols. 1 & 2). New York, NY: Free Press.

Fishman, H. C., Andes, F., & Knowlton, R. (2001). Enhancing family therapy: The addition of a community resource specialist. *Journal of Marital and Family Therapy, 27*(1), 111–116.

Fitzgerald, P., & Leudar, I. (2010). On active listening in person-centered, solution-focused psychotherapy. *Journal of Pragmatics, 42*(12), 3188–3198.

Fitzsimons, S., & Fuller, R. (2002). Empowerment and its implications for clinical practice in mental health: A review. *Journal of Mental Health, 11*(5), 481–499. doi:10.1080/09638230020023

Fleming, B., Freeman, A., Pretzer, J., & Simon, K. M. (2004). The treatment of depression. In *Clinical applications of cognitive therapy* (2nd ed., pp. 97–127). New York, NY: Kluwer Academic/Plenum.

Florin, P., & Wandersman, A. (1990). An introduction to citizen participation, voluntary organizations, and community development: Insights for empowerment through research. *American Journal of Community Psychology, 18*(1), 41–54.

Forster, R. (1998). Patient advocacy in psychiatry: The Austrian and Dutch model. *International Social Work, 41*(2), 155–167.

Fortner, J., & Walsh, S. R. (2002). Coming full circle: Family therapy and psychiatry reunite in a training program. *Families, Systems, & Health 20*(1), 105–111.

Fortune, A. E. (Ed.). (1985). *Task centered practice with families and groups.* New York, NY: Springer.

Foster-Fishman, P. G., Salem, D. A., Chibnall, S., Legler, R., & Yapchai, C. (1998). Empirical support for the critical assumptions of empowerment theory. *American Journal of Community Psychology, 26*(4), 507–536. doi:10.1023/A:1022188805083

Fox, R. (1982). The personal log: Enriching clinical practice. *Clinical Social Work Journal,10*, 94–102.

Fox, R. (1983). Contracting in supervision: A goal oriented process. *The Clinical Supervisor, 1*(1), 37–49.

Foxx, R. M., McMorrow, M. J., & Bittle, R. G. (1985). Teaching social skills to psychiatric inpatients. *Behaviour Research and Therapy, 23*(5), 531–537.

Frame, M. W. (2000). The spiritual genogram in family therapy. *Journal of Marital & Family Therapy, 26*(2), 211–216.

France, K. (1975). Evaluation of lay volunteer crisis telephone workers. *American Journal of Community Psychology, 3*, 197–217.

Frank, J. D., & Frank, J. B. (1993). *Persuasion and healing: A comparative study of psychotherapy* (3rd ed.). Baltimore, MD: Johns Hopkins University Press.

Frank, S. (2000). *Public speaking.* Holbrook, MA: Adams Media.

Franklin, C., Moore, K., & Hopson, L. (2008). Effectiveness of solution-focused brief therapy in a school setting. *Children & Schools, 30*(1), 15–26.

Franklin, M., & Politsky, R. (1992). The problem of interpretation: Implications and strategies for the field of art therapy. *Arts in Psychotherapy, 19*, 163–175.

Franko, D. L. (1993). The use of a group meal in the brief group therapy of bulimia nervosa. *International Journal of Group Psychotherapy, 43*(2), 237–242.

Franz, C. E., Barker, J. C., Kim, K., Flores, Y., Jenkins, C., Kravitz, R. L., & Hinton, L. (2010). When help becomes a hindrance: Mental health referral systems as barriers to care for primary care physicians treating patients with Alzheimer's disease. *The American Journal of Geriatric Psychiatry, 18*(7), 576–585.

Franzen, S., Morrel-Samuels, S., Reischl, T. M., & Zimmerman, M. A. (2009). Using process evaluation to strengthen intergenerational partnerships in the youth empowerment solutions program. *Journal of Prevention & Intervention in the Community, 37*(4), 289–301.

Freddolino, P. P. (1998). Building on experience: Lessons from a distance education MSW program. *Computers in Human Services, 15*(2/3), 39–50.

Fredrickson, B. L., Cohn, M. A., Coffey, K. A., Pek, J., & Finkel, S. M. (2008). Open hearts build lives: Positive emotions, induced through loving-kindness meditation, build consequential personal resources. *Journal of Personality & Social Psychology, 95*(5), 1045–1062.

Freed, A. (1988). Interviewing through an interpreter. *Social Work, 33*(4), 315–319.

Freeman, A. (2007). The use of homework in cognitive behavior therapy: Working with complex anxiety and insomnia. *Cognitive and Behavioral Practice 14*(3), 261–267.

French, J. R., & Raven, B. (1959). The bases of social power. In D. Cartwright (Ed.), *Studies in social power* (pp. 150–167). Ann Arbor, MI: Institute for Social Research.

Fretz, B. R., Corn, R., Tuemmler, J. M., & Bellet, W. (1979). Counselor nonverbal behavior and client evaluation. *Journal of Counseling Psychology, 26*(4), 304–311.

Frey, A. (2002). Enhancing children's social skills through classroom meetings. *School Social Work Journal, 26*(2), 46–57.

Friedberg, D., McClure, J. M., & Hillwig, G. (2009). *Cognitive therapy techniques for children and adolescents: Tools for enhancing practice.* New York, NY: Guilford Press.

Friedberg, R. D. (1994). Storytelling and cognitive therapy with children. *Journal of Cognitive Psychotherapy, 8*(3), 209–217.

Friedländer, W. A. (1976). *Concepts and methods of social work.* (2nd ed.). Englewood Cliffs, NJ: Prentice Hall.

Friedman, N. (1993). Fritz Perls's "layers" and the empty chair: A reconsideration. *Gestalt Journal, 16*(2), 95–119.

Friedmann, E., Katcher, A. H., Thomas, S. A., Lynch, J. J., & Messent, P. R. (1983). Social interaction and blood pressure. Influence of animal companions. *Journal of Nervous and Mental Disorder, 171*(8), 461–465.

Fromme, D. K., & Beam, D. C. (1974). Dominance and sex differences in nonverbal responses to differential eye contact. *Journal of Research in Personality, 8*, 76–87.

Fuat, U. (2003). *Movie therapy, moving therapy!* Victoria, British Columbia: Trafford.

Furman, B., & Ahola, T. (1992). *Solution talk: Hosting therapeutic conversations.* New York, NY: Norton.

Furman, R. (2003/2004). Poetry as a tool for self-reflection in social work education. *Arete, 27*(2), 65–70.

Furman, R., Coyne, A., & Negi, N. J. (2008). An international experience for social work students: Self-reflection through poetry and journal writing exercises. *Journal of Teaching in Social Work, 28*(1/2), 71–85.

Furman, R., Downey, E. P., Jackson, R. L., & Bender, K. (2002). Poetry therapy as a tool for strengths-based practice. *Advances in Social Work, 3*(2), 146–157.

Fusco, L. C. (1997). The techniques of intervention. In F. J. Turner (Ed.), *Social work practice: A Canadian perspective.* Toronto, Ontario: Prentice Hall.

Fusco, L. (2002). Mediation in social work practice. In F. J. Turner (Ed.), *Social work practice: A Canadian perspective.* Toronto, Ontario: Pearson.

Fusco, L. (2002). The techniques of intervention. In F. Turner (Ed.), *Social work practice: A Canadian perspective.* Toronto, Ontario: Pearson.

Fusco, L. (2002). The techniques of interviewing. In F. Turner (Ed.), *Social work practice: A Canadian perspective.* Toronto, Ontario: Pearson.

Gafner, G. (2005). *Clinical applications of hypnosis.* New York, NY: Norton Professional Books.

Galinsky, M. J., Schopler, J. H., & Abell, M. D. (1997). Connecting group members through telephone and computer groups. *Health and Social Work, 22*(3), 181–188.

Gallagher-Thompson, D., Wang, P., Liu, W., Cheung, V., Peng, R., China, D., & Thompson, L. W. (2010). Effectiveness of a psychoeducational skill training DVD program to reduce stress in Chinese American dementia caregivers. *Aging & Mental Health, 14*(3), 263–273.

Galvin, K., Sharples, A., & Jackson, D. (2002). Citizens Advice Bureaux in general practice: An illuminative evaluation. *Health and Social Care in the Community, 8*(4), 277–282.

Gambrill, E. (1997). *Social work practice.* New York, NY: Oxford University Press.

Gambrill, E. (2001). Social work: An authority-based profession. *Research on Social Work Practice, 11*(2), 166–175. doi:10.1177/104973150101100203

Gannon, L. (1982). The role of power in psychotherapy. *Women & Therapy, 1*(2), 3–11.

Gantt, L. M. (1998). A discussion of art therapy as a science. *Art Therapy: Journal of the American Art Therapy Association, 15*(1), 3–12.

Garcia, C. L. (1986). Extending reading tradition: An educational therapy approach. *Reading Psychology*, *7*(4), 305–311.

Garcia-Ramirez, M., Martinez, M. F., Balcazar, F. E., Suarez-Balcazar, Y., Albar, M.-J., Domínguez, E., & Santolaya, F. J. (2005). Psychosocial empowerment and social support factors associated with the employment status of immigrant welfare recipients. *Journal of Community Psychology*, *33*(6), 673–690. doi:10.1002/jcop.20072

Gardiner, J. C., Furois, M., Tansley, D. P., & Morgan, B. (2000). Music therapy and reading as intervention strategies for disruptive behavior in dementia. *Clinical Gerontologist: The Journal of Aging and Mental Health*, *22*(1), 31–46.

Garvin, C. D., & Seaberg, B. A. (1984). *Interpersonal practice in social work* (2nd ed.). Toronto, Ontario: Allyn & Bacon.

Gazzola, N., & Stalikas, A. (1997). An investigation of counselor interpretations in client centered therapy. *Journal of Psychotherapy Integration*, *7*(4), 313–327.

Gazzola, N., & Stalikas, A. (2004). Social worker interpretations and client processes in three therapeutic modalities: Implications for psychotherapy integration. *Journal of Psychotherapy Integration*, *14*(4), 397–418.

Gehart, D., & Lucas, B. (2007). Client advocacy in marriage and family therapy: A qualitative case study. *Journal of Family Psychotherapy*, *18*(1), 39–56.

Gellis, Z. D., & Bruce, M. L. (2010). Problem-solving therapy for subthreshold depression in home healthcare patients with cardiovascular disease. *The American Journal of Geriatric Psychiatry*, *18*(6), 464–474.

Gelso, C. J., Hill, C. E., & Kivlighan, D. M. (1991). Transference, insight, and the counselor's intentions during a counseling hour. *Journal of Counseling and Development*, *69*(5), 428–433.

Gelso, C. J., Hill, C. E., Mohr, J. J., Rochlen, A. B., & Zack, J. (1999). Describing the face of transference: Psychodynamic social workers' recollections about transference in cases of successful long-term therapy. *Journal of Counseling Psychology*, *46*(2), 257–267.

Gelso, C. J., Kivlighan, D. M., Wine, B., Jones, A., & Friedman, S. C. (1997). Transference, insight, and the course of time-limited therapy. *Journal of Counseling Psychology*, *44*(2), 209–217.

Germain, A., & Nielsen, T. (2003). Impact of imagery rehearsal treatment on distressing dreams, psychological distress, and sleep parameters in nightmare patients. *Behavioral Sleep Medicine*, *1*(3), 140–154.

Gfeller, K. E. (2002). Music as therapeutic agent: Historical and sociocultural perspectives. In R. G. Unkefer & M. H. Thaut (Eds.), *Music therapy in the treatment of adults with mental disorders: Theoretical bases and clinical interventions* (2nd ed., pp. 60–67). St. Louis, MO: MMB Music.

Gibbs, J. T., & Fuery, D. (1994). Mental health and well-being of Black women: Toward strategies of empowerment. *American Journal of Community Psychology*, *22*(4), 559–582.

Gil, E. (1991). *The healing power of play: Working with abused children*. New York, NY: Guilford Press.

Gil., E. (1994). *Play in family therapy*. New York, NY: Guilford Press.

Gilbert, M. C. (2000). Spirituality in social work groups: Practitioners speak out. *Social Work With Groups*, *22*(4), 67–84.

Gillman, M. (1996). Empowering professionals in higher education. In B. Humphries (Ed.), *Critical perspectives on empowerment* (pp. 99–116). Birmingham: Venture Press.

Gilroy, A., & Lee, C. (1995). *Art and music: Therapy and research*. London: Routledge.

Gingerich, W. J., & Eisengart, S. (2000). Solution-focused brief therapy: A review of the outcome research. *Family Process*, *39*(4), 477–498.

Gitterman, A., & Germain, C. B. (2008). *The life model of social work practice: Advances in theory and practice*. Chichester, England: Columbia University Press.

Gittleman, M. (1965). Behavior rehearsal as a technique in child treatment. *Journal of Child Psychology and Psychiatry, 6*(3–4), 251–255.

Glasser, I. (1983). Guidelines for using an interpreter in social work. *Child Welfare, 57,* 468–470.

Glueckauf, R. L., Fritz, S. P., Eckland, J., Eric, P., Liss, H. J., & Dages, P. (2002). Videoconferencing-based counseling for rural teenagers with epilepsy: Phase 1 findings. *Rehabilitation Psychology, 47*(1), 49–72.

Goellity, A. (2001). Dreaming their way into life: Group experience with oncology patients. A group experience with oncology patients. *Social Work with Groups, 24*(1), 53–68.

Goelitz, A. (2001). Nurturing life with dreams: Therapeutic dream work with cancer patients. *Clinical Social Work Journal, 29*(4), 375–385. doi:10.1023/A:1012219314370

Gold, C., Wigram, T., & Voracek, M. (2007). Predictors of change in music therapy with children and adolescents: The role of therapeutic techniques. *Psychology and Psychotherapy: Theory, Research and Practice, 80,* 577–589.

Goldberg, B. (2002). Unwrapping the secrets of the gift: Gift giving and psychotherapy. *Psychoanalysis & Contemporary Thought, 25*(4), 465–490.

Goldberg, D. (2000). "Emplotment": Letter writing with troubled adolescents and their families. *Clinical Child Psychology and Psychiatry, 5*(1), 63–76.

Goldfried, M. R., & Davison, G. C. (1994). *Clinical behavior therapy.* New York, NY: Wiley.

Goldman, R. S., Axelrod, B. N., & Tompkins, L. M. (1992). Effect of instructional cues on schizophrenic patients' performance on the Wisconsin Card Sorting Test. *The American Journal of Psychiatry, 149*(12), 1718–1722.

Goldsmith, M. (2001). When words are no longer necessary: The gift of ritual. *Journal of Religions Gerontology, 12*(3/4), 139–150.

Goldstein, E. G. (2007). Social work education and clinical learning: Yesterday, today, tomorrow. *Clinical Social Work Journal, 35,* 15–23.

Goldstein, H. (1973). *Social work practice: A unitary approach.* Columbia: University of South Carolina Press.

Goldstein, H. (2001). Poetry and practice. *Families in Society, 81*(3), 235–237.

Goldstein, M. (1989). Poetry and therapeutic factors in group therapy. *Journal of Poetry Therapy, 2*(4), 231–241.

Goodman, K. D. (2007). *Music therapy groupwork with special needs children: The evolving process.* Springfield, IL: Charles C. Thomas.

Gordon. E., & Hodge, D. R. (2010). Helping child welfare workers improve cultural competence by utilizing spiritual genograms with Native American families and children. *Children and Youth Services Review, 32*(2), 239–245.

Gottman, J. M. (1981). *Time-series analysis: A comprehensive introduction for social scientists.* New York, NY: Cambridge University Press.

Grafanaki, S., & McLeod, J. (1999). Narrative processes in the construction of helpful and hindering events in experiential psychotherapy. *Psychotherapy Research, 9*(3), 289–303.

Graff, H., & Luborsky, L. L. (1977). Long-term trends in transference and resistance: A report on a quantitative-analytic method applied to four psychoanalyses. *Journal of the American Psychoanalytic Association, 25*(2), 471–490.

Graham, J. R., & Barter, K. (1999). Collaboration a social work practice method. *Families in Society, 80*(1), 6–13.

Greenberg, I. A. (1974). *Psychodrama: Theory and therapy.* New York, NY: Behavioral Publications.

Greenberg, L. S. (1983). Toward a task analysis of conflict resolution in Gestalt therapy. *Psychotherapy, 20,* 190–201.

Greenberg, L. S. (1984). Task analysis: The general approach. In L. N. Rice & L. S. Greenberg (Eds.), *Patterns of change* (pp. 124–148). New York, NY: Guilford Press.

Greenberg, L. S., & Malcolm, W. (2002). Resolving unfinished business: Relating process to outcome. *Journal of Consulting & Clinical Psychology, 70*(2), 406–416.

Greenberg, L. S., Warwar, S. H., & Malcolm, W. M. (2008). Differential effects of emotion-focused therapy and psychoeducation in facilitating forgiveness and letting go of emotional injuries. *Journal of Counseling Psychology, 55*(2), 185–196.

Greene, G. J. (1989). Using the written contract for evaluating and enhancing practice effectiveness. *Journal of Independent Social Work, 4*(2), 135–155.

Greene, G. J., Lee, M., Mentzer, R. A., Pinnell, S. R., & Niles, D. (1998). Miracles, dreams, and empowerment: A brief therapy practice note. *Families in Society, 79*(4), 395–399.

Greene, R., & Greene, R. R. (2008). *Human behavior theory & social work practice.* (3rd ed.). New Brunswick, NJ: Transaction.

Greenhalgh, T. (1999). Writing as therapy. *British Medical Journal, 319,* 270–271.

Grinnell, R. M., & Unrau, Y. A. (2007). *Social work research and evaluation: Foundations of evidence-based practice* (8th ed.). New York, NY: Oxford University Press.

Grocke, D., & Wigram, T. (2007). *Receptive methods in music therapy: Techniques and clinical applications for music therapy clinicians, educators, and students.* London, England: Jessica Kingsley.

Grove, D. S. (2002). Strategic family therapy. In A. J. Roberts & G. J. Greene (Eds.), *Social workers' desk reference (pp. 406–412).* New York, NY: Oxford Press.

Grumet, G. W. (1983). Eye contact: The core of interpersonal relatedness. *Psychiatry, 46*(2), 172–180.

Guilfoyle, M. (2003). Dialogue and power: A critical analysis of power in dialogical therapy. *Family Process, 42*(3), 331–343.

Gursansky, D., Harvey, J., & Kennedy, R. (2003). *Case management: Policy, practice and professional business.* New York, NY: Columbia University Press.

Haber, D., & Looney, C. (2000). Health contract calendars: A tool for health professionals with older adults. *The Gerontologist, 40*(2), 235–239

Hardcastle, D. A., Powers, P. R., & Wenocur, S. (2004). *Community practice: Theories and skills for social workers* (2nd ed.). New York, NY: Oxford University Press.

Holloway, F., & Carson, J. (2001). Case management: An update. *International Journal of Social Psychiatry 47*(3), 21–31.

Gustafson, D. H., Hawkins, R., Boberg, E., Pingree, S., Serlin, R. E., Graziano, F., & Chan, C. L. (1999). Impact of a patient-centered, computer-based health information/support system. *American Journal of Preventive Medicine, 16*(1), 1–9.

Gustavan, C. B. (2000). In-versing your life: Using poetry as therapy. *Families in Society, 81*(3), 328–331.

Gutheil, I. A. (1993). Rituals and termination procedures. *Smith College Studies in Social Work, 63*(2), 163–176.

Gutiérrez, L. (1991). Empowering women of color: A feminist model. In M. B. Jenkins, N. R. Hooyman, & N. Gottlieb (Eds.), *Feminist social work practice in clinical settings* (pp. 199–214). Newbury Park, CA: Sage.

Gutierrez, L. M., Parson, R. J., & Cox, E. O. (1998). *Empowerment in work practice: A source-book.* Pacific Grove, CA: Brooks/Cole.

Gyorky, Z. K., Royalty, G. M., & Johnson, D. H. (1994). Time-limited therapy in university counseling centers: Do time-limited and time-unlimited centers differ? *Professional Psychology—Research & Practice, 25*(1), 50–54.

Haber, D. (1993). Health contracts with older adults. *Clinical Gerontologist, 14*(2), 44–49.

Haber, D. (2001). Promoting readiness to change behavior through health assessments. *Clinical Gerontologist, 23*(1–2), 152–158.

Haber, D. (2003). *Health promotion and aging: Practical applications for health professionals* (3rd ed.). New York, NY: Springer.

Haber, D., & Looney, C. (2000). Health contract calendars: A tool for health professionals with older adults. *Gerontologist, 40*(2), 235–239.

Haber, D., & Rhodes, D. (2004). Health contract with sedentary older adults. *The Gerontologist, 44*(6), 827–835.

Hackney, H., & Cormier, L. S. (1979). *Counselling strategies and objectives*. Englewood Cliffs, NJ: Prentice Hall.

Hackstaff, G. L., & House, S. T. (1990). Development of a collaborative geriatric program between the legal system and a social work-directed program of a community hospital. *Social Work in Health Care, 14*(3), 1–16.

Hadas-Lidor, N., Naveh, E., & Weiss, P. (2006). From social worker to teacher: Development of professional identity and the issue of mediation. *Journal of Cognitive Education and Psychology, 6*(1), 100–114.

Hagood, M. M. (1990, Spring). Art therapy research in England: Impressions of an American art social worker. *Arts in Psychotherapy, 17*(1), 75–79.

Hahn, R. A., & Kleist, D. M. (2000). Divorce mediation: Research and implications for family and couples counseling. *The Family Journal, 8*(2), 165–171.

Hahn, W. K. (1998). Gifts in psychotherapy: An intersubjective approach to patient gifts. *Psychotherapy: Theory, Research, Practice, Training, 35*(1), 78–86.

Hajal, F. (1978). Using tape recorders in the treatment of latency-age children. *Social Casework, 59*, 371–374.

Halbrook, B., & Duplechin, R. (1994). Rethinking touch in psychotherapy: Guidelines for practitioners. *Psychotherapy in Private Practice, 13*(3), 43–53.

Halevy, J. (1998). A genogram with an attitude. *Journal of Marital & Family Therapy, 24*(2), 233–242.

Haley, J. (1976). *Problem-solving therapy*. San Francisco, CA: Jossey Bass.

Haley, J. (1987). *Problem-solving therapy* (2nd ed). San Francisco, CA: Jossey-Bass.

Haley, J., & Richeport-Haley, M. (2007). *Directive family therapy*. Binghamton, NY: Haworth Press.

Halperin, D. (2001). The play's the thing: How social group work and theatre transformed a group into a community. *Social Work with Groups. 24*(2), 27–46.

Hammer, E. F. (1968). Interpretation: What is it? In E. F. Hammer (Ed.), *Use of interpretation in treatment: Technique and art* (pp. 1–4). New York, NY: Grune & Stratton.

Hanna, K., & Rodger, S. (2002). Towards family-centred practice in paediatric occupational therapy: A review of the literature on parent-social worker collaboration. *Australian Occupational Therapy Journal, 49*(1), 14–24.

Hanson, J. (2005). Should your lips be zipped? How social worker self-disclosure and non-disclosure affects clients. *Counselling & Psychotherapy Research, 5*(2), 96–104.

Hanson, W. E., Razzhavaikina, T. I., & Scheel, M. J. (2004). The process of recommending homework in psychotherapy: A review of social worker delivery methods, client acceptability, and factors that affect compliance. *Psychotherapy: Theory, Research, Practice, Training, 41*(1), 38–55.

Hardiman, E. R. (2007). Referral to consumer-run programs by mental health providers: A national survey. *Community Mental Health Journal, 43*(3), 197–210.

Hardy, G. E., & Shapiro, D. A. (1985). Social worker response modes in prescriptive vs. exploratory psychotherapy. *British Journal of Clinical Psychology, 24*(4), 235–245.

Hardy, K. V., & Sasyloffy, T. A. (1995). The cultural genogram: Key to training culturally competent family social workers. *Journal of Marital and Family Therapy, 21*(3), 221–237.

Hartman, A. (1978). Diagrammatic assessment of family relationships. *Social Casework, 59*(10), 465–478.

Harwood, T. M., Sulzner, J. M., & Beutier, L. E. (2006). *Handbook of homework assignments in psychotherapy.* New York, NY: Springer.

Hayes, F. D. (1969). The use of authority. *Australian Social Work, 22*(2), 13–18.

Hayes, J. A., McCracken, J. E., McClanahan, M. K., Hill, C. E., Harp, J. S., & Carozzoni, P. (1998). Social worker perspectives on countertransference: Qualitative data in search of a theory. *Journal of Counseling Psychology, 45*(4), 468–482.

Haynes, K., & Mickelson, J. (2000). *Affecting change: Social work in the political arena* (4th ed.). New York, NY: Songman.

Heatherington, L., & Friedlander, M. L. (1990). Applying task analysis to structural family therapy. *Journal of Family Psychology, 4*(1), 36–48.

Heimberg, R. G. (2002). Cognitive-behavioral therapy for social anxiety disorder: Current status and future directions. *Biological Psychiatry, 51*(1), 101–108.

Heinonen, T., & Spearman, L. (2006). *Social work practice: Problem solving and beyond* (2nd ed.). Toronto, Ontario: Thomson/Nelson.

Helling, M. K., & Stovers, R. G. (2005). Genogram as a research tool. *Great Plains Sociologist, 17*(1), 78–85.

Henzell, J. (1995). Research and the particular: Epistemology in art and psychotherapy. In A. Gilroy & C. Lee (Eds.), *Art and music: Therapy and research* (pp. 185–205). London, England: Routledge.

Hepworth, D. H., Rooney, R. H. & Larsen, J. (1997). *Direct social work practice* (5th ed.). Toronto, Ontario: Brooks/Cole.

Hepworth, D. H., Rooney, R. H., & Larsen, J. A. (2002). *Direct social work practice: Theory and skills* (6th ed.). Pacific Grove, CA: Brooks/Cole.

Hepworth, D. H. Rooney, R. J., & Larsen, J. A. (2009). *Direct social work practice: Theory and skills* (8th ed.). Belmont, CA: Pacific Grove, CA: Brooks/Cole.

Hepworth, D. H., Rooney, R. J., & Larsen, J. A. (2010). *Direct social work practice: Theory and skills* (8th ed.). Pacific Grove, CA: Brooks/Cole.

Herbert, M., & Levin, R. (1996). The advocacy role in hospital social work. *Social Work in Health Care, 22*(3), 71–83.

Herbert, M., & Mould, J. (1992). The advocacy role in public child welfare. *Child Welfare, 71*(2), 114–130.

Heritage, J., & Sefi, S. (1992). Dilemmas of advice: Aspects of delivery and reception of advice in interactions between health visitors and first time mothers. In P. Drew & J. Heritage (Eds.), *Talk at work: Interactions in institutional settings* (pp. 359–417). Cambridge, England: Cambridge University Press.

Herron, W., & Welt, S. (1992). *Money matters: The fee in psychotherapy and psychoanalysis.* New York and London: Guilford Press.

Hesley, J. W., & Hesley, J. G. (1998). *Rent two films and let's talk in the morning: Using popular movies in psychotherapy.* New York, NY: Wiley.

Hibel, J., & Polanco, M. (2010). Tuning the ear: Listening in narrative therapy. *Journal of Systemic Therapies, 29*(1), 51–66.

Higgins, W. H., Ivey, A. E., & Uhlemann, M. R. (1970). Media therapy: A programmed approach to teaching behavioral skills. *Journal of Counseling Psychology, 17*(1), 20–26.

Hill, C. E. (1975). Sex of client and sex and experience level of counselor. *Journal of Counseling Psychology*, *22*(1), 6–11.

Hill, C. E. (2003). *Dream work in therapy: Facilitating exploration, insight, and action*. Washington, DC: American Psychological Association.

Hill, C. E. (2005). Social worker techniques, client involvement, and the therapeutic relationship: Inextricably intertwined in the therapy process. *Psychotherapy: Theory, Research, Practice, Training*, *42*(4), 431–442.

Hill, C. E., Mahalik, J. R., & Thompson, B. J. (1989). Social worker self-disclosure. *Psychotherapy*, *26*(3), 290–295.

Hill, C. E., Thompson, B. J., & Ladany, N. (2003). Social worker use of silence in therapy. *Journal of Clinical Psychology*, *59*(4), 513–524.

Hill, C. E., Thompson, B. J., & Mahalik, J. R. (1989). Social worker interpretation. In C. E. Hill (Ed.), *Social worker techniques and client outcomes: Eight cases of brief psychotherapy* (pp. 284–310). Newbury Park, CA: Sage.

Hill, F. E., & Harmon, M. (1976). The use of telephone tapes in a telephone counseling program. *Crisis Intervention*, *7*, 88–96.

Hill, K. A. (1987). Meta-analysis of paradoxical interventions. *Psychotherapy*, *24*(2), 266–270.

Hilliard, R. E. (2007). The effects of Orff-based music therapy and social work groups on childhood grief symptoms and behaviors. *Journal of Music Therapy*, *44*, 123–138.

Hodge, D. R. (2005). Spiritual ecograms: A new assessment instrument for identifying clients' spiritual strengths in space and across time. *Families in Society: The Journal of Contemporary Social Services*, *86*(2), 287–296.

Hodge, D. R. (2005). Spiritual lifemaps: A client centered pictorial instrument for spiritual assessment, planning and intervention. *Social Work*, *50*(1), 77–87.

Hoefer, R. (2006). *Advocacy practice for social justice*. Chicago, IL: Lyceum Books.

Hoffer, A. (2006). What does the analyst want? Free association in relation to the analyst's activity, ambition, and technical innovation. *American Journal of Psychoanalysis*, *66*(1), 1–23.

Hofmann, S. G., & DiBartolo, P. M. (2000). An instrument to assess self-statements during public speaking: Scale development and preliminary psychometric properties. *Behaviour Therapy*, *31*(3), 499–515.

Hokkanen, H., Häggman-Laitila, A., & Eriksson, E. (2006). Resources and support of home-dwelling elderly people—Literature review. *Gerontologia*, *20*, 12–21.

Hollingsworth, L. D., Allen-Meares, P., Shanks, T. R., & Gant, L. M. (2009). Using the miracle question in community engagement and planning. *Families in Society*, *90*(3), 332–335.

Hollis, F. (1964). *Casework: A psychosocial therapy*. New York, NY: Random House.

Holloway, E. L., Freund, R. D., Gardner, S. L., Nelson, M. L., & Walker, B. R. (1989). Relation of power and involvement to theoretical orientation in supervision: An analysis of discourse. *Journal of Counseling Psychology*, *36*(1), 88–102.

Holmes, E. (2007). Sound and song as hypnotherapy: A holistic approach for transformation through the use of sound and song. *Australian Journal of Clinical Hypnotherapy and Hypnosis*, *28*, 12–18.

Holmes, S. (2006). Becoming "the best possible" family counselor or family mediator: What expertise research has to say. *Journal of Family Studies*, *12*(1), 113–122.

Hope, D. A., Heimberg, R. G., & Turk, C. L. (2010). *Managing social anxiety: A cognitive-behavioral therapy approach: Social worker guide* (2nd ed.). New York, NY: Oxford University Press.

Hornblow, A. R. (1986). Does telephone counselling have preventive value? *Australian and New Zealand Journal of Psychiatry*, *20*(1), 23–28.

Hornblow, A. R., & Sloane, H. R. (1980). Evaluating the effectiveness of telephone counselling services. *British Journal of Psychiatry, 137*, 377–378.

Hough, M., & Paisley, K. (2008). An empowerment theory approach to adventure programming for adults with disabilities. *Therapeutic Recreation Journal, 42*, 89–102.

Houlding, C., Schmidt, F., & Walker, D. (2010). Youth social worker strategies to enhance client homework completion. *Child and Adolescent Mental Health, 15*(2), 103–110.

Hover-Krame, M. D. (1996). *Healing touch: A resource for health care professionals.* Albany, NY: Delmar.

Hudson, W. W. (1982). *The clinical measurement package: A field manual.* Chicago, IL: Dorsey Press.

Huerta-Wong, J. E., & Schoech, R. (2010). Experiential learning and learning environments: The case of active listening skills. *Journal of Social Work Education, 46*(1), 85–102.

Hull, G. H., & Mather, J. H. (2005). *Understanding generalist practice with families.* Belmont, CA: Thomson Brooks/Cole.

Humphries. B. (Ed.). (1996). *Critical perspectives on empowerment.* Birmingham: Venture Press.

Hundert, E. M. (1998). Looking a gift horse in the mouth: The ethics of gift-giving in psychiatry. *Harvard Review of Psychiatry, 6*(2), 114–117.

Hundert, E. M., & Appelbaum, P. S. (1995). Boundaries in psychotherapy: Model guidelines. *Psychiatry, 58*(4), 345–356.

Hunsley, J. (1988). Conceptions and misconceptions about the context of paradoxical therapy. *Professional Psychology: Research and Practice, 19*(5), 553–559.

Hunt, C. (2000). *The therapeutic dimensions of autobiography in creative writing.* London, England: Jessica Kingsley.

Hunt, P. A. (1993). Relateline: An evaluation of a telephone helpline counselling service for marital problems. *British Journal of Guidance and Counselling, 21*(3), 277–289.

Hunt, R. (2009). *Introduction to community-based nursing* (4th ed.). Philadelphia, PA: Wolters Kluwer/ Lippincott Williams & Wilkins.

Hur, M. H. (2006). Empowerment in terms of theoretical perspectives: Exploring a typology of the process and components across disciplines. *Journal of Community Psychology, 34*(5), 523–540. doi:10.1002/ jcop.20113

Hurn, R. (2003). Butterflies in possibility land: An example of the miracle question when counselling briefly. *Counselling Psychology Review, 18*(4), 17–27.

Hutchison, E. D. (1987). Use of authority in direct social work practice with mandated clients. *The Social Service Review, 61*(4), 581–598.

Hyden, M. (2001). For the child's sake: Parents and social workers discuss conflict-filled parental relations after divorce. *Child & Family Social Work, 6*(2), 115–128.

Imber-Black, E. (1991). Rituals and the healing process. In F. Walsh & M. McGoldrick (Eds.), *Living beyond loss: Death in the family* (pp. 207–223). New York, NY: Norton.

Imber-Black, E., & Roberts,J. (1992). *Rituals for our times: Celebrating, healing, and changing our lives and our relationships.* New York, NY: HarperCollins.

Imber-Black, E., Roberts, J., & Whiting, R. (Eds.). (1988). *Rituals in families and family therapy.* New York, NY: Norton.

Inagaki, T. (2004). When the seal was revealed: The process that TV games mediated between the social worker and the client. *Psychiatry and Clinical Neuroscience, 58*(5), 533–534.

Ingram, R. E., & Scott, W. D. (1990). Cognitive behavior therapy. In A. S. Bellack, M. Hersen, & A. E. Karzin (Eds.), *International handbook of behavior modification and therapy* (2nd ed., pp. 53–65). New York, NY: Plenum.

Ivey, A., Gluckstern, N., & Ivey, M. B. (1993). *Basic attending skills.* Amherst, MA: Microtraining Associates.

Ivings, K., & Khardaji, S. (2007). Cognitive reframing of positive beliefs about smoking: A pilot study. *Behavioural and Cognitive Psychotherapy, 35*(1), 117–120.

Ivory, J. J., & McCollum, J. A. (1999). Effects of social and isolate toys on social play in an inclusive setting. *The Journal of Special Education, 32*(4), 238–243.

Jacobs, E. A., Chen, A. H., Karliner, L. S., Agger-Gupta, N., & Mutha, S. (2006). The need for more research on language barriers in health care: A systematic review and proposed research agenda. *Milbank Quarterly, 84*(1), 111–133.

Jacobs, J. T. (2005). Treatment of depressive disorders in split versus integrated therapy and comparisons of prescriptive practices of psychiatrists and advanced practice registered nurses. *Archives of Psychiatric Nursing, 19*(6), 256–263.

Jacobson, N. S., Dobson, K. S., Truax, P. A., Addis, M. E., Koerner, K., Gollan, J. K., … Prince, S. E. (1996). A component analysis of cognitive-behavioral treatment for depression. *Journal of Consulting and Clinical Psychology, 64*, 295–304.

James, R. K. (2008). *Crisis intervention strategies* (6th ed.). Belmont, CA: Brooks/Cole.

Jarvik, L. F. (1990). Role reversal: Implications for therapeutic intervention. *Journal of Gerontological Social Work, 15*(1/2), 23–34.

Jefferson, C. (1978). Some notes on the use of family sculpture in therapy. *Family Process, 17*(1), 69–76.

Jennings, L. B., Parra-Medina, D. M., Messias, D. K., & McLoughlin, K. (2006). Toward a critical social theory of youth empowerment. *Journal of Community Practice, 14*(1/2), 31–55.

Jerome, L. W., & Zaylor, C. (2000). Cyberspace: Creating a therapeutic environment for telehealth applications. *Professional Psychology: Research and Practice, 31*(5), 478–483.

Jerome, L. W., DeLeon, P. H., James, L. C., Folen, R., Earles, J., & Gedney, J. J. (2000). The coming of age of telecommunications in psychological research and practice. *American Psychologist, 51*, 407–421.

Jessee, E. H., Jurkovic, G. J., Wilkie, J., & Chiglinsky, M. (1982). Positive reframing with children: Conceptual and clinical considerations. *American Journal of Orthopsychiatry, 52*(2), 314–322.

Johnson, B. (2000). Using video vignettes to evaluate childrens' personal safety knowledge: Methodological and ethical issues. *Child Abuse and Neglect, 24*(6), 811–827.

Johnson, C., Nicklas, T., Arbeit, M., Webber, L., & Berenson, G. (1992). Behavioral counseling and contracting as methods for promoting cardiovascular health in families. *Journal of the American Dietetic Association, 92*(4), 479–481.

Johnson, D. M., Worell, J., & Chandler, R. K. (2005). Assessing psychological health and empowerment in women: The Personal Progress Scale revised. *Women and Health, 41*(1), 109–129.

Johnson, J. E., & Ershler, J. L. (1985). Social and cognitive play forms and toy use by nonhandicapped and handicapped preschoolers. *Topics in Early Childhood Special Education, 5*(3), 69–82.

Johnson, J. E., Christie, J. F., & Yawkey, T. D. (1987). *Play and early childhood development.* New York, NY: HarperCollins.

Johnson, L. C. (1986). *Social work practice: A generalist approach* (2nd ed., pp. 312–314). Toronto, Ontario: Allyn & Bacon.

Johnson, L. C. (1997). *Social work practice* (6th ed., pp. 335–337). Toronto, Ontario: Allyn & Bacon.

Johnson, M. (1986). Paradoxical interventions: From repugnance to cautious curiosity. *The Counseling Psychologist, 14*(2), 297–302.

Johnson, S. L. (2009). *Social worker's guide to posttraumatic stress disorder intervention.* Burlington, MA: Elsevier.

Johnson, W. R., & Smith, E. W. L. (1997). Gestalt empty-chair dialogue versus systematic desensitization in the treatment of a phobia. *Gestalt Review, 1*(2), 150–162.

Jones, E. J., Ghannam, J., Nigg, J. T., & Dyer, J. F. P. (1993). A paradigm for single-case research: The time-series study of a long-term psychotherapy for depression. *Journal of Consulting and Clinical Psychology, 61*(3), 381–394.

Jones, R. E., & Cooper, J. (1971). Mediation of experimenter effects. *Journal of Personality and Social Psychology, 20*(1), 70–74.

Joseph, L. M., & Hunter, A. D. (2001). Differential application of a cue card strategy for solving fraction problems: Exploring instructional utility of the Cognitive Assessment System. *Child Study Journal, 31*(2), 123–136.

Julliard, K. (1998). Outcomes research in health care: Implications for art therapy. *Art Therapy: Journal of the American Art Therapy Association, 15*(1), 13–21.

Julliard, K., Gujral, J., Hamil, S., Oswald, E., Smyk, A., & Testa, N. (2000). Art-based evaluation in research education. *Art Therapy: Journal of the American Art Therapy Association, 17*(2), 118–124.

Junge, M. (1989). The heart of the matter. *Arts in Psychotherapy, 16*, 77–78.

Junge, M. B., & Linesch, D. (1993). Our own voices: New paradigms for art therapy research. *Arts in Psychotherapy, 20*(1), 61–67.

Kabat-Zinn, J. (2005). *Coming to our senses: Healing ourselves and the world through mindfulness.* New York, NY: Hyperion.

Kadushin, A. (1977). *Social work consultation.* New York, NY: Columbia University Press.

Kadushin, A. (1990). *The social work interview.* New York, NY: Columbia University Press.

Kadushin, A., & Buckman, M. (1978). Practice of social work consultation: A survey. *Social Work, 23*(3), 372–379.

Kadushin, A., & Harkness, D. (2002). *Supervision in social work.* New York, NY: Columbia University Press.

Kadushin, A., & Kadushin, G. (1997). *The social work interview* (4th edition). New York, NY: Columbia University Press.

Kahn, S. R. (1993). Reflections upon the functions of food in a children's psychotherapy group. *Journal of Child and Adolescent Group Therapy, 3*(3), 143–153. doi:10.1007/BF00999845

Kanter, J. S. (1983). Reevaluation of task-centered social work practice. *Clinical Social Work Journal, 11*(3), 228–244.

Kapitan, L. (1998). In pursuit of the irresistible: Art therapy research in the hunting tradition. *Art Therapy: Journal of the American Art Therapy Association, 15*(1), 22–28.

Kaplan, F. (1998). Scientific art therapy: An integrative and research-based approach. *Art Therapy: Journal of the American Art Therapy Association, 15*(2), 93–98.

Kaplan, F. (2000). *Art, science, and art therapy: Repainting the picture.* London, England: Jessica Kingsley.

Kaplan, F. (2001). Areas of inquiry for art therapy research. *Art Therapy: Journal of the American Art Therapy Association, 18*(3), 142–147.

Kapust, L. R., & Weintraub, S. (1988). The home visit: Field assessment of mental status impairment in the elderly. *The Gerontologist, 28*(1), 112–115.

Kar, S. B., Pascual, C. A., & Chickering, K. L. (1999). Empowerment of women for health promotion: A meta-analysis. *Social Science & Medicine, 49*(11), 1431–1460. doi:10.1016/S0277-9536(99)00200-2

Karliner, L. S., Jacobs, E. A., Chen, A. H., & Mutha, S. (2007). Do professional interpreters improve clinical care for patients with limited English proficiency? A systematic review of the literature. *Health Services Research, 42*(2), 727–754.

Kashyn, M. (1999). Telephone group work: Challenges for practice. *Social Work With Groups, 22*(1), 63–77.

Kasius, C. (Ed.). (1951). *Principles and techniques in social casework*. New York, NY: Family Association of America.

Kaslow, F. W., & Friedman, J. (1977). Utilization of family photos and movies in family therapy. *Journal of Marital and Family Therapy, 3*(1), 19–25. doi:10.1111/j.1752-0606.1977.tb00441.x

Kaslow, F. W., Magnavita, J. J., Massey, R. F., Patterson, T., & Massey, S. D. (2002). *Comprehensive handbook of psychotherapy: Interpersonal/humanistic/existential*. New York, NY: Wiley.

Kasturirangan, A. (2008). Empowerment and programs designed to address domestic violence. *Violence Against Women, 14*(12), 1465–1475. doi:10.1177/1077801208325188

Kaufert, J. M., & Putsch, R. W. (1997). Communication through interpreters in health care: Ethical dilemas arising from difference in class, culture, language and power. *Journal of Clinical Ethics, 8*(1), 71–87.

Kavanaugh, J. (2000). *Worldwide gestures*. Phoenix, AZ: Waterford Press.

Kazantzis, N., & Ronan, K. R. (2006). Can between-session (homework) activities be considered a common factor in psychotherapy? *Journal of Psychotherapy Integration, 16*(2), 115–127.

Kazantzis, N., Deane, F. P., Ronan, K. R., & L'Abate, L. (2005). *Using homework assignments in cognitive behavior therapy*. New York, NY: Routledge.

Keefe, T. (1996). Meditation and social work treatment. In F. J. Turner (Ed.), *Social work treatment: Interlocking theoretical approaches* (pp. 434–460). New York, NY: Free Press.

Keiley, M. K., Dolbin, M., Hill, J., Karuppaswamy, N., Liu, T., Natrajan, R., Poulsen, S., ... Robinson, P. (2002). The cultural genogram: Experiences from within a marriage and family therapy training program. *Journal of Marital & Family Therapy, 28*(2), 165–178.

Kellett, U., Moyle, W., McAllister, M., King, C., & Gallagher, F. (2010). Life stories and biography: A means of connecting family and staff to people with dementia. *Journal of Clinical Nursing, 19*(11–12), 1707–1715.

Kelly, E. W. (1978). Effects of counselor's eye contact on student-clients' perceptions. *Perceptual and Motor Skills, 46*(2), 627–632.

Kelly, E. W., & True. J. H. (1980). Eye contact and communication of facilitation conditions. *Perceptual and Motor Skills, 51*, 815–820.

Kember, D., Leung, D., Jones, A., Loke, A. Y., McKay, J., Sinclair, K., ... Yeung, E. (2000). Development of a questionnaire to measure the level of reflective thinking. *Assessment and Evaluation in Higher Education, 25*(4), 381–389.

Kendon, A. (1967). Some functions of gaze-direction in social interaction. *Acta Psychologica, 26*, 22–63.

Kestenbaum, C. J. (1985). The creative process in child psychotherapy. *American Journal of Psychotherapy, 39*(4), 479–489.

Khan-Bourne, N., & Brown, R. G. (2003). Cognitive behaviour therapy for the treatment of depression in individuals with brain injury. *Neuropsychological Rehabilitation, 13*(1), 89–107.

Kieffer, C. H. (1984). Citizen empowerment: A developmental perspective. *Prevention in Human Services, 3*(2), 9–36. doi:10.1300/ J293v03n02_03

Kilgussk, A. F. (1977). Therapeutic use of a soap opera discussion group with psychiatric in-patients. *Clinical Social Work Journal, 5*(1), 58–65.

Kim, M., & Tomaino, C. M. (2008). Protocol evaluation for effective musitc therapy for persons with nonfluent aphasia. *Topics in Stroke Rehabilitation, 15*, 555–569.

Kim, S., Crutchfield, C., Williams, C., & Hepler, N. (1998). Toward a new paradigm in substance abuse and other problem behavior prevention for youth: Youth development and empowerment approach. *Journal of Drug Education, 28*(1), 1–17.

Kimball, R. O. (1990). Empowerment: How and why they work: Special Report: Challenging teens in treatment. *Adolescent Counselor, 4*(2): 18–22.

King, G. D. (1977). An evaluation of the effectiveness of a telephone counselling centre. *American Journal of Community Psychology, 5*(1), 75–83.

Kingston, G., Gray, M. A., & Williams, G. (2010). A critical review of the evidence on the use of video-tapes or DVD to promote patient compliance with home programmes. *Disability and Rehabilitation: Assistive Technology, 5*(3), 153–163.

Kipper, D. A. (1988). The differential effect of role-playing conditions on the accuracy of self-evaluation. *Group Psychotheapy, Psychodrama and Sociometry, 41*, 30–35.

Kirschenbaum, H., & Henderson, V. L. (1989). *Carl Rogers reader.* Boston, MA: Houghton Mifflin.

Kirschenbaum, H., & Jourdan, A. (2005) . The current status of Carl Rogers and the person-centered approach. *Psychotherapy: Theory, Research, Practice, Training, 42*(1), 37–51.

Kirst-Ashman, K. K. (1993). *Understanding generalist practice.* Chicago, IL: Nelson-Hall.

Kirst-Ashman, K. K., & Hull, G. H. (2006). *Understanding generalist practice* (4th ed.). Belmont, CA: Thomson Brooks/Cole.

Kirst-Ashman, K. K., & Hull, G. H. (2009). *Understanding generalist practice* (5th ed.). Belmont, CA: Brooks/Cole.

Kiselica, M. S., & Robinson, M. (2001). Bringing advocacy counseling to life: The history, issues, and human dramas of social justice work in counseling. *Journal of Counseling & Development, 79*(4), 387–397.

Kissman, K. (1989). Poetry and feminist social work. *Journal of Poetry Therapy, 2*(4), 221–230.

Kitayama, S., Park, H., Sevincer, T. A., Karasawa, M., & Uskul, A. K. (2009). A cultural task analysis of implicit independence: Comparing North America, Western Europe, and East Asia. *Journal of Personality & Social Psychology, 97*(2), 236–255.

Kitler, J. (1994). *Advance group leadership.* Pacific Grove, CA: Brooks/Cole.

Klebenow, S. (1991). Power gender and money. In S. Klebanow & E. L. Lowenkopf (Eds.), *Money and minds* (pp. 3–14). New York, NY: Plenum Press.

Kleck, R. E. (1968). Physical stigma and nonverbal cues emitted in face-to-face interactions. *Human Relations, 21*, 19–28.

Kleck, R. E., & Nuessle, W. (1968). Congruence between indicative and communicative functions of eye contact in interpersonal relations. *British Journal of Social and Clinical Psychology, 7*(4), 241–246.

Knapp, M. L., & Daly, J. A. (2002). *Handbook of interpersonal communication.* (3rd ed.). Thousand Oaks, CA: Sage.

Knez, I., & Enmarker, I. (1998). Effects of office lighting on mood and cognitive performance and a gender effect in work-related judgment. *Environment and Behavior, 30*(4), 553–567.

Know, R., Butow, P. N., Devine, R., & Tattersall, M. H. N. (2002). Audiotapes of oncology consultations: Only for the first consultation? *Annals of Oncology, 13*, 622–627.

Knox, S. (2008). Gifts in psychotherapy: Practice review and recommendations. *Psychotherapy: Theory, Research, Practice, Training, 45*(1), 103–110.

Knox, S., Hess, S. A., Williams, E. N., & Hill, C. E. (2003). Here's a little something for you: How social workers respond to client gifts. *Journal of Counseling Psychology, 50*(2), 199–210.

Kobak, R. R., & Waters, D. B. (1984). Family therapy as a rite of passage: Play's the thing. *Family Process, 23*(1), 89–100.

Koenig, H. (1997). *Is religion good for your health? The effects of religion on physical and mental health.* New York, NY: Haworth Press.

Koenig, H. G., Meador, K., & Parkerson, G. (1997). Religion index for psychiatric research: A 5-item measure for use in health outcome studies. *American Journal of Psychiatry, 154*(6), 885–886.

Kolko, D. J., & Milan, M. A. (1983). Refraining and paradoxical instruction to overcome "resistance" in the treatment of delinquent youths: A multiple baseline analysis. *Journal of Consulting and Clinical Psychology, 51*(5), 655–660.

Kolko, D. J., & Milan, M. A. (1986). Acceptability of paradoxical interventions: Some paradoxes of psychotherapy research. *Professional Psychology: Research and Practice, 17*(6), 524–527.

Kossly, S. M. (2005). Reflective thinking and mental imagery: A perspective on the development of posttraumatic stress disorder. *Development and Psychopathology, 17*(3), 851–863.

Kosutic, I., Garcia, M., Graves, T., Barnett, F., Hall, J., Haley, E., Rock, J., Bathon, A., & Kaiser, B. (2009).The critical genogram: A tool for promoting critical consciousness. *Journal of Feminist Family Therapy: An International Forum, 21*(3), 151–176.

Kozloff, M. (1978). *Photography and fascination.* New York, NY: Addison House.

Krakow, B., Hollifield, M., Johnston, L., Koss, M., Warner, T. D., Tandberg, D., … Prince, H. (2001). Imagery rehearsal therapy for chronic nightmares in sexual assault survivors with posttraumatic stress disorder: A randomized controlled trial. *JAMA: Journal of the American Medical Association, 286,* 537–545.

Krakow, B., Kellner, R., Neidhart, J., Pathak, D., & Lambert, L. (1993). Imagery rehearsal treatment of chronic nightmares: With a thirty month follow-up. *Journal of Behavior Therapy and Experimental Psychiatry, 24*(4), 325–330.

Krakow, B., & Zadra, A. (2006). Clinical management of chronic nightmares: Imagery rehearsal therapy. *Behavioral Sleep Medicine, 4*(1), 45–70.

Kramer, B. J., & Gibson, J. W. (1991). The cognitively impaired elderly's response to touch: A naturalistic study. *Journal of Gerontological Social Work, 18*(1/2), 175–193.

Kreider, D. G., & Motto, J. A. (1970). Parent-child role reversal and suicidal states in adolescence. *Adolescence, 9*(35), 365–370.

Kreisberg, S. (1992). *Transforming power: Domination, empowerment and education.* Albany, NY: State University of New York Press.

Kressel, K. (1987). Clinical implications of existing research on divorce mediation. *American Journal of Family Therapy, 15*(1), 69–74.

Krietemeyer, B. C., & Heiney, S. P. (1992). Storytelling as a therapeutic technique in a group for school-aged oncology patients. *Children's Health Care, 21*(1), 14–20.

Kris, A. O. (1982). *Free association method and process.* New Haven, CT: Yale University Press.

Kris, A. O. (1992). Interpretation and the method of free association. *Psychoanalytic Inquiry, 12*(2), 208–224.

Kritzberg, N. I. (1980). On patients' gift-giving. *Contemporary Psychoanalysis, 16*(1), 98–118.

Kroeker, C. J. (1995). Individual, organizational, and societal empowerment: A study of the processes in a Nicaraguan agricultural cooperative. *American Journal of Community Psychology, 23*(5), 749–764. doi:10.1007/BF02506990

Kuelz, A. K., Stotz, U., Riemann, D., Schredl, M., & Voderholzer, U. (2010). Dream recall and dream content in obsessive-compulsive patients: Is there a change during exposure treatment? *Journal of Nervous and Mental Disease, 198*(8), 593–596.

Kurtz, L. F. (1997). *Self-help and support groups: A handbook for practitioners.* Thousand Oaks, CA: Sage.

Kurtz, P. D., Lindsey, E. W., Jarvis, S., & Nackerud, L. (2000). How runaway and homeless youth navigate troubled waters: The role of formal and informal helpers. *Child and Adolescent Social Work Journal, 17*(5), 381–402.

Kurtz, S., Stone, J. L., & Holbrook, T. (2002). Clinically sensitive peer-assisted mediation in mental health settings. *Health and Social Work, 27*(2), 155–159.

LaClave, L. J., & Brack, G. (1989). Reframing to deal with patient resistance: Practical application. *American Journal of Psychotherapy, 43*(1), 68–76.

Ladany, N., Hill, C. E., Thompson, B. J., & O'Brien, K. M. (2004). Social worker perspectives on using silence in therapy: A qualitative study. *Counselling & Psychotherapy Research, 4*(1), 80–89.

Laird, J. (1984). Sorcerers, shamans, and social workers—The use of ritual in social work practice. *Social Work, 29*(2), 123–129.

Laird, J. (1988). Women and rituals in family therapy. In E. Imber-Black, J. Roberts, & R. A. Whiting (Eds.), *Rituals in families and family therapy* (pp. 331–362). New York, NY: Norton.

Laitila, A., & Aaltonen, J. (1998). Application of the assimilation model in the context of family therapy: A case study. *Contemporary Family Therapy, 20*(3), 277–290.

Laken, A. (1973). *How to get control of your time and your life.* New York, NY: New American Library.

Lambe, L. (1995). Gardening a multisensory experience. In J. Hogg & J. Court (Eds.), *Making leisure provision for people with profound learning and multiple disabilities* (pp. 160–177). London: Chapman & Hall.

Landreth, G. (2002). *Play therapy: The art of the relationship* (2nd ed.). Muncie, IN: Accelerated Development, Inc.

Lange, R. (1994). *Empowered psychotherapy: Teaching self processing.* London, England: Karnac.

Lantz, J., & Gyamarah, J. (2002, Spring–Summer). Using art in short term existential psychotherapy. *Journal of Brief Therapy, 1*(2), 155–162.

Largo-Marsh, L., & Spates, C. R. (2002). The effects of writing therapy in comparison to EMD/R on traumatic stress: The relationship between hypnotizability and client expectancy to outcome. *Professional Psychology: Research & Practice, 33*(6), 581–586.

Lash, S. J., & Blosser, S. L. (1999). Increasing adherence to substance abuse aftercare group therapy. *Journal of Substance Abuse Treatment, 16*(1), 55–60.

Laverack, G., & Wallerstein, N. (2001). Measuring community empowerment: A fresh look at organizational domains. *Health Promotion International, 16*(2), 179–185.

Lawson, D. M. (1988). Using family sculpting and choreography in a student growth group. *Journal of Counseling & Development, 66*(5), 246–247.

Lazarus, A. A. (1966). Behaviour rehearsal vs. non-directive therapy vs. advice in effecting behaviour change. *Behaviour Research and Therapy, 4*(3), 209–212.

Leathard, A. (2003). *Interprofessional collaboration: From policy to practice in health and social care.* New York, NY: Brunner-Routledge.

Lee, B. R., Munson, M. R., Ware, N. C., Ollie, M. T., Scott, L. D., & McMillen, J. C. (2006). Experiences of and attitudes toward mental health services among older youths in foster care. *Psychiatric Services, 57*(4), 487–492.

Lee, J. (1996). The empowerment approach to social work practice. In F. J. Turner (Ed.), *Social work treatment: Interlocking theoretical approaches* (pp. 218–249). New York, NY: Free Press.

Lee., J. A. (2001). *The empowerment approach to social work practice* (2nd ed.). Chichester, England: Columbia University Press.

Leece, J., & Leece, D. (2010). Personalisation: Perceptions of the role of social work in a world of brokers and budgets. *The British Journal of Social Work, 40*(7), 1–20. doi: 10.1093/bjsw/bcq087.

Leger, F. J., & Lazurus, A. A. (1998). *Behavioural biological and cognitive foundations of psychotherapy.* New York, NY: Haworth Press.

Leigh, A. (1998). *Referral and termination issues for counselors.* London, England: Sage.

Lemon, E.C., & Goldstein, S. (1978). The use of time limits in planned brief casework. *Social Casework*, *59*(10), 588–596.

Lens, V., & Gibelman, M. (2000). Advocacy, be not forsaken: Retrospective lessons from welfare reform. *Families in Society*, *18*(6), 611–620.

Leonard, P. J. (1996). Consciousness-raising groups as a multicultural awareness approach: An experience with counselor trainees. *Cultural Diversity & Mental Health*, *2*(2), 89–98.

Leonardsen, D. (2007). Empowerment in social work: An individual vs. a relational perspective. *International Journal of Social Welfare*, *16*(1), 3–11. doi:10.1111/j.1468–2397.2006.00449.x

Lepore, S. (1997). Expressive writing moderates the relation between intrusive thoughts and depressive symptoms. *Journal of Personality and Social Psychology*, *73*(5), 1030–1037.

Leslie, M., & Schuster, P. (1991). The effect of contingency contracting on adherence and knowledge of exercise regimen. *Patient Education and Counseling*, *18*(3), 231–241.

Lethem, J. (2002). Brief solution focused therapy. *Child and Adolescent Mental Health*, *7*(4), 189–192.

Levenson, R. L., & Herman, J. (1991). The use of role playing as a technique in the psychotherapy of children. *Psychotherapy: Theory, Research, Practice, Training*, *28*(4), 660–666.

Levin, J. S. (1994). Religion and health: Is there an association, is it valid, and is it causal? *Social Science & Medicine*, *38*(11), 1475–1482.

Levin, S., & Wermer, H. (1966). The significance of giving gifts to children in therapy. *Journal of the Academy of Child Psychiatry*, *5*, 630–652.

Levinson, B. (1972). *Pets and human development* Springfield, IL: Charles C. Thomas.

Levinson, B. M., & Mallon, G. P. (1997). *Pet oriented child psychotherapy* (2nd ed.). Springfield, IL: Charles C. Thomas.

Lewis, A., Newton, H., & Vials, S. (2008). Realising child voice: The development of cue cards. *Support for Learning*, *23*(1), 26–31.

Lietz, C. A. (2010). Critical thinking in child welfare supervision. *Administration in Social Work*, *34*(1), 68–78.

Ligon, J. (2002). Fundamentals of brief treatment: Principles and practices. In A. R. Roberts & G. J. Greene (Eds). *Social workers' desk reference* (pp. 96–100). Oxford, England: Oxford University Press.

Lim, S., & Nakamoto, T. (2008). Genograms: Use in therapy with Asian families with diverse cultural heritages. *Contemporary Family Therapy: An International Journal*, *30*(4), 199–219.

Linesch, D. (1992). Research approaches within master's level art therapy training programs. *Art Therapy: Journal of the American Art Therapy Association*, *9*(3), 129–134.

Linesch, D. (1995). Art therapy research: Learning from experience. *Art Therapy: Journal of the American Art Therapy Association*, *12*(4), 261–265.

Liu, C., Leung, C. A., Li, S., Chi, I., & Chow, W. N. (2004). An experience of social work case management for frail elders in Hong Kong. *Geriatrics & Gerontology International*, *4*(Supp. 1), S173–S177.

Livingston, P. M., White, V. M., Hayman, J., Maunsell, E., Dunn, S. M., & Hill, D. (2010). The psychological impact of a specialist referral and telephone intervention on male cancer patients: A randomised controlled trial. *Psycho-Oncology*, *19*(6), 617–625.

Llewelyn, S. P., Elliot, R., Shapiro, D. A., Hardy, G., & Firth-Cozens, J. (1988). Client perceptions of significant events in prescriptive and exploratory periods of individual therapy. *British Journal of Clinical Psychology*, *27*(2), 105–114.

Loomis, M. (1982). Contracting for change. *Transactional Analysis Journal*, *12*(1), 51–55.

Lounsbury, J. W., & Hall, D. Q. (1976). Supervision and consultation conflicts in the day-care licensing role. *The Social Service Review*, *50*(3), 515–523.

Lowenstein, R. (1951). The problem of interpretation. *Psychoanalytic Quarterly, 20*, 1–14.

Lowenstein, R. (1957). Some thoughts on interpretation in the theory and practice of psychoanalysis. *The Psychoanalytic Study of the Child, 12*, 127–150.

Lowery, C. T., & Mattaini, M. A. (2001). Shared power in social work: A Native American perspective of change. In H. Briggs & K. Corcoran (Eds.), *Social work practice* (pp. 109–124). Chicago, IL: Lyceum.

Lown, N., & Britton, B. (1991). Engaging families through the letter writing technique. *Journal of Strategic and Systemic Therapies, 10*(2), 43–48.

Luborsky, L., Singer, B., & Luborsky, L. (1975). Comparative studies of psychotherapies: Is it true that "everyone has won and all must have prizes"? *Archives of General Psychiatry, 32*, 995–1008.

Lucas, S. E. (2005). *The art of public speaking.* New York, NY: McGraw-Hill.

Ludman, E. J., Simon, G. E., Tutty, S., & Von Korff, M. (2007). A randomized trial of telephone psychotherapy and pharmacotherapy for depression: Continuation and durability of effects. *Journal of Consulting & Clinical Psychology, 75*(2), 257–266.

Lusebrink, V. B., Rosal, M. L., & Campanelli, M. (1993). Survey of doctoral work by art social workers. *Art Therapy: Journal of the American Art Therapy Association, 10*(4), 226–234.

Macfie, J., Toth, S. L., Rogosch, F. A., Robinson, J., Emde, R. N., & Cicchetti, D. (1999). Effect of maltreatment on preschoolers' narrative representations of responses to relieve distress and of role reversal. *Developmental Psychology, 35*(2), 460–465.

MacInnis, C. C., Mackinnon, S. P., & MacIntyre, P. D. (2010). The illusion of transparency and normative beliefs about anxiety during public speaking. *Research in Social Psychology, 15*, 42–52.

MacKinnon, D. (2006). Music, madness and the body: Symptom and cure. *History of Psychiatry, 17*, 9–21.

Maddalena, C. J. (2009). The resolution of internal conflict through performing poetry. *The Arts in Psychotherapy, 36*(4), 222–230.

Mahon, E. J. (1992). Dreams: A developmental and longitudinal perspective. *The Psychoanalytic Study of the Child, 47*, 49–65.

Mair, F., & Whitten, P. (2000). Systematic review of studies of patient satisfaction with telemedicine. *British Medical Journal, 320*, 1517–1520.

Major, B. (1981). Gender patterns in touching behavior. In C. Mayo & N. M. Henley (Eds.), *Gender and nonverbal behavior* (pp.15–37). New York, NY: Springer-Verlag.

Major, B., & O'Brien, L. T. (2005). The social psychology of stigma. *Annual Review of Psychology, 56*(1), 393–421. doi:10.1146/annurev-psych.56.091103.070137

Major, B., Schmidlin, A. M., & Williams, L. (1990). Gender patterns in social touch: The impact of setting and age. *Journal of Personality and Social Psychology, 58*(4), 634–643.

Makaskill, N. D. (1996). Improving clinical outcomes in REBT/CBT: The therapeutic uses of tape-recording. *Journal of Rational-Emotive and Cognitive Behavior, 14*(3), 199–207

Malchiodi, C. A. (1995). Does a lack of art therapy research hold us back? *Art Therapy: Journal of the American Art Therapy Association, 12*(4), 218–219.

Malchiodi, C. A. (Ed.). (1998). Art therapy and research [Special issues]. *Art Therapy: Journal of the American Art Therapy Association, 15*(1 & 2).

Mallery, B., & Navas, M. (1982). Engagement of preadolescent boys in group therapy: Videotape as a tool. *International Journal of Group Psychotherapy, 32*(4), 453–467.

Maluccio, A., & Marlow, W. (1974). The case for contract. *Social Work, 19*(1), 28–35.

Maluccio, A., & Marlow, W. (1975). The case for the contract. In B. Compton & B. Galaway (Eds.), *Social work processes.* Homewood, IL: Dorsey.

Maly, R. C., Stein, J. A., Umezawa, Y., Leake, B., & Anglin, M. D. (2008). Racial/ethnic differences in breast cancer outcomes among older patients: Effects of physician communication and patient empowerment. *Health Psychology, 27*(6), 728–736. doi:10.1037/0278–6133.27.6.728

Mandel, D. R., Baron, R. M., & Fisher, J. D. (1980). Room utilization and dimensions of density: Effects of height and view. *Environment and Behavior, 12*(3), 308–319.

Mandel, S. E., Hanser, S. B., Secic, M., & Davis, B. A. (2007). Effects of music therapy on health-related outcomes in cardiac rehabilitation: A randomized controlled trial. *Journal of Music Therapy, 44,* 176–197.

Manning, B. H. (1991). *Cognitive self-instruction for classroom processes.* Albany, NY: State University of New York Press.

Manning, P. (1965). *Office design: A study of environment.* Liverpool, England: University of Liverpool.

Mannino, F., MacLennan, B., & Shore, M. (1975). *The practice of mental health consultation.* Adelphi, MD: National Institute of Mental Health.

Manzoni, G. M., Pagnini, F., Castelnuovo, G., & Molinari, E. (2008). Relaxation training for anxiety: A ten-year systematic review with meta-analysis. *BMC Psychiatry, 8*(41), 8–41.

Marchetti-Mercer, M. C., & Cleaver, G. (2000). Genograms and family sculpting: An aid to cross-cultural understanding in the training of psychology students in South Africa. *The Counseling Psychologist, 28*(1), 61–80.

Marcos, L. R. (1979). Effects of interpreters on the evaluation of psychopathology in non-English-speaking patients. *American Journal of Psychiatry, 136*(2), 171–174.

Marner, T. (2000). *Letters to children in family therapy: A narrative approach.* London, England: Jessica Kingsley.

Marra, T. (2005). *Dialectical behavior therapy: A practical and comprehensive guide.* Oakland, CA: New Harbinger.

Martin, F., & Farnum, J. (2002). Animal-assisted therapy for children with pervasive developmental disorders. *Journal of Nursing Research, 24*(6), 657–670.

Marziali, E., & Donahue, P. (2006). Caring for others: Internet video-conferencing group intervention for family caregivers of older adults with neurodegenerative disease. *The Gerontologist, 46*(3), 398–403.

Mason, J., & Rice, D. (2008). Does a business-like letter written for a general practitioner meet the standards for patients? *Psychiatric Bulletin, 32*(7), 259–262.

Massie, D. K. (2004). Psychosocial issues for the elderly with cancer: The role of social work. *Topics in Geriatric Rehabilitation Cancer Issues Related to the Older Person, 20*(2), 114–119.

Masterson, S., & Owen, S. (2006). Mental health service user's social and individual empowerment: Using theories of power to elucidate far-reaching strategies. *Journal of Mental Health, 15*(1), 19–34. doi:10.1080/ 09638230500512714

Matlo, H. C. (2002). Integrating art therapy methodology in brief inpatient substance abuse treatment for adults. *Journal of Social Work Practice in the Addictions, 2*(2), 69–83.

Matsumoto, M., & Smith, J. C. (2001). Progressive muscle relaxation, breathing exercises, and ABC relaxation theory. *Journal of Clinical Psychology, 57*(12), 1551–1557.

Matthews, M., Fawcett, S., & Stephen, B. (1981). *Referral for psychological testing. Matching clients and services: Information and referral.* Beverly Hills, CA: Sage.

Mausbach, B. T., Moore, R., Roesch, S., Cardenas, V., & Patterson, T. L. (2010). The relationship between homework compliance and therapy outcomes: An updated meta-analysis. *Cognitive Therapy and Research, 34*(5), 429–438.

Mayseless, O., Bartholomew, K., Henderson, A., & Trinke, S. (2004). I was more her mom than she was mine. Role reversal in a community sample. *Family Relations, 53,* 78–86.

Mazza, N. (1996). Poetry therapy: A framework and synthesis of techniques for family social work. *Journal of Family Social Work, 1*(3), 3–18.

Mazza, N. (1999). The poetic in family social work. *Journal of Family Social Work, 3*(3), 69–73.

McCaffrey, R. (2007). The effect of healing gardens and art therapy on older adults with mild to moderate depression. *Holistic Nursing Practice, 21*(2), 79–84.

McClary, R. (2007). Healing the psyche through music, myth, and ritual. *Psychology of Aesthetics, Creativity, and the Arts, 1,* 155–159.

McComb, J. J. R., & Clopton, J. R. (2003). The effects of movement, relaxation, and education on the stress levels of women with subclinical levels of bulimia. *Eating Behaviors, 4*(1), 79–88.

McCoyd, J. L. M. (2010). The implicit contract: Implications for health social work. *Health & Social Work, 35*(2), 99–106.

McFall, R. M., & Marston, A. R. (1970). An expert-mental investigation of behavior rehearsal in assertive training. *Journal of Abnormal Psychology, 76*(2), 295–303.

McGoldrick, M., Gerson, R., & Shellenberger, S. (1999). *Genograms: Assessment and intervention* (2nd ed.). New York, NY: Norton.

McGuinness, T. M., Noonan, P., & Dyer, J. G. (2005). Family history as a tool for psychiatric nurses. *Archives of Psychiatric Nursing, 19*(3), 116–124.

McLaughlin, A. M. (2009). Clinical social workers: Advocates for social justice. *Advances in Social Work, 10*(1), 51–68.

McLean, L. S. (2002). Overcoming obstacles: Therapeutic success despite external barriers. *Primary Care Companion Journal of Clinical Psychiatry, 4*(1), 27–29.

Mclennan, J., Culkin, K., & Courtney, P. (1994). Telephone counsellors' conceptualising abilities and counselling skills. *British Journal of Guidance and Counselling, 22*(2), 183–195.

McLoughlin, D. (2000). Transition, transformation and the art of losing: Some uses of poetry in hospice care for the terminally ill. *Psychodynamic Counselling, 6*(2), 215–234.

McMillan, B., & Callicutt, J. W. (1981). Fees for counseling services: Why charge them? *Administration in Mental Health, 9*(2), 100–122.

McNamee, S., & Gergen, S. (Eds.). (1992). *Therapy as social construction.* Newbury Park, CA: Sage.

McNiff, S. (1986). Freedom of research and artistic inquiry. *The Arts in Psychotherapy, 13*(4), 279–284.

McNiff, S. (1987). Research and scholarship in the creative arts therapies. *The Arts in Psychotherapy, 14*(2), 285–292.

McNiff, S. (1993). The authority of experience. *The Arts in Psychotherapy, 20*(1), 3–9.

McNiff, S. (1998). *Art-based research.* London, England: Jessica Kingsley.

McNiff, S. (1998). Enlarging the vision of art therapy research. *Art Therapy: Journal of the American Art Therapy Association, 15*(2), 86–92.

McQuade, S. (1999). Using psychodynamic, cognitive behavioral, and solution based questioning to co-construct a new narrative. *Clinical Social Work Journal, 24*(4), 339–353.

McWhirter, E. H. (1991). Empowerment in counseling. *Journal of Counseling & Development, 69*(3), 222–227.

McWhirter, E. H. (1998). An empowerment model of counsellor education. *Canadian Journal of Counselling, 32*(1), 12–26.

Media (*The Wall Street Journal*). (2012). [Walk&Talk website]. Retrieved from http://www.walkandtalk.com/media.html#twsj

Meichenbaum, D., & Gilmore, J. B. (1984). The nature of unconscious processes: A cognitive- behavioral perspective. In K. Bowers & D. Meichenbaum (Eds.), *The unconscious reconsidered* (pp. 273–298). New York, NY: Wiley.

Meissner, W. W. (2000). On analytic listening. *The Psychoanalytic Quarterly*, *69*(2), 317–367.

Mercer, S. O., & Garner, J. D. (1981). Social work consultation in long-term care facilities. *Health & Social Work*, *6*(2) 5–13.

Meyer, J. A., & Mann, M. B. (2006). Teachers' perceptions of the benefits of home visits for early elementary children. *Early Childhood Education Journal*, *34*(1), 93–97.

Meyers, J., Parsons, R., & Martin, R. (1979). *Mental health consultation in the schools*. San Francisco, CA: Jossey-Bass.

Michalshi, J. H., Mishna, F., Worthington, C., & Cummings, R. A. (2003). Multi-method impact evaluation of a therapeutic summer camp program. *Child and Adolescent Social Work Journal*. *20*(1), 53–76.

Middleman, R. R., & Wood, G. G. (1990). *Skills for direct practice in social work*. New York, NY: Columbia University Press.

Milewski-Hertlein, K. (2001). The use of a socially constructed genogram in clinical practice. *The American Journal of Family Therapy*, *29*(1), 23–38.

Miley, K. K., O'Melia, M., & DuBois, B. (2007). *Generalist social work practice: An empowerment approach* (5th ed.). Boston, MA: Allyn & Bacon.

Miller, A. A. (1961). Diagnostic evaluation for determining the use of psychiatric resources or family casework resources. *American Journal of Orthopsychiatry*, *31*, 598–611.

Miller, G. (1997). *Becoming miracle workers: Language and meaning in brief therapy*. New York, NY: Aldine de Gruyter.

Miller, J., Fletcher, K., & Kabat-Zinn, J. (1995). Three year follow-up and clinical implications of a mindfulness meditation-based stress reduction intervention in the treatment of anxiety disorders. *General Hospital Psychiatry*, *17*(3), 192–200.

Miller, K., Martel, Z., Pazdirek, L., Caruth, M., & Lopez, D. (2005). The role of interpreters in psychotherapy with refugees: An exploratory study. *American Journal of Orthopsychiatry*, *75*(1), 27–39.

Miller, M. (2002). How much should psychosocial workers tell about themselves? *Harvard Mental Health Letter*, *19*(4), 3–6.

Miller, P. A. (1985). Professional use of lay resources. *Social Work*, *30*(5), 409–416.

Miller, P. H. (2002). *Theories of developmental psychology* (4th ed.). New York, NY: Worth.

Miscall, B. K., & Sorter, D. (2008). Voice and cure: The significance of voice in repairing early patterns of disregulation. *Clinical Social Work Journal*, *36*(1), 31–39.

Mishna, F., Michalshi, J., & Cummings, R. (2001). Camps as social work intervention: Returning to our roots. *Social Work With Groups*, *24*(3/4), 153.

Mishna, F., Muskat, B., & Shamess, G. (2002). Food for thought: The use of food in group therapy with children and adolescents. *International Journal for Group Psychotherapy*. *52*(1), 27–47.

Mitchell, J., Howell, C., Turnbull, D., & Murphy, M. (2005). Computer-assisted group therapy for the treatment of depression and anxiety in general practice. *Primary Care Mental Health*, *3*, 27–39.

Mitchell, J., & Lynch, R. S. (2003). Beyond the rhetoric of social and economic justice: Redeeming the social work advocacy role. *Race, Gender & Class*, *10*(2), 8–26.

Moldofsky, Z. (2000). Meals made easy: A group program at a food bank. *Social Work With Groups*, *23*(1), 83–96.

Monnickendam, M., & Markus, E. J. (1997). Effects of a practice-centered, cognitive-oriented computer course on computer attitudes: Implications for course content. *Social Work & Social Sciences Review*, *6*(3), 175–185.

Montenegro, M. (2002). Ideology and community social psychology: Theoretical considerations and practical implications. *American Journal of Community Psychology*, *30*(4), 511–527.

Montoya, L. A., Giardino, A. P., & Leventhal, J. M. (2010). Mental health referral and services for maltreated children and child protection evaluations of children with special needs: A national survey of hospital- and community-based medically oriented teams. *Child Abuse & Neglect, 34*(8), 593–601.

Moore, T. E. (1995) Subliminal self-help auditory tapes: An empirical test of perceptual consequences. *Canadian Journal of Behavioural Science, 27*(1), 9–20.

Moraes, E., de Campos, G. M., Figlie, N. B., Ferraz, M. B., & Laranjeira, R. (2009). Home visits in the outpatient treatment of individuals dependent on alcohol: Randomized clinical trial. *Addictive Disorders & Their Treatment, 9*(1), 18–31.

Moreira, P., Beutler, L. E., Gonçalves, O. F. (2008). Narrative change in psychotherapy: Differences between good and bad outcome cases in cognitive, narrative, and prescriptive therapies. *Journal of Clinical Psychology, 64*(10), 1181–1194.

Morris, J. (2003). The home visit in family therapy. *Journal of Family Psychotherapy, 14*(3), 95–99.

Mosak, H., & Maniacci, M. P. (1998). *Tactics in counseling and psychotherapy.* Itasca, IL: Peacock.

Moxley, D. (1989). *The practice of case management.* Newbury Park, CA: Sage.

Moynihan, S. K. (1974). Home visits for family treatment. *Social Casework, 55*(10), 612–616.

Mozdzierz, G. J., Peluso, P. R., & Lisiecki, J. (2008). *Principles of counseling and psychotherapy: Learning the essential domains and nonlinear thinking of master practitioners.* New York, NY: Routledge.

Muff, J. (1996). Images of life on the verge of death: Dreams and drawings of people with AIDS. *Perspectives in Psychiatric Care, 32*(3), 10–23.

Mulroy, E. A., & Shay, S. (1997). Nonprofit organizations and innovation: A model of neighborhood-based collaboration to prevent child maltreatment. *Social Work, 42*(5), 515–524.

Multon, K. D., Patton, M. J., & Kivlighan, D. M. (1996). Development of the Missouri Identifying Transference Scale. *Journal of Counseling Psychology, 43*, 243–252.

Munford, R., & Sanders, J. (2007). Drawing out strengths and building capacity in social work with troubled young women. *Child & Family Social Work, 13*(1), 2–11.

Munson, C. E. (2002). *Handbook of clinical social work supervision* (3rd ed.). Binghamton, NY: Haworth.

Murphy, M. J., & Wright, D. W. (2005). Supervisees' perspectives of power use in supervision. *Journal of Marital and Family Therapy, 31*(3), 283–295.

Muschel, I. (1984). Pet therapy with terminal cancer patients. *Social Casework, 65*(8), 451–458.

Myers, D., & Hayes, J. A. (2006). Effects of social worker general self-disclosure and countertransference disclosure on ratings of the social worker and session. *Psychotherapy: Theory, Research, Practice, Training, 43*(2), 173–185.

Myers, S. (2000). Empathic listening: Reports on the experience of being heard. *Journal of Humanistic Psychology, 40*(2), 148–173.

Nakaya, N., Kumano, H., Minoda, K., Koguchi, T., Tanouchi, K., Kanazawa, M., & Fukudo, S. (2004). Preliminary study: Psychological effects of muscle relaxation on juvenile delinquent. *International Journal of Behavioral Medicine, 11*(3), 176–180.

National Association of Social Workers. (1997). *Third-party reimbursement for clinical social work services.* Washington, DC: Author.

Nau, D. S. (1997). Andy writes to his amputated leg: Utilizing letter writing as an interventive technique in brief family therapy. *Journal of Family Psychotherapy, 8*(1), 1–12.

Needleman, J. (1991). *Money and the meaning of life.* New York, NY: Doubleday.

Nesbitt, L. L., & Tabatt-Haussmann, K. (2008). The role of the creative arts therapies in the treatment of pediatric hematology and oncology patients. *Primary Psychiatry, 15*, 56–62.

Netting. F. E., & Williams, F. G. (1996). Case manager–physician collaboration: Implications for professional identity, roles, and relationships. *Health and Social Work, 21*(3), 216–224.

Neumann, J. K. (1981). Self-help depression treatment: An evaluation of an audio cassette program with hospitalized residents. *The Behavior Therapist, 4,* 15–16.

Newman, S. S. (2005). Considering fees in psychodynamic psychotherapy: Opportunities for residents. *Academic Psychiatry, 29*(1), 21–28.

Nezu, A. M., Nezu, C. M., & Lombardo, E. (2003). Problem-solving therapy. In W. T. O'Donohue, J. E. Fisher, & S. C. Hayes (Eds.), *Cognitive behavior therapy: Applying empirically supported techniques in your practice* (pp. 301–307). Hoboken, NJ: Wiley.

Nicholson, J. M., Berthelsen, D., Abad, V., Williams, K., & Bradley, J. (2008). Impact of music therapy to promote positive parenting and child development. *Journal of Health Psychology, 13,* 226–238.

Nickerson, P. R. (1995). Solution-focused group therapy. *Social Work, 40*(1), 132–133.

Norcross, J. C. (2002). *Psychotherapy relationships that work: Social worker contributions and responsiveness to patients.* New York, NY: Oxford University Press.

Norcross, J. C., & Beutler, L. E. (2000). A prescriptive eclectic approach to psychotherapy training. *Journal of Psychotherapy Integration, 10*(3), 247–261. doi:10.1023/A:1009444912173

Norcross, J. C., & Goldfried, M. R. (2005). *Handbook of psychotherapy integration* (2nd ed.). New York, NY: Oxford University Press.

Northcut, T. B. (2000). Constructing a place for religion and spirituality in psychodynamic practice. *Clinical Social Work Journal, 28*(2), 155–169.

Northen, H. (1995). *Clinical social work knowledge and skills* (2nd ed.). New York, NY: Columbia University Press.

Novak, T. (1996). Empowerment and the politics of poverty. In B. Humphries (Ed.), *Critical perspectives on empowerment* (pp. 85–98). Birmingham: Venture Press.

Nugent, W. (1996). The use of hypnosis in social work practice. In F. J. Turner (Ed.), *Social work treatment: Interlocking theoretical approaches* (pp. 362–388). New York, NY: Free Press.

Nugent, W. (2001). Mediation techniques for persons in dispute. In H. Briggs & K. Corcoran (Eds.), *Structuring change* (pp. 311–323). Chicago, IL: Lyceum Books.

Nugent, W. R. (1995). Testing the effects of active listening. *Research on Social Work Practice, 5*(2), 152–175. doi:10.1177/104973159500500202

Nye, E. F. (1997). Writing as healing. *Qualitative Inquiry, 3*(4), 439–452.

O'Callaghan, C.C. (1997). Therapeutic opportunities associated with the music when using song writing in palliative care. *Music Therapy Perspectives, 15,* 32–38.

O'Conner, K. (2002). The value and use of interpretation in play therapy. *Professional Psychology: Research and Practice, 33*(6), 523–528.

O'Connor, K., & Braverman, L. (Eds.). (1997). *Play therapy theory and practice—A comparative presentation.* New York, NY: Wiley.

O'Connor, K. (2000). *The play therapy primer.* New York, NY: Wiley.

O'Donohue, W. T., & Fisher, J. E. (2009). *Cognitive behavior therapy: Applying empirically supported techniques in your practice* (2nd ed.). Hoboken, NJ: Wiley.

O'Hanlon, W. H., & Weiner-Davis, M. (1989). *In search of solutions: A new direction in psychotherapy.* New York, NY: Norton.

O'Neal, G. S. (1993). Preventing conflict: Encouraging collaboration among students, faculty, and family. *Social Work in Education, 15*(2), 83–89.

O-Neil McMahon, M. (1996). *The general method of social work practice: A generalist perspective* (3rd ed., pp. 217–218). Boston, MA: Allyn & Bacon.

O'Callaghan, C. (2005). Qualitative data-mining through reflexive journal analysis: Implications for music therapy practice development. *Journal of Social Work Research and Evaluation*, 6(2), 217–229.

O'Connor, P. J., Pronk, N. P., Tan, A., & Whitebird, R. R. (2005). Characteristics of adults who use prayer as an alternative therapy. *American Journal of Health Promotion*, 19(5), 369–375.

Oldfield, A. (2006). *Interactive music therapy in child and family psychiatry: Clinical practice, research and teaching*. London, England: Jessica Kinglsey.

Olin, S. S., Hoagwood, K. E., Rodriguez, J., Ramos, B., Burton, G., Penn, M., Crowe, M., Radigan, M., & Jensen, P. S. (2010). The application of behavior change theory to family-based services: Improving parent empowerment in children's mental health. *Journal of Child and Family Studies*, 19(4), 462–470.

Olsen, S., Dudley-Brown, S., & McMullen, P. (2004). Case for blending pedigrees, genograms and eco-maps: Nursing's contribution to the "big picture." *Nursing and Health Sciences*, 6(4), 295–308.

Olson, D. H., Portner, J., & Lavee, Y. (1985). *FACES III manual and norms*. D. H. Olson, *Family Social Science*, University of Minnesota, St. Paul, MN.

Olson, F. (1993). The development and impact of ritual in couple counseling. *Counseling and Values*, 38, 12–21.

Ontario College of Social Workers and Social Service Workers. (2000). *Code of ethics and standards of practice*. Toronto: Author.

Oppawsky, J. (2000). Utilizing drawings when working with adults in therapy. *Journal of Psychotherapy in Independent Practice*, 2(1), 49–61.

Oppawsky J. (2001). Client writing. An important psychotherapy tool when working with adults and children. *Journal of Clinical Activities, Assignments and Handouts in Psychotherapy Practice*, 1(4), 29–40.

Orcutt, B. A., Flowers, L. C., & Seinfeld, J. (1990). *Science and inquiry in social work practice*. New York, NY: Columbia University Press.

Osborn, A. F. (1963). *Applied imagination: Principles and procedures of creative problem solving* (3rd ed., rev.). New York, NY: Scribner's.

Osborn, M., & Osborn, S. (1991). *Public speaking* (2nd ed.). Boston, MA: Houghton Mifflin.

Ost, L.-G., Westling, B., & Hellström, K. (1993). Applied relaxation, exposure in-vivo, and cognitive methods in the treatment of panic disorder with agoraphobia. *Behaviour Research and Therapy*, 31(4), 383–394.

Oznobishin, O., & Kurman, J. (2009). Parent-child role reversal and psychological adjustment among immigrant youth in Israel. *Journal of Family Psychology*, 23(3), 405–415.

Paat, E. R., Shadden, E. B., & Miller, E. C. (1988). Time therapy technique: The use of time as a catalyst for treatment. *Hospital & Community Psychiatry*, 39(2), 177–185.

Padilla, A. M., & Salgado de Snyder, V. N. (1992). Hispanics: What the culturally informed evaluator needs to know. In M. A. Orlandi, R. Weston, & L. G. Epstein (Eds.), *Cultural competence for evaluators: A guide for alcohol and other drug abuse prevention practitioners working with ethnic/racial communities* (pp. 117–146). Rockville, MD: U.S. Department of Health and Human Services, Substance Abuse and Mental Health Services Administration, Office for Substance Abuse Prevention.

Paivo, S. C. (1995). Resolving "unfinished business": Efficacy of experiential therapy using empty-chair dialogue. *Journal of Consulting and Clinical Psychology*, 63(3), 419–425.

Papp, P., Silverstein, O., & Carter, E. (1973). Family sculpting in preventative work with well families. *Family Process*, 12(2), 197–212.

Pardeck J. T., & Musich, J. A. (2005). Recommended children's books on disabilities. *Journal of Social Work and Rehabilitation*, 1(2), 53–72.

Parker, L. (1997). Unraveling power issues in couples therapy. *Journal of Feminist Family Therapy, 9*(2), 3–18.

Parker, L. (2009). Disrupting power and privilege in couples therapy. *Clinical Social Work Journal, 37*(3), 248–255.

Parker, W. M. (1998). *Consciousness raising: A primer for multicultural counseling* (2nd ed.). Springfield, IL: Charles C. Thomas.

Parsloe, P. (Ed.). (1996). *Pathways to empowerment.* Birmingham: Venture Press.

Parsons, R. J. (2002). Guidelines for empowerment-based social work practice. In A. R. Roberts & G. J. Greene (Eds.), *Social worker's desk reference* (pp. 396–401). Oxford, England: Oxford University Press.

Parton, N., & O'Byrne, P. (2000). *Constructive social work: Towards a new practice.* New York, NY: St. Martin's Press.

Pattillo, M. (2002). Assessing the gifts, talents, and skills of nursing home residents. *Geriatric Nursing, 23*(1), 48–50.

Pavlov, I. P. (1927). *Conditioned reflexes.* New York, NY: Oxford University Press.

Payne, H. (1993). *Handbook of inquiry in the arts therapies: One river, many currents.* London, England: Jessica Kingsley.

Payne, K. L., Prentice, D. S., & Allen, R. S. (2010). *A comparison of two interventions to increase completion of advance directives. Clinical Gerontologist, 33*(1), 49–61.

Pearlmutter, S. (2002). Archiving political practice: Interpreting individual need and social action. *Journal of Progressive Human Services, 13*(1), 31–51.

Peeks, A. L. (1999). Conducting a social skills group with Latina adolescents. *Journal of Child and Adolescent Group Therapy, 9*(3), 139–153.

Peluso, P. R. (2006). Expanding the use of the ethical genogram: Incorporating the ethical principles to help clarify counselors' ethical decision-making styles. *The Family Journal: Counseling and Therapy for Couples and Families, 14*(2), 158–163.

Pennebaker, J. (1993). Putting stress into words: Health, linguistic, and therapeutic implications. *Behavior Research and Therapy, 31*(6), 539–548.

Pennebaker, J. W. (1990). *Opening up: The healing power of expressing emotions.* New York, NY: Guilford.

Pepper, R. S. (2003). Be it ever so humble: The controversial issue of psychotherapy groups in the home office setting. *Group, 27*(1), 41–52.

Perez-de-Albeniz, A., & Holmes, J. (2000). Meditation: Concepts, effects and uses in therapy. *International Journal of Psychotherapy, 5*(1), 49–58.

Perlman, H. H. (1957). *Social casework: A problem-solving process.* Chicago, IL: University of Chicago Press.

Perlman, H. H. (1968). *Persona: Social role and personality.* Chicago, IL: University of Chicago Press.

Perr, H. M. (1985). The use of audiotapes in psychotherapy. *Journal of the American Academy of Psychoanalysis, 13,* 391–398.

Perry, C. W. (2002). Basic counselling technique: A beginning social worker's toolkit. Bloomington, IN: First Books Library.

Peterson, C. L. (1977). Consultation with community care facilities. *Social Work in Health Care, 2*(2), 181–191.

Peterson, M. L. (2002) Treatment planning with individuals. In A. R. Roberts & G. J. Greene (Eds.), *Social workers' desk reference* (pp. 320–323). New York, NY: Oxford University Press.

Peterson, N. A., & Hughey, J. (2004). Social cohesion and intrapersonal empowerment: Gender as moderator. *Health Education Research, 19*(5), 533–542. doi:10.1093/her/cyg057

Peterson, N. A., Hamme, C. L., & Speer, P. W. (2002). Cognitive empowerment of African Americans and Caucasians: Differences in understandings of power, political functioning, and shaping ideology. *Journal of Black Studies, 32*(3), 336–351.

Peterson, N. A., Lowe, J. B., Aquilino, M. L., & Schneider, J. E. (2005). Linking social cohesion and gender to intrapersonal and interactional empowerment: Support and new implications for theory. *Journal of Community Psychology, 33*(2), 233–244.

Peterson, N. A., Lowe, J. B., Hughey, J., Reid, R. J., Zimmerman, M. A., & Speer, P. W. (2006). Measuring the intrapersonal component of psychological empowerment: Confirmatory factor analysis of the Sociopolitical Control Scale. *American Journal of Community Psychology, 38*(3/4), 287–297. doi:10.1007/s10464-006-9070-3

Peterson, Z. D. (2002). More than a mirror: The ethics of social worker self-disclosure. *Psychotherapy: Theory, Research, Practice, Training, 39*(1), 21–31.

Petr, C. G. (2004). *Social work with children and their families: Pragmatic foundations* (2nd ed.). New York, NY: Oxford University Press.

Pfirman, E. S. M. (1988). The effects of a wilderness challenge course on victims of rape in locus-of-control, self-concept, and fear. *Dissertation Abstracts International, 49*/07-B, 2870. (UMI No. AAD88–18574)

Phan. H. P. (2009). Exploring students' reflective thinking practice, deep processing strategies, effort, and achievement goal orientations. *Educational Psychology, 29*(3), 297–313.

Phan, H. P. (2009). Reflective thinking, effort, persistence, disorganization, and academic performance: A mediational approach. *Journal of Research in Educational Psychology, 7*(3), 927–952.

Phillips, B. (1999). Reformulating dispute narratives through active listening. *Mediation Quarterly, 17*(2), 161–180.

Pinson, B. M. (2002). Touch in therapy: An effort to make the unknown known. *Journal of Contemporary Psychotherapy, 32*(2–3), 179–196.

Piska, S. (2005, November/December). Helping to heal: Therapeutic garden design. *Interscope Magazine.*

Pole, N., & Jones, E. E. (1998). The talking cure revisited: Content analyses of a two-year psychodynamic psychotherapy. *Psychotherapy Research, 8*(2), 171–189.

Polgar, A.T. (2005) *Conducting parenting capacity assessments: A manual for mental health practitioners.* Hamilton, Ontario: Sandrian.

Poon, V. H. K. (1996). The effects of immigration on family health for Hong Kong Chinese emigrating to North America. *Hong Kong Practitioner, 18*(12), 647–654.

Poulan, J. (2002). *Collaborative social work: Strengths based generalist practice.* Itascda, IL: Peacock.

Poulin, J. (2005). *Strength-based generalist practice: A collaborative approach.* Belmont, CA: Brooks/Cole-Thompson Learning.

Presser, H. B., & Sen, G. (Eds.). (2000). *Women's empowerment and demographic processes: Moving beyond Cairo.* New York, NY: Oxford University Press.

Price, R. H. (1990). Whither participation and empowerment? *American Journal of Community Psychology, 18*(1), 163–167.

Priester, P. E., Scherer, J., Steinfeldt, J. A., Jana-Masri, A., Jashinsky, T., Jones, J. E., & Vang, C. (2009). The frequency of prayer, meditation and holistic interventions in addictions treatment: A national survey. *Pastoral Psychology, 58*(3), 315–322.

Prochaska, J. O., & Norcross, J. C. (2003). *Systems of psychotherapy: A transtheoretical analysis* (5th ed.). Pacific Grove, CA: Brooks/Cole.

Provost, J. A. (1999). A dream focus for short-term growth groups. *Journal for Specialists in Group Work, 24*(1), 74–87.

Puskar, K., & Nerone, M. (1996). Genogram: A useful tool for nurse practitioners. *Journal of Psychiatric and Mental Health Nursing, 3*(1), 55–60.

Putsch, R. W. (1985). Cross-cultural communication: The special case of interpreters in health care. *Journal of the American Medical Association, 254*(23), 3344–3348.

Pyle, N. R. (2009). Therapeutic letters as relationally responsive practice. *Journal of Family Nursing, 15*(1), 65–82.

Rait, D., & Glick, I. (2008). A model for reintegrating couples and family therapy training in psychiatric residency programs. *Academic Psychiatry, 32*(2), 81–86.

Rajski, P. (2003). Finding God in the silence: Contemplative prayer and therapy. *Journal of Religion & Health, 42*(3), 181–190.

Ramirez, A., Ekselius, L., & Ramklint, M. (2009). Mental disorders among young adults self-referred and referred by professionals to specialty mental health care. *Psychiatric Services, 60*(12), 1649–1655.

Rapoport, L. (1995). Consultation in social work. In R. Edwards (Ed.), *Encyclopedia of social work* (17th ed., Vol. 1, pp. 193–196). Washington, DC: National Association of Social Workers.

Rappaport, J. (1981). In praise of paradox: A social policy of empowerment over prevention. *American Journal of Community Psychology, 9*(1), 1–25. doi:10.1007/BF00896357

Rappaport, J. (1987). Terms of empowerment/exemplars of prevention: Toward a theory for community psychology. *American Journal of Community Psychology, 15*(2), 121–148. doi:10.1007/BF00919275

Rappaport, J. (1995). Empowerment meets narrative: Listening to stories and creating settings. *American Journal of Community Psychology, 23*(5), 795–807. doi:10.1007/BF02506992

Rasmusen, P., & Tomm, K. (1992). Guided letter-writing: A long brief therapy method. *Journal of Strategic and Systemic Therapies, 11*(4), 1–18.

Ray, R. A., & Street, A. F. (2005). Ecomapping: An innovative research tool for nurses. *Journal of Advanced Nursing, 50*(5), 545–552.

Reamer, F. G. (2006). *Social work values and ethics.* (3rd ed.). Chichester, England: Columbia University Press.

Reandeau, S. G., & Wampold, B. E. (1991). Relationship of power and involvement to working alliance: A multiple-case sequential analysis of brief therapy. *Journal of Counseling Psychology, 38*(2), 107–114.

Recupero, P., & Rainey, S. E. (2005). Forensic aspects of e-therapy. *Journal of Psychiatric Practice, 11*(6), 405–410.

Reed, A. (1969, December). Using a tape recorder in counseling alcoholics. *Pastoral Psychology, 20,* 45–49.

Rees, C. S., & Haythornthwaite, S. C. (2004). Telepsychology and videoconferencing: Issues, opportunities, and guidelines for psychologists. *Australian Psychologist, 39*(3), 212–220.

Rees, L., & Clark, S. S. (2006). Can collaboration between education and health professionals improve the identification and referral of young people with eating disorders in schools? A pilot study. *Journal of Adolescence, 29*(1), 137–151.

Reger, J. (2004). Organizational "emotion work" through consciousness-raising: An analysis of a feminist organization. *Qualitative Sociology, 27*(2), 205–222.

Reid, W. J. (1996) Task-centered social work. In F. J. Turner (Ed.), *Social work treatment: Interlocking theoretical approaches* (pp. 617–640). New York, NY: Free Press.

Reiff, H. B. (2004). Reframing the learning disabilities experience redux. *Learning Disabilities Research & Practice, 19*(3), 185–198.

Reik, T. (1948). *Listening with the third ear.* New York, NY: Grove Press.

Rempel, G. R., Neufeld, A., & Kushner, K. E. (2007). Interactive use of genograms and ecomaps in family caregiving research. *Journal of Family Nursing, 13*(4), 403–419.

Renk, K. P. D., Roddenberry, A. B. S., & Oliveros, A. B. A. (2004). A cognitive reframing of ghosts in the nursery. *Journal of Child & Family Studies, 13*(4), 377–384.

Restifo, S. (2009). Writing a letter to patients. *Australasian Psychiatry, 17*(2), 123–125.

Rhoads, J. M., & Feather, B. F. (1972). Transference and resistance observed in behavior therapy. *Journal of Medical Psychology, 45*(2), 99–103.

Rhue, J. W., Lynn, S. J., & Kirsch, I. (Eds.). (1993). *Handbook of clinical hypnosis.* Washington, DC: American Psychological Association.

Rice, L. N., & Saperia, E. P. (1984). Task analysis of the resolution of problematic reactions. In L. N. Rice & L. S. Greenberg (Eds.), *Patterns of change* (pp. 29–66). New York, NY: Guilford Press.

Richeson, J. A., & Ambady, N. (2001). When roles reverse: Stigma, status, and self-evaluation. *Journal of Applied Social Psychology, 31*(7), 1350–1378.

Richmond, M. (1917). *Social diagnosis.* Philadelphia, PA: The Russell Sage Foundation.

Riedel Bowers, N. (2001). *A journey within a journey: A naturalistic inquiry of the early relationship development process of non-directive play therapy* (Unpublished doctoral dissertation). Wilfrid Laurier University, Waterloo, Ontario.

Riedel Bowers, N. (2009). A naturalistic inquiry of the early relationship development process of non-directive play therapy. *International Journal of Play Therapy, 18*(3), 176–189.

Riger, S. (1993). What's wrong with empowerment. *American Journal of Community Psychology, 21*(3), 279–292. doi:10.1007/BF00941504

Risley-Curtiss, C. (2010). Social work practitioners and the human-companion animal bond: A national study. *Social Work, 55*(1), 38–46.

Robbins, A., & Erismann, M. (1992). Developing therapeutic artistry: A joint countertransference supervisory seminar/stone sculpting workshop. *The Arts in Psychotherapy, 19*(5), 367–377.

Robbins, S. B., & Jolkovski, M. P. (1987). Managing countertransference feelings: An interactional model using awareness of feeling and theoretical framework. *Journal of Counseling Psychology, 34*(3), 276–282.

Robbins, S. P. (1983) *Organization theory: The structure and design of organizations.* Englewood Cliffs, NJ: Prentice Hall.

Robert, H. E. (1990). *Robert's rules of order* (9th ed.). Glenview, IL: Scott Foresman.

Roberts, A. R. (1998). *Battered women and their families: intervention strategies and treatment programs* (2nd ed.). New York, NY: Springer.

Roberts, A. R,. & Watkins, J. M. (Eds.). (2009). *Social workers' desk reference* (2nd ed.). New York, NY: Oxford University Press.

Roberts, V. (1994). Conflict and collaboration, managing intergroup relations. In A. Obholzer & V. Roberts (Eds.), *The unconscious at work: Individual and organizational stress in the human services/by members of the Tavistock Clinic "Consulting to Institutions" Workshop* (pp. 187–196). London, England: Routledge.

Robertson, M., & Barford, F. (1970). Story-making in psychotherapy with a chronically ill child. *Psychotherapy: Theory, Research, and Practice, 7*(2), 104–107.

Robin, M., ten Bensel, R. W., Quigley, J., & Anderson, R. K. (1984). Abused children and their pets. In R. K. Anderson, B. L. Hart, & L. A. Hart (Eds.), *The pet connection* (pp.111–130). Minneapolis: University of Minnesota Press.

Rocha, E. M. (1997). A ladder of empowerment. *Journal of Planning Research, 17*(1), 31–44.

Rodebaugh, T. L., Holaway, R. M., & Heimberg, R. G. (2004). The treatment of social anxiety disorder. *Clinical Psychology Review, 24*(7), 883–908.

Rodgers, N. (2009). Therapeutic letters: A challenge to conventional notions of boundary. *Journal of Family Nursing, 15*(1), 50–64.

Roes, N. A. (2002). *Therapeutic techniques for engaging challenging clients*. New York, NY: Haworth Press.

Rogers, C. R. (1951). *Client-centered therapy*. London, England: Constable.

Rombach, M. (2003). An invitation to therapeutic letter writing. *Journal of Systemic Therapies, 22*(1), 15–32.

Ronen, T., & Freeman, A. (2007). *Cognitive behavior therapy in clinical social work practice*. New York, NY: Springer.

Rosal, M. L. (1989). Co-perspective: Master's papers in art therapy: Narrative or research case studies? *The Arts in Psychotherapy, 16*(1), 71–75.

Rosal, M. L. (1998). Research thoughts: Learning from the literature and from experience. *Art Therapy: Journal of the American Art Therapy Association, 15*(1), 47–50.

Rose, M. (1987). The function of food in residential treatment. *Journal of Adolescence, 10*(2), 149–162.

Rose, S. M. (1992). *Case management and social work practice*. New York, NY: Longman.

Rosen, A., & Teesson, M. (2001). Does case management work? The evidence and the abuse of evidence-based medicine. *Australian and New Zealand Journal of Psychiatry 35*, 731–746.

Rosenberg, B. (2000). Mandated clients and solution focused therapy: "It's not my miracle." *Journal of Systemic Therapies, 19*(1), 90–99.

Rosenberg, E. B., & Nitzberg, H. (1980). *The clinical social worker becomes a consultant. Social Work in Health Care, 5*(3), 305–312.

Rosenthal, H. G. (1998). *Favorite counseling and therapy techniques*. New York, NY: Brunner-Routledge.

Rossiter, C. (2001). Long ago and far away: On the use of classical Chinese poetry in poetry therapy. *Journal of Poetry Therapy, 15*(1), 37–39.

Rotering, L. H. (1994). *A comparison of professional disciplines' utilization of self-help groups as client resources*. Albany State University of New York Press.

Rothery, M. A. (1980). Contracts and contracting. *Clinical Social Work Journal, 8*(3), 179–187.

Rothman, J. (1991). Guidelines for case management: Toward empirically based practice. *Social Work, 35*, 520–528.

Rothman, J. (1992). *Guidelines for case management: Putting research to professional use*. Itasca, IL: Peacock.

Rothman, J. (1998) Contracting in clinical social work. Chicago: Nelson Hall Seabury, B. A. (1974) The contract: Uses and abuses, and limitations. *Social Work, 21*(1), 16–21.

Rubin, L., & Livesay, H. (2006). Look, up in the sky!! Using superheroes in play therapy. *International Journal of Play Therapy, 15*(1), 117–133.

Russell, K. C. (2000). Exploring how the wilderness therapy process relates to outcomes. *The Journal of Experiential Education, 23*(3), 170–176.

Ruth, J. A. (1996). It's the feeling that counts: Toward an understanding of emotion and its influence on gift exchange processes. In C. Otnes & R. F. Beltramini (Eds.), *Gift-giving: A research anthology* (pp. 195–214). Bowling Green, OH: Bowling Green State University Popular Press.

Ruysschaert, N. (2009). (Self) hypnosis in the prevention of burnout and compassion fatigue for caregivers: Theory and induction. *Contemporary Hypnosis, 26*(3), 159–172.

Ryan, V. L., & Gizynski, M. N. (1971). Behavior therapy in retrospect: Patients' feelings about their behavior therapy. *Journal of Consulting and Clinical Psychology, 37*, 1–9.

Sable, P. (1995). Pets, attachment and well-being across the life cycle. *Social Work, 40*(3), 334–341.

Saintonge, S., Achille, P. A., & Lachance, L. (1998). The influence of Big Brothers on the separation–individuation of adolescents from single-parent families. *Adolescence, 33*(130), 343–353.

Sakiyama, Y., & Koch, N. (2003). Touch in dance therapy in Japan. *American Journal of Dance Therapy*, 25(2), 79–95.

Saleebey, D. (2011). Strengths perspective in social work practice. In Francis J. Turner (Ed.), *Social work: Interlocking theoretical perpspectives* (5th ed., pp. 477–485) New York, NY: Oxford University Press.

Salvatore, G., Dimaggio, G., & Semerari, A. (2004). A model of narrative development: Implications for understanding psychopathology and guiding therapy. *Psychology & Psychotherapy: Theory, Research & Practice*, 77(2), 231–254.

Santa Rita, E. J. (1998). What do you do after asking the miracle question in solution-focused therapy? *Family Therapy*, 25(3), 189–195.

Sauer, R. J. (1984). Family therapy in a partial hospitalization setting. *Family Therapy*, 11(3), 211–215.

Sax, P. R. (1978). An inquiry into fee setting and its determinants. *Clinical Social Work Journal*, 6(4), 305–312.

Schade, M., Hruza, T., Washburne, A., & Carns, M. (2006). Relaxation as an adjunct to psychotherapy. *Journal of Clinical Psychology*, 8, 338–346.

Schafer, R. (1983). *The analytic attitude*. New York, NY: Basic Books.

Scharf, A. (1968). *Art & photography*. London, England: Allen Lane.

Schauer, M., & Mauritz, K. H. (2003). Musical motor feedback (MMF) in walking hemiparetic stroke patients: Randomized trials of gait improvement. *Clinical Rehabilitation*, 17(7), 713–722.

Schauer, M., Neuner, F. & Elbert, T. (2005). *Narrative exposure therapy (NET)*. Cambridge, MA: Hogrefe and Huber.

Schaverien, J. (1995). Researching the esoteric: Art therapy research. In A. Gilroy & C. Lee (Eds.), *Art and music: Therapy and research* (pp. 21–34). London, England: Routledge.

Schlachet, P. J. (1992). The dream in group therapy: A reappraisal of unconscious processes in groups. *Group*, 16(4), 195–209.

Schneider, R. L., & Lester, L. (2000). Social work advocacy: A new framework for action. Belmont: Brooks/Cole.

Schneider, S., Schönle, P. W., Altenmüller, E., & Münte, T. F. (2007). Using musical instruments to improve motor skill recovery following a stroke. *Journal of Neurology*, 254, 1339–1346.

Schopp, L., Johnstone, B., & Merrell, D. (2000). Telehealth and neuropsychological assessment: New opportunities for psychologists. *Professional Psychology: Research and Practice*, 31, 179–183.

Schredl, M. (2010). Explaining the gender difference in dream recall frequency. *Dreaming*, 20(2), 96–106.

Schredl, M., & Sartorius, H. (2010). Dream recall and dream content in children with attention deficit/hyperactivity disorder. *Child Psychiatry and Human Development*, 41(2), 230–238.

Schultz, K. (1988). Money as an issue in therapy. *Journal of Independent Social Work*, 3(1), 7–21.

Schulz, A. J., Israel, B. A., Zimmerman, M. A., & Checkoway, B. N. (1995). Empowerment as a multi-level construct: Perceived control at the individual, organizational and community levels. *Health Education Research*, 10(3), 309–327.

Schuman, E. (2004). Family therapy and family mediation. *Psychology and Education: An Interdisciplinary Journal*, 41(2), 38–39.

Schut, A. J., Castonguay, L. G., Flanagan, K. M., Yamasaki, A. S., Barber, J. P., Bedics, J. D., & Smith, T. L. (2005). Social worker interpretation, patient-social worker interpersonal process, and outcome in psychodynamic psychotherapy for avoidant personality disorder. *Psychotherapy: Theory, Research, Practice, Training. Special Issue: The Interplay of Techniques and the Therapeutic Relationship in Psychotherapy*, 42(4), 494–511.

Scott, D. (2005). Inter-organisational collaboration in family-centred practice: A framework for analysis and action. *Australian Social Work, 58*(2), 132–141.

Scourfield, P. (2010). Going for brokerage: A task of "independent support" or social work? *The British Journal of Social Work, 40*(3), 858–877. doi:10.1093/bjsw/bcn141.

Searight, H. R., & Searight, B. K. (2009). Working with foreign language interpreters: Recommendations for psychological practice. *Professional Psychology: Research and Practice, 40*(5), 444–451.

Segal, E., Gerdes, K., & Steiner, S., (2007). *An introduction to the profession of social work: Becoming a change agent.* Belmont, CA: Brooks/Cole Publishing.

Sellers, D. M. (2006). The evaluation of an animal assisted therapy intervention for elders with dementia in long-term care. *Activities, Adaptation & Aging, 30*(1), 61–77.

Seltzer, L. F. (1983). Influencing the "shape" of resistance: An experimental exploration of paradoxical directives and pscyological reactance. *Basic and Applied Social Psychology, 4*(1), 47–71.

Selvini-Pazzololi, M. S., Boscolo, L., Cecchin, G. F., & Prata, G. (1977). Family rituals: A powerful tool in family therapy. *Family Process, 16*, 445–453.

Shapiro, S. L., & Walsh, R. (2003). An analysis of recent meditation research and suggestions for future directions. *Humanistic Psychologist, 31*(2–3), 86–114.

Sheafor, B. W., Horejsi, C. R., & Horejsi, G. A. (1997). *Techniques and guidelines for social work practice* (4th ed.). Toronto, Ontario: Allyn & Bacon.

Sheafor, B. W., & Horejsi, C. R. (2003). *Techniques and guidelines for social work practice* (6th ed.). Boston, MA: Allyn & Bacon.

Sheafor, B. W., & Horejsi, C. R. (2008). *Techniques and guidelines for social work practice* (8th ed.). Boston, MA: Allyn & Bacon.

Shearer, R., & Davidhizar, R. (2003). Using role play to develop cultural competence. *Journal of Nursing Education, 42*(6), 273–276.

Shebib, B. (2000). *Choices: Practical interviewing and counseling skills.* Needham Heights, MA: Allyn & Bacon.

Shechtman, Z., Vurembrand, N., & Hertz-Lazarowitz, R. (1994). A dyadic and gender-specific analysis of close friendships of preadolescents receiving group psychotherapy. *Journal of Social and Personal Relationships, 11*(3), 443–448.

Shellenberger, S., Dent, M. M., Davis-Smith, M., Seale, J. P., Weintraut, R., & Shelton, J., & Levy, R. (1981). *Behavioral assignments and treatment compliance.* Champaign, IL: Research Press.

Shilts, L., & Gordon, A. B. (1996). What to do after the miracle occurs. *Journal of Family Psychotherapy, 7*(1), 15–22.

Shohet, C., & Klein, P. S. (2010). Effects of variations in toy presentation on social behaviour of infants and toddlers in childcare. *Early Child Development and Care, 180*(6), 823–834.

Shorr, S. I., & Jason, L. A. (1982). A comparison of men's and women's consciousness raising groups. *Groups, 6*(4), 51–55.

Shulman, L. (2008). *The skills of helping individuals, families, groups, and communities* (6th ed.). Belmont, CA: Brooks/Cole.

Simon, B. L. (1994). *Empowerment traditions: History of empowerment in social work.* New York, NY: Columbia University Press.

Simon, J. (1990). The single parent: Power and the integrity of parenting. *The American Journal of Psychoanalysis, 50*(2), 187–198.

Simon, W. E. (1973). Age, sex, and title of social worker as determinants of patient preferences. *Journal of Psychology, 83*(1), 145–149.

Simpson, G. A., Williams, J. C., & Segall, A. B. (2007). Social work education and clinical learning. *Clinical Social Work Journal, 35*, 3–14.

Singh, A. M. (1999). Shamans, healing and mental health. *Journal of Child and Family Studies, 8*(2), 131–134.

Singh, N. N., McKay, J. D., & Singh, A. N. (1999). The need for cultural brokers in mental health services. *Journal of Child and Family Studies, 8*(1), 1–10. doi:10.1023/A:1022949225965.

Sitkowski, S., & Herron, W. G. (1991). Attitudes of social workers and their patients toward money. *Psychotherapy in Private Practice, 8*(4), 27–37.

Skinner, B. F. (1938). *The behavior of organisms*. New York, NY: Appleton-Century-Crofts.

Slavson, S. R. (1966). The phenomenology and dynamics of silence in psychotherapy groups. *International Journal of Group Psychotherapy, 16*(4), 395–404.

Sloan, R. P., Bagiella, E., Powell, T. (1999). Religion, spirituality, and medicine. *Lancet, 353*(9153), 664–667.

Smith, G. G., & Celano, M. (2000). Revenge of the mutant cockroach: Culturally adapted storytelling in the treatment of a low-income African American boy. *Cultural Diversity and Ethnic Minority Psychology, 6*(2), 220–227.

Smith, J. C., Cumming, A., & Xeros-Constantinides, S. (2010). A decade of parent and infant relationship support group therapy programs. *International Journal of Group Psychotherapy, 60*(1), 59–90.

Smith, M. A. (2000). The use of poetry therapy in the treatment of an adolescent with borderline personality disorder: A case study. *Journal of Poetry Therapy, 14*(1), 3–14.

Smolar, A. I. (2002). Reflections on gifts in the therapeutic setting: The gift from patient to social worker. *American Journal of Psychotherapy, 56*(1), 27–45.

Smyth, J. (1998). Written emotional expression, effect sizes, outcome types, and moderating variables. *Journal of Consulting and Clinical Psychology, 66*(1), 174–184.

Smyth, J. M., Stone, A. A., Hurewitz, A., & Kaell, A. (1999). Effects of writing about stressful experiences on symptom reduction in patients with asthma or rheumatoid arthritis: A randomized trial. *Journal of the American Medical Association, 281*(14), 130–149.

Solli, H. P. (2008). "Shut up and play!" Improvisational use of popular music for a man with schizophrenia. *Nordic Journal of Music Therapy, 17*, 67–77.

Solomon, B. B. (1987). Empowerment: Social work in oppressed communities. *Journal of Social Work Practice, 2*(4), 79–91. doi:10.1080/ 02650538708414984

Sontag, S. (1977/1980). *On photography*. New York, NY: Dell.

Souchay, C., Moulin, C. J. A., Isingrini, M., & Conway, M. A. (2008). Rehearsal strategy use in Alzheimer's disease. *Cognitive Neuropsychology, 25*(6), 783–797.

Sowards, S. K., & Renegar, V. R. (2004). The rhetorical functions of consciousness-raising in third wave feminism. *Communication Studies, 55*(4), 535–552.

Sowers, K. M., White, B. W., & Dulmus, C. N. (2008). *Comprehensive handbook of social work and social welfare: The profession of social work*. Hoboken, NJ: Wiley.

Spandler, H., Burman, E., Goldberg, G., Margison, F., & Amos, T. (2000). "A double-edged sword": Understanding gifts in psychotherapy. *European Journal of Psychotherapy, Counseling and Health, 3*(1), 77–101.

Speer, P. W. (2000). Intrapersonal and interactional empowerment: Implications for theory. *Journal of Community Psychology, 28*(1), 51–61.

Speer, P. W., & Hughey, J. (1995). Community organizing: An ecological route to empowerment and power. *American Journal of Community Psychology, 23*(5), 729–748.

Speer, P. W., Jackson, C. B., & Peterson, N. A. (2001). The relationship between social cohesion and empowerment: Support and new implications for theory. *Health Education & Behavior, 28*(6), 716–732. doi:10.1177/109019810102800605

Spence, S. H. (2003). Social skills training with children and young people: Theory, evidence and practice. *Child & Adolescent Mental Health, 8*(2), 84–96.

Speraw, S. (2010). *Review of genograms: Assessment and intervention* (3rd ed.). *Issues in Mental Health Nursing, 31*(8), 550.

Spreckelmeyer, K. F. (1993). Office relocation and environmental change: A case study. *Environment and Behavior, 25*(2), 181–204.

Staples, L. (1984). *Roots to power: A manual for grassroots organizing.* New York, NY: Praeger.

Star, B. (1979). Expanding the boundaries of videotape self-confrontation. *Journal of Education for Social Work, 15*(1), 87–94.

Starr, A. (1977). *Rehearsal for living: Psychodrama: Illustrated therapeutic techniques.* Chicago, IL: Nelson-Hall.

Startup, M., & Shapiro, D. A. (1993). Social worker treatment fidelity in prescriptive vs. exploratory psychotherapy. *British Journal of Clinical Psychology, 32*(4), 443–456.

Stein, H. (1965). The gift in therapy. *American Journal of Psychotherapy, 19*(3), 480–486.

Steinburg, D. (2000). *Letters from the clinic: Letter writing in clinical practice for mental health professionals.* London, England: Routledge.

Steinmetz, H. C. (2006). Directive psychotherapy: Freeing from the dilemma. *Journal of Clinical Psychology, 3*(3), 288–293.

Stewart, D. (1979). Photo therapy: Theory & practice. *Art Psychotherapy, 6*(1), 41–46.

Stirtzinger, R. M. (1983). Story telling: A creative therapeutic technique. *The Canadian Journal of Psychiatry/La Revue canadienne de psychiatrie, 28*(7), 561–565.

St-Onge, M., Mercier, P., & De Koninck, J. (2009). Imagery rehearsal therapy for frequent nightmares in children. *Behavioral Sleep Medicine, 7*(2), 81–98.

Stover, C. S., Poole, G., & Marans, S. (2009). The domestic violence home-visit intervention: Impact on police-reported incidents of repeat violence over 12 months. *Violence & Victims, 24*(5), 591–606.

Strand, V. C., & Badger, L. (2007). A clinical consultation model for child welfare supervisors. *Child Welfare, 86*(1), 79–96.

Strean, H. (1979). *Psychoanalytic theory and social work practice* (pp. 66–70). New York, NY: Free Press.

Strean, H. S. (1996). Psychoanalytic theory and social work treatment. In F. J. Turner (Ed.), *Social work treatment: Interlocking theoretical approaches* (4th ed., pp. 544–546). New York, NY: Free Press.

Stricker, G., & Gold, J. R. (1993). *Comprehensive handbook of psychotherapy integration.* New York, NY: Plenum Press.

Strom, K. (1992). Reimbursement demands and treatment decisions: A growing dilemma for social workers. *Social Work, 37*(5), 398–403.

Strong, T. (2002). Poetic possibilities in conversations about suffering. *Contemporary Family Therapy, 24*(3), 457–473.

Strong, T., & Pyle, N. R. (2009). Constructing a conversational "miracle": Examining the "miracle question" as it is used in therapeutic dialogue. *Journal of Constructivist Psychology, 22*(4), 328–353.

Strong, T., Pyle, N. R., & Sutherland, O. (2009). Scaling questions: Asking and answering them in counselling. *Counselling Psychology Quarterly, 22*(2), 171–185.

Suárez-Orozco, C., Todorova, I. L. G., & Louie, J. (2002). Making up for lost time: The experience of separation and reunification among immigrant families. *Family Process, 41*(4), 625–643.

Sue, S., & Zane, N. (1897). The role of culture and cultural techniques in psychotherapy: A critique and reformulation. *American Psychologist, 42*(1), 37–45.

Sullivan, K., Marshall, S. K., & Schonert-Reichl, K. A. (2002). Do expectancies influence choice of help-giver? Adolescents' criteria for selecting an informal helper. *Journal of Adolescent Research, 17*(5), 509–531.

Swoboda, J. S., Dowd, E. T., & Wise, S. L. (1990). Reframing and restraining directives in the treatment of clinical depression. *Journal of Counseling Psychology, 37*(3), 254–260.

Szalay, L. B., Carroll, J. F. X., & Tims, F. (1993). Rediscovering free associations for use in psychotherapy. *Psychotherapy: Theory, Research, Practice, Training, 30*(2), 344–356.

Tahan, H. A. (2005). Essentials of advocacy in case management. *Lippincott's Case Management, 10*(3), 136–145.

Talan, K. H. (1989). Gifts in psychoanalysis: Theoretical and technical issues. *Psychoanalytic Study of the Child, 44,* 149–163.

Talerico, C. J. (1986). The expressive arts and creativity as a form of therapeutic experience in the field of mental health. *The Journal of Creative Behavior, 20*(4), 229–247.

Tallman, K., & Bohart, A. C. (1999). The client as a common factor: Clients as self-healers. In M. A. Hubble, B. L. Duncan, & S. D. Miller (Eds.), *The heart and soul of change: What works in therapy* (pp. 91–131). Washington, DC: American Psychological Association.

Tan, S. Y. (2007). Use of prayer and scripture in cognitive-behavioral therapy. *Journal of Psychology and Christianity, 26*(2), 101–111.

Tannous, C. (2000). Social workers as advocates for their clients with disabilities: A conflict of roles? *Australian Occupational Therapy Journal, 47*(1), 41–46.

Tapper, D., Kleinman, P., & Nakashian, M. (1997). An interagency collaboration strategy for linking schools with social and criminal justice services. *Social Work in Education, 19,* 176–188.

Tavernier, D. L. (2009). The genogram: Enhancing student appreciation of family genetics. *Journal of Nursing Education, 48*(4), 222–225.

Taylor, E. R. (2009). Sandtray and solution-focused therapy. *International Journal of Play Therapy, 18*(1), 56–68.

Teevan, K. G., & Gabel, H. (1978). Evaluation of modeling—role-playing and lecture—discussion training techniques for college student mental health paraprofessionals. *Journal of Counseling Psychology, 25*(2), 169–171.

Tengland, P. (2008). Empowerment: A conceptual discussion. *Health Care Analysis, 16*(2), 77–96.

Tharp, R. G. (1999). Social worker as teacher. *Human Development, 42,* 18–25.

Thomas, A. J. (1998). Understanding culture and worldview in family systems: Use of the multicultural genogram. *The Family Journal: Counseling and Therapy for Couples and Families, 6*(1), 24–32.

Thomsen, D. K. (2009). There is more to life stories than memories. *Memory, 17*(4), 445–457.

Thorne, F. C. (1948). Theoretical foundations of directive psychotherapy. *Annals of the New York Academy of Sciences, 49*(6), 869–877.

Thorne, F. C. (2006). Directive psychotherapy: XVI, situational analysis. *Journal of Clinical Psychology, 4*(3), 290–298.

Tibbetts, T. J. (1995). Art therapy at the crossroads: Art and science. *Art Therapy: Journal of the American Art Therapy Association, 12*(4), 257–260.

Tolson, E. R., Reid, W. J., & Garvin, C. D. (1994). *Generalist practice: A task-centered approach.* New York, NY: Columbia University Press.

Torrance, J. (2003). Autism, aggression, and developing a therapeutic contract. *American Journal of Dance Therapy, 25*(2), 97–109.

Torres, L., & Ong, A. D. (2010). A daily diary investigation of Latino ethnic identity, discrimination, and depression. *Cultural Diversity and Ethnic Minority Psychology, 16*(4), 561–568.

Tosone, C. A. (1993). *Impact of the level of patient functioning on the content and frequency of social worker interpretation.* New York, NY: NYU Press.

Tourse, R., & Mooney, J. F. (Eds.). (1999). *Collaborative practice.* Westport, CT: Praeger.

Tower, K. D. (2000). Fashionable late? Social work and television. *Journal of Technology in Human Services, 16*(2/3), 175–192.

Trachtman, R. (1999). The money taboo: Its effects in everyday life and in the practice of psychotherapy. *Clinical Social Work Journal, 27*(3), 275–288.

Trepper, T. S. (1993). *101 interventions in family therapy.* New York, NY: Haworth Press.

Treseder, P. (1997). *Empowering children & young people: Promoting involvement in decision-making.* London, England: Save the Children.

Trexler, L. D., & Karst, T. O. (1972). Rational-emotive therapy, placebo, and no-treatment effects on public-speaking anxiety. *Journal of Abnormal Psychology, 79*(1), 60–67.

Trickett, E. J. (1991). *Living an idea: Empowerment and the evolution of an alternative high school.* Cambridge, MA: Brookline Books.

Troester, J. D., & Darby, J. A. (1976). The role of the mini-meal in therapeutic play groups. *Social Casework, 57*(2), 97–103.

Tuber, S. (2009). *Attachment, play and authencity: A Winnicott primer.* Lanham, MD: Jason Aronson.

Tubman, J. G., Montgomery, M. J., & Wagner, E. F. (2001). Letter writing as a tool to increase client motivation to change: Application to an inpatient crisis unit. *Journal of Mental Health Counseling, 23*(4), 295–311.

Turner, F. J. (1996). *Social work treatment: Interlocking theoretical approaches.* (4th ed.) New York, NY: The Free Press.

Turner, F. J. (2002). Psychosocial therapy. In R. A. Roberts & G. J. Greene (Eds.), *Social work desk reference* (p. 111). New York, NY: Oxford University Press.

Turner, F. J. (2002). The role of interpreters in contemporary practice. In F. J. Turner (Ed.), *Social work practice* (2nd ed., pp. 545–552). Scarborough, Ontario: Prentice Hall, Allyn & Bacon Canada.

Turner, J., & Rose-Marie, J. (1996). Problem-solving theory and social work treatment. In F. J. Turner (Ed.), *Social work treatment: Interlocking theoretical approaches* (4th ed., pp. 503–522). New York, NY: Free Press.

Tussing, H. L., & Valentine, D. P. (2001). Helping adolescents cope with the mental illness of a parent through bibliotherapy. *Child & Adolescent Social Work Journal, 18*(6), 455–469.

Twersky, R. K., & Cole, W. M. (1976). Social work fees in medical care. *Social Work in Health Care, 2*(1), 77–84.

Umphress, E. E., Simmons, A. L., Boswell, W. R., & Triana, M. C. (2008). Managing discrimination in selection: The influence of directives from an authority and social dominance orientation. *Journal of Applied Psychology, 93*(5), 982–993.

Unger, R. K. (2001). *Handbook of the psychology of women and gender.* New York, NY: Wiley.

Van der Oord, S., Lucassen, S., Van Emmerik, A. A. P., & Emmelkamp, P. M. G. (2010). Treatment of post-traumatic stress disorder in children using cognitive behavioural writing therapy. *Clinical Psychology & Psychotherapy, 17*(3), 240–249.

Van Deurzen, A. (1998). *Paradox and passion in psychotherapy.* New York, NY: Wiley.

Van Voorhis, R., & Hostetter, C. (2006). The impact of MSW education on social worker empowerment and commitment to client empowerment through social justice advocacy. *Journal of Social Work Education, 42*(1), 105–121.

VandenBos, G. R., & Williams, S. (2000). The Internet versus the telephone: What is telehealth, anyway? *Professional Psychology: Research and Practice, 31*(5), 490–492.

Vanderplasschen, W., Rapp, R. C., Wolf, J. R., & Broekaert, E. (2004). The development and implementation of case management for substance use disorders in North America and Europe. *Psychiatric Services, 55*(8), 913–922.

Vasquez, C., & Javier, R. A. (1991). The problem with interpreters: Communicating with Spanish-speaking patients. *Hospital and Community Psychiatry, 42*(2), 163–165.

Vehviläinen, S. (2001). Evaluative advice in educational counseling: The use of disagreement in the "stepwise entry" to advice. *Research on Language and Social Interaction, 34,* 371–398.

Venberg, B., & Schum, M. J. (2002). Internet bibliotherapy: A narrative analysis of a reading simulated support group. *Journal of Social Work and Disability and Rehabilitation, 1*(1), 81–97.

Venter, C. A. (1993). Graphic family sculpting as a technique in family therapy. *Social Worker-Research-Practitioner, 6*(2), 12–15.

Vidgen, A., & Williams, R. (2001). Letter-writing practices in a child and family service. *Journal of Family Therapy, 23*(3), 317–326. doi:10.1111/1467–6427.00186

Von Hug-Helllmuth, H. (1921). On the technique of child-analysis. *International Journal of Psychoanalysis, 2,* 286–305.

Vourlekis, B. S., & Robert, R. G. (Eds.). (1992). *Social work case management.* New York, NY: Aldine.

Wade, S. L., Walz, N. C., Carey, J. C. P., & Williams, K. M. (2008). Preliminary efficacy of a web-based family problem-solving treatment program for adolescents with traumatic brain injury. *Journal of Head Trauma Rehabilitation. Focus on Clinical Research and Practice, Part 2, 23*(6), 369–377.

Wadeson, H. (1980). Art therapy research. *Art Education, 33*(4), 31–35.

Wadeson, H. (Ed.). (1992). *A guide to conducting art therapy research.* Mundelein, IL: The American Art Therapy Association.

Wadeson, H. (2010). *Art psychotherapy* (2nd ed.). Hoboken, NJ: Wiley.

Wadeson, H. (2010). *Art therapy practice: Innovative approaches with diverse populations.* New York, NY: Wiley.

Wagner-Moore, L. E. (2004). Gestalt therapy: Past, present, theory, and research. *Psychotherapy: Theory, Research, Practice, Training, 41*(2), 180–189.

Walker, S. (2004). Community work and psychosocial practice: Chalk and cheese or birds of a feather? *Journal of Social Work Practice, 18*(2), 161–175.

Wall, M. D., Kleckner, T., Amendt, J. H., & Bryant, R. D. (1989). Therapeutic compliments: Setting the stage for successful therapy. *Journal of Marital and Family Therapy, 15*(2), 159–167.

Wallach, H. S., Safir, M. P., & Bar-Zvi, M. (2009). Virtual reality cognitive behavior therapy for public speaking anxiety: A randomized clinical trial. *Behavior Modification, 33*(3), 314–338.

Wallerstein, N. (1992). Powerlessness, empowerment, and health: Implications for health promotion programs. *American Journal of Health Promotion, 6*(3), 197–205.

Wallerstein, N., & Bernstein, E. (1988). Empowerment education: Freire's ideas adapted to health-education. *Health Education Quarterly, 15*(4), 379–394.

Walrath, C., dosReis, S., Miech, R., Liao, Q., Holden, E. W., De Carolis, G., … Leaf, P. (2001). Referral source differences in functional impairment levels for children served in the comprehensive community mental health services for children and their families program. *Journal of Child & Family Studies, 10*(3), 385–397.

Walsh, J. (2010). *Theories for direct social work practice* (2nd ed.). Belmont, CA: Wadsworth.

Walsh, J. A. (1990). Using external consultants in social service agencies. *The Journal of Contemporary Social Services, 71*(5), 291–295.

Walters, K., Buszewicz, M., Russell, J., & Humphrey, C. (2003). Teaching as therapy: Cross sectional and qualitative evaluation of patients' experiences of undergraduate psychiatry teaching in the community. *British Medical Journal, 326*(7392), 740.

Waltman, G. H. (1989). Social work consultation services in rural areas. *Human Services in the Rural Environment, 12*(3), 17–21.

Ward, G., Woodward, G., Stevens, A., & Stinson, C. (2003). Using overt rehearsals to explain word frequency effects in free recall. *Journal of Experimental Psychology: Learning, Memory, and Cognition, 29*(2), 186–210.

Wardhaugh, R. (2009). *An introduction to sociolinguistics* (6th ed.). Malden, MA: Blackwell.

Warner, S. L. (1989). Sigmund Freud and money. *Journal of the American Academy of Psychoanalysis, 17*(4), 609–622.

Washington, O., & Moxley, D. (2001). The use of prayer in group work with African American women recovering from chemical dependency. *Families in Society, 82*(1), 49–59.

Wasik, B. (1990). *Home visiting: Procedures for helping families*. Newbury, CA: Sage.

Waters, J. A., & Finn, E. (1995). Handling client crises effectively on the telephone. In A. R. Roberts (Ed.), *Crisis intervention and time-limited cognitive treatment* (pp. 251–289). Thousand Oaks, CA: Sage.

Watts, C., & Shrader, E. (1998). The genogram: A new research tool to document patterns of decision-making, conflict and vulnerability within households. *Health Policy & Planning, 13*(4), 459–464.

Watts-Jones, D. (1997). Toward an African American genogram. *Family Process, 36*(4), 375–383.

Watzlawick, P., Bavelas, J. B., & Jackson, D. (1967). *Pragmatics of human communication: A study of interactional patterns, pathologies, and paradoxes*. New York, NY: Norton.

Watzlawick, P., Weakland, J., & Fisch, R. (1974). *Change: Principles of problem resolution*. New York, NY: Norton.

Weber, L. A. (1980). The effect of videotape and playback on an in-patient adolescent group. *International Journal of Group Psychotherapy, 30*, 213–227.

Weeks, G., & L'Abate, L. (1978). A bibliography of paradoxical methods in psychotherapy of family systems. *Family Process, 17*(1), 95–98.

Weingarten, K. (1992). A consideration of intimate and non-intimate interactions in therapy. *Family Process, 31*(1), 45–59.

Weinstein, J., Whittington, C., & Leiba, T. (2003). *Collaboration in social work practice*. New York, NY: Jessica Kinglsey.

Weinter, C., & Cartwright, R.T. (1999) *Descripto-cards for adult aphasia*. New York, NY: Psychological Corporation.

Weiser, J. (1990). More than meets the eye. Using ordinary snapshots as tools for therapy In T. Laidlaw, C. Malmo, & Associates (Eds.). *Healing voices: Feminist approaches to therapy with women* (pp. 83–117). San Francisco, CA: Jossey-Bass.

Weiser, J. (2001). Phototherapy techniques: Using clients' personal snapshots and family photos as counseling and therapy tools. *The Journal of Media Arts and Cultural Criticism, 29*(3), 10–15.

Weiser, J. (2003). A picture is worth a thousand words: Using phototherapy techniques in counselling practice. *Bulletin of the Private Practitioners Chapter Newsletter (Canadian Counselling Association), 3*(2), 3–4.

Weiser, J. (2004). Phototherapy techniques in counseling and therapy: Using ordinary snapshots and photo-interactions to help clients heal their lives. *The Canadian Art Therapy Association Journal, 17*(2), 23–53.

Weiss, M. Using house calls in a psychotherapy practice. In P. Keller & S. Heyman (Eds.), Innovation in clinical practice: A sourcebook (Vol. 9, pp. 229–238). Sarasota, FL: Professional Resource Exchange.

Weiss, Y. (1993). Teaching bedside interviewing skills in a social work training programme. *Social Work in Health Care, 18*(314), 201–219.

Weiss-Gal, I., & Welbourne, P. (2008). The professionalization of social work: A cross-national exploration. *International Journal of Social Welfare, 17*(4), 281–290.

Weitz, R. (1982). Feminist consciousness raising, self-concept, and depression, *Sex Roles, 8*(3), 231–241.

Welch, I. D. (1998). *The path of psychotherapy. Matters of the heart* (pp. 33–38). New York, NY: Brooks/Cole.

Whisman, M. A., & Jacobson, N. S. (1990). Power, marital satisfaction, and response to marital therapy. *Journal of Family Psychology, 4*(2), 202–212.

White, M., & Epston, D. (1990). *Narrative means to therapeutic ends.* New York, NY: Norton.

White, V. E., & Murray, M. A. (2002). Passing notes: The use of therapeutic letter writing in counseling adolescents. *Journal of Mental Health Counseling, 24*(2), 166–176.

Whitehead-Pleaux, A. M., Zebrowski, N., Baryza, M. J., & Sheridan, R. L. (2007). Exploring the effects of music therapy on pediatric pain: Phase 1. *Journal of Music Therapy, 44*, 217–241.

Widen, H. A. (2000). Using dreams in brief therapy. *Psychoanalytic Social Work, 7*(2), 1–4.

Wieser, M. J., Pauli, P., Alpers, G. W., & Mühlberger, A. (2009). Is eye to eye contact really threatening and avoided in social anxiety?—An eye-tracking and psychophysiology study. *Journal of Anxiety Disorders, 23*(1), 93–103.

Wilkes, J. K. (2009). *The role of companion animals in counseling and psychology: Discovering their use in the therapeutic process.* Springfield, IL: Charles C. Thomas.

Willard, C. (1996). The nurse's role as patient advocate: Obligation or imposition? *Journal of Advanced Nursing, 24*, 60–66.

Williams, C., Soydan, H., Johnson, M. (1998). *Social work and minorities: European perspectives.* New York, NY: Routledge.

Williams, M. (1971). The problem profile technique in consultation. *Social Work, 16*(3), 52–59.

Willow, R. A., Tobin, D. J., & Toner, S. (2009). Assessment of the use of spiritual genograms in counselor education. *Counseling and Values, 53*(3), 214–223.

Wilson, J. M. (1982). The value of touch in psychotherapy. *American Journal of Orthopsychiatry, 52*(1), 65–72.

Winnicott, D. (1971). *Playing and reality.* London: Routledge Press.

Wolf, D., & Abbell, N. (2003). Examining the effects of meditation techniques on psychosocial functioning. *Research on Social Work Practice, 13*(1), 27–42.

Wolfson, E. R. (1999). The fee in social work: Ethical dilemmas for practitioners. *Social Work, 44*(3), 269–273.

Wolin, S. J., & Bennett, L. A. (1984). Family rituals. *Family Process, 23*(3), 401–420.

Wolin, S. J., Bennett, L. A., Noonan, D. L., & Teitelbaum, M. A. (1980). Disrupted family rituals: A factor in the intergenerational transmission of alcoholism. *Journal of Studies on Alcohol, 41*(3), 199–214.

Wolock, I., Sherman, P., Feldman, L. H., & Metzger, B. (2001). Child abuse and neglect referral patterns: A longitudinal study. *Children and Youth Services Review, 23*(1), 21–47.

Wolpe, J. (1958). *Psychotherapy by reciprocal inhibition.* Stanford, CA: Stanford University Press.

Wolpe, J. (1973). *Practice of behavior therapy* (2nd ed.). New York, NY: Pergamon Press.

Wong, N. T., Zimmerman, M. A., & Parker, E. A. (2010). A typology of youth participation and empowerment for child and adolescent health promotion. *American Journal of Community Psychology, 46*(1–2), 100–114.

Wood, M. R. (2010). What makes for successful speaker–listener technique? Two case studies. *The Family Journal, 18*(1), 50–54.

Wood, T. E., Englander-Golden, P., Golden, D. E., & Pillai, V. K. (2010). Improving addictions treatment outcomes by empowering self and others. *International Journal of Mental Health Nursing, 19*(5), 363–368.

Woods, L. J. (1988). Home-based family therapy. *Social Work, 33*(3), 211–214.

Woods, M. (1964). *Casework: A psychosocial therapy* (4th ed.). New York, NY: McGraw-Hill.

Woods, M. E., & Hollis, F. (1981). *Casework: A psychosocial therapy* (3rd ed.). New York, NY: McGraw-Hill.

Woods, M. E., & Hollis, F. (1990). *Casework: A psychosocial therapy* (4th ed.). New York, NY: McGraw-Hill.

Woods, M. E., & Hollis, F. (2000). *Casework: A psychosocial therapy* (5th ed.). New York, NY: McGraw-Hill.

Word, C. O., Zanna, M. P., & Cooper, J. (1974). The nonverbal mediation of self-fulfilling prophecies in interracial interaction. *Journal of Experimental Social Psychology, 10*(2), 109–120.

Worell, J., & Remer, P. (2003). *Feminist perspectives in therapy: Empowering diverse women* (2nd ed.). New York, NY: Wiley.

Wright, C. V., Perez, S., & Johnson, D. M. (2010). The mediating role of empowerment for African American women experiencing intimate partner violence. *Psychological Trauma: Theory, Research, Practice, and Policy.* Advance online publication. doi: 10.1037/a0017470

Wright, T. (2007). Cultural genogram: A tool for teaching and practice. *Families, Systems & Health, 25*(4), 367–382.

Wu, C., & Honig, A. S. (2010). Taiwanese mothers' beliefs about reading aloud with preschoolers: Findings from the Parent Reading Belief Inventory. *Early Child Development and Care, 180*(5), 647–669.

Yakushko, O. (2010). Clinical work with limited English proficiency clients: A phenomenological exploration. *Professional Psychology: Research and Practice, 41*(5), 449–455.

Yelaja, S. A. (1971). *Authority and social work: Concept and use.* Toronto, Ontario: University of Toronto Press.

Yoder, J. D., & Kahn, A. S. (1992). Toward a feminist understanding of women and power. *Psychology of Women Quarterly, 16*(2), 381–388. doi:10.1111/j.1471–6402.1992.tb00263.x

Young, S. (2009). Professional relationships and power dynamics between urban community-based nurses and social work case managers. *Professional Case Management, 14*(6), 312–320.

Yu, D. S. F., Lee, D. T. F., & Woo, J. (2010). Improving health-related quality of life of patients with chronic heart failure: Effects of relaxation therapy. *Journal of Advanced Nursing, 66*(2), 392–403.

Zamparo, J. (2005). Meditation. In F. Turner (Ed.), *Encyclopedia of Canadian social work* (pp. 233–234). Waterloo, Ontario: Wilfrid Laurier Press.

Zastrow, C. (1993). *Social work with groups* (3rd ed.). Chicago, IL: Nelson-Hall.

Zastrow, C. (2009). *The practice of social work: A comprehensive worktext* (9th ed.). Belmont, CA: Brooks/Cole.

Zastrow, C. (2009). *Social work with groups: A comprehensive workbook* (7th ed.). Belmont, CA: Brooks/Cole.

Zastrow, C. (2010). *Introduction to social work and social welfare: Empowering people* (10th ed.). Belmont, CA: Brooks/Cole.

Zastrow, C. H. (2008). *Social work with groups: A comprehensive workbook* (7th ed.). Belmont, CA: Brooks/Cole.

Zayas, L. H., & Katch, M. (1989). Contracting with adolescents: An ego psychological approach. *Social Casework, 70*(1), 3–9.

Zayfert, C., & Becker, C. B. (2007). *Cognitive-behavioral therapy for PTSD: A case formulation approach.* New York, NY: Guilford Press.

Zeig, J. K. (1997). *The evolution of psychotherapy: The third conference.* New York, NY: Brunner/Mazel.

Zeligs, M. A. (1961). The psychology of silence: Its role in transference, counter-transference and the psychoanalytic process. *Journal of the American Psychoanalytic Association, 9*(1), 7–43.

Ziguras, S. J., & Stuart, G. W. (2000). A meta-analysis of the effectiveness of mental health case management over 20 years. *Psychiatric Services 51,* 1410–1421.

Zimmerman, M. A. (1995). Psychological empowerment: Issues and illustrations. *American Journal of Community Psychology, 23*(5), 581–599. doi:10.1007/BF02506983

Zimmerman, M. A. (2000). Empowerment theory: Psychological, organizational, and community levels of analysis. In J. Rappaport & E. Seidman (Eds.), *Handbook of community psychology* (pp. 43–63). New York, NY: Kluwer Academic/Plenum.

Zimmerman, M. A., & Rappaport, J. (1988). Citizen participation, perceived control, and psychological empowerment. *American Journal of Community Psychology, 16*(5), 725–750. doi:10.1007/BF00930023

Zimmerman, M. A., & Warschausky, S. (1998). Empowerment theory for rehabilitation research: Conceptual and methodological issues. *Rehabilitation Psychology, 43*(1), 3–16.

Zischka, P., & Fox, R. (1985). Consultation as a function of school social work. *Social Work in Education, 7*(2), 69–79.

Index